Resources for the Writing Process

As you write you may wish to review advice on various aspects of the writing process. This selective list provides a quick reference.

Planning

Determining purpose, subject, and audience: 2–6, 12–15, 30–49, 194–196

Generating ideas (brainstorming techniques): 62–64, 181–183, 313–316

Formulating a plan and a thesis: 6–7, 8–15, 83, 85–86, 91, 129–138, 181

Outlining (formal and informal): 494–497, 503–506

Avoiding writer's block: 56–59

Drafting

Drafting opening paragraphs: 520–525, 527

Developing paragraphs: 57–60, 65–67, 82–83

Organizing paragraphs: 494–497, 500, 505–506

Considering paragraph length and unity: 500–503

Drafting a conclusion and title: 525–527

Revising

Revising for content and logic: 55–59, 68–76, 353–361

Revising for coherence, style, and tone: 495–497, 500–503, 522–525, 540–549; in handbook: 578–579, 584–585, 620–622, 631–632

Editing and proofreading: 59; in handbook: 577–684, 616–619, 639–660, 683–684

Please see the inside back cover for a list of reading selections in *The Riverside Guide to Writing.*

THE RIVERSIDE GUIDE TO WRITING

SECOND EDITION

DOUGLAS HUNT
University of Missouri

HOUGHTON MIFFLIN COMPANY Boston Toronto
Geneva, Illinois Palo Alto Princeton, New Jersey

Sponsoring Editor: George Kane
Basic Book Editor: Martha Bustin
Associate Editor: Nandana Sen
Editorial Assistant: Bruce Cantley
Senior Project Editor: Janet Young
Editorial Assistant: Marybeth Griffin
Associate Production/Design Coordinator: Caroline Ryan Morgan
Senior Manufacturing Coordinator: Priscilla Bailey

Credits

Cover and Part Opener photos: Gelatin-silver prints by Lee Friedlander, courtesy Fraenkel Gallery, San Francisco: Cover—*Tokyo, 1977;* p. xxvi—*Kentucky, 1977;* p. 76—*East Chatham, New York, 1974;* p. 178—*New York City, 1962;* p. 290—*New York City, 1979;* p. 414, *Wilmington, Delaware, 1965;* p. 492—*Estes Park, Colorado, 1984;* p. 575—*San Francisco, 1984.* For more information about Lee Friedlander, see p. 685.

Text credits appear on pages 687–690, which constitute an extension of the copyright page.

Printed in the U.S.A.

Library of Congress Catalog Card Number: 94-76511

ISBN: Student Edition 0-395-68623-7
      Examination Copy 0-395-71714-0

99 00 01-DH-10 9 8 7 6 5 4 3

THE RIVERSIDE
GUIDE TO
WRITING

BRIEF CONTENTS

CONTENTS

CHAPTER 3

Drafting and Revising   50

PART II

Observation and Experience   77

CHAPTER 4

Eyewitness Reports   78

CHAPTER 5

Autobiographical Writing   123

PART III   # RESEARCH   179

CHAPTER 6

Short Research Reports   180

CHAPTER 7

Longer Research Papers   246

PART IV

PERSUASION 291

CHAPTER 8

Proposals 292

PART V

CHAPTER 11

INTERPRETATION AND EVALUATION 415

Writing About Literature 416

CHAPTER 12 *Reviews and Evaluations*   458

PART VI   MATTERS OF FORM AND STYLE   493

CHAPTER 13 *Organization*   494

Introductions and Conclusions   520

CHAPTER 14

A Practical Approach to Style   538

CHAPTER 15

PART VII

HANDBOOK OF GRAMMAR AND USAGE   575

SECTION 1

Grammar and Sentence Structure   576

SECTION 2

Usage and Diction   620

SECTION 3

Punctuation and Mechanics   661

PREFACE

Like every job, writing textbooks has its frustrations, but no one can complain that it lacks opportunities for on-the-job training. The textbook author does his or her best with a first edition, receives abundant feedback from users, revises, gets more feedback from reviewers, revises again, and again, and eventually a second edition emerges. The process so resembles a good writing class that in revising *The Riverside Guide to Writing* I felt myself becoming a student again, benefitting from the process as I hope students will benefit.

CHANGES IN THE SECOND EDITION

The most gratifying response to the first edition came from veteran instructors who say that, for whatever reason, students who use the *Guide* write better papers—more interesting, more thoughtful, developed with greater care. When we undertook the second edition, one reviewer advised us to "CHANGE NOTHING; I don't know exactly why the book works as it is, but it works." No advice could have been more tempting. Nonetheless, anyone who used the first edition will notice scores of changes—many of them noted in the "transition guide" printed in the Instructor's Resource Manual. Most of these are simply attempts to improve on features of the first edition: the new first chapter, for example, presents more clearly than the old one did the idea that the writer's task is to help the reader see a subject—even the most familiar subject—in a fresh way. The new chapter on writing short research papers supplements the chapter on writing longer reports. Other changes were made for the sake of instructors who have used the first edition for several semesters and felt the need for new readings (forty-six of the book's 104 selections are new), new writing assignments (over half of the sixty-five assignments are new), and new exercises. Changes in the book's structure and sequence are described on the next page under "Organization."

Perhaps the most significant change is a new emphasis on the audience. The emphasis shows most visibly in the addition of Chapter 2 ("Writing for an Audience"), but concern about the writer's relationship with readers pervades the entire book. The new emphasis pays dividends particularly in the persuasion section, with its stress on arguments that grow out of assumptions shared by the audience and the writer.

ORGANIZATION

The second edition divides into six parts. The first part, *Composing,* presents the three themes that will recur throughout the book: the obligation of the writer to present a fresh interpretation of a subject, the necessity for the writer to envision readers' responses, and the mental leverage that drafting and revision create. The second part, *Observation and Experience,* gives students models, practical guidance, and assignments that encourage them to create fresh interpretations of the world they see through their own eyes. The third, *Research,* gives the same sort of support to students as they undertake essays based on library research, interviews, surveys, or systematic forms of direct observation. The fourth part, *Persuasion,* begins with a chapter on proposal writing that teachers of the first edition found particularly appealing to students, then presents in two rather challenging chapters a more detailed treatment of arguments about facts and arguments about rules. The fifth, *Interpretation and Evaluation,* includes chapters on writing about literature and evaluation of products ranging from books to backpacks. The sixth part, *Matters of Form and Style,* is a practical discussion of ways that writers achieve coherence, write workable introductions and conclusions, and help the reader navigate the page safely and pleasurably. Users of the hardcover edition will find a seventh part: a brief *Handbook of Grammar and Usage.*

FEATURES

The principal features of *The Riverside Guide to Writing* are these:

● Varied Assignments.   Sixty-five full-length assignments and several dozen shorter assignments prepare students for the kinds of writing they will do throughout their college careers. Modeled on assignments used in courses across the curriculum, the assignments allow students to practice in simplified form the skills in research and analysis that they will use in courses in history, sociology, literature, biology, and other disciplines. The number and variety of assignments should allow instructors to choose their own emphases and to tailor their course to their students' abilities and interests.

● Chapters Organized to Support Assignments.   Nine of the book's chapters present a particular type of paper (e.g., the proposal). Each of these chapters analyzes student and/or professional examples and concludes with a compact statement of "Points to Consider" while composing, followed by "Questions for Peer Review."

● An Extensive Reading Program.   The book contains 104 diverse, cross-curricular readings (forty-six of them new to this edition). Some, especially among the fifty-three end-of-chapter readings, are long enough to serve as lessons for analysis and summary. Many of the fifty-one in-chapter readings are short enough to serve as models for student essays. The reading program for the *Guide* is so complete that many instructors will feel no need to use an additional reader.

● **Versatile Exercises.**   Exercises scattered through the chapters prepare students for the writing assignments. These exercises can often serve as a focal point for an entire class period. Almost all of them are designed with a dual purpose: not only to help students digest the information in the chapter, but to allow them to practice critical thinking skills they will use in a variety of classes. Instructors committed to collaborative learning will find these exercises particularly helpful.

● **A Chapter on Writing about Literature.**   Emphasizing both close reading and legitimate differences in interpretation, this chapter should be useful in programs where the composition course serves as a prerequisite to literature courses.

● **A New Chapter on Writing Short Research Reports.**   For those instructors who are moving away from the long, formal research paper, but who still want to cover basic research skills, this chapter treats the short research report in a brief, practical manner.

The abundance of readings and assignments in *The Riverside Guide* make it appropriate not only for one-term composition courses, but also for sequences that stretch over two or three courses with somewhat varied emphases. It would be possible, for example, to use it for a series of courses that focus on (1) the writing process and personal writing, (2) writing from research, and (3) argumentation and persuasion.

ANCILLARIES

Also available are the following support materials:

● **An Instructor's Resource Manual.**   This manual offers commentary on the chapters and on each full-length reading, an alternate table of contents for the readings (rhetorical and cross-curricular), a transition guide for users of the first edition, suggested course plans, techniques for teaching, and ideas for working through the assignments.

● **New—An Instructor's Support Package.**   This packet contains useful information in an easily reproduced form (loose-leaf, $8\frac{1}{2}'' \times 11''$). It includes supplemental assignments, sample student papers, transparency masters of key checklists and overviews, and exercises and answers to accompany the grammar handbook included in the hardcover edition.

● **Practical English Exercises and Review (PEER) Software.**   This easy-to-use program offers computerized review and practice in six areas: grammar, sentence errors, sentence structure, punctuation, mechanics, and diction and style. Students are able to practice at their own pace. PEER software is available to instructors free upon adoption, with no restrictions on copying, in a Macintosh or IBM-compatible format.

- *The American Heritage College Dictionary,* **Third Edition.**   This popular college dictionary is available at a very low price when ordered in a shrink-wrapped package with the *Guide*.

ACKNOWLEDGMENTS

Like many textbook writers, I am tempted to acknowledge the contribution of every rhetorician, old and new, who ever lived and wrote. Writers of rhetorics today stand on some massive shoulders and hope that this perch allows them to take in a broad horizon.

I will, however, avoid the long list that begins with Aristotle and ends with the most recent issue of *College Composition and Communication*. My more immediate debts are three. First, I owe thanks to an able set of reviewers who contributed to my understanding of what the first edition did and what the second needed to do:

Priscilla Bellairs, Northern Essex Community College (MA); Louise Berry, University of Tennessee; Patricia E. Connors, Memphis State University (TN); Sarah T. Dangelantonio, Franklin Pierce College (NH); Joan Fitch, Mississippi Gulf Coast Community College; Fritz Fleischmann, Babson College (MA); Christopher Gould, University of North Carolina, Wilmington; Diana J. Grahn, Longview Community College (MO); Romana Hilebrand (student), University of Idaho; Maureen Hourigan, University of Nevada, Las Vegas; Steve Kerby (student), University of North Texas; Phyllis Klein (student); University of Denver; Mary Beth Lake, Normandale Community College (MN); Tim Morris, Southwest Missouri State University; Gary A. Olson, University of South Florida; Virginia Randolph, Pepperdine University (CA); Barry L. Richins, Northland Pioneer College (AZ); Joyce Rivers-Fritch, Indiana University of Pennsylvania; Trina Ruth (student), University of Florida; John Schilb, University of Maryland; Patrick Scott, University of South Carolina; Peter Vanderhoof, Peninsula College (WA); Heidemarie Z. Weidner, Tennessee Technological University; and Mark Withrow, Columbia College, Chicago.

Second, for their detailed critique of Chapter 9's treatment of the Shakespeare/Oxford controversy, special thanks is due to Richard Whalen and to Charleton and Vera Ogburn. Third, I want to thank the editorial staff at Houghton Mifflin, especially Martha Bustin, whose energy and intelligence have improved every page.

Doug Hunt
University of Missouri

THE RIVERSIDE
GUIDE TO
WRITING

PART I

COMPOSING

"In many ways writing is the act of saying I,
of imposing oneself upon other people, of saying,
listen to me, see it my way, change your mind."

JOAN DIDION

Finding a Perspective

I HAVE BEEN ASKING MY FRIENDS LATELY—VETERAN WRITERS AND EAGER beginners alike—to name *the first thing* a writer needs to do to produce a good essay or report. The answers have varied: be confident, have an idea, find conviction, consider the audience, balance doubt and belief, know the material. That a handful of people can answer the question in so many ways reminds me that any single answer is likely to sound foolish. But since every book must put *something* first, let me propose my own answer: the first thing writers must do is put themselves in a position to say something. In this chapter we will concentrate on that problem alone, letting other things that must be said about writing stand to one side, waiting their turn.

How do you put yourself in a position to say something about a subject? In a broad sense, there are two ways. (1) You can gather esoteric experience or knowledge. Travel to a remote region of New Guinea, infiltrate the training camp of a white supremacist army, study every scrap of information you can find on the making of *The Wizard of Oz*. Then you will be in a position to give your readers information that would not otherwise be available to them. *Or* (2) you can deal with material that is familiar to both you and your readers, but look at it from a fresh angle. Show your readers that the fast-food hamburger is a remarkable example of what division of labor can accomplish or that *Jurassic Park* is better understood as a film about marketing than as a film about dinosaurs.

Of course, most successful writing combines elements of both methods. Developing a fresh angle on the familiar subject often requires research, and a research report falls flat if the writer can't stir the reader to fresh thinking. In this book, we will deal with both research and rethinking, but with somewhat more emphasis on the latter, for three reasons:

1. As a student writer, you can't travel to a lamasery in Tibet to find material for a paper on Buddhism. If you are writing an essay on foreign

2

policy, you probably won't be granted an interview with the Secretary of State. Lacking the time and resources some writers can devote to research, you must find a way to make the most of the material that is available to you.

2. A college education is less about learning esoteric facts than about beginning to see facts from new angles: to see as a sociologist does, as a biologist does, as an artist or engineer does. Therefore, writing in college puts a premium on mental flexibility.

3. To see something *different* is an opportunity life will occasionally send your way, but to see something *differently* is part of the writer's discipline, whether the writer is developing a proposal for a new product or offering a fresh understanding of our nation's history. We could go further and say that seeing differently—breaking the grip of unexamined, habitual views—is part of the thinker's discipline.

SAYING SOMETHING: AN EXAMPLE WITHOUT WORDS

To clarify our approach, let's begin with a visual example, one where *seeing* is very literally the issue. Please look at the photograph that follows and spend a minute telling yourself what you see, before you go on.

© Tana Hoban, from *Circles, Triangles and Squares*, Macmillan Publishing Company, New York, 1974

If your response is like most I've heard, it runs something like this one, given by a Midwestern graduate student in her mid-twenties: "It's a boat with a lot of tires hanging off the side. Maybe it's a tugboat, and the tires serve as bumpers. It's tied up to a dock somewhere, probably in an industrial or commercial area that's not too well kept up, since there are broken windows in the building. The cabin of the boat seems very white, as if it had been freshly painted." Some of you who live in port cities may have seen the photo a bit differently. Even as viewers, we can't disentangle ourselves from our pasts. Sailors or landlubbers, we see what we are prepared to see.

Now let's put the photo in the context photographer Tana Hoban chose for it and think about what she is encouraging us to see. It is from Hoban's *Circles, Triangles and Squares,* a book that contains no words except the title. The book has twenty-six photos, including the two that follow.

If we let the book do its work on us, it will change the way we view the pictures it contains. In addition to seeing everyday objects in a real-world setting ("a boat . . . tied up to a dock"), we will see a number of circles, triangles, and squares. In addition to seeing objects that have three dimensions and weight and practical uses, we will see each photograph as a flat surface covered with a two-dimensional design, like a jigsaw puzzle made out of geometric pieces. If the book *really* gets to us, the change in perception it causes may linger after we put it down. We may go out into the world and discover that everywhere we look, we find a visual field crowded with circles, triangles, and squares. (The great French painter Cézanne said that all around him he saw "the cylinder, the sphere, the cone, all put into perspective").

Hoban's book (which we could call a photo essay) shows that she has put herself in a position to say something, to help people see a subject in a way they aren't accustomed to seeing it. And yet from another perspective, there is nothing really *new* in Hoban's "essay." People have taken photos of boats and girls and baby carriages since the camera was invented. Nor are circles, triangles, and squares her invention. What Hoban has done is encourage us to *see one thing* (objects in the world) *in terms of another* (geometric shapes). And this bringing together of things usually kept separate is a good example of what we ordinarily mean by taking a fresh view of the subject.

SUBJECTS AND FRAMEWORKS

Implicit in the example of Tana Hoban's photography is a procedure that many successful writers seem to follow, consciously or not. They recognize what we might call the "default" or "natural" or "general" view people tend to take of a subject, and they modify this expected view by bringing another perspective to bear. We could put it like this: the writer puts the familiar *subject* into a *framework* the audience would not have been inclined to apply to it. In effect, Tana Hoban's photo is a paragraph that says to the reader, "I know you are accustomed to viewing a tugboat tied up to a dock as a 'boat'—a solid object that takes up space and has uses. Now I want you to see it differently, as an example of the way our visual world is made up of circles and squares that are just as real, just as present, as boats and docks. Usually you ignore the circles and squares, but you can see them. See!" Or to put it telegraphically, "Subject: tugboat. Framework: geometric shapes." In fact, visualizing Hoban's photo inside a frame labeled "Geometric Shapes" may help you fix in your mind the definitions we are giving to subject and framework.

The subject is there, open to everyone's inspection; the framework tells the reader what to make of it, how to view it. The framework answers the often impolite but always present questions "So what?" or "What's the point?" When the subject is "framed" in a thought-provoking way, the writer has said something.

To clarify the meaning of subject and framework, we might consider some synonyms used in various contexts. For *subject,* we sometimes say

facts	details
data	phenomenon
raw material	event
experience	observations
instances	examples
case	evidence

For *framework,* we use the following synonyms, some of which emphasize logic and some, emotion:

hypothesis	concept
frame of reference	principle
point of view	rule
theory	context
model	feeling
generalization	predisposition
drift	archetype
bias	gist
thesis	paradigm
idea	world view
premise	insight

All of us constantly put subjects (or "sets of facts" or "phenomena") into frameworks (or "perspectives" or "models" or "theses"); it's the way we make sense of our world. Unfortunately, the frameworks we use are often unexamined and unproductive—mere prejudices, really. One of the great services a writer can do for readers is force them to reconsider the way they habitually frame a subject.

Sometimes writers work inductively—"up" from the subject to find a framework that will help interpret it. Sometimes they work "down," deductively fleshing out a predetermined framework by setting new subjects in it. This, surely, is what Tana Hoban did when she took some of the photos for *Circles, Triangles and Squares*. Political columnists typically fill their conservative or liberal frameworks each day or week with examples drawn from current events. From the reader's perspective, it may not make much difference whether the writer is moving from subject to framework or vice versa. What counts is that the relation between subject and framework is thought-provoking. The writer ordinarily hopes that it is more than this, of course: the writer hopes that it is also persuasive, moving, charming, clever, profound, and more. But to be any of these things, it must first be thought-provoking.

♦ *Identifying Frameworks for a Photograph.* The following photograph is from another of Tana Hoban's books. To sharpen your understanding of the distinction between subject and framework, name three possible frameworks for it, three statements of what it might be "about." Don't worry about seeing the picture as Hoban would see it: the graduate student who saw in the tugboat photo a contrast between negligence (the run-down warehouse) and maintenance (the freshly painted boat) was as "right" as Hoban herself. Write a brief explanation of why your interpretation seems to fit the photo and how it makes the photo more meaningful.

EXERCISE 1

© Tana Hoban, from *Look Again!*, Macmillan Publishing Company, New York, 1971

THREE EXAMPLES WITH WORDS

To get a sense of how writers bring subjects and frameworks together to form fresh interpretations, let's begin with a pair of passages about John F. Kennedy written by Theodore White, a Pulitzer Prize–winning journalist. Before we do, we should note some information about White that helps us see how writers build frameworks from the whole of their experience, from emotion as well as logic.

White was a third-generation American, born into a poor family in Boston's Jewish ghetto, which had not long before been a ghetto for Irish Catholic immigrants. He rose in the world through scholarship, distinguishing himself at the Boston Public Latin School, which meant steeping himself not only in the Latin language, but in the history and politics of ancient Rome. In fact, when poverty forced him to leave school and sell newspapers on street corners, he sometimes shouted the headlines in Latin or belted out a quotation from a Roman orator. All this background affects the frameworks in which he puts Kennedy, a fellow Bostonian of his own generation.

In the following passage from *In Search of History*, White reminds readers that Kennedy, a Catholic, was a member of a minority group that had been excluded from the highest political offices. We might label the passage "Gatekeeper":

> He was the man who ruptured the silent understanding that had governed American politics for two centuries—that this was a country of white Protestant gentry and yeomen who offered newer Americans a choice for leadership only within their clashing rivalries. He made us look at ourselves afresh. Kennedy ended many other myths and fossil assumptions, and with him, an old world of politics and government came to a close.
>
> But how the new world that he ushered in will take shape remains yet to be seen—and thus we cannot finally measure him.
>
> Kennedy was, whether for good or bad, an enormously large figure. Historically, he was a gatekeeper. He unlatched the door, and through the door marched not only Catholics, but blacks, and Jews, and ethnics; women, youth, academics, newspersons, and an entirely new breed of young politicians who did not think of themselves as politicians—all demanding their share of the action and the power in what is now called participatory democracy.

Some people are in the habit of distinguishing between informative and "creative" writing. If we look at what is happening here, though, we can see that White's informative writing is creative: it develops a fresh interpretation of Kennedy partly from the stuff of White's own experience. The subject is the same Kennedy about whom millions of words have been written, but the framework comes from White; comes from being poor, being part of an excluded minority, being nearly shut out from the American dream—and then discovering that there was a way for outsiders like him to succeed.

Just after White's "gatekeeper" passage comes one that we might call the *"gravitas"* passage:

> Liberals, generally, could not see the weight and dignity in Kennedy until well on into the campaign year of 1960; with such outstanding exceptions as Arthur M. Schlesinger, Jr., they considered him a lightweight who had bought his Senate seat with his father's money. Practical politicians saw him more clearly. John Bailey, the "boss" of Connecticut, a veteran of the regular ranks of old politics, once described to me his movement in four years from Stevenson to Kennedy. He had supported Stevenson in both 1952 and 1956, said Bailey, because Stevenson had "heft," and that's what voters wanted in their Presidents. Bailey had probably never heard of the Roman civic phrase *gravitas*, the weightiness that is so becoming to a man of public affairs. But by 1958 Bailey could feel the "heft" he wanted in John F. Kennedy and was mobilizing for him. And by the time he was killed, John Kennedy was accepted fully

for his *gravitas* by liberals, just as much as by politicians and common people who had elected him chiefly because he was elegant, gay, witty, young and attractive.

Here is White at age 63, doing what he had done at age 18: announcing the headlines of his times in Latin, presenting contemporary America in the framework of Roman political thought. This, again, is a personal and creative act: White's lifelong mission was to show that American current events during his lifetime had the "heft" of classical history.

White puts himself in a position to say something by assuming that people have a standard "take" on Kennedy ("witty, young and attractive"), then encouraging them to see Kennedy in frameworks where they probably have not been accustomed to seeing him. Other writers could give us other frameworks. Some might say that Kennedy—white, male, and very rich—unlatched no doors, but instead showed that it was possible to outspend all opponents and buy an election. Some might say that *gravitas* was exactly what Kennedy lacked, that he was a playboy president who loved politics just because he loved every high-stakes game. Consider this passage from Richard Reeve's *President Kennedy: Profile of Power:*

A WRITER AT WORK

"President Kennedy: Profile of Power"
RICHARD REEVE

In hundreds of interviews with the men and women who were around John Kennedy, the story that I tend to remember first was told by Abram Chayes, a Harvard Law School professor who became counsel to the Department of State. He was waiting for the candidate at Washington National Airport one hot August afternoon in 1960, on board the *Caroline,* a twin-engined Convair that was the campaign plane. The two-year-old daughter for whom the plane was named was there along with a half dozen other small children, two pregnant women—Jacqueline Kennedy and Jean Kennedy Smith—and another professor, Walt Rostow, an economist from the Massachusetts Institute of Technology.

Kennedy arrived two hours late for the short flight to a weekend at Hyannis Port. The pilot cranked the propellers into action as soon as he saw Kennedy walk into the airport's private North Terminal. Inside the plane, the passengers watched him at the pay telephones, make one more call, then another and another.

Finally, he came up the stairway to the plane, kissing his wife and sister then strapping them into the plane's two beds, buckling the children into their seats with a flash of conversation for each, leaving lighted little faces in his busy wake. He did the same with the men, focusing on each for a moment. Then, surrounded by smiles and happy chatter, he settled into his seat, a large swivel chair in the center. The stewardess came back with a bowl of his favorite fish chowder, someone handed him the afternoon newspapers, and his barber began to cut his hair as the professors reported to him on their specialties and the issues of the day.

It was almost as if those around him were figures in tableaux,[1] who came alive only when John Kennedy was in place in the center. He was an artist who painted with other people's lives. He squeezed people like tubes of paint, gently or brutally, and the people around him—family, writers, drivers, ladies-in-waiting—were the indentured inhabitants serving his needs and desires.

Each framework brought to bear on the subject may reveal something about the writer as well as about the subject. Not being Theodore White, Reeves can see what White couldn't—and vice versa.

Which is the *real* Kennedy? The question won't leave us alone, but we know that it is in many ways unanswerable, since the truth that every writer gives us is created by an interaction between the subject and frameworks that not everyone shares. In such a case, it is fruitless to talk about *the* truth. At most the writer knows some reliable facts from which he or she constructs *a* truth or *some* truths. The most important writing you will do in college and in your professional life will almost certainly have to do with subjects that can be interpreted in more than one way. "Having something to say" means encouraging readers to set aside, at least briefly, the view they have been inclined to take and to consider, at least briefly, the view you offer in its place.

◆ *Shifting to Thought-Provoking Frameworks.* Implicit in our definition of what makes writing fresh is the idea of a framework shift. We might express this shift with a sentence on the following pattern: "Although people are inclined to see X [the subject] as Y [the common view], it may be better seen as Z [the fresh framework]." The point of departure for this chapter, for example, might be stated as "Although people are inclined to see 'having something to say' as a matter of having fresh data or experiences, it may be better seen as viewing a subject in an unaccustomed way." Imagine that you are assigned essays on each of the ten subjects below:

EXERCISE 2

1. childhood
2. winter
3. homelessness
4. Hillary Rodham Clinton
5. Roseanne Arnold
6. Abraham Lincoln
7. the automobile
8. skin
9. nuclear power
10. soap

For each subject, write a sentence on the "Although people are inclined to see X as Y, it may be better to see it as Z" pattern. Your sentences should assume an audience of general readers that includes your

---

[1] **tableaux:** "Living pictures" created on a stage by actors who remain motionless until they are released by the director's cue.

classmates, and your aim should be to propose a shift in framework that could produce a paper interesting to them.

THREE STANCES FOR WRITERS

As we have seen, essays often grow out of a tension between two ways of viewing the same subject. The writer struggles against an "old" framework, a habitual way of thinking. He or she presents a "new" framework for the reader's consideration. With a little thought we can see that this struggle between habit and freshness accounts for three stances writers often take in successful essays.

The Contrary-to-Popular-Opinion Stance.   This may be the key stance for most undergraduate writing, for the simple reason that it shows the writer is doing the business higher education prepares people to do. The writer recognizes the inadequacies of a framework popular with those who have thought superficially about the subject, and he or she offers another in its place. In recent years, for example, British comedian John Cleese has been delivering a speech that counters the commonplace view that mistakes are indications of weakness. His view is that mistakes, if they are openly made and freely acknowledged, are part of a valuable feedback system: "I suggest that unless we have a tolerant attitude toward mistakes—I might almost say a *positive* attitude toward them—we shall be behaving irrationally, unscientifically, and unsuccessfully."

The writer of a more academic essay might cite an expert who has developed a new idea with which to challenge a familiar assumption: "Although most American workers in the 1990s see themselves as the beneficiaries of labor-saving technology, economist Juliet Schor has demonstrated that today's Americans are caught in a system that has them working more and earning less than their parents did."

The writer stands as someone who has thought harder about the subject than the average person or has taken time to learn what the experts say. There is, of course, a danger of arrogance: to say to the reader, "I know more than you do" can be offensive. The skillful writer finds ways to combine boldness with tact.

The Now-I-Know-Better Stance.   Writers adopting this stance seem to be encountering earlier selves. They contrast their early impressions of the subject with their later, more thoughtful judgment; their naive view with their more mature view. The stance might seem to ignore the audience entirely, but it doesn't. Suppose a writer says, "I used to think that overt racism had become unstylish in the United States, but then I began to listen to the way many college students talk about Arabs." Isn't the writer tactfully assuming that the readers believe overt racism *is* out of fashion and that they have *not* listened to college students talking about Arabs? Only such an audience would feel the full impact of what the writer is about to say. Or suppose a writer says, "The first dozen times I saw *The Wizard of Oz,* I thought it was scary or funny or corny, but definitely kid stuff. Now I've come to think of it as a work of art, goofier than most films and novels intended for adults, but at least as meaningful." The writer is assuming (or inventing) an audience inclined to view the film as "kid stuff." Otherwise, there would be no news to deliver.

The Expert-Opinion-Notwithstanding Stance.   This is the typical stance of experts writing for other experts. Scholars generally take it when they write articles for other scholars; lawyers, when they write briefs for courtroom argument. The writer may review the framework (or frameworks) that influential experts have applied to the subject, then argue that another framework is preferable. This "new" framework may be entirely the writer's own, but it will more likely be grounded in the work of other investigators. The statement below is a fair specimen of the stance:

> Psychoanalyst Bruno Bettelheim sees "Cinderella" primarily as a story about sibling rivalry; feminist Madonna Kolbenschlag sees it primarily as a story about the attractiveness of abasement in women. Both views have obvious merit, but neither adequately takes into account the social history of the tale. What we have here is a story that assures readers that nobility is something that has to do with bloodlines rather than circumstances.

Notice that the writer's setting aside of Bettelheim and Kolbenschlag is not a high-handed dismissal, but an explanation of why their truth doesn't exhaust all Truth about the story. Implied in the expert-opinion-notwithstanding approach is the writer's understanding of the frameworks he or she rejects. Understanding generally produces appreciation, even admiration.

I certainly wouldn't claim that *all* essays and articles use one of these three stances, though if you begin to read with the stances in mind, you'll be surprised how many do. What I will claim is that writing and framework shifting go hand in hand.

AN INTERNAL TEST FOR STANCE

Stance has such a stagey sound to it—like *posture* or *pose*—that I feel compelled to offer a way of distinguishing those stances you or I might adopt as a mere rhetorical trick from those with a deeper legitimacy. The test requires us to ignore the audience for a time and have a conversation with ourselves.

When I think about homelessness in our society, for example, I realize that I alternate between two frameworks. At some moments I believe that all behavior has causes the individual can't control: our genes and our environment are in the driver's seat. At others, I believe we have free will and are responsible for our own conditions in life. One set of beliefs inclines me to charity; one inclines me to hardheartedness. Or if you see the subject differently, one inclines me to be condescending toward the homeless, and one inclines me to treat them as my equals. You could say that on this question, I am involved in an argument with myself. So are millions of other people.

Questions about which people can reasonably disagree even *with themselves*—these are the richest seedbeds for essays. Eventually, successful essayists develop a keen sense for what aspects of a subject are likely to produce this sort of mental division in the reader. I suspect that they do so by attending carefully to the divisions in their own thinking.

A good method of finding your most productive stance is to search for a conflict of frameworks that you feel yourself. If the "old" framework you attribute to your readers has *no* appeal for you, if you can't remember why it was *ever* appealing, it is unlikely to be the common-sense view of your audience. Nor is it likely to stimulate you to produce your best thinking and writing. If, however, the "old" framework has so much appeal for you that you are sometimes tempted to backslide into it, your essay is more likely to succeed. If I were writing an essay on homelessness, I would focus on the question of whether the homeless have somehow chosen their condition. I don't *think* they have, but it is a close and difficult call—the sort of difficult call that might keep me and my readers mentally engaged, with the subject and with one another.

EXERCISE 3

♦ *Developing Stances and Narrowing Topics.* A writer's stance necessarily varies according to audience and circumstance. When the writer aims to address the audience in a casual, modest, unassertive way, the now-I-know-better stance may be best. When he or she formally addresses an academic or professional group, the expert-opinion-notwithstanding stance may be best. Many cases in between are well served by the contrary-to-popular-opinion stance. The subject can be defined (narrowed) in a way that makes the chosen stance workable. If, for instance, the general subject is Texans, a writer might take the contrary-to-popular-opinion stance with a statement like this:

> "Don't mess with Texas," a popular bumper sticker reads, and the witless arrogance it seems to express is what many people expect to find in Texans. In actuality, Texans find Texans an inexhaustible source of humor.

Or the writer could take the now-I-know-better stance with a statement like this:

> Growing up in a military family that moved every few years, I used to doubt that there was any dramatic connection between geography and character; then I moved to West Texas and learned how wrong I had been.

Or the writer might adopt the expert-opinion-notwithstanding stance with a statement like the next, with scholarly articles cited in parentheses:

> Several researchers have noted that the self-images of Texas men are connected with such "masculine" icons as the truck (Spearit 1983, Johnson 1978), the cowboy hat (Jones 1991, Argentary 1984, Wills 1957), and the game of football (Wilson 1989). What these studies have overlooked is that the self-image of Texas *women* is connected almost as strongly with the same "masculine" icons.

For each subject listed below, develop statements comparable to those above. Try to write statements that could produce an effective essay. For the purposes of this exercise, feel free to invent articles by experts, as I have done in my example about masculine icons.

a. baseball
b. motherhood
c. religion
d. the president
e. railroads

Assignments for Chapter 1

ASSIGNMENT 1: **A Short Essay with a Reconsidered Subject**

The process of completing exercises 2 and 3 in this chapter should have provided you with some ideas worth developing into an essay. Choose the most promising of these ideas and develop it into an essay about 500 words long.

ASSIGNMENT 2: **Sow's Ears**

One of the home truths about writing is that the writer rarely has an absolutely free choice of subjects and that many assigned subjects leave the writer cold. Faced with this unhappy situation, successful writers manage to make a silk purse out of a sow's ear. Finding a framework in which the subject will come to life is the key.

Listed below are four classic sow's ears, subjects that for decades have produced mountains of bad student writing. Write a short essay (your instructor will specify the length) that redeems one of those subjects by putting it into a context that brings it to life.

1. An unforgettable character.
2. A memorable book or movie.
3. An event that changed my life.
4. School days.

VARIATION: In the hands of good writers, these sow's ears have produced a number of silk purses. Listed below are essays or chapters that redeem one of the subjects above.

1. *An unforgettable character.*
   Joan Didion, "Quiet Days at Malibu" (p. 100)
   Annie Dillard, "Mother" (p. 110)

2. *A memorable book, movie, or lecture.*
   Henry Louis Gates Jr., "Malcolm, the Aardvark and Me" (p. 26)
   David Denby, "Emotional Rescue" (p. 490)

3. *An event that changed my life.*
   Samuel Scudder, "Learning to See" (p. 23)
   George Orwell, "Shooting an Elephant" (p. 143)

4. *School days.*
   Anna Quindlen, "Nuns" (p. 28)
   Roger Wilkins, "Confessions of a Blue-Chip Black" (p. 157)

Read one of these essays and write a paragraph explaining how the writer brings it to life by putting it in an unusual or important framework.

ASSIGNMENT 3   ## INFORMAL SUMMARIES

A standard assignment in many college courses is a short essay summarizing an article or book assigned for class. These essays may be "formal" in the sense that they attempt to reflect precisely the structure of the work they summarize. More often they are informal, allowing the reader to recast the information in whatever way seems most useful. Your assignment here is to write an informal summary of any of the essays collected in *The Riverside Guide to Writing.* Among the likely candidates are these:

Alan Dershowitz, "The Old Itch to Censor" (p. 412)
Margaret Mead, "Warfare Is Only an Invention, Not a Biological
   Necessity" (p. 377)
Annie Dillard, "Singing with the Fundamentalists" (p. 568)
Jessica Mitford, "Let Us Now Appraise Famous Writers" (p. 227)

There are innumerable ways to handle such assignments, but the three modeled below are particularly useful in helping you assimilate what you have read. Your instructor may ask you either to follow one of the models or to write three summaries of the same essay, each following a different model.

MODEL 1:
A DETAIL/
FRAMEWORK
SUMMARY
As we have seen, writers do their work largely by finding a relationship between small details of a subject and the larger framework into which the subject fits. One way to summarize a chapter or essay is by writing a paragraph that begins with a small detail from the passage you are summarizing, moves quickly to the largest generalization in the essay, and then moves back to other details. The aim in such a summary is not to alter the author's interpretation, but to encapsulate it. This encapsulated summary should give an undistorted view of the essay to someone who has not read it or should serve you as a reliable reminder after the essay itself has faded in your memory. The following 200-word distillation of Joan Didion's "Marrying Absurd" (p. 20) is a fairly typical detail/framework summary.

> In "Marrying Absurd" Joan Didion quotes James A. Brennan, Justice of the Peace in Las Vegas, who says that when he performed sixty-seven weddings in three hours, "I got it down from five to three minutes. . . . I could've married them en masse, but they're people, not cattle.

People expect more when they get married." The quotation is typical of the essay, which discusses Las Vegas weddings as extreme examples of both the American "devotion to instant gratification" and the American desire for a "niceness" that instant gratification isn't likely to produce. The essay concentrates on the speed and impersonality of the weddings, carried out in a city so devoted to gambling and pleasure that events there seem to have "no connection with 'real' life," let alone to the consecration of lifetime unions. "Services" (including the providing of rings and witnesses) that ought to make a wedding seem solid and traditional can be rented or purchased on the spot, at any time of the day or night, "presumably on the assumption that marriage, like craps, is a game to be played when the table seems hot." On the other hand, Didion points out that for many who are married in Las Vegas, speed and convenience are not the only issues. Las Vegas wedding chapels sell "'niceness,' the facsimile of proper ritual, to children who do not know how else to find it."

MODEL 2: A SUMMARY IN THE FRAMEWORK OF THE AUTHOR'S LIFE AND WORK

More difficult than the detail/framework summary, but often more enlightening, is a summary that begins by identifying a dominant theme in the writer's life and work and then shows how a particular essay (down to its particular details) is a part of his or her larger "project" as a writer. Such a summary requires a trip to the library, but not necessarily a prolonged one. If the author is well known, you should be able to find adequate information in a good encyclopedia, in *Current Biography,* or in *Contemporary Authors,* which is the source primarily relied on in the following example.

A critic once said of Joan Didion (1934–) that "ghastliness and pointlessness" are her "invariable themes." Born into a stable family with conventional values, Didion seems to favor tradition, conservatism, and control. Until she lost interest in political labels, she called herself a Republican, and she has written essays criticizing the women's liberation movement and praising John Wayne's adherence, on screen and off, to "the Code" of old-fashioned decencies. Confronted by the social chaos of the 1960s, Didion became curious and alarmed. In fact, she began *Slouching Toward Bethlehem,* her 1969 collection of essays, by quoting W. B. Yeats's poem "The Second Coming": "Things fall apart; the center cannot hold;/Mere anarchy is loosed upon the world."

"Marrying Absurd" (1966), one of the essays in that collection, shows traditional marriage reduced to a ghastly and almost pointless parody in the wedding chapels of Las Vegas. Didion emphasizes the extreme impersonality of what should be a most personal ceremony. One Justice of the Peace, she points out, married sixty-seven couples in three hours, getting the "ceremony" down from five minutes to three. The chapels advertise their services with the sort of garishness that the casinos do, and they offer them around the clock "presumably on the premise that marriage, like craps, is a game to be played when the table is hot." In Las Vegas, Didion sees a typical sight, a drunken bride "in an orange mini-dress and flame-colored hair." More depressing still is the sight of a pregnant bride sitting in a Strip restaurant after her hurried wedding: "'It was just as nice,' she sobbed, 'as I hoped and dreamed it would be.'" The Las Vegas version of "niceness," "the facsimile of proper ritual," is for Didion another sign that things are falling apart.

MODEL 3:
A SUMMARY IN
A FRAMEWORK
THE READER
PROVIDES

A reader who is also a thinker and writer will sometimes want to pluck the subject of an essay or chapter out of the author's framework and place it in a context that comes from his or her own mind. The following example shows how someone skeptical about the economic specialization in twentieth-century life (not a major concern of Didion's) brings Didion's subject into his context. Notice that the summary characterizes the essay accurately, though from an angle Didion might think slightly odd.

Nearly a century and a half ago, Henry David Thoreau said that our tendency to turn aspects of our lives over to specialists could get us into trouble. "Where is this division of labor to end? and what object does it finally serve? No doubt another may also think for me, but it is not therefore desirable that he should do so to the exclusion of my thinking for myself." In her essay "Marrying Absurd" Joan Didion gives us an example of specialization producing results that are sad and disturbing. The essay describes Las Vegas, "the most extreme and allegorical of American settlements," a place that stands in the middle of the desert and has no traditional industry, but has developed two "service industries." The town supports itself by offering entertainment (notably gambling) or weddings, products that in the nineteenth century were made at home with very little specialized assistance. Though Didion touches on entertainment, her primary subject is the weddings performed in the city's nineteen "wedding chapels." These weddings are produced with great efficiency: one Justice of the Peace, faced with high demand for his eight-dollar ceremony, squeezed it down to three minutes. The services the chapels offer are remarkably complete. For a price, they can provide rings, witnesses, transportation, music—all the things that once had to be produced laboriously by those who cared about the bride and groom and wanted to see their marriage properly launched. A ceremony that once belonged to the community and family has been turned over to strangers. It isn't, as Didion points out, merely a matter of convenience. It is also that many rootless people have lost the old knowledge of how to make a wedding. Las Vegas is "merchandising 'niceness,' the facsimile of proper ritual, to children who do not know how else to find it, how to make the arrangements, how to do it 'right.'"

MARRYING ABSURD

Joan Didion

From 1967 to 1969 Joan Didion and her husband, the novelist and screenwriter John Gregory Dunne, alternately wrote a column ("Points West") for the *Saturday Evening Post*. The subjects for Didion's columns were often places, seen in the framework of the cultural upheaval of the 1960s. "Marrying Absurd" appeared in the *Post* on December 16, 1967, and was collected in her book *Slouching Towards Bethlehem* in 1968.

1 TO BE MARRIED IN LAS VEGAS, CLARK County, Nevada, a bride must swear that she is eighteen or has parental permission and a bridegroom that he is twenty-one or has parental permission. Someone must put up five dollars for the license. (On Sundays and holidays, fifteen dollars. The Clark County Courthouse issues marriage licenses at any time of the day or night except between noon and one in the afternoon, between eight and nine in the evening, and between four and five in the morning.) Nothing else is required. The State of Nevada, alone among these United States, demands neither a premarital blood test nor a waiting period before or after the issuance of a marriage license. Driving in across the Mojave from Los Angeles, one sees the signs way out on the desert, looming up from that moonscape of rattlesnakes and mesquite, even before the Las Vegas lights appear like a mirage on the horizon: "GETTING MARRIED? Free License Information First Strip Exit." Perhaps the Las Vegas wedding industry achieved its peak operational efficiency between 9:00 P.M. and midnight of August 26, 1965, an otherwise unremarkable Thursday which happened to be, by Presidential order, the last day on which anyone could improve his draft status merely by getting married. One hundred and seventy-one couples were pronounced man and wife in the name of Clark County and the State of Nevada that night, sixty-seven of them by a single justice of the peace, Mr. James A. Brennan. Mr. Brennan did one wedding at the Dunes and the other sixty-six in his office, and charged each couple eight dollars. One bride lent her veil to six others. "I got it down from five to three minutes," Mr. Brennan said later of his feat. "I could've married them *en masse,* but they're people, not cattle. People expect more when they get married."

2 What people who get married in Las Vegas actually do expect—what, in the largest sense, their "expectations" are—strikes one as a curious and self-contradictory business. Las Vegas is the most extreme and allegorical of American settlements, bizarre and beautiful in its venality and in its devotion to immediate gratification, a place the tone of which is set by mobsters and call girls and ladies' room attendants with amyl nitrite poppers in their uniform pockets. Almost everyone notes that there is no "time" in Las Vegas, no night and no day and no past and no future (no Las Vegas casino, however, has taken the obliteration of the ordinary time sense quite so far as Harold's Club in Reno, which for a while issued, at odd intervals in the day and night, mimeographed "bulletins" carrying news from the world outside); neither is there any logical

sense of where one is. One is standing on a highway in the middle of a vast hostile desert looking at an eighty-foot sign which blinks "STARDUST" or "CAESAR'S PALACE." Yes, but what does that explain? This geographical implausibility reinforces the sense that what happens there has no connection with "real" life; Nevada cities like Reno and Carson are ranch towns, Western towns, places behind which there is some historical imperative. But Las Vegas seems to exist only in the eye of the beholder. All of which makes it an extraordinarily stimulating and interesting place, but an odd one in which to want to wear a candlelight satin Priscilla of Boston wedding dress with Chantilly lace insets, tapered sleeves and a detachable modified train.

3   And yet the Las Vegas wedding business seems to appeal to precisely that impulse. "Sincere and Dignified Since 1954," one wedding chapel advertises. There are nineteen such wedding chapels in Las Vegas, intensely competitive, each offering better, faster, and, by implication, more sincere services than the next: Our Photos Best Anywhere, Your Wedding on A Phonograph Record, Candlelight with Your Ceremony, Honeymoon Accommodations, Free Transportation from Your Motel to Courthouse to Chapel and Return to Motel, Religious or Civil Ceremonies, Dressing Rooms, Flowers, Rings, Announcements, Witnesses Available, and Ample Parking. All of these services, like most others in Las Vegas (sauna baths, payroll-check cashing, chinchilla coats for sale or rent), are offered twenty-four hours a day, seven days a week, presumably on the premise that marriage, like craps, is a game to be played when the table seems hot.

4   But what strikes one most about the Strip chapels, with their wishing wells and stained-glass paper windows and their artificial bouvardia, is that so much of their business is by no means a matter of simple convenience, of late-night liaisons between show girls and baby Crosbys.[1] Of course there is some of that. (One night about eleven o'clock in Las Vegas I watched a bride in an orange minidress and masses of flame-colored hair stumble from a Strip chapel on the arm of her bridegroom, who looked the part of the expendable nephew in movies like *Miami Syndicate.* "I gotta get the kids," the bride whimpered. "I gotta pick up the sitter, I gotta get to the midnight show." "What you gotta get," the bridegroom said, opening the door of a Cadillac Coupe de Ville and watching her crumple on the seat, "is sober.") But Las Vegas seems to offer something other than "convenience"; it is merchandising "niceness," the facsimile of proper ritual, to children who do not know how else to find it, how to make the arrangements, how to do it "right." All day and evening long on the Strip, one sees actual wedding parties, waiting under the harsh lights at a crosswalk, standing uneasily in the parking lot of the Frontier while the photographer hired by The Little Church of the West ("Wedding Place of the Stars") certifies the occasion, takes the picture: the bride in a veil and white satin pumps, the bridegroom usually in a white dinner jacket, and even an attendant or two, a sister or a best friend in hot-pink *peau de soie,* a flirtation veil, a carnation nosegay. "When I Fall in Love It Will Be Forever," the organist plays, and then a few bars of *Lohengrin.* The mother cries; the stepfather, awkward in his role, invites the chapel hostess to join them for a drink at the Sands. The hostess declines with a professional smile; she has already transferred her interest to the group waiting outside. One bride out, another in, and again the sign goes up on the chapel door: "One moment please— Wedding."

5   I sat next to one such wedding party in a Strip restaurant the last time I was in Las Vegas. The marriage had just taken place; the

---

[1] **baby Crosbys:** Male singers; the name alludes to crooner Bing Crosby (1904–77).

bride still wore her dress, the mother her corsage. A bored waiter poured out a few swallows of pink champagne ("on the house") for everyone but the bride, who was too young to be served. "You'll need something with more kick than that," the bride's father said with heavy jocularity to his new son-in-law; the ritual jokes about the wedding night had a certain Panglossian[2] character, since the bride was clearly several months pregnant. Another round of pink champagne, this time not on the house, and the bride began to cry. "It was just as nice," she sobbed, "as I hoped and dreamed it would be." ◆

_____

[2] **Panglossian:** Pangloss, a philosopher in Voltaire's novel *Candide* (1758), often expressed a foolish optimism in the face of dire situations.

LEARNING TO SEE

Samuel Scudder

Samuel Scudder (1837–1911) was one of the most productive scientists of his time, specializing in the discovery and description of insect species, living or fossilized. In the essay below, he recalls a turning point in his education: his study under the great naturalist Louis Agassiz, who made Harvard University the center for natural history instruction and research during the mid-nineteenth century.

1   IT WAS MORE THAN FIFTEEN YEARS AGO THAT I entered the laboratory of Professor Agassiz, and told him I had enrolled my name in the Scientific School as a student of natural history. He asked me a few questions about my object in coming, my antecedents generally, the mode in which I afterwards proposed to use the knowledge I might acquire, and, finally, whether I wished to study any special branch. To the latter I replied that, while I wished to be well grounded in all departments of zoology, I purposed to devote myself specially to insects.

2   "When do you wish to begin?" he asked.

3   "Now," I replied.

4   This seemed to please him, and with an energetic "Very well!" he reached from a shelf a huge jar of specimens in yellow alcohol.

5   "Take this fish," said he, "and look at it; we call it a haemulon; by and by I will ask what you have seen."

6   With that he left me, but in a moment returned with explicit instructions as to the care of the object entrusted to me.

7   "No man is fit to be a naturalist," said he, "who does not know how to take care of specimens."

8   I was to keep the fish before me in a tin tray, and occasionally moisten the surface with alcohol from the jar, always taking care to replace the stopper tightly. Those were not the days of ground-glass stoppers and elegantly shaped exhibition jars; all the old students will recall the huge neckless glass bottles with their leaky, wax-besmeared corks, half eaten by insects, and begrimed with cellar dust. Entomology was a cleaner science than ichthyology, but the example of the Professor, who had unhesitatingly plunged to the bottom of the jar to produce the fish, was infectious; and though this alcohol had a "very ancient and fishlike smell,"[1] I really dared not show any aversion within these sacred precincts, and treated the alcohol as though it were pure water. Still I was conscious of a passing feeling of disappointment, for gazing at a fish did not commend itself to an ardent entomologist. My friends at home, too, were annoyed when they discovered that no amount of eau-de-Cologne would drown the perfume which haunted me like a shadow.

9   In ten minutes I had seen all that could be seen in that fish, and started in search of the Professor—who had, however, left the Museum; and when I returned, after lingering over some of the odd animals stored in the upper apartment, my specimen was dry all over. I dashed the fluid over the fish as if to resuscitate the beast from a fainting-fit, and looked with anxiety for a return of the normal sloppy

_____
[1] "a very ancient and fishlike smell": Shakespeare, *The Tempest*, II, ii, 25.

appearance. This little excitement over, nothing was to be done but to return to a steadfast gaze at my mute companion. Half an hour passed—an hour—another hour; the fish began to look loathsome. I turned it over and around; looked it in the face—ghastly; from behind, beneath, above, sideways, at a three-quarters' view—just as ghastly. I was in despair; at an early hour I concluded that lunch was necessary; so, with infinite relief, the fish was carefully replaced in the jar, and for an hour I was free.

10   On my return, I learned that Professor Agassiz had been at the Museum, but had gone, and would not return for several hours. My fellow-students were too busy to be disturbed by continued conversation. Slowly I drew forth that hideous fish, and with a feeling of desperation again looked at it. I might not use a magnifying-glass; instruments of all kinds were interdicted. My two hands, my two eyes, and the fish; it seemed a most limited field. I pushed my finger down its throat to feel how sharp the teeth were. I began to count the scales in the different rows, until I was convinced that that was nonsense. At last a happy thought struck me—I would draw the fish; and now with surprise I began to discover new features in the creature. Just then the Professor returned.

11   "That is right," said he; "a pencil is one of the best of eyes. I am glad to notice, too, that you keep your specimen wet, and your bottle corked."

12   With these encouraging words, he added:

13   "Well, what is it like?"

14   He listened attentively to my brief rehearsal of the structure of parts whose names were still unknown to me: the fringed gill-arches and movable operculum; the pores of the head, fleshy lips and lidless eyes; the lateral line, the spinous fins and forked tail; the compressed and arched body. When I had finished, he waited as if expecting more, and then, with an air of disappointment:

"You have not looked very carefully; why,"   15 he continued more earnestly, "you haven't even seen one of the most conspicuous features of the animal, which is as plainly before your eyes as the fish itself; look again, look again!" and he left me to my misery.

I was piqued; I was mortified. Still more of   16 that wretched fish! But now I set myself to my task with a will, and discovered one new thing after another, until I saw how just the Professor's criticism had been. The afternoon passed quickly; and when, toward its close, the Professor inquired:

"Do you see it yet?"   17

"No," I replied, "I am certain I do not, but   18 I see how little I saw before."

"That is next best," said he, earnestly, "but   19 I won't hear you now; put away your fish and go home; perhaps you will be ready with a better answer in the morning. I will examine you before you look at the fish."

This was disconcerting. Not only must I   20 think of my fish all night, studying, without the object before me, what this unknown but most visible feature might be; but also, without reviewing my discoveries, I must give an exact account of them the next day. I had a bad memory; so I walked home by Charles River in a distracted state, with my two perplexities.

The cordial greeting from the Professor the   21 next morning was reassuring; here was a man who seemed to be quite as anxious as I that I should see for myself what he saw.

"Do you perhaps mean," I asked, "that the   22 fish has symmetrical sides with paired organs?"

His thoroughly pleased "Of course! of   23 course!" repaid the wakeful hours of the previous night. After he had discoursed most happily and enthusiastically—as he always did—upon the importance of this point, I ventured to ask what I should do next.

"Oh, look at your fish!" he said, and left   24 me again to my own devices. In a little more than an hour he returned, and heard my new catalogue.

25   "That is good, that is good!" he repeated; "but that is not all; go on"; and so for three long days he placed that fish before my eyes, forbidding me to look at anything else, or to use any artificial aid. "Look, look, look," was his repeated injunction.

26   This was the best entomological lesson I ever had—a lesson whose influence has extended to the details of every subsequent study; a legacy the Professor has left to me, as he has left it to many others, of inestimable value, which we could not buy, with which we cannot part.

27   A year afterward, some of us were amusing ourselves with chalking outlandish beasts on the Museum blackboard. We drew prancing starfishes; frogs in mortal combat; hydra-headed worms; stately crawfishes, standing on their tails, bearing aloft umbrellas; and grotesque fishes with gaping mouths and staring eyes. The Professor came in shortly after, and was as amused as any at our experiments. He looked at the fishes.

28   "Haemulons, every one of them," he said; "Mr. _____ drew them."

29   True; and to this day, if I attempt a fish, I can draw nothing but haemulons.

30   The fourth day, a second fish of the same group was placed beside the first, and I was bidden to point out the resemblances and differences between the two; another and another followed, until the entire family lay before me, and a whole legion of jars covered the table and surrounding shelves; the odor had become a pleasant perfume; and even now, the sight of an old, six-inch, worm-eaten cork brings fragrant memories.

31   The whole group of haemulons was thus brought in review; and, whether engaged upon the dissection of the internal organs, the preparation and examination of the bony framework, or the description of the various parts, Agassiz's training in the method of observing facts and their orderly arrangement was ever accompanied by the urgent exhortation not to be content with them.

32   "Facts are stupid things," he would say, "until brought into connection with some general law."

33   At the end of eight months, it was almost with reluctance that I left these friends and turned to insects; but what I had gained by this outside experience has been of greater value than years of later investigation in my favorite groups. ◆

MALCOLM, THE AARDVARK AND ME

Henry Louis Gates Jr.

No less than boats and baby carriages, books have different meanings in the eyes of different readers. In the brief essay that follows, Henry Louis Gates Jr., now a professor at Harvard University, recalls the way that *The Autobiography of Malcolm X* struck him when he was a 17-year-old high school student "in a village in the hills of West Virginia."

1 ONE OF THE MOST GRATIFYING EFFECTS of Spike Lee's film *Malcolm X* is that its success has prompted the restoration of Malcolm's autobiography to the best-seller lists. The country is *reading* the 1965 book once again, as avidly, it seems, as it is seeing Mr. Lee's movie. For 17 weeks *The Autobiography of Malcolm X*, written with the assistance of Alex Haley, has been on the *New York Times* paperback best-seller list, and for 10 of those weeks it was No. 1. Today, on the 28th anniversary of his assassination, Malcolm's story has become as American—to borrow H. Rap Brown's famous aphorism—as violence and cherry pie.

2 Malcolm first came into my life some three decades ago, when I was nine years old and Mike Wallace and CBS broadcast a documentary about the Nation of Islam. It was called *The Hate That Hate Produced,* and it showed just about the scariest black people I had ever seen: black people who talked right into the faces of white people, telling them off without even blinking. While I sat in our living room, I happened to glance over at my mother. A certain radiance was slowly transforming her soft brown face, as she listened to Malcolm naming the white man as the devil. "Amen," she said, quietly at first, "All right, now," she continued, much more emphatically. All this time and I had not known just how deeply my mother despised white people. The revelation was terrifying but thrilling.

3 The book came into my life much later.

4 I was almost 17, a junior in high school, and I was slowly and pleasurably devouring *Ebony* magazine. More precisely, I was reading a profile of the Roman Catholic basketball player Lew Alcindor, who was then a star at UCLA and who later became a legend with the Los Angeles Lakers as the Muslim basketball player Kareem Abdul-Jabbar. In the profile he said that *The Autobiography of Malcolm X* had meant more to him than any other book, and that *all* black Americans should read it—*today.*

5 Today was not possible for me, since I lived in a village in the hills of West Virginia where nobody carried such things. I had to go down to Red Bowl's newsstand, make a deposit and wait while they sent away for it. But when the book arrived, I read it straight through the night, as struck by its sepia-colored photograph of a dangerous-looking, gesticulating Malcolm as I was by the contents, the riveting saga of a man on the run, from whites (as the son of a Garveyite father) and blacks (his former mentors and colleagues at the Nation of Islam, after his falling-out with Elijah Muhammad).

6 I loved the hilarious scene in which Malcolm is having his hair "conked," or "pro-

26

cessed" ("relaxed" remains the euphemism); unable to rinse out the burning lye because the pipes in his home are frozen, he has no recourse but to dunk his head in a toilet bowl. A few months before, the benignly parochial principal of our high school had "paddled" my schoolmate Arthur Galloway when Arthur told him that his processed hairstyle was produced by a mixture of eggs, mashed potatoes, and lye. "Don't lie to me, boy," the principal was heard saying above Arthur's protests.

7   What I remembered most, though, is Malcolm's discussion of the word "aardvark".

8   "I saw that the best thing I could do was get hold of a dictionary—to study. . . . I spent two days just riffling uncertainly through the dictionary's pages. I'd never realized so many words existed! . . . Funny thing, from the dictionary first page right now, that 'aardvark' springs to my mind. The dictionary had a picture of it, a long-tailed, long-eared, burrowing African mammal, which lives off termites caught by sticking out its tongue as an anteater does for ants."

9   Years later, near the end of his life, Malcolm found himself heading to the American Museum of Natural History in New York to learn more about that exotic creature, even while trying to figure out how to avoid an almost certain Muslim death sentence. "Boy! I never will forget that old aardvark!" he had mused to Alex Haley. What manner of politician was this, I wondered, in this the year that Stokely Carmichael and Rap Brown, Eldridge Cleaver and Huey P. Newton, Ron Karenga

and Amiri Baraka, simultaneously declared themselves to be the legitimate sons of Malcolm the father, to linger with aardvarks when his world was collapsing around him?

Although Malcolm proudly avowed that he 10 read no fiction (he says he read only one novel "since I started serious reading," and that was *Uncle Tom's Cabin*), he still loved fiction— "fiction" defined as a making, a creating, with words. His speeches—such as the oft-repeated "Ballot or the Bullet" or "Bandung Conference"—are masterpieces of the rhetorical arts. More than Martin Luther King Jr., more than any of the black nationalists or the neo-Marxists, Malcolm X was a *writer,* a wordsmith.

In 1968, my English teacher told me that in 11 years to come, long after the civil rights struggle was a footnote in history, this man would be remembered—like St. Augustine, like Benjamin Franklin, like Henry Adams—because of his gift with words. High praise: and yet the teacher's observation, I must confess, didn't go down well with me at the time. Imagining the book stretched on the autopsy slab of purely literary analysis, I somehow felt that the overriding immediacy of Malcolm's experience— and my special relation to it—had been diminished. Despite Malcolm's cautious if heartfelt moves toward universalism, I felt that part of him would always belong to African mammals like aardvarks, like me. ◆

Nuns

Anna Quindlen

Anna Quindlen's "Life in the 30's" column appeared in the *New York Times* and other newspapers from 1986 through 1988. In a sense, the column was a "retreat to the home front" for a reporter who had previously written about more public matters; but as "Nuns" illustrates, Quindlen's essays about her individual life are framed by social and political concerns. Quindlen continues to be an active and popular columnist. In 1992 her work won her a Pulitzer Prize.

1   THE MOST COMPELLING QUESTION OF MY girlhood was whether nuns had hair. Occasionally, when we were taken by Mother Thérèse to the yard beside the school, as we eddied about her long black legless skirts in our duffle coats and saddle shoes, a strong wind would lift the heavy black serge of her veil, and one of us—that day's celebrity— would glimpse a strand or two at the nape of her neck. For days we would conjecture whether it was merely the popular pixie cut under there, or whether her entire scalp had been shaved and what we had seen was just an oversight. A few girls of a Jesuitical turn of mind suggested that perhaps she had hair just like ours and that it was braided or pinned up. No one ever took them very seriously.

2   The nuns were, with the exception of my family and one or two fast friends, the most important force in my formative years. It is popular now to think of them as a joke or an anachronism, to suggest that the nuns taught little more than that a well-placed ruler hurt like the dickens and that boys were only after one thing, but that was not what I learned from them at all. I learned that women were smart and capable, could live in community to- gether without men, and in fact did not need men much.

3   I am sure that being under the constant sway of human beings living in a state of enforced employment and chastity must have had some blacker reverberations, and I know

the nuns attached too much value to our being well behaved, to sitting with backs straight and hands folded. But today it is the good things I remember. I suspect, deep down, that some of those women turned me into a femi- nist. I wonder what they would think of that? For the nuns were intelligent, most of them, and they seemed in charge. The place where they lived smelled of furniture polish and horse- hair-stuffed brocade and reeked of order, and if in the morning there was chalk on their sim- ple yet majestic habits, by afternoon it was gone.

4   I attended Catholic school just as the sover- eignty of the church over the lives of its citi- zens was beginning, very slowly, to crumble. It was still a time when the Roman Catholic son who chose the priesthood beat the one who went to medical school hands down, when a Catholic daughter chose habitual pregnancy or the convent. Often it was the brightest and the most ambitious who took the latter course, which offered, in some orders, the opportunity for education and advancement. But it must have also seemed an attractive life when faced with the alternatives. I know that what I found most seductive about the convent was the place itself. Growing up in and among families where children—in various stages of undress, distress, and toilet training—outnumbered adults, I thought it was a place of wonderful peace and quiet. There were no fingerprints on the mahogany table tops.

5   My recollection is that the woman who founded the order that taught me, a somewhat upper-crusty group that ran private rather than mere parochial schools, had even been a wife and mother and had thrown it over for the convent. The story was that her husband decided he had a calling for the priesthood and somehow got a dispensation to follow it despite a sizable family, and his wife then decided to enter religious life. He changed his mind—that's men for you—but she refused to change hers. When I was a schoolgirl, the founder was being pushed very heavily for sainthood. No mixed messages in that story. The religious life was a higher way.

6   Nuns seemed sure of themselves. Perhaps, in order to style oneself a bride of Christ, self-confidence must be part of the costume. It was not their supremacy but their vulnerability that we found most disturbing. On those rare occasions when Mother Thérèse wept, it seemed to me now, of course, that she was high-strung, quite young, and very pretty, and that seventh grade combined with poverty, chastity, and obedience must have been heavy going. And we often gave her good reason to cry.

7   I never heard a word about sex from the nuns. I learned that clunker about patent-leather shoes reflecting up from a fat girl who had older sisters when both of us were in fifth grade. There were only two kinds of men I ever saw the sisters with: the priests, upon whom they danced attendance with an air both deferential and slightly flirtatious, and our fathers, who were either hangdog and very proper, or embarrassingly jovial and jokey. I know now that the sisters were in masculine thrall, both to Rome and to various philanthropists, relying on one for the rules by which they lived and the other for the money and the clothes and the house in which to do the living. But it seemed to me that they took good care of themselves.

8   I always thought the nuns were somehow sterner and less warm with the boys than with the girls, although my husband says he had a teacher who thought the girls were second-rate because they could never become priests. And there was always one—I remember mine as vividly as if she were glaring over the top of this page, hissing, "Miss Quindlen, is that you whispering in the back of my classroom?"—who was mean and angry and sadistic. But most of them were like Sister Mary Luke, tall, pale, her enfolding embrace exaggerated by her uniform capelet, who was wonderful with playground spills and played a mean game of volleyball; or Mother Mary Ephrem, who made me learn a new, arcane word from the dictionary every day of eighth grade so that someday I would be doing precisely what I am doing now.

9   I remember the sisters running down a hockey field or out on the polished wood of the basketball court, driving or dribbling, their voluminous skirts held up by huge safety pins that they always kept pinned to their bodices. I was amazed to hear from other girls that *athletics* were only for boys; a Catholic schoolgirl learns *sports,* led by a nun.

10   Above all it seemed to me that the nuns who taught us had their own lives—much more so than my mother, who was parceled out to many others, our family's community property. I always pictured the sisters, each with a cool white bedroom in the top reaches of their stone house, no rug on the floor, a crucifix over the bed, books on the bureau. One of my most enduring memories is the last day of school each year, when we would fly down the street and they would stand on the steps and wave, waiting until the last child was gone before turning back and readying the classrooms for their long rest. I never saw the nuns during the summer months. I always wondered if they went swimming, and, if so, what they wore. I imagined this community of capable women gathered at a beach house somewhere, in white habits instead of their workaday black, playing volleyball, batting the ball back and forth over the net, their ankles flashing. ◆

2 Writing for an Audience

IN RECENT YEARS VISUALIZATION HAS BECOME AN IMPORTANT PART OF sports psychology. The tennis player is encouraged to imagine herself, feet planted firmly, hands gripping the racquet in just the right position, driving a perfect cross-court backhand. Or the basketball player is urged to visualize himself rising, wrist cocked, eyes on the back of the rim, sending his jump shot over the hands of a defender—perfect follow-through, nothing but net. Creating a mental picture of the successful act is one key to finding the "groove" all athletes look for. Without the picture, practice is merely exercise. The more time I spend writing and teaching writing, the more I become convinced that visualization is a key to success here, too. But what needs to be visualized? Not the fingers curling perfectly over the keyboard, certainly.

Perhaps what writers visualize most often is the moment when someone reads the page. The exact scenario will vary from writer to writer and from situation to situation. It may be a picture of an instructor sitting at a desk cluttered with papers, laughing aloud when she encounters a comic passage. It may be a picture of the boss reading a memo, realizing how clear and persuasive it is, and immediately taking the time to read it through again, slowly. It may be a picture of a man reading a newspaper column at the breakfast table and saying to his wife, "Listen to this!" Your visualization defines your ambition as a writer. When the poet Tennyson was eleven years old, he began to collect his writing in a notebook labeled

Vol. I   The Poetry of Tennyson
Vol. II   The Lyrical Poetry of Tennyson
Vol. III   The Prose Writings of Tennyson

Though the notebook contained only sixty-three pages, young Tennyson clearly visualized the moment when future readers would pull thick volumes from their library shelves to do some serious reading.

I certainly don't want to urge Tennyson's vision on anyone, but I do often tell students that they have reached the point in their careers where they need to see themselves as writing for a *public*. Until we reach college, most of us write for readers we know quite well—papers for teachers we see every day, letters for family members and friends. Important as these readers may be, they aren't often the kind of audience that encourages a writer to grow and experiment. A high school student writing about a Shakespeare play for a teacher who seems to worship Shakespeare may feel enormous pressure to echo her enthusiasm: " 'Shakespeare's *Macbeth* is truly one of the greatest plays ever written.'—That should show Ms. Gulch that I'm on her side." A niece writing her aunt and uncle to thank them for a birthday gift is rarely in a position to be candid and insightful. "Frankly, I think *The Prophet* is about the sappiest book I've ever read, but thanks for giving me a copy" is an unlikely beginning for a thank-you note; and even if it were followed by a brilliant critique of the book, the brilliance would be out of place.

Ordinarily, writing for audiences we know well means writing in a way that does no damage to existing relationships. Writing for an audience of strangers—a public—means visualizing a new relationship, one where we have more freedom and more power. As E. B. White put it, "The essayist arises in the morning and, if he has work to do, selects his garb from an unusually extensive wardrobe: he can pull on any sort of shirt, be any sort of person, according to his mood and his subject matter—philosopher, scold, jester, raconteur, confidant, pundit, devil's advocate, enthusiast." When you visualize yourself writing for a public, you give yourself the sort of freedom people sometimes experience when they move out of the old neighborhood and into a strange city. The slate is wiped clean. You have no reputation, so you escape from who you *were* in the eyes of friends, family, and teachers, and make fresh decisions about who you *are* and *will become*.

VISUALIZING THE AUDIENCE FOR COLLEGE WRITING

"But wait," you might object. "Writing in college is *not* writing for an audience of strangers, any more than writing in high school is. It is writing for an instructor or—if there is peer review—writing for an instructor and some classmates."

True, a paper written for a college class is not as public a document as a column written for the *New York Times,* not as separated from face-to-face relationships. Nevertheless, the "rule" of anonymity applies. A college essay is usually read as if it had to stand entirely on its own, addressed to strangers. Instructors and professors read as if they were members of an imaginary "target" audience whose tastes and backgrounds are not precisely their own. If a composition assignment requires you to write a letter to the members of a city school board, for example, your instructor may say of a given passage, "I find this joke about football coaches and air bags very funny, but I think some of the board members might find it tasteless and insulting" or "I am not particularly irritated by misspellings, but some of them might be." Like the student, the instructor must visualize the moment of reception.

College professors often assume that when no particular audience is specified, students will visualize and write for the "general educated reader." This target audience is a truly remarkable invention: a mythological creature with some college education in no particular subject and a very strange life. The general reader is both male and female; both old and young; both rich and poor; simultaneously left, right, and centrist in politics; and by turns a member of every conceivable ethnic and racial minority. He or she is, in short, both everyone and no one. I always have trouble conceiving of the general reader in the singular, and so am inclined to visualize a crowd. The key in dealing with this crowd-creature is not to confuse it with either yourself or your instructor. A sociology professor who is a sexist himself may quite properly take you to task for writing a sentence potentially offensive to women, even though no women will actually read the paper. An economics professor might praise you for an essay that clearly explains the principle of decreasing marginal utility. But to whom did you explain it? Not to her, really, but to an audience of general readers that both of you visualized as needing and wanting the information.

The artificiality of writing for professors who are pretending they are not themselves may wear on your nerves and make you long to get out into the real world where the only audience is the target audience. The real world, however, turns out to be filled with comparable situations. A lawyer writing an important brief will normally show it to an intermediate audience of colleagues in the firm before submitting it to the target audience, the court. An engineer's proposal ordinarily passes across several friendly desks before it is mailed to a potential client. This chapter passed by no fewer than fifteen intermediate readers before it went to the typesetter. Intermediate audiences don't read to see whether they are *personally* pleased with a draft. Mine were reading, as far as they were able, not for their own sakes but for yours. Every stage of composing, critiquing, and revising was punctuated by speculations about how you would react to this example or that, whether you would find a given approach intriguing or boring, whether you would smile at a wisecrack or be offended by it.

Once you escape the limitations (and the safety) of writing for very familiar audiences, your true audience is always absent and to some degree mysterious. Your growth as a writer depends on your ability to develop a healthy and productive relationship with these absent strangers.

ONE WRITER INVENTS HER AUDIENCE AND HERSELF

A good piece of writing creates a clear picture of an audience, a writer, and a relationship between them. Consider the following paragraph, written by a composition student named Valerie Sinzdak. Her assignment was to write a profile of a person or a group that the general public might be interested in reading about, the sort of human interest story that could appear in a local newspaper or magazine. Sinzdak's profile begins with a contrast between *hearing* her subject and *seeing* it.

> On the telephone, Mike and Mary Gerard, barely thirtysomething, can communicate traditional middle American values. They grow things, and they sell them. They pay their taxes. The name of their business, Heavenly Harvest Sprouts, represents not religious fanaticism but only convenient alliteration. Only in the Gerards' home can a true middle-class American discover the subtle subversive details: the tufts of hair under Mary's arms, the Amish stove instead of a Whirlpool, the lack of real milk, and the kitchen drawers that hold not only silverware but also research papers listing the number of children who will starve to death this year and the number who could be saved if farmers converted grazing land to grain fields. Papers on their coffee table tell them the percentage of American food that contains pesticide residue. Organic farmers, the Gerards may be the only area farmers to know this information, and they seem to be the only ones who act on it, raising food without pesticides or chemical fertilizers. In a rented house on rented land at the end of a dirt road on the edge of Columbia, the Gerards, disenchanted consumers who now produce their own food, envision and begin a revolution in American farming, complete with propaganda.

A WRITER AT WORK

"Mike and Mary Gerard"
VALERIE SINZDAK

This is a strong introduction to a strong essay. We could notice any number of things that Sinzdak has done well, but we'll concentrate on the way she visualizes both an audience and a self to address that audience. We needn't read her mind to do this. The essay provides the evidence.

Some of Sinzdak's assumptions about her audience would interest anthropologists more than they need interest us: she clearly visualizes readers who know what a telephone does, for example, and what silverware is. More significantly for our purposes, she imagines readers

1. who will recognize *thirtysomething* as an allusion to yuppyish baby boomers.[1]

---

[1] boomers: And as I write this sentence, I am obviously visualizing readers who know that "yuppies" are "young, upwardly-mobile professionals" and "baby boomers" are people born between the end of World War II and the beginning of the Vietnam War. Does the fact that I am adding this note tell you that I am slightly uneasy about this visualization? How does the danger of including the note compare to the danger of omitting it?

2. who know the meaning of the word *alliteration.*

3. who know what an Amish stove is and how it contrasts with a Whirlpool.

4. who know that when she says, "Real milk," she is implying a contrast to something like soy milk.

5. who know why people are alarmed by pesticide residue.

6. who know that when she says, "Columbia," she is referring to the city with that name in Missouri, not to one of the other fifteen Columbias in the United States.

7. who *don't* know the Gerards.

These seven we might describe as assumptions about the audience's store-house of factual information. They tell us that Sinzdak has visualized an audience of well-educated people who watched some television in the late 1980s and early 1990s, who are aware of environmental and health issues, and who are quite familiar with Columbia, Missouri. Not all Sinzdak's assumptions about her audience are about their store of factual information, however. She seems also to visualize readers

8. who are not only familiar with but *comfortable* with middle-class American values (so that, for instance, they will find the unshaven hair under Mary Gerard's arms slightly foreign).

9. who are interested in and potentially sympathetic to people that strike them as eccentric.

10. who enjoy touches of irony, like the way the Gerards' coffee table (a very traditional middle-class bit of furniture) is covered not with glossy magazines, but with papers about pesticide residues.

These assumptions of Sinzdak's are intelligent ones, given that her assigned final audience is a readership like that of a local newspaper or magazine, but they are not *inevitable.* She visualized a bright, educated set of readers who are engaged with the issues of their times. She might have visualized a set of readers who normally read nothing but *Hustler* or the *National Enquirer.* She might have visualized a set of intolerant readers with no use for vegetarians or for women with hair under their arms. Or she might have visualized a set of readers that share the Gerards' world view so completely that they would find nothing peculiar about it. She chose to see her readers as flexible thinkers willing to hesitate, at least while reading her essay, between the world of "traditional American values" and the "subversive" world of the Gerards. Whether we fit into this audience precisely or not, we may feel slightly flattered by the way we are addressed, and we may be willing to imagine ourselves, at least briefly, as the sort of people Sinzdak wants us to be.

One lesson we can take from Sinzdak is that the wise writer is generous in visualizing a target audience. A writer asked to address an essay or speech to members of the clergy, for instance, might imagine them as sanctimonious, narrow-minded killjoys and then try to find an interesting way to address *that* group. On the other hand, the writer could visualize them as a group of highly educated people interested in community affairs and eager to lend their support to any good cause. Making the choice would call up different aspects of the writer's personality. Successful writers learn that no matter how specific the target audience is, there is room for visualization. Visualize an intelligent, alert group of readers—even if those readers are children—and you put yourself in a position to stretch your own intelligence and capability. Visualize dunderheads and you will write prose suited to dunderheads.

What image did Sinzdak create of herself in this piece of writing? For one thing, she presented herself as a person who *prefers* to address an alert, intelligent audience like the one we've just described. If we judge writers by the company they imagine themselves in, we would assume that she is broad-minded, well read, alive to irony, concerned about environmental and health issues, and willing to entertain the idea that people who appear to be eccentric may provide a valuable critique of middle-class values. She gives us the impression that she is a sharp observer, one who will snoop in a silverware drawer to see what it actually contains. She doesn't lecture or preach; in White's terms, she seems more a "philosopher" than an "enthusiast." She avoids taking the spotlight in the essay, avoids talking directly about herself, and so develops a demeanor of detachment that we often see in professional reporters. There's no "I was so nervous when I went to interview the Gerards" talk in this essay. Sinzdak has visualized herself as a confident writer more eager to talk about her subject than about herself. Is this the person Sinzdak sees in the mirror every morning? Perhaps not. Is this the Valerie Sinzdak I met face to face in class three days a week? Not exactly, I suppose. For one thing, Valerie-in-class was silent as the Sphinx. Sinzdak-on-paper has a great deal to say. She is good company, and who is to say that she is less real than the silent student in the second row?

♦ *Describing Visualized Audiences and Created Selves in Four Student Essays.* Write a page describing the visualized audience and created selves of each of the following student essays. The following questions may help focus your thinking: What background does the writer assume readers have? What attitudes will they bring to the subject? What do

EXERCISE 1

they know and not know? Do you feel included in the audience, or excluded from it? To what extent, and why? What attitude does the writer take toward the audience? What does the passage seem to reveal about the writer's mental habits? How much does the writer reveal about her or his situation in life (age, educational level, social class, race, politics, and so on)? How do you respond to this writer's "created self"? With liking or distaste, with trust or distrust, or in some other way? Why?

A.   Seat Belts (complete)

A major problem in the United States is death in traffic accidents. The number of deaths would be reduced if everyone used seat belts. Therefore, everyone should use seat belts.

Young people should use seat belts. People between sixteen and twenty-five are more likely to be in accidents than any other group. Because they are so often in accidents, it is important that they buckle their seat belts.

Older people should also use seat belts. Although they are not in accidents as often as younger people, their lives are very valuable. Older people have responsible jobs and are often parents. If they are killed, others suffer from the loss. Therefore, they too should take the time to fasten their seat belts,

The very young should use seat belts. Children and young teen-agers have their whole lives in front of them. Their parents should teach them to buckle up. Infants should be placed in carriers that can be strapped in with a seat belt.

As we have seen, all people should use seat belts. Young people need to be careful because they are in so many accidents. Older people need to think how their deaths would affect others. Infants and children need to have their lives protected so that they will not die before they have experienced life.

B.   Sorority Sisters (excerpt)

On just about any Friday night in a sorority, you can walk into the television room and find a group of girls watching a movie, or some program. The favorite in my sorority is *Picket Fences*. We usually crowd into the room at 9:00 to see what crazy crimes will come to the town of Rome, Wisconsin. At our sorority it is no surprise when the doorbell rings and it's the Domino's pizza man. If necessary you can always find a willing friend to massage your aching back caused from a hectic week just completed. If you need someone to talk to, you can single out the one person you wish to confide your most secretive thoughts to. When you live in a sorority you share a house and all its facilities with approximately sixty other girls. There are always times when you will think back to less complicated days, when you had your own bathroom and bedroom. However, it is the situations such as on a Friday night that help you realize that living in a sorority gives you so many friends, each who means something different. In a sorority there are three types of friendships to develop: (1) Good, (2) Better, and (3) Best, which all mean something different.

C.   Richard English (excerpt)

In the middle of his lecture, Dr. Richard English begins to choke. He clasps one hand around his throat, and with the other, makes a fist to cover his mouth as he coughs. As the students in the lecture hall move to the edge of their seats in concern for the middle-aged professor, whose grimacing face is now beet red, Dr. English finally reaches deep inside his mouth and pulls out a green rubber toy. "Excuse me," he says apologetically to the class, "I guess I had a frog in my throat." Then he lets out a goofy, sheepish laugh as his students sigh and moan. This is a typical classroom antic Dr. English uses to "make [class] interesting, to make it fun."

   Dr. English tries to make his classes fun because he feels it enables him to motivate his students. "I want to motivate them—in college and in life—to have fun. If it isn't fun, it's just one of those hurdles you jump." On the first day of his learning and instruction class, he tells his students to raise a hand if they have a grade point average below two point five. He feels that anyone accepted to a university is capable of maintaining at least a B average and concludes that those who are not successful are not enjoying learning.

D.   The Meaning of the Misfit's Final Words (excerpt)

At the end of "A Good Man Is Hard to Find," the Misfit says about the dead grandmother, "She would of been a good woman . . . if it had been somebody there to shoot her every minute of her life." By this he means that only on the verge of death has this woman come to know the importance of life, and that if she had had a similar threat throughout her life, she could have realized this moment much sooner.

   Throughout the first part of the story, the grandmother is completely preoccupied by her own world, viewing everything in relation to her past, almost to the point of losing touch with the actual world in which she lives. The story is told through her eyes, and from that viewpoint, none of the other characters seems very vivid or worth remembering. Bailey is simply described as "the son she lived with," the mother barely says anything at all and never establishes a personality, and the characterization of the children doesn't reach beyond their typically bratty banter. The grandmother continually ignores those around her, focusing on herself and her past; instead of living for each moment, she dwells on times gone by which she remembers as somehow being "better." Unless they remind her of the past or unless she wants something from them, the self-centered grandmother never notices anyone, even her own family. No one distracts her from her past—until she meets the Misfit.

Assignments
for Chapter 2

ASSIGNMENT 1: **A PERSONAL AD**

As Bonnie Auslander's essay "In Search of Mr. Write" shows, writing a personal ad forces a person to face in compressed form all the difficulties of inventing an audience and a self. Write an ad on your own behalf; then write a brief essay explaining the choices you made in writing the ad. Though personal ads are ordinarily written in search of (ISO) romance, yours need not be. What you are ISO may be a key part of your self-characterization.

ASSIGNMENT 2: **A "PERSONAL" FOR AN ESSAY**

The visualized relationship between reader and writer could be expressed in language that echoes that of the personal ad. Valerie Sinzdak's essay, for instance, might be characterized this way: "NOSEY, self-effacing writer interested in alternative lifestyles ISO well-educated middle-class reader capable of detecting irony and questioning own values." Write comparable ads for each of the four passages in exercise 1 (p. 35).

ASSIGNMENT 3: **AN ANALYSIS OF THE WRITER-AUDIENCE RELATIONSHIP**

In an essay 300 to 500 words long, describe the invented audience and writer in Barbara Ehrenreich's "Stop Ironing the Diapers." Attach to your essay a brief note commenting on the audience *you* invented in the process of writing your essay and the "self" that you presented to the audience.

ASSIGNMENT 4: **A COMPARISON OF READING WITH EXPERIENCE**

Richard Rodriguez's "Mr. Secrets" presents readers with a dilemma. Should we read it as an essay about *his* particular problems and progress as a writer, or should we read it as an essay that shows in an extreme form *every* writer's problems and progress? To explore this question and help others explore it, write an essay in which you compare your experiences as a writer with those of Rodriguez.

ASSIGNMENT 5:   **A LETTER TO THE AUTHOR**

Write a letter to the author of *The Riverside Guide to Writing,* evaluating his relationship with his audience. To judge from the first two or three chapters, including the readings and assignments, what sort of person does he think you are? What sort of person is he asking you to be? What sort of person does he present himself as being? Does this invention of an audience and a self *work* for you, or do you have problems with it? Please explain and give examples in your reply.

Your letter could obviously affect the way I do my work—as both a teacher and a writer—in the future. I would appreciate receiving a copy at the following address:

Doug Hunt
Department of English
310 Tate Hall
University of Missouri
Columbia, MO 65211

IN SEARCH OF MR. WRITE

Bonnie Auslander

A free-lance writer and a poet, Bonnie Auslander also teaches English and directs the writing center at Converse College in Spartanburg, South Carolina. "In Search of Mr. Write" first appeared in *College English* in September 1993.

1   MY MOTHER'S FIRST PERSONAL AD didn't sound like my mother at all. "Hello, my-daughter-the-writing-teacher," she'd said to me on the phone. "Do you have a moment? How does this sound? 'DW'—that's, you know, divorced woman—'pretty, professional, young 50s, likes classical music, long walks, literature, ISO SM, 50s.' That's—"

2   "I know," I interrupted. "In search of a single man."

3   A pause. "So what do you think?" she asked.

4   I traced the pattern in the carpet with my toe. I was excited that my mother was considering dating, let alone placing a personal ad. But how could I tell her I didn't think much of her ad? I thought of conferences with my student writers. *Begin with sincere praise.*

5   "I like the word 'pretty,'" I said at last. It was self-assured yet modest. Just like her, in fact.

6   "But I wonder," I continued, "if, um, you could be a little more specific. You sound kind of general."

7   I was hoping my mother wouldn't notice my conversation so far was nothing but writing teacher clichés. *Ask writers to use specifics to illustrate their ideas.*

8   She wanted to know what I meant by general, so I plowed on. "How about, oh, 'DW etc., likes Schubert—'"

9   "What if there's some wonderful man out there who likes Bach more than Schubert?"

10   "But Mom, I bet he'll still answer the ad. Schubert will grab his attention and show him you're a true music lover. Besides, everyone always says they love long walks and music. You have to be different. You have to show them *which* long walks and what *kinds* of music."

11   "These ads cost you by the word. I don't have room for a novel!"

12   "I know. That's why you have to—I mean, why you might want to—use specifics to make your point."

13   We began to rewrite. Schubert was a good choice to represent her taste in music, but what about books? Tolstoy? Too big. Virginia Woolf? Too wild. Grace Paley? Too obscure.

14   We were stuck. We decided to get off the phone and talk later. Another rule: *Get the writer to put the piece aside for a while.* (Fortunately my mother likes to get a head start on things. The deadline wasn't for another two weeks.)

15   The next day I carried my mother's ad around with me in a little notebook. I studied it indoors while waiting for the microwave to beep. I took it outdoors while waiting for the dog to pee. I was starting to worry.

16   "Mom," I said to her that night on the phone, "this ad is sounding a little pretentious. I wish we could inject some humor."

17   "Yeah," she said. "I'll just say I have a sense of humor just like I said I liked literature. You know, 'DW with wonderful sense of humor—'"

18   We giggled, recalling reading ads that contained exactly those words. You had to wonder about people who claimed to be funny but couldn't come up with any better way of expressing it. *Show, don't tell.*

19   "You know what would be great?" I said. "Something clever and Jewish (my mother was particularly interested in meeting Jewish men) that will catch his eye . . ." *Strong beginnings—what journalists call leads—grab the reader's attention and set the tone.*

20   That's when she came up with the inspired phrase, "non-kvetch." (*Kvetch* is Yiddish for someone who gripes all the time.) After that the writing of the ad clicked: "NON-KVETCH. Pretty DJW, professional, young 50s, likes Schubert, Chekhov, All Things Considered, and Matisse, ISO DM, 50s." *Help the writer find her voice.*

21   Two months later my mother received a batch of "Dear Non-Kvetch" letters. She answered some of them, and eventually went out with two men. They didn't work out. The retired doctor was much too old for her, and after several weeks the civil engineer admitted he preferred Stephen King to Chekhov. But she hasn't given up. Every few months she rewrites her ad, tinkering with the authors and artists in it for a different effect. "Maybe put in Jane Austen?" she mutters, more to herself than to me. "No, wait—what about George Eliot?"

22   These days I'm thinking about writing my own personal ad. I've got a draft here scribbled on a paper placemat: "SW, writer, energetic reader . . ." Sounds kind of flat. Should I mention my dog? Describe my appearance?

23   I think I'll give my mother a call. ♦

MR. SECRETS

Richard Rodriguez

The parents of Richard Rodriguez were Mexican-American immigrants living in the San Francisco area. When Rodriguez started school in Sacramento, he spoke little English. He became an excellent student, taking a B.A. from Stanford University and an M.A. from Columbia University. He seemed destined to become a college professor, but while studying English Renaissance literature in London, he abruptly gave up his academic work to write *Hunger of Memory: The Education of Richard Rodriguez*. In the following excerpt, he discusses one of the difficult lessons of that education: learning to address an audience of strangers.

1 WHEN MY FOURTH-GRADE TEACHER made our class write a paper about a typical evening at home, it never occurred to me actually to do so. "Describe what you do with your family," she told us. And automatically I produced a fictionalized account. I wrote that I had six brothers and sisters; I described watching my mother get dressed up in a red-sequined dress before she went with my father to a party; I even related how the imaginary baby sitter ("a high school student") taught my brother and sisters and me to make popcorn and how, later, I fell asleep before my parents returned. The nun who read what I wrote would have known that what I had written was completely imagined. But she never said anything about my contrivance. And I never expected her to either. I never thought she *really* wanted me to write about my family life. In any case, I would have been unable to do so.

2 I was very much the son of parents who regarded the most innocuous piece of information about the family to be secret. Although I had, by that time, grown easy in public, I felt that my family life was strictly private, not to be revealed to unfamiliar ears or eyes. Around the age of ten, I was held by surprise listening to my best friend tell me one day that he "hated" his father. In a furious whisper he said that when he attempted to kiss his father before going to bed, his father had laughed: "Don't you think you're getting too old for that sort of thing, son?" I was intrigued not so much by the incident as by the fact that the boy would relate it to *me*.

3 In those years I was exposed to the sliding-glass-door informality of middle-class California family life. Ringing the doorbell of a friend's house, I would hear someone inside yell out, "Come on in, Richie; door's not locked." And in I would go to discover my friend's family undisturbed by my presence. The father was in the kitchen in his underwear. The mother was in her bathrobe. Voices gathered in familiarity. A parent scolded a child in front of me; voices quarreled, then laughed; the mother told me something about her son after he had stepped out of the room and she was sure he couldn't overhear; the father would speak to his children and to me in the same tone of voice. I was one of the family, the parents of several good friends would assure me. (Richie.)

4 My mother sometimes invited my grammar school friends to stay for dinner or even to stay overnight. But my parents never treated such visitors as part of the family, never told

43

them they were. When a school friend ate at our table, my father spoke less than usual. (Stray, distant words.) My mother was careful to use her "visitor's voice." Sometimes, listening to her, I would feel annoyed because she wouldn't be more herself. Sometimes I'd feel embarrassed that I couldn't give to a friend at my house what I freely accepted at his.

5   I remained, nevertheless, my parents' child. At school, in sixth grade, my teacher suggested that I start keeping a diary. ("You should write down your personal experiences and reflections.") But I shied away from the idea. It was the one suggestion that the scholarship boy couldn't follow. I would not have wanted to write about the minor daily events of my life; I would never have been able to write about what most deeply, daily, concerned me during those years: I was growing away from my parents. Even if I could have been certain that no one would find my diary, even if I could have destroyed each page after I had written it, I would have felt uncomfortable writing about my home life. There seemed to me something intrinsically public about written words.

6   Writing, at any rate, was a skill I didn't regard highly. It was a grammar school skill I acquired with comparative ease. I do not remember struggling to write the way I struggled to learn how to read. The nuns would praise student papers for being neat—the handwritten letters easy for others to read; they promised that my writing style would improve as I read more and more. But that wasn't the reason I became a reader. Reading was for me the key to "knowledge"; I swallowed facts and dates and names and themes. Writing, by contrast, was an activity I thought of as a kind of report, evidence of learning. I wrote down what I heard teachers say. I wrote down things from my books. I wrote down all I knew when I was examined at the end of the school year. Writing was performed after the fact; it was

not the exciting experience of learning itself. In eighth grade I read several hundred books, the titles of which I still can recall. But I cannot remember a single essay I wrote. I only remember that the most frequent kind of essay I wrote was the book report.

7   In high school there were more "creative" writing assignments. English teachers assigned the composition of short stories and poems. One sophomore story I wrote was a romance set in the Civil War South. I remember that it earned me a good enough grade, but my teacher suggested with quiet tact that next time I try writing about "something you know more about—something closer to home." Home? I wrote a short story about an old man who lived all by himself in a house down the block. That was as close as my writing ever got to my house. Still, I won prizes. When teachers suggested I contribute articles to the school literary magazine, I did so. And when I was asked to join the school newspaper, I said yes. I did not feel any great pride in my writings, however. (My mother was the one who collected my prize-winning essays in a box she kept in her closet.) Though I remember seeing my by-line in print for the first time, and dwelling on the printing press letters with fascination: RICHARD RODRIGUEZ. The letters furnished evidence of a vast public identity writing made possible.

8   When I was a freshman in college, I began typing all my assignments. My writing speed decreased. Writing became a struggle. In high school I had been able to handwrite ten- and twenty-page papers in little more than an hour—and I never revised what I wrote. A college essay took me several nights to prepare. Suddenly everything I wrote seemed in need of revision. I became a self-conscious writer. A stylist. The change, I suspect, was the result of seeing my words ordered by the even, impersonal, anonymous typewriter print. As arranged by a machine, the words that I typed no longer seemed mine. I was able to see them

with a new appreciation for how my reader would see them.

9   From grammar school to graduate school I could always name my reader. I wrote for my teacher. I could consult him or her before writing, and after. I suppose that I knew other readers could make sense of what I wrote—that, therefore, I addressed a general reader. But I didn't think very much about it. Only toward the end of my schooling and only because political issues pressed upon me did I write, and have published in magazines, essays intended for readers I never expected to meet. Now I am struck by the opportunity. I write today for a reader who exists in my mind only phantasmagorically. Someone with a face erased; someone of no particular race or sex or age or weather. A gray presence. Unknown, unfamiliar. All that I know about him is that he has had a long education and that his society, like mine, is often public (*un gringo*).

• • •

10   I write very slowly because I write under the obligation to make myself clear to someone who knows nothing about me. It is a lonely adventure. Each morning I make my way along a narrowing precipice of written words. I hear an echoing voice—my own resembling another's. Silent! The reader's voice silently trails every word I put down. I reread my words, and again it is the reader's voice I hear in my mind, sounding my prose.

11   When I wrote my first autobiographical essay, it was no coincidence that, from the first page, I expected to publish what I wrote. I didn't consciously determine the issue. Somehow I knew, however, that my words were meant for a public reader. Only because of that reader did the words come to the page. The reader became my excuse, my reason for writing.

12   It had taken me a long time to come to this address. There are remarkable children who very early are able to write publicly about their personal lives. Some children confide to a diary those things—like the first shuddering of sexual desire—too private to tell a parent or brother. The youthful writer addresses a stranger, the Other, with "Dear Diary" and tries to give public expression to what is intensely, privately felt. In so doing, he attempts to evade the guilt of repression. And the embarrassment of solitary feeling. For by rendering feelings in words that a stranger can understand—words that belong to the public, this Other—the young diarist no longer need feel all alone or eccentric. His feelings are capable of public intelligibility. In turn, the act of revelation helps the writer better understand his own feelings. Such is the benefit of language: By finding public words to describe one's feelings, one can describe oneself to oneself. One names what was previously only darkly felt.

13   I have come to think of myself as engaged in writing graffiti. Encouraged by physical isolation to reveal what is most personal; determined at the same time to have my words seen by strangers. I have come to understand better why works of literature—while never intimate, never individually addressed to the reader—are so often among the most personal statements we hear in our lives. Writing, I have come to value written words as never before. One can use *spoken* words to reveal one's personal self to strangers. But *written* words heighten the feeling of privacy. They permit the most thorough and careful exploration. (In the silent room, I prey upon that which is most private. Behind the closed door, I am least reticent about giving those memories expression.) The writer is freed from the obligation of finding an auditor in public. (As I use words that someone far from home can understand, I create my listener. I imagine her listening.)

14   My teachers gave me a great deal more than I knew when they taught me to write public English. I was unable then to use the skill for deeply personal purposes. I insisted upon writing impersonal essays. And I wrote always

with a specific reader in mind. Nevertheless, the skill of public writing was gradually developed by the many classroom papers I had to compose. Today I *can* address an anonymous reader. And this seems to me important to say. Somehow the inclination to write about my private life in public is related to the ability to do so. It is not enough to say that my mother and father do not want to write their autobiographies. It needs also to be said that they are unable to write to a public reader. They lack the skill. Though both of them can write in Spanish and English, they write in a hesitant manner. Their syntax is undertain. Their vocabulary limited. They write well enough to communicate "news" to relatives in letters. And they can handle written transactions in institutional America. But the man who sits in his chair so many hours, and the woman at the ironing board—"keeping busy because I don't want to get old"—will never be able to believe that any description of their personal lives could be understood by a stranger far from home. ♦

Stop Ironing the Diapers

Barbara Ehrenreich

An essayist whose work appears with some regularity in such magazines as the *New Republic, Mother Jones,* and the *Atlantic,* Barbara Ehrenreich is often described as "irreverent" or "witty." As you read the following essay, first published in *Ms.* magazine in 1989, consider the assumptions she seems to make about her readers and the relationship she attempts to forge with them.

1 I WAS SADDENED TO READ, A FEW WEEKS AGO, that a group of young women is planning a conference on that ancient question: is it possible to raise children and have a career at the same time? A group of young *men*—now that would be interesting. But I had thought that among women the issue had been put to rest long ago with the simple retort, Is it possible to raise children *without* having some dependable source of income with which to buy them food, clothing, and Nintendo?

2 Of course, what the young women are worried about is whether it's possible to raise children *well* while at the same time maintaining one's membership in the labor force. They have heard of "quality time." They are anxious about "missing a stage." They are afraid they won't have the time to nudge their offsprings' tiny intellects in the direction of the inevitable SATs.

3 And no wonder they are worried: while everything else in our lives has gotten simpler, speedier, more microwavable and user-friendly, child-raising seems to have expanded to fill the time no longer available for it. At least this is true in the trendsetting, postyuppie class, where it is not uncommon to find busy young lawyers breast-feeding until the arrival of molars, reserving entire weekdays for the company of five-year-olds, and feeling guilty about not ironing the diapers.

4 This is not only silly but dangerous. Except under the most adverse circumstances—such as homelessness, unsafe living conditions, or lack of spouse and child care—child-raising was not *meant* to be a full-time activity. No culture on earth outside of mid-century suburban America has ever deployed one woman per child without simultaneously assigning her such major productive activities as weaving, farming, gathering, temple maintenance, and tent building. The reason is that full-time one-on-one child-raising is not good for women *or* children. And it is on the strength of that anthropological generalization, as well as my own two decades of motherhood, that I offer you my collected tips on *how to raise your children at home in your spare time.*

5 1. *Forget the "stages."* The women who are afraid to leave home because they might "miss a stage" do not realize that all "stages" last more than ten minutes. Sadly, some of them last fifteen years or more. Even the most cursory parent, who drops in only to change clothes and get the messages off the answering machine, is unlikely to miss a "stage." Once a "stage" is over—and let us assume it is a particularly charming one, involving high-pitched squeals of glee and a rich flow of spittle down the chin—the best thing you can do is *forget it* at once. The reason for this is that no self-respecting six-year-old wants to be reminded

that she was once a fat little fool in a high chair; just as no thirteen-year-old wants to be reminded that she was ever, even for a moment, a six-year-old.

6   I cannot emphasize this point strongly enough: the parent who insists on remembering the "stages"—and worse still, bringing them up—risks turning that drool-faced little darling into a *lifelong enemy*. I mean, try to see it from the child's point of view: suppose you were condemned to being two and a half feet tall, unemployed, and incontinent for an indefinite period of time. Would you want people reminding you of this unfortunate phase for the rest of your life?

7   2. *Forget "quality time."* I tried it once on May 15, 1978. I know because it is still penciled into my 1978 appointment book. "Kids," I announced, "I have forty-five minutes. Let's have some quality time!" They looked at me dully in the manner of rural retirees confronting a visitor from the Census Bureau. Finally, one of them said, in a soothing tone, "Sure, Mom, but could it be after *Gilligan's Island*?"

8   The same thing applies to "talks," as in "Let's sit down and have a little talk." In response to that—or the equally lame "How's school?"—any self-respecting child will assume the demeanor of a prisoner of war facing interrogation. The only thing that works is *low-quality* time: time in which you—and they—are ostensibly doing something else, like housework. Even a two-year-old can dust or tidy and thereby gain an exaggerated sense of self-importance. In fact, this is the only sensible function of housework, the other being to create the erroneous impression that you do not live with children at all.

9   Also, do not underestimate the telephone as a means of parent-child communication. Teenagers especially recognize it as an instrument demanding full disclosure, in infinite detail, of their thoughts, ambitions, and philosophical outlook. If you want to know what's on their minds, call them from work. When you get home, they'll be calling someone else.

3. *Do not overload their intellects.* Many parents, mindful of approaching nursery-school entrance exams, PSATs, GREs, and so forth, stay up late into the night reading back issues of *Scientific American* and the *Cliff's Notes* for the *Encyclopaedia Britannica*. This is in case the child should ask a question, such as "Why do horses walk on their hands?" The *overprepared* parent answers with a twenty-minute disquisition on evolution, animal husbandry, and DNA, during which the child slinks away in despair, determined never to ask a question again, except possibly the indispensable "Are we there yet?"

The part-time parent knows better, and responds only in vague and elusive ways, letting her voice trail off and her eyes wander to some mythical landscape, as in: "Well, they don't when they fight. . . . No, then they rear up. . . . Or when they fly . . . like Pegasus . . . mmmm." This system invariably elicits a stream of eager questions, which can then be referred to a more reliable source.

4. *Do not attempt to mold them.* First, because it takes too much time. Second, because a child is not a salmon mousse. A child is a temporarily disabled and stunted version of a larger person, whom you will someday know. Your job is to help them overcome the disabilities associated with their size and inexperience so that they get on with being that larger person, and in a form that you might *like* to know.

Hence the part-time parent encourages self-reliance in all things. For example, from the moment my children mastered Pidgin English, they were taught one simple rule: Never wake a sleeping adult. I was mysterious about the consequences, but they became adept, at age two, at getting their own cereal and hanging out until a reasonable hour. Also, contrary to widespread American myth, no self-respecting toddler enjoys having wet and clammy buns. Nor is the potty concept alien to the one-year-old mind. So do not make the common mistake of withholding the toilet facilities until the crisis of nursery-school matriculation forces the issue.

14   *5. Do not be afraid they will turn on you, someday, for being a lousy parent.* They *will* turn on you. They will also turn on the full-time parents, the cookie-making parents, the Little League parents, and the all-sacrificing parents. If you are at work every day when they get home from school, they will turn on you, eventually, for being a selfish, neglectful careerist. If you are at home every day, eagerly awaiting their return, they will turn on you for being a useless, unproductive layabout. This is all part of the normal process of "individuation," in which one adult ego must be trampled into the dust in order for one fully formed teenage ego to emerge. Accept it.

15   Besides, a part-time parent is unlikely to ever harbor that most poisonous of all parental thoughts: "What I gave up for you . . . !" No child should have to take the rap for wrecking a grown woman's brilliant career. The good part-time parent convinces her children that they are positive assets, without whose wit and insights she would never have gotten the last two promotions.

16   *6. Whether you work outside the home or not, never tell them that being a mommy is your "job."* Being a mommy is a relationship, not a profession. Nothing could be worse for a child's self-esteem than to think that you think that being with her is *work*. She may come to think that you are involved in some obscure manufacturing process in which she is only the raw material. She may even come to think that her real mom was switched at birth, and that you are the baby-sitter. Which leads to my final tip:

17   *7.* Even if you are not a part-time parent, even if you haven't the slightest intention of entering the wide world of wage earning, *pretend that you are one.* ◆

3 Drafting and Revising

EVERY WRITER, SOONER OR LATER, REALIZES THAT WRITING IS AN unnatural act. The body was not designed to sit essentially motionless for hours on end. The mind, designed to dart in many directions, rebels when we command it to produce orderly sentences and paragraphs. We may be communicative creatures by nature, but the communication we crave is talk rather than writing, which requires us to isolate ourselves for hours from our friends. Many people, probably most people, even in a generally literate country like the United States, are so uncomfortable with the process of writing that they avoid it whenever possible, to the delight of shareholders in telephone companies.

This chapter concerns itself with what happens to the person who decides (or is forced) to write rather than call. It divides into two parts, the first dealing with the general problem of having a brain ill-suited to the job, the second with the special problem of coaxing the brain back to work if it goes on strike. In both parts the point is the same: when we address any but the most trivial subjects, the process of writing not only *communicates* thought, it also *improves* thinking.

FOGGINESS: THE DAIN CURSE

Our starting point in understanding this improvement will be disorder—the near chaos that overtakes us all when we attempt to pursue a train of thought. One of the clearest descriptions of this disorder comes from the mouth of Gabrielle Dain, a character in Dashiell Hammett's mystery novel *The Dain Curse*. Gabrielle, convinced that she has inherited a family curse that produces madness, describes her symptoms to Hammett's hard-boiled detective:

A WRITER AT WORK

"The Dain Curse"
DASHIELL HAMMETT

> "I've not ever been able to think clearly, as other people do, even the simplest thoughts. Everything is always so confused in my mind. No matter what I try to think about, there's a fog that gets between me and

it, and other thoughts get between us, so I barely catch a glimpse of the thought I want before I lose it again, and have to hunt through the fog, and at last find it, only to have the same thing happen again and again and again. Can you understand how horrible that can become: going through life like that—year after year—knowing you will always be like that—or worse?"

To which the detective replies:

"I can't. It sounds normal as hell to me. Nobody thinks clearly, no matter what they pretend. Thinking's a dizzy business, a matter of catching as many of those foggy glimpses as you can and fitting them together the best you can. That's why people hang on so tight to their beliefs and opinions; because, compared to the haphazard way in which they're arrived at, even the goofiest opinion seems wonderfully clear, sane, and self-evident. And if you let it get away from you, then you've got to dive back into that foggy muddle to wangle yourself out another to take its place."

One way of describing the Dain Curse, a curse shared by almost all of us, is to say that the mind's capacity for focused attention is very small. Our skulls may contain a great deal of information, but we can be conscious of only a small portion of it at a time. A person trying to think coherently, trying to match various memories, facts, and perceptions to an interpretive framework, is like a person with a small flashlight trying to reorganize a dark warehouse.

WHAT COGNITIVE PSYCHOLOGY TELLS US ABOUT FOGGINESS

Cognitive psychologists have given us a rough idea of how small the flashlight is: people are capable of retaining in the forefront of their consciousness only five to nine separate items at a time, whether those items are numbers, letters, words, or short sentences. Having what is usually called a "great memory" doesn't help. Suppose that we meet a woman who has memorized an entire book of limericks—150 poems, each identified by a short title. We ask her to recite a dozen of the poems in an arbitrary order: "Parrot," "Irish Priest," "Socks," "Jumbo," "Raincoat," etc. Clearly this woman has a good long-term memory, but unless we allow her to write down our list of requests, she will forget some or most of them. Old information (the 150 limericks) may be safely stored in our minds, but fresh information evaporates quickly, like ether from an open bottle.

George Miller, a pioneer researcher in this area, points out that any shift in the focus of our attention will speed the evaporation.

Give a person three consonants—CHS, or MXB, for instance—and then immediately have him count backward by threes until you are ready to test his recall. The counting breaks up his normal processes of transfer from temporary to more permanent memory, so that twenty seconds later the string of consonants, which would ordinarily be perfectly recalled, is forgotten more than 90 percent of the time.

Experiments of this sort have led cognitive psychologists to see "working memory," the pot we keep on the brain's front burner, as a half-pint affair always ready to overflow. Even modest attempts to process information can crowd out the very information we are trying to process.

The implications for anyone attempting an ambitious mental chore like writing are alarming. We find ourselves trying—all in the same minute—to fit subject to framework, to consider our relation to our readers, to evaluate the quality of a metaphor we are using, and to remember whether *i* comes before *e* in *receive*. Inevitably, something slips. Typically, what slips is the most difficult part of the job. Our head begins to spin, our stomach to growl, and our wonderfully clear vision of the subject seen in a new framework begins to slip away. The old way of seeing it seems, after all, "wonderfully clear, sane, and self-evident."

THE STABILIZING INFLUENCE OF WRITING

To understand how writing helps us overcome the limitations of our minds, let's return to an image introduced a few paragraphs ago: the metaphor of the flashlight and the warehouse. Suppose you were actually given a flashlight and told to rearrange a darkened warehouse. You would find yourself facing difficulties on at least three levels. At the lowest level, there is the problem of identifying individual objects: what are these flat metal gizmos with the hole in the center? At the highest level, there is the problem of defining your goal: what would a sensible arrangement of the whole warehouse be? In between, there is the problem of sorting: do the widgets belong in the same bay as the blodgetts, or would it make more sense to put them in the bin next to the thingamajigs? These three levels of difficulty, unfortunately, intertwine. Until you know what sort of objects you are dealing with, you can't come up with a sensible arrangement of the whole. Until you know what the arrangement of the whole is, you can't make rational decisions about how to group widgets and blodgetts. But if you wander around the warehouse trying to examine and identify all the objects one at a time in your flashlight's beam, you will get nothing done. Every attempt to think about organizing the objects will cloud your memory of what the objects are.

But suppose you are carrying a notebook and pencil. Now you can make lists of objects, write yourself notes about plans for organization, draw maps of the various bins and bays. It will still be a hard task, but time is on your side. You can still only see a few inches in front of your face, and your capacity for concentration is no better than it was before, but the ability to record information and ideas securely keeps them from evaporating and *allows you to think about one thing at a time,* confident that even if your progress is slow, it is sure.

♦ *A Test of Working Memory.* To test the effect of thinking about a complex problem, both by and without writing about it, work with a partner on the following project. One of you will be allowed to write; the other will not. Each of you should think of nine types of fasteners, arrange the list of nine fasteners alphabetically according to the *final* letter, and think of an unconventional use for each of the fasteners. Do not list the same unconventional use for two different fasteners. One item on your list could be the zipper, which could be used to light a match. The first person finished should immediately dictate his or her list to the other, who should then dictate his or her incomplete list back.

WRITING AND THINKING IN STAGES

The notebook that is useful in helping us organize the physical world is even more useful in helping us organize our mental worlds. It allows us to overcome some of the limitations of our minds and memories. Some scholars go so far as to say that writing makes our mental engines more powerful, but this claim is disputable. It is enough to say that writing creates a kind of mechanical advantage, a leverage, that allows us to do more work with the same mental engine. We can see this leverage at work by looking at a piece of writing passing through several drafts. Consider, for example, the passage in which the flashlight metaphor was first introduced:

> One way of describing the Dain Curse, a curse shared by almost all of us, is to say that the mind's capacity for focused attention is very small. Our skulls may contain a great deal of information, but we can be conscious of only a small portion of it at a time. A person trying to think coherently, trying to match various memories, facts, and perceptions to an interpretive framework, is like a person with a small flashlight trying to reorganize a dark warehouse.

These three sentences evolved through three stages, which I can reproduce and date accurately, since each was saved on a computer disk. The story of my struggles with them is a fair illustration of the way that writing and revision can help us think.

Version 1. 4:35 P.M., December 31. The original version of this passage, though it contained only two sentences, was the result of a good deal of thought:

> One way of describing the Dain Curse, which is a curse shared by almost all of us, is to say that the mind's capacity for focused attention is very small. When we try to concentrate on a complex question or situation, we seem to be bailing with a leaky bucket.

When I wrote this, I was nervous about equating the Dain Curse with the mind's limited "capacity for focused attention"; Dashiell Hammett and psychologists like George Miller (to whom I wanted to build a bridge) speak very different languages. It took me some weeks to decide that he and they are discussing the same problem, and I hesitated before committing myself on paper to this connection. The metaphor about "bailing with a leaky bucket" was the one that made the connection clear to me, so I put it in.

Version 2. 6:31 P.M., December 31.   As I wrote further into the chapter, however, I became unhappy with that leaky bucket. It was certainly a clear image for memory loss, but it wasn't particularly helpful when I wanted to discuss the relation of writing to thinking. In Version 2, I doubled back to reconsider the metaphor, producing the following draft:

> One way of describing the Dain Curse, which is a curse shared by almost all of us, is to say that the mind's capacity for focused attention is very small. Our minds may contain a great deal of information, but we can be conscious of only a small portion of it at a time. A person trying to think coherently, trying to create a match between various facts and the framework that will interpret them, is like a person exploring a vast dark building with a penlight they can illuminate only a few inches at a time.

It seemed to me that though the writer's problem might actually *be* a memory problem (the leaky bucket), it *feels* like a problem of limited vision ("I barely catch a glimpse of the thought I want before I lose it"). This gave me the idea of a flashlight in a large building. I liked this image, too, because the beam of the flashlight seems to correspond to the "focused attention" that the psychologists are concerned with. After some hesitation, I chose *penlight* rather than *flashlight* because I liked the idea of the tiniest possible flashlight mismatched with a vast building. It also occurred to me that I could help my readers make the connection to college-level thinking and writing by referring to the idea of interpretation via framework from Chapter 1, so I added this reference in the third sentence. Then, it being New Year's Eve and my mental flashlight dimming, I quit.

You'll notice, by the way, that the typographical error in the last sentence of Version 2 (*they* for *that*) escaped my attention. Obviously, I am too pea-brained to be constantly aware of what is going on at every level of even a short passage. So, probably, are you.

Version 3. 7:50 A.M., January 2.   Back at work on January 2, I printed out a draft of the chapter and penciled changes in the margin. In the passage we are considering, I began to realize that the flashlight-and-building metaphor wasn't quite specific enough: it didn't suggest that the person with the flashlight, like the thinker or writer, has a job to do. So I changed the building to a warehouse to be rearranged—a change that has obviously affected the rest of the chapter.

> One way of describing the Dain Curse, a curse shared by almost all of us, is to say that the mind's capacity for focused attention is very small. Our skulls may contain a great deal of information, but we can be conscious of only a small portion of it at a time. A person trying to think coherently, trying to match various memories, facts, and perceptions to an interpretive framework, is like a person with a small flashlight trying to reorganize a dark warehouse.

Worried that not every reader would know what a penlight is, I had checked the word in my dictionary and failed to find it. Perhaps it was a brand name? At any rate, I decided that *small flashlight,* though it pleased me less, might communicate better. Then I turned my attention to issues of style and correctness. I dropped the *which is* from the first sentence to make it move somewhat faster and considered dropping the *almost.* I changed *minds* to *skulls* in the second sentence because *mind* seems too dull and abstract a word to repeat in back-to-back sentences. Some philosophers, I realized, would object to locating the mind so securely in the skull, but I decided in this case to choose the more graphic word rather than to be mincingly correct. In the third sentence, I hit on a problem that was more than stylistic. I didn't want to suggest that it is only facts that lie around in the warehouse of our mind and can be misplaced. Memories that aggregate hundreds of separate facts may be temporarily lost, and so—especially—may the little flashes of insight that have not quite formed themselves into fixed ideas. So may whole ideas, whole systems of thought. As a compromise between oversimplifying and overelaborating, I simply added *memories* and *perceptions.* The third sentence was now becoming cumbersome, so I found a way to shorten it: "interpretive framework" for "framework that will interpret them." Finally, I eliminated the adjective *vast,* a word that seemed rather snooty in this context and was probably unnecessary, since warehouses are rarely small.

THE ADVANTAGE OF REVISION: MENTAL REPROCESSING

It won't have escaped your attention that I have now written more than thirty sentences explaining the evolution of three. Even this ten-to-one ratio is deceptively low, since I have left much out of the account to avoid boring you more than necessary. It won't have escaped your attention, either, that there is a rough correspondence between the levels at which I was forced to think and the levels mentioned in the warehouse problem. At the highest level, I was struggling with what I ought to say, with what I could understand, about how the mind works. At the lowest level, I was checking for typographical errors and wondering whether *penlight* was a word my audience would recognize. In between were such decisions as whether to talk about a *vast dark building* or a *dark warehouse*. By writing as I thought my way through the passage, rather than trying to compose it in my head, I was able to bring the penlight of my attention to bear on one problem at a time.

It is the recursiveness of writing, the ability it gives us to return to our earlier thoughts and hone them, that makes the unnatural act of writing valuable not only to the reader but to the writer. Writing and revising bring our diffuse thoughts together in a compact form. The process allows us to think more efficiently than we would otherwise be able to do. Certainly the end product is "smarter" than the products of the early steps. The linguist Martin Joos compares this mental reprocessing to careful packing of a suitcase:

> The rewriter is as one who packs his thought for a long journey. Having packed the garment, he does not merely straighten out the folds and close the paragraph. Instead, he unpacks completely and repacks again. And again; and again and again. Each time, he tucks one more thought into this or that pocket. When he quits, there are more of them than of words. So many labors of love on a single sentence, that many rewards for the rereader. On the surface, one teasing half-reward; others at successively greater and greater depths, so that each reading finds one more.

Joos's point is not that each revision will add bulk to a passage (who doesn't prefer a light suitcase to a heavy one?), but that each revision condenses more consideration into each word. The person who learns to unpack and repack a paragraph has learned a way of dealing with the Dain Curse.

TRUSTING THE PROCESS: HOW TO AVOID WRITER'S BLOCK

The benefits of drafting and redrafting come to us only when we can get something on the page to begin with. The next few pages are intended for writers who have sat for long periods in front of a blank page or a blank computer screen. (If you are part of that happy minority of writers who are never blocked, you may want to close your eyes till the scary part is over.)

Professional writers can't afford long unproductive periods. A difficult passage may send them for a brief walk or a talk with a sympathetic friend, but they return and produce. Memoirist and poet Maya Angelou goes to her workroom at 6:30 every morning and stays until afternoon, always producing something she can edit in the evening. The journalist Theodore White, like many others, followed a similar routine. In interviews, professional writers talk far less than amateurs about inspiration, and far more about staying on the job, regardless of whether it feels like a productive day or an unproductive one. Even E. B. White, a less methodical worker than Angelou, rejected the notion that the writer should wait for the inspired moment: "I think that writing is mainly work. Like a mechanic's job. A mechanic might as well say he was waiting for inspiration before he greased your car because if he didn't feel just right he'd miss a lot of the grease points. . . ."

One advantage that experienced professionals have over inexperienced amateurs is that they have learned how to trust the writing process. The inexperienced writer may labor for hours on an opening paragraph—writing the first sentence, erasing it, rewriting it. When the clock finally forces her to get something done, right or wrong, she writes her paragraph at one burst, looks it over, and pronounces it dead on arrival: "No. You can't say that. You'll bore them to death."[1] Experienced writers may find getting started just as unpleasant, but, knowing that the process of writing and revising will eventually rescue them, they start. They don't have to rely on inspiration because they have the confidence to produce drivel, if necessary, in the early going. "In my own case," says economist and writer John Kenneth Galbraith, "there are days when the result is so bad that no fewer than five revisions are required. However, when I'm greatly inspired, only four are needed . . . ." Like other experienced writers, Galbraith knows that no one ever gets to the top of the stairs in a single leap.

◆ *Rules for Writers.* One problem that may create writer's block is a too hasty and too rigid adherence to "rules" of good writing. Writers may block on an opening paragraph, for example, if they have constantly in their minds the "rule" that the introduction should grab the reader's attention. Trying to invent a "grabber" at the same time you are trying to project the general shape of your essay can be an impossibly large task. Sometimes you may have to ignore for a draft or two the rule about grabbing attention.

EXERCISE 2

The preoccupation with rules is particularly damaging if the rules aren't important ones. List a few rules of good writing that you try to follow. Don't list rules of punctuation or spelling. Share your list with your classmates and your instructor to get their reactions. How important do they feel these rules are? How early in the writing process should they be observed?

FRONT AREAS AND BACK AREAS

Because of the rule she had on her mind, the blocked writer we have been discussing was composing as if her page were in full view of her audience. Awareness of an audience is one of the psychological conditions that creates logical, coherent prose, but it can also be one of the obstacles to writing. A person preoccupied with the audience may have no attention left for the hard thinking necessary to bring a subject and framework together.

---

[1] "bore them to death": This account of the behavior of a blocked writer is based on a case study described in Mike Rose's "Rigid Rules, Inflexible Plans, and the Stifling of Language: A Cognitive Analysis of Writer's Block," *College Composition and Communication,* December 1980.

Sociologists have provided us with a useful way of talking about this problem. They point out that workers in most occupations that involve an audience have "back areas" as well as front areas. Onstage, actors are in a front area, where everything they do will be scrutinized. But backstage is the green room, where they can shed cumbersome costumes, rehearse lines, complain about the audience, chew gum, or do whatever is necessary to get them through the performance. And before opening night were early read-throughs and rehearsals where the actors could temporarily forget about the audience and concentrate on the difficult business of making sense of characters and situations. A friend of mine once visited a powerful executive whose "office" was as uncluttered and composed as a room in a museum. But a small door at the rear led to the real office, where the executive worked amid stacks of papers and open books. People seem to need a space, physical or psychological, where they concentrate on their work without worrying about appearances.

Some writers create back areas by freewriting. Others, like Theodore White and Joan Didion, keep journals: Didion says that hers is filled with "bits of the mind's string too short to use, an indiscriminate and erratic assemblage with meaning only for its maker." Others begin a project by writing their thoughts in a letter to a friend. Personal letters, as Garrison Keillor points out, don't feel like performances: "When you have a True True Friend to write to, a *compadre,* a soul sibling, then it's like driving a car down a country road, you get behind the keyboard and press on the gas."

Even when writers don't freewrite, keep a private journal, or begin with a letter, they may spend a good deal of time writing essentially for themselves or for a friendly audience before they attend closely to the needs of a more public audience. Communicating with an audience of strangers is an important function of writing, but it isn't the *only* function. Sometimes we write to straighten things out in our minds. The public is not invited.

DEALING WITH THE ERRORMONGER

The antithesis of Keillor's "True True Friend" is a figure we might call the errormonger. For him, the first interest of a piece of writing is the errors it contains. Typographical, factual, grammatical—all errors are equally important in his eyes, even variations from standard usage so slight that most competent writers would not regard them as errors at all, but as stylistic choices.

You will probably do well to banish all thought of this character from the "back areas" in which you do your initial drafting. When you are first getting words on the page, you shouldn't spend much time worrying about whether *immediate* has one *m* or two, or whether to use a comma after *therefore,* or whether Lincoln was 6′4″ or 6′5″. Get the sentence wrong if necessary, but get it *down.* If you are afraid of losing track of a possible error, make a mark in the margin or type a "flag" (I use @@@) into the text. Don't—please—stop in midthought to start reading through a handbook or encyclopedia. The errormonger can't see the draft, can't circle the error and embarrass you. He has no pass to go backstage.

As you approach the final draft, though, you'll want to remember that there are errormongers in almost every "target" audience and that to win their respect, you must be as fastidious as they are. If you are writing on a computer, run a spell check. If you have access to a computerized proofreading program, learn to use it (but don't trust it too much). Besides these mechanical aids, try some of the techniques that professional proofreaders use. You might, for example, read through the text three times, concentrating each time on something different.

> *Reading One:* Concentrate exclusively on coherence ("flow") between sentences. Examine each sentence with a single question in mind: Is the relationship between this sentence and the material that comes before it clear?

> *Reading Two:* Concentrate on the quality of the sentences judged in isolation from one another. Do they seem to be well formed, economical, properly punctuated, clear in their wording? For this reading, some proofreaders begin with the last sentence of the paper and work backward to the beginning.

> *Reading Three:* Concentrate on individual words, spaces, and marks of punctuation. Have you typed *there* for *their, it's* for *its, Mrs. Groundhog* for *Mrs. Grundy?* Are the paragraph breaks where they should be? Are all the spaces intentional? Are marks of punctuation that work in pairs (parentheses, quotation marks, sometimes commas) properly paired?

Most people who compose on a computer find it difficult to proofread on screen. Proofread from hard copy whenever possible. If you must proofread onscreen, consider narrowing your margins temporarily so that you are looking at only three or four words per line.

All the techniques we've discussed create some psychological distance between you and what you have written. Only when you look at the text with the cold eye of a stranger do you see all its blemishes. Time, of course, is the best distancer of all, which is why it is best to delay proofreading until the heat of composition has cooled. The cold eye that allows us to edit copy well can stop composition in its tracks.

A Cautious Overview of the Writing Process

The textbooks of earlier generations sometimes contained lists that told the student writer what to do step-by-step, as though writing an essay were as straightforward as assembling a bookcase. Research conducted in the last twenty-five years has shown that these lists don't describe methods of successful writers, methods that are so various and complex that *no* list can describe them. Nonetheless, we can hazard a few generalizations about how experienced writers work in the early, middle, and late stages of the writing process.

Early on, these writers concentrate on their goals and procedures. They consider who their ultimate audience is, what that audience needs or wants to know, what reactions they hope to inspire in the audience. They define their subject and framework tentatively, and they may produce a preliminary outline. If the subject demands research, they may delay drafting until they have enough information to be confident of their direction.

Drafting, however, is the essential business. Sometimes, for some writers, drafting is a tidy process that goes according to plan. For most writers, it is not. Drafting provokes new planning, new planning requires redrafting, which provokes yet more planning, which . . . but you get the idea. During this creative stage of preliminary drafting, writers may ignore their target audience for a time, writing primarily for themselves (or a "True True Friend"). In later drafts, the ultimate readers return to mind, and the writer shapes the material in a way that is more appropriate for an audience of strangers.

After two or three (or more) drafts, the writer will often produce one for reading by colleagues or editors. This semipublic reading can be an exciting stage in the paper's development, comparable to the dress rehearsal of a play, but the writer's work is not done. He or she has to consider readers' comments, positive and negative, and read the draft again, ready— if necessary—to go back to square one.

PEER REVIEW: A CHECKLIST

Students in composition classes often act as "peer editors" or "peer reviewers" of each other's papers, just as engineers, lawyers, managers, and other professionals often act as peer reviewers of each other's work. To get the maximum benefit from peer review, you and your reviewers need to act on three assumptions. First, your reviewers need to know that the draft you offer represents your best effort. You waste your reviewers' time and talent by presenting them with material you have not attempted to organize and present clearly. The appropriate draft for peer review is rarely the first one; it should be one that you would not be embarrassed to present to a stranger. Second, your reviewers should agree to be as frank as courtesy will allow in reporting on the essay's strengths and weaknesses. Third, you and your reviewers should acknowledge that even the most painstaking and intelligent peer review leaves responsibility for the draft in *your* hands. Peer review rarely solves a writer's problems: reviewers frequently contradict one another and often make suggestions that would do more harm than good. The process is valuable not because it allows the writer to *rely* on the judgments of others, but because it leaves the writer with reactions to weigh and consider.

To get the fullest and frankest criticism, be certain that your reviewer understands exactly what the assignment is and exactly who your target audience is. To get your reviewer to think about the essay's general effect, you might ask him or her to follow some of the procedures listed here:

1. Describe the reader who would most enjoy or benefit from what I have written.

2. State (in *your* words rather than mine) the essay's central point. Would readers from the intended audience think this point too obvious to need making, or have I encouraged them to see the subject in an unaccustomed way? Please explain.

3. Tell me what you believe to be the two or three greatest strengths of the essay.

4. Tell me what you believe to be the two or three greatest weaknesses of the essay.

5. Tell me what you would do next if this were your essay.

To focus your reviewer's attention on the particulars, you might ask him or her to follow these procedures:

6. Underline with a straight line particularly valuable sentences and phrases in the essay. I will interpret these underlines as advice not to rewrite these passages substantially or delete them in a subsequent draft.

7. Underline with a jagged underline ($\sim$) particularly ineffective or unclear sentences or phrases. I will interpret these jagged underlines as advice to rewrite these passages or delete them.

8. Mark with a thunderbolt ($\lessgtr$) any points where a sentence does not seem logically connected to the one before it.

9. Circle any plain errors of spelling, punctuation, or grammar that you see. These circles will help me proofread.

10. Write a brief marginal note on any passage that you think might offend, confuse, or bore my intended audience.

You'll find additional procedures and questions for peer review at the end of several of the following chapters.

Having friends give you independent reactions of this sort is obviously a great advantage. If you can't find someone to serve as a reviewer, you may want to follow the advice of the Roman poet Horace: leave the essay in a desk drawer for a few days, then draw it out and try to read it with the eye of a stranger. Actually, Horace recommended nine years. He was not at that time an undergraduate.

Assignments
for Chapter 3

FREEWRITING AND LOOPING

A technique some writers use to create a psychological "back area" is freewriting. As its name implies, this technique is an exercise in unruliness. In freewriting, you write headlong about your topic for a fixed period of time (perhaps ten minutes); the only rule is that you must keep your pencil moving forward constantly. You mustn't *pause* to take stock or to consider whether what you are saying makes sense or would bore a reader. You mustn't go back to correct. You may, of course, *write* that you don't think you are making sense or that you think what you are saying is boring. You may find yourself writing for some seconds, "I can't think what to say, I can't think what to say." Eventually, though, you will say something: freewriting tends to turn up nuggets of thought that can later be developed in a more thoughtful way.

Some writing teachers now recommend a technique called "looping" that systematically exploits this tendency of freewriting to produce nuggets. In looping, the writer first freewrites (perhaps for ten minutes), then stops to read through the result, looking for a nugget—about a sentence long—that appears to be the best observation the writing has turned up. Transferring that sentence to the top of a new page, the writer then launches into another freewriting. In all probability, this second freewriting will produce better material than the first because the writer's head is now clearer, the attention better focused. Obviously the process can be repeated any number of times: the second freewriting can produce a nugget for the third, the third produce a nugget for the fourth, and so on. Eventually, the writer will weary of looping because he or she is ready to develop the essay more systematically.

Try a twenty-minute looping exercise on a topic you are considering for an upcoming paper. Use five minutes on the first freewriting, then one minute reading the result, choosing the nugget, and writing the nugget at the top of another page; use five minutes for the second freewriting, then one minute reading, choosing, and writing the nugget at the top of another page; use five minutes to freewrite, then three minutes to consider the whole exercise and decide whether looping seems to be a technique useful to you.

ASSIGNMENT 2:   **LISTING**

Like freewriting, listing can be a useful "back area" activity. Unlike the systematic outliner, the lister refuses to think too early about coherence or selectivity. He or she merely makes a list—at first in no particular order—of ideas or details that *might* find their way into the paper. If you are writing a memoir in a historical framework (an assignment from Chapter 5), you might begin with a list of times when, as a child, you began to sense that you were living inside history. One of the items ("the day Gorbachev came to town") on this list might lead you to make another list, of events that happened to you that day; and perhaps a third, of historic events that the Gorbachev visit brought to mind. List builds on list in much the same way that "loop" builds on "loop."

What form these lists take varies from writer to writer. Some of us automatically number lists, some leave them unnumbered; some prefer lists that line up neatly, others prefer the sort of free-form list that is often called an "idea map" (see illustration p. 64). If you are using lists to start a writing project or to restart it when it stalls, the key is to avoid rigidity. At first you needn't concern yourself about whether a given item is good or bad, or about whether it belongs on this list or that. The list is merely an aid to memory, like the notebook in the metaphor of the warehouse. It allows the writer to capture a thought before it can disappear.

Take ten minutes to list as rapidly as possible ideas and details that might be useful to you in an upcoming paper. Then take ten minutes to write yourself a note about the most interesting items on the list.

ASSIGNMENT 3:   **ANALYSIS OF E. B. WHITE'S REVISION PROCESS**

Studying the trail of drafts an accomplished writer leaves behind can give us some hints about how his or her mind works. White's note to his editor midway through the revision process indicates that he was greatly concerned about the tone of his essay. Examine his drafts carefully and write a short essay (300 to 500 words) in which you explain what he seems to have disliked about the tone of the early drafts, and how he altered this tone in the later ones.

ASSIGNMENT 4:   **ANALYSIS OF YOUR OWN REVISION PROCESS**

Search through drafts of your old papers until you find a short passage that changed fairly dramatically from first draft to last. Write an analysis of the changes, comparable to the one on pages 53–55. If you do not have drafts of earlier papers, begin to collect some for the next paper you write, so that you can return to this assignment later.

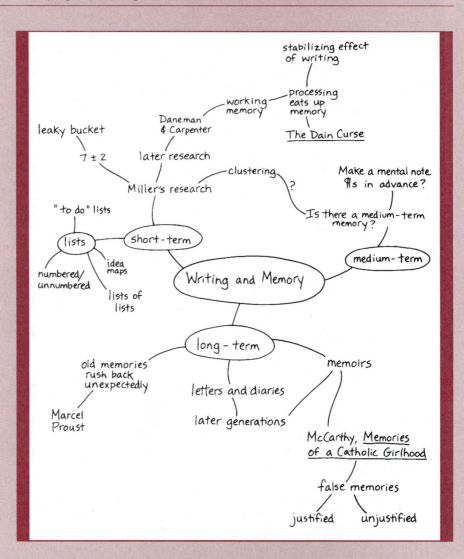

ERASE YOUR TRACKS

Annie Dillard

One of America's most prolific essayists, Annie Dillard has been unusually eager to explain how she does her work. In interviews and written comments, she has discussed the way she conceived and wrote particular essays. In *The Writing Life* (1989), from which the following passage is taken, she gives readers a more general view of the writer's work, throwing in a good deal of practical advice along the way.

1 WHEN YOU WRITE, YOU LAY OUT A LINE of words. The line of words is a miner's pick, a woodcarver's gouge, a surgeon's probe. You wield it, and it digs a path you follow. Soon you find yourself deep in new territory. Is it a dead end, or have you located the real subject? You will know tomorrow, or this time next year.

2 You make the path boldly and follow it fearfully. You go where the path leads. At the end of the path, you find a box canyon. You hammer out reports, dispatch bulletins.

3 The writing has changed, in your hands, and in a twinkling, from an expression of your notions to an epistemological tool. The new place interests you because it is not clear. You attend. In your humility, you lay down the words carefully, watching all the angles. Now the earlier writing looks soft and careless. Process is nothing; erase your tracks. The path is not the work. I hope your tracks have grown over; I hope birds ate the crumbs; I hope you will toss it all and not look back.

4 The line of words is a hammer. You hammer against the walls of your house. You tap the walls, lightly, everywhere. After giving many years' attention to these things, you know what to listen for. Some of the walls are bearing walls; they have to stay, or everything will fall down. Other walls can go with impunity; you can hear the difference. Unfortu-

nately, it is often a bearing wall that has to go. It cannot be helped. There is only one solution, which appalls you, but there it is. Knock it out. Duck.

5 Courage utterly opposes the bold hope that this is such fine stuff the work needs it, or the world. Courage, exhausted, stands on bare reality: this writing weakens the work. You must demolish the work and start over. You can save some of the sentences, like bricks. It will be a miracle if you can save some of the paragraphs, no matter how excellent in themselves or hard-won. You can waste a year worrying about it, or you can get it over with now. (Are you a woman, or a mouse?)

6 The part you must jettison is not only the best-written part; it is also, oddly, that part which was to have been the very point. It is the original key passage, the passage on which the rest was to hang, and from which you yourself drew the courage to begin. Henry James knew it well, and said it best. In his preface to *The Spoils of Poynton*, he pities the writer, in a comical pair of sentences that rises to a howl: "Which is the work in which he hasn't surrendered, under dire difficulty, the best thing he meant to have kept? In which indeed, before the dreadful *done*, doesn't he ask himself what has become of the thing all for the sweet sake of which it was to proceed to that extremity?"

7   So it is that a writer writes many books. In each book, he intended several urgent and vivid points, many of which he sacrificed as the book's form hardened. "The youth gets together his materials to build a bridge to the moon," Thoreau noted mournfully, "or perchance a palace or temple on the earth, and at length the middle-aged man concludes to build a wood-shed with them." The writer returns to these materials, these passionate subjects, as to unfinished business, for they are his life's work.

8   It is the beginning of a work that the writer throws away.

9   A painting covers its tracks. Painters work from the ground up. The latest version of a painting overlays earlier versions, and obliterates them. Writers, on the other hand, work from left to right. The discardable chapters are on the left. The latest version of a literary work begins somewhere in the work's middle, and hardens toward the end. The earlier version remains lumpishly on the left; the work's beginning greets the reader with the wrong hand. In those early pages and chapters anyone may find bold leaps to nowhere, read the brave beginnings of dropped themes, hear a tone since abandoned, discover blind alleys, track red herrings, and laboriously learn a setting now false.

10   Several delusions weaken the writer's resolve to throw away work. If he has read his pages too often, those pages will have a necessary quality, the ring of the inevitable, like poetry known by heart; they will perfectly answer their own familiar rhythms. He will retain them. He may retain those pages if they possess some virtues, such as power in themselves, though they lack the cardinal virtue, which is pertinence to, and unity with, the book's thrust. Sometimes the writer leaves his early chapters in place from gratitude; he cannot contemplate them or read them without feeling again the blessed relief that exalted him when the words first appeared—relief that he was writing anything at all. That beginning served to get him where he was going, after all; surely the reader needs it, too, as groundwork. But no.

11   Every year the aspiring photographer brought a stack of his best prints to an old, honored photographer, seeking his judgment. Every year the old man studied the prints and painstakingly ordered them into two piles, bad and good. Every year the old man moved a certain landscape print into the bad stack. At length he turned to the young man: "You submit this same landscape every year, and every year I put it on the bad stack. Why do you like it so much?" The young photographer said, "Because I had to climb a mountain to get it."

12   A cabdriver sang his songs to me, in New York. Some we sang together. He had turned the meter off; he drove around midtown, singing. One long song he sang twice; it was the only dull one. I said, You already sang that one; let's sing something else. And he said, "You don't know how long it took me to get that one together."

13   How many books do we read from which the writer lacked courage to tie off the umbilical cord? How many gifts do we open from which the writer neglected to remove the price tag? It is pertinent, is it courteous, for us to learn what it cost the writer personally? . . .

14   It takes years to write a book—between two and ten years. Less is so rare as to be statistically insignificant. One American writer has written a dozen major books over six decades. He wrote one of those books, a perfect novel, in three months. He speaks of it, still, with awe, almost whispering. Who wants to offend the spirit that hands out such books?

15   Faulkner wrote *As I Lay Dying* in six weeks; he claimed he knocked it off in his spare time from a twelve-hour-a-day job performing manual labor. There are other

examples from other continents and centuries, just as albinos, assassins, saints, big people, and little people show up from time to time in large populations. Out of a human population on earth of four and a half billion, perhaps twenty people can write a book in a year. Some people lift cars, too. Some people enter week-long sled-dog races, go over Niagara Falls in barrels, fly planes through the Arc de Triomphe. Some people feel no pain in childbirth. Some people eat cars. There is no call to take human extremes as norms.

16 Writing a book, full time, takes between two and ten years. The long poem, John Berryman said, takes between five and ten years. Thomas Mann was a prodigy of production. Working full time, he wrote a page a day. That is 365 pages a year, for he did write every day—a good-sized book a year. At a page a day, he was one of the most prolific writers who ever lived. Flaubert wrote steadily, with only the usual, appalling strains. For twenty-five years he finished a big book every five to seven years. My guess is that full-time writers average a book every five years; sev-enty-three usable pages a year, or a usable fifth of a page a day. The years that biographers and other nonfiction writers spend amassing and mastering materials are well matched by the years novelists and short-story writers spend fabricating solid worlds that answer to immaterial truths. On plenty of days the writer can write three or four pages, and on plenty of other days he concludes he must throw them away.

17 Octavio Paz cites the example of "Saint-Pol-Roux, who used to hang the inscription 'The poet is working' from his door while he slept."

18 The notion that one can write better during one season of the year than another Samuel Johnson labeled, "Imagination operating upon luxury." Another luxury for an idle imagination is the writer's own feeling about the work. There is neither a proportional relationship, nor an inverse one, between a writer's estimation of a work in progress and its actual quality. The feeling that the work is magnificent, and the feeling that it is abominable, are both mosquitoes to be repelled, ignored, or killed, but not indulged. ◆

Moon-Walk

E. B. White

In his biography of E. B. White, Professor Scott Elledge of Cornell University has given us a useful tool for examining the process by which a good writer works through a series of drafts, improving both style and thought. In the collection of White's papers at Cornell, Elledge found six drafts of a one-paragraph comment White wrote for the *New Yorker* after the July 20, 1969, moon-walk by astronauts Neil Armstrong and Edwin Aldrin, Jr. The six drafts are reproduced on the following pages.

Elledge notes that White watched the moon-walk on television in his Maine home until about 1:00 A.M. on Monday, July 21, and that he wrote "under some pressure," since his paragraph had to be ready for typesetting in New York at noon the same day. When White completed the third draft, he believed he had done the job and telegraphed the result to the *New Yorker*. He soon decided that he didn't like what he had sent, however, and took the piece through three more drafts before sending William Shawn, editor of the *New Yorker,* the following telegram: "My comment no good as is. I have written a shorter one on the same theme but different in tone. If you want to hear it, I'll read it to you." Shawn phoned White back, listened to the new version, and agreed that it was better. White then dictated it to Shawn, who rushed it to the printer.

DRAFT 1, PAGE 1

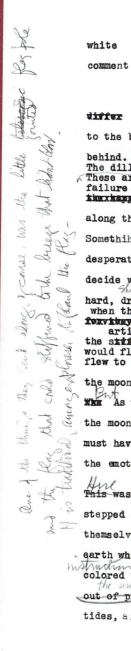

[handwritten top right:] astronaut would never have reached their goal. But they sent along something that might better have been left behind—

white

comment

Planning a trip to the moon ~~isxunsmktdityme~~

~~differ~~ differs in no esstial respect from planning a trip
to the beach. You have to decide what to take, *along,* what to leave

behind. Should the thermos jug go? The child's rubber horse?
The dill pickles?
These are sometimes fateful decisions, on which the success or
failure *outing*
~~thexhappinsss~~ of the whole ~~expxition~~ turns. Something goes

along that spoils everything because it is always in the way.

Something gets left behind that spoils everything because it is
for   were saddled with the
desperately needed for comfort or, safety. The men who had to
send
decide what to take along /to the moon must have pondered long and
Should the vacuum cleaner go? The peanut butter?   fully
hard, drawn up many a list. We're not sure they planned well, ~~or m~~
when they included the
~~fxrxkhxyxxextxdxxxxxxxxxxxxxx~~ the little telescoped flagpole and
artificially stiffened
the ~~stiffendx~~ American flag, ~~artifisallyxxstiffenad~~ so that it
would fly to the breeze that didn't blow.
flew to the breeze that didn't blow. The Stars and Stripes on

the moon undoubtedly gave untold satisfaction to millions of
But
~~Xhe~~ As we watched the Stars and Stripes planted on the surface of

the moon, we experienced the same sensations of pride ~~and~~ that

must have filled the hearts of millions of Americans. But it

the emotion soon turned to *stone in our stomach*
Here a   to do something new, and unparalleled in all history,
~~This~~ was ~~our~~ great chance, and we muffed it. The ~~nsxn~~ men who
were
stepped out onto the surface of the moon are, in a class by
the sum age of the   of men & women everywhere
themselves---pioneers of what is universal. They saw the
dark sky
earth whole---hust as it is, a round ball in a   But they *followed*
instruction &
colored the moon red, white, and blue0---~~good colors all---but~~
the moon that is out of the purview of nationality by its very position
~~out of place in that setting~~. The moon still ~~influences~~ the
still
tides, and the tides lap on every shore, right around the globe.

DRAFT 1, PAGE 2

still holds the key to madness

Kiss in every land

The moon stil belongs to lovers, and lovers are everywhere--not

just in America. What a pity we couldn't have planted some

emblem that ~~exactly~~ expressed the occasion, even if it were
          precisely   this unique, this incredible

nothing more than a white banner, with the legend: ~~xMakexyourxbet~~-y."
          that simply said =

"At last!"

handkerchief, symbol of the common colt
which, like the moon, belongs to all.
mankind

DRAFT 2

white

comment

Planning a trip to the moon differs in no essential respect from planning a trip to the beach. You have to decide what to take along, what to leave behind. Should the thermos jug go? The child's rubber horse? The dill pickles? These are sometimes fateful decisions on which the success or failure of the whole outing turns. Something ~~gaix~~ goes along that spoils everything because it is always in the way. Something gets left behind that is desperately needed for comfort or for safety. The men who drew up the moon list for the astronauts planned long and hard and well. (Should the vacuum cleaner go? *to suck up moondust and save the world?*) Among the items they sent along, of course, was the little jointed flagpole and the flag that could be stiffened to the breeze that didn't blow. (It is traditional among explorers to plant the flag.) Yet the two men who stepped out on the surface of the moon were in a class by themselves: they were of the new race of men, those who hadseen the earth whole. When, following instructions, they colored the moon red, white, and blue, they were ~~stepping out of character~~ *trembling with the past* ---or so it seemed to us who watched, trembling with awe and admiration and pride. This was the last scene in the long book of nationalism, and ~~they followed the book.~~ ~~But~~ the moon still holds the key to madness, which is universal, still controls the tides, that lap on ~~every shore~~ everywhere, and ~~xhi~~ blesses *still speaks but the wide sky* lovers that kiss in every land, under no ~~particular~~ banner. What a pity we ~~couldn't have played the scene as it should been played~~ planting, perhaps, a simple white handkerchief, symbol of the common cold, that belongs to ~~mankind impartially~~ and ~~knows no borders~~ *all and recongnizes no*

What would have been acceptable to them explorationce—

Which like the moon,

is and trembles

DRAFT 3

white

comment

Planning a trip to the moon differs in no essential respect from planning a trip to the beach. You have to decide what to take along, what to leave behind. Should the thermos jug go? The child's rubber horse? The dill pickles? These are sometimes fateful decisions on which the success or failure of the whole outing turns. Something goes along that spoils everything because it is always in the way; something gets left behind that is desperately needed for comfort or for safety. The men who drew up the moon list for the astronauts planned long and hard and well. (Should the vacuum cleaner go, to suck up moondust?) Among the *inevitable* items they sent along, of course, was the little jointed flagpole and the flag that could be stiffened to the breeze that did not blow. (It is traditional among explorers to plant the flag.) Yet the two men who stepped out on the surface of the moon were in a class by themselves and should have been equipped accordingly: they were of the new breed of men, those who had seen the earth whole. When, following instructions, they colored the moon red, white, and blue, they were fumbling with the past---or so it seemed to us, who watched, trembling with awe and admiration and pride. This moon plant was the last scene in the long book of nationalism, one that could well have been omitted. The moon still holds the key to madness, which is universal, still controls the tides that lap on shores everywhere, still guards lovers that kiss in every land under no banner but the sky. What a pity we couldn't have forsworn our little Iwo Jima scene and planted instead a banner acceptable to all---a simple white handkerchief, perhaps, symbol of the common cold, which, like the moon, affects us all.

DRAFT 4

it tusn out;

The moon is a great place for men, and when

Armstrong and Aldrin danced from sheer exuberance, it was
                                           a poor place for
a sight to see. But the moon is ~~no place for banners~~ flags.
                          ~~for the breeze~~ doesn't blow   a flag is out
~~They~~ cannot float on the breeze, and ~~theyxdmntt~~ belong there
 of place on the moon anyway.
anyway. Like every great river, every great sea, the moon

belongs to ~~no one~~ and belongs to all. What a pity we

couldn't have forsworn our little Iwo Jima flag-lanting

scene and planted instead a universal banner acceptable

to all---a limp white handkerchief, perhaps, symbol of the

common cold, which, like the moon, affects us all.

Of course, it is traditional that explorers plant the flag,

and it was inevitable that our astronauts should follow thw

custom. But the act was the last chapter in the long book

of nationalism, one that could well have been omitted---or

~~so it seemed to us.~~ The moon still holds the key to madness,

still controls the tides that lap on shores everywhere, still

guards the lovers that kiss in every land under no banner but th

the sky. What a pity ~~wxxxxxidmtt~~ that, in our triumph, we

couldn't have forsworn the little Iwo Jima scene and planted

a banner acceptable to all---a ~~simple~~ white handkerchief,

perhaps, symbol of the common cold, whcih, like the moon, affects
us all.

DRAFT 5

white

comment

like two happy children

The moon, it turns out, is a great place for men. One-sixth gravity must be a lot of fun, and when Armstrong and Aldrin went into their little dance, it was a moment not only of triumph but of gaiety. The moon, on the other hand, is a poor place for flags. Ours looked stiff and dopey, trying to float on the breeze that does not blow. (There must be a lesson here somewhere.) It is traditional, of course, for explorers to plant the flag, but it struck us, as we watched with awe and admiration and pride, that our two men were universal men, not national men, and should have been equipped accordingly. The moon, like every great river, every great sea, belongs to none and belongs to all; It still holds the key to madness, still controls the tides that lap on shores everywhere, still guards the lovers that kiss in every land under no banner but the sky. What a pity that, in our moment of triumph, we couldn't have forsworn the Iwo Jima scene and planted instead a device acceptable to all: a limp white handkerchief, perhaps, symbol of the common cold, which, like the moon, affects us all, unites us all.

DRAFT 6

white

comment

       The moon, it turns out, is a great place for men. One-sixth gravity must be a lot of fun, and when Armstrong and Aldrin went into their bouncy little dance, like two happy children, it was a moment not only of triumph but of gaiety. The moon, on the other hand, is a poor place for flags. Ours looked stiff and awkward, trying to float on the breeze that does not blow. (There must be a lesson here somewhere.) It is traditional, of course, for explorers to plant the flag, but it struck us, as we watched with awe and admiration and pride, that our two fellows were universal men, not national men, and should have been equipped accordingly. Like every great river and every great sea, the moon belongs to none and belongs to all. It still holds the key to madness, still controls the tides that lap on shores everywhere, still guards the lovers that kiss in every land under no banner but the sky. What a pity that in our moment of triumph we did not forswear the familiar Iwo Jima scene and plant instead a device acceptable to all: a limp white handkerchief, perhaps, symbol of the common cold, which, like the moon, affects us all, unites us all!

Courtesy of the Division of Rare Books and Manuscript Collections, Cornell University Library

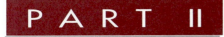

PART II

OBSERVATION AND EXPERIENCE

"He [Charles Darwin] often said that no one could be a good observer unless he was an active theorizer."

Francis Darwin

Eyewitness Reports

WHY IS IT THAT SOME PEOPLE CAN HAVE FASCINATING EXPERIENCES but produce dull accounts of them, while other people seem to find the seed of an engaging report every time they walk around the block?

John Henry Newman raised this question in *The Idea of a University*, complaining that too often, "seafaring men" who traveled around the globe had nothing to say about what they had seen:

> They sleep, and they rise up, and they find themselves, now in Europe, now in Asia; they see visions of great cities and wild regions; they are in the marts of commerce, or amid the islands of the South; they gaze on Pompey's pillar, or on the Andes; and nothing which meets them carries them forward or backward, to any idea beyond itself. Nothing has drift or relation; nothing has a history or a promise. Everything stands by itself, and comes and goes in its turn, like the shifting scenes of a show, which leave the spectator where he was.

Newman's statement brings us back to a point made in Chapter 1, that writing worth reading freshens a subject by putting it into a meaningful framework. Whether you are writing an essay for class, a business report, or a magazine article, to offer nothing but a collection of details in which "everything stands by itself" will disappoint your readers. A successful report is not a neutral attempt to record whatever passes before the writer's eyes; it is an attempt to *characterize* the subject—to find (or create) something significant in it. Charles Darwin, from whom we will hear momentarily, used to say that "no one could be a good observer unless he was an active theorizer."

The heart of this chapter will be several short reports on places, events, and people. Sandwiched between these examples you'll find some comments on ways the writers bring subjects and frameworks together and a few

From *Description de l' Egypte*, by Vivant Denon, 1809

Pompey's pillar was a gigantic column (88 feet high) in Alexandria, Egypt, raised about A.D. *300 to honor the Roman emperor Diocletian.*

comments on style. The intelligent way to read the chapter, however, is to pay twice as much attention to the reports as you do to my commentary. You are more likely to write a good report by imitating the techniques of a good reporter than by following the suggestions of a textbook writer.

THE LITERAL PLACE AND THE IDEA OF A PLACE

Imagine what would happen if you took a notebook to a restaurant for an hour and attempted to record in detail everything you saw, heard, smelled, tasted, or touched in the place. That man sitting over in the corner, for example. It would not be enough to describe his face, with its spots of acne and its drooping mustache. You would have also to describe his clothes minutely, down to the smudge of mud on the instep of his right shoe. And, of course, you would have to describe his actions: the way he held his fork, what he did when his napkin fell off his lap, what vegetables he ate in what order. And then there would be the other two people at the table, and the other ten tables in the room, and the room itself, and your own meal. The task would be simply impossible. And if it could be completed, the result would be useless and dull—probably to you and certainly to anyone else.

What keeps a successful report out of this mire is a strong idea that organizes observations and tells the writer which details to emphasize, which to mention only in passing, and which to ignore. In this respect, every well-focused report tells readers not only about the subject but about the writer's view of the world. Send a devoted shopper to a foreign city and you will tend to get a report on bargains; send a devoted police officer and you will tend to get a report on crime.

The first report we'll look at is a paragraph from Darwin's *Voyage of the Beagle,* one of the most popular travel books of all time. Darwin wrote this paragraph long before he began *The Origin of Species,* and in it you will find not the voice of the middle-aged scientist but that of the young Englishman curious about life in the cattle-ranching region of Banda Oriental (southern Uruguay) during a visit in 1832:

A WRITER AT WORK

"Banda Oriental"
CHARLES DARWIN

On the first night we slept at a retired little country-house; and there I soon found out that I possessed two or three articles, especially a pocket compass, which created unbounded astonishment. In every house I was asked to show the compass, and by its aid, together with a map, to point out the direction of various places. It excited the liveliest admiration that I, a perfect stranger, should know the road (for direction and road are synonymous in this open country) to places where I had never been. At one house a young woman, who was ill in bed, sent to entreat me to come and show her the compass. If their surprise was great, mine was greater, to find such ignorance among people who possessed their thousands of cattle, and "estancias"[2] of great extent. It can only be accounted for by the circumstance that this retired part of the country is seldom visited by foreigners. I was asked whether the earth or sun moved; whether it was hotter or colder in the north; where Spain was, and many other such questions. The greater number of the inhabitants had an indistinct idea that England, London, and North America were different names for the same place; but the better informed well knew that London and North America were separate countries close together,

---

2 **estancia:** Latin American Spanish for *ranch*

and that England was a large town in London! I carried with me some promethean matches,[3] which I ignited by biting; it was thought so wonderful that a man should strike fire with his teeth, that it was usual to collect the whole family to see it: I was once offered a dollar for a single one. Washing my face in the morning caused much speculation at the village of Las Minas; a superior tradesman closely cross-questioned me about so singular a practice; and likewise why on board we wore our beards; for he had heard from my guide that we did so. He eyed me with suspicion; perhaps he had heard of ablutions in the Mahomadan religion, and knowing me to be a heretick,[4] probably he came to the conclusion that all heretics were Turks. It is the general custom in this country to ask for a night's lodging at the first convenient house. The astonishment at the compass, and my other feats of jugglery, was to a certain degree advantageous, as with that, and the long stories my guides told of my breaking stones, knowing venomous from harmless snakes, collecting insects &c, I repaid them for their hospitality.

Portrait by George Richmond, by permission of the Darwin Museum, Down House, Courtesy of Mr. G.P. Darwin

There can be no mistaking the "drift" of this passage. While there must have been other things to report about the life of the villagers Darwin met, he chose to emphasize (and be amused by) their ignorance of Europe and its ways. You might detect a note of arrogance here: who but an Englishman would find it so odd that people living 7,000 miles from London knew so little about it? But there is something more at work. In South America, Darwin was observing people of European origin who had become so separated from Europe that they had become a new people, with a new culture. As anyone who has read *The Origin of Species* knows, he had a mind disposed to be fascinated by differences among creatures that share a common ancestry. Variation, difference, divergence—these and the ways they can be "accounted for" fascinated Darwin from the time he was a young man, and they are also, more often than not, the glue that holds his reports together.

◆ *Action as an Element of Description.* When they describe a place, some writers stop all action. People and things are described as if they were in a still photograph, and the result can be tedious. Darwin, however, includes a good deal of action in his description of Banda Oriental. Examine his paragraph closely and identify at least ten separate actions reported in it.

EXERCISE 1

---

[3] **promethean match:** The promethean match, ignited by breaking a small glass bead wrapped in paper, was first manufactured in London in 1828.
[4] heretic: The people of Banda Oriental called Darwin a "heretic" because he was not a Catholic.

SCRAPBOOKS AND SCENES

We could describe Darwin's method of reporting on Banda Oriental as a "scrapbook" technique. His paragraph collects a series of short episodes and observations that took place on separate days but are connected by a common theme. Compare Darwin's method to the method of George Orwell describing a scene in Marrakech, Morrocco, in 1939:

A WRITER AT WORK

*"Marrakech
Ghetto"*
GEORGE ORWELL

When you go through the Jewish quarters you gather some idea of what the medieval ghettos were probably like. Under their Moorish rulers the Jews were only allowed to own land in certain restricted areas, and after centuries of this kind of treatment they have ceased to bother about overcrowding. Many of the streets are a good deal less than six feet wide, the houses are completely windowless, and sore-eyed children cluster everywhere in unbelievable numbers, like clouds of flies. Down the centre of the street there is generally running a little river of urine. In the bazaar huge families of Jews, all dressed in the long black robe and little black skull cap, are working in dark fly-infested booths that look like caves. A carpenter sits crosslegged at a prehistoric lathe, turning chair-legs at lightning speed. He works the lathe with a bow in his right hand and guides the chisel with his left foot, and thanks to a lifetime of sitting in this position his left leg is warped out of shape. At his side his grandson, aged six, is already starting on the simpler parts of the job. I was just passing the coppersmiths' booths when somebody noticed that I was lighting a cigarette. Instantly, from the dark holes all around, there was a frenzied rush of Jews, many of them old grandfathers with flowing gray beards, all clamouring for a cigarette. Even a blind man somewhere at the back of one of the booths heard a rumour of cigarettes and came crawling out, groping in the air with his hand. In about a minute I had used up the whole packet. None of these people, I suppose, works less than twelve hours a day, and every one of them looks on a cigarette as a more or less impossible luxury.

Here we don't have the impression of looking through a scrapbook but the impression of viewing a continuous scene, as if we were walking with Orwell through the marketplace and listening to his comments. Though it is possible that the passage contains details gathered from several visits to the bazaar, it reads as if Orwell observed all of them at once, perhaps in the space of an hour. Reports written by Darwin's scrapbook method have the advantage of allowing the writer to fit material in more easily, but reports using Orwell's scenic method sometimes have a stronger impact because they give the impression of immediacy, of "being there."

Though his technique is different from Darwin's, Orwell, too, has written a report that has "drift or relation . . . a history and a promise." Without seeming to take his eyes off the present place, Orwell connects it to the past—to the eight centuries of Moorish rule in North Africa and to the medieval ghettos in Europe. He also, disturbingly, suggests the "promise" of the future: the grandson, aged six, will soon have a warped leg to match his grandfather's. Orwell once said that his starting point as a writer was "always a feeling of partisanship, a sense of injustice." Whether he is reporting on Marrakech or London or Paris, his idea of a place is shaped by his concern for oppressed people. Those out of sympathy with Orwell's views might say that his political and moral concerns *distort* his vision; those who are in sympathy might say that they *sharpen* it, allowing him to notice details like the sores on the eyes of children and the crooked leg of the carpenter. One way or another, his concerns give his report the kind of "drift" and "relation" Newman prized.

♦ *Objective and Subjective Language in Reporting.* Orwell's characterization of the Marrakech ghetto includes several words and phrases that seem to be both accurate ("objective") and emotionally charged ("subjective"). Locate six examples of such words and phrases and explain how they serve both a subjective and an objective function.

EXERCISE 2

FINDING SUBJECTS AND FRAMEWORKS FOR A REPORT ON A PLACE

The passages from Orwell and Darwin touch on a fascinating theme: the effect of place on character. If you are searching for a way of approaching a report on a place, you might begin by considering the same theme. Think about how the people in the place you report on (whether a foreign country or a building on the next block) differ from the people in your own family and neighborhood. Then consider ways in which the cultural and natural environment may account for this difference. Darwin attributes the ignorance of the villagers of Banda Oriental to isolation from foreign influences. Orwell attributes the poverty and misery of the Jews of Marrakech to laws that denied them ownership of land and forced them into crowded ghettos. What comparable factors (positive or negative) did you find at work in the place you visited? Thinking about the effect of one of these factors may help create "drift" and "relation."

Another way of approaching the report, particularly if you are writing about a place you are quite familiar with, is to assume the role of a guide for the less informed. To be successful, you'll need to think about the range of your intended audience: what do your best-informed and worst-informed readers already know about the place? What are their motives for wanting to know more? Your classmates may be a good audience for such an essay, especially if some are relative strangers to the city in which your college is located. Can you think of a place they ought to visit or ought to avoid? The reasons you have for visiting or avoiding that place may become frameworks for an essay.

EVENTS AND THEIR SIGNIFICANCE

The passages we have just examined report the relatively constant qualities of a place. That is, though Orwell describes Marrakech as it appeared to him at a particular time, his aim is not to record a passing hour in that city's history. Presumably a traveler who came to the city a week, a month, or a year later would find matters essentially unchanged. Darwin, likewise, reports not on a given event in Banda Oriental but on conditions that had existed before his visit and would persist for some time after. Often, however, writers want to report an event that passes quickly. Their goals are to help readers get a sense of what it was like to be present at the event and to help them understand the significance of what happened.

When events involve famous people, reporters may have half their work done for them: readers don't need to be told why the president's visit to a local high school is significant. Ordinarily, though, writers have to show that the event they have witnessed is interesting and significant. And ordinarily they aren't content with creating just *any* sort of interest: they are reporting the event to illustrate a particular point, and they want to focus interest on this point. Consider the following passage from Jane Jacobs's *The Life and Death of Great American Cities,* a book about urban crime and urban safety. Jacobs's point in the second chapter is that the business activity that keeps streets and sidewalks lively makes them safer. This thesis shapes her report on what she saw one day as she looked out her window and into the adjacent street.

A WRITER AT WORK

"Street Scene"
JANE JACOBS

The incident that attracted my attention was a suppressed struggle going on between a man and a little girl eight or nine years old. The man seemed to be trying to get the girl to go with him. By turns he was directing a cajoling attention to her, and then assuming an air of nonchalance. The girl was making herself rigid, as children do when they resist, against the wall of one of the tenements across the street.

As I watched from our second-story window, making up my mind how to intervene if it seemed advisable, I saw it was not going to be necessary. From the butcher shop beneath the tenement had emerged the woman who, with her husband, runs the shop; she was standing within earshot of the man, her arms folded and a look of determination on her face. Joe Cornacchia, who with his sons-in-law keeps the delicatessen, emerged about the same moment and stood solidly to the other side. Several heads poked out of the tenement windows above, one was withdrawn quickly and its owner reappeared a moment later in the doorway behind the man. Two men from the bar next to the butcher shop came to the doorway and waited. On my side of the street, I saw that the locksmith, the fruit man and the laundry proprietor had all come out of their shops and that the scene was being surveyed from a number of windows besides ours. That man did not know it, but he was surrounded. Nobody was going to allow a little girl to be dragged off, even if nobody knew who she was.

I am sorry—sorry for purely dramatic purposes—to have to report that the little girl turned out to be the man's daughter.

The details in this little narrative create interest by giving us a sense of seeing a particular action that happened on a particular day. But the details also reinforce Jacobs's thesis by showing the kinds of activities that keep the eyes of law-abiding citizens on the street. A street without a delicatessen, a butcher shop, a locksmith, a laundry, a fruit vendor, and (yes) a bar would not be as safe a street for a little girl to walk on. The absence of neighborhood businesses, as Jacobs says a few paragraphs before this passage, creates a Great Blight of Dullness that keeps streets empty, unwatched, and unsafe.

◆ *The Role of Verbs in a Report on Events.* An event is essentially a bundle of related actions with a well-defined beginning and end. Jacobs's narrative begins with her seeing a struggle between a man and a girl and ends with her learning that the man is the girl's father. Between the first sentence and the last are thirty-five verbs or verb forms (participles, gerunds, and infinitives). Find them; then answer the following questions:

EXERCISE 3

1. How many of the verbs describe a definite physical action?
2. How many actions per sentence does Jacobs average?

These calculations will provide you with a benchmark against which you can measure the amount of action packed into your own reporting. (Jacobs sets a high standard.)

FINDING SUBJECTS AND FRAMEWORKS FOR A REPORT ON AN EVENT

As the example from Jane Jacobs shows, the ideal subject for a report on an event has some of the elements of drama:

- a situation that creates tension (the sight of a little girl struggling with a man)

- actions that grow out of the tension (the neighbors positioning themselves to intervene)

- an end to the tension (the discovery that the man is the girl's father).

The drama that makes a report effective, however, is generated as much by the framework as by the subject. Had Jacobs not been thinking about the way businesses on the street contribute to safety, she might have focused her attention on the struggle between the man and the girl, not even noticing the more subtle drama created by the reactions of the shopkeepers and their customers.

When you choose a subject to report on, therefore, you'll want to choose one that is *naturally* dramatic and action-filled, but also one about which you have a *theory* of meaningful drama. If you go to a baseball game intending to report on it, for instance, you may theorize beforehand that the real drama will lie in the ability of the home team's pitcher, still mending from an injury, to muster the confidence to pitch well. If you are reporting on a concert, you may theorize that the real story will be the performer's attempt to introduce the audience to a kind of music they have never heard before. Of course, the event may surprise you; a good reporter is nimble enough to change theories when the subject takes an unexpected turn.

EXERCISE 4

◆ *A Brainstorming Session on Reportable Events.* Typically, reporters for local newspapers gather for daily or weekly editorial conferences where they either receive assignments for stories from an autocratic editor or discuss assignments democratically. Following the democratic pattern, meet for a few minutes with a group of your classmates and make a list of at least six upcoming events that could be subjects of interesting reports. For each event, try to think of at least two theories the reporter might have about where the drama will lie.

THE CHARACTER TYPE AND THE REPORT ON A PERSON

When we discuss people, we almost automatically use language like "You know the type" or "What kind of woman is she?" We all have theories about character types—pigeonholes into which a new acquaintance or a public figure can be put. At its worst, this way of thinking produces crude and unrealistic stereotypes, stereotyping so offensive that we might wish we could forget about types altogether and deal with each individual *as* an individual. As an ethical position, refusal to deal in types has merit; but as a practical matter, we confront so many people every day that our minds would be overwhelmed if we didn't form some categories. If only for convenience, we learn to see some people as flatterers, some as perfectionists, some as bigots, some as liberals, and so forth. Recognizing the type helps us know how to act, even how to feel, when we confront the individual.

Seeing two ways at once is a key to reporting on personalities. We look at the individual (our subject) through one eye and at a familiar character type (our framework) through the other. We are interested in finding correspondences between the individual and the type, but—as in all reporting—flexibility is crucial. We may need to show ways our subject escapes the type, as well as ways he or she fits it, and close observation may convince us that he or she belongs to another type altogether.

THE THEOPHRASTAN CHARACTER

To get a clearer picture of how character types work in reporting, let's begin by examining a short essay that presents a "pure" type—one that doesn't pretend to represent an individual. The author is Theophrastus, an ancient Greek philosopher.

A WRITER AT WORK

"The Faultfinder"
THEOPHRASTUS

Faultfinding is being unreasonably critical of your portion in life. For example, a friend sends over a serving of the main dinner course with his compliments: the faultfinder is the kind who says to the messenger, "You can go tell your master I said that he didn't want me to have a taste of his soup and his third-rate wine—that's why he wouldn't give me a dinner invitation." And even while his mistress is kissing him he will complain, "I wonder if you really love me the way you say you do." He gets angry with the weather, too, not because it rained but because it didn't rain soon enough.

If he comes on a wallet in the street, his comment is "Always this—never a real find!" Let him get a slave at bargain prices, moreover, after begging and pleading, and what does he say but "I really wonder if the fellow can be in sound shape, seeing that he was so cheap." Or supposing somebody announces, "You've got a baby boy!" He meets this good news with: "You might as well have told me half my estate's down the drain—that's what it really means." What's more, he can win a case with every single ballot in his favor; he will still claim that his lawyer passed over a lot of sound arguments. And when friends have raised a loan to help him out and one of them asks him, "Aren't you pleased?" his answer is "How can I be, when I have to pay everybody back and then act grateful besides?"

Theophrastus wrote thirty such characters, memorable because of the author's eye and ear for details. His Flatterer, for instance, dispenses compliments while "he is pulling a loose thread from your coat or picking a piece of chaff the wind has blown onto your hair." When it is the Pinchpenny's turn to have neighbors over for a meal, he has the meat cut into tiny slices. On shipboard the Coward is the one "who mistakes a rocky headland for a pirate brig, and who asks if there are unbelievers on board when a big wave hits the side."

The formula for a Theophrastan character is very simple. It begins with a sentence defining the character type and then presents a series of details, as precise as possible and with as little commentary as possible. Though they are sometimes humorous, Theophrastus's characters were written for the purpose of moral instruction. By presenting his students with clear pictures of various character faults, he was giving them, indirectly, a series of lessons in morality and psychology. The composition of the characters was an essentially scientific project. Like Aristotle, Theophrastus was a great botanist who delighted in collecting specimens of plants and categorizing them by species, genus, and family according to their similarities. The writing of the characters was, so to speak, human botanizing—an attempt to identify the different species of men who could be found in Athens.

EXERCISE 5

◆ *A List of Character Types.* Theophrastus left us thirty characters, suggesting that he had observed thirty distinct species of Athenians. Consider the community around you. Name at least half a dozen character types that you think are common in the population. Keep this list as a basis for Assignment 3 at this chapter's end.

EXERCISE 6

◆ *A Rewrite of "The Faultfinder."* Theophrastus illustrates "The Faultfinder" with examples drawn from daily life in ancient Athens. Retaining his first sentence, rewrite the character using examples drawn from the daily life of your own community.

THE INDIVIDUAL PERSONALITY IN THE CONTEXT OF THE GENERAL CHARACTER

Since it is about a type rather than an individual, the "Theophrastan character" keeps writers out of some kinds of trouble. They may gather details from the study of actual people, but since no one is mentioned by name in the sketch itself, no one would dare to complain. Who would have threatened to sue Theophrastus by claiming to be the model for "The Faultfinder" or "The Absent-Minded Man"? Only someone who wanted to appear, unnamed, in "The Dunce."

But readers are usually eager to learn about "real people" rather than about types. Or, rather, they are eager to learn about real people *as* types. When we analyze the profiles that appear in books, newspapers, and magazines, we discover that the individuals in them are usually portrayed as examples of familiar character types. Consider, for example, the way that Kenneth Walsh opened a story about Hillary Rodham Clinton for *U.S. News and World Report:*

A WRITER AT WORK

"Hillary Clinton"
KENNETH WALSH

Ever the diligent scholar, Hillary Clinton has immersed herself in a crash course on being first lady. In the last two months, advisers say, she surveyed a host of opinion leaders, conferred with scores of friends and read the biographies of every one of her 43 predecessors. Typically, Mrs. Clinton wanted to know exactly what made past first ladies successful, where they might have gone wrong and how she could put her imprimatur on the job and the country. Her meticulous research even included reading a collection of mystery novels written by Franklin D.

Roosevelt's son Elliott, in which Eleanor Roosevelt appears as an amateur sleuth.

A passage like this gives the reader information on two levels at once. Walsh may help us understand Hillary Clinton as an individual by associating her with a type we have encountered before—the Scholar. At the same time, he may help us understand the type better by giving us an example of the way such a person behaves in a particular instance. (It surprises me that *anyone* could be "diligent scholar" enough to read all those biographies.)

The writer may choose to present a subject as a positive type or as a negative one, a perfect representative of the species or an odd one that breaks the mold in surprising ways. The important thing is for the writer to tap into the audience's catalogue of character types. The writer who begins *there* has a good chance of helping the reader connect new information with old.

Often a writer knows the person he or she is writing about far better than Kenneth Walsh knows Hillary Clinton and can see a dozen aspects of the subject's character in every gesture. Nonetheless, for the reader's sake, a careful reporter will ordinarily focus on one aspect at a time, as E. B. White does in this portrait of his wife, Katharine:[1]

I seldom saw her *prepare* for gardening, she merely wandered out into the cold and the wet, into the sun and the warmth, wearing whatever she had put on that morning. Once she was drawn into the fray, once involved in transplanting or weeding or thinning or pulling deadheads, she forgot all else; her clothes had to take things as they came. I, who was the animal husbandryman on the place, in blue-jeans and an old shirt, used to marvel at how unhesitatingly she would kneel in the dirt and begin grubbing about, garbed in a spotless cotton dress or a handsome tweed skirt and jacket. She simply refused to dress *down* to a garden: she moved in elegantly and walked among her flowers as she walked among her friends—nicely dressed, perfectly poised. If when she arrived back indoors the Ferragamos were encased in muck, she kicked them off. If the tweed suit was a mess, she sent it to the cleaner's.

The only moment in the year when she actually got herself up for gardening was on the day in fall that she had selected, in advance, for the laying out of the spring bulb garden—a crucial operation, carefully charted and full of witchcraft. The morning often turned out to be raw and overcast, with a searching wind off the water—an easterly that finds its way quickly to your bones. The bad weather did not deter Katharine: the hour had struck, the strategy of spring must be worked out according to plan. . . .

---

[1] portrait: From his introduction to her collection of horticultural essays, *Onward and Upward in the Garden* (1979).

Armed with a diagram and a clipboard, Katharine would get into a shabby old Brooks raincoat much too long for her, put on a little round wool hat, pull on a pair of overshoes, and proceed to the director's chair—a folding canvas thing—that had been placed for her at the edge of the plot. There she would sit, hour after hour, in the wind and the weather, while Henry Allen produced dozens of brown paper packages of new bulbs and a basketful of old ones, ready for the intricate interment. As the years went by and age overtook her, there was something comical yet touching in her bedraggled appearance on this awesome occasion— the small, hunched-over figure, her studied absorption in the implausible notion that there would be yet another spring, oblivious to the ending of her own days, which she knew perfectly well was near at hand, sitting there with her detailed chart under those dark skies in the dying October, calmly plotting the resurrection.

A man writing within two years of the death of his wife must have a thousand images of her in his mind, particularly if the marriage is as happy as White's was and the wife as talented and complex as Katharine Sergeant Angell White. But White, knowing from long practice that a writer must find a way to simplify and focus, chooses to portray her *in this passage* as *one* thing, a devoted gardener. The framework allows him to *suggest* Katharine's stylishness, her intensity, her optimism, her self-forgetfulness, and many other memorable qualities without producing a blur of form-less description.

EXERCISE 7

◆ *Preparation to write a memory-based portrait.* E. B. White, who chose in the passage above to portray his wife as a devoted gardener, might have chosen to portray her as a brilliant fiction editor for the *New Yorker* or as a woman who found a way to balance the demands of career and family. Writing about someone you know well means making decisions like this. Think of someone you know quite well and about whom you might be able to write an interesting essay. List (and briefly explain) three different character types you might employ to make your portrait work.

EXERCISE 8

◆ *Preparation to write an interview-based portrait.* Name five people who could interest readers in your community or on your campus *and whom you might be able to interview.* (These might be nameable individuals, like the men's basketball coach, or members of an interesting group, like Act Up.) For each person, state in a sentence what type of character your potential readers might expect to encounter. Then create a list of five key questions that would help you confirm or refute the accuracy of the public's perception.

RESEARCHING AND WRITING AN EYEWITNESS REPORT

POINTS TO CONSIDER

Begin with a hypothesis (or two).   Because almost every subject will confront you with more details than you can possibly notice and use, you need to begin with some ideas that can direct your attention. Reporting on a local athletic star, you might begin with the hypothesis (acquired from rumor) that she is an example of a compulsive worker, someone who constantly drives herself to succeed. If you begin your research with this hypothesis in mind, you may notice that when you interview her, she is compulsively tidying her desk, and you may recognize this as a detail pertinent to the framework of your report. Even hypotheses that are overthrown by research are valuable because they focus writers' attention.

Gather more material than you can use.   When you begin your research, gather more details than you can possibly use. Only a fraction of these may appear in your essay; but in the process of drafting, you may change your mind about which details are most important. Begin with an oversupply and you will be able to pick and choose.

Be prepared to simplify.   The more you learn about your subject, the more uncomfortable you may be with presenting it in a single framework. If your subject is a person, for instance, you may feel that it would be truer to present her as twelve things than one: she is a mother, a doctor, a swimmer, a faultfinder, a sports fan, a political conservative, an agnostic, an audiophile, the product of a broken home, an overachiever, a liar on petty issues, and an example of someone who got one good break and ran with it. The problem is that attempting to say everything about a subject can become a way of saying nothing in particular and boring the reader in the process.

Occasionally, you may encounter a subject you simply can't "put together" in a single framework. Theodore White, for instance, found Jimmy Carter an unfathomable "mystery" and was forced to present him in a series of frameworks or "layers" (see pages 107–109). If you read White's description, however, you'll see that he emphasizes Carter the Christian and Carter the engineer and that he barely mentions other aspects of the president's personality. Effective writers know that even when they want to make the point that their subject is complex, they must choose where they will place their emphasis.

QUESTIONS FOR PEER REVIEW

If you have an opportunity for peer review, ask your reviewer both for general comments (see the checklist on page 61) and for answers to four particular questions:

1. Do all my examples contribute to one impression, or do they point in different directions and so blur the impression? Which examples seem most to the point? Which seem farthest from the point?

2. Are my examples graphic? That is, do they give you a sense of *being there*, seeing with your own eyes and hearing with your own ears? Which examples are most lively? Which are least lively?

3. Have I stereotyped my subject in a way that is offensive or clearly false?

4. Do you know more about my subject now than when you started reading? What have you found out? What do you think my ultimate readers are likely to learn?

There is another question, one that no reviewer can answer for you: did the process of writing the report alter your understanding of the subject? Like other kinds of writing, the eyewitness report seems to succeed best when the writer becomes part of his or her own audience. George Orwell became the conscience of his generation because he *wrote* his way to a sharper and sharper perception of injustice. Surely Jane Jacobs's own vision of the activity on city streets changed when she began to write *The Life and Death of Great American Cities*. An excellent report is generally an eye opener for the writer as well as the reader.

Assignments for Chapter 4

ASSIGNMENT 1: **A REPORT ON A PLACE**

For this assignment you will act as a journalist whose job is to characterize a place you presume your readers have not seen. Since you are probably not able to travel far while classes are in session, you may have to rely on memory for your report. The memory of a recent journey may serve you best, since success will depend largely on recalling precise details. Don't overlook the possibility of traveling locally and reporting on a place unfamiliar to many of your classmates. You might produce an interesting report on a club or restaurant, a neighborhood, a museum, or some other public building. A visit to the city jail may provide you with more to write about than a vacation trip to Paris would.

ASSIGNMENT 2: **A REPORT ON AN EVENT**

In this case your assignment is a very common one for reporters on local papers, to attend an event and write a report that gives those who did not attend it a sense of what they missed. Jane Jacobs's description of the scene outside her window reminds us that an event needn't be newsworthy to be interesting. The key is that it should arouse curiosity, that people should wonder what such an occasion is like. A concert by a well-known artist might, therefore, be a good subject, but an amateur barbershop quartet contest might be more interesting still. Those who have never been present at a livestock auction, a political protest rally, or a beauty contest may be interested in a report that gives them a strong impression of what such events are like.

ASSIGNMENT 3: **A THEOPHRASTAN CHARACTER**

Following as precisely as possible the formula used by Theophrastus himself, write a "character" that exemplifies a vice or a virtue and also gives a lively and accurate picture of how we live today.

ASSIGNMENT 4: **A REPORT ON AN ACQUAINTANCE**

Write a report on someone you know well and whose personality you believe will interest your classmates. The challenge here will be two-fold, to show that your acquaintance embodies a "type" worth discussing and to illustrate your characterization with graphic details: actions, words, appearances, contrasts, and so forth.

ASSIGNMENT 5:

AN INTERVIEW-BASED REPORT ON A "PUBLIC FIGURE"

For this assignment, your mission is to characterize a person who by vocation, avocation, or name is likely to arouse the sort of interest that might result in a story in a local newspaper. Your primary sources of information should be *not* other published reports but direct observation and interviews with the subject and perhaps with others who know the subject. You will want to choose a subject likely to grant you an interview, of course. You might interview a musician, an artist, an actor or actress (amateur or professional), an especially popular teacher, the writer of a book, a dedicated athlete, a politician in the community or a student politician, or someone committed to a controversial cause. Write for an audience curious to know what makes such a person tick.

ASSIGNMENT 6:

A REPORT ON A CHARACTER IN A SHORT STORY OR POEM

The people we encounter in literature often approach the complexity of those we meet in life, and they are often presented with little or no commentary by the author. To practice both the close reading of a literary work and your ability to write a focused report, write a 250-word description of one of the following characters.

1. The Duke or the Duchess in "My Last Duchess" (p. 449)
2. The narrator in "The Hammer Man" (p. 445)
3. Jack in "No One's a Mystery" (p. 443)
4. The narrator in "No One's a Mystery" (p. 443)
5. Either of the parents in "Blackberries" (p. 440)

MY SOJOURN IN THE LANDS OF MY ANCESTORS

Maya Angelou

Maya Angelou's report on her weekend in a village in the West African country of Ghana is part of her book *All God's Children Need Traveling Shoes*. She added the italicized introduction when she published the report in *Ms.* magazine in August 1986.

1   *DURING THE EARLY SIXTIES IN NEW YORK City, I met, fell in love with, and married a South African Freedom Fighter who was petitioning the United Nations over the issue of apartheid. A year later, my 15-year-old son, Guy, and I followed my new husband to North Africa.*

2   *I worked as a journalist in Cairo and managed a home that was a haven to Freedom Fighters still trying to rid their countries of colonialism. I was a moderately good mother to a growingly distant teenager and a faithful, if not loving, wife. I watched my romance wane and my marriage end in the shadows of the Great Pyramid.*

3   *In 1962, my son and I left Egypt for Ghana, where he was to enter the university and I was to continue to a promised job in Liberia. An automobile accident left Guy with a broken neck and me with the responsibility of securing work and a place for him to recover. Within months I did have a job, a house, and a circle of black American friends who had come to Africa before me. With them I, too, became a hunter for that elusive and much longed-for place the heart could call home.*

4   *Despite our sincerity and eagerness, we were often rebuffed. The pain of rejection in Africa caused the spiritual that black slaves sang about their oppressors to come to my mind:*

*I'm going to tell God
How you treat me
when I get home.*

5   *On the delicious and rare occasions when we were accepted, our ecstasy was boundless, and we could have said with our foreparents in the words of another spiritual:*

*My soul got happy
When I came out of the wilderness
Came out of the wilderness
Came out of the wilderness.
My soul got happy
When I came out of the wilderness
And up to the welcome table.*

6   I had a long weekend, money in my purse, and working command of Fanti. After a year in Accra, I needed country quiet, so I decided to travel into the bush. I bought roasted plantain stuffed with boiled peanuts, a quart of Club beer, and headed my little car west. The stretch was a highway from Accra to Cape Coast, filled with trucks and private cars passing from lane to lane with abandon. People hung out of windows of the crowded mammie lorries, and I could hear singing and shouting when the drivers careened those antique vehicles up and down hills as if each was a little train out to prove it could.

7   I stopped in Cape Coast only for gas. Although many black Americans had headed for the town as soon as they touched ground in Ghana, I successfully avoided it for a year. Cape Coast Castle and the nearby Elmina Castle had been holding forts for captured slaves. The captives had been imprisoned in dungeons beneath the massive buildings, and friends of mine who had felt called upon to make the trek reported that they felt the thick stone walls still echoed with old cries.

8   The palm-tree-lined streets and fine white-stone buildings did not tempt me to remain any longer than necessary. Once out of the town and again onto the tarred roads, I knew I had not made a clean escape. Despite my hurry, history had invaded my little car. Pangs of self-pity and a sorrow for my unknown relatives suffused me. Tears made the highway waver and were salty on my tongue.

9   What did they think and feel, my grandfathers, caught on those green savannas, under the baobab trees? How long did their families search for them? Did the dungeon wall feel chilly and its slickness strange to my grandmothers, who were used to the rush of air against bamboo huts and the sound of birds rattling their green roofs?

10   I had to pull off the road. Just passing near Cape Coast Castle had plunged me back into the eternal melodrama.

11   There would be no purging, I knew, unless I asked all the questions. Only then would the spirits understand that I was feeding them. It was a crumb, but it was all I had.

12   I allowed the shapes to come to my imagination; children passed, tied together by ropes and chains, tears abashed, stumbling in a dull exhaustion, then women, hair uncombed, bodies gritted with sand, and sagging in defeat. Men, muscles without memory, minds dimmed, plodding, leaving bloodied footprints in the dirt. The quiet was awful. None of them cried, or yelled, or bellowed. No moans came from them. They lived in a mute territory,

dead to feeling and protest. These were the legions, sold by sisters, stolen by brothers, bought by strangers, enslaved by the greedy, and betrayed by history.

13   For a long time I sat as in an open-air auditorium watching a troupe of tragic players enter and exit the stage.

14   The visions faded as my tears ceased. Light returned and I started the car, turned off the main road, and headed for the interior. Using rutted track roads, and lanes a little larger than footpaths, I found the River Pra. The black water moving quietly, ringed with the tall trees, seemed enchanted. A fear of snakes kept me in the car, but I parked and watched the bright sun turn the water surface into a rippling cloth of lamé. I passed through villages that were little more than collections of thatch huts, with goats and small children wandering in the lanes. The noise of my car brought smiling adults out to wave at me.

15   In the late afternoon I reached the thriving town that was my destination. A student whom I had met at Legon (where the University of Ghana is located) had spoken to me often of the gold-mining area, of Dunkwa, his birthplace. His reports had so glowed with the town's virtues, I had chosen that spot for my first journey.

16   My skin color, features, and the Ghana cloth I wore would make me look like any young Ghanaian woman. I could pass if I didn't talk too much.

17   As usual, in the towns of Ghana, the streets were filled with vendors selling their waves of tinned pat milk, hot spicy Killi Willis (fried, ripe plantain chips), Pond's cold cream, and antimosquito incense rings. Farmers were returning home, children returning from school. Young boys grinned at mincing girls, and always there were the market women, huge and impervious. I searched for a hotel sign in vain and as the day lengthened, I started to worry. I didn't have enough gas to get to Koforidua, a large town east of Dunkwa, where there would

certainly be hotels, and I didn't have the address of my student's family. I parked the car a little out of the town center and stopped a woman carrying a bucket of water on her head and a baby on her back.

18   "Good day." I spoke in Fanti and she responded. I continued, "I beg you, I am a stranger looking for a place to stay."

19   She repeated, "Stranger?" and laughed. "You are a stranger? No. No."

20   To many Africans, only whites could be strangers. All Africans belonged somewhere, to some clan. All Akan[1]-speaking people belong to one of eight blood lines (Abosua) and one of eight spirit lines (Ntoro).

21   I said, "I am not from here."

22   For a second, fear darted in her eyes. There was the possibility that I was a witch or some unhappy ghost from the country of the dead. I quickly said, "I am from Accra." She gave me a good smile. "Oh, one Accra. Without a home," she laughed. The Fanti word *Nkran*, for which the capital was named, means the large ant that builds 10-foot-high domes of red clay and lives with millions of other ants.

23   "Come with me." She turned quickly, steadying the bucket on her head, and led me between two corrugated tin shacks. The baby bounced and slept on her back, secured by the large piece of cloth wrapped around her body. We passed a compound where women were pounding the dinner *foo foo*[2] in wooden bowls.

24   The woman shouted, "Look what I have found. One Nkran which has no place to sleep tonight." The women laughed and asked, "One Nkran? I don't believe it."

25   "Are you taking it to the old man?"

26   "Of course."

27   "Sleep well, alone, Nkran, if you can." My guide stopped before a small house. She put the water on the ground and told me to wait while she entered the house. She returned immediately, followed by a man who rubbed his eyes as if he had just been awakened.

28   He walked close and peered hard at my face. "This is the Nkran?" The woman was adjusting the bucket on her head.

29   "Yes, Uncle. I have brought her." She looked at me, "Good-bye, Nkran. Sleep in peace. Uncle, I am going." The man said, "Go and come, child," and resumed studying my face. "You are not Ga.[3]" He was reading my features.

30   A few small children had collected around his knees. They could barely hold back their giggles as he interrogated me.

31   "Aflao?"

32   I said, "No."

33   "Brong-ahafo?"

34   I said, "No. I am . . ." I meant to tell him the truth, but he said, "Don't tell me. I will soon know." He continued staring at me. "Speak more. I will know from your Fanti."

35   "Well, I have come from Accra and I need to rent a room for the night. I told that woman that I was a stranger . . ."

36   He laughed. "And you are. Now, I know. You are Bambara from Liberia. It is clear you are Bambara." He laughed again. "I always can tell. I am not easily fooled." He shook my hand. "Yes, we will find you a place for the night. Come." He touched a boy at his right. "Find Patience Aduah and bring her to me."

37   The children laughed, and all ran away as the man led me into the house. He pointed me to a seat in the neat little parlor and shouted, "Foriwa, we have a guest. Bring beer." A small black woman with an imperial air entered the room. Her knowing face told me that she had witnessed the scene in her front yard.

---

[1] **Akan:** The Akan languages include Fanti, Ashanti, and five or six others principally spoken in Ghana.

[2] **foo foo (fufu):** a bread made of pounded plantain and cassava.

[3] **Ga:** The Ga, Aflao; Brong-ahafo, and Bambara are West African ethnic groups.

38   She spoke to her husband. "And, Kobina, did you find who the stranger was?" She walked to me. I stood and shook her hand. "Welcome, stranger." We both laughed. "Now don't tell me, Kobina, I have ears, also. Sit down, sister, beer is coming. Let me hear you speak."

39   We sat facing each other while her husband stood over us smiling. "You, Foriwa, you will never get it."

40   I told her my story, adding a few more words I had recently learned. She laughed grandly. "She is Bambara. I could have told you when Abaa first brought her. See how tall she is? See her head? See her color? Men, huh. They only look at a woman's shape."

41   Two children brought beer and glasses to the man, who poured and handed the glasses around. "Sister, I am Kobina Artey; this is my wife, Foriwa, and some of my children."

42   I introduced myself, but because they had taken such relish in detecting my tribal origin I couldn't tell them that they were wrong. Or, less admirably, at that moment I didn't want to remember that I was an American. For the first time since my arrival, I was very nearly home. Not a Ghanaian, but at least accepted as an African. The sensation was worth a lie.

43   Voices came to the house from the yard.

44   "Brother Kobina," "Uncle," "Auntie."

45   Foriwa opened the door to a group of people, who entered, speaking fast and looking at me.

46   "So this is the Bambara woman? The stranger?" They looked me over and talked with my hosts. I understood some of their conversation. They said that I was nice-looking and old enough to have a little wisdom. They announced that my car was parked a few blocks away. Kobina told them that I would spend the night with the newleyweds, Patience and Kwame Duodu. Yes, they could see clearly that I was a Bambara.

47   "Give us the keys to your car, sister; someone will bring your bag."

48   I gave up the keys and all resistance. I was either at home with friends or I would die wishing that to be so.

49   Later, Patience, her husband, Kwame, and I sat out in the yard around a cooking fire near to their thatched house, which was much smaller than the Artey bungalow. They explained that Kobina Artey was not a chief, but a member of the village council, and all small matters in that area of Dunkwa were taken to him. As Patience stirred the stew in the pot that was balanced over the fire, children and women appeared sporadically out of the darkness carrying covered plates. Each time Patience thanked the bearers and directed them to the house, I felt the distance narrow between my past and present.

50   In the United States, during segregation, black American travelers, unable to stay in hotels restricted to white patrons, stopped at churches and told the black ministers or deacons of their predicaments. Church officials would select a home and then inform the unexpecting hosts of the decision. There was never a protest, but the new hosts relied on the generosity of their neighbors to help feed and even entertain their guests. After the travelers were settled, surreptitious knocks would sound on the back door.

51   In Stamps, Arkansas, I heard so often, "Sister Henderson, I know you've got guests. Here's a pan of biscuits."

52   "Sister Henderson, Mama sent a half a cake for your visitors."

53   "Sister Henderson, I made a lot of macaroni and cheese. Maybe this will help with your visitors."

54   My grandmother would whisper her thanks and finally when the family and guests sat down at the table, the offerings were so different and plentiful, it appeared that days had been spent preparing the meal.

55   Patience invited me inside, and when I saw the table I was confirmed in my earlier impression. Groundnut stew, garden egg stew, hot pepper soup, *kenke, kotomre,* fried plantain,

dukuno,[4] shrimp, fish cakes, and more, all crowded together on variously patterned plates.

56   In Arkansas, the guests would never suggest, although they knew better, that the host had not prepared every scrap of food, especially for them.

57   I said to Patience, "Oh, sister, you went to such trouble."

58   She laughed, "It is nothing, sister. We don't want our Bambara relative to think herself a stranger anymore. Come let us wash and eat."

59   After dinner, I followed Patience to the outdoor toilet; then they gave me a cot in a very small room.

60   In the morning, I wrapped my cloth under my arms, sarong fashion, and walked with Patience to the bathhouse. We joined about 20 women in a walled enclosure which had no ceiling. The greetings were loud and cheerful as we soaped ourselves and poured buckets of water over our shoulders.

61   Patience introduced me. "This is our Bambara sister."

62   "She's a tall one, all right. Welcome, sister."

---

4   **kenke, kotomre . . . dukuno:** *kenke,* corn dough, a staple food of the Fanti people is called *dukuno* in Ashanti; *kotomre (kantomire)* is a green vegetable.

"I like her color."   63

"How many children, sister?" The woman was looking at my breasts.   64

I apologized, "I only have one."   65

"One?"   66

"One?"   67

"One!" Shouts reverberated over the splashing water. I said, "One, but I'm trying."   68

They laughed. "Try hard, sister. Keep trying."   69

We ate leftovers from the last night feast, and I said a sad good-bye to my hosts. The children walked me back to my car, with the oldest boy carrying my bag. I couldn't offer money to my hosts, Arkansas had taught me that, but I gave change to the children. They bobbed and jumped and grinned.   70

"Good-bye, Bambara Auntie."   71

"Go and come, Auntie."   72

"Go and come."   73

I drove into Cape Coast before I thought of the gruesome castle and out of its environs before the ghosts of slavery caught me. Perhaps, their attempts had been halfhearted. After all, in Dunkwa, although I let a lie speak for me, I had proved that one of their descendants, at least one, could just briefly return to Africa, and that despite cruel betrayals, bitter ocean voyages, and hurtful centuries, we were still recognizable. ◆   74

QUIET DAYS IN MALIBU

Joan Didion

Joan Didion's report on the community she lived in for seven years is made up of four sections that were composed over a period of two years. These were put together, like pieces of a jigsaw puzzle, for publication as one essay in *The White Album* (1979). Each part seems to make its own statement, but you may find that when joined together they acquire more meaning than they would have if they were read and considered separately.

1.

IN A WAY IT SEEMS THE MOST IDIOSYNCRATIC of beach communities, twenty-seven miles of coastline with no hotel, no passable restaurant, nothing to attract the traveler's dollar. It is not a resort. No one "vacations" or "holidays," as those words are conventionally understood, at Malibu. Its principal residential street, the Pacific Coast Highway, is quite literally a highway, California 1, which runs from the Mexican border to the Oregon line and brings Greyhound buses and refrigerated produce trucks and sixteen-wheel gasoline tankers hurtling past the front windows of houses frequently bought and sold for over a million dollars. The water off Malibu is neither as clear nor as tropically colored as the water off La Jolla. The beaches at Malibu are neither as white nor as wide as the beach at Carmel. The hills are scrubby and barren, infested with bikers and rattlesnakes, scarred with cuts and old burns and new R.V. parks. For these and other reasons Malibu tends to astonish and disappoint those who have never before seen it, and yet its very name remains, in the imagination of people all over the world, a kind of shorthand for the easy life. I had not before 1971 and will probably not again live in a place with a Chevrolet named after it.

2.

Dick Haddock, a family man, a man twenty-six years in the same line of work, a man who has on the telephone and in his office the crisp and easy manner of technological middle management, is in many respects the prototypical Southern California solid citizen. He lives in a San Fernando Valley subdivision near a freshwater marina and a good shopping plaza. His son is a high-school swimmer. His daughter is "into tennis." He drives thirty miles to and from work, puts in a forty-hour week, regularly takes courses to maintain his professional skills, keeps in shape and looks it. When he discusses his career he talks, in a kind of politely impersonal second person, about how "you would want like any other individual to advance yourself," about "improving your rating" and "being more of an asset to your department," about "really knowing your business." Dick Haddock's business for all these twenty-six years has been that of a professional lifeguard for the Los Angeles County Department of Beaches, and his office is a $190,000 lookout on Zuma Beach in northern Malibu.

It was Thanksgiving morning, 1975. A Santa Ana wind was just dying after blowing in off the Mojave for three weeks and setting

69,000 acres of Los Angeles County on fire. Squadrons of planes had been dropping chemicals on the fires to no effect. Querulous interviews with burned-out householders had become a fixed element of the six o'clock news. Smoke from the fires had that week stretched a hundred miles out over the Pacific and darkened the days and lit the nights and by Thanksgiving morning there was the sense all over Southern California of living in some grave solar dislocation. It was one of those weeks when Los Angeles seemed most perilously and breathtakingly itself, a cartoon of natural disaster, and it was a peculiar week in which to spend the day with Dick Haddock and the rest of the Zuma headquarters crew.

4 Actually I had wanted to meet the lifeguards ever since I moved to Malibu. I would drive past Zuma some cold winter mornings and see a few of them making their mandatory daily half-mile swims in open ocean. I would drive past Zuma some late foggy nights and see others moving around behind the lookout's lighted windows, the only other souls awake in all of northern Malibu. It seemed to me a curious, almost beatified career choice, electing to save those in peril upon the sea forty hours a week, and as the soot drifted down around the Zuma lookout on that Thanksgiving morning the laconic routines and paramilitary rankings of these civil servants in red trunks took on a devotionary and dreamlike inevitability. There was the "captain," John McFarlane, a man who had already taken his daily half-mile run and his daily half-mile swim and was putting on his glasses to catch up on paperwork. Had the water been below 56 degrees he would have been allowed to swim in a wet suit, but the water was not below 56 degrees and so he had swum as usual in his red trunks. The water was 58 degrees. John McFarlane is 48. There was the "lieutenant," Dick Haddock, telling me about how each of the Department's 125 permanent lifeguards (there are also 600 part-time or "recurrent" lifeguards) learns

crowd control at the Los Angeles County Sheriff's Academy, learns emergency driving techniques at the California Highway Patrol Academy, learns medical procedures at the U.S.C. Medical Center, and, besides running the daily half-mile and swimming the daily half-mile, does a monthly 500-meter paddle and a monthly pier jump. A "pier jump" is just what it sounds like, and its purpose is to gain practice around pilings in heavy surf.

5 There was as well the man out on patrol.

6 There were as well the "call-car personnel," two trained divers and cliff-climbers "ready to roll at any time" in what was always referred to as "a Code 3 vehicle with red light and siren," two men not rolling this Thanksgiving morning but sitting around the lookout, listening to the Los Angeles Rams beat the Detroit Lions on the radio, watching the gray horizon and waiting for a call.

7 No call came. The radios and the telephones crackled occasionally with reports from the other "operations" supervised by the Zuma crew: the "rescue-boat operation" at Paradise Cove, the "beach operations" at Leo Carrillo, Nicholas, Point Dume, Corral, Malibu Surfrider, Malibu Lagoon, Las Tunas, Topanga North and Topanga South. Those happen to be the names of some Malibu public beaches but in the Zuma lookout that day the names took on the sound of battle stations during a doubtful cease-fire. All quiet at Leo. Situation normal at Surfrider.

8 The lifeguards seemed most comfortable when they were talking about "operations" and "situations," as in "a phone-watch situation" or "a riptide situation." They also talked easily about "functions," as in "the function of maintaining a secure position on the beach." Like other men at war they had charts, forms, logs, counts kept current to within twelve hours: *1405 surf rescues off Zuma between 12:01 A.M. January 1, 1975 and 11:59 P.M. Thanksgiving Eve 1975*. As well as: *36,120 prevention rescues, 872 first aids, 176 beach*

emergency calls, 12 resuscitations, 8 boat distress calls, 107 boat warnings, 438 lost-and-found children, and *0 deaths.* Zero. No body count. When he had occasion to use the word "body" Dick Haddock would hesitate and glance away.

9   On the whole the lifeguards favored a diction as flat and finally poetic as that of Houston Control. Everything that morning was "real fine." The headquarters crew was "feeling good." The day was "looking good." Malibu surf was "two feet and shape is poor." Earlier that morning there had been a hundred or so surfers in the water, a hundred or so of those bleached children of indeterminate age and sex who bob off Zuma and appear to exist exclusively on packaged beef jerky, but by ten they had all pocketed their Thanksgiving jerky and moved on to some better break. "It heats up, we could use some more personnel," Dick Haddock said about noon, assessing the empty guard towers. "That happened, we might move on a decision to open Towers One and Eleven, I'd call and say we need two recurrents at Zuma, plus I might put an extra man at Leo."

10   It did not heat up. Instead it began to rain, and on the radio the morning N.F.L. game gave way to the afternoon N.F.L. game, and after a while I drove with one of the call-car men to Paradise Cove, where the rescue-boat crew needed a diver. They did not need a diver to bring up a body, or a murder weapon, or a crate of stolen ammo, or any of the things Department divers sometimes get their names in the paper for bringing up. They needed a diver, with scuba gear and a wet suit, because they had been removing the propeller from the rescue boat and had dropped a metal part the size of a dime in twenty feet of water. I had the distinct impression that they particularly needed a diver in a wet suit because nobody on the boat crew wanted to go back in the water in his trunks to replace the propeller, but there seemed to be some tacit agreement that the lost part was to be considered the point of the dive.

11   "I guess you know it's fifty-eight down there," the diver said.

12   "Don't need to tell me how cold it is," the boat lieutenant said. His name was Leonard McKinley and he had "gone permanent" in 1942 and he was of an age to refer to Zuma as a "bathing" beach. "After you find that little thing you could put the propeller back on for us, [if] you wanted. As long as you're in the water anyway? In your suit?"

13   "I had a feeling you'd say that."

14   Leonard McKinley and I stood on the boat and watched the diver disappear. In the morning soot from the fires had coated the surface but now the wind was up and the soot was clouding the water. Kelp fronds undulated on the surface. The boat rocked. The radio sputtered with reports of a yacht named *Ursula* in distress.

15   "One of the other boats is going for it," Leonard McKinley said. "We're not. Some days we just sit here like firemen. Other days, a day with rips, I been out ten hours straight. You get your big rips in the summer, swells coming up from Mexico. A Santa Ana, you get your capsized boats, we got one the other day, it was overdue out of Santa Monica, they were about drowned when we picked them up."

16   I tried to keep my eyes on the green-glass water but could not. I had been sick on boats in the Catalina Channel and in the Gulf of California and even in San Francisco Bay, and now I seemed to be getting sick on a boat still moored at the end of the Paradise Cove pier. The radio reported the *Ursula* under tow to Marina del Rey. I concentrated on the pilings.

17   "He gets the propeller on," Leonard McKinley said, "you want to go out?"

18   I said I thought not.

19   "You come back another day," Leonard McKinley said, and I said that I would, and although I have not gone back there is no day when I do not think of Leonard McKinley and Dick Haddock and what they are doing, what situations they face, what operations, what

green-glass water. The water today is 56 degrees.

3.

20 Amado Vazquez is a Mexican national who has lived in Los Angeles County as a resident alien since 1947. Like many Mexicans who have lived for a long time around Los Angeles he speaks of Mexico as "over there," remains more comfortable in Spanish than in English, and transmits, in his every movement, a kind of "different" propriety, a correctness, a cultural reserve. He is in no sense a Chicano. He is rather what California-born Mexicans sometimes call "Mexican-from-Mexico," pronounced as one word and used to suggest precisely that difference, that rectitude, that personal conservatism. He was born in Ahualulco, Jalisco. He was trained as a barber at the age of ten. Since the age of twenty-seven, when he came north to visit his brother and find new work himself, he has married, fathered two children, and become, to the limited number of people who know and understand the rather special work he found for himself in California, a kind of legend. Amado Vazquez was, at the time I first met him, head grower at Arthur Freed Orchids, a commercial nursery in Malibu founded by the late motion-picture producer Arthur Freed, and he is one of a handful of truly great orchid breeders in the world.

21 In the beginning I met Amado Vazquez not because I knew about orchids but because I liked greenhouses. All I knew about orchids was that back in a canyon near my house someone was growing them *in greenhouses*. All I knew about Amado Vazquez was that he was the man who would let me spend time alone in these greenhouses. To understand how extraordinary this seemed to me you would need to have craved the particular light and silence of greenhouses as I did: all my life I had been try-

ing to spend time in one greenhouse or another, and all my life the person in charge of one greenhouse or another had been trying to hustle me out. When I was nine I would deliberately miss the school bus in order to walk home, because by walking I could pass a greenhouse. I recall being told at that particular greenhouse that the purchase of a nickel pansy did not entitle me to "spend the day," and at another that my breathing was "using up the air."

22 And yet back in this canyon near my house twenty-five years later were what seemed to me the most beautiful greenhouses in the world—the most aqueous filtered light, the softest tropical air, the most silent clouds of flowers—and the person in charge, Amado Vazquez, seemed willing to take only the most benign notice of my presence. He seemed to assume that I had my own reasons for being there. He would speak only to offer a nut he had just cracked, or a flower cut from a plant he was pruning. Occasionally Arthur Freed's brother Hugo, who was then running the business, would come into the greenhouse with real customers, serious men in dark suits who appeared to have just flown in from Taipei or Durban and who spoke in hushed voices, as if they had come to inspect medieval enamels, or uncut diamonds.

23 But then the buyers from Taipei or Durban would go into the office to make their deal and the silence in the greenhouse would again be total. The temperature was always 72 degrees. The humidity was always 60 per cent. Great arcs of white phalaenopsis trembled overhead. I learned the names of the crosses by studying labels there in the greenhouse, the exotic names whose value I did not then understand. *Amabilis* × *Rimestadiana* = *Elisabethae*. *Aphrodite* × *Rimestadiana* = *Gilles Gratiot*. *Amabilis* × *Gilles Gratiot* = *Katherine Siegwart* and *Katherine Siegwart* × *Elisabethae* = *Doris*. *Doris* after Doris Duke. *Doris* which first flowered at Duke Farms in 1940. At least

once each visit I would remember the nickel pansy and find Amado Vazquez and show him a plant I wanted to buy, but he would only smile and shake his head. "For breeding," he would say, or "not for sale today." And then he would lift the spray of flowers and show me some point I would not have noticed, some marginal difference in the substance of the petal or the shape of the blossom. "Very beautiful," he would say. "Very nice you like it." What he would not say was that these plants he was letting me handle, these plants "for breeding" or "not for sale today," were stud plants, and that the value of such a plant at Arthur Freed could range from ten thousand to more than three-quarters of a million dollars.

24   I suppose the day I realized this was the day I stopped using the Arthur Freed greenhouses as a place to eat my lunch, but I made a point of going up one day in 1976 to see Amado Vazquez and to talk to Marvin Saltzman, who took over the business in 1973 and is married to Arthur Freed's daughter Barbara. (As in *Phal. Barbara Freed Saltzman* "Jean McPherson," *Phal. Barbara Freed Saltzman* "Zuma Canyon," and *Phal. Barbara Freed Saltzman* "Malibu Queen," three plants "not for sale today" at Arthur Freed.) It was peculiar talking to Marvin Saltzman because I had never before been in the office at Arthur Freed, never seen the walls lined with dulled silver awards, never seen the genealogical charts on the famous Freed hybrids, never known anything at all about the actual business of orchids.

25   "Frankly it's an expensive business to get into," Marvin Saltzman said. He was turning the pages of *Sander's List*, the standard orchid studbook, published every several years and showing the parentage of every hybrid registered with the Royal Horticultural Society, and he seemed oblivious to the primeval silence of the greenhouse beyond the office window. He had shown me how Amado Vazquez places the pollen from one plant into the ovary of a flower on another. He had explained that the best times to do this are at full moon and high tide, because phalaenopsis plants are more fertile then. He had explained that a phalaenopsis is more fertile at full moon because in nature it must be pollinated by a night-flying moth, and over sixty-five million years of evolution its period of highest fertility began to coincide with its period of highest visibility. He had explained that a phalaenopsis is more fertile at high tide because the moisture content of every plant responds to tidal movement. It was all an old story to Marvin Saltzman. I could not take my eyes from the window.

26   "You bring back five-thousand seedlings from the jungle and you wait three years for them to flower," Marvin Saltzman said. "You find two you like and you throw out the other four-thousand-nine-hundred-ninety-eight and you try to breed the two. Maybe the pollenization takes, eighty-five percent of the time it doesn't. Say you're lucky, it takes, you'll still wait another four years before you see a flower. Meanwhile you've got a big capital investment. An Arthur Freed could take $400,000 a year from M.G.M. and put $100,000 of it into getting this place started, but not many people could. You see a lot of what we call back-yard nurseries—people who have fifty or a hundred plants, maybe they have two they think are exceptional, they decide to breed them—but you talk about major nurseries, there are maybe only ten in the United States, another ten in Europe. That's about it. Twenty."

27   Twenty is also about how many head growers there are, which is part of what lends Amado Vazquez his legendary aspect, and after a while I left the office and went out to see him in the greenhouse. There in the greenhouse everything was operating as usual to approximate that particular level of a Malaysian rain forest—not on the ground but perhaps a hundred feet up—where epiphytic orchids grow wild. In the rain forest these orchids get broken by wind and rain. They get pollinated ran-

domly and rarely by insects. Their seedlings are crushed by screaming monkeys and tree boas and the orchids live unseen and die young. There in the greenhouse nothing would break the orchids and they would be pollinated at full moon and high tide by Amado Vazquez, and their seedlings would be tended in a sterile box with sterile gloves and sterile tools by Amado Vazquez's wife, Maria, and the orchids would not seem to die at all. "We don't know how long they'll live," Marvin Saltzman told me. "They haven't been bred under protected conditions that long. The botanists estimate a hundred and fifty, two hundred years, but we don't know. All we know is that a plant a hundred years old will show no signs of senility."

28   It was very peaceful there in the greenhouse with Amado Vazquez and the plants that would outlive us both. "We grew in osmunda then," he said suddenly. Osmunda is a potting medium. Amado Vazquez talks exclusively in terms of how the orchids grow. He had been talking about the years when he first came to this country and got a job with his brother tending a private orchid collection in San Marino, and he had fallen silent. "I didn't know orchids then, now they're like my children. You wait for the first bloom like you wait for a baby to come. Sometimes you wait four years and it opens and it isn't what you expected, maybe your heart wants to break, but you love it. You never say, 'that one was prettier.' You just love them. My whole life is orchids."

29   And in fact it was. Amado Vazquez's wife, Maria (as in *Phal. Maria Vasquez* "Malibu," the spelling of Vazquez being mysteriously altered by everyone at Arthur Freed except the Vazquezes themselves), worked in the laboratory at Arthur Freed. His son, George (as in *Phal. George Vasquez* "Malibu"), was the sales manager at Arthur Freed. His daughter, Linda (as in *Phal. Linda Mia* "Innocence"), worked at Arthur Freed before her marriage. Amado Vazquez will often get up in the night to check a heater, adjust a light, hold a seed pod in his hand and try to sense if morning will be time enough to sow the seeds in the sterile flask. When Amado and Maria Vazquez go to Central or South America, they go to look for orchids. When Amado and Maria Vazquez went for the first time to Europe a few years ago, they looked for orchids. "I asked all over Madrid for orchids," Amado Vazquez recalled. "Finally they tell me about this one place. I go there, I knock. The woman finally lets me in. She agrees to let me see the orchids. She takes me into a house and . . ."

Amado Vazquez broke off, laughing.   30

"She has three orchids," he finally managed   31 to say. "Three. One of them dead. All three from Oregon."

We were standing in a sea of orchids, an ex-   32 travagance of orchids, and he had given me an armful of blossoms from his own cattleyas to take to my child, more blossoms maybe than in all of Madrid. It seemed to me that day that I had never talked to anyone so direct and unembarrassed about the things he loved. He had told me earlier that he had never become a United States citizen because he had an image in his mind which he knew to be false but could not shake: the image was that of standing before a judge and stamping on the flag of Mexico. "And I love my country," he had said. Amado Vazquez loved his country. Amado Vazquez loved his family. Amado Vazquez loved orchids. "You want to know how I feel about the plants," he said as I was leaving. "I'll tell you. I will die in orchids."

4.

In the part of Malibu where I lived from Janu-   33 ary of 1971 until quite recently we all knew one another's cars, and watched for them on the highway and at the Trancas Market and at the Point Dume Gulf station. We exchanged information at the Trancas Market. We left packages and messages for one another at the Gulf station. We called one another in times of wind and fire and rain, we knew when one another's septic tanks needed pumping, we watched for ambulances on the highway and helicopters on the beach and worried about one another's dogs and horses and children and corral gates and Coastal Commission permits. An accident on the highway was likely to involve someone we knew. A rattlesnake in my driveway meant its mate in yours. A stranger's campfire on your beach meant fire on both our slopes.

34   In fact this was a way of life I had not expected to find in Malibu. When I first moved in 1971 from Hollywood to a house on the Pacific Coast Highway I had accepted the conventional notion that Malibu meant the easy life, had worried that we would be cut off from "the real world," by which I believe I meant daily exposure to the Sunset Strip. By the time we left Malibu, seven years later, I had come to see the spirit of the place as one of shared isolation and adversity, and I think now that I never loved the house on the Pacific Coast Highway more than on those many days when it was impossible to leave it, when fire or flood had in fact closed the highway. We moved to this house on the highway in the year of our daughter's fifth birthday. In the year of her twelfth it rained until the highway collapsed, and one of her friends drowned at Zuma Beach, a casualty of Quaaludes.

35   One morning during the fire season of 1978, some months after we had sold the house on the Pacific Coast Highway, a brush fire caught in Agoura, in the San Fernando Valley. Within two hours a Santa Ana wind had pushed this fire across 25,000 acres and thirteen miles to the coast, where it jumped the Pacific Coast Highway as a half-mile fire storm generating winds of 100 miles per hour and temperatures up to 2500 degrees Fahrenheit. Refugees huddled on Zuma Beach. Horses caught fire and were shot on the beach, birds exploded in the air. Houses did not explode but imploded, as in a nuclear strike. By the time this fire storm had passed 197 houses had vanished into ash, many of them houses which belonged or had belonged to people we knew. A few days after the highway reopened I drove out to Malibu to see Amado Vazquez, who had, some months before, bought from the Freed estate all the stock at Arthur Freed Orchids, and had been in the process of moving it a half-mile down the canyon to his own new nursery, Zuma Canyon Orchids. I found him in the main greenhouse at what had been Arthur Freed Orchids. The place was now a range not of orchids but of shattered glass and melted metal and the imploded shards of the thousands of chemical beakers that had held the Freed seedlings, the new crosses. "I lost three years," Amado Vazquez said, and for an instant I thought we would both cry. "You want today to see flowers," he said then, "we go down to the other place." I did not want that day to see flowers. After I said goodbye to Amado Vazquez my husband and daughter and I went to look at the house on the Pacific Coast Highway in which we had lived for seven years. The fire had come to within 125 feet of the property, then stopped or turned or been beaten back, it was hard to tell which. In any case it was no longer our house. ◆

Jimmy Carter

Theodore White

By the time Theodore White published the following passage in *America in Search of Itself: The Making of the President 1956–1980* (1982), he had reported on the career of Presidents Eisenhower, Kennedy, Johnson, Nixon, and Ford. He had seen and evaluated, therefore, a diverse set of presidential personalities. Reading his report on Jimmy Carter, however, one feels that he is struggling to understand a nature very different from his own. His struggle produces a report that puts Carter's personality into several conflicting frameworks.

1 JIMMY CARTER WAS ALWAYS A MYSTERY, THIS man with the straw-colored hair and clear blue eyes, whose enemies came to despise him while those who would be friends could not understand him. Carter fit no mold nor any of those familiar journalistic diagrams by which political writers try to explore the nature of a presidency through the personality of the President. He could not describe himself, as Roosevelt so jauntily did, as having passed from being "Dr. New Deal" to "Dr. Win the War." Nor could he be described, as was Richard Nixon by so many of us, in the twenty years of Nixon's eminence, as being the "Old Nixon" or the "New Nixon," with new Nixons succeeding one another every two or three years in the public print.

2 The personality of Jimmy Carter was the same from the day he decided to run for the presidency until he lost it. And that personality, rather than changing from an "old" to a "new" Carter, had to be examined as a set of layers of faith, of action, even of unpleasantnesses. What made it most difficult was that the most important layer of the personality was a Christianity so devout and concerned that political writers found it awkward to write about.

3 That layer—of true belief—was uppermost and undermost. I encountered it initially before he became President, when I had my first long talk with Carter in Plains, Georgia, in his pleasant middle-class home, surrounded by oak trees—a home comfortable by any standards but by no means the style of mansion so many presidential candidates had acquired. At that time, in 1976, I was pursuing the candidates with a single-track question that might possibly be useful if I was to write a book on that year's campaign. "Where did modern American history really begin?" I would ask, and all had different answers. Jimmy Carter began with civil rights, "the most profound sociological change that's taken place in the country." It was the law as well as Martin Luther King that brought the change in the South, he said. So long as civil rights had been something administered by HEW, and while local and state laws contradicted federal laws, there was this question: "Whose laws do you obey?" But once the federal courts took over, everything changed. The South *wanted* to change, and the federal courts forced it along. Carter rambled on in answering my question and then got to family life. "When I grew up, the family was my community," he said. "I always knew where my mother and father were, they always knew where I was. I never had a problem where there was any doubt or fear except . . . disappointing my family . . . and there was a

greater centering of the life in the community, for which our schools and church were the center." He has since been called a "dispassionate President," but when he talked quietly, he could be passionate. And on black rights he was most passionate of all. Sumter County is one of the most segregationist counties of the Old South; but he had led the fight there for integration, had refused flatly, publicly, to join the White Citizens Council or the "segs." To give the blacks their open and equal opportunity was a matter of faith—of Christianity. Somewhere Carter had crossed a line in his past; blacks as well as whites were the children of God.

4   Much could be said about the archaic fundamentalist underpinning of his Christianity. But it was real. He believed. No other candidate could write, as did Carter, an open letter to a newspaper declaring his belief in creationism.[1] He taught Sunday school in Plains, held prayer breakfasts in the White House, began lunch, even with such amused big-city politicians as Ed Koch, mayor of New York, by asking permission to say grace. "Why not?" Koch, who had come to plead for aid for his city, is reported to have replied. "We can all use a little extra help."

5   It was impossible to ignore that motivation of love and mercy which Christianity brought to the administration of Jimmy Carter. He tried to make real all the promises that a generation of liberal programs had substituted for old faith. He ticked off to me the record of previous Presidents, their shortcomings, their lack of faith. Of Kennedy, he said, he "lacked boldness."

6   Then there was a second layer of the Carter personality—Jimmy Carter the engineer. He

had answered my first question by talking of civil rights. Then he gave me an alternative beginning for his reflection on where modern American history began: Sputnik.[2] "Sputnik shook people," he said, "the first dawning of the belief that the Soviets were actually able to challenge us in a world that we thought was uniquely ours from a scientific and technological [view]."

7   No journalist ever gets to know a President, unless he has known him years before on his way up. Presidents are too busy to spend time on any but those who are useful to them. So a writer must invent the outline of the man he fitfully glimpses. And it seemed to me that one could invent a Jimmy Carter on the model of Sir Isaac Newton. Newton was also a man of science and of God; Newton thought the universe was a clockwork mechanism fashioned by God with some ultimate unfathomed design, and that by exploring the mechanics of things he could bare the larger design.

8   These two layers of Jimmy Carter's personality intersected. A pilot named Peterson had flown me down to Plains for my first visit. I sat beside him and we talked of Carter. Peterson was devoted to him. He had flown Carter from Atlanta to Plains several times. On their flights Carter would sit beside him, ask him how the plane worked, had learned to understand and operate the instruments in the cockpit. Then Peterson added a catching observation. He and Carter attended the same Baptist church in Plains and Carter would say occasionally, "Saw you in church on Sunday." But Mrs. Peterson did not go to services. Peterson recalled Carter asking whether he could call on her someday to talk about it. But he could not have been more surprised when Carter did indeed call (this in the midst of a presidential campaign), to talk with Mrs. Peterson about church, prayer, God, and the importance of Sunday services.

---

[1] creationism: "The article in Monday's *Atlanta Constitution* incorrectly states," he wrote in the summer of 1976, "that I do not 'believe in such biblical accounts as Eve being created from Adam's rib and other such miracles.' I have never made any such statement and have no reason to disbelieve Genesis 2:21, 22 or other biblical miracles. . . ." [author's note].

[2] **Sputnik:** The first artificial earth satellite, launched by the USSR on October 4, 1957.

9   The engineer Carter was quite distinct from the Carter of faith. He would rise at five-thirty every morning at the White House and be at his desk before any of his staff. And he worked hard. He seemed to believe that if he could grasp all the facts and figures of a problem, he would understand its dynamics. A prominent New York Democrat, one of the major contributors to the party, visited Carter in midterm and was asked into the private study adjacent to the Oval Office. There sat Carter at his desk, with a pile of papers knee-high beside him. "Do you know what that is?" he asked the visitor. "That's the Air Force budget," said Carter. "I've read every page of it." The astonished executive talked briefly with the President, then made his exit through the office of Hamilton Jordan, who acted as chief of staff. There he sat down to enjoy a good conversation on politics and policy. It was as if, said the businessman later, Carter was the chief researcher, Jordan the chief policymaker. This appetite for swallowing detail went with Carter always. At his summit conference with Brezhnev[3] in Vienna, both were invited to a performance of Mozart's *The Abduction from the Seraglio*. Brezhnev, in his box, tired and restless, would doze, nod, occasionally chat and joke with his attendants. But Carter in his box had brought with him the full libretto of the opera and, turning the pages, followed the score act by act, scene by scene, even making notes in the margins. "Carter," said one of those with the President, "is not exactly a bundle of laughs."

10   There were also all the other layers of Carter. Carter the yeoman, for example. He knew the name of every tree he saw, and loved them all. I mentioned to him, on my first visit, that I had seen a stand of Southern cypress a few miles south of his home, near the town of Americus. The observation caught him. "That's a climatological line," he said. "North of that stand of cypress you won't find any more . . . all the way to the North Pole." He pulled the last phrase out with characteristic melancholy of tone, for he loved his Southern homeland. Then there was Carter of the primaries of 1976, a first-class mechanic of politics, aware of every county, city, voting bloc he must deal with, enjoying the adventure. Yet however much the public Carter on the stump, at the town meeting, in a student dormitory, seemed warm and outgoing, there was the other, prickly, private man—shy, soft-spoken, occasionally vindictive, withdrawn, unable to entertain give-and-take except with his Georgians, his wife, and Pat Caddell. This was a wary, small-town Carter, peering at the world and the barons of Washington with the skepticism of a country visitor, fearful of being taken in by them as much as they, on his arrival, feared him.

11   "You have to understand," said one of Carter's White House guard, "that Carter simply did not *like* politicians. He had set his mind on being governor of Georgia, and he got to be governor by politics; he set his mind on being President, and he got that job done using politicians. But he didn't *like* them. He asked Russell Long over to the White House once to ask for his help on a tax bill, gave Long half an hour, and when the half hour was over, he simply got up and said, 'Thank you.' He wasn't offering friendship. We tried to get him to see the older Democrats, the wise men, people like Clifford and Harriman. He tried that twice and then just stopped. We told him he had to make friends in Congress. Of course, he didn't drink, but he played tennis. So we made a list of congressmen and senators to be invited over for a game. He went through the names, played once with each of them, checked them off the list. And that was that." . . . ◆

---

[3] **Brezhnev:** Leonid Brezhnev (1906–82), a Communist party official considered the leader of the Soviet Union for eighteen years.

MOTHER

Annie Dillard

Annie Dillard's memoir *An American Childhood* contains the following much-praised chapter about her mother. Sketching the character of a private person presents problems that Theodore White never faced when he wrote about public figures like Jimmy Carter. Why, after all, should anyone care what kind of person Annie Dillard's mother was? Is there anything noteworthy to say about a suburban housewife? As the essay progresses, the reasons for writing (and reading) become clearer and clearer.

1 ONE SUNDAY AFTERNOON MOTHER wandered through our kitchen, where Father was making a sandwich and listening to the ball game. The Pirates were playing the New York Giants at Forbes Field. In those days, the Giants had a utility infielder named Wayne Terwilliger. Just as Mother passed through, the radio announcer cried—with undue drama—"Terwilliger bunts one!"

2 "Terwilliger bunts one?" Mother cried back, stopped short. She turned. "Is that English?"

3 "The player's name is Terwilliger," Father said. "He bunted."

4 "That's marvelous," Mother said. "'Terwilliger bunts one.' No wonder you listen to baseball. 'Terwilliger bunts one.'"

5 For the next seven or eight years, Mother made this surprising string of syllables her own. Testing a microphone, she repeated, "Terwilliger bunts one"; testing a pen or a typewriter, she wrote it. If, as happened surprisingly often in the course of various improvised gags, she pretended to whisper something else in my ear, she actually whispered, "Terwilliger bunts one." Whenever someone used a French phrase, or a Latin one, she answered solemnly, "Terwilliger bunts one." If Mother had had, like Andrew Carnegie, the opportunity to cook up a motto for a coat of arms, hers would have read simply and tellingly, "Terwilliger bunts one." (Carnegie's was "Death to Privilege.")

6 She served us with other words and phrases. On a Florida trip, she repeated tremulously, "That . . . is a royal poinciana." I don't remember the tree; I remembered the thrill in her voice. She pronounced it carefully, and spelled it. She also liked to say "portulaca."

7 The drama of the words "Tamiami Trail" stirred her, we learned on the same Florida trip. People built Tampa on one coast, and they built Miami on another. Then—the height of visionary ambition and folly—they piled a slow, tremendous road through the terrible Everglades to connect them. To build the road, men stood sunk in muck to their armpits. They fought off cottonmouth moccasins and six-foot alligators. They slept in boats, wet. They blasted muck with dynamite, cut jungle with machetes; they laid logs, dragged drilling machines, hauled dredges, heaped limestone. The road took fourteen years to build up by the shovelful, a Panama Canal in reverse, and cost hundreds of lives from tropical, mosquito-carried diseases. Then, capping it all, some genius thought of the word Tamiami: they called the road from Tampa to Miami, this very road under our spinning wheels, the Tamiami Trail. Some called it Alligator Alley. Anyone could drive over this road without a thought.

8 Hearing this, moved, I thought all the suf-

fering of road building was worth it (it wasn't my suffering), now that we had this new thing to hang these new words on—Alligator Alley for those who liked things cute, and, for connoisseurs like Mother, for lovers of the human drama in all its boldness and terror, the Tamiami Trail.

9 Back home, Mother cut clips from reels of talk, as it were, and played them back at leisure. She noticed that many Pittsburghers confuse "leave" and "let." One kind relative brightened our morning by mentioning why she'd brought her son to visit: "He wanted to come with me, so I left him." Mother filled in Amy and me on locutions we missed. "I can't do it on Friday," her pretty sister told a crowded dinner party, "because Friday's the day I lay in the stores."

10 (All unconsciously, though, we ourselves used some pure Pittsburghisms. We said "tele pole," pronounced "telly pole," for that splintery sidewalk post I loved to climb. We said "slippy"—the sidewalks are "slippy." We said, "That's all the farther I could go." And we said, as Pittsburghers do say, "This glass needs washed," or "The dog needs walked"—a usage our father eschewed; he knew it was not standard English, nor even comprehensible English, but he never let on.)

11 "Spell 'poinsettia,'" Mother would throw out at me, smiling with pleasure. "Spell 'sherbet.'" The idea was not to make us whizzes, but, quite the contrary, to remind us—and I, especially, needed reminding—that we didn't know it all just yet.

12 "There's a deer standing in the front hall," she told me one quiet evening in the country.

13 "Really?"

14 "No. I just wanted to tell you something once without your saying, 'I know.'"

15 Supermarkets in the middle 1950s began luring, or bothering, customers by giving out Top Value Stamps or Green Stamps. When, shopping with Mother, we got to the head of the checkout line, the checker, always a young man, asked, "Save stamps?"

16 "No," Mother replied genially, week after week, "I build model airplanes." I believe she originated this line. It took me years to determine where the joke lay.

17 Anyone who met her verbal challenges she adored. She had surgery on one of her eyes. On the operating table, just before she conked out, she appealed feelingly to the surgeon, saying, as she had been planning to say for weeks, "Will I be able to play the piano?" "Not on me," the surgeon said. "You won't pull that old one on me."

18 It was, indeed, an old one. The surgeon was supposed to answer, "Yes, my dear, brave woman, you will be able to play the piano after this operation," to which Mother intended to reply, "Oh, good, I've always wanted to play the piano." This pat scenario bored her; she loved having it interrupted. It must have galled her that usually her acquaintances were so predictably unalert; it must have galled her that, for the length of her life, she could surprise everyone so continually, so easily, when she had been the same all along. At any rate, she loved anyone who, as she put it, saw it coming, and called her on it.

19 She regarded the instructions on bureaucratic forms as straight lines. "Do you advocate the overthrow of the United States government by force or violence?" After some thought she wrote, "Force." She regarded children, even babies, as straight men. When Molly learned to crawl, Mother delighted in buying her gowns with drawstrings at the bottom, like Swee'pea's, because, as she explained energetically, you could easily step on the drawstring without the baby's noticing, so that she crawled and crawled and crawled and never got anywhere except into a small ball at the gown's top.

20 When we children were young, she mothered us tenderly and dependably; as we got older, she resumed her career of anarchism. She collared us into her gags. If she answered the phone on a wrong number, she told the caller, "Just a minute," and dragged the receiver to Amy or me, saying, "Here, take this, your name is Cecile," or, worse, just, "It's for you." You had to think on your feet. But did you want to perform well as Cecile, or did you want to take pity on the wretched caller?

21 During a family trip to the Highland Park Zoo, Mother and I were alone for a minute. She approached a young couple holding hands on a bench by the seals, and addressed the young man in dripping tones: "Where have you been? Still got those baby-blue eyes; always did slay me. And this"—a swift nod at the dumbstruck young woman, who had removed her hand from the man's—"must be the one you were telling me about. She's not so bad, really, as you used to make out. But listen, you know how I miss you, you know where to reach me, same old place. And there's Ann over there—see how she's grown? See the blue eyes?"

22 And off she sashayed, taking me firmly by the hand, and leading us around briskly past the monkey house and away. She cocked an ear back, and both of us heard the desperate man begin, in a high-pitched wail, "I swear, I never saw her before in my life. . . ."

23 On a long, sloping beach by the ocean, she lay stretched out sunning with Father and friends, until the conversation gradually grew tedious, when without forethought she gave a little push with her heel and rolled away. People were stunned. She rolled deadpan and apparently effortlessly, arms and legs extended and tidy, down the beach to the distant water's edge, where she lay at ease just as she had been, but half in the surf, and well out of earshot.

24 She dearly loved to fluster people by throwing out a game's rules at whim—when she was getting bored, losing in a dull sort of way, and when everybody else was taking it too seriously. If you turned your back, she moved the checkers around on the board. When you got them all straightened out, she denied she'd touched them; the next time you turned your back, she lined them up on the rug or hid them under your chair. In a betting rummy game called Michigan, she routinely played out of turn, or called out a card she didn't hold, or counted backward, simply to amuse herself by causing an uproar and watching the rest of us do double takes and have fits. (Much later, when serious suitors came to call, Mother subjected them to this fast card game as a trial by ordeal; she used it as an intelligence test and a measure of spirit. If the poor man could stay a round without breaking down or running out, he got to marry one of us, if he still wanted to.)

25 She excelled at bridge, playing fast and boldly, but when the stakes were low and the hands dull, she bid slams for the devilment of it, or raised her opponents' suit to bug them, or showed her hand, or tossed her cards in a handful behind her back in a characteristic swift motion accompanied by a vibrantly innocent look. It drove our stolid father crazy. The hand was over before it began, and the guests were appalled. How do you score it, who deals now, what do you do with a crazy person who is having so much fun? Or they were down seven, and the guests were appalled. "Pam!" "Dammit, Pam!" He groaned. What ails such people? What on earth possesses them? He rubbed his face.

26 She was an unstoppable force; she never let go. When we moved across town, she persuaded the U.S. Post Office to let her keep her old address—forever—because she'd had stationery printed. I don't know how she did it.

Every new post office worker, over decades, needed to learn that although the Doaks' mail is addressed to here, it is delivered to there.

27   Mother's energy and intelligence suited her for a greater role in a larger arena—mayor of New York, say—than the one she had. She followed American politics closely; she had been known to vote for Democrats. She saw how things should be run, but she had nothing to run but our household. Even there, small minds bugged her; she was smarter than the people who designed the things she had to use all day for the length of her life.

28   "Look," she said. "Whoever designed this corkscrew never used one. Why would anyone sell it without trying it out?" So she invented a better one. She showed me a drawing of it. The spirit of American enterprise never faded in Mother. If capitalizing and tooling up had been as interesting as theorizing and thinking up, she would have fired up a new factory every week, and chaired several hundred corporations.

29   "It grieves me," she would say, "it grieves my heart," that the company that made one superior product packaged it poorly, or took the wrong tack in its advertising. She knew, as she held the thing mournfully in her two hands, that she'd never find another. She was right. We children wholly sympathized, and so did Father; what could she do, what could anyone do, about it? She was Samson in chains. She paced.

30   She didn't like the taste of stamps so she didn't lick stamps; she licked the corner of the envelope instead. She glued sandpaper to the sides of kitchen drawers, and under kitchen cabinets, so she always had a handy place to strike a match. She designed, and hounded workmen to build against all norms, doubly wide kitchen counters and elevated bathroom sinks. To splint a finger, she stuck it in a lightweight cigar tube. Conversely, to protect a pack of cigarettes, she carried it in a Band-Aid box. She drew plans for an over-the-finger toothbrush for babies, an oven rack that slid up and down, and—the family favorite—Lendalarm. Lendalarm was a beeper you attached to books (or tools) you loaned friends. After ten days, the beeper sounded. Only the rightful owner could silence it.

31   She repeatedly reminded us of P. T. Barnum's dictum: You could sell anything to anybody if you marketed it right. The adman who thought of making Americans believe they needed underarm deodorant was a visionary. So, too, was the hero who made a success of a new product, Ivory soap. The executives were horrified, Mother told me, that a cake of this stuff floated. Soap wasn't supposed to float. Anyone would be able to tell it was mostly whipped-up air. Then some inspired adman made a leap: Advertise that it floats. Flaunt it. The rest is history.

32   She respected the rare few who broke through to new ways. "Look," she'd say, "here's an intelligent apron." She called upon us to admire intelligent control knobs and intelligent pan handles, intelligent andirons and picture frames and knife sharpeners. She questioned everything, every pair of scissors, every knitting needle, gardening glove, tape dispenser. Hers was a restless mental vigor that just about ignited the dumb household objects with its force.

Torpid conformity was a kind of sin; it was   33
stupidity itself, the mighty stream against which Mother would never cease to struggle. If you held no minority opinions, or if you failed to risk total ostracism for them daily, the world would be a better place without you.

34   Always I heard Mother's emotional voice asking Amy and me the same few questions: Is that your own idea? Or somebody else's? "*Giant* is a good movie," I pronounced to the family at dinner. "Oh, really?" Mother warmed to these occasions. She all but rolled

up her sleeves. She knew I hadn't seen it. "Is that your considered opinion?"

35 She herself held many unpopular, even fantastic, positions. She was scathingly sarcastic about the McCarthy hearings while they took place, right on our living-room television; she frantically opposed Father's wait-and-see calm. "We don't know enough about it," he said. "I do," she said. "I know all I need to know."

36 She asserted, against all opposition, that people who lived in trailer parks were not bad but simply poor, and had as much right to settle on beautiful land, such as rural Ligonier, Pennsylvania, as did the oldest of families in the finest of hidden houses. Therefore, the people who owned trailer parks, and sought zoning changes to permit trailer parks, needed our help. Her profound belief that the country-club pool sweeper was a person, and that the department-store saleslady, the bus driver, telephone operator, and housepainter were people, and even in groups the steelworkers who carried pickets and the Christmas shoppers who clogged intersections were people—this was a conviction common enough in democratic Pittsburgh, but not altogether common among our friends' parents, or even, perhaps, among our parents' friends.

37 Opposition emboldened Mother, and she would take on anybody on any issue—the chairman of the board, at a cocktail party, on the current strike; she would fly at him in a flurry of passion, as a songbird selflessly attacks a big hawk.

38 "Eisenhower's going to win," I announced after school. She lowered her magazine and looked me in the eyes: "How do you know?" I was doomed. It was fatal to say, "Everyone says so." We all knew well what happened. "Do you consult this Everyone before you make your decisions? What if Everyone decided to round up all the Jews?" Mother knew there was no danger of cowing me. She simply tried to keep us all awake. And in fact it was always clear to Amy and me, and to Molly when she grew old enough to listen, that if our classmates came to cruelty, just as much as if the neighborhood or the nation came to madness, we were expected to take, and would be each separately capable of taking, a stand. ♦

MATH CLASS

Tracy Kidder

By now Tracy Kidder may have established himself as America's foremost reporter on everyday life. His method is painstaking observation. He will watch people at work for a period of several months, systematically taking notes, supplementing these notes with interviews and reading, and finally producing a book that gives a remarkably clear picture of a way of life. Thus far, he has produced best-selling books about computer programmers, house builders, a fifth-grade teacher, and the residents of a retirement home. In the following passage from *Among Schoolchildren*, you'll see how his patient observation allows him to understand and recreate the world of Massachusetts teacher Chris Zajac and her homeroom class.

1   THE LEAVES HAD BEGUN TO TURN ON THE distant trees on the Chicopee bank of the invisible river. The days had grown cooler. Out on the playground, along with the usual incidental trash blowing around in the fall winds, were many small pieces of what must have been a huge jigsaw puzzle mixed in with the grass. The puzzle pieces had lain there since school started and were now soggy bits of brown cardboard. Maybe a frustrated child had dumped the puzzle last summer. Out on the playground, a boy from another homeroom cavorted around on a dirt bike, doing wheelies. He was playing hooky, but evidently couldn't stay away. He waved and shouted whenever he saw a child's face in the windows.

2   Inside, math was in progress. Clarence went to the room next door for math, but Chris kept Robert, her second most difficult student, and she received from the homeroom next door lanky, mischievous Manny. Math was almost always lively. Chris sat at the spindly-legged table at the front of the room. The top math group, five girls and only three boys, but a nearly equal mixture of white and Puerto Rican children and one Filipino, also from next door, sat at desks on the side of the room by the window, wrestling with word problems in bright morning sunlight. That top group's heads were bowed over open textbooks, their lips bunched up in great concentration. The low math group looked different. Children from next door made up half of this group, too. The low group surrounded Mrs. Zajac: three fidgety children at the table, before her and beside her; Felipe a little behind her on the right; three children standing at the board, working on multiplication problems; and the rest of the fifteen in the low group at desks on the doorway side of the room, behind Mrs. Zajac's back. Some eyes in the low group were darting and furtive. There were always whispers among them, also grins, and a few stifled yawns.

3   This year's low math group wasn't like last year's, which was entirely remedial. It contained a gang of five boys, who, whenever she turned her back, threw snots and erasers and made armpit farts at the children who were trying to work, and among them was the boy— this was one of her favorite teacher stories— who decided one day to start barking in class. Not, Chris knew, because of Tourette Syndrome, some of whose victims bark involuntarily. This boy barked in order to get suspended, so he'd have a holiday. She

thought, "No way, buster. I can wait you out." The boy yipped. She ordered him to stop. He growled. She tried to embarrass him by describing what he was doing. He laid his head back and bayed. So she decided to ignore him, and went on teaching: "Ten times five is what?" "Ruff ruff." And carry the five." "Aro-ooo!" Afterward Chris and her math aide found an empty room off the principal's office, went inside, and laughed for a good five minutes. Tears flowed down their cheeks.

4   Now from the group of low math students behind Chris came the sound of muffled, tuneless singing: "Cha, cha, cha. Cha, cha, cha."

5   "Robert, would you like to sing for the class?" said Chris, glancing over her shoulder at the burly child. "No? Then why don't you get busy. You still owe me yesterday's math."

6   The singing stopped.

7   She held up a flash card, aiming the question "4 × 6 =" backward over her shoulder, for Felipe, who still hadn't learned his times tables, while with her left hand Chris corrected Jorge's paper, then paused and, leaning farther left, examined sleepy Jimmy's work, which wasn't going well. "How much is seven times seven, Jimmy?"

8   "Forty. Forty-nine."

9   "And what do you carry?"

10   "Forty-nine?"

11   "No. Think, Jimmy." She turned back to Jorge's paper. "Excellent, Jorge!" Then back to Jimmy. "And carry the what?" That question left hanging, another flash card held aloft for Felipe, she looked toward the children who stood at the board. "Very good, Mariposa. Margaret, look at the problem. See if you can figure out where you went wrong."

12   "The nine?" said Jimmy at her side.

13   "No, Jimmy. *Think.*" More noise from the low group behind her. Without turning around, she extended her left hand back, snapped her fingers, and, leaving her index finger extended said, "Manny. Henrietta. Settle down."

"*Diablo!*"   14

That was Manny's voice. Sometimes when   15
he said that, Chris would bop Manny on his gorgeously curly black-haired head with a sheaf of papers, and Manny would leer up at her, and she'd try not to laugh. Sometimes from behind her she'd hear muffled sounds of an argument. Once, she turned to Manny and Henrietta, a tall black girl from the homeroom next door, and said, "Why do you two have to bicker?" A little smile slid over to one side of Chris's mouth. "If you tease each other, it must mean you *like* each other." "Like," to the children of Kelly School, implied matrimony.

Henrietta gasped.   16

"*Diablo!*" said Manny.   17

"No, it don't!" said Henrietta. "I'd rather   18
die than like him!"

"Oh, yes, it does!" sang Chris. "When I   19
was in school, if a boy and girl were always bickering, it meant they liked each other." That shut Manny up, but only for a while.

Chris turned her eyes to the children solving   20
problems on the board. "Very good, Margaret. Do you understand it now?" There was more whispering behind her. Again, her left hand shot back. "Horace, your own work." Another flash card for Felipe while she called over her other shoulder, "Henrietta, come on up here." Then she turned her head all the way around, toward the low math scholars at their desks behind her. "Horace, are you all done?"

"No."   21

"Then why are you talking to Jorge?"   22

She turned back around and said to Felipe   23
and Jimmy, "What's the matter with you two? The minute I turn my head, you have to talk? What number do you carry, Jimmy?"

"The four."   24

"Very good. Got it now? Okay, Jimmy, you   25
can go back to your desk."

"*Ocho,*" said a voice behind Chris, unmis-   26
takably Manny's hoarse whiskey voice. Manny was trying to whisper to one of his buddies, but he just couldn't do it quietly.

27   Chris turned. "Why don't you try Chinese, Manny? You can say it in Swahili, Manny. I still know you're giving him the answer." Chris liked them to help each other, but today she wanted to find out just how each one was faring in multiplication, so she kept saying, "Your own work."

28   "*Diablo!*"

29   "You keep it up, Manny, and I'll show you what a *diablo* I can be."

30   Henrietta, who just a moment ago was sticking out her long, pink tongue at Manny, sat down in Jimmy's place, on Mrs. Zajac's left.

31   "Okay, Henrietta, let's see what you've done," said Chris.

32   "I wanta quit. It's too hard."

33   Mrs. Zajac stopped everything else, and looked the girl in the eye. "Wouldn't it be great, Henrietta, if I turned around and said, 'Manny doesn't get multiplication, so I quit'?"

34   Henrietta nodded in perverse agreement.

35   "No, Henrietta. You can't quit. You have to keep trying. You can't just quit in life, Henrietta. Believe me, there are times when I'd like to."

36   Sometimes, at such moments, feeling altogether calm, Chris would think, "In my next life, I'm coming back as an air-traffic controller." But there was always a child somewhere in the room who waited for her. If, in the afternoon during writing time, she sat at the table, bright red fingertips applied to her temples, trying to help Pedro or Julio put his ideas for a story into unscrambled English, Felipe might get jealous, even though she gave him ten minutes just ten minutes ago. Felipe would come up and stand at her side, holding his own story, saying, "Mrs. Zajac, Mrs. Zajac." She'd stick out her arm at him, the traffic cop gesture, and say, still gazing at Pedro's tangled story, "Felipe, I'm with Pedro now." Felipe would travel back to his desk looking like a little storm, and say to his neighbor Irene, "See, she hates me. I told you." Others waited more quietly. Judith always finished assignments early. She killed time by working on her novel, a feminist tale called *Shana and the Warriors,* or she read a published novel—Judith favored stories of teen-age romance. Sometimes Judith stopped reading or writing, and lifted her eyes toward the narrow, train-like windows, and she thought about boys—handsome, religious, serious, chivalrous boys she hadn't met yet.

37   Chris felt them waiting around her. She thought how much fun it would be to sit for a long time with Judith and discuss her novel. She glanced at the clock, up on the wall above the closets. Its minute hand stood still. She had a few minutes before science. But the minute hand was one of those which stored up time and then sprang the news on her all at once. It leaped. She absolutely had to help poor Pedro. "Slow learner" was the kindly term for many of these children. It implied what she knew to be true, that they *could* learn, but she also knew that in this time-bound world, a slow learner might not learn at all if she didn't hurry up. And if she didn't hurry, she wouldn't get to keep her promise to Arabella, who was waiting patiently for Chris to help her fix up her story about becoming a hairdresser someday.

38   Usually, Chris could manage to keep most of them busy, but that was pure engineering. They always had time on their hands, and she never had much to spare.

39   This is an era of blossoming research in techniques for teaching math. The new wisdom was supposed to arrive at Kelly School in the person of a representative of the publisher of the new math textbooks. He gave the teachers a lecture in a classroom after school one fall day, the representative at a slide projector and the teachers in chairs made for children. The change in perspective seemed to inspire in the teachers a form of revenge. There was a lot of whispering in the audience. Talking fast and nervously, the representative allowed that the

new math texts contained "objectives" that had been "correlated" to "a computer management program." "And we've correlated them to specific objectives. So that the management guide, ad nauseam, I'm going to get this point across, it correlates the specific objectives. . . . Subject integration is whereby math is integrated with other subjects. . . . We do it through means of verbiage and through the actual algorithm itself."

40   Chris sighed.

41   "When you see 'Think,' that's for the above average youngster."

42   "Well, I have *two* of those," murmured Chris to Bob, a sixth-grade teacher.

43   "These are minimum assignment guides, so please follow them. . . . We have masters for chapter readiness. Testing. We have three forms of tests. . . . Computational error analysis. It not only diagnoses. It offers some remediation."

44   Bob whispered to Chris, "It slices and it dices."

45   The teachers didn't ask many questions. The representative seemed disappointed but not surprised. "We're not saying that this is the end-all or know-all," he said.

46   Chris and Candy, another teacher friend, giggled behind their hands.

47   Chris felt she could use some help. For the low math group especially, solving the simplest word problems seemed insuperable. She'd had trouble with math herself in school, but she'd been good at reading, and most of her low group weren't good readers. She taught them what she called "clue words." She made stacks of books to illustrate the meanings of those words, of "more than" and "less than" and "equal to." To make word problems palpable, she dumped change on their desks, along with the cookie crumbs that her daughter had dropped in her purse during Chris's last expedition to the grocery store. At the first marking period, Chris had noticed that another fifth-grade teacher's math students had made much

better grades than hers in problem solving. She had gone to that teacher and asked how she did it. But the method mainly consisted of the teacher's solving the first two-thirds of the problems herself.

48   Chris faced a bigger problem, one that looked impossibly far beyond her control. One Monday morning Chris asked Jimmy what time he went to bed last night. Jimmy, whose eyes looked glassy, with little bags beneath them, said he didn't know. Well, said Chris, what time did the last show he watched on TV begin?

49   Jimmy said eleven-thirty.

50   "Eleven-thirty?" she cried.

51   Yeah, said Jimmy, but it was a special, a really good movie called *Cobra*.

52   Mrs. Zajac had just started in on her usual speech about bedtimes, the I-don't-care-what-show-it-was-eleven-thirty's-too-late-even-Mrs.-Zajac-can't-stay-up-*that*-late lecture, when from the class rose several other voices.

53   "I saw that!"

54   "Yeah, bro, that was fresh!"

55   "Remember that part where the guy . . ."

56   "This is what I'm up against," said Chris, slowly turning her head from one child to the other to make sure each got to see her stupefied look, and finally letting her gaze fall on Judith, who smiled back and shook her head.

57   Maybe the worst thing about TV is not violence or licentiousness but the fact that some children stay up until around midnight to watch it. About half of Chris's class did, at one time or another, and came to school with fewer than six hours of sleep.

58   It was a Wednesday morning, the dead middle of a week in late fall. Bracing air came in the cracked-open casement behind Chris's desk, the sort of air that ought to make children frisky. The clock read a little past eight. She stood in front of her low math group. As

planned, she had begun to go over last night's homework, but Felipe had no idea how many pumpkins *in all* were bought if two people had bought fourteen pumpkins each; Horace said he'd forgotten his book; Manny and Henrietta admitted they hadn't done the homework; Robert just shrugged when she asked where his was; and Alan, of all people, a schoolteacher's son, had a note from his mother saying that he'd lost the assignment. "I think that you think your mother fell off the turnip cart yesterday, too," Chris said to Alan. Then she came to a dead stop.

59   The day was overcast. Jimmy's skin looked gray under fluorescent light. He lay with his head down on his desk, shifting his stick-like forearms around under his cheek as if rearranging a pillow. The usually high-spirited Manny gazed open-mouthed toward the window. Felipe had slid halfway down the back of his chair and scowled at his lap. "You can't make me do it. I'm not going to do anything unless you give me more attention," Felipe seemed to be saying to her. It would feel good and constructive to spank him, but that would have to wait for the pretext of his birthday. Robert was dismantling another pen. Soon he'd have ink all over his hands and his pants. His mother could worry about that. Horace was trying to do his homework now, by copying from Margaret's. At least he seemed awake. Jorge's eyes were shut, literally shut. Jorge was staying back. He had told his homeroom teacher, who had told the story in the Teachers' Room, that he'd get even by not doing any work this year, and she couldn't make him, because his mother didn't care. He wore the same set of clothes as on the first days of school.

60   Chris had seen progress in this group. They would start long division fairly soon. But today even the well-behaved ones, such as Margaret, looked sleepy. Bring back Clarence from the room next door. Clarence, at least, never looked sleepy.

61   Chris considered telling them she couldn't teach *celery*, but the eyes that were open and looking at her seemed to say that they didn't want to hear it all from her again: they'd need to know this if they wanted to move on to something new; if they didn't want to get cheated at the grocery store; if they wanted to learn how to design cars and rocket ships. They did not want to hear that Mrs. Zajac couldn't drill holes in their heads and pour in information, that they had to help, which meant, first of all, paying attention. Jimmy yawned. He didn't even bother to cover his mouth. A paper fell off a child's desk and floated down, gently arcing back and forth like a kite without a tail. She'd try something different. An old trick might work.

62   Chris turned and wrote on the board:

$$\begin{array}{r} 296 \\ \times 78 \\ \hline \end{array}$$

63   "All right Jimmy, you go to the board."

64   Jimmy arose slowly, twisting his mouth. He slouched up to the green board and stared at the problem.

65   Chris sat down in Jimmy's seat. "I want you to pretend you're the teacher, and you're going to show me how to multiply, and I don't know how." So saying, and in one abandoned movement, Chris collapsed on Jimmy's desk, one cheek landing flat on the pale brown plastic top and her arms hanging lifelessly over the sides.

66   A child giggled.

67   "Gonna get my attention first, Jimmy?" called Mrs. Zajac.

68   Several children giggled. Jorge's eyes opened, and he grinned. All around the little room, heads lifted. Chris's mouth sagged open. Her tongue protruded. Her head lay on the desk top. Up at the board, Jimmy made a low, monotonic sound, which was his laugh.

69   Abruptly, Chris sat up. "Okay, Jimmy," she called. "I'm awake now. What do I do first? Seven times six is . . ."

70   Jimmy was shaking his head.

71   "No? Why can't I multiply seven times six first?" she said, and she pouted.

72   There was a lot more light in the room now. It came from smiles. The top group had all lifted their eyes from their papers. Judith smiled at Mrs. Zajac from across the room.

73   Jimmy got through the first step, and Chris turned around in Jimmy's chair and said to Manny, "You're next. You're a teacher, too."

74   "*Diablo!*" Manny looked up toward the ceiling.

75   Chris climbed into Manny's seat as he sauntered to the board.

76   "I'm gonna give you a hard time, like you give me," Chris called at Manny's back. She looked around at the other children. They were all looking at her. "When you sit in this seat, see, you've got to sit like this." She let her shoulders and her jaw droop, and she stared at the window.

77   "Look out in space!" declared Felipe.

78   "Look out in space," she agreed.

79   The clock over the closets jumped and rested, jumped and rested. The smell of pencil shavings was thick in the air. Giggles came from all sides.

80   "Boy, do I have a lot of friends helping me out! Now who wants to teach Mrs. Zajac?

81   "Me!" cried most of the class in unison.

82   Crying "No!" and "No way!" at Chris's wrong answers and "Yes!" when the child at the board corrected her and she turned to the others to ask if the correction was right, the low group found their way to the end of the problem. Arising from the last child's chair she had occupied, her black hair slightly infused with the new redness in her cheeks, her skirt rustling, she turned back into Mrs. Zajac. "Okay, thank you. Now that I know how to do it, I hope you know how to do it. I'm going to put examples on the board," she said. "You are going to work on them." ◆

YO, RAPPERS! BETTER NOT CALL THIS WOMAN A 'HO'

Rosalind Bentley

One convention of "straight news" reporting is that reporters never mention their own presence at an event or their own reaction to it. Occasionally, however, the event provokes such a strong reaction that the reporter drops the pose of objectivity and decides that his or her reaction to an event may be an important part of the story. This seems to have happened when Rosalind Bentley of the *Minneapolis-St. Paul Star Tribune* attended a 1993 symposium on Hip Hop culture.

1   I'M A BLACK WOMAN. I'M A JOURNALIST. I'm a big rap fan. And I'd like to think I'm an unwavering, unconditional supporter of the right to free speech.

2   But maybe it's time for me to turn in my objectivity card because damned if I'm gonna co-sign another young black man calling a black woman a bitch or a 'ho' in the name of artistic freedom.

3   Colleagues would say I'm traipsing into dangerous territory, way too far to the right. Walking hand-in-hand with Tipper Gore down censorship lane. But as a friend of mine likes to say, "Right is right," and it seems to me that it just ain't right to call a woman a bitch or a 'ho' (slang for whore), then laugh about it and get paid thousands of dollars for doing it.

4   Picture this: A room full of newspaper, television and radio reporters gathered for the kickoff symposium at the National Association of Black Journalists' conference in Houston. The topic is "Hip Hop: The Medium, Its Message and Responsibility."

5   On stage are rappers from the group RUN DMC; Bushwick Bill, a former member of the Houston-based rap group the Geto Boys; and Reg E. Gaines, self-proclaimed hip-hop poet. Also present are two women editors of music magazines, Mimi Valdez of Vibe and Kierna Mayo of Source, and New York University sociologist David Dent. Our moderator is hip-hop columnist Darryl Dawsey of the Detroit News.

6   At least 300 of us sit waiting to be enlightened about a music form and lifestyle that originated in inner-city black neighborhoods and now has infiltrated suburbs, Burger King commercials and clothing displays.

7   As infectious as the rap beat is, often the lyrics are misogynistic and nihilistic. Songs like *I Need a Gangsta Bitch*, *Bitch Better Have My Money* and *My Ex-Girlfriend's a 'Ho'* aren't about how to build strong black male and female relationships. But I am sitting here hungry to hear the reasons for the rage.

8   After all, I know black men are perhaps the most despised and feared group of people in this country, and hey, I'm looking for a reason to defend my brothers' anger.

9   So here is Bushwick Bill, standing on stage spouting off 1960s rhetoric: "Black people need to return to African values, we need to work together."

10   The audience, including me, applauds. When you're really hungry, even leftovers taste good.

11   Soon the discussion turns to the derogatory descriptions of women prevalent in "gangsta"

121

(read gangster) rap. Then Bushwick, my brother in dreadlocks, stands up and says that the reason he refers to women as bitches and 'ho's in his music is because the only women he's ever dealt with are bitches and 'ho's. Suddenly I'm not hungry any more.

12   Karyn Collins of the Asbury Park Press in New Jersey steps to the microphone and asks the question that has started many a schoolyard fight and landed many in a hospital bed or a grave.

13   "What about your mother?" Collins asks.

14   "My mother's a woman, but I'm not (expletive) her," Bushwick begins. "And if I was just (expletive) you, then you would be a bitch or a 'ho.'"

15   Bushwick goes on to insult the woman about her looks and her weight. So much for African values.

16   Scores of women and a few men walk out, including me.

17   When asked to apologize by immediate-past NABJ president Sidmel Estes-Sumpter, Bushwick isn't sorry for what he said, but only sorry he has offended people by speaking his mind.

18   After the NABJ walkout, a few of my colleagues tell me to try to understand Bushwick's reasoning. They say he's a product of his environment, that he represents the failure of his parents' generation to raise a responsible tribe of freedom fighters.

19   I try very hard to become the objective journalist again, but Bushwick has offended two things I was born with—my gender and my race. Instead of getting me to be more understanding of his plight as a young American black man, he has made me indifferent to it. At a time when the never-ending struggle against racism requires black men and black women to stand side by side, attitudes like Bushwick's make the toiling more tedious.

20   Sad thing about it is, Bushwick isn't alone. There are some female rappers who get big money for calling themselves names they'd curse a man for calling them. As for the argument that we can expect as much from someone of his generation and background, well, Bushwick and I are both in our 20s. We both grew up in the projects. I suspect one of the biggest differences between the two of us is that he suffers from a lack of home training. And although it's disappointing that someone didn't teach him to respect women, it doesn't mean he can't learn.

21   He's an intelligent man. He knows record companies will pay him well to talk about shooting someone and to call women names. He just isn't an evolved man.

22   Perhaps more women need to say to the Bushwicks of the world, "Until you learn how to speak to us in a respectful manner, we'll continue to walk on by." ◆

5 *Autobiographical Writing*

I N CHAPTER 4 WE EXAMINED EYEWITNESS WRITING THAT LOOKS OUTWARD to report on the world as the writer sees it. If the writer appears as a character in an essay, it is only incidentally: "I was just passing the coppersmith's booth when . . . ," George Orwell says, but he immediately shifts his attention to the actions of the inhabitants of the Marrakech ghetto. In this chapter we will be looking at essays different in two respects:

1. They are structured as stories. They begin, that is, by showing a person caught in a troublesome situation, and they end when the trouble ends. Though we saw stories used in Chapter 4, they were short illustrations tucked inside larger structures. Here the story gets fuller development.

2. The writers are characters in the stories they tell.

This kind of narrative fills many personal letters and is one of the oldest literary forms, but it has academic uses as well. Increasingly, professors of history, sociology, and psychology ask students to write narratives that connect their lives with their studies, and researchers in several fields now recognize that personal narratives, honestly told, can provide information no one could quarry from the massed data of "objective" research.

THE WRITER AS CHARACTER AND THE WRITER AS INTERPRETER

The writer has a double presence in narratives about personal experience. On the one hand, there is the "writer as character," moving around in the story, acting and thinking about events as they occur. The experience of this person, what it was like to be *there, then,* is the *subject* of the memoir. On the other hand, there is the "writer as interpreter," a somewhat older and presumably wiser person who establishes the *framework* in which the experience is *now* interpreted.

Textbook authors don't ordinarily turn to their great-aunts' memoirs to illustrate a point, but in this case I can't resist. Consider the following passage from my great-aunt Alberta Carr's handwritten memoir of growing up on a farm just south of the Texas-Oklahoma border. The year was 1897. Oklahoma was then not a state but a U.S. territory made up almost entirely of Indian reservations. The Carr family had hopes of moving into the Indian Territory as soon as it was opened for settlement by whites.

Dad bought a small farm where they resided for 5 yrs before moving into the Okla. Territory. It was a well settled community but—just north of the river only Indians, outlaws & thieves. They preyed on farmers stealing their live stock, food, in fact anything they wanted then crossing the river where the citizens had no recourse. As a result an Anti Horse Thief Society was formed and did much to protect their interests. Dad belonged of course and was active altho we always had a sense of uneasiness. They would come in groups into Nacona on wk.ends and make much trouble for law enforcement officials.

My Dad could plant the straightest rows I ever saw in a field. They were beautiful and every one noticed and admired them. Late one Sat. 5 or 6 of the river bunch came riding by and noticed the beautiful field of young cotton. The house set up about a block from the road there was a fence and a front gate. They whirled their horses and came galloping up in a cloud of dust, shouting with much profanity. They wanted to see the man who could run such straight rows. We were all petrified. Mom was begging Dad not to go out but you don't know my Dad. He kept a revolver (a British Bulldog) laying on top of the cupboard (loaded). He reached up got it and put it in his hip pocket and walked out to the front gate as tho it was nothing out of the ordinary. The leader pulled out a bottle and said By God, I want to drink with the man who ran those rows. Dad said I don't drink fellows whereupon they whirled and galloped away. I was hiding under Mom's apron, but I saw it all and you can bet it made a profound impression on me.

This brief passage, unedited, shows the memoirist's dual perspective at work. Aunt Bert is present "as character," hiding behind her mother's apron and telling us what she sees and what she knows. Part of the pleasure of reading the story is that it takes us back almost a hundred years and shows us what the world then looked like to a six-year-old girl. On the other hand, we feel the presence of the other Aunt Bert, the seventy-three-year-old woman who looks back on the event and sees meaning in it that a six-year-old could not. The "writer as interpreter" knows that this confrontation is between two types of men, each presented through carefully chosen details: the outlaw and the solid citizen. She knows that such a confrontation belongs to the history of the period and, in fact, epitomizes the period.

As you read through the examples in this chapter and as you write your own memoir, be aware of the two authors who are present—one as the subject, one as the discoverer or inventor of the framework that will give the subject meaning.

The Importance of Frameworks for the Memoir

The writer of a memoir has one special advantage but also faces a peculiar difficulty. The advantage—an enormous one—is that he or she knows the subject intimately. A historian or biographer laboring for decades couldn't possibly amass the amount of information about your life that you are capable of recalling at will. On this subject, you are the world's greatest expert. Most of your research can be conducted in a comfortable chair, with a pencil and paper as aids.

The difficulty is that none of this knowledge is likely to be *in itself* interesting to an audience of strangers. As Annie Dillard says, "You have to take pains in a memoir not to hang on the reader's arm, like a drunk, and say 'And then I did this and it was so interesting.'" To some degree, you may be able to create interest by the charm or energy of your writing style, but style alone is rarely enough. The most successful memoirs are generally those in which the author presents private events in frameworks that give them more than personal interest. A memoirist like Maya Angelou, writing about an event from her girlhood in Stamps, Arkansas, can evoke the framework of America's troubled race relations. A memoirist like Mary McCarthy, writing about her girlhood in Minneapolis, can evoke every child's struggle to find out what her "self" is like. The *subject* of the memoir comes from the world of individual experience—the world of *I;* the *framework* comes from the world of shared experience—the world of *we.*

The world of shared experience is so large that it provides an inexhaustible supply of frameworks. In the following pages, we will look at some examples of memoirs that present the writer's personal experience in three broadly defined kinds of frameworks: the historical, the social, and the psychological.

Historical Frameworks

At some point in growing up we discover that we are a part of history, that the events of our private lives connect with the events that form the headlines today and will appear in the history books our children will read.

As a boy growing up in Jacksonville, Florida, in the 1870s, James Weldon Johnson made a collection of brass buttons and rusty bayonets that he dug up from yards and fields. When Ulysses S. Grant came to the city to deliver a speech, Johnson found a way to shake his hand. At the time both the collection and the handshake were merely exciting, but later Johnson realized that he was literally in touch with an earlier period in American history: slavery, the Civil War, and Reconstruction.

Annie Dillard, looking back on her childhood in Pittsburgh, realized that her city "like Rome, or Jericho" was "a sliding pile of cities built ever nearer the sky."

> City workers continually paved the streets: they poured asphalt over the streetcar tracks, streetcar tracks their fathers had wormed between the old riverworn cobblestones, cobblestones laid smack into the notorious nineteenth-century mud. Long stretches of that mud were the same pioneer roads that General John Forbes's troops had hacked over the mountains from Carlisle, or General Braddock's troops had hacked for the Chesapeake and the Susquehanna, widening with their axes the woodland paths the Indians had worn on deer trails.

The sense of connection with the past that this passage reveals is the essence of memoirs in historical frameworks. The memoirist discovers a way in which his or her life connects with General Grant or with "the woodland paths the Indians had worn on deer trails." He or she communicates this discovery in a way that helps readers understand the great web of such connections that makes up history.

At the same time, of course, the memoirist is telling what he or she hopes will be an engaging story. Here, for example, is Theodore White's memoir of his sixth grade year in a public school in the Jewish ghetto in Boston. As you will see, it was a year full of history lessons, some planned by his history teacher, Miss Fuller, who was, White says, "probably the first Protestant I ever met."

A WRITER AT WORK

"History Lessons"
THEODORE WHITE

She decided we would have a play the day before Thanksgiving, a free-form play in the classroom, in which we would all together explore the meeting of Puritans and Indians, and the meaning of Thanksgiving. She divided the class, entirely Jewish, into those children who were American-born and spoke true English, and those who were recent arrivals and spoke only broken English or Yiddish. I was Elder William Bradford because I spoke English well. "Itchie" Rachlin, whose father was an unemployed trumpet player recently arrived from Russia, and who spoke vivid Yiddish, was Squanto, our Indian friend. Miss Fuller hoped that those who could not speak English would squawk strange Indian sounds while I, translating their sounds to the rest of the Puritans, all of us in black cardboard cone hats, would offer good will and brotherhood. "Itchie" and the other recently arrived immigrant children played the game of being "Indian" for a few minutes, then fell into Yiddish, pretending it was Indian talk. Miss Fuller could not, of course, understand them, but I tried to clean up their Yiddish vulgarities in my translation to the other little Puritans, who could not help but giggle. ("*Vos is dos vor traef?*" said Itchie, meaning: "You want us to eat pig food?" and I would translate in English: "What kind of strange food is this before us?") Miss Fuller became furious as we laughed our way through the play; and when I tried to explain, she was hurt and upset. Thanksgiving was sacred to her.

But she was a marvelous teacher. Once we had learned the names and dates from 1630[1] to the Civil War, she let us talk and speculate, driving home the point that history connected to "now," to "us." America for her was all about freedom, and all the famous phrases from "Give me liberty or give me death" to the Gettysburg Address had to be memorized by her classes—and understood.

She was also a very earnest, upward-striving teacher. I realize now that she must have been working for an advanced degree, for she went to night school at Boston University to take education courses. This, too, reached from outside to me. One day she told my mother about a project her night-school seminar was conducting in how much independent research a youngster of ten or eleven could do on his own—one of those projects now so commonplace in progressive schools. Would my mother mind, she asked, if I was given such an assignment, and then reported on it to her seminar? My mother said yes after Miss Fuller promised to bring me home herself afterward.

My assignment was to study immigration, and then to speak to the seminar about whether immigrants were good or bad for America. Her seminar mates would question me to find out how well I had mastered the subject. The Immigration Act of 1924—the "Closing of the Gates"—had just been passed; there was much to read in both papers and magazines about the controversy, but my guide was my father. He put it both ways: the country had been built by immigrants, so immigrants were not bad. He had been an immigrant himself. On the other hand, as a strong labor man, he followed the A.F. of L. line of those days. The National Association of Manufacturers (the capitalists) wanted to continue unrestricted immigration so they could sweat cheap labor. But the American Federation of Labor wanted immigration restricted to keep the wages of American workingmen from being undercut by foreigners. This was a conundrum for my father: he was against the capitalists and for the A.F. of L.; but he was an immigrant himself, as were all our friends and neighbors. He helped me get all the facts, and I made a speech on the platform of a classroom at Boston University Teachers

---

[1] 1630: The date the first English settlers arrived in Boston.

College at nine one night, explaining both sides of the story and taking no position. I enjoyed it all, especially when the teachers began asking me questions; I had all the dates and facts, and an attentive audience, but no answers then just as I have none now. I must have done well, for Miss Fuller kissed me and bought me candy to eat on the streetcar. It became clear to me, as we talked on our way home, that immigrants were history, too. History was happening now, all about us, and the gossip of Erie Street and the problem of whether someone's cousin could get a visa back in the old country and come here were really connected to the past, and to Abraham Lincoln, Henry Clay, Sam Adams, Patrick Henry and the Elder William Bradford.

Viewed as a piece of storytelling, White's memoir takes him from his confusion and embarrassment during the play to his confidence and understanding after his seminar presentation. Viewed as a piece of essay writing, it connects the subject of White's early education with the framework of the immigrant experience in America. If history is an enormous web, White's memoir helps us understand one strand.

Notice the assumptions that White makes about what his readers know and what they want to know. He doesn't explain, for instance, the circumstances of the first Thanksgiving, assuming that his readers will understand them better than Itchie Rachlin did. He does translate Itchie's statement "*Vos is dos vor traef?*" because he knows few of his readers will understand Yiddish, and he words his discussion of the A.F. of L. and the National Association of Manufacturers so that someone who has only a vague notion of what these organizations are will not be confused. He assumes that his readers will be interested in what it was like to grow up in an immigrant community where few people spoke English. He assumes they will be interested in how the children of immigrant families come to see themselves as Americans. He doesn't assume that they will want to hear his lecture on the intricacies of the Immigration Act of 1924. No less than Miss Fuller, White is teaching a lesson about American history. Like Miss Fuller, he must be careful to suit the lesson to the audience.

SEARCHING FOR HISTORICAL FRAMEWORKS FOR YOUR OWN MEMOIR

A first step for writing an effective historical memoir is to think of your life as belonging to history. Theodore White knew that he was a product of one of the great periods of immigration to the United States. James Weldon Johnson learned early that his life belonged to a chapter of America's racial history. The following exercises are intended to help you think about the historical frameworks into which your own life fits and to help you find a topic for a historical memoir.

♦ *Identifying a Key Historical Event.* Name an event that occurred during your childhood or adolescence that was so obviously historic that you remember the moment you first heard about it. Make notes on at least three ways the event affected the course of your life thereafter.

EXERCISE 1

♦ *Identifying a Process of Historical Change.* Think about at least two groups (ethnic, sexual, economic, social, political, or other) to which you belong. Make notes on how the status of each of these groups has changed from the day that you were born to the present. Note any widely known events associated with this change. Note any events you have witnessed that can be associated with this change.

EXERCISE 2

♦ *Identifying Historical Themes from Late Childhood.* To a surprising degree, childhood memoirs seem to focus on events that happened to the writer when he or she was ten to fourteen years old. Consider this period in your own life. List at least three major "themes" in the public history of those years. Were any of those themes echoed in your own life?

EXERCISE 3

♦ *Remembering History Lessons.* Recall a specific occasion when someone attempted to show you, as Miss Fuller showed Theodore White, that history is connected to "us." Describe your reaction to the lesson then and your reaction now.

EXERCISE 4

SOCIAL FRAMEWORKS

No definite line separates social frameworks from historical ones, but what we will call social frameworks are more dramatically concerned with *difference*. Most of us remember occasions when we became uncomfortably aware that the customs and values of our immediate family and friends were not the *only* customs and values. We learned that not all people were like "us," and we speculated on what kind of people "they" were. The following passage from Maya Angelou's *I Know Why the Caged Bird Sings* recaptures her childhood feeling about the oddness of "whitefolks."

In Stamps[2] the segregation was so complete that most Black children didn't really, absolutely know what whites looked like. Other than that they were different, to be dreaded, and in that dread was included the hostility of the powerless against the powerful, the poor against the rich, the worker against the worked for and the ragged against the well dressed.

    I remember never believing that whites were really real.

A WRITER AT WORK

"Whitefolks"
MAYA ANGELOU

---

[2] Stamps: Angelou grew up in Stamps, Arkansas.

Many women who worked in their kitchens traded at our Store, and when they carried their finished laundry back to town they often set the big baskets down on our front porch to pull a singular piece from the starched collection and show either how graceful was their ironing hand or how rich and opulent was the property of their employers.

I looked at the items that weren't on display. I knew, for instance, that white men wore shorts, as Uncle Willie did, and that they had an opening for taking out their "things" and peeing, and that white women's breasts weren't built into their dresses, as some people said, because I saw their brassieres in the baskets. But I couldn't force myself to think of them as people. People were Mrs. LaGrone, Mrs. Hendricks, Momma, Reverend Sneed, Lillie B, and Louise and Rex. White folks couldn't be people because their feet were too small, their skin too white and see-throughy, and they didn't walk on the balls of their feet the way people did—they walked on their heels like horses.

People were those who lived on my side of town. I didn't like them all, or, in fact, any of them very much, but they were people. These others, the strange pale creatures that lived in their alien unlife, weren't considered folks. They were whitefolks.

Notice how important the memoirist's dual perspective is here. If the adult Angelou believed that "white folks couldn't be people," she would be the ugliest kind of bigot. What makes the passage palatable is our sense that the narrator has grown up and can tell about her childhood misconceptions with a smile. What makes it interesting is that Angelou helps us understand how the misconceptions were created.

Wonderful as the "whitefolks" passage is, Angelou chooses not to develop it into a story with a beginning, middle, and end. For an example of a fully developed narrative that builds on a sense of differing social customs, let's look at an excerpt from James Weldon Johnson's autobiography *Along This Way*. In this case, the "different" people are not as separated from the narrator as Angelou's "whitefolks." Johnson's own grandmother is one of them.

A WRITER AT WORK

"Revival Meeting"
JAMES WELDON
JOHNSON

After John Barton[3] died I spent a good deal of time at my grandmother's house to keep her company. I made myself handy, especially in the shops, where I served a part of each day as clerk. I often slept at her house. On those evenings, after the shop was closed, she usually read to me for an hour or so. She read from the Bible and from a thick, illustrated book in green cloth called *Home Life in the Bible*. She also read me stories from books that she drew from the library of Ebenezer Church Sunday School. These stories were better written and slightly less juvenile than those in the "library" my father had given me, but they were of the same genre. My grandmother had had very little school-

---

[3] **John Barton:** The second husband of Johnson's grandmother.

ing, and could not read as my mother did; that, however, did not daunt her, she read a great deal, and more and more as she grew older. When she read Bible stories aloud to me she came across many names difficult to pronounce, especially in the stories from the Old Testament, but I never knew her to be stumped by a single one; she'd call it something and pass right on. In this way she coined, I am sure, a number of wonderful words.

It was during this period that she disclosed her consuming ambition, her ambition for me to become a preacher. She lived until I was thirty years old, and I believe she never felt that I had done other than choose the lesser part. She took me to Sunday school each week and to some of the church services. I was practically living at my grandmother's when there came a revivalist to Ebenezer. She attended the meetings every night, taking me along with her, always walking the distance of about a mile each way. Sometimes that homeward mile for my short legs seemed without end. In these revival meetings the decorum of the regular Sunday service gave way to something primitive. It was hard to realize that this was the same congregation which on Sunday mornings sat quietly listening to the preacher's exegesis of his text and joining in singing conventional hymns and anthems led by a choir. Now the scene is changed. The revivalist rants and roars, he exhorts and implores, he warns and threatens. The air is charged. Overlaid emotions come to surface. A woman gives a piercing scream and begins to "shout"; then another, and another. The more hysterical ones must be held to be kept from "shouting" out of their clothes. Sinners crowd to the mourners' bench. Prayers and songs go up for the redemption of their souls. Strapping men break down in agonizing sobs, and emotionally strained women fall out in a rigid trance. A mourner "comes through" and his testimony of conversion brings a tumult of rejoicing.

I was only about nine years old but younger souls had been consecrated to God; and I was led to the mourners' bench. I knelt down at the altar. I was so wedged in that I could hardly breathe. I tried to pray. I tried to feel a conviction of sin. I, finally, fell asleep. . . . The meeting was about to close; somebody shook me by the shoulder. . . . I woke up but did not open my eyes or stir. . . . Whence sprang the whim, as cunning as could have occurred to one of the devil's own imps? The shaking continued, but I neither opened my eyes nor stirred. They gathered round me. I heard, "Glory to God, the child's gone off!" But I did not open my eyes or stir. My grandmother got a big, strong fellow who took me on his back and toted me that long mile home. Several people going our way accompanied us, and the conversation reverted to me, with some rather far-fetched allusions to the conversion of Saul of Tarsus. The situation stirred my sense of humor, and a chuckle ran round and round inside of me, because I did not dare to let it get out. The sensation was a delicious one, but it was suddenly chilled by the appalling thought that I could not postpone my awakening indefinitely. Each step home-ward, I knew, brought the moment of reckoning nearer. I needed to think and think fast; and I did. I evolved a plan that I thought was good; when I reached home and "awoke" I recounted a vision. The vision was based on a remembered illustration in *Home Life in the Bible* that purported to be the artist's conception of a scene in heaven. To that conception I added some original embellishments. Apparently my plan worked out to the satisfaction of everybody concerned. Indeed, for me, it worked out almost too satisfactorily, for I was called upon to repeat the vision many times thereafter—to my inward shame.

Readers needn't know who James Weldon Johnson was to find this passage interesting. Its eyewitness description of a revival service makes it worth reading, and the dilemma of the nine-year-old Johnson reminds readers of the enormous pressure children feel to meet the expectations of adults—no matter how uneasy they may be with those expectations. Those who *do* know Johnson will recognize that the story fits into one of the major frameworks of his autobiography and his other writings: the quest to "strike an emotional and intellectual balance" in the practice of religion. Like many social memoirs, Johnson's shows a piece of the writer's struggle to *choose* the customs that will define his life.

SEARCHING FOR SOCIAL FRAMEWORKS FOR YOUR OWN MEMOIR

A key to writing a memoir in a social framework is learning to think of yourself as a creature shaped by the society around you. This shaping may take the form of instructions from family members about the ways that "we" are different from "them." It may come directly from an institution that attempts to "socialize" the young: the school; the church, synagogue, or mosque; the athletic team; the Girl Scouts or Boy Scouts; and so forth. In some cases, it may come less from deliberate instruction than from the example of an adult who lives according to such definite values that we feel an unspoken pressure to adopt those values as our own. Think of yourself as a malleable substance and try to identify the forces that have shaped you—or attempted to.

The following exercises may help you find social frameworks and subjects for a memoir.

EXERCISE 5

◆ *Recalling Negative Stereotypes.* Adults sometimes try to shape the characters of children by holding up a group as a negative example, an example of what *not* to be. Describe a time when you had a group presented to you as a negative stereotype.

EXERCISE 6

◆ *Recalling Rejected Social Lessons.* Social lessons that you refuse to learn are sometimes more memorable than those you accept. Describe instances from your childhood when you recognized a lesson about social differences and resisted it.

◆ *Recalling Lessons About Sex Roles.* Among the most universal (often indirect) "lessons" of childhood is the teaching of feminine and masculine roles. Describe the ways you received clues about how men's behavior should differ from women's (or vice versa).

EXERCISE 7

◆ *Recalling an Outsider's Influence.* One common crisis in growing up is falling under the influence of a person outside the family whose values and style of life directly conflict with much of what the family has attempted to inculcate in us. Describe such a crisis in your own life.

EXERCISE 8

PSYCHOLOGICAL FRAMEWORKS

Eventually most of us find in our character an element that can't be entirely accounted for by the times we live in or by the attempts of society to mold us. We discover that (for better or worse) we have a nature, a personality. The discovery of this nature is one of the richest themes in memoir writing. Often writers will recall an event from early life that captures the essence of their personality, not only as it was at that moment but as it will continue to be until the day they die. In the passage that follows, Mark Twain describes such an incident.

A WRITER AT WORK

"Cadet of Temperance"
MARK TWAIN

In Hannibal when I was about fifteen I was for a short time a Cadet of Temperance, an organization which probably covered the whole United States during as much as a year—possibly even longer. It consisted in a pledge to refrain, during membership, from the use of tobacco; I mean it consisted partly in that pledge and partly in a red merino sash, but the red merino sash was the main part. The boys joined in order to be privileged to wear it—the pledge part of the matter was of no consequence. It was so small in importance that, contrasted with the sash, it was in effect nonexistent. The organization was weak and impermanent because there were not enough holidays to support it. We could turn out and march and show the red sashes on May Day with the Sunday schools and on the Fourth of July with the Sunday schools, the independent fire company and the militia company. But you can't keep a juvenile moral institution alive on two displays of its sash per year. As a private I could not have held out beyond one procession but I was Illustrious Grand Worthy Secretary and Royal Inside Sentinel and had the privilege of inventing the passwords and of wearing a rosette on my sash. Under these conditions I was enabled to remain steadfast until I had gathered the glory of two displays—May Day and the Fourth of July. Then I resigned straightway and straightway left the lodge.

I had not smoked for three full months and no words can adequately describe the smoke appetite that was consuming me. I had been a smoker from my ninth year—a private one during the first two years and a public one after that—that is to say, after my father's death. I was smoking and entirely happy before I was thirty steps from the lodge door. I do not know what the brand of the cigar was. It was probably not choice, or the previous smoker would not have thrown it away so soon. But I realized that it was the best cigar that was ever made. The previous smoker would have thought the same if he had been without a smoke for three months. I smoked that stub without shame. I could not do it now without shame, because now I am more refined than I was then. But I would smoke it just the same. I know myself and I know the human race well enough to know that.

Unlike the memoirs by Angelou and Johnson, this one does not attempt to recreate the feeling of being a child: we barely enter the mind of the "writer as character"; the "writer as interpreter" dominates. As Twain grew older, his conviction that the conventional morality of groups like the Cadets of Temperance was hypocrisy grew stronger. The contrariness of the nine-year-old in the story foreshadows the cynicism of the old man who wrote it and dozens of other stories filled with skeptical humor. And notice that even though Twain writes to make us smile, he also wants to inform: to show us by revealing *his* nature what human nature is *really* like.

Not every memoirist shares Twain's confidence that his nature is representative of all of human nature. Some writers, like Mary McCarthy, see themselves as particular types:

. . . in St. Stephen's School, I was not devout just to show off; I felt my religion very intensely and longed to serve God better than anyone else. This, I thought, was what He asked of me. I lived in fear of making a poor confession or of not getting my tongue flat enough to receive the Host reverently. One of the great moral crises of my life occurred on the morning of my first Communion. I took a drink of water. Unthinkingly, of course, for had it not been drilled into me that the Host must be received fasting, on the penalty of mortal sin? It was only a sip, but that made no difference, I knew. A sip was as bad as a gallon; I *could not* take Communion. And yet I had to. My Communion dress and veil and prayer book were laid out for me, and I was supposed to lead the girls' procession; John Klosick, in a white suit, would be leading the boys'. It seemed to me that I would be failing the school and my class, if, after all the rehearsals, I had to confess what I had done and drop out. The sisters would be angry; my guardians would be angry, having paid for the dress and veil. I thought of the procession without me in it, and I could not bear it. To make my first Communion later, in ordinary clothes, would not be the same. On the other hand, if I took my first Communion in a state of mortal sin, God would never forgive me; it would be a fatal beginning. I went through a ferocious struggle with my conscience, and all the while, I think, I knew the devil was going to prevail; I was going to take Communion, and only God and I would know the real facts. So it came about: I received my first Communion in a state of outward holiness and inward horror, believing I was damned, for I could not imagine that I could make a true repentance—

the time to repent was now, before committing the sacrilege; afterward, I could not be really sorry for I would have achieved what I had wanted.

I suppose I must have confessed this at my next confession, scarcely daring to breathe it, and the priest must have treated it lightly: my sins, as I slowly discovered, weighed heavier on me than they did on my confessors. Actually, it is quite common for children making their first Communion to have just such a mishap as mine: they are so excited on that long-awaited morning that they hardly know what they are doing, or possibly the very taboo on food and water and the importance of the occasion drive them into an unconscious resistance. I heard a story almost identical with mine from Ignazio Silone. Yet the despair I felt that summer morning (I think it was Corpus Christi Day) was in a certain sense fully justified: I *knew myself,* how I was and would be forever; such dry self-knowledge is terrible. Every subsequent moral crisis of my life, moreover, has had precisely the pattern of this struggle over the first Communion; I have battled, usually without avail, against a temptation to do something which only I knew was bad, being swept on by a need to preserve outward appearances and to live up to other people's expectations of me. The heroine of one of my novels, who finds herself pregnant, possibly as the result of an infidelity, and is tempted to have the baby and say nothing to her husband, is in the same fix, morally, as I was at eight years old, with that drink of water inside me that only I knew was there. When I supposed I was damned, I was right—damned, that is, to a repetition or endless re-enactment of that conflict between excited scruples and inertia of will.

Is the Mary McCarthy type—the person trapped "between excited scruples and inertia of will"—common or uncommon? If it is common, then readers are learning about the psychological workings of millions of people, including perhaps themselves. If it is uncommon, they are learning about the range of possibilities open to human nature. Every memoir that is honestly written can teach us something about human psychology.

SEARCHING FOR PSYCHOLOGICAL FRAMEWORKS FOR YOUR OWN MEMOIR

Psychological memoirs may be more difficult to manage than historical or social ones because they require us to have a clear view of ourselves. It is not easy to pluck out of childhood experience an incident that epitomizes our personalities, to say "I know myself and I know the human race well enough to know that" or "I *knew myself,* how I was and would be forever." It is probably best to start by recollecting who we are at present before we search our earlier lives. The following exercises may help you with that recollection.

◆ *The Battle of the Virtues and Vices.* In a long poem called the *Psychomachia*, Aurelius Clemens Prudentius (348–404 A.D.) presented the personality as a battleground on which seven sins fought seven virtues. The idea was a catchy one and became one of the standard ways of thinking about personality during the Middle Ages. On the chart below (and with slight modifications) Prudentius's vices are arranged on the left, his virtues on the right. If you can imagine a hand-to-hand battle between each vice and its corresponding virtue in your own personality, where on the following scale would you say the battle now stands?

This exercise may help you think of incidents from your childhood that showed the battle turning in favor of one of your besetting "sins" (which you may not now think of as sinful at all) or one of your redeeming "virtues" (which you may not think of as entirely good things).

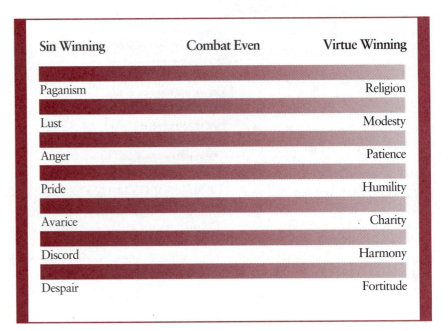

Sin Winning	Combat Even	Virtue Winning
Paganism		Religion
Lust		Modesty
Anger		Patience
Pride		Humility
Avarice		Charity
Discord		Harmony
Despair		Fortitude

◆ *Positive and Negative Personality Traits.* Since the time of Aristotle, at least, those who think about personality traits have noticed that virtues and vices are often flip sides of the same coin. Courage in one situation becomes foolhardiness in another. Honesty can become rude bluntness. Psychologists and philosophers sometimes create tables that link personality strengths with their corresponding weaknesses. The following table has been constructed over the centuries by those ancient students of personality types, the astrologers. Ignoring the astrological sign you were born under, decide which set of traits matches your personality best and which matches your personality worst.

Aries ♈	+	**Assertive, energetic, courageous, ardent**
	−	**Aggressive, angry, egotistical, impulsive**
Taurus ♉	+	**Conservative, reliable, steadfast, patient, deliberate**
	−	**Greedy, stodgy, possessive, obstinate**
Gemini ♊	+	**Intellectual, versatile, communicative, alert**
	−	**Nervous, undependable, impatient, unable to concentrate**
Cancer ♋	+	**Protective, domestic, emotional, patriotic**
	−	**Oversensitive, oblique, crabby, moody, acquisitive**
Leo ♌	+	**Creative, vital, commanding, expansive, regal**
	−	**Pleasure seeking, conceited, domineering, lazy**
Virgo ♍	+	**Practical, modest, analytical, unassuming**
	−	**Reticent, overdiscriminating, aloof, overcritical**
Libra ♎	+	**Harmonious, affable, diplomatic, balanced, thoughtful**
	−	**Indecisive, vapid, discontented**
Scorpio ♏	+	**Intense, passionate, penetrating, genuine**
	−	**Blunt, cruel, lustful, vindictive**
Sagittarius ♐	+	**Expansive, free, enthusiastic, profound**
	−	**Reckless, outspoken, excessive, boisterous**
Capricorn ♑	+	**Cautious, ambitious, serious, stable, orderly**
	−	**Cold, limited, miserly, fearful**
Aquarius ♒	+	**Instructive, inventive, aspiring, changeable, unconventional**
	−	**Revolutionary, detached, cool, rebellious**
Pisces ♓	+	**Intuitive, inspired, sensitive, intangible**
	−	**Vague, oversentimental, confused, self-pitying**

You may find that the cluster of adjectives associated with one of the signs of the zodiac describes you well and provides the right framework for a memoir. Perhaps you will find it useful instead to produce a comparable cluster that doesn't pretend to be written in the stars.

POINTS TO

CONSIDER

WRITING A MEMOIR

Look for a Compact Story Line.   Thinking about your life historically, socially, and psychologically is a good technique for turning up material for a memoir. A good story, however, is the heart of the matter. *Story* implies a struggle with a definite beginning and a definite end. Recall occasions when you found yourself in conflict with people or institutions (think of James Weldon Johnson at the mourners' bench) or with yourself (think of Mary McCarthy taking her first communion "in a state of outward holiness and inward horror"). A sharply focused incident that begins and ends on the same day is more likely to succeed than one that extends over weeks and is complicated by many events and characters.

Don't Lose Track of Your Framework.   Some of us, when we start talking about our own experience, tend to see all details as equally important (or unimportant). Don't forget that you are addressing an audience of strangers. These strangers want only those details that are intriguing in themselves or that are pertinent to an interesting framework. Let them know that there is a *point* to your story.

Be Modest.   If you think back on the memoirs included in this chapter, you'll realize that none of the writers looks back on himself or herself with smug self-satisfaction. More often, they look back with humor or with horror. One reason for this is simply that the writers know what bores readers: self-justification and self-aggrandizement. It is worth remembering, too, that the now-I-know-better stance is one of the three classic postures described in Chapter 1. When the writer-as-character knows less than the writer-as-narrator, we get a sense of growth and development.

QUESTIONS FOR PEER REVIEW

If you have an opportunity for peer review, ask your reviewer both for general comments (see the checklist on page 60) and for answers to three particular questions:

1. Have I shown you anything about how my earlier life connects with history? (With social customs?) (With my personality?)

2. Are there details or incidents vivid enough that you will remember them a week from now? What are they?

3. Are there details or events that are unnecessary or dull? What are they?

You may also want to ask the question Annie Dillard clearly asked herself while she was writing *An American Childhood:* Did I "hang on the reader's arm, like a drunk, and say 'And then I did this and it was so interesting.'"

GROWING UP IN AMERICA: 10 LIVES

While some memoirs of childhood and youth are intended only for friends and relatives, others are widely read and help shape a nation's image of itself. The ten examples below could serve as a short course on what it means, and has meant, to grow up in America.

1.   Frederick Douglass (1813–95) *Narrative of the Life of Frederick Douglass: An American Slave* (1845). The first of three volumes of Douglass's autobiography, this book combines eloquence and historical importance. It traces Douglass's life from early childhood to his escape North in 1837.

2.   Helen Keller (1880–1968) *The Story of My Life* (1903). Written in Keller's sophomore year at Radcliffe, this autobiography tells the story of her struggle, despite blindness and deafness, to become an educated woman. The book is also a tribute to her teacher, Anne Sullivan.

3.   Richard Wright (1908–60) *Black Boy* (1945). The story of Wright's coming of age amid racial repression and violence is a milestone in both social history and literature. Like Douglass's autobiography, Wright's ends with an escape North.

4.   Mary McCarthy (1912–89) *Memories of a Catholic Girlhood* (1957). McCarthy's memoirs of living as an orphan among unsympathetic relatives in Minneapolis, then as an uneasy boarder in Catholic schools in Washington state, is sometimes hilarious and sometimes grim.

5.   Theodore White (1915–86), *In Search of History: A Personal Adventure* (1979). The first section of White's autobiography is a story of pluck and luck—White's childhood in an immigrant family, his struggles during the Depression, and his success at Harvard.

6.   Russell Baker (1925–), *Growing Up* (1982). Baker's autobiography covers the first twenty-four years of his life, including his childhood in a proud Virginia family suffering the hardships of the Depression. The book includes memorable portraits of people who influenced Baker, notably his mother who had "a passion for improving the male of the species."

7.   Maya Angelou (1928–), *I Know Why the Caged Bird Sings* (1970). The first of Angelou's several memoirs, this book includes remarkable pictures of life in the highly segregated town of Stamps, Arkansas. It ends in Angelou's sixteenth year, with her graduation from high school and the birth of her son.

8.   Richard Rodriguez (1944–), *Hunger of Memory* (1982). Controversial because of Rodriguez's opposition to bilingual education, this autobiography focuses on the tension between the life of the author's Mexican-American family and his new life as a "scholarship boy" increasingly separated from the family's traditions and language.

9.   Annie Dillard (1945–), *An American Childhood* (1987). Dillard's memoir recreates a child's life in Pittsburgh in the 1950s and includes fine portraits of her eccentric family, but its chief interest lies in the way it traces the awakening of her own mind and spirit.

10.   Patricia Hampl (1946–), *A Romantic Education* (1981). Hampl is a poet, and her memoir—full of arresting images and metaphors—is a meditation on the forces that have shaped her own (and her generation's) sense of identity, history, and beauty. It begins in St. Paul, Minnesota, and ends in Prague, Czechoslovakia, in 1975. ◆

Assignments
for Chapter 5

ANALYSIS OF A MEMOIR

Because memoirs are often many-faceted, they give us an excellent opportunity to practice one of the most common assignments in college classes, the analysis of a reading passage. An analysis is different from any of the three types of summaries discussed in Chapter 1 (pp. 17–19), because it requires you to break down your subject (the passage) by viewing it in *several* frameworks. Often the frameworks are built into the assignment: they are major themes of the course you are studying, and you are expected to show your mastery of these themes in the process of analysis. In a sociology or psychology class, for example, you might study five forces that affect self-esteem and then be asked to analyze Maya Angelou's *I Know Why the Caged Bird Sings* to show these forces at work. The terms of analysis become frameworks for your examination of the text.

Such assignments are not easy. You will sometimes feel that you have been handed a block of wood and told to put it into a glove in such a way that all five fingers are filled. Angelou did not, after all, write her book as an illustration of the five forces that affect self-esteem, and you would have to do considerable mental rearrangement of her material to make the analyis work. Remember that this difficult rearrangement is precisely the purpose of such assignments. The professor who assigns the paper hopes that you will discover how his or her discipline can alter your view of a subject. To analyze a text successfully, you will have to see it in a somewhat different way than the author saw it and perhaps in a way that would not entirely please the author. On the other hand, you are intellectually and ethically obliged to treat the text fairly, not altering the essence of what it says and not misrepresenting any details.

In this chapter we have a fairly simple set of terms of analysis: the three frameworks for memoir (historical, social, and psychological). The following example uses all three terms in its analysis of Theodore White's memoir about early history lessons (p. 107).

> Theodore White presents a pair of sixth-grade memories: one of participating in a "free-form" play about the first Thanksgiving, one of delivering a paper to a group of teachers in a night-school education class at Boston University. These memories connect his life to the larger context of immigration in American history. The play was, of course,

140

about an immigrant group (the Puritans) meeting with native-born Americans, and it was presented by a mixed cast of American-born students and newly arrived immigrant children. Thus it gave White a double exposure to the American traditions of cooperation and misunderstanding among various immigrant groups. The paper White later delivered to his teacher's night-school class discussed the Immigration Act of 1924, clearly a part of the same 300-year-old story.

Though this historical framework dominates the memoir, we can also see young White getting an early exposure to serious conflicts between groups with different values and ideologies. This social lesson comes from his conversations with his father, who, because he was an immigrant himself, had reason to oppose "The Closing of the Gates" by the Immigration Act. White's father did not express opposition, however. Being a socialist and a union man, he saw that the importation of cheap labor served the interests of the capitalists by keeping the wages of American workers low. This discussion with his father about the conflict between the trade unions and the capitalists must have been one of White's earliest exposures to politics outside the family and the neighborhood.

On the psychological level, White was learning what he was good at, what he enjoyed, and what abilities would allow him to make his way in the world. In the play, it is his ability to bridge the cultural gap between his American teacher and his immigrant classmates that puts him in a position of responsibility. In the night-school class he learned that he enjoyed explaining contemporary history, enjoyed having "all the dates and facts" and an "attentive audience." The play and speech might be seen as the beginnings of White's career as a writer about American politics.

Almost all extended memoirs and many short ones lend themselves to this three-part analysis. Your assignment is to analyze one of the readings at the end of this chapter using *at least two* of our frameworks (historical, social, and psychological) as the terms of analysis.

ASSIGNMENT 2:   **ANALYSIS OF AN INITIATION STORY**

The transition from childhood or adolescence into the adult world is so common a theme in literature that the "initiation story" is sometimes thought of as a special literary genre. Like the memoirs we have read, the initiation story shows a protagonist gaining self-understanding and knowledge of the world. Analyze the protagonist's learning in one of the following stories:

Leslie Norris, "Blackberries," p. 440
Elizabeth Tallent, "No One's a Mystery," p. 443
Toni Cade Bambara, "The Hammer Man," p. 445

You may elect to use one or more of this chapter's categories—historical, social, and psychological—in your analysis. You may find other terms more suitable.

ASSIGNMENT 3:   **A MEMOIR**

Write a memoir that puts an experience from your past into at least one of the three general frameworks mentioned in the chapter: historical, social, and psychological.

SHOOTING AN ELEPHANT

George Orwell

"Shooting an Elephant" (1936) is the only memoir collected in this group that treats an episode from the writer's adult life. Like the other memoirs, however, it looks backward on an earlier self: the Orwell who writes the essay is clearly a different man from the Orwell who served as a policeman in Burma. As you read the essay, think especially about its historical setting and what that implies about the younger Orwell's predicament and the older Orwell's perspective.

1 IN MOULMEIN, IN LOWER BURMA, I WAS hated by large numbers of people—the only time in my life that I have been important enough for this to happen to me. I was sub-divisional police officer of the town, and in an aimless, petty kind of way anti-European feeling was very bitter. No one had the guts to raise a riot, but if a European woman went through the bazaars alone somebody would probably spit betel juice over her dress. As a police officer I was an obvious target and was baited whenever it seemed safe to do so. When a nimble Burman tripped me up on the football field and the referee (another Burman) looked the other way, the crowd yelled with hideous laughter. This happened more than once. In the end the sneering yellow faces of young men that met me everywhere, the insults hooted after me when I was at a safe distance, got badly on my nerves. The young Buddhist priests were the worst of all. There were several thousands of them in the town and none of them seemed to have anything to do except stand on street corners and jeer at Europeans.

2 All this was perplexing and upsetting. For at that time I had already made up my mind that imperialism was an evil thing and the sooner I chucked up my job and got out of it the better. Theoretically—and secretly, of course—I was all for the Burmese and all against their oppressors, the British. As for the job I was doing, I hated it more bitterly than I can perhaps make clear. In a job like that you see the dirty work of Empire at close quarters. The wretched prisoners huddling in the stinking cages of the lock-ups, the grey, cowed faces of the long-term convicts, the scarred buttocks of the men who had been flogged with bamboos—all these oppressed me with an intolerable sense of guilt. But I could get nothing into perspective. I was young and ill-educated and I had to think out my problems in the utter silence that is imposed on every Englishman in the East. I did not even know that the British Empire is dying, still less did I know that it is a great deal better than the younger empires that are going to supplant it. All I knew was that I was stuck between my hatred of the empire I served and my rage against the evil-spirited little beasts who tried to make my job impossible. With one part of my mind I thought of the British Raj as an unbreakable tyranny, as something clamped down, in *saecula saeculorum*,[1] upon the will of prostrate peoples; with another part I thought that the greatest joy in the world would be to drive a bayonet into a Buddhist priest's guts. Feelings like these are the normal by-products of imperi-

---

1 **saecula saeculorum**: "For ages of ages"; until the end of time.

alism; ask any Anglo-Indian official, if you can catch him off duty.

3   One day something happened which in a roundabout way was enlightening. It was a tiny incident in itself, but it gave me a better glimpse than I had had before of the real nature of imperialism—the real motives for which despotic governments act. Early one morning the sub-inspector at a police station the other end of the town rang me up on the 'phone and said that an elephant was ravaging the bazaar. Would I please come and do something about it? I did not know what I could do, but I wanted to see what was happening and I got on to a pony and started out. I took my rifle, an old .44 Winchester and much too small to kill an elephant, but I thought the noise might be useful *in terrorem*. Various Burmans stopped me on the way and told me about the elephant's doings. It was not, of course, a wild elephant, but a tame one which had gone "must." It had been chained up, as tame elephants always are when their attack of "must" is due, but on the previous night it had broken its chain and escaped. Its mahout, the only person who could manage it when it was in that state, had set out in pursuit, but had taken the wrong direction and was now twelve hours' journey away, and in the morning the elephant had suddenly reappeared in the town. The Burmese population had no weapons and were quite helpless against it. It had already destroyed somebody's bamboo hut, killed a cow and raided some fruit-stalls and devoured the stock; also it had met the municipal rubbish van and, when the driver jumped out and took to his heels, had turned the van over and inflicted violences upon it.

4   The Burmese sub-inspector and some Indian constables were waiting for me in the quarter where the elephant had been seen. It was a very poor quarter, a labyrinth of squalid bamboo huts, thatched with palm-leaf, winding all over a steep hillside. I remember that it was a cloudy, stuffy morning at the beginning of the rains. We began questioning the people as to where the elephant had gone and, as usual, failed to get any definite information. That is invariably the case in the East; a story always sounds clear enough at a distance, but the nearer you get to the scene of events the vaguer it becomes. Some of the people said that the elephant had gone in one direction, some said that he had gone in another, some professed not even to have heard of any elephant. I had almost made up my mind that the whole story was a pack of lies, when we heard yells a little distance away. There was a loud scandalized cry of "Go away, child! Go away this instant!" and an old woman with a switch in her hand came round the corner of a hut, violently shooing away a crowd of naked children. Some more women followed, clicking their tongues and exclaiming; evidently there was something that the children ought not to have seen. I rounded the hut and saw a man's dead body sprawling in the mud. He was an Indian, a black Dravidian coolie, almost naked, and he could not have been dead many minutes. The people said that the elephant had come suddenly upon him round the corner of the hut, caught him with its trunk, put its foot on his back and ground him into the earth. This was the rainy season and the ground was soft, and his face had scored a trench a foot deep and a couple of yards long. He was lying on his belly with arms crucified and head sharply twisted to one side. His face was coated with mud, the eyes wide open, the teeth bared and grinning with an expression of unendurable agony. (Never tell me, by the way, that the dead look peaceful. Most of the corpses I have seen look devilish.) The friction of the great beast's foot had stripped the skin from his back as neatly as one skins a rabbit. As soon as I saw the dead man I sent an orderly to a friend's house nearby to borrow an elephant rifle. I had already sent back the pony, not wanting it to go mad with fright and throw me if it smelt the elephant.

5   The orderly came back in a few minutes with a rifle and five catridges, and meanwhile some Burmans had arrived and told us that the elephant was in the paddy fields below, only a few hundred yards away. As I started forward practically the whole population of the quarter flocked out of the houses and followed me. They had seen the rifle and were all shouting excitedly that I was going to shoot the elephant. They had not shown much interest in the elephant when he was merely ravaging their homes, but it was different now that he was going to be shot. It was a bit of fun to them, as it would be to an English crowd; besides they wanted the meat. It made me vaguely uneasy. I had no intention of shooting the elephant—I had merely sent for the rifle to defend myself if necessary—and it is always unnerving to have a crowd following you. I marched down the hill, looking and feeling a fool, with the rifle over my shoulder and an ever-growing army of people jostling at my heels. At the bottom, when you got away from the huts, there was a metalled road and beyond that a miry waste of paddy fields a thousand yards across, not yet ploughed but soggy from the first rains and dotted with coarse grass. The elephant was standing eight yards from the road, his left side towards us. He took not the slightest notice of the crowd's approach. He was tearing up bunches of grass, beating them against his knees to clean them and stuffing them into his mouth.

6   I had halted on the road. As soon as I saw the elephant I knew with perfect certainty that I ought not to shoot him. It is a serious matter to shoot a working elephant—it is comparable to destroying a huge and costly piece of machinery—and obviously one ought not to do it if it can possibly be avoided. And at that distance, peacefully eating, the elephant looked no more dangerous than a cow. I thought then and I think now that his attack of "must" was already passing off; in which case he would merely wander harmlessly about until the ma-

hout came back and caught him. Moreover, I did not in the least want to shoot him. I decided that I would watch him for a little while to make sure that he did not turn savage again, and then go home.

7   But at that moment I glanced round at the crowd that had followed me. It was an immense crowd, two thousand at the least and growing every minute. It blocked the road for a long distance on either side. I looked at the sea of yellow faces above the garish clothes—faces all happy and excited over this bit of fun, all certain that the elephant was going to be shot. They were watching me as they would watch a conjurer about to perform a trick. They did not like me, but with the magical rifle in my hands I was momentarily worth watching. And suddenly I realized that I should have to shoot the elephant after all. The people expected it of me and I had got to do it; I could feel their two thousand wills pressing me forward, irresistibly. And it was at this moment, as I stood there with the rifle in my hands, that I first grasped the hollowness, the futility of the white man's dominion in the East. Here was I, the white man with his gun, standing in front of the unarmed native crowd—seemingly the leading actor of the piece; but in reality I was only an absurd puppet pushed to and fro by the will of those yellow faces behind. I perceived in this moment that when the white man turns tyrant it is his own freedom that he destroys. He becomes a sort of hollow, posing dummy, the conventionalized figure of a sahib. For it is the condition of his rule that he shall spend his life in trying to impress the "natives," and so in every crisis he has got to do what the "natives" expect of him. He wears a mask, and his face grows to fit it. I had got to shoot the elephant. I had committed myself to doing it when I sent for the rifle. A sahib has got to act like a sahib; he has got to appear resolute, to know his own mind and do definite things. To come all that way, rifle in hand, with two thousand people

marching at my heels, and then to trail feebly away, having done nothing—no, that was impossible. The crowd would laugh at me. And my whole life, every white man's life in the East, was one long struggle not to be laughed at.

8   But I did not want to shoot the elephant. I watched him beating his bunch of grass against his knees, with that preoccupied grandmotherly air that elephants have. It seemed to me that it would be murder to shoot him. At that age I was not squeamish about killing animals, but I had never shot an elephant and never wanted to. (Somehow it always seems worse to kill a *large* animal.) Besides, there was the beast's owner to be considered. Alive, the elephant was worth at least a hundred pounds; dead, he would only be worth the value of his tusks, five pounds, possibly. But I had got to act quickly. I turned to some experienced-looking Burmans who had been there when we arrived, and asked them how the elephant had been behaving. They all said the same thing; he took no notice of you if you left him alone, but he might charge if you went too close to him.

9   It was perfectly clear to me what I ought to do. I ought to walk up to within, say, twenty-five yards of the elephant and test his behavior. If he charged, I could shoot; if he took no notice of me, it would be safe to leave him until the mahout came back. But also I knew that I was going to do no such thing. I was a poor shot with a rifle and the ground was soft mud into which one would sink at every step. If the elephant charged and I missed him, I should have about as much chance as a toad under a steamroller. But even then I was not thinking particularly of my own skin, only of the watchful yellow faces behind. For at that moment, with the crowd watching me, I was not afraid in the ordinary sense, as I would have been if I had been alone. A white man mustn't be frightened in front of "natives"; and so, in general, he isn't frightened. The sole thought in my

mind was that if anything went wrong those two thousand Burmans would see me pursued, caught, trampled on and reduced to a grinning corpse like that Indian up the hill. And if that happened it was quite probable that some of them would laugh. That would never do. There was only one alternative. I shoved the cartridges into the magazine and lay down on the road to get a better aim.

The crowd grew very still, and a deep, low,   10 happy sigh, as of people who see the theatre curtain go up at last, breathed from innumerable throats. They were going to have their bit of fun after all. The rifle was a beautiful German thing with cross-hair sights. I did not then know that in shooting an elephant one would shoot to cut an imaginary bar running from ear-hole to ear-hole. I ought, therefore, as the elephant was sideways on, to have aimed straight at his ear-hole; actually I aimed several inches in front of this, thinking the brain would be further forward.

When I pulled the trigger I did not hear the   11 bang or feel the kick—one never does when a shot goes home—but I heard the devilish roar of glee that went up from the crowd. In that instant, in too short a time, one would have thought, even for the bullet to get there, a mysterious, terrible change had come over the elephant. He neither stirred nor fell, but every line of his body had altered. He looked suddenly stricken, shrunken, immensely old, as though the frightful impact of the bullet had paralysed him without knocking him down. At last, after what seemed a long time—it might have been five seconds, I dare say—he sagged flabbily to his knees. His mouth slobbered. An enormous senility seemed to have settled upon him. One could have imagined him thousands of years old. I fired again into the same spot. At the second shot he did not collapse but climbed with desperate slowness to his feet and stood weakly upright, with legs sagging and head drooping. I fired a third time. That was the shot that did for him. You could see the agony of it jolt his whole body and knock the last remnant of strength from his legs. But in falling he seemed for a moment to rise, for as his hind legs collapsed beneath him he seemed to tower upward like a huge rock toppling, his trunk reaching skywards like a tree. He trumpeted, for the first and only time. And then down he came, his belly towards me, with a crash that seemed to shake the ground even where I lay.

12   I got up. The Burmans were already racing past me across the mud. It was obvious that the elephant would never rise again, but he was not dead. He was breathing very rhythmically with long rattling gasps, his great mound of a side painfully rising and falling. His mouth was wide open—I could see far down into caverns of pale pink throat. I waited a long time for him to die, but his breathing did not weaken. Finally I fired my two remaining shots into the spot where I thought his heart must be. The thick blood welled out of him like red velvet, but still he did not die. His body did not even jerk when the shots hit him, the tortured breathing continued without a pause. He was dying, very slowly and in great agony, but in some world remote from me where not even a bullet could damage him further. I felt that I had got to put an end to that dreadful noise. It seemed dreadful to see the great beast lying there, powerless to move and yet powerless to die, and not even to be able to finish him. I sent back for my small rifle and poured shot after shot into his heart and down his throat. They seemed to make no impression. The tortured gasps continued as steadily as the ticking of a clock.

13   In the end I could not stand it any longer and went away. I heard later that it took him half an hour to die. Burmans were bringing dahs and baskets even before I left, and I was told they had stripped his body almost to the bones by the afternoon.

14   Afterwards, of course, there were endless discussions about the shooting of the elephant. The owner was furious, but he was only an Indian and could do nothing. Besides, legally I had done the right thing, for a mad elephant has to be killed, like a mad dog, if its owner fails to control it. Among the Europeans opinion was divided. The older men said I was right, the younger men said it was a damn shame to shoot an elephant for killing a coolie, because an elephant was worth more than any damn Coringhee coolie. And afterwards I was very glad that the coolie had been killed; it put me legally in the right and it gave me a sufficient pretext for shooting the elephant. I often wondered whether any of the others grasped that I had done it solely to avoid looking a fool. ◆

To Everest

Jan Morris

Jan Morris was born James Morris. He served in the British army from 1943 to 1947, then became a reporter and editor for the *Times* of London. In 1953 he was the *Times* correspondent who accompanied Sir Edmund Hillary on the first successful climb of Mount Everest. Thereafter, he became a foreign correspondent, reporting on wars and rebellions and writing travel books. Despite his success and despite being the father of five children, he knew he was not comfortable with his male identity. "I was 3 or perhaps 4 years old when I realized I had been born into the wrong body," Morris wrote in *Conundrum*, the autobiography from which the following chapter is taken. Eventually, he began a series of medical procedures that changed his sex. In 1972, these changes were completed, and James began to live and publish as Jan.

1 THOUGH I RESENTED MY BODY, I DID NOT dislike it. I rather admired it, as it happened. It might not be the body beautiful, but it was lean and sinewy, never ran to fat, and worked like a machine of quality, responding exuberantly to a touch of the throttle or a long haul home. Women, I think, never have quite this feeling about their bodies, and I shall never have it again. It is a male prerogative, and contributes no doubt to the male arrogance. In those days, though for that very reason I did not want it, still I recognized the merits of my physique, and had pleasure from its exercise.

2 I first felt its full power, as one might realize for the first time the potential of a run-in car, in 1953, when I was assigned by *The Times* to join the British expedition shortly to make the first ascent of Mount Everest. This was essentially a physical undertaking. The paper had exclusive rights to dispatches from the mountain, and I was to be the only correspondent with the team, my job being partly to see that dispatches from the expedition's leader got safely home to London, but chiefly to write dispatches of my own. The competition would be intense and very likely violent, communica-tions were primitive to a degree, and the only way to do the job was to climb fairly high up the mountain myself and periodically, to put a complex operation simply, run down it again with the news. It was not particularly to my credit that I was given the assignment—at an agile twenty-six I was patently better suited for it than most of my colleagues at Printing House Square. I took exercise daily (as I still do), did not smoke (and still don't), and though excessively fond of wine, seldom drank spirits, not much liking the taste of them.

3 I was also, being some years out of the 9th Lancers, furiously keen.[1] There is something about the newspaper life, however specious its values and ridiculous its antics, that brings out the zest in its practitioners. It may be nonsense, but it is undeniably fun. I was not especially anxious to achieve fame in the trade, for I already felt instinctively that it would not be my life's occupation, but even so I would have stooped to almost any skulduggery to achieve

---

[1] furiously keen: Morris soldiered with this British regiment from 1943 to 1947, rising to the rank of second lieutenant. Among these highly professional soldiers, shows of enthusiasm, or "keenness," were considered bad form.

148

what was, self-consciously even then, quaintly called a scoop. The news from Everest was to be mine, and anyone who tried to steal it from me should look out for trouble.

4   In such a mood, at such an age, at the peak of a young man's physical condition, I found myself in May, 1953, high on the flank of the world's greatest mountain.

5   Let me try to describe the sensation for my readers, as it seems to me today—and especially for my women readers, who are unlikely I now see to have experienced such a conjunction of energies.

6   Imagine first the setting. This is theatrically changeable. In the morning it is like living, reduced to minuscule proportions, in a bowl of broken ice cubes in a sunny garden. Somewhere over the rim, one assumes, there are green trees, fields, and flowers; within the bowl everything is a brilliant white and blue. It is silent in there. The mountain walls deaden everything and cushion the hours in a disciplinary hush. The only noise is a drip of water sometimes, the howl of a falling boulder or the rumble of a distant avalanche. The sky above is a savage blue, the sun glares mercilessly off the snow and ice, blistering one's lips, dazzling one's eyes, and filling that mountain declivity with its substance.

7   In the afternoon everything changes. Then the sky scowls down, high snow-clowds billow in from Tibet, a restless cruel wind blows up, and before long the snow is falling in slanted parallel across the landscape, blotting out sky, ridges, and all, and making you feel that your ice-bowl has been put back into the refrigerator. It is terribly cold. The afternoon is filled with sounds, the rush of wind, the flapping of tent-canvas, the squeak and creak of guy-ropes; and as the evening draws on the snow piles up around your tent, half burying it infinitesimally in the hulk of Everest, as though you have been prematurely incarcerated, or perhaps trapped in a sunken submarine—for you can see the line of snow slowly rising through the nylon walls of the tent, like water rising to submerge you.

8   But imagine now the young man's condition. First, he is constant against this inconstant background. His body is running not in gusts and squalls, but at a steady high speed. He actually tingles with strength and energy, as though sparks might fly from his skin in the dark. Nothing sags in him. His body has no spare weight upon it, only muscles made supple by exercise. When, in the bright Himalayan morning, he emerges from his tent to make the long trek down the mountain to the Khumbu glacier below, it is as though he could leap down there in gigantic strides, singing as he goes. And when, the same evening perhaps, he labors up again through the driving snow, it is not a misery but a challenge to him, something to be outfaced, something actually to be enjoyed, as the deep snow drags at his feet, the water trickles down the back of his neck, and his face thickens with cold, ice, and wind.

9   There is no hardship to it, for it is not imposed upon him. He is the master. He feels that anything is possible to him, and that his relative position to events will always remain the same. He does not have to wonder what his form will be tomorrow, for it will be the same as it is today. His mind, like his body, is tuned to the job, and will not splutter or falter. It is this feeling of unfluctuating control, I think, that women cannot share, and it springs of course not from the intellect or the personality, nor even so much from upbringing, but specifically from the body. The male body may be ungenerous, even uncreative in the deepest kind, but when it is working properly it is a marvelous thing to inhabit. I admit it in retrospect more than I did at the time, and I look back to those moments of supreme male fitness as one remembers champagne or a morning swim. Nothing could beat me, I knew for sure; and nothing did.

10   I think for sheer exuberance the best day of my life was my last on Everest. The mountain had been climbed, and I had already begun my race down the glacier towards Katmandu, leaving the expedition to pack its gear behind me. By a combination of cunning and ingenuity I had already sent a coded message through an Indian Army radio transmitter at Namche Bazar, twenty miles south of Everest, its operators being unaware of its meaning; but I did not know if it had reached London safely, so I was myself hastening back to Katmandu and the cable office with my own final dispatch. How brilliant I felt, as with a couple of Sherpa porters I bounded down the glacial moraine towards the green below! I was brilliant with the success of my friends on the mountain, I was brilliant with my knowledge of the event, brilliant with muscular tautness, brilliant with conceit, brilliant with awareness of the subterfuge, amounting very nearly to dishonesty, by which I hoped to have deceived my competitors and scooped the world. All those weeks at high altitude had suited me, too, and had given me a kind of heightened fervor, as though my brain had been quickened by drugs to keep pace with my body. I laughed and sang all the way down the glacier, and when next morning I heard from the radio that my news had reached London providentially on the eve of Queen Elizabeth's coronation, I felt as though I had been crowned myself.

11   I never mind the swagger of young men. It is their right to swank, and I know the sensation!

12   Once more on Everest I was the outsider—formally this time, as well as tacitly. None of the climbers would have guessed, I am sure, how irrevocably distinct I felt from them; but they were aware that I was not a climber, and had been attached to the expedition only to watch. At first I was supposed to provide my own victuals and equipment, but it seemed rather silly to maintain such segregation twenty thousand feet above nowhere, so I soon pooled my resources with theirs, and pitched my tent amont them.

13   On Everest, nevertheless, I realized more explicitly some truths about myself. Though I was as fit as most of those men, I responded to different drives. I would have suffered almost anything to get those dispatches safely back to London, but I did not share the mountaineers' burning urge to see that mountain climbed. Perhaps it was too abstract an objective for me—certainly I was not animated by any respect for inviolate nature, which I have always disliked, preferring like George Leigh-Mallory a blend of tame and wild. I was pleased when they did climb Everest, but chiefly for a less than elevated reason—patriotic pride, which I knew to be unworthy of their efforts, but which I could not suppress.

14   I well understood the masochistic relish of challenge which impelled them, and which stimulated me too, but the blankness of the achievement depressed me. One of the older Everesters, H. W. Tilman, once quoted G. K. Chesterton to illustrate the urge of alpinism: "I think the immense act has something about it human and excusable; and when I endeavor to analyze the reason of this feeling I find it to lie, not in the fact that the thing was big or bold or successful, but in the fact that the thing was perfectly useless to everybody, including the person who did it." Leigh-Mallory presumably meant much the same, when he talked of climbing Everest simply "because it was there." But this elusive prize, this snatching at air, this nothingness, left me dissatisfied, as I think it would leave most women. Nothing had been discovered, nothing made, nothing improved.

15   I have always discounted the beauty of clouds, because their airy impermanence seems to me to disqualify them from the truest beauty, just as I have never responded to kinetic art, and love the shifting light of nature only because it reveals new shapes and meaning in the solids down below. Nor do I like sea views, unless there is land to be seen beyond

them. A similar distrust of the ephemeral or the un-finite weakened my response to the triumph of Everest in 1953. It was a grand adventure, I knew, and my part in relaying its excitements to the world was to transform my professional life, and dog me ever after; yet even now I dislike that emptiness at its climax, that perfect uselessness, and feel in a slightly ashamed and ungrateful way that it was really all rather absurd.

16   For it was almost like a military expedition—the colonel in command, not so long from Montgomery's staff, the little army of porters who wound their way bent-back with their loads over the hills from Katmandu, the meticulously packed and listed stores, the briefings, the air of ordered determination. It was a superbly successful expedition—nobody killed, nobody disgraced—and looking back upon it now I see its cohesion as a specifically male accomplishment. Again constancy was the key. Men more than women respond to the team spirit, and this is partly because, if they are of an age, of a kind, and in a similar condition, they work together far more like a mechanism. Elations and despondencies are not so likely to distract them. Since their pace is more regular, all can more easily keep to it. They are distinctly more rhythm than melody.

17   In 1953 the rhythm was steadier than it might be now, for it was conscious then as well as constitutional. Stiff upper lip and fair play were integral to the British masculine ethos, and shame was a powerful impulse towards achievement. Social empathy, too, strongly reinforced the sense of maleness. The functional efficiency of class I had already discovered in the Army, and it was the same on Everest. Hunt's climbers were men of the officer class, as they would then have been called, and they were bound by common tastes and values. They spoke the same language, shared the same kind of past, enjoyed the same pleasures. Three of them had been to the same school. In a social sense they formed a kind of

club; in an imperial sense, and this was almost the last of the imperial adventures, they were a company of sahibs attended by their multitudinous servants.

18   One could not, I think, apply these categories to women of equal intelligence in similar circumstances, and less and less can one now apply them to men. Class has lost its binding function; patriotism has lost its elevating force; young men are no longer ashamed of weaknesses; the stiff upper lip is no longer an ideal, only a music hall sally. The barrier between the genders is flimsier now, and no expedition will ever again go to the Himalayas so thoroughly masculine as Hunt's. It embarrasses me rather to have to admit that from that day to this, none has gone there more successfully.

19   I need not belabor my sense of alienation from this formidable team. I liked most of its members very much, and have remained friends with some to this day, but my sense of detachment was extreme, and though I shamelessly accepted their help throughout the adventure, still I was always at pains to cherish my separateness. I hated to think of myself as one of them, and when in England we were asked to sign menus, maps, or autograph books, I used carefully to sign myself James Morris of *The Times*—until the climbers, fancying I fear altogether different motives in me, asked me not to. At the same time a wayward self-consciousness—for I was a child of the age, too—compelled me to keep up male appearances, perhaps as much for my own persuasion as for anyone else's. I even overdid it rather. I grew a beard, and when at the end of the expedition I walked into the communications room at the British Embassy in Katmandu with my tin mug jangling from the belt of my trousers, the wireless operator asked acidly if I *had* to look so jungly. He did not know how cruelly the jibe hurt, for in a few words it cut this way and that through several skins of self-protection.

20   Everest taught me new meanings of maleness, and emphasized once more my own inner dichotomy. Yet paradoxically my most evocative memory of the experience haunts me with a truth of an altogether different kind. Often when there was a lull on the mountain I would go down the glacier and wander among the moraines. Sometimes I went south, towards the distant Buddhist temple at Thyangboehe where the deodars shaded the green turf, and the bells, gongs, and trumpets of the monks sounded from their shambled refectory. Sometimes I clambered into the snows of the north, towards the great wall of the Lho La, over whose ominous white ridge stood the peaks of Tibet. I vaguely hoped to catch a glimpse of an abominable snowman, and I was looking too for traces of the lemurs and mountain hares which sometimes, I had been told, penetrated those high deserts.

21   I saw no animals ever. What I found instead was a man. I saw him first in the extreme distance, across an absolutely blank snowfield at about nineteen thousand feet, to which I had climbed from the glacier below for the sake of the view. At first I was frightened, for I could not make out what he was—only a small black swaying speck, indescribably alone in the desolation. As he came closer I saw that he could only be human, so I plunged through the loose snow to meet him, and presently, there near the top of the world, thousands of feet and many miles above the trees, the streams, or human habitation, we met face to face. It was the strangest encounter of my life.

22   He was a holy man, wandering in the mountains, I suppose, for wandering's sake. His brown, crinkled, squashed-up face looked back at me expressionless from beneath a yellow hood, and found it seemed nothing strange in my presence there. He wore a long yellow cloak and hide boots, and from his waist there hung a spoon and a cloth satchel. He carried nothing else, and he wore no gloves. I greeted him as best I could, but he did not answer, only smiling at me distantly and without surprise. Perhaps he was in a trance. I offered him a piece of chocolate, but he did not take it, simply standing there before me, slightly smiling, almost as though he were made of ice himself. Presently we parted, and without a word he continued on his unfaltering journey, apparently making for Tibet without visible means of survival, and moving with a proud, gliding, and effortless motion that seemed inexorable. He did not appear to move fast, but when I looked around he had almost disappeared, and was no more than that small black speck again, inexplicably moving over the snows.

23   I envied him his insouciant speed, and wondered if he too felt that tingling of the body, that sense of mastery, which had so deepened my sense of duality upon the slopes of Everest. But the more I thought about it, the more clearly I realized that he had no body at all. ◆

POWHITETRASH

Maya Angelou

When Maya Angelou's parents were divorced in 1931, she was sent to Stamps, Arkansas, to be raised by her grandmother, Annie Henderson, whom she soon began to call "Momma." In the rigidly segregated town, Annie Henderson was a pillar of the black community. She owned a store and considerable property, some of it rented to whites. In the following chapter from Angelou's autobiography *I Know Why the Caged Bird Sings* (1969), we see an encounter between this formidable grandmother and some of the town's least distinguished white citizens.

1 "THOU SHALL NOT BE DIRTY" AND "Thou shall not be impudent" were the two commandments of Grandmother Henderson upon which hung our total salvation.

2 Each night in the bitterest winter we were forced to wash faces, arms, necks, legs and feet before going to bed. She used to add, with a smirk that unprofane people can't control when venturing into profanity, "and wash as far as possible, then wash possible."

3 We would go to the well and wash in the ice-cold, clear water, grease our legs with the equally cold stiff Vaseline, then tiptoe into the house. We wiped the dust from our toes and settled down for schoolwork, cornbread, clabbered milk, prayers and bed, always in that order. Momma was famous for pulling the quilts off after we had fallen asleep to examine our feet. If they weren't clean enough for her, she took the switch (she kept one behind the bedroom door for emergencies) and woke up the offender with a few aptly placed burning reminders.

4 The area around the well at night was dark and slick, and boys told about how snakes love water, so that anyone who had to draw water at night and then stand there alone and wash knew that moccasins and rattlers, puff adders and boa constrictors were winding their way to the well and would arrive just as the person washing got soap in her eyes. But Momma convinced us that not only was cleanliness next to Godliness, dirtiness was the inventor of misery.

5 The impudent child was detested by God and a shame to its parents and could bring destruction to its house and line. All adults had to be addressed as Mister, Missus, Miss, Auntie, Cousin, Unk, Uncle, Buhbah, Sister, Brother, and a thousand other appellations indicating familial relationship and the lowliness of the addressor.

6 Everyone I knew respected these customary laws, except for the powhitetrash children.

7 Some families of powhitetrash lived on Momma's farm land behind the school. Sometimes a gaggle of them came to the Store, filling the whole room, chasing out the air and even changing the well-known scents. The children crawled over the shelves and into the potato and onion bins, twanging all the time in their sharp voices like cigar-box guitars. They took liberties in my Store that I would never dare. Since Momma told us that the less you say to white-folks (or even powhitetrash) the better, Bailey and I would stand, solemn, quite, in the displaced air. But if one of the playful apparitions got close to us, I pinched it. Partly out of angry frustration and partly because I didn't believe in its flesh reality.

8 They called my uncle by his first name and ordered him around the Store. He, to my crying shame, obeyed them in his limping dip-straight-dip fashion.

9   My grandmother, too, followed their orders, except that she didn't seem to be servile because she anticipated their needs.

10   "Here's sugar, Miz Potter, and here's baking powder. You didn't buy soda last month, you'll probably be needing some."

11   Momma always directed her statement to the adults, but sometimes, Oh painful sometimes, the grimy, snotty-nosed girls would answer her.

12   "Naw, Annie . . ."—to Momma? Who owned the land they lived on? Who forgot more than they would ever learn? If there was any justice in the world, God should strike them dumb at once!—"Just give us some extry sody crackers, and some more mackerel."

13   At least they never looked in her face, or I never caught them doing so. Nobody with a smidgen of training, not even the worst roustabout, would look right in a grown person's face. It meant the person was trying to take the words out before they were formed. The dirty little children didn't do that, but they threw their orders around the Store like lashes from a cat-o'-nine-tails.

14   When I was around ten years old, those scruffy children caused me the most painful and confusing experience I had ever had with my grandmother.

15   One summer morning, after I had swept the dirt yard of leaves, spearmint-gum wrappers and Vienna-sausage labels, I raked the yellow-red dirt, and made half-moons carefully, so that the design stood out clearly and mask-like. I put the rake behind the Store and came through the back of the house to find Grandmother on the front porch in her big, wide white apron. The apron was so stiff by virtue of the starch that it could have stood alone. Momma was admiring the yard, so I joined her. It truly looked like a flat redhead that had been raked with a big-toothed comb. Momma didn't say anything but I knew she liked it. She looked over toward the school principal's house and to the right at Mr. McElroy's. She

was hoping one of those community pillars would see the design before the day's business wiped it out. Then she looked upward to the school. My head had swung with hers, so at just about the same time we saw a troop of the powhitetrash kids marching over the hill and down by the side of the school.

16   I looked to Momma for direction. She did an excellent job of sagging from her waist down, but from the waist up she seemed to be pulling for the top of the oak tree across the road. Then she began to moan a hymn. Maybe not to moan, but the tune was so slow and the meter so strange that she could have been moaning. She didn't look at me again. When the children reached halfway down the hill, halfway to the Store, she said without turning, "Sister, go on inside."

17   I wanted to beg her, "Momma, don't wait for them. Come on inside with me. If they come in the Store, you go to the bedroom and let me wait on them. They only frighten me if you're around. Alone I know how to handle them." But of course I couldn't say anything, so I went in and stood behind the screen door.

18   Before the girls got to the porch I heard their laughter crackling and popping like pine logs in a cooking stove. I suppose my lifelong paranoia was born in those cold, molasses-slow minutes. They came finally to stand on the ground in front of Momma. At first they pretended seriousness. Then one of them wrapped her right arm in the crook of her left, pushed out her mouth and started to hum. I realized that she was aping my grandmother. Another said, "Naw, Helen, you ain't standing like her. This here's it." Then she lifted her chest, folded her arms and mocked that strange carriage that was Annie Henderson. Another laughed, "Naw, you can't do it. Your mouth ain't pooched out enough. It's like this."

19   I thought about the rifle behind the door, but I knew I'd never be able to hold it straight, and the .410, our sawed-off shotgun, which stayed loaded and was fired every New Year's

night, was locked in the trunk and Uncle Willie had the key on his chain. Through the fly-specked screen-door, I could see that the arms of Momma's apron jiggled from the vibrations of her humming. But her knees seemed to have locked as if they would never bend again.

20 She sang on. No louder than before, but no softer either. No slower or faster.

21 The dirt of the girls' cotton dresses continued on their legs, feet, arms and faces to make them all of a piece. Their greasy uncolored hair hung down, uncombed, with a grim finality. I knelt to see them better, to remember them for all time. The tears that had slipped down my dress left unsurprising dark spots, and made the front yard blurry and even more unreal. The world had taken a deep breath and was having doubts about continuing to revolve.

22 The girls had tired of mocking Momma and turned to other means of agitation. One crossed her eyes, stuck her thumbs in both sides of her mouth and said, "Look here, Annie." Grandmother hummed on and the apron strings trembled. I wanted to throw a handful of black pepper in their faces, to throw lye on them, to scream that they were dirty, scummy peckerwoods, but I knew I was as clearly imprisoned behind the scene as the actors outside were confined to their roles.

23 One of the smaller girls did a kind of puppet dance while her fellow clowns laughed at her. But the tall one, who was almost a woman, said something very quietly, which I couldn't hear. They all moved backward from the porch, still watching Momma. For an awful second I thought they were going to throw a rock at Momma, who seemed (except for the apron strings) to have turned into stone herself. But the big girl turned her back, bent down and put her hands flat on the ground— she didn't pick up anything. She simply shifted her weight and did a hand stand.

24 Her dirty bare feet and long legs went straight for the sky. Her dress fell down around her shoulders, and she had on no drawers. The slick pubic hair made a brown triangle where her legs came together. She hung in the vacuum of that lifeless morning for only a few seconds, then wavered and tumbled. The other girls clapped her on the back and slapped their hands.

25 Momma changed her song to "Bread of Heaven, bread of Heaven, feed me till I want no more."

26 I found that I was praying too. How long could Momma hold out? What new indignity would they think of to subject her to? Would I be able to stay out of it? What would Momma really like me to do?

27 Then they were moving out of the yard, on their way to town. They bobbed their heads and shook their slack behinds and turned, one at a time:

28 "'Bye, Annie."

29 "'Bye, Annie."

30 "'Bye, Annie."

31 Momma never turned her head or unfolded her arms, but she stopped singing and said, "'Bye, Miz Helen, 'bye, Miz Ruth, 'bye, Miz Eloise."

32 I burst. A firecracker July-the-Fourth burst. How could Momma call them Miz? The mean nasty things. Why couldn't she have come inside the sweet, cool store when we saw them breasting the hill? What did she prove? And then if they were dirty, mean and impudent, why did Momma have to call them Miz?

33 She stood another whole song through and then opened the screen door to look down on me crying in rage. She looked until I looked up. Her face was a brown moon that shone on me. She was beautiful. Something had happened out there, which I couldn't completely understand, but I could see that she was happy. Then she bent down and touched me as mothers of the church "lay hands on the sick and afflicted" and I quieted.

34 "Go wash your face, Sister." And she went behind the candy counter and hummed,

"Glory, glory, hallelujah, when I lay my burden down."

35   I threw the well water on my face and used the weekday handkerchief to blow my nose. Whatever the contest had been out front, I knew Momma had won.

36   I took the rake back to the front yard. The smudged footprints were easy to erase. I worked for a long time on my new design and laid the rake behind the wash pot. When I came back in the Store, I took Momma's hand and we both walked outside to look at the pattern.

37   It was a large heart with lots of hearts growing smaller inside, and piercing from the outside rim to the smallest heart was an arrow. Momma said, "Sister, that's right pretty." Then she turned back to the Store and resumed, "Glory, glory, hallelujah, when I lay my burden down." ♦

CONFESSIONS OF A BLUE-CHIP BLACK

Roger Wilkins

Born in Kansas City, Roger Wilkins lived there, in Harlem, and in Grand Rapids, Michigan, as he was growing up. Trained as a lawyer, Wilkins served briefly as a welfare worker and an attorney in private practice in New York. He then went to Washington, D.C., to serve in various government posts before becoming director of the Ford Foundation's domestic programs. In 1972, disturbed because he saw the Foundation as part of a white power structure safely isolated from the reality of the urban poverty around him, he resigned and began contributing editorials and articles to the *New York Times* and other publications. Wilkins is now a professor of history at George Mason University.

1   EARLY IN THE SPRING OF 1932—SIX months after Earl's brother, Roy, left Kansas City to go to New York to join the national staff of the National Association for the Advancement of Colored People, and eight months before Franklin Roosevelt was elected president for the first time—Earl and Helen Wilkins had the first and only child to be born of their union. I was born in a little segregated hospital in Kansas City called Phillis Wheatley.[1] The first time my mother saw me, she cried. My head was too long and my color, she thought, was blue.

2   My parents never talked about slavery or my ancestors. Images of Africa were images of backwardness and savagery. Once, when I was a little boy, I said to my mother after a friend of my parents left the house: "Mr. Bledsoe is black, isn't he, mama."

3   "Oh," she exclaimed. "Never say anybody is black. That's a terrible thing to say."

4   Next time Mr. Bledsoe came to the house, I commented, "Mama, Mr. Bledsoe is navy blue."

5   When I was two years old and my father was in the tuberculosis sanitarium, he wrote me a letter, which I obviously couldn't read, but which tells a lot about how he planned to raise his Negro son.

Friday, March 22, 1934

Dear Roger—

Let me congratulate you upon having reached your second birthday. Your infancy is now past and it is now that you should begin to turn your thoughts upon those achievements which are expected of a brilliant young gentleman well on his way to manhood.

During the next year, you should learn the alphabet; you should learn certain French and English idioms which are a part of every cultivated person's vocabulary: you should gain complete control of those natural functions which, uncontrolled, are a source of worry and embarrassment to even the best of grandmothers: you should learn how to handle table silver so that you will be able to eat gracefully and conventionally: and you should learn the fundamental rules of social living—politeness, courtesy, consideration for others, and the rest.

This should not be difficult for you. You have the best and most patient of mothers in your sterling grandmother and your excellent mother. Great things are expected of you. Never, never forget that.

Love,
Your Father

---

[1] **Phillis Wheatley:** A black American poet (1753?—1784).

6 We lived in a neat little stucco house on a hill in a small Negro section called Roundtop. I had no sense of being poor or of any anxiety about money. At our house, not only was there food and furniture and all the rest, there was even a baby grand piano that my mother would play sometimes. And there was a cleaning lady, Mrs. Turner, who came every week.

7 When it was time for me to go to school, the board of education provided us with a big yellow bus, which carried us past four or five perfectly fine schools down to the middle of the large Negro community, to a very old school called Crispus Attucks.[2] I have no memories of those bus rides except for my resentment of the selfishness of the whites who wouldn't let us share those newer-looking schools near to home.

8 My father came home when I was four and died when I was almost nine. He exuded authority. He thought the women hadn't been sufficiently firm with me, so he instituted a spanking program with that same hard hairbrush that my grandmother had used so much to try to insure that I didn't have "nigger-looking" hair.

9 After my father's death, the family moved to New York. Our apartment was in that legendary uptown area called Sugar Hill, where blacks who had it made were said to live the sweet life. I lived with my mother, my grandmother, and my mother's younger sister, Zelma. My Uncle Roy and his wife, Minnie, a New York social worker, lived on the same floor. My Aunt Marvel and her husband, Cecil, lived one floor down.

10 As life in New York settled into a routine, my life came to be dominated by four women: my mother, her sisters, and her mother. Nobody else had any children, so everybody concentrated on me.

---

[2] **Crispus Attucks:** An American mulatto who led the mob in the "Boston Massacre" and was killed by British troops (1723?—1770).

---

11 Sometime early in 1943 my mother's work with the YMCA took her to Grand Rapids, Michigan, where she made a speech and met a forty-four-year-old bachelor doctor who looked like a white man. He had light skin, green eyes, and "good hair"—that is, hair that was as straight and as flat as white people's hair. He looked so like a white person that he could have passed for white. There was much talk about people who had passed. They were generally deemed to be bad people, for they were not simply selfish, but also cruel to those whom they left behind. On the other hand, people who could pass, but did not, were respected.

12 My mother remarried in October 1943, and soon I was once more on a train with my grandmother, heading toward Grand Rapids and my new home. This train also took me, at the age of twelve, beyond the last point in my life when I would feel totally at peace with my blackness.

13 My new home was in the north end of Grand Rapids, a completely white neighborhood. This would be the place I would henceforth think of as home. And it would be the place where I would become more Midwestern than Harlemite, more American than black, and more complex than was comfortable or necessary for the middle-class conformity that my mother had in mind for me.

14 Grand Rapids was pretty single-family houses and green spaces. The houses looked like those in *Look* magazine or in *Life*. You could believe, and I did, that there was happiness inside. To me, back then, the people seemed to belong to the houses as the houses belonged to the land, and all of it had to do with being white. They moved and walked and talked as if the place, the country, and the houses were theirs, and I envied them.

15 I spent the first few weeks exploring Grand Rapids on a new bike my stepfather had bought for me. The people I passed would look back at me with intense and sometimes

puzzled looks on their faces as I pedaled by. Nobody waved or even smiled. They just stopped what they were doing to stand and look. As soon as I saw them looking, I would look forward and keep on riding.

16   One day I rode for miles, down and up and down again. I was past Grand Rapids' squatty little downtown, and farther south until I began to see some Negro people. There were black men and women and some girls, but it was the boys I was looking for. Then I saw a group: four of them. They were about my age, and they were dark. Though their clothes were not as sharp as the boys' in the Harlem Valley, they were old, and I took the look of poverty and the deep darkness of their faces to mean that they were like the hard boys of Harlem.

17   One of them spotted me riding toward them and pointed. "Hey, lookit that bigole skinny bike," he said. Then they all looked at my bike and at me. I couldn't see expressions on their faces; only the blackness and the coarseness of their clothes. Before any of the rest of them had a chance to say anything, I stood up on the pedals and wheeled the bike in a U-turn and headed back on up toward the north end of town. It took miles for the terror to finally subside.

18   Farther on toward home, there was a large athletic field. As I neared the field, I could see some large boys in shorts moving determinedly around a football. When I got to the top of the hill that overlooked the field, I stopped and stood, one foot on the ground and one leg hanging over the crossbar, staring down at them. All the boys were white and big and old—sixteen to eighteen. I had never seen a football workout before, and I was fascinated. I completely forgot everything about color, theirs or mine.

19   Then one of them saw me. He pointed and said, "Look, there's the little coon watchin us."

20   I wanted to be invisible. I was horrified. My heart pounded, and my arms and legs shook,

but I managed to get back on my bike and ride home.

21   The first white friend I made was named Jerry Schild. On the second day of our acquaintance, he took me to his house, above a store run by his parents. I met his three younger siblings, including a very little one toddling around in bare feet and a soiled diaper.

22   While Jerry changed the baby, I looked around the place. It was cheap, all chintz and linoleum. The two soft pieces of furniture, a couch and an overstuffed chair, had gaping holes and were hemorrhaging their fillings. And there were an awful lot of empty brown beer bottles sitting around, both in the kitchen and out on the back porch. While the place was not dirty, it made me very sad. Jerry and his family were poor in a way I had never seen people be poor before, in Kansas City or even in Harlem.

23   Jerry's father wasn't there that day and Jerry didn't mention him. But later in the week, when I went to call for Jerry, I saw him. I yelled for Jerry from downstairs in the back and his father came to the railing of the porch on the second floor. He was a skinny man in overalls with the bib hanging down crookedly because it was fastened only on the shoulder. His face was narrow and wrinkled and his eyes were set deep in dark hollows. He had a beer bottle in his hand and he looked down at me. "Jerry ain't here," he said. He turned away and went back inside.

24   One day our front doorbell rang and I could hear my mother's troubled exclamation. "Jerry! What's wrong?" Jerry was crying so hard he could hardly talk. "My father says I can't play with you anymore because you're not good enough for us."

25   Creston High School, which served all the children from the north end of Grand Rapids, was all white and middle-class. Nobody talked to me that first day, but I was noticed. When I left school at the end of the day I found my bike leaning up against the fence where I had

left it, with a huge glob of slimy spit on my shaggy saddle cover. People passed by on their way home and looked at me and spit. I felt a hollowness behind my eyes, but I didn't cry. I just got on the bike, stood up on the pedals, and rode it home without sitting down. And it went that way for about the first two weeks. After the third day, I got rid of the saddle cover because the plain leather was a lot easier to clean.

26   But the glacier began to thaw. One day in class, the freckle-faced kid with the crewcut sitting next to me was asking everybody for a pencil. And then he looked at me and said, "Maybe you can lend me one." Those were the best words I had heard since I first met Jerry. This kid had included me in the human race in front of everybody. His name was Jack Waltz.

27   And after a while when the spitters had subsided and I could ride home sitting down, I began to notice that little kids my size were playing pickup games in the end zones of the football field. It looked interesting, but I didn't know anybody and didn't know how they would respond to me. So I just rode on by for a couple of weeks, slowing down each day, trying to screw up my courage to go in.

28   But then one day, I saw Jack Waltz there. I stood around the edges of the group watching. It seemed that they played forever without even noticing me, but finally someone had to go home and the sides were unbalanced. Somebody said, "Let's ask him."

29   As we lined up for our first huddle, I heard somebody on the other side say, "I hope he doesn't have a knife." One of the guys on my side asked me, "Can you run the ball?" I said yes, so they gave me the ball and I ran three quarters of the length of the field for a touchdown. And I made other touchdowns and other long runs before the game was over. When I thought about it later that night, I became certain that part of my success was due to the imaginary knife that was running interference for me. But no matter. By the end of the game, I had a

group of friends. Boys named Andy and Don and Bill and Gene and Rich. We left the field together and some of them waved and yelled, "See ya tomorra, Rog."

30   And Don De Young, a pleasant round-faced boy, even lived quite near me. So, after parting from everybody else, he and I went on together down to the corner of Coit and Knapp. As we parted, he suggested that we meet to go to school together the next day. I had longed for that but I hadn't suggested it for fear of a rebuff for overstepping the limits of my race. I had already learned one of the great tenets of Negro survival in America: to live the reactive life. It was like the old Negro comedian who once said, "When the man asks how the weather is, I know nuff to look keerful at his face 'fore even I look out the window." So, I waited for him to suggest it, and my patience was rewarded. I was overjoyed and grateful.

31   I didn't spend all my time in the north end. Soon after I moved to Grand Rapids, Pop introduced me to some patients he had with a son my age. The boy's name was Lloyd Brown, and his father was a bellman downtown at the Pantlind Hotel. Lloyd and I often rode bikes and played basketball in his backyard. After a while, my mother asked me why I never had Lloyd come out to visit me. It was a question I dreaded, but she pressed on. "After all," she said, "you've had a lot of meals at his house and it's rude not to invite him back." I knew she was right and I also hated the whole idea of it.

32   With my friends in the north, race was never mentioned. Ever. I carried my race around with me like an open basket of rotten eggs. I knew I could drop one at any moment and it would explode with a stench over everything. This was in the days when the movies either had no blacks at all or featured rank stereotypes like Stepin Fetchit,[3] and the popular magazines like *Life, Look,* the *Saturday*

---

3 **Stepin Fetchit:** A lazy black character in the film *Hearts in Dixie* (1929).

Evening Post, and *Collier's* carried no stories about Negroes, had no ads depicting Negroes, and generally gave the impression that we did not exist in this society. I knew that my white friends, being well brought up, were just too polite to mention this disability that I had. And I was grateful to them, but terrified, just the same, that maybe someday one of them would have the bad taste to notice what I was.

33   It seemed to me that my tenuous purchase in this larger white world depended on the maintenance between me and my friends in the north end of our unspoken bargain to ignore my difference, my shame, and their embarrassment. If none of us had to deal with it, I thought, we could all handle it. My white friends behaved as if they perceived the bargain exactly as I did. It was a delicate equation, and I was terrified that Lloyd's presence in the North End would rip apart the balance.

34   I am so ashamed of that shame now that I cringe when I write it. But I understand that boy now as he could not understand himself then. I was an American boy, though I did not fully comprehend that either. I was fully shaped and formed by America, where white people had all the power in sight, and they owned everything in sight except our house. Their beauty was the real beauty; there wasn't any other beauty. A real human being had straight hair, a white face, and thin lips. Other people, who looked different, were lesser beings.

35   No wonder, then, that most black men desired the forbidden fruit of white loins. No wonder, too, that we thought that the most beautiful and worthy Negro people were those who looked most white. We blacks used to have a saying: "If you're white, you're all right. If you're brown, stick around. If you're black, stand back." I was brown.

36   It was not that we in my family were direct victims of racism. On the contrary, my stepfather clearly had a higher income than the parents of most students in my high school. Unlike those of most of my contemporaries,

black and white, my parents had college degrees. Within Grand Rapids' tiny Negro community, they were among the elite. The others were the lawyer, the dentist, the undertaker, and the other doctor.

37   But that is what made race such exquisite agony. I did have a sense that it was unfair for poor Negroes to be relegated to bad jobs—if they had jobs at all—and to bad or miserable housing, but I didn't feel any great sense of identity with them. After all, the poor blacks in New York had also been the hard ones: the ones who tried to take my money, to beat me up, and to keep me perpetually intimidated. Besides, I had heard it intimated around my house that their behavior, sexual or otherwise, left a good deal to be desired.

38   So I thought that maybe they just weren't ready for this society, but that I was. And it was dreadfully unfair for white people to just look at my face and lips and hair and decide that I was inferior. By being a model student and leader, I thought I was demonstrating how well Negroes could perform if only the handicaps were removed and they were given a chance. But deep down I guess I was also trying to demonstrate that I was not like those other people; that I was different. My message was quite clear: I was *not nigger.* But the world didn't seem quite ready to make such fine distinctions, and it was precisely that fact—though at the time I could scarcely even have admitted it to myself—that was the nub of the race issue for me.

39   I would sometimes lie on my back and stare up at passing clouds and wonder why God had played a dirty trick by making me a Negro. It all seemed so random. So unfair to me. To *me!* But in school I was gaining more friends, and the teachers respected me. It got so that I could go for days not thinking very much about being Negro, until something made the problem unavoidable.

40   One day in history class, for instance, the teacher asked each of us to stand and tell in

turn where our families had originated. Many of the kids in the class were Dutch with names like Vander Jagt, De Young, and Ripstra. My pal Andy was Scots-Irish. When it came my turn, I stood up and burned with shame and when I would speak, I lied. And then I was even more ashamed because I exposed a deeper shame. "Some of my family was English," I said—Wilkins is an English name—"and the rest of it came from . . . Egypt." Egypt!

41   One Saturday evening after one of our sandlot games, I went over to Lloyd's. Hearing my stories, Lloyd said mildly that he'd like to come up and play some Saturday. I kept on talking, but all the time my mind was repeating: "Lloyd wants to play. He wants to come up to the North End on Saturday. Next Saturday. Next Saturday." I was trapped.

42   So, after the final story about the final lunge, when I couldn't put it off any longer, I said, "Sure. Why not?" But, later in the evening, after I had had some time to think, I got Lloyd alone. "Say, look," I said. "Those teams are kinda close, ya know. I mean, we don't switch around. From team to team. Or new guys, ya know?"

43   Lloyd nodded, but he was getting a funny look on his face . . . part unbelieving and part hurt. So I quickly interjected before he could say anything, "Naw, man. Naw. Not like you shouldn't come and play. Just that we gotta have some good reason for you to play on our team, you dig?"

44   "Yeah," Lloyd said, his face still puzzled, but no longer hurt.

45   "Hey, I know," I said. "I got it. We'll say you're my cousin. If you're my cousin, see, then you gotta play. Nobody can say you can't be on my team, because you're family, right?"

46   "Oh, right. Okay," Lloyd said, his face brightening. "Sure, we'll say we're cousins. Solid."

47   I felt relieved as well. I could have a Negro cousin. It wasn't voluntary. It wouldn't be as if I had gone out and made a Negro friend deliberately. A person couldn't help who his cousins were.

48   There began to be a cultural difference between me and other blacks my age too. Black street language had evolved since my Harlem days, and I had not kept pace. Customs, attitudes, and the other common social currencies of everyday black life had evolved away from me. I didn't know how to talk, to banter, to move my body. If I was tentative and responsive in the North End, where I lived, I was tense, stiff, and awkward when I was with my black contemporaries. One day I was standing outside the church trying, probably at my mother's urging, to make contact. Conversational sallies flew around me while I stood there stiff and mute, unable to participate. Because the language was so foreign to me, I understood little of what was being said, but I did know that the word used for a white was *paddy*. Then a boy named Nickerson, the one whom my mother particularly wanted me to be friends with, inclined his head slightly toward me and said, to whoops of laughter, "technicolor paddy." My feet felt rooted in stone, and my head was aflame. I never forgot that phrase.

49   I have rarely felt so alone as I did that day riding home from church. Already partly excluded by my white friends, I was now almost completely alienated from my own people as well. But I felt less uncomfortable and less vulnerable in the white part of town. It was familiar enough to enable me to ward off most unpleasantness.

50   And then there was the problem of girls. They were everywhere, the girls. They all had budding bosoms, they all smelled pink, they all brushed against the boys in the hall, they were all white, and, in 1947–49, they were all inaccessible.

51   There were some things you knew without ever knowing how you knew them. You knew that Mississippi was evil and dangerous, that New York was east, and the Pacific ocean was

west. And in the same way you knew that white women were the most desirable and dangerous objects in the world. Blacks were lynched in Mississippi and such places sometimes just for looking with the wrong expression at white women. Blacks of a very young age knew that white women of any quality went with the power and style that went with the governance of America—though, God knows, we had so much self-hate that when a white woman went with a Negro man, we promptly decided she was trash, and we also figured that if she would go with him she would go with any Negro.

52   Nevertheless, as my groin throbbed at fifteen and sixteen and seventeen, *they* were often the only ones there. One of them would be in the hallway opening her locker next to mine. Her blue sweater sleeve would be pushed up to just below the elbow, and as she would reach high on a shelf to stash away a book, I would see the tender dark hair against the white skin of her forearm. And I would ache and want to touch that arm and follow that body hair to its source.

53   Some of my friends, of course, did touch some of those girls. My friends and I would talk about athletics and school and their loves. But they wouldn't say a word about the dances and the hayrides they went to.

54   I perceived they liked me and accepted me as long as I moved aside when life's currents took them to where I wasn't supposed to be. I fit into their ways when they talked about girls, even their personal girls. And, indeed, I fit into the girls' lives when they were talking about boys, most particularly their own personal boys. Because I was a boy, I had insight. But I was also Negro, and therefore a neuter.

So a girl who was alive and sensuous night after night in my fantasies would come to me earnestly in the day and talk about Rich or Gene or Andy. She would ask what he thought about her, whether he liked to dance, whether, if she invited him to her house for a party, he would come. She would tell me her fears and her yearnings, never dreaming for an instant that I had yearnings too and that she was their object.

55   There may be few more powerful obsessions than a teenage boy's fixation on a love object. In my case it came down to a thin brunette named Marge McDowell. She was half a grade behind me, and she lived in a small house on a hill. I found excuses to drive by it all the time. I knew her schedule at school, so I could manage to be in most of the hallways she had to use going from class to class. We knew each other, and she had once confided a strong but fleeting yearning for my friend Rich Kippen. I thought about her constantly.

56   Finally, late one afternoon after school, I came upon her alone in a hallway. "Marge," I blurted, "can I ask you something?"

57   She stopped and smiled and said, "Sure, Roger, what?"

58   "Well I was wondering," I said. "I mean. Well, would you go to the hayride next week with me."

59   Her jaw dropped and her eyes got huge. Then she uttered a small shriek and turned, hugging her books to her bosom the way girls do, and fled. I writhed with mortification in my bed that night and for many nights after.

60   In my senior year, I was elected president of the Creston High School student council. It was a breakthrough of sorts.◆

THE MESMERIZER

Mark Twain

When Mark Twain died, he left behind hundreds of pages of autobiographical writing. Portions of this autobiography have appeared in various forms; the most complete version is *The Autobiography of Mark Twain* (1959, edited by Charles Neider). In the excerpt below, Twain recalls the introduction of mesmerism to his home town, Hannibal, Missouri. Mesmerism, based on a theory of "animal magnetism," had been denounced as a hoax as early as 1784. Only in the middle of the nineteenth century did investigators begin to understand the true nature of hypnotism.

1   AN EXCITING EVENT IN OUR VILLAGE WAS the arrival of the mesmerizer. I think the year was 1850. As to that I am not sure but I know the month—it was May; that detail has survived the wear of fifty years. A pair of connected little incidents of that month have served to keep the memory of it green for me all this time; incidents of no consequence and not worth embalming, yet my memory has preserved them carefully and flung away things of real value to give them space and make them comfortable. The truth is, a person's memory has no more sense than his conscience and no appreciation whatever of values and proportions. However, never mind those trifling incidents; my subject is the mesmerizer now.

2   He advertised his show and promised marvels. Admission as usual: 25 cents, children and negroes half price. The village had heard of mesmerism in a general way but had not encountered it yet. Not many people attended the first night but next day they had so many wonders to tell that everybody's curiosity was fired and after that for a fortnight the magician had prosperous times. I was fourteen or fifteen years old, the age at which a boy is willing to endure all things, suffer all things short of death by fire, if thereby he may be conspicuous and show off before the public; and so, when I saw the "subjects" perform their foolish antics on the platform and make the people laugh and shout and admire I had a burning desire to be a subject myself.

3   Every night for three nights I sat in the row of candidates on the platform and held the magic disk in the palm of my hand and gazed at it and tried to get sleepy, but it was a failure; I remained wide awake and had to retire defeated, like the majority. Also, I had to sit there and be gnawed with envy of Hicks, our journeyman; I had to sit there and see him scamper and jump when Simmons the enchanter exclaimed, "See the snake! See the snake!" and hear him say, "My, how beautiful!" in response to the suggestion that he was observing a splendid sunset; and so on—the whole insane business. I couldn't laugh, I couldn't applaud; it filled me with bitterness to have others do it and to have people make a hero of Hicks and crowd around him when the show was over and ask him for more and more particulars of the wonders he had seen in his visions and manifest in many ways that they were proud to be acquainted with him. Hicks—the idea! I couldn't stand it; I was getting boiled to death in my own bile.

4   On the fourth night temptation came and I was not strong enough to resist. When I had gazed at the disk a while I pretended to be sleepy and began to nod. Straightway came the professor and made passes over my head and

164

down my body and legs and arms, finishing each pass with a snap of his fingers in the air to discharge the surplus electricity; then he began to "draw" me with the disk, holding it in his fingers and telling me I could not take my eyes off it, try as I might; so I rose slowly, bent and gazing, and followed that disk all over the place, just as I had seen the others do. Then I was put through the other paces. Upon suggestion I fled from snakes, passed buckets at a fire, became excited over hot steamboat-races, made love to imaginary girls and kissed them, fished from the platform and landed mud cats that outweighed me—and so on, all the customary marvels. But not in the customary way. I was cautious at first and watchful, being afraid the professor would discover that I was an impostor and drive me from the platform in disgrace; but as soon as I realized that I was not in danger, I set myself the task of terminating Hicks's usefulness as a subject and of usurping his place.

5   It was a sufficiently easy task. Hicks was born honest, I without that incumbrance—so some people said. Hicks saw what he saw and reported accordingly, I saw more than was visible and added to it such details as could help. Hicks had no imagination; I had a double supply. He was born calm, I was born excited. No vision could start a rapture in him and he was constipated as to language, anyway; but if I saw a vision I emptied the dictionary onto it and lost the remnant of my mind into the bargain.

6   At the end of my first half-hour Hicks was a thing of the past, a fallen hero, a broken idol, and I knew it and was glad and said in my heart, "Success to crime!" Hicks could never have been mesmerized to the point where he could kiss an imaginary girl in public or a real one either, but I was competent. Whatever Hicks had failed in, I made it a point to succeed in, let the cost be what it might, physically or morally. He had shown several bad defects and I had made a note of

them. For instance, if the magician asked, "What do you see?" and left him to invent a vision for himself, Hicks was dumb and blind, he couldn't see a thing nor say a word, whereas the magician soon found out that when it came to seeing visions of a stunning and marketable sort I could get along better without his help than with it.

7   Then there was another thing: Hicks wasn't worth a tallow dip on mute mental suggestion. Whenever Simmons stood behind him and gazed at the back of his skull and tried to drive a mental suggestion into it, Hicks sat with vacant face and never suspected. If he had been noticing he could have seen by the rapt faces of the audience that something was going on behind his back that required a response. Inasmuch as I was an impostor I dreaded to have this test put upon me, for I knew the professor would be "willing" me to do something, and as I couldn't know what it was, I should be exposed and denounced. However, when my time came, I took my chance. I perceived by the tense and expectant faces of the people that Simmons was behind me willing me with all his might. I tried my best to imagine what he wanted but nothing suggested itself. I felt ashamed and miserable then. I believed that the hour of my disgrace was come and that in another moment I should go out of that place disgraced. I ought to be ashamed to confess it but my next thought was not how I could win the compassion of kindly hearts by going out humbly and in sorrow for my misdoings, but how I could go out most sensationally and spectacularly.

8   There was a rusty and empty old revolver lying on the table among the "properties" employed in the performances. On May Day two or three weeks before there had been a celebration by the schools and I had had a quarrel with a big boy who was the school bully and I had not come out of it with credit. That boy was now seated in the middle of the house, halfway down the main aisle. I crept stealthily

and impressively toward the table, with a dark and murderous scowl on my face, copied from a popular romance, seized the revolver suddenly, flourished it, shouted the bully's name, jumped off the platform and made a rush for him and chased him out of the house before the paralyzed people could interfere to save him. There was a storm of applause, and the magician, addressing the house, said, most impressively—

9   "That you may know how really remarkable this is and how wonderfully developed a subject we have in this boy, I assure you that without a single spoken word to guide him he has carried out what I mentally commanded him to do, to the minutest detail. I could have stopped him at a moment in his vengeful career by a mere exertion of my will, therefore the poor fellow who has escaped was at no time in danger."

10   So I was not in disgrace. I returned to the platform a hero and happier than I have ever been in this world since. As regards mental suggestion, my fears of it were gone. I judged that in case I failed to guess what the professor might be willing me to do, I could count on putting up something that would answer just as well. I was right, and exhibitions of unspoken suggestion became a favorite with the public. Whenever I perceived that I was being willed to do something I got up and did something—anything that occurred to me—and the magician, not being a fool, always ratified it. When people asked me, "How *can* you tell what he is willing you to do?" I said, "It's just as easy," and they always said admiringly, "Well, it beats *me* how you can do it."

11   Hicks was weak in another detail. When the professor made passes over him and said "his whole body is without sensation now—come forward and test him, ladies and gentlemen," the ladies and gentlemen always complied eagerly and stuck pins into Hicks, and if they went deep Hicks was sure to wince, then that poor professor would have to explain that Hicks "wasn't sufficiently under the influence." But I didn't wince; I only suffered and shed tears on the inside. The miseries that a conceited boy will endure to keep up his "reputation"! And so will a conceited man; I know it in my own person and have seen it in a hundred thousand others. That professor ought to have protected me and I often hoped he would, when the tests were unusually severe, but he didn't. It may be that he was deceived as well as the others, though I did not believe it nor think it possible. Those were dear good people but they must have carried simplicity and credulity to the limit. They would stick a pin in my arm and bear on it until they drove it a third of its length in, and then be lost in wonder that by a mere exercise of will power the professor could turn my arm to iron and make it insensible to pain. Whereas it was not insensible at all; I was suffering agonies of pain.

12   After that fourth night, that proud night, that triumphant night, I was the only subject. Simmons invited no more candidates to the platform. I performed alone every night the rest of the fortnight. Up to that time a dozen wise old heads, the intellectual aristocracy of the town, had held out as implacable unbelievers. I was as hurt by this as if I were engaged in some honest occupation. There is nothing surprising about this. Human beings feel dishonor the most, sometimes, when they most deserve it. That handful of overwise old gentlemen kept on shaking their heads all the first week and saying they had seen no marvels there that could not have been produced by collusion; and they were pretty vain of their unbelief too and liked to show it and air it and be superior to the ignorant and the gullible. Particularly old Dr. Peake, who was the ringleader of the irreconcilables and very formidable; for he was an F.F.V.,[1] he was learned, white-

_____
1 F.F.V.: First Families of Virginia, an elite social organization.

haired and venerable, nobly and richly clad in the fashions of an earlier and a courtlier day, he was large and stately, and he not only seemed wise but was what he seemed in that regard. He had great influence and his opinion upon any matter was worth much more than that of any other person in the community. When I conquered him at last, I knew I was undisputed master of the field; and now after more than fifty years I acknowledge with a few dry old tears that I rejoiced without shame.

13 In 1847 we were living in a large white house on the corner of Hill and Main Streets—a house that still stands but isn't large now although it hasn't lost a plank; I saw it a year ago and noticed that shrinkage.[2] My father died in it in March of the year mentioned but our family did not move out of it until some months afterward. Ours was not the only family in the house; there was another, Dr. Grant's. One day Dr. Grant and Dr. Reyburn argued a matter on the street with sword canes and Grant was brought home multifariously punctured. Old Dr. Peake calked the leaks and came every day for a while to look after him.

14 The Grants were Virginians, like Peake, and one day when Grant was getting well enough to be on his feet and sit around in the parlor and talk, the conversation fell upon Virginia and old times. I was present but the group were probably unconscious of me, I being only a lad and a negligible quantity. Two of the group—Dr. Peake and Mrs. Crawford, Mrs. Grant's mother—had been of the audience when the Richmond theater burned down thirty-six years before, and they talked over the frightful details of that memorable tragedy. These were eyewitnesses, and with their eyes I saw it all with an intolerable vividness: I saw the black smoke rolling and tumbling toward the sky, I saw the flames burst through it and turn red, I heard the shrieks of the despairing, I glimpsed their faces at the windows, caught fitfully through the veiling smoke, I saw them jump to their death or to mutilation worse than death. The picture is before me yet and can never fade.

15 In due course they talked of the colonial mansion of the Peakes, with its stately columns and its spacious grounds, and by odds and ends I picked up a clearly defined idea of the place. I was strongly interested, for I had not before heard of such palatial things from the lips of people who had seen them with their own eyes. One detail, casually dropped, hit my imagination hard. In the wall by the great front door there was a round hole as big as a saucer—a British cannon ball had made it in the war of the Revolution. It was breathtaking; it made history real; history had never been real to me before.

16 Very well, three or four years later, as already mentioned, I was king bee and sole "subject" in the mesmeric show; it was the beginning of the second week; the performance was half over; just then the majestic Dr. Peake with his ruffled bosom and wristbands and his gold-headed cane entered, and a deferential citizen vacated his seat beside the Grants and made the great chief take it. This happened while I was trying to invent something fresh in the way of vision, in response to the professor's remark—

17 "Concentrate your powers. Look—look attentively. There—don't you see something? Concentrate—concentrate! Now then—describe it."

18 Without suspecting it, Dr. Peake, by entering the place, had reminded me of the talk of three years before. He had also furnished me capital and was become my confederate, an accomplice in my frauds. I began on a vision, a vague and dim one (that was part of the game at the beginning of a vision; it isn't best to see it too clearly at first, it might look as if you had come loaded with it). The vision

---

[2] a year ago: Written in 1903. [author's note]

developed by degrees and gathered swing, momentum, energy. It was the Richmond fire. Dr. Peake was cold at first and his fine face had a trace of polite scorn in it; but when he began to recognize that fire, that expression changed and his eyes began to light up. As soon as I saw that, I threw the valves wide open and turned on all the steam and gave those people a supper of fire and horrors that was calculated to last them one while! They couldn't gasp when I got through—they were petrified. Dr. Peake had risen and was standing—and breathing hard. He said, in a great voice:

19   "My doubts are ended. No collusion could produce that miracle. It was totally impossible for him to know those details, yet he has described them with the clarity of an eyewitness—and with what unassailable truthfulness God knows I know!"

20   I saved the colonial mansion for the last night and solidified and perpetuated Dr. Peake's conversion with the cannon-ball hole. He explained to the house that I could never have heard of that small detail, which differentiated this mansion from all other Virginian mansions and perfectly identified it, therefore the fact stood proven that I had *seen* it in my vision. Lawks!

21   It is curious. When the magician's engagement closed there was but one person in the village who did not believe in mesmerism and I was the one. All the others were converted but I was to remain an implacable and unpersuadable disbeliever in mesmerism and hypnotism for close upon fifty years. This was because I never would examine them, in after life. I couldn't. The subject revolted me. Perhaps it brought back to me a passage in my life which for pride's sake I wished to forget; though I thought, or persuaded myself I thought, I should never come across a "proof" which wasn't thin and cheap and probably had a fraud like me behind it.

22   The truth is I did not have to wait long to get tired of my triumphs. Not thirty days, I think. The glory which is built upon a lie soon becomes a most unpleasant incumbrance. No doubt for a while I enjoyed having my exploits told and retold and told again in my presence and wondered over and exclaimed about, but I quite distinctly remember that there presently came a time when the subject was wearisome and odious to me and I could not endure the disgusting discomfort of it. I am well aware that the world-glorified doer of a deed of great and real splendor has just my experience; I know that he deliciously enjoys hearing about it for three or four weeks and that pretty soon after that he begins to dread the mention of it and by and by wishes he had been with the dammed before he ever thought of doing that deed. I remember how General Sherman used to rage and swear over "While we were marching through Georgia," which was played at him and sung at him everywhere he went; still, I think I suffered a shade more than the legitimate hero does, he being privileged to soften his misery with the reflection that his glory was at any rate golden and reproachless in its origin, whereas I had no such privilege, there being no possible way to make mine respectable.

23   How easy it is to make people believe a lie and how hard it is to undo that work again! Thirty-five years after those evil exploits of mine I visited my old mother, whom I had not seen for ten years; and being moved by what seemed to me a rather noble and perhaps heroic impulse, I thought I would humble myself and confess my ancient fault. It cost me a great effort to make up my mind; I dreaded the sorrow that would rise in her face and the shame that would look out of her eyes; but after long and troubled reflection, the sacrifice seemed due and right and I gathered my resolution together and made the confession.

24   To my astonishment there were no sentimentalities, no dramatics, no George Washington effects; she was not moved in the least degree; she simply did not believe me and said so! I

was not merely disappointed, I was nettled to have my costly truthfulness flung out of the market in this placid and confident way when I was expecting to get a profit out of it. I asserted and reasserted, with rising heat, my statement that every single thing I had done on those long-vanished nights was a lie and a swindle; and when she shook her head tranquilly and said she knew better, I put up my hand and *swore* to it—adding a triumphant, "*Now* what do you say?"

25   It did not affect her at all; it did not budge her the fraction of an inch from her position. If this was hard for me to endure, it did not begin with the blister she put upon the raw when she began to put my sworn oath out of court with *arguments* to prove that I was under a delusion and did not know what I was talking about. Arguments! Arguments to show that a person on a man's outside can know better what is on his inside than he does himself. I had cherished some contempt for arguments before, I have not enlarged my respect for them since. She refused to believe that I had invented my visions myself; she said it was folly: that I was only a child at the time and could not have done it. She cited the Richmond fire and the colonial mansion and said they were quite beyond my capacities. Then I saw my chance! I said she was right—I didn't invent those, I got them from Dr. Peake. Even this great shot did not damage. She said Dr. Peake's evidence was better than mine, and he had said in plain words that it was impossible for me to have heard about those things. Dear, dear, what a grotesque and unthinkable situation: a confessed swindler convicted of honesty and condemned to acquittal by circumstantial evidence furnished by the swindled!

26   I realized with shame and with impotent vexation that I was defeated all along the line. I had but one card left but it was a formidable one. I played it and stood from under. It seemed ignoble to demolish her fortress after she had defended it so valiantly but the defeated know not mercy. I played that master card. It was the pin-sticking. I said solemnly—

27   "I give you my honor, a pin was never stuck into me without causing me cruel pain."

28   She only said—

29   "It is thirty-five years. I believe you do think that now but I was there and I know better. You never winced."

30   She was so calm! and I was so far from it, so nearly frantic.

31   "Oh, my goodness!" I said, "let me *show* you that I am speaking the truth. Here is my arm; drive a pin into it—drive it to the head—I shall not wince."

32   She only shook her gray head and said with simplicity and conviction—

33   "You are a man now and could dissemble the hurt; but you were only a child then and could not have done it."

34   And so the lie which I played upon her in my youth remained with her as an unchallengeable truth to the day of her death. Carlyle[3] said "a lie cannot live." It shows that he did not know how to tell them. If I had taken out a life policy on this one the premiums would have bankrupted me ages ago. ◆

---

[3] **Carlyle:** Thomas Carlyle (1795–1881), the Victorian prose writer.

MEMORY AND IMAGINATION

Patricia Hampl

Patricia Hampl is a poet, an essayist, and the author of the award-winning memoir *A Romantic Education*. She also teaches a course in autobiographical writing at the University of Minnesota. In the following essay, she offers a fragment of her own autobiographical writing, then turns back to answer a hard question about it: "Why do I—why should anybody—write memoir at all?"

1   WHEN I WAS SEVEN, MY FATHER, WHO played the violin on Sundays with a nicely tortured flair which we considered artistic, led me by the hand down a long, unlit corridor in St. Luke's School basement, a sort of tunnel that ended in a room full of pianos. There many little girls and a single sad boy were playing truly tortured scales and arpeggios in a mash of troubled sound. My father gave me over to Sister Olive Marie, who did look remarkably like an olive.

2   Her oily face gleamed as if it had just been rolled out of a can and laid on the white plate of her broad, spotless wimple. She was a small, plump woman; her body and the small window of her face seemed to interpret the entire alphabet of olive: her face was a sallow green olive placed upon the jumbo ripe olive of her black habit. I trusted her instantly and smiled, glad to have my hand placed in the hand of a woman who made sense, who provided the satisfaction of being what she was: an Olive who looked like an olive.

3   My father left me to discover the piano with Sister Olive Marie so that one day I would join him in mutually tortured piano-violin duets for the edification of my mother and brother who sat at the table meditatively spooning in the last of their pineapple sherbet until their part was called for: they put down their spoons and clapped while we bowed, while the sweet ice in their bowls melted, while the music melted, and we all melted a little into each other for a moment.

4   But first Sister Olive must do her work. I was shown middle C, which Sister seemed to think terribly important. I stared at middle C and then glanced away for a second. When my eye returned, middle C was gone, its slim finger lost in the complicated grasp of the keyboard. Sister Olive struck it again, finding it with laughable ease. She emphasized the importance of middle C, its central position, a sort of North Star of sound. I remember thinking, "Middle C is the belly button of the piano," an insight whose originality and accuracy stunned me with pride. For the first time in my life I was astonished by metaphor. I hesitated to tell the kindly Olive for some reason; apparently I understood a true metaphor is a risky business, revealing of the self. In fact, I have never, until this moment of writing it down, told my first metaphor to anyone.

5   Sunlight flooded the room; the pianos, all black, gleamed. Sister Olive, dressed in the colors of the keyboard, gleamed; middle C shimmered with meaning and I resolved never —never—to forget its location: it was the center of the world.

6   Then Sister Olive, who had had to show me middle C twice but who seemed to have drawn no bad conclusions about me anyway, got up and went to the windows on the opposite wall. She pulled the shades down, one after the other. The sun was too bright, she said. She sneezed as she stood at the windows with the sun shedding its glare over her. She sneezed and sneezed, crazy little convulsive sneezes,

one after another, as helpless as if she had the hiccups.

7   "The sun makes me sneeze," she said when the fit was over and she was back at the piano. This was odd, too odd to grasp in the mind. I associated sneezing with colds, and colds with rain, fog, snow and bad weather. The sun, however, had caused Sister Olive to sneeze in this wild way, Sister Olive who gleamed benignly and who was so certain of the location of the center of the world. The universe wobbled a bit and became unreliable. Things were not, after all, necessarily what they seemed. Appearance deceived: here was the sun acting totally out of character, hurling this woman into sneezes, a woman so mild that she was named, so it seemed, for a bland object on a relish tray.

8   I was given a red book, the first Thompson book, and told to play the first piece over and over at one of the black pianos where the other children were crashing away. This, I was told, was called practicing. It sounded alluringly adult, practicing. The piece itself consisted mainly of middle C, and I excelled, thrilled by my savvy at being able to locate that central note amidst the cunning camouflage of all the other white keys before me. Thrilled too by the shiny red book that gleamed, as the pianos did, as Sister Olive did, as my eager eyes probably did. I sat at the formidable machine of the piano and got to know middle C intimately, preparing to be as tortured as I could manage one day soon with my father's violin at my side.

9   But at the moment Mary Katherine Reilly was at my side, playing something at least two or three lessons more sophisticated than my piece. I believe she even struck a chord. I glanced at her from the peasantry of single notes, shy, ready to pay homage. She turned toward me, stopped playing, and sized me up.

10   Sized me up and found a person ready to be dominated. Without introduction she said, "My grandfather invented the collapsible opera hat."

11   I nodded, I acquiesced, I was hers. With that little stroke it was decided between us—that she should be the leader, and I the sidekick. My job was admiration. Even when she added, "But he didn't make a penny from it. He didn't have a patent"—even then, I knew and she knew that this was not an admission of powerlessness, but the easy candor of a master, of one who can afford a weakness or two.

12   With the clairvoyance of all fated relationships based on dominance and submission, it was decided in advance: that when the time came for us to play duets, I should always play second piano, that I should spend my allowance to buy her the Twinkies she craved but was not allowed to have, that finally, I should let her copy from my test paper, and when confronted by our teacher, confess with convincing hysteria that it was I, I who had cheated, who had reached above myself to steal what clearly belonged to the rightful heir of the inventor of the collapsible opera hat. . . .

13   There must be a reason I remember that little story about my first piano lesson. In fact, it isn't a story, just a moment, the beginning of what could perhaps become a story. For the memoirist, more than for the fiction writer, the story seems already *there,* already accomplished and fully achieved in history ("in reality," as we naively say). For the memoirist, the writing of the story is a matter of transcription.

14   That, anyway, is the myth. But no memoirist writes for long without experiencing an unsettling disbelief about the reliability of memory, a hunch that memory is not, after all, *just* memory. I don't know why I remembered this fragment about my first piano lesson. I don't, for instance, have a single recollection of my first arithmetic lesson, the first time I studied Latin, the first time my grandmother tried to teach me to knit. Yet these things occurred too, and must have their stories.

15   It is the piano lesson that has trudged forward, clearing the haze of forgetfulness, showing itself bright with detail more than thirty years after the event. I did not choose to remember the piano lesson. It was simply there, like a book that has always been on the shelf, whether I ever read it or not, the binding and title showing as I skim across the contents of my life. On the day I wrote this fragment I happened to take that memory, not some other, from the shelf and paged through it. I found more detail, more event, perhaps a little more entertainment than I had expected, but the memory itself was there from the start. Waiting for me.

16   Or was it? When I reread what I had written just after I finished it, I realized that I had told a number of lies. I *think* it was my father who took me the first time for my piano lesson—but maybe he only took me to meet my teacher and there was no actual lesson that day. And did I even know then that he played the violin—didn't he take up his violin again much later, as a result of my piano playing, and not the reverse? And is it even remotely accurate to describe as "tortured" the musicianship of a man who began every day by belting out "Oh What a Beautiful Morning" as he shaved?

17   More: Sister Olive Marie did sneeze in the sun, but was her name Olive? As for her skin tone—I would have sworn it was olive-like; I would have been willing to spend the better part of an afternoon trying to write the exact description of imported Italian or Greek olive her face suggested: I wanted to get it right. But now, were I to write that passage over, it is her intense black eyebrows I would see, for suddenly they seem the central fact of that face, some indicative mark of her serious and patient nature. But the truth is, I don't remember the woman at all. She's a sneeze in the sun and a finger touching middle C. That, at least, is steady and clear.

18   Worse: I didn't have the Thompson book as my piano text. I'm sure of that because I remember envying children who did have this wonderful book with its pictures of children and animals printed on the pages of music.

19   As for Mary Katherine Reilly. She didn't even go to grade school with me (and her name isn't Mary Katherine Reilly—but I made that change on purpose). I met her in Girl Scouts and only went to school with her later, in high school. Our relationship was not really one of leader and follower; I played first piano most of the time in duets. She certainly never copied anything from a test paper of mine: she was a better student, and cheating just wasn't a possibility with her. Though her grandfather (or someone in her family) did invent the collapsible opera hat and I remember that she was proud of that fact, she didn't tell me this news as a deft move in a childish power play.

20   So, what was I doing in this brief memoir? Is it simply an example of the curious relation a fiction writer has to the material of her own life? Maybe. That may have some value in itself. But to tell the truth (if anyone still believes me capable of telling the truth), I wasn't writing fiction. I was writing memoir—or was trying to. My desire was to be accurate. I wished to embody the myth of memoir: to write as an act of dutiful transcription.

21   Yet clearly the work of writing narrative caused me to do something very different from transcription. I am forced to admit that memoir is not a matter of transcription, that memory itself is not a warehouse of finished stories, not a static gallery of framed pictures. I must admit that I invented. But why?

22   Two whys: why did I invent, and then, if a memoirist must inevitably invent rather than transcribe, why do I—why should anybody—write memoir at all?

23   I must respond to these impertinent questions because they, like the bumper sticker I saw the other day commanding all who read it to QUESTION AUTHORITY, challenge my authority as a memoirist and as a witness.

24   It still comes as a shock to realize that I don't write about what I know: I write in order to find out what I know. Is it possible to convey to a reader the enormous degree of blankness, confusion, hunch and uncertainty lurking in the act of writing? When I am the reader, not the writer, I too fall into the lovely illusion that the words before me (in a story by Mavis Gallant, an essay by Carol Bly, a memoir by M. F. K. Fisher), which *read* so inevitably, must also have been *written* exactly as they appear, rhythm and cadence, language and syntax, the powerful waves of the sentences laying themselves on the smooth beach of the page one after another faultlessly.

25   But here I sit before a yellow legal pad, and the long page of the preceding two paragraphs is a jumble of crossed-out lines, false starts, confused order. A mess. The mess of my mind trying to find out what it wants to say. This is a writer's frantic, grabby mind, not the poised mind of a reader ready to be edified or entertained.

26   I sometimes think of the reader as a cat, endlessly fastidious, capable, by turns, of mordant indifference and riveted attention, luxurious, recumbent, and ever poised. Whereas the writer is absolutely a dog, panting and moping, too eager for an affectionate scratch behind the ears, lunging frantically after any old stick thrown in the distance.

27   The blankness of a new page never fails to intrigue and terrify me. Sometimes, in fact, I think my habit of writing on long yellow sheets comes from an atavistic fear of the writer's stereotypic "blank white page." At least when I begin writing, my page isn't utterly blank; at least it has a wash of color on it, even if the absence of words must finally be faced on a yellow sheet as truly as on a blank white one. Well, we all have our ways of whistling in the dark.

28   If I approach writing from memory with the assumption that I know what I wish to say, I assume that intentionality is running the show. Things are not that simple. Or perhaps writing is even more profoundly simple, more telegraphic and immediate in its choices than the grating wheels and chugging engine of logic and rational intention. The heart, the guardian of intuition with its secret, often fearful intentions, is the boss. Its commands are what a writer obeys—often without knowing it. Or, I do.

29   That's why I'm a strong adherent of the first draft. And why it's worth pausing for a moment to consider what a first draft really is. By my lights, the piano lesson memoir is a first draft. That doesn't mean it exists here exactly as I first wrote it. I like to think I've cleaned it up from the first time I put it down on paper. I've cut some adjectives here, toned down the hyperbole there, smoothed a transition, cut a repetition—that sort of housekeeperly tidying-up. But the piece remains a first draft because I haven't yet gotten to know it, haven't given it a chance to tell me anything. For me, writing a first draft is a little like meeting someone for the first time. I come away with a wary acquaintanceship, but the real friendship (if any) and genuine intimacy—that's all down the road. Intimacy with a piece of writing, as with a person, comes from paying attention to the revelations it is capable of giving, not by imposing my own preconceived notions, no matter how well-intentioned they might be.

30   I try to let pretty much anything happen in a first draft. A careful first draft is a failed first draft. That may be why there are so many inaccuracies in the piano lesson memoir: I didn't censor, I didn't judge. I kept moving. But I would not publish this piece as a memoir on its own in its present state. It isn't the "lies" in the piece that give me pause, though a reader has a right to expect a memoir to be as accurate as the writer's memory can make it. No, it isn't the lies themselves that makes the piano lesson memoir a first draft and therefore "unpublishable."

31   The real trouble: the piece hasn't yet found its subject; it isn't yet about what it wants to

be about. Note: what *it* wants, not what I want. The difference has to do with the relation a memoirist—any writer, in fact—has to unconscious or half-known intentions and impulses in composition.

32   Now that I have the fragment down on paper, I can read this little piece as a mystery which drops clues to the riddle of my feelings, like a culprit who wishes to be apprehended. My narrative self (the culprit who has invented) wishes to be discovered by my reflective self, the self who wants to understand and make sense of a half-remembered story about a nun sneezing in the sun. . .

33   We only store in memory images of value. The value may be lost over the passage of time (I was baffled about why I remembered that sneezing nun, for example), but that's the implacable judgment of feeling: *this,* we say somewhere deep within us, is something I'm hanging on to. And of course, often we cleave to things because they possess heavy negative charges. Pain likes to be vivid.

34   Over time, the value (the feeling) and the stored memory (the image) may become estranged. Memoir seeks a permanent home for feeling and image, a habitation where they can live together in harmony. Naturally, I've had a lot of experiences since I packed away that one from the basement of St. Luke's School; that piano lesson has been effaced by waves of feeling for other moments and episodes. I persist in believing the event has value—after all, I remember it—but in writing the memoir I did not simply relive the experience. Rather, I explored the mysterious relationship between all the images I could round up and the even more impacted feelings that caused me to store the images safely away in memory. Stalking the relationship, seeking the congruence between stored image and hidden emotion—that's the real job of memoir.

35   By writing about that first piano lesson, I've

come to know things I could not know otherwise. But I only know these things as a result of reading this first draft. While I was writing, I was following the images, letting the details fill the room of the page and use the furniture as they wished. I was their dutiful servant—or thought I was. In fact, I was the faithful retainer of my hidden feelings which were giving the commands.

36   I really did feel, for instance, that Mary Katherine Reilly was far superior to me. She was smarter, funnier, more wonderful in every way—that's how I saw it. Our friendship (or she herself) did not require that I become her vassal, yet perhaps in my heart that was something I wanted; I wanted a way to express my feeling of admiration. I suppose I waited until this memoir to begin to find the way.

37   Just as, in the memoir, I finally possess that red Thompson book with the barking dogs and bleating lambs and winsome children. I couldn't (and still can't) remember what my own music book was, so I grabbed the name and image of the one book I could remember. It was only in reviewing the piece after writing it that I saw my inaccuracy. In pondering this "lie," I came to see what I was up to: I was getting what I wanted. At last.

38   The truth of many circumstances and episodes in the past emerges for the memoirist through details (the red music book, the fascination with a nun's name and gleaming face), but these details are not merely information, not flat facts. Such details are not allowed to lounge. They must work. Their work is the creation of symbol. But it's more accurate to call it the *recognition* of symbol. For meaning is not "attached" to the detail by the memoirist; meaning is revealed. That's why a first draft is important. Just as the first meeting (good or bad) with someone who later becomes the beloved is important and is often reviewed for signals, meanings, omens, and indications.

39   Now I can look at that music book and see it not only as "a detail," but for what it is,

how it *acts*. See it as the small red door leading straight into the dark room of my childhood longing and disappointment. That red book *becomes* the palpable evidence of that longing. In other words, it becomes symbol. There is no symbol, no life-of-the-spirit in the general or the abstract. Yet a writer wishes—indeed all of us wish—to speak about profound matters that are, like it or not, general and abstract. We wish to talk to each other about life and death, about love, despair, loss, and innocence. We sense that in order to live together we must learn to speak of peace, of history, of meaning and values. Those are a few.

40   We seek a means of exchange, a language which will renew these ancient concerns and make them wholly and pulsingly ours. Instinctively, we go to our store of private images and associations for our authority to speak of these weighty issues. We find, in our details and broken and obscured images, the language of symbol. Here memory impulsively reaches out its arms and embraces imagination. That is the resort to invention. It isn't a lie, but an act of necessity, as the innate urge to locate personal truth always is.

41   All right. Invention is inevitable. But why write memoir? Why not call it fiction and be done with all the hashing about, wondering where memory stops and imagination begins? And if memoir seeks to talk about "the big issues," about history and peace, death and love—why not leave these reflections to those with expert and scholarly knowledge? Why let the common or garden variety memoirist into the club? I'm thinking again of that bumper sticker: why Question Authority?

42   My answer, of course, is a memoirist's answer. Memoir must be written because each of us must have a created version of the past. Created: that is, real, tangible, made of the stuff of a life lived in place and in history. And the down side of any created thing as well: we must live with a version that attaches us to our limitations, to the inevitable subjectivity of our points of view. We must acquiesce to our experience and our gift to transform experience into meaning and value. You tell me your story, I'll tell you my story.

43   If we refuse to do the work of creating this personal version of the past, someone else will do it for us. That is a scary political fact. "The struggle of man against power," a character in Milan Kundera's novel *The Book of Laughter and Forgetting* says, "is the struggle of memory against forgetting." He refers to willful political forgetting, the habit of nations and those in power (Question Authority!) to deny the truth of memory in order to disarm moral and ethical power. It's an efficient way of controlling masses of people. It doesn't even require much bloodshed, as long as people are entirely willing to give over their personal memories. Whole histories can be rewritten. As Czeslaw Milosz said in his 1980 Nobel Prize lecture, the number of books published that seek to deny the existence of the Nazi death camps now exceeds one hundred.

44   What is remembered is what *becomes* reality. If we "forget" Auschwitz,[1] if we "forget" My Lai,[2] what then do we remember? And what is the purpose of our remembering? If we think of memory naively, as a simple story, logged like a documentary in the archive of the mind, we miss its beauty but also its function. The beauty of memory rests in its talent for rendering detail, for paying homage to the senses, its capacity to love the particles of life, the richness and idiosyncrasy of our existence. The function of memory, on the other hand, is intensely personal and surprisingly political.

---

[1] **Auschwitz:** Polish site in World War II of the concentration camp Auschwitz-Birkenau, where more than a million prisoners, most of them Jews, were exterminated.

[2] **My Lai:** Incident in 1968 during the Vietnam war, in which American troops massacred unarmed Vietnamese civilians, including women and children.

45   Our capacity to move forward as developing beings rests on a healthy relation with the past. Psychotherapy, that widespread method of mental health, relies heavily on memory and on the ability to retrieve and organize images and events from the personal past. We carry our wounds and perhaps even worse, our capacity to wound, forward with us. If we learn not only to tell our stories but to listen to what our stories tell us—to write the first draft and then return for the second draft—we are doing the work of memoir.

46   Memoir is the intersection of narration and reflection, of storytelling and essay-writing. It can present its story *and* reflect and consider the meaning of the story. It is a peculiarly open form, inviting broken and incomplete images, half-recollected fragments, all the mass (and mess) of detail. It offers to shape this confusion—and in shaping, of course it necessarily creates a work of art, not a legal document. But then, even legal documents are only valiant attempts to consign the truth, the whole truth and nothing but the truth to paper. Even they remain versions.

47   Locating touchstones—the red music book, the olive Olive, my father's violin playing—is deeply satisfying. Who knows why? Perhaps we all sense that we can't grasp the whole truth and nothing but the truth of our experience. Just can't be done. What can be achieved, however, is a version of its swirling, changing wholeness. A memoirist must acquiesce to selectivity, like any artist. The version we dare to write is the only truth, the only relationship we can have with the past. Refuse to write your life and you have no life. At least, that is the stern view of the memoirist.

48   Personal history, logged in memory, is a sort of slide projector flashing images on the wall of the mind. And there's precious little order to the slides in the rotating carousel. Beyond that confusion, who knows who is running the projector? A memoirist steps into this darkened room of flashing, unorganized images and stands blinking for a while. Maybe for a long while. But eventually, as with any attempt to tell a story, it is necessary to put something first, then something else. And so on, to the end. That's a first draft. Not necessarily the truth, not even *a* truth sometimes, but the first attempt to create a shape.

49   The first thing I usually notice at this stage of composition is the appalling inaccuracy of the piece. Witness my first piano lesson draft. Invention is screamingly evident in what I intended to be transcription. But here's the further truth: I feel no shame. In fact, it's only now that my interest in the piece truly quickens. For I can see what isn't there, what is shyly hugging the walls, hoping not to be seen. I see the filmy shape of the next draft. I see a more acute version of the episode or—this is more likely—an entirely new piece rising from the ashes of the first attempt.

50   The next draft of the piece would have to be a true re-vision, a new seeing of the materials of the first draft. Nothing merely cosmetic will do—no rouge buffing up the opening sentence, no glossy adjective to lift a sagging line, nothing to attempt covering a patch of gray writing. None of that. I can't say for sure, but my hunch is the revison would lead me to more writing about my father (why was I so impressed by that ancestral inventor of the collapsible opera hat? Did I feel I had nothing as remarkable in my own background? Did this make me feel inadequate?). I begin to think perhaps Sister Olive is less central to this business than she is in this draft. She is meant to be a moment, not a character.

51   And so I might proceed, if I were to undertake a new draft of the memoir. I begin to feel a relationship developing between a former self and me.

52   And, even more compelling, a relationship between an old world and me. Some people think of autobiographical writing as the precious occupation of a particularly self-absorbed person. Maybe, but I don't buy that. True

memoir is written in an attempt to find not only a self but a world.

53   The self-absorption that seems to be the impetus and embarrassment of autobiography turns into (or perhaps always was) a hunger for the world. Actually, it begins as hunger for *a* world, one gone or lost, effaced by time or a more sudden brutality. But in the act of remembering, the personal environment expands, resonates beyond itself, beyond its "subject," into the endless and tragic recollection that is history.

54   We look at old family photographs in which we stand next to black, boxy Fords and are wearing period costumes, and we do not gaze fascinated because there we are young again, or there we are standing, as we never will again in life, next to our mother. We stare and drift because there we are . . . historical. It is the dress, the black car that dazzle us now and draw us beyond our mother's bright arms which once caught us. We reach into the attractive impersonality of something more significant than ourselves. We write memoir, in other words. We accept the humble position of writing a version rather than "the whole truth."

55   I suppose I write memoir because of the radiance of the past—it draws me back and back to it. Not that the past is beautiful. In our communal memoir, in history, the death camps *are* back there. In intimate life too, the record is usually pretty mixed. "I could tell you stories . . ." people say and drift off, meaning terrible things have happened to them.

56   But the past is radiant. It has the light of lived life. A memoirist wishes to touch it. No one owns the past, though typically the first act of new political regimes, whether of the left or the right, is to attempt to re-write history, to grab the past and make it over so the end comes out right. So their power looks inevitable.

57   No one owns the past, but it is a grave error (another age would have said a grave sin) not to inhabit memory. Sometimes I think it is all we really have. But that may be a trifle melodramatic. At any rate, memory possesses authority for the fearful self in a world where it is necessary to have authority in order to Question Authority.

58   There may be no more pressing intellectual need in our culture than for people to become sophisticated about the function of memory. The political implications of the loss of memory are obvious. The authority of memory is a personal confirmation of selfhood. To write one's life is to live it twice, and the second living is both spiritual and historical, for a memoir reaches deep within the personality as it seeks its narrative form and also grasps the life-of-the-times as no political treatise can.

59   Our most ancient metaphor says life is a journey. Memoir is travel writing, then, notes taken along the way, telling how things looked and what thoughts occurred. But I cannot think of the memoirist as a tourist. This is the traveller who goes on foot, living the journey, taking on mountains, enduring deserts, marveling at the lush green places. Moving through it all faithfully, not so much a survivor with a harrowing tale to tell as a pilgrim, seeking, wondering. ◆

PART III

RESEARCH

"Nothing is so difficult but that it can be found out by seeking."

TERENCE

Short Research Reports

ALMOST ALL WRITING INVOLVES RESEARCH. EVEN MEMOIRISTS, IF they take their jobs seriously, generally consult some source besides their own recollections. Mary McCarthy, in the process of writing *Memories of a Catholic Girlhood,* interviewed members of her family and searched for newspaper accounts of her mother's and father's lives. In writing his autobiography, James Weldon Johnson used reference books, family photographs, and letters; he even found and quoted from a book of children's stories that he had read as a child. Some of the advice given in this chapter could apply to any type of essay. We'll be concentrating, however, on short reports where investigation is the heart of the matter, where the writer knows from the outset that the success or failure of the work will depend largely on the quality of the research. We will discuss field notebooks, interviews, and questionnaires, as well as library research. The longer research paper, with its more ambitious research program and its special problems of manuscript form, will be the subject of Chapter 7.

Though it is easy for a textbook writer to suggest that research is an orderly, predictable process, the truth is more complex. Effective research requires a clear vision of an intellectual goal, the ability to distinguish quickly between information useful in pursuing that goal and information that can safely be ignored, and a cool head in the face of stubborn and unpredictable problems—temperamental interviewees, magazines with missing pages, books not on the shelves, indexes put together by people who clearly didn't have your problem in mind. A good portion of a researcher's time is spent working around obstacles, and it is often in the process of improvising an alternative route that the researcher stumbles on information more useful than anything he or she could have imagined.

The hints below should, therefore, be taken only as hints, intended to save you some time. In practice, research is a skill that you learn on the job, first as a student writer, then as a member of a profession. You'll probably find that the best way to use this chapter is to read it through quickly to get an overview of some research methods. Later, when you start work on your report documenting the level of violence in schools (see page 198) or your explication of an editorial cartoon (page 199), you can return to these hints for guidance.

SOME HINTS ON RESEARCH

HINT 1:

Develop hypotheses early.

The very idea of research suggests to some people that the truth about a given subject is out there somewhere and that the researcher's task is essentially to find and record it. But as this book stresses repeatedly, writing involves interpretation: the joining of a subject and a framework. Unless you have a framework, a thesis, your research is likely to produce a mass of data that says nothing.

Objectivity seems to demand that you form no thesis before your research is complete. But if you have no thesis, you have no way of formulating questions for interviews or of evaluating the importance of what you read. A better approach is to form a thesis—perhaps it would be better to call it a hypothesis—as early as possible and be prepared to change it as often as an honest interpretation of the data demands. In fact, you may find it useful to begin work on a project by drafting a one-page summary, based on entirely imaginary research, of what you hope your final essay will be. This exercise focuses your search for authentic information. Sometimes you may find that your final paper reverses the thesis of your anticipatory summary. The flexibility that allows such reversal is far more valuable in research than mere objectivity is.

HINT 2:

If you plan to write from direct observation, keep a journal or field notebook.

Field notebooks are standard equipment for newspaper and magazine reporters, sociologists and anthropologists, and natural scientists who do their work out-of-doors. A mammalogist at my university, for example, makes systematic daily observations of mammal behavior in the field, beginning each entry by carefully noting the location, the time and date, and the weather conditions, then precisely describing anything that strikes him as novel or thought-provoking about the animals he is watching. For practical reasons, he prefers spiral-bound notebooks (from which no pages can escape) with backs stiff enough to serve as a firm working surface.

Spiral notebooks were not invented when Charles Darwin sailed as a naturalist on the *Beagle* in 1831–1836, but we find in Darwin's journal of the voyage evidence of the scientist's habit of daily, scrupulous observation. Here, for example, is material adapted from an observation off the southeastern coast of South America:

A WRITER AT WORK

"Gossamer Spiders"
CHARLES DARWIN

On several occasions, when the *Beagle* has been within the mouth of the Plata,[1] the rigging has been coated with the web of the Gossamer Spider. One day (November 1st, 1832) I paid particular attention to this subject. The weather had been fine and clear, and in the morning the air was full of patches of the flocculent web, as on an autumnal day in England. The ship was sixty miles distant from the land, in the direction of a steady though light breeze. Vast numbers of a small spider, about one-tenth of an inch in length, and of a dusky red color, were attached to the webs. There must have been, I should suppose, some thousands on the ship. The little spider, when at first coming in contact with the rigging, was always seated on a single thread, and not on the flocculent mass. This latter seems merely to be produced by the entanglement of the single threads. The spiders were all of one species, but of both sexes, together with young ones. These latter were distinguished by their smaller size and more dusky colour. . . . The little aeronaut as soon as it arrived on board was very active, running about, sometimes letting itself fall, and then reascending on the same thread; sometimes employing itself in making a small and very irregular mesh in the corners between the ropes. It could run with facility on the surface of the water. When disturbed it lifted up its front legs, in the attitude of attention. On its first arrival it appeared very thirsty, and with exserted maxillae drank eagerly of drops of water; this same circumstance has been observed by Stack: may it not be the consequence of the little insect having passed through a dry and rarefied atmosphere? Its stock of web seems inexhaustible. While watching some that were suspended by a single thread, I several times observed that the slightest breath of air bore them away out of sight, in a horizontal line.

The journal serves two purposes, the more obvious being that it becomes a record of details on which the writer can later draw at will. Observations as close as those that Darwin made are very perishable, and only someone who writes daily can expect to preserve them. A good night's sleep can be fatal to the memory of details. The second advantage of the journal is that it improves the writer's powers of observation, just as a pencil in hand seems to improve the artist's. Darwin's descriptions show the alertness of someone used to asking, "How can I describe this?" and "Have I missed anything worth recording?" A similar alertness can be seen in the entries

---

[1] **The Plata:** The Río de la Plata or River Plate, the estuary formed by the confluence of the Paraná and Uruguay rivers.

Joan Didion makes in her daily notebook: "'That woman Estelle . . . is partly the reason why George Sharp and I are separated today.' *Dirty crêpe-de-Chine wrapper, hotel bar, Wilmington RR, 9:45 A.M. August Monday morning.*" Unlike Darwin, Didion does not attempt to make her notebook an accurate and complete record. Instead she makes it a repository for the odd details that bring a moment back into memory. Though Didion says that she does not mine this notebook when she writes an essay or novel, no doubt the practice it has given her in noticing unexpected details produces some of the rich texture of her writing. For the writer who works directly from life rather than from books, the daily notebook is one of the principal sources of such details.

HINT 3:

If you interview, plan questions in advance, put your subject at ease, and verify your notes when possible.

The interview—an important source of information for reporters, social scientists, and some businesspeople—ought to be used by student writers more often than it is. A skillfully conducted interview gives you fresh information to work with, information that no other writer has touched. Unfortunately, television has created an image of the interview as something that derives its interest from the fame of the person interviewed. In fact, interviews with relatively unknown people uncover information odder and more interesting than anything you are likely to hear from a celebrity, as Joan Didion proves in such essays as "Marrying Absurd" and "Quiet Days in Malibu."

What makes interviews hard is precisely what makes them valuable: they involve face-to-face contact with people. Since the person you are interviewing is donating time to your project, you are under a stronger-than-normal obligation to observe the ordinary courtesies, making an appointment at a time convenient for the interviewee, not overstaying your welcome, being generous with your thanks. At the same time, the interview is not an entirely social occasion; you need to be as prepared and focused as you would be for a job interview or an important business meeting.

One of the most accomplished interviewers of the century is Jessica Mitford, author of books and articles that uncovered abuses in the Famous Writers School, the funeral industry, prison management, and the criminal justice system. Her advice on interviewing is valuable.

A WRITER AT WORK

"Conducting the Interview"
JESSICA MITFORD

The individuals to be interviewed will usually fall into two categories: Friendly Witnesses, those who are sympathetic to your point of view, such as the victim of a racket you are investigating, or an expert who is clarifying for you technical matters within his field of knowledge; and Unfriendlies, whose interests may be threatened by your investigation and who therefore will be prone to conceal rather than reveal the information you are seeking.

While your approach to each of these will differ, some general rules hold good for *all* interviews. Prepare your approach as a lawyer would for an important cross-examination. Take time to think through exactly what it is that you want to learn from the interview; I write out and number in order the questions I intend to ask. That way I can number the answer, keyed to the number of the question, without interrupting the flow of conversation, and if the sequence is disturbed (which it probably will be, in the course of the interchange), I have no problem reconstructing the Q. and A. as they occurred. Naturally other questions may arise that I had not foreseen, but I will still have my own outline as a guide to the absolute essentials.

Immediately after the interview, I type up the Q.s and A.s before my notes get cold. If, in the course of doing this, I discover that I have missed something, or another question occurs to me, I call up the person immediately while the subject is still freshly in mind.

In the case of the Friendly Witness, it often helps to send him a typescript of the interview for correction or elaboration. I did this to good effect after interviews with defense lawyers from whom I was seeking information about the conspiracy law for *The Trial of Dr. Spock,* and with Dr. Margen and other physicians who revealed the nature of drug experiments on prisoners for *Kind and Usual Punishment.* In each case the expert whom I had consulted not only saved me from egregious error but in correcting my transcription of the interview enriched and strengthened the points to be made.

For Unfriendly Witnesses—which in my experience have included undertakers, prosecutors, prison administrators, Famous Writers—I list the questions in graduated form from Kind to Cruel. Kind questions are designed to lull your quarry into a conversational mood: "How did you first get interested in funeral directing as a career?" "Could you suggest any reading material that might help me to understand more about problems of Corrections?" and so on. By the time you get to the Cruel questions—"What is the wholesale cost of your casket retailing for three thousand dollars?" "How do you justify censoring a prisoner's correspondence with his lawyer in violation of the California law?"—your interlocutor will find it hard to duck and may blurt out a quotable nugget.

The portable tape recorder can obviously be useful to interviewers, allowing them to capture the interviewee's precise words. It has not, however, replaced the notebook. Some people are reluctant to talk in the presence of a tape recorder, and some portions of even a carefully taped interview may turn out inaudible. Should you have the good fortune to get ninety minutes of audible tape, you will face the difficult task of finding and transcribing the key quotations. Experienced reporters who use tape recorders generally take notes to serve as a backup and as a visual reminder of the key points of the conversation. Some treat the tape as the backup and rely primarily on the notebook.

HINT 4:

If you use a questionnaire, design it carefully and justify your interpretation of its results.

Interviews are useful in situations where the opinions of one individual or a few individuals count. They are cumbersome in situations where the opinions of large numbers of people are important. Suppose that a student on a twenty-thousand-student campus is writing a proposal that the library should be kept open around the clock, except for Friday and Saturday nights. She believes, from conversations with her friends, that a large portion of the student body has been inconvenienced by the library's present schedule, and she would like to prove to the administration the extent of this inconvenience. A questionnaire seems to be the best solution: if she could produce data indicating that a large number of students would benefit from extended hours, her case would surely be strengthened.

But administering a questionnaire properly is not an easy task. There is, in the first place, the difficulty of constructing the questions properly. Consider the following alternatives:

1. Do you believe that as many as 25% of students lose ten or more hours of research each semester because of the library's being closed from midnight to 8:00 A.M. on weekday (Sunday through Thursday) nights?

2. Should the library be open at night on weekdays?

3. The university library closes from midnight to 8:00 A.M. Monday through Thursday. If the library were open all night these nights, how many more hours would you have spent there this week?

Each of these questions is flawed. Number 1 is unnecessarily difficult and asks respondents about the lives of people they have never met. Number 2 is ambiguous. Not every respondent will take *at night* to mean "midnight to 8:00 A.M." and *weekdays* to mean "Monday through Thursday." Some will say that the library should (or should not) be open at night for their *personal* benefit. Some will say that it *should* be open for the sake of others or even for the university's reputation, even though they would never use it themselves.

Number 3 has things to be said for it. It gives respondents the essential information in short, clear sentences, and it asks respondents to examine only their own behavior and opinions rather than the opinions of others. By limiting the time frame to the week immediately past, it avoids speculation about the future and doesn't ask for impossible feats of memory. Even this question has weaknesses, however. Different respondents may interpret "week" differently: Does it mean the last seven days, including today? Does it mean the seven days prior to this one? Does it mean last calendar week? Perhaps the questioner should specify a range of dates. Even then, there would be problems to consider. Not every week in a school term, for example, produces the same level of library use. Such difficulties can (and should) be discussed in any report that uses survey data.

I don't mean to exaggerate the difficulty of framing good questions for surveying groups of people, but I do want to warn that the difficulties are considerable—so considerable that one ought to be skeptical about the validity of even professionally constructed questionnaires. A wise researcher will at least have each question scrutinized by several readers attuned to the kinds of problems we have been discussing.

As crucial as the writing of good questions is the selection of people who will complete the questionnaire. On some occasions it is possible to survey everyone in a given group, but in the example we are working with, this would clearly be impossible. Even if our investigator could afford to mail questionnaires to twenty thousand students, only a fraction of them would respond, and this fraction would probably not be very representative of the whole population. Presumably, people irritated by the library's closing would be more likely to return the form than those who had never even considered going to a library at night. Researchers who can't afford mass mailings ordinarily must hand their questionnaires directly to respondents, then hover in the area until a significant[2] number of questionnaires is returned.

Such handing and hovering must happen somewhere, and the location may affect the result. Suppose the researcher on the library question decides to poll students as they enter or leave the library. Would the sample be representative? No, because students in the library at any given time are probably more-frequent-than-average users of the library. Suppose the researcher does a 2:00 A.M. survey or a 7:00 A.M. survey in a twenty-four-hour diner near campus. Would the sample be representative? Probably not. The 2:00 A.M. survey of night owls would exaggerate the inconvenience of the library's closing, and the 7:00 A.M. survey of larks would probably underestimate it. A better time and place might be noon on a weekday at the student union snack bar.

If you intend to use questionnaires extensively in your research, I suggest that you consult a faculty member (perhaps from the sociology or psychology department) who can discuss with you such issues as the form of questions, the format of responses, and the appropriate size and composi-

---

[2] Significant: "Statistical significance," an important concept in survey research, is too complex to discuss here. Common sense should tell you, however, that a large sample is more likely to produce credible data than a small one. When samples smaller than twenty are offered as representative of large populations, statisticians tend to show acute anxiety or downright amusement.

tion of your sample of respondents. A good short discussion of these issues can be found in Chapter 9 of *The Practice of Social Research* (Earl Babbie), in Chapters 9 and 10 of *The Science of Educational Research* (George J. Mouly), and in *The Survey Research Handbook* (Pamela L. Alreck and Robert B. Settle).

HINT 5:

For the best advice on library research, consult your librarian.

Professional reference librarians, trained in research techniques and familiar with the peculiarities of their own libraries, are a valuable resource. If your campus library conducts tours, attend one so that you can hear from your local experts such information as what computerized indexes are available to you, how your computer on-line catalogue works, and how the reference area is arranged. When you find yourself at your wits' end on a research project, go to the reference librarian for help and treat him or her well: this is a relationship worth cultivating.

My favorite reference librarian, Wayne Barnes, recommended Jean Key Gates's *Guide to the Use of Books and Libraries* as my best resource when I undertook this chapter. I can, in turn, recommend it to you as a thoroughly useful book. But I also want to recommend Mr. Barnes himself—or whichever of his colleagues sits at the reference desk of your own library.

HINT 6:

Search for primary sources.

To put the matter colloquially, a *primary* source is one that gets you close to the horse's mouth. If you are writing about women's lives during the siege of Vicksburg (1862–63), for instance, documents such as diaries, letters, and official documents written during the siege would be primary sources. A book written in 1994 by a historian relying on those Civil War documents is clearly a secondary source. Primary sources are the "hard data" on which credible scholarship is built. The distinction between primary and secondary sources is not absolute, of course: unless written by an eyewitness, a newspaper account of the siege published in 1863 would be less "primary" than the diary of a Vicksburg woman involved in it, but would be more "primary" than a historian's account written in 1994. The reporter presumably had face-to-face contact with people involved in the siege. The historian was facing only documents.

On some subjects, you'll find yourself forced to rely on secondary sources for most of your information, but your writing will gain credibility and force if occasionally, at least, you can bypass the interpreters and scholars and take readers back to a document that has a living connection to the event itself.

HINT 7:

Use indexes to search for articles in magazines, newspapers, and other periodicals.

Tens of thousands of magazines, scholarly publications, and newspapers print millions of articles each year in the United States alone. The total output of information is so great that indexing has become a considerable business in its own right. Indexes and bibliographies (discussed in Chapter 7) overlap somewhat in their definition and function, but when reference librarians talk about indexes, they usually mean publications that list articles from current periodicals by author, subject, and title. Don't be confused by the fact that some indexes are also bibliographies and vice versa. There are now so many indexes available in large libraries that it would be foolish to attempt to list them all, but we will discuss three representative ones: *Readers' Guide to Periodical Literature, New York Times Index,* and *Essay and General Literature Index.*

Readers' Guide indexes more than 180 periodicals and manages to do so at remarkable speed. Every two weeks it publishes a slim paperback of publications for the two weeks before, arranged by author, title, and subject. These biweekly accumulations are combined to produce thicker paperback accumulations by month and still thicker ones by quarter (three months). At the end of a publication year, all the citations are combined in a single bound volume. Many libraries have the complete set of yearly indexes, stretching back to 1905. This is a truly remarkable resource. For material published in popular (as opposed to scholarly) magazines, it allows the researcher both a long reach back into time and an opportunity to bring research very near the present moment. Someone interested in the growing "professionalization" of college sports, for example, can trace the story through hundreds of articles and essays distributed over more than eight decades and extending to the current month. There are now dozens of indexes like *Readers' Guide,* most of them somewhat more specialized in their coverage. Some typical titles are:

Applied Science and Technology Index, which specializes in scientific, technical, and engineering journals.

Bibliographic Index, an annual publication that lists major bibliographies published during the previous year.

Humanities Index, which covers scholarly periodicals in such fields as philosophy, history, anthropology, and religion.

Social Sciences Index, which covers scholarly periodicals in such fields as psychology, sociology, economics, and law.

Subject heading ──── **BIRMINGHAM, Ala.**
Birmingham: we can say things in the open.
il Newsweek 64:23 D 14 '64
Case history of a sick city. il Newsweek
62:23-4+ S 30 '63
Coming home from Birmingham: reflections
on tragic southern city. W. Hamilton.
Christian Cent 80:1302-3 O 23 '63
In defense of two cities. R. Moley. News-
week 63:110 Ap 27 '64
Root of the trouble in Birmingham. M. Mc-
Grory. America 109:411 O 12 '63

Sub-heading ──── **Crime**
Birmingham church bomber. G. McMillan. il
Sat Eve Post 237:15-19 Je 6 '64
Article title ──── Farce in Birmingham. il Time 82:27-8 O 18
'63
Publication infor- ──── Half-cocked. il Newsweek 62:35 O 14 '63
mation: magazine   New bombing terrorists of the South call
title, volume num- themselves Nacirema: American spelled
ber, page numbers, backward. G. McMillan. Life 55:39-40 O 11
'63
month, day, year,
Author of article ────   Hotels, restaurants, etc.
Barbecue and the bar; Ollie's in Birmingham
resists public-accommodations section of
Civil rights act. il Newsweek 64:32 S 28 '64
Beyond a doubt; Negroes served at Ollie's
barbecue. il Time 84:13-14 D 25 '64
Ollie McClung's big decision. M. Durham.
Life 57:31 O 9 '64

                    Negroes
After Birmingham riots, troubles linger on.
il U S News 54:40-2 My 27 '63
Special informa- ──── After Birmingham riots: who has gained? il
tion: illustrations U S News 54:46-7 Je 17 '63
Alabama bombers kill four Negro girls. Christian Cent 80:1160 S 25 '63
As racial troubles broke loose in Alabama.
il U S News 54:8 My 13 '63
Battle hymn in Birmingham. C. G. Bell. Nation 196:370-3 My 4 '63
Beginning in Birmingham. V. Harding. il Reporter 28:13-19 Je 6 '63; Discussion. 29:5 Jl 4
'63

Sample entry from the Reader's Guide to Periodical Literature.

Public Affairs Information Service Bulletin, which lists articles by public and private agencies on social, economic, and political topics.

MLA [Modern Language Association] *International Bibliography of Books and Articles on the Modern Languages and Literature,* an index whose title speaks for itself.

New York Times Index would at first seem to be a limited tool, since it indexes only a single newspaper. The publication has, however, covered current affairs thoroughly since 1851, and the indexing is unusually complete. Like *Readers' Guide, New York Times Index* is issued initially in small pamphlets covering two weeks and eventually accumulated into annual volumes. These volumes create, as the publishers say, "A Book of Record" in which newsworthy events can be traced day by day, sometimes in the most minute detail. A researcher needing to know when and where President Ford bumped his head on the door frame of *Air Force One* could find the information in the *New York Times Index*. Other important newspaper indexes are the *National Newspaper Index, Christian Science Monitor Index,* [London] *Times Index,* and *Wall Street Journal Index*.

Subject heading

Abstract of a
news story

News stories of
special interest
are printed in
boldface.

Note on length of article:
(L) means over three
columns, (M) means one to
two, and (S) means less than
one column.

Publication information:
month, day, section number,
pagenumber, and column
number.

UNITED STATES POLITICS AND GOVERNMENT-Cont
Jl I.I7:I

Russell Baker Op-Ed column on Pres. Bush's demand for constitutional amendment to prohibit flag-buring: wonders why he is not fighting for amber waves of grain, spacious skies and shining seas, all threatened by profit-making schemers (S) Jl 1.1.23:1

Ken Philmus, manager of George Washington Bridge, says that when American flag is lowered into position on bridge on Fourth of July, maintenance crew and staff are filled with pride; 60-by-90 foot flag, reputedly largest free-flying banner in world, has hung from bridge's western arch on national holidays since 1947 (S) Jl 2.1.6:6

Congressional leaders and some Bush Administration officials say President's popularity will be put to serious test when he makes some hard decisions on budget and cloud of other issues now facing him (M). Jl 2.1 17:1

Supreme Court ruling that burning American flag as politcal protest is protected by First Amendment produces patriotic uproar and demands for constitutional amendment; cartoon (M) Jl 2.IV. 1:1

Editorial on American attachment to the flag, its virtues and the sad extreme to which it is being pushed in aftermath of Supreme Court decision extending First Amendment protection to those who would burn flag as act of political protest. Jl 2.IV.12:1

Anthony Lewis column opposes Pres. Bush's call for constitutional amendment to prevent desecration of the American flag, saying it would amount to an exception to Bill of Rights Jl 2.IV.13:1

Garrision Keillor Op-Ed article attacking Pres. Bush's proposal for constitutional amendment to outlaw buring the flag. Jl 2.IV.13.4

Sample page from the New York Times Index.

The *Essay and General Literature Index* deserves special mention because it indexes essays and articles that are collected in books. Without such an index, being "collected in" a book would amount almost to being "hidden in" one, since sections of books do not receive special listings in either periodical indexes or the card catalogue.

Included in your library's research collection will be many volumes of *digests* or *abstracts,* which are essentially indexes expanded to include substantial information about the items indexed. *Book Review Digest,* for example, reprints short extracts from book reviews and gives the locations of complete reviews. It is a valuable resource for researchers who want a quick overview of a book they are considering as a possible source. *Facts on File* summarizes press coverage of major news stories. *Biological Abstracts, Psychology Abstracts,* and other similarly titled volumes summarize the articles they index and are great aids for the busy researcher.

HINT 8:

Take advantage of CD-ROM *and other data-base searches.*

Computer technology has had a dramatic impact on indexing in recent years. Some of the resources discussed in the last section (like the *MLA Bibliography* and *Readers' Guide*) are now available in CD-ROM form in most college libraries. Other indexes (like *Infotrac,* which specializes in widely read magazines) are available on CD-ROM only and are updated frequently, so it is possible to locate articles published in the last few weeks.

The features of *Infotrac* are fairly typical of most data bases. Suppose, for instance, that you are interested in writing about homelessness. The most straightforward method of research would be to use *Infotrac's* subject guide and, when the screen asks you to type in a topic, type "homelessness." The next screen that appears will tell you how many articles on the subject are in the data base. The number is probably well over a hundred, too many for you to consider systematically. On the same screen, however, you will find a line that says ">subtopics." Move the cursor to that line

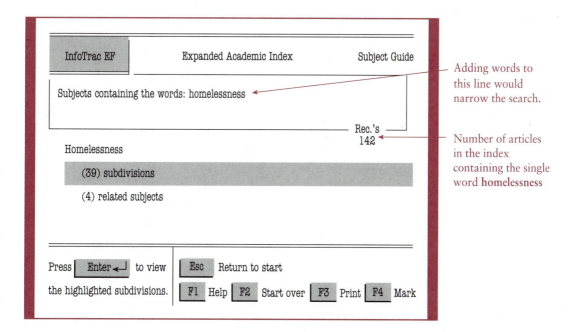

InfoTrac EF	Expanded Academic Index	Subject Guide

Subdivisions of: Homelessness

	Rec.'s
– analysis	7
– bibliography	1
– case studies	2
– causes of	7
– communication systems	1
– demographic aspects	1
– economic aspects	1
– economic policy	1
– england	1
– europe	2
– florida	1
– health aspects	5
– history	3
– international aspects	1
– investigations	1
– laws, regulations, etc.	13

Select a subdivision by moving the highlight bar with the keyboard's arrow keys

Press   Enter ⏎   to view the citation(s) for the highlighted subject

Esc   Return to subject list

F1   Help   F2   Start over   F3   Print   F4   Mark

and press the Enter key. You will find a long list of subtopics, or categories, into which the "homelessness" articles have been divided, followed by a notation of the number of articles on each subtopic. The subtopic "causes of" might list about twenty articles—a far more manageable number, if your real interest is the causes.

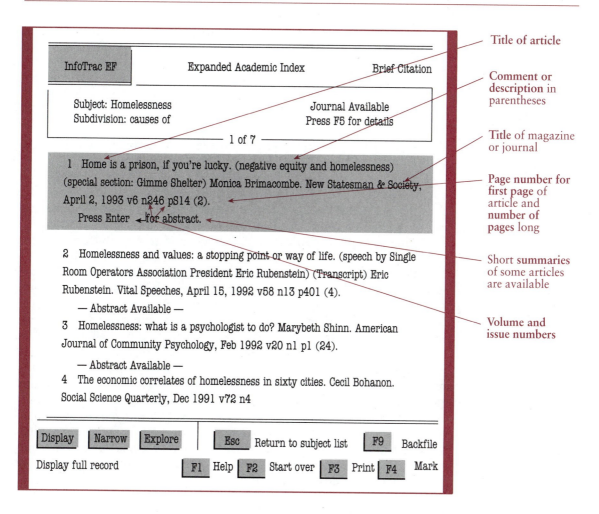

Title of article

Comment or description in parentheses

Title of magazine or journal

Page number for first page of article and number of pages long

Short summaries of some articles are available

Volume and issue numbers

A somewhat more sophisticated way of using *Infotrac* is to select the key word search rather than the subject guide. This feature allows you to narrow a search very quickly by specifying two or more key words (separated by commas) that should appear in the title or in the subject description. You could, for example, type "homelessness, causes" to go directly to the twenty or so articles listed. Or you could type "homelessness, clinton" to try to locate articles on the president's attitude toward the homeless. Or you could type, "homelessness, california, clinton, causes" to see if you can locate an article that records a statement by the president on the causes of homelessness in California. *Infotrac* has convenient features that allow you to broaden your search to related topics or to narrow it by adding key words. Learning to use such features on this data base or on another is a good investment of time because they allow you to navigate through an index efficiently. When you have learned to use one data base well, you'll see that other data bases follow much the same principles and can be mastered easily.

WRITING THE REPORT

Respect your readers' knowledge—and their ignorance.   Writing from research can create special problems in the relationship between you and your audience. After researching a topic intensively for some time, you may find yourself in a perilous situation: you don't have the deep knowledge of a true expert, but you have learned enough to lose touch with the general public. It then becomes possible for you to fall between chairs, writing something too simple to interest the expert and too complicated for the ordinary reader.

You need, therefore, to visualize your target audience clearly. If you have any doubts, consult your instructor. In most circumstances, he or she will probably encourage you to write more for general readers than for experts. But even among general readers, there can be a considerable range of knowledge. The top-level reader may be someone as well informed as you are at the *end* of your research; the bottom-level reader may be someone as ill informed as you were at the *beginning*. Good research-based writing manages to accommodate itself tactfully to the needs of both ends of this spectrum. The least-informed readers will sometimes encounter phrases clearly intended for people who know more than they do, but these phrases won't be essential to the meaning of a passage. Better-informed readers will frequently find phrases giving information that seems obvious to them, but because these overexplanations are connected to fresh information or fresh insight, they don't lead to boredom.

Show your readers where your information comes from.   To evaluate the reliability of your conclusions, readers need to know what sources of information you are using: a fact drawn from the *New York Times* might be questioned, but most readers will accept it before they will accept a "fact" drawn from the *National Inquirer*. As your sources become less familiar to them, you need to give the readers enough information to allow them to evaluate each source. This returns us to the problem of helping the least-informed reader without irritating the best-informed. Consider the following examples drawn from essays in this book.

> Some constitutional theorists (Justice Douglas was one) have maintained that any obscenity law is a serious abridgment of free speech. Others (and Justice Earl Warren was one) have maintained that the First Amendment was never intended to protect obscenity.
> —Susan Brownmiller, "Let's Put Pornography Back in the Closet"

Chivalry's famous celebrator Ramon Lull, a contemporary of St. Louis, could now state as his thesis that "God and chivalry are in concord."

—Barbara Tuchman, "Chivalry"

Writing a book, full time, takes between two and ten years. The long poem, John Berryman said, takes between five and ten years.

—Annie Dillard, *The Writing Life*

You'll notice that the three writers are forced to make assumptions about their readers' level of background knowledge. Susan Brownmiller, writing for *Newsday,* assumes that even her bottom-level readers know what a justice of the Supreme Court is and that—with a slight nudge, at least—they will recognize the names of two of the most famous justices. She avoids explaining too much, as you can see by comparing her sentences to this cumbersome rewrite:

Some constitutional theorists (Justice William O. Douglas, who sat on the U.S. Supreme Court—the court ultimately responsible for interpretation of the U.S. Constitution—from 1939 to 1975 and was one of its most liberal members, was one) have maintained that any obscenity law is a serious abridgment of free speech. Others (and Justice Earl Warren, Chief Justice of the U.S. Supreme Court from 1953 to 1969, and another famous liberal, was one) have maintained that the First Amendment was never intended to protect obscenity.

Her use of the title *Justice* before the names of Douglas and Warren, however, helps the reader make the connection to the Supreme Court.

Barbara Tuchman, writing a book about the fourteenth century for a general audience, pauses to give some information about Ramon Lull, a name that might otherwise mean nothing to many readers. Notice, though, that she assumes that all readers will know perfectly well who St. Louis is. A bottom-level reader, one who doesn't recognize St. Louis as the great crusader-king who ruled France in the middle of the thirteenth century, will miss some information here, but not much. Even this reader will know that Lull lived *sometime* in the Middle Ages and that he was famous for his writings on chivalry.

Annie Dillard, clearly assuming that most of the readers of *The Writing Life* will be people interested in literature, does not pause to identify John Berryman as a major modern American poet, winner of a Pulitzer Prize and a National Book Award; but even the reader who has never heard of Berryman can follow the sense of the passage well enough to *assume* that he is a poet of some importance. In this context, Dillard is right to treat Berryman's identity as a matter of common knowledge, even though her bottom-level readers may never have heard his name before.

Deciding how much information to give with a quotation is one of the dozens of small gestures that define your relationship with your audience. As is generally true in the research paper, your goal is to write in a way that keeps your bottom-level reader tolerably well informed while offering your middle- and top-level readers uncluttered access to material they will find fresh and interesting.

QUESTIONS FOR PEER REVIEW

Obviously, running a draft by intermediate readers before submitting the finished product can help you gauge whether you have underexplained or overexplained. If you can, find one reader who can fairly represent the least-informed end of your intended range of readers and another who can fairly represent the best-informed. In addition to asking the general peer review questions listed on pp. 60–61, ask this pair of readers two more:

Where have I underexplained, creating the possibility of confusion?

Where have I overexplained, wasting the reader's time and attention by repeating what should be treated as common knowledge?

If you have a single reviewer, describe the range of your audience and ask him or her to be alert for anything that seems wrong for readers at either end. I have had good luck giving my reviewer a red pencil to highlight any phrase or clause that overexplains and a blue pencil to highlight any that underexplains. Every spot of color gave me reason to reconsider; every stretch of white reassured me.

AVOIDING PLAGIARISM

Though the mechanics of acknowledging sources can be complex (See "Some General Comments on Citation Form," pp. 284–289), the general principles are simple enough: the words and ideas of other writers are their property—legally and ethically. The legal question doesn't arise until you publish your work, but the ethical question is always present. In our society, particularly in an academic community, people expect to be paid for their intellectual labors—if not with money, at least with the increase in reputation that comes from being cited by other writers and researchers. The rule, then, is that when you use *ideas, facts, or words* produced by the labors of someone else, you give your source credit.

General Knowledge. The obligation to acknowledge sources doesn't mean that every piece of information you get from a book needs to be tagged with the name of its owner. Many facts and ideas are "general knowledge," even though you don't know them yourself. You might begin your research for a paper on Charles Darwin not knowing that *The Origin of Species* was published in 1859 or that Sir Charles Lyell's writings on geology shaped Darwin's thinking, but both the fact and the idea are "general knowledge": no one could name a *particular* person who "came up" with them. These details, therefore, can be worked into your paper without a citation. But if you mentioned that Darwin's famous illness was caused by the bite of a South American beetle, you would be benefiting from the work of a particular scholar, Saul Adler. To use this idea without mentioning Adler's name is to deprive him of due credit.

How do you know whether an idea or fact belongs to the body of general knowledge? When in doubt, see how the information is treated in standard reference sources, such as encyclopedias. Information that appears in an *unsigned* encyclopedia entry and is not attributed to a particular source is being treated by the editors as general knowledge. You may treat it the same way. Information in a *signed* magazine article may not be "general knowledge"; it may reflect original work by the author. But if two or three signed articles give the same information without naming a source, then you may consider it general knowledge. If you are unable to decide whether a piece of information is general knowledge, err on the side of courtesy and honesty: give credit to the source.

Taking Language from a Source. When you put the words of another writer into your paper, you owe that writer an acknowledgment, even if the idea expressed is commonplace. You must enclose the passage you take in quotation marks[1] *and* name the source. To give the name of the writer without the quotation marks would imply that you are paraphrasing (putting the idea into your own words). If the words are not yours, this constitutes a type of theft. Writing on the same subject as another writer, you will sometimes use identical phrasing for a few words at a stretch. But when the stretch exceeds four or six words, or when the organization of whole paragraphs is virtually identical and the verbal similarity strong, you can be accused of plagiarism.

---

[1] Quotation marks: If the quotation is more than four lines long, quotation marks are usually not used. Instead, the block of quotation is indented one inch from the left margin. See page 268 for an example.

Assignments
for Chapter 6

ASSIGNMENT 1: **WOMEN'S TALK VERSUS MEN'S TALK**

In a series of popular books, articles, and interviews during the late 1980s and early 1990s, linguist Deborah Tannen has claimed that there are distinct differences between the conversational styles of men and women. After acquainting yourself with Tannen's theory, test some aspect of it by systematic observation, keeping a field notebook like that described on pages 180–183. Then write an essay about one thousand words long in which you explain Tannen's theory and show how your observations confirm it or raise questions about it. Write for a general audience, as if you were a columnist for a newspaper or news magazine.

ASSIGNMENT 2: **GENDER AND CLASSROOM INTERACTION**

Studies conducted at various levels in the American educational system have suggested that teachers interact differently with male students than with female students, calling on male students more often in class, for instance, or asking them more probing follow-up questions. After locating and reading enough information about such studies to understand their methods and implications, conduct a study of your own by systematically recording interactions in one or more of your classes. Write an essay about one thousand words long discussing both your study and the issue in general. You may choose to write an essay appropriate for an audience of teachers or for a general audience.

ASSIGNMENT 3: **VIOLENCE IN THE SCHOOLS**

Violence in high schools continues to be a source of great concern to educators, parents, and students. Like many issues in education, however, it affects different schools very differently. After locating and reading enough information on the issue to give yourself a sense of the national picture, use surveys, interviews, or both to investigate local effects of school violence. You may want to concentrate on violence in a single school, in two contrasting schools, or in the schools of a single city. Use your reading and your field research to write an essay about one thousand words long on the subject. Your essay should be appropriate for publication in a local newspaper.

ASSIGNMENT 4:

SEX EDUCATION IN THE SCHOOLS

Partly because of the spread of AIDS, the role of American schools in sex education has expanded dramatically in the last decade, sometimes alarming citizens who feel that the school has no business usurping the family or church in this matter. Students who have been in high school during this period are in some ways in the best possible position to evaluate how much sex education is actually going on in the schools and what its effects are. Using surveys, interviews, or both with recent high school graduates, gather information and write an essay about one thousand words long evaluating the situation. You may choose to address your essay to a general audience (such as readers of a newspaper or magazine), to an audience associated with the educational system (such as high school principals), or to an audience alarmed by the expansion of sex education (such as members of a conservative religious group).

ASSIGNMENT 5:

EXPLICATING EDITORIAL CARTOONS

This assignment gives you an opportunity to practice a research-and-writing skill required in many college classes. Presented with a "text," the writer is asked to put it into a "context." In a history class, for instance, the text might be a speech by Abraham Lincoln, and the context might be the controversy over slavery in the Western territories. In an art class, the text might be a painting, and the context might be an artistic movement like expressionism or cubism.

Your mission in this assignment is to select one of the following cartoons and write an essay that (1) explains the historical situation the cartoon addresses and (2) explains the cartoonist's commentary on the situation. If you wish, you may also (3) evaluate the commentary briefly. The sample paper on pages 204–206 may help you see some possibilities.

Imagine, if you like, that the cartoon and your accompanying essay will appear in an album with the title *Events and Comments: What Editorial Cartoons Tell Us About Who We Were*. Assume that you are writing for an audience with the same level of general knowledge your classmates have. In some cases, you will need (for the sake of that audience) to discuss the historical subject at some length; in some cases you will want to spend most of your space helping your audience understand the cartoonist's attitude and showing that it is (or is not) representative of its period. Remember that your job goes beyond being "right" about the cartoon: your essay should become an interesting minilesson in the history of an era.

Writing the paper will involve you in some detective work. Look closely at the cartoon and its date for clues. You will find such simple indexes as *Infotrac,* the *Readers' Guide to Periodical Literature,* and the *New York Times Index* useful in locating background material. *Facts on File* and yearbooks published by such encyclopedias as *Britannica* and *World Book* may also be helpful. You should, of course, cite any sources you use—either informally, by listing them at the end, or formally, as the sample paper does. (See "Some General Notes on Citation Form," pp. 284–289).

Eight Cartoons for Explication

by John Chase. The John Chase Collection, Tulane University Library

John Chase, New Orleans Times-Picayune, *October, 1962*

Pat Oliphant, Denver Post, *April, 1968*

Craig MacIntosh, Minneapolis Star, *October, 1976*

Gene Basset, Scripps-Howard Newspapers, *June, 1978*

Paul Conrad, Los Angeles Times, *October, 1981*

Tony Auth, Philadelphia Inquirer, *March, 1987*

Signe Wilkinson, Philadelphia Daily News, *October, 1991*

Dana Summers, Orlando Sentinel, *September, 1992.*

Sample Essay
MAULDIN'S REDNECKS

In September of 1962, southwest Georgia was the center of the battle over desegregation. In the city of Albany, Martin Luther King, Jr., led a coalition of black and white clergymen in a series of highly publicized protests that local authorities answered with restraint ("Trouble" 47). On the outskirts of Albany, however, a Ku Klux Klan rally drew 4000 spectators to hear Imperial Wizard Robert M. Shelton declare, "We don't want no violence, but we ain't gonna let the niggers spit in our faces, either" ("School Bells" 31–32).

In rural areas outside the spotlight of the national media, violence was nearer the surface. In Terrell County, Georgia, a county in which 64% of the residents were black and 98% of the registered voters were white, the Student Non-violent Coordinating Committee (SNCC) was sponsoring a voter-registration drive for black citizens ("3 Shot" 22). Some whites resisted the drive with intimidation and violence.

"See you in church."

September 1962

by Bill Mauldin, reprinted with special permission of North American Syndicate

Sheriff Z. T. Mathews and his deputies "badgered and harassed" SNCC workers and black residents at a rally in July; and in August the Shady Grove Baptist Church, site of SNCC rallies, was destroyed by fire (Sitton, "Negro Churches" 21). On September 2 "night riders" fired several bullets into the home of a black family active in the voter-registration campaign in neighboring Lee County (Sitton, "Night Riders" 20), and on September 5, three shotgun blasts were fired into another Negro home, injuring two white college students and one black child ("3 Shot" 1). Before dawn on September 9, Mount Olive Baptist Church and Mount Mary Baptist Church, both of which had been used by SNCC as rallying points, were burned to the ground. Sheriff Mathews told reporters that he found no evidence of arson and that he did not believe that the burnings were associated with the registration drive. If arson was involved, he said, the cause was probably not the registration drive itself, but the outrage Terrell County residents felt when they saw white SNCC workers living in the same houses with blacks: "It's unusual for white folks to go down there living with niggers—pretty unusual. . . . The niggers are upset about it, too—the better niggers" (Sitton, "Night Riders" 1, 21).

These ugly events are the subject of Bill Mauldin's cartoon captioned "See you in church." In the cartoon Mauldin, drawing for the *Chicago Sun-Times*, expressed attitudes that were probably typical of the northern white liberals of the time. President Kennedy had called the burning of the churches "cowardly as well as outrageous" (Loftus 1), and Mauldin's cartoon seems to second this judgment and to add *benighted* and *hypocritical* to the list of adjectives. The crescent moon at the upper right reminds us that the church-bombers did their dirty work under cover of darkness. The portrayal of the two men passes a judgment on their state of civilization. Notice the clothing of the man on the left: the untied boots, the ill-fitting, beltless pants with a half-buttoned fly, the undershirt stretched by a potbelly, the battered hat. Only a person this backward, Mauldin seems to be saying, would be capable of such an act. That the men who are on their way to burn a church are themselves church-goers makes them hypocrites, or perhaps even something lower. A hypocrite is someone who consciously professes one set of values and acts on another, but the men Mauldin draws may not have self-consciousness enough to be hypocrites: they may not understand the contradiction between Christianity and violent repression.

Mauldin presents the episode in the framework of Southern backwardness and unconscious hypocrisy. His rural white Southerners are stereotyped to the point of being almost ape-like. Thirty-five years later, we can look at this cartoon and see the Northern stereotyping of white Southerners as unfair, almost as troubling as white stereotyping of blacks. But in the heat of the times, the advocates of civil rights needed an image of the enemy, and the stereotypical Southern redneck was an ideal target.

Works Cited

Loftus, Joseph A. "Kennedy Decries Church Burning in Racial Dispute." *New York Times* 14 Sept. 1962, late edition: 1.

Sitton, Claude. "Night Riders Fire on 4 Negro Homes." *New York Times* 1 Sept. 1962, late edition: 20.

--- "2 Negro Churches Burned in Georgia; F.B.I. Man Attacked." *New York Times* 10 Sept. 1962, late edition: 1, 21.

"Then School Bells Rang." *Newsweek* 17 Sept. 1962: 31–32.

"Trouble, Trouble." *Newsweek* 10 Sept. 1962: 47.

"3 Shot in Georgia by Night Riders." *New York Times* 6 Sept. 1962, late edition: 1, 22.

ASSIGNMENT 6: **EDITORIAL CARTOONS FROM THE PRESENT DAY**

Locate an editorial cartoon published within the last two months and write an essay that puts it into context. Since you are now dealing with a period fresh in the mind of your readers, you must be especially alert to your responsibility to tell them something new about the events or the cartoonist's interpretation of them. Because indexes like *Readers' Guide* and *Infotrac* can't be updated instantaneously, you may have to do much of your research without their assistance, scanning recent newspapers and magazines for pertinent information or using an on-line data service such as *Nexus*.

ASSIGNMENT 7:   ## POEMS IN THEIR HISTORICAL CONTEXT

Some poems, like editorial cartoons, comment on current events, personalities, or social circumstances. Choose one of the poems below and write an essay in which you explain both its historical context and the writer's interpretation of that context. Assume that since your audience will read the poem along with your commentary, you don't need to quote from it extensively but can easily refer to particular lines. Assume that your audience is about as knowledgeable about the events or conditions alluded to as your classmates are.

ELIZABETH BARRETT BROWNING

To George Sand: A Desire

Thou large-brained woman and large-hearted man,
Self-called George Sand! whose soul, amid the lions
Of thy tumultuous senses, moans defiance
And answers roar for roar, as spirits can:
I would some mild miraculous thunder ran
Above the applauded circus, in appliance
Of thine own nobler nature's strength and science,
Drawing two pinions, white as wings of swan,
With holier light! that thou to woman's claim
And man's mightst join beside the angel's grace
Of a pure genius sanctified from blame,
Till child and maiden pressed to thine embrace
To kiss upon thy lips a stainless fame.

1844

EDNA ST. VINCENT MILLAY

Justice Denied in Massachusetts

Let us abandon then our gardens and go home
And sit in the sitting-room.
Shall the larkspur blossom or the corn grow under this cloud?

Sour to the fruitful seed
Is the cold earth under this cloud,
Fostering quack and weed, we have marched upon but cannot conquer;
We have bent the blades of our hoes against the stalk of them.

Let us go home, and sit in the sitting-room.
Not in our day
Shall the cloud go over and the sun rise as before,
Beneficent upon us
Out of the glittering bay,
And the warm winds be blown inward from the sea
Moving the blades of corn
With a peaceful sound.
Forlorn, forlorn,
Stands the blue hay-rack by the empty mow.
And the petals drop to the ground,
Leaving the tree unfruited.
The sun that warmed our stooping backs and withered the weed
    uprooted—
We shall not feel it again.
We shall die in darkness, and be buried in the rain.

What from the splendid dead
We have inherited—
Furrows sweet to the grain, and the weed subdued—
See now the slug and the mildew plunder.
Evil does overwhelm
The larkspur and the corn;
We have seen them go under.

Let us sit here, sit still,
Here in the sitting-room until we die;
At the step of Death on the walk, rise and go;
Leaving to our children's children this beautiful doorway,
And this elm,
And a blighted earth to till
With a broken hoe.

                                                            1927

COUNTEE CULLEN

Scottsboro, Too, Is Worth Its Song
(A poem to American poets)

I said:
Now will the poets sing,—
Their cries go thundering

Like blood and tears
Into the nation's ears,
Like lightning dart
Into the nation's heart.
Against disease and death and all things fell,
And war,
Their strophes rise and swell
To jar
The foe smug in his citadel.

Remembering their sharp and pretty
Tune for Sacco and Vanzetti,
I said:
Here too's a cause divinely spun
For those whose eyes are on the sun,
Here in epitome
Is all disgrace
And epic wrong,
Like wine to brace
The minstrel heart, and blare it into song.

Surely, I said,
Now will the poets sing.
          But they have raised no cry.
          I wonder why.

                                                        1935

JOY DAVIDMAN [1]

Snow in Madrid

Softly, so casual
Lovely, so light, so light,
The cruel sky lets fall
Something one does not fight.

How tenderly to crown
The brutal year
The clouds send something down
That one need not fear.

Men before perishing
See with unwounded eye
For once a gentle thing
Fall from the sky.

                              1938

---

[1] From Joy Davidman, Letter to a Comrade, copyright © 1938. Reprinted by permission of the publisher, Yale University Press.

GWENDOLYN BROOKS

The Chicago Defender Sends a Man to Little Rock
Fall, 1957

In Little Rock the people bear
Babes and comb and part their hair
And watch the want ads, put repair
To roof and latch. While wheat toast burns
A woman waters multiferns.

Time upholds and overturns
The many, tight, and small concerns.

In Little Rock the people sing
Sunday hymns like anything,
Through Sunday pomp and polishing.

And after testament and tunes,
Some soften Sunday afternoons
With lemon tea and Lorna Doones.

I forecast
And I believe
Come Christmas Little Rock will cleave
To Christmas tree and trifle, weave,
From laugh and tinsel, texture fast.

In Little Rock is baseball; Barcarolle.
That hotness in July . . . the uniformed figures raw and implacable
And not intellectual,
Batting the hotness or clawing the suffering dust.
The Open Air Concert, on the special twilight green. . . .
When Beethoven is brutal or whispers to lady-like air.
Blanket-sitters are solemn, as Johann troubles to lean
To tell them what to mean. . . .

There is love, too, in Little Rock. Soft women softly
Opening themselves in kindness.
Or, pitying one's blindness,
Awaiting one's pleasure
In azure
Glory with anguished rose at the root. . . .
To wash away old semi-discomfitures.
They re-teach purple and unsullen blue.
The wispy soils go and certain
Half-havings have they clarified to sures.

In Little Rock they know
Not answering the telephone is a way of rejecting life,

That it is our business to be bothered, is our business
To cherish bores or boredom, be polite
To lies and love and many-faceted fuzziness.

I scratch my head, massage the hate-I-had.
I blink across my prim and pencilled pad.
The saga I was sent for is not down.
Because there is a puzzle in this town.
The biggest News I do not dare
Telegraph to the Editor's chair:
"They are like people everywhere."

The angry Editor would reply
In hundred harryings of Why.

And true, they are hurling spittle, rock,
Garbage and fruit in Little Rock.
And I saw coiling storm a-writhe
On bright madonnas. And a scythe
Of men harassing brownish girls.
(The bows and barrettes in the curls
And braids declined away from joy.)

I saw a bleeding brownish boy. . . .

The lariat lynch-wish I deplored.

The loveliest lynchee was our Lord.

1960

MARKET RESEARCH IN THE GENERAL STORE

Noel Perrin

Noel Perrin teaches English at Dartmouth College. He also ranches, farms, and writes essays for a variety of publications. He makes syrup from his own sugar maples, which accounts for his interest in researching Best Foods Company's claims about the virtues of a synthetic product called Golden Griddle.

1   ABOUT FIFTEEN MONTHS AGO, THE BEST Foods Company made a big splash with a series of TV ads about pancake syrup. They filmed the ads in Vermont. In them, native after native was shown tucking into two samples of pancake, and then saying that he or she preferred the one soaked in a Best Foods product called Golden Griddle to the one soaked in Vermont maple syrup.

2   These ads upset a lot of people in Vermont, including the Attorney General, who got an injunction against them. They also upset me. Because if Golden Griddle was really better, why was I working so hard every spring? Why was I hanging sap buckets, gathering, boiling, falling into snow drifts, when I could just as well be down working at a Best Foods factory in New Jersey? So I decided to check this matter out.

3   The first thing I did was to buy a bottle of Golden Griddle. That is, I bought a plastic container filled with a mixture of sugar, dextrose syrup, corn syrup, sodium benzoate, potassium sorbate, natural and artificial flavors, and caramel coloring. Plus 3% maple syrup. The next Sunday morning I had my wife serve me two identical pancakes, just as in the TV ads. One was covered with Golden Griddle and one with my own maple syrup.

4   I had no trouble telling them apart. The Golden Griddle had a nice color, and it's certainly sweet enough. But it had quite a perceptible chemical taste. I voted the maple syrup first by a wide margin. Then I gave the test to her and our daughters. Same results.

5   This was such fun that the following Sunday morning we decided to do it again. We invited two couples to breakfast, old friends who happen to be fellow sugarers. Four more votes for maple syrup. Maple syrup now ahead eight to nothing.

6   By now it looked pretty suspicious. How come all the Vermonters in the TV ads like Golden Griddle better, and all the ones we tried like maple syrup better? But before deciding that Best Foods was pulling a fast one, we decided to wait one more Sunday. This time we invited some other old friends—father, mother, and two teenage children—who must be something like eighth and ninth generation Vermonters. We were not expecting the result. Three votes for Golden Griddle, one for maple syrup.

7   The three who had picked Golden Griddle were pretty unhappy about it, being good Vermonters. Naturally we spent the rest of breakfast discussing what made them choose it, and doing more tasting. All three finally decided it

212

was because Golden Griddle has such a strong flavor.

8   At this point I developed a theory. As anyone who has read this far knows, maple syrup comes in three grades called Fancy, A, and B, with progressively stronger tastes. There's also a fourth variety, stronger still, which never appears in retail stores. Officially, it's called 'ungraded syrup,' but locally everyone calls it Grade C.

9   I had been using Fancy at the three Sunday breakfasts. What if I had used B or C? Would the father and the two kids in that family have still preferred Golden Griddle? I decided I would run a much bigger test, this time using two kinds of maple syrup as well as Golden Griddle. But first I would find out exactly what Best Foods had done, so I could compare my results to theirs as accurately as possible.

10   After quite a lot of writing and phoning, I learned that they had hired a New York market research company called Decisions Center, Inc., to come to Vermont and do the whole thing. Decisions Center had done a good and careful job. They spent three days testing 223 people, of whom 58% had preferred Golden Griddle, 40% had chosen maple syrup, and 2% hadn't been able to decide. And, sure enough, they had used a mild Grade A syrup from a big producer down in Windsor County. I know him. The only possibly sneaky thing in the whole operation was done by Best Foods itself, not the market researchers. The tests were given in a shopping center in the little industrial city of Springfield, Vermont. The people tested were naturally mostly from Springfield. But when it came time to make the folksy commercials, all these city people were taken over to Newfane, a picture-postcard village, so the background would look more rural and authentic. But that's probably normal advertising technique.

11   The first free day I had, I hustled down to Windsor County and bought a quart of the identical Grade A syrup they had used. Then I opened an old mayonnaise jar of my own Grade C, picked up the bottle of Golden Griddle, and set off for the shopping center in my town. That is, I walked over to the general store. All one morning, my daughter Amy and I sat at a table in the Village Store in Thetford Center and ran tests. Forty people tried our three samples. That represents everyone who came into the store that morning, except a few on diets and two who have diabetes.

12   What we found was fascinating. About a quarter of the human race have naturally good palates—or, at any rate, a quarter of the people in our test did. That is, about a quarter of the people we tested not only had a preference, but could identify the different syrups by taste. After the test they'd say Sample 1 is early-run maple, Sample 2 ain't maple syrup at all, and Sample 3 must be end of the season. They were right.

13   All nine people who could identify the samples put the Grade A first. All but one of them put the Golden Griddle last. They hated it. Elmer Brown, for example, who runs Brown's Nursery, and is a native of northern Vermont. The minute he tasted Sample 2, he looked at me accusingly and said, 'Why, Noel, that one's got Karo in it.'

14   Of the other 31, three liked the Grade A best, thirteen liked Grade C best, and fifteen liked Golden Griddle best. So my test results are as follows. One hundred per cent of the people with good palates preferred maple syrup, and so did 52% of the people without good palates.

15   But I don't see any great surprise in that. Why wouldn't they? Maple syrup is free from potassium sorbate and sodium benzoate; it has absolutely no synthetic smell. The important finding, as I see it, is that 90.3% of the people with untrained palates wanted a powerful flavor. Something really strong. What I interpret this to mean is that if you're a gourmet, it's well worth getting Fancy or Grade A maple syrup. Maybe even if you just *want* to be one.

But if you're not and don't care whether you ever are, you're wasting your money. Being a maple producer, I am hardly going to suggest that you therefore get Golden Griddle or Log Cabin or Vermont Maid (which seems actually to be made in Winston-Salem, North Carolina). Instead I suggest you get a good hearty grade B, and save $2 a gallon. Or since you won't find it in any store, write to some farmer and get a gallon of Grade C direct from him. It currently costs about $9 a gallon, which isn't all that much more than the supermarket stuff. Golden Griddle, Log Cabin, etc., if you ever bought a whole gallon at once, would run you between $6.50 and $7.50.

You don't know a farmer to write? I know lots, and I have an obliging publisher. If you write me care of him, I will undertake to pass orders on. For Fancy, A, B, or C. After all, I'm not plugging my own syrup. What with those tests and my regular customers, not to mention making 300 maple sugar hearts for our village fair last summer,[1] I'm sold out. ♦

16

---

[1] Maple sugar hearts: I made them out of the rest of my Grade C. Personally, I wouldn't dream of putting C on pancakes. As syrup, I only like Fancy, A, and B. [author's note]

LET US NOW APPRAISE FAMOUS WRITERS

Jessica Mitford

Jessica Mitford's "Let Us Now Appraise Famous Writers," first published in the *Atlantic Monthly* in 1970, has become a minor classic in the world of investigative reporting. To appreciate the skill, humor, and importance of the piece, you need to have a sense of the status of the authors who became associated with the Famous Writers School, a learn-by-mail "college" that was advertising heavily in several major magazines: Paul Engle, one of the fifteen "famous writers" on the faculty, was the winner of prestigious poetry prizes and the founder of the University of Iowa's internationally famous Writers' Workshop. Rod Serling was an award-winning screenwriter and the creative force behind *The Twilight Zone,* one of America's most successful television series. Red Smith was the dean of American sportswriters. Bennet Cerf was president of the publishing firm Random House and was a household name because of his appearances on the game show "What's My Line?" Yet somehow, the advertisements implied, these men and their equally famous colleagues would take time to read and comment on the work of anyone who passed the "talent test" and paid the considerable tuition. Mitford, famous herself for a book exposing abuses in the funeral industry, smelled a rat and used her formidable skills as a researcher to expose it.

Beware of the scribes who like to go about in long robes, and love salutations in the market-places . . . and the places of honor at feasts; who devour widows' houses . . .

LUKE 20:46, 47

IN RECENT YEARS I HAVE BECOME AWARE OF fifteen Famous Faces looking me straight in the eye from the pages of innumerable magazines, newspapers, fold-out advertisements, sometimes in black-and-white, sometimes in living color, sometimes posed in a group around a table, sometimes shown singly, pipe in hand in book-lined study or strolling through a woodsy countryside: the Guiding Faculty of the Famous Writers School.[1]

Here is Bennett Cerf, most famous of them all, his kindly, humorous face aglow with sincerity, speaking to us in the first person from a mini-billboard tucked into our Sunday newspaper: "If you want to write, my colleagues and I would like to test your writing aptitude. We'll help you find out whether you can be trained to become a successful writer." And Faith Baldwin, looking up from her typewriter with an expression of ardent concern for that vast, unfulfilled sisterhood of nonwriters: "It's a shame more women don't take up writing. Writing can be an ideal profession for women. . . . Beyond the thrill of that first sale, writing brings intangible rewards." J. D. Ratcliff, billed in the ads as "one of America's highest-paid freelance authors," thinks it's a shame, too: "I can't understand why more beginners don't take the short road to publication by writing articles for magazines and newspapers. It's a wonderful life."

The short road is attained, the ads imply, via the aptitude test which Bennett Cerf and

---

[1] Guiding Faculty of the Famous Writers School: They are: Faith Baldwin, John Caples, Bruce Catton, Bennett Cerf, Mignon G. Eberhart, Paul Engle, Bergen Evans, Clifton Fadiman, Rudolf Flesch, Phyllis McGinley, J. D. Ratcliff, Rod Serling, Max Shulman, Red Smith, Mark Wiseman. [author's note]

his colleagues would like you to take so they may "grade it free of charge." If you are one of the fortunate ones who do well on the test, you may "enroll for professional training." After that, your future is virtually assured, for the ads promise that "Fifteen Famous Writers will teach you to write successfully at home."

4   These offers are motivated, the ads make clear, by a degree of altruism not often found in those at the top of the ladder. The Fifteen have never forgotten the tough times—the "sheer blood, sweat and rejections slips," as J. D. Ratcliff puts it—through which they suffered as beginning writers; and now they want to extend a helping hand to those still at the bottom rung. "When I look back, I can't help thinking of all the time and agony I would have saved if I could have found a real 'pro' to work with me," says Ratcliff.

5   How can Bennett Cerf—Chairman of the Board of Random House, columnist, television personality—and his renowned colleagues find time to grade all the thousands of aptitude tests that must come pouring in, and on top of that fulfill their pledge to "teach you to write successfully at home"? What are the standards for admission to the school? How many graduates actually find their way into the "huge market that will pay well for pieces of almost any length" which, says J. D. Ratcliff, exists for the beginning writer? What are the "secrets of success" that the Famous Fifteen say they have "poured into a set of specially created textbooks"? And how much does it cost to be initiated into these secrets?

6   My mild curiosity about these matters might never have been satisfied had I not learned, coincidentally, about two candidates for the professional training offered by the Famous Writers who passed the aptitude test with flying colors: a seventy-two-year-old foreign-born widow living on Social Security, and a fictitious character named Louella Mae Burns.

7   The adventures of these two impelled me to talk with Bennett Cerf and other members of the Guiding Faculty, to interview former students, to examine the "set of specially created textbooks" (and the annual stockholders' reports, which proved in some ways more instructive), and eventually to visit the school's headquarters in Westport, Connecticut.

8   An Oakland lawyer told me about the seventy-two-year-old widow. She had come to him in some distress: a salesman had charmed his way into her home and at the end of his sales pitch had relieved her of $200 (her entire bank account) as down payment on a $900 contract, the balance of which would be paid off in monthly installments. A familiar story, for like all urban communities ours is fertile ground for roving commission salesmen skilled in unloading on the unwary housewife anything from vacuum cleaners to deep freezers to encyclopedias to grave plots, at vastly inflated prices. The unusual aspect of this old lady's tale was the merchandise she had been sold. No sooner had the salesman left than she thought better of it, and when the lessons arrived she returned them unopened.

9   To her pleas to be released from the contract, the Famous Writers replied: "Please understand that you are involved in a legal and binding contract," and added that the school's policy requires a doctor's certificate attesting to the ill health of a student before she is permitted to withdraw.

10   There was a short, sharp struggle. The lawyer wrote an angry letter to the school demanding prompt return of the $200 "fraudulently taken" from the widow, and got an equally stiff refusal in reply. He then asked the old lady to write out in her own words a description of the salesman's visit. She produced a garbled, semiliterate account, which he forwarded to the school with the comment, "This is the lady whom your salesman found to be 'very qualified' to take your writing course. I wonder if Mr. Cerf is aware of the cruel deceptions to which he lends his name?" At the bottom of his letter, the lawyer wrote

the magic words "Carbon copies to Bennett Cerf and to Consumer Fraud Division, U.S. Attorney's Office." Presto! The school suddenly caved in and returned the money in full.

11   Louella Mae Burns, the other successful candidate, is the brainchild of Robert Byrne and his wife. I met her in the pages of Byrne's informative and often hilarious book *Writing Rackets* (Lyle Stuart, 1969, $3.95), which treats of the lures held out to would-be writers by high-priced correspondence schools, phony agents who demand a fee for reading manuscripts, the "vanity" presses that will publish your book for a price.

12   Mrs. Byrne set out to discover at how low a level of talent one might be accepted as a candidate for "professional training" by the Famous Writers. Assuming the personality of a sixty-three-year-old widow of little education, she tackled the aptitude test.

13   The crux of the test is the essay, in which the applicant is invited to "tell of an experience you have had at some time in your life." Here Louella Mae outdid herself: "I think I can truthfully say to the best of my knowledge that the following is truly the most arresting experience I have ever undergone. My husband, Fred, and I, had only been married but a short time. . . ." Continuing in this vein, she describes, "one beautiful cloudless day in springtime" and "a flock of people who started merging along the sidewalk . . . When out of the blue came a honking and cars and motorcycles and policemen. It was really something! Everybody started shouting and waving and we finally essayed to see the reason of all this. In a sleek black limousine we saw real close Mr. Calvin Coolidge, the President Himself! It was truly an unforgettable experience and one which I shall surely long remember."

14   The effort drew a two-and-a-half-page typewritten letter from Donald T. Clark, registrar of Famous Writers School, which read in part: "Dear Mrs. Burns, Congratulations! The enclosed Test unquestionably qualifies you for enrollment . . . only a fraction of our students receive higher grades. . . . In our opinion, you have a basic writing aptitude which justifies professional training." And the clincher: "You couldn't consider breaking into writing at a better time than today. Everything indicates that the demand for good prose is growing much faster than the supply of trained talent. Just consider how a single article can cause a magazine's newsstand sales to soar; how a novel can bring hundreds of thousands in movie rights. . . ."

15   There is something spooky about this exchange, for I later found out that letters to successful applicants are written not by a "registrar" but by copywriters in the Madison Avenue office of the school's advertising department. Here we have Donald T. Clark's ghost writer in earnest correspondence with ghost Louella Mae Burns.

16   Perhaps these two applicants are not typical of the student body. What of students who show genuine promise, those capable of "mastering the basic skills" and achieving a level of professional competence? Will they, as the school suggests, find their way into "glamorous careers" and be "launched on a secure future" as writers?

17   Robert Byrne gives a gloomy account of the true state of the market for "good prose" and "trained talent." He says that of all lines of work free-lance writing is one of the most precarious and worst paid (as who should know better than Bennett Cerf & Co.?). He cites a survey of the country's top twenty-six magazines. Of 79,812 unsolicited article manuscripts, fewer than a thousand were accepted. Unsolicited fiction manuscripts fared far worse. Of 182,505 submitted, only 560 were accepted. Furthermore, a study based on the earnings of established writers, members of the Authors League with published books to their credit, shows that the average free-lance earns just over $3,000 a year—an income which, Byrne points out, "very nearly qualifies him for emergency welfare assistance."

18   What have the Famous Fifteen to say for themselves about all this? Precious little, it turns out. Most of those with whom I spoke were quick to disavow any responsibility for the school's day-to-day operating methods and were unable to answer the most rudimentary questions: qualifications for admission, teacher-student ratio, cost of the course. They seemed astonished, even pained, to think people might be naïve enough to take the advertising at face value.

19   "If anyone thinks we've got time to look at the aptitude tests that come in, they're out of their mind!" said Bennett Cerf. And Phyllis McGinley: "I'm only a figurehead. I thought a person had to be qualified to take the course, but since I never see any of the applications or the lessons, I don't know. Of course, somebody with a real gift for writing wouldn't have to be taught to write."

20   One of the FWS brochures says, "On a short story or novel you have at hand the professional counsel of Faith Baldwin . . . all these eminent authors in effect are looking over your shoulder as you learn." Doesn't that mean in plain English, I asked Miss Baldwin, that she will personally counsel students? "Oh, that's just one of those things about advertising; most advertisements are somewhat misleading," she replied. "Anyone with common sense would know that the fifteen of us are much too busy to read the manuscripts the students sent in."

21   Famous Writer Mark Wiseman, himself an ad man, explained the alluring promises of "financial success and independence," the "secure future as a writer" held out in the school's advertising. "That's just a fault of our civilization," he said. "You have to overpersuade people, make it all look optimistic, not men-

---

OBJECT LESSON

"Every writer worth his salt develops, after a time, his own style."
—Faith Baldwin, *Principles of Good Writing*, FWS textbook.

But famous writers write alike:

If you want to write, my colleagues and I would like to test your writing aptitude. We'll help you find out if you can be trained to become a successful writer. We know that many men and women who could become writers—and *should* become writers—never do. Some are uncertain of their talent and have no reliable way of finding out if it's worth developing. Others simply can't get topnotch professional training without leaving their homes or giving up their jobs.

by Faith Baldwin

If you want to write and see your work published, my colleagues and I would like to test your writing aptitude. We'll help you find out whether you can be trained to become a successful writer.

We know that many men and women who could become writers—and *should* become writers—never do. Some are uncertain of their talent and have no reliable way of finding out if it's worth developing. Others simply can't get topnotch professional training without leaving their homes or giving up their jobs.

by Bennett Cerf

(Reprinted from postcard inserts circulated in millions of paperback books.)

tion obstacles and hurdles. That's true of all advertising." Why does the school send out fleets of salesmen instead of handling all applications by mail? "If we didn't have salesmen, not nearly as many sales would be made. It's impossible, you see, to explain it all by mail, or answer questions people may have about the course." (It seems strange that while the school is able to impart the techniques requisite to become a best-selling author by mail, it cannot explain the details of its course to prospects and answer their questions in the same fashion; but perhaps that is just another fault of our civilization.)

22   Professor Paul Engle, a poet who directed the Writers' Workshop at the University of Iowa, is the only professional educator among the fifteen. But like his colleagues he pleads ignorance of the basics. The school's admissions policy, its teaching methods and selling techniques are a closed book to him. "I'm the least informed of all people," he said. "I only go there once in a great while. There's a distinction between the *Guiding* Faculty, which doesn't do very much, and the *Teaching* Faculty, which actually works with the students— who've spent really quite a lot of money on the course!" Professor Engle has only met once with the Guiding Faculty, to pose for a publicity photograph: "It was no meeting in the sense of gathering for the exchange of useful ideas. But I think the school is not so much interested in the work done by the Guiding Faculty as in the prestige of the names. When Bennett Cerf was on *What's My Line?* his name was a household word!"

23   How did Professor Engle become a member of the Guiding Faculty in the first place? "That fascinated *me!*" he said. I got a letter from a man named Gordon Carroll, asking me to come to Westport the next time I was in New York. So I did go and see him. He asked me if I would join the Guiding Facuty. I said, 'What do I guide?' We talked awhile, and I said well it seems all right, so I signed on." How could

it come about that the Oakland widow and Louella Mae Burns were judged "highly qualified" to enroll? "I'm not trying to weasel out, or evade your questions, but I'm so very far away from all that."

24   Bennett Cerf received me most cordially in his wonderfully posh office at Random House. Each of us was (I think, in retrospect) bent on putting the other thoroughly at ease. "May I call you Jessica?" he said at one point. "I don't see why not, *Mortuary Management* always does." We had a good laugh over that. He told me that the school was first organized in the late fifties (it opened for business in February, 1961) as an offshoot of the immensely profitable Famous Artists correspondence school, after which it was closely modeled. Prime movers in recruiting Famous Writers for the Guiding Faculty were the late Albert Dorne, an illustrator and president of Famous Artists; Gordon Carroll, sometime editor of *Coronet* and *Reader's Digest;* and Mr. Cerf. "We approached representative writers, the best we could get in each field: fiction, advertising, sportswriting, television. The idea was to give the school some prestige."

25   Like his colleagues on the Guiding Faculty, Mr. Cerf does no teaching, takes no hand in recruiting instructors or establishing standards for the teaching program, does not pass on advertising copy except that which purports to quote him, does not supervise the school's business practices: "I know *nothing* about the business and selling end and I care *less*. I've nothing to do with how the school is run, I can't put that too strongly to you. But it's been run extremely cleanly. I mean that from my heart, Jessica." What, then, is his guiding role? "I go up there once or twice a year to talk to the staff." The Guiding Faculty, he said, helped to write the original textbooks. His own contribution to these was a section on how to prepare a manuscript for publication: "I spent about a week talking into a tape machine about how a manuscript is turned into a

book—practical advice about double-spacing the typescript, how it is turned into galleys, through every stage until publication." How many books by FWS students has Random House published? "Oh, come on, you must be pulling my leg—no person of any sophistication whose book we'd publish would have to take a mail order course to learn how to write."

26   However, the school does serve an extremely valuable purpose, he said, in teaching history professors, chemistry professors, lawyers, and businessmen to write intelligibly. I was curious to know why a professor would take a correspondence course in preference to writing classes available in the English Department of his own university—who are all these professors? Mr. Cerf did not know their names, nor at which colleges they were presently teaching.

27   While Mr. Cerf is by no means uncritical of some aspects of mail order selling, he philosophically accepts them as inevitable in the cold-blooded world of big business—so different, one gathers, from his own cultured world of letters. "I think mail order selling has several built-in deficiencies," he said. "The crux of it is a very hard sales pitch, an appeal to the gullible. Of course, once somebody has signed a contract with Famous Writers he can't get out of it, but that's true with every business in the country." Noticing that I was writing this down, he said in alarm, "For God's sake, don't quote me on that 'gullible' business—you'll have all the mail order houses in the country down on my neck!" "Then would you like to paraphrase it?" I asked, suddenly getting very firm. "Well—you could say in general I don't like the hard sell, yet it's the basis of all American business." "Sorry, I don't call that a paraphrase, I shall have to use both of them," I said in a positively governessy tone of voice. "Anyway, why do you lend your name to this hard-sell proposition?" Bennett Cerf (with his melting grin): "Frankly, if you must know, I'm an awful ham—I love to see my name in the papers!"

28   On the delicate question of their compensation, the Famous ones are understandably reticent. "That's a private matter," Bennett Cerf said, "but it's quite generous and we were given stock in the company, which has enhanced a great deal." I asked Phyllis McGinley about a report in *Business Week* some years ago that in addition to their substantial stock holdings each member of the Guiding Faculty receives 1.6 percent of the school's annual gross revenue, which then amounted to $4,400 apiece. "Oh? Well, I may have a price on my soul, but it's not *that* low, we get a lot more than that!" she answered gaily.

29   With one accord the Famous Writers urged me to seek answers to questions about advertising policy, enrollment figures, costs, and the like from the director of the school, Mr. John Lawrence, former president of William Morrow publishing company. Mr. Lawrence invited me to Westport so that I could see the school in operation, and meet Mr. Gordon Carroll, who is now serving as director of International Famous Writers schools.

30   The Famous Schools are housed in a row of boxlike buildings at the edge of Westport ("It's Westport's leading industry," a former resident told me), which look from the outside like a small modern factory. Inside, everything reflects expansion and progress. The spacious reception rooms are decorated with the works of Famous Artists, the parent school, and Famous Photographers, organized in 1964.

31   The success story, and something of the *modus operandi*,[2] can be read at a glance in the annual shareholders' reports and the daily stock market quotations. (The schools have gone public and are now listed on the New York Stock Exchange as FAS International.)

32   Tuition revenue for the schools zoomed from $7,000,000 in 1960 to $48,000,000 in

—————

[2] **modus operandi:** method of working.

1968. During this period, the price per share of common stock rose from $5 to $40. (It has fallen sharply, however, in recent months.)

33   The schools' interest in selling as compared with teaching is reflected more accurately in the corporate balance sheets than in the brochures sent to prospective students. In 1966 (the last time this revealing breakdown was given), when total tuition revenue was $28,000,000, $10,800,000 was spent on "advertising and selling" compared with $4,800,000 on "cost of grading and materials."

34   The Famous Schools have picked up many another property along the way: they now own the Evelyn Wood Speed Reading Course, Welcome Wagon, International Accountants Society (also a correspondence school), Linguaphone Institute, Computer College Selection Service. Their empire extends to Japan, Australia, Sweden, France, Germany, Switzerland, Austria. An invasion of Great Britain is planned (the report warns) as soon as the English prove themselves worthy of it by stabilizing the currency situation. In the "market testing stage" are plans for a Famous Musicians School, Business Courses for Women, a Writing for Young Readers Course.

35   Summarizing these accomplishments, the shareholders' report states: "We are in the vanguard of education throughout the world, the acknowledged leader in independent study and an innovator in all types of learning. We will continue to think boldly, to act with wisdom and daring, to be simultaneously visionary and effective." The schools, mindful of "the deepening of the worldwide crisis in education," are casting predatory looks in the direction of "the total educational establishment, both academic and industrial." The shareholders' report observes sententiously, "As grave times produce great men to cope with them, so do they produce great ideas."

36   From Messrs. Lawrence and Carroll I learned these salient facts about Famous Writers School:

37   The cost of the course (never mentioned in the advertising, nor in the letters to successful applicants, revealed only by the salesman at the point where the prospect is ready to sign the contract): $785, if the student makes a one-time payment. But only about 10 percent pay in a lump sum. The cost to the 90 percent who make time payments, including interest, is about $900, or roughly twenty times the cost of extension and correspondence courses offered by universities.

38   Current enrollment is 65,000, of which three-quarters are enrolled in the fiction course, the balance in nonfiction, advertising, business writing. Almost 2,000 veterans are taking the course at the taxpayers' expense through the GI Bill. Teaching faculty: 55, for a ratio of $1,181\frac{4}{5}$ students per instructor.

39   There are 800 salesmen deployed throughout the country (for a ratio of $14\frac{3}{5}$ salesmen for every instructor) working on a straight commission basis. I asked about the salemen's kits: might I have one? "You'd need a dray horse to carry it!" Mr. Carroll assured me. He added that they are currently experimenting with a movie of the school, prepared by Famous Writer Rod Serling, to show in prospects' homes.

40   I was surprised to learn that despite the fact the schools are accredited by such public agencies as the Veterans Administration and the National Home Study Council, they preserve considerable secrecy about some sectors of their operation. Included in the "confidential" category, which school personnel told me could not be divulged, are:

The amount of commission paid to salesmen.

Breakdown of the $22,000,000 "sales and advertising" item in the shareholders' report as between sales commissions and advertising budget.

Breakdown of the $48,000,000 income from tuition fees as between Writers, Artists, Photographers.

Terms of the schools' contract with Guiding Faculty members.

41   If Bennett Cerf and his colleagues haven't time to grade the aptitude tests, who has? Their stand-ins are two full-timers and some forty pieceworkers, mostly housewives, who "help you find out whether you can be trained to become a successful writer" in the privacy of their homes. There are no standards for admission to FWS, one of the full-timers explained. "It's not the same thing as a grade on a college theme. The test is designed to indicate your *potential* as a writer, not your present ability." Only about 10 percent of the applicants are advised they lack this "potential," and are rejected.

42   The instructors guide the students from cheerful little cubicles equipped with machines into which they dictate the "two-page letter of criticism and advice" promised in the advertising. They are, Gordon Carroll told me, former free-lance writers and people with editorial background: "We never hire professional teachers, they're too *dull!* Deadly dull. Ph.D.s are the worst of all!" (Conversely, a trained teacher accustomed to all that the classroom offers might find an unrelieved diet of FWS students' manuscripts somewhat monotonous.) The annual starting salary for instructors is $8,500 for a seven-hour day, something of a comedown from the affluent and glamorous life dangled before their students in the school's advertising.

43   As I watched the instructors at work, I detected a generous inclination to accentuate the positive in the material submitted. Given an assignment to describe a period in time, a student had chosen 1933. Her first paragraph, about the election of F.D.R. and the economic situation in the country, could have been copied out of any almanac. She had followed this with "There were breadlines everywhere." I watched the instructor underline the breadlines in red, and write in the margin: "Good work,

Mrs. Smith! It's a pleasure working with you. You have recaptured the atmosphere of those days."

44   Although the key to the school's financial success is its huge dropout rate ("We couldn't make any money if all the students finished," Famous Writer Phyllis McGinley had told me in her candid fashion), the precise percentage of dropouts is hard to come by. "I don't know exactly what it is, or where to get the figures," said Mr. Lawrence. "The last time we analyzed it, it related to the national figure for high-school and college dropouts, let's say about two-thirds of the enrollments."

45   However, according to my arithmetic based on figures furnished by the school, the dropout rate must be closer to 90 percent. Each student is supposed to send in 24 assignments over a three-year period, an average of 8 a year. With 65,000 enrolled, this would amount to more than half a million lessons a year, and the 55 instructors would have to race along correcting these at a clip of one every few minutes. But in fact (the instructors assured me) they spend an hour or more on each lesson, and grade a total of only about 50,000 a year. What happens to the other 470,000 lessons? "That's baffling," said Mr. Carroll. "I guess you can take a horse to water, but you can't make him drink."

46   These balky nags are, however, legally bound by the contract whether or not they ever crack a textbook or send in an assignment. What happens to the defaulter who refuses to pay? Are many taken to court? "None," said Mr. Lawrence. "It's against our policy to sue in court." Why, if the school considers the contract legally binding? "Well— there's a question of morality involved. You'd hardly take a person to court for failing to complete a correspondence course."

47   Mrs. Virginia Knauer, the President's Assistant for Consumer Affairs, with whom I discussed this later, suspects there is another question involved. "The Famous Writers would never win in court," she said indig-

nantly. "A lawsuit would expose them—somebody should take *them* to court. Their advertising is reprehensible, it's very close to being misleading." Needless to say, the debtors are not informed of the school's moral scruples against lawsuits. On the contrary, a Finnish immigrant, whose husband complained to Mrs. Knauer that although she speaks little English she had been coerced into signing for the course by an importunate salesman, was bombarded with dunning letters and telegrams full of implied threats to sue.

48   A fanciful idea occurred to me: since the school avers that it does not sue delinquents, I could make a fortune by advertising in the literary monthlies: For $10 I will tell you how to take the Famous Writers' course for nothing." To those who sent in their ten dollars, I would return a postcard saying merely, "Enroll in the course and make no payments." I tried this out on Mr. Carroll, and subsequently on Bennett Cerf. Their reaction were identical. "You'd find yourself behind bars if you did that!" "Why? Whom would I have defrauded?" A question they were unable to answer, although Bennett Cerf, in mock horror, declared that the inventive mail order industry would certainly find *some* legal means to frustrate my iniquitous plan.

49   Both Mr. Lawrence and Mr. Carroll were unhappy about the case of the seventy-two-year-old widow when I told them about it—it had not previously come to their attention. It was an unfortunate and unusual occurrence, they assured me, one of those slip-ups that may happen from time to time in any large corporation.

50   On the whole, they said, FWS salesmen are very carefully screened; only one applicant in ten is accepted. They receive a rigorous training in ethical salesmanship; every effort is made to see that they do not "oversell" the course or stray from the truth in their home presentation.

51   Eventually I had the opportunity to observe the presentation in the home of a neighbor who conjured up a salesman for me by sending in the aptitude test. A few days after she had mailed it in, my neighbor got a printed form letter (undated) saying that a field representative of the school would be in the area next week for a very short while and asking her to specify a convenient time when he might telephone for an appointment. There was something a little fuzzy around the edges here—for she had not yet heard from the school about her test—but she let that pass.

52   The "field representative" (like the cemetery industry, the Famous Writers avoid the term "salesman") when he arrived had a ready explanation: the school had telephoned to notify him that my neighbor had passed the test, and to tell him that luckily for her there were "a few openings still left in this enrollment period"—it might be months before this opportunity came again!

53   The fantasy he spun for us, which far outstripped anything in the advertising, would have done credit to the school's fiction course.

54   Pressed for facts and figures, he told us that two or three of the Famous Fifteen are in Westport at all times working with "a staff of forty or fifty experts in their specialty" evaluating and correcting student manuscripts. . . . Your Guiding Faculty member, could be Bennett Cerf, could be Rod Serling depending on your subject, will review at least one of your manuscripts, and may suggest a publisher for it. . . . There are 300 instructors for 3,000 students ("You mean, one teacher for every ten students?" I asked. "That's correct, it's a ratio unexcelled by any college in the country," said the field representative without batting an eye). . . . Hundreds of university professors are currently enrolled . . . 75 percent of the students publish in their first year, and the majority more than pay for the course through their sales. . . . There are very few dropouts because only serious, qualified applicants (like my neighbor) are permitted to enroll. . . .

55   During his two-hour discourse, he casually mentioned three books recently published by students he personally enrolled—one is already being made into a movie! "Do tell us the names, so we can order them?" But he couldn't remember, offhand: "I get so darn many announcements of books published by our students."

56   Oh, clean-cut young man, does your mother know how you earn your living? (And, Famous Fifteen, do yours?)

57   The course itself is packaged for maximum eye-appeal in four hefty "two-toned, buckram-bound" volumes with matching loose-leaf binders for the lessons. The texbooks contain all sorts of curious and disconnected matter: examples of advertisements that "pull"; right and wrong ways of ending business letters; paragraphs from the *Saturday Evening Post, This Week, Reader's Digest;* quotations from successful writers like William Shakespeare, Faith Baldwin, Mark Twain, Mark Wiseman, Winston Churchill, Red Smith; and elementary grammar lesson ("*Verbs* are action words. A *noun* is the name of a person, place or thing"); a glossary of commonly misspelled words; a standard list of printer's proof-marking symbols.

58   There is many a homespun suggestion for the would-be Famous Writer on what to write about, how to start writing: "Writing ideas—ready-made aids for the writer—are available everywhere. In every waking hour you hear and see and feel. . . ." "How do you get started on a piece of writing? One successful author writes down the word 'The' the moment he gets to the typewriter in the morning. He follows 'The' with another word, then another. . . ." (But the text writer, ignoring his own good advice, starts a sentence with "As," and trips himself in an imparsable sentence: "As with so many professional writers, Marjorie Holmes keeps a notebook handy. . . .)

59   Throughout the course the illusion is fostered that the student is, or soon will be, writing for publication: "Suppose you're sitting in the office of a magazine editor discussing an assignment for next month's issue. . . ." The set of books includes a volume entitled "How to Turn Your Writing Into Dollars," which winds up on a triumphal note with a sample publisher's contract and a sample agreement with a Hollywood agent.

60   In short, there is really nothing useful in these books that could not be found in any number of writing and style manuals, grammar texts, marketing guides, free for the asking in the public library.

61   Thrown in as part of the $785–$900 course is a "free" subscription to *Famous Writers* magazine, a quarterly in which stories written by students appear under this hyperbolic caption: "Writers Worth Watching: In this section, magazine editors and book publishers can appraise the quality of work being done by FWS students." According to the school's literature, "Each issue of the magazine is received and read by some 2,000 editors, publishers and other key figures in the writing world." However, Messrs. Carroll and Lawrence were unable to enlighten me about these key figures—who they are, how it is known that they read each issue, whether they have ever bought manuscripts from students after appraising the quality of their work.

62   The student sales department of the magazine is also worth watching. Presumably the school puts its best foot forward here, yet the total of all success stories recorded therein each year is only about thirty-five, heavily weighted in the direction of small denominational magazines, local newspapers, pet-lovers' journals, and the like. Once in a while a student strikes it rich with a sale to *Reader's Digest, Redbook, McCall's,* generally in "discovery" departments of these magazines that specifically solicit first-person anecdotes by their readers as distinct from professional writers: Most Unforgettable Character, Turning-Point, Suddenly It Happens to You.

63   The school gets enormous mileage out of

these few student sales. The same old successful students turn up time and again in the promotional literature. Thus an ad in the January 4, 1970, issue of *The New York Times* Magazine features seven testimonials: "I've just received a big, beautiful check from the *Reader's Digest.* . . ." "I've just received good news and a check from *Ellery Queen's Mystery Magazine.* . . ." "Recently, I've sold three more articles. . . ." How recently? Checking back through old copies of *Famous Writers* magazine, I found the latest of these success stories had appeared in the student sales department of a 1968 issue; the rest had been lifted from issues of 1964 and 1965.

64   As for the quality of individual instruction, the reactions of several former FWS students with whom I spoke varied. Only one—a "success story" lady featured in FWS advertising who has published four juvenile books—expressed unqualified enthusiasm. Two other successes of yesteryear, featured in the school's 1970 ad, said they had never finished the course and had published nothing since 1965.

65   A FWS graduate who had completed the entire course (and has not, to date, sold any of her stories) echoed the views of many: "It's tremendously overblown, there's a lot of busywork, unnecessary padding to make you think you're getting your money's worth. One peculiar thing is you get a different instructor for each assignment, so there's not much of the 'personal attention' promised in the brochures." However, she added, "I have to be fair. It did get me started, and it did make me keep writing."

66   I showed some corrected lessons that fell into my hands to an English professor. One assignment: "To inject new life and color and dimension into a simple declarative sentence." From the sentence "The cat washed its paws," the student had fashioned this: "With fastidious fussiness, the cat flicked his pink tongue over his paws, laying the fur down neatly and symmetrically." The instructor had crossed out "cat" and substituted "the burly gray tomcat." With fastidious fussiness, the lanky, tweed-suited English professor clutched at his balding, pink pate and emitted a low, agonized groan of bleak, undisguised despair: "Exactly the sort of wordy stuff we try to get students to *avoid.*"

67   The staggering dropout rate cannot, I was soon convinced, be laid entirely at the door of rapacious salesmen who sign up semiliterates and other incompetents. Many of those who told me of their experience with the school are articulate, intelligent people, manifestly capable of disciplined self-study that could help them to improve their prose style. Why should adults of sound mind and resolute purpose first enroll in FWS and then throw away their substantial investment? One letter goes far to explain:

My husband and I bought the course for two main reasons. The first was that we were in the boondocks of Arkansas and we truly felt that the Famous Writers School under the sponsorship of Bennett Cerf etc. was new in concept and would have more to offer than other courses we had seen advertised. The second was the fact that we had a definite project in mind: a fictionalized account of our experiences in the American labor movement.

I guess the worst part of our experience was the realization that the school could not live up to its advertised promise. It is in the area of the assignments and criticism that the course falls down. Because you get a different instructor each time, there is no continuity. This results in the student failing to get any understanding of story and structure from the very beginning.

My husband completed about eight assignments, but felt so intensely frustrated with the course that he could not go on. He couldn't get any satisfaction from the criticism.

While the school is careful to advise that no one can teach writing talent they constantly encourage their students towards a belief in a market that doesn't exist for beginning writers. For us, it was an expensive and disappointing experience.

68   The phenomenal success of FWS in attracting students (if not in holding them) does point to an undeniable yearning on the part of large numbers of people not only to see their work published, but also for the sort of self-improvement the school purports to offer. As Robert Byrne points out, what can be learned about writing from a writing course can be of great value in many areas of life, "from love letters to suicide notes." For shut-ins, people living in remote rural areas, and others unable to get classroom instruction, correspondence courses may provide the only opportunity for supervised study.

69   Recognizing the need, some fifteen state universities offer correspondence courses that seem to me superior to the Famous Writers course for a fraction of the cost. True, the universities neither package nor push their courses, they provide no handsome buckram-bound two-tone loose-leaf binders, no matching textbooks, no sample Hollywood contract.

70   Unobtrusively tucked away in the *Lifelong Learning* bulletin of the University of California Extension at Berkeley are two such offerings: Magazine Article Writing, 18 assignments, fee $55; and Short Story Theory and Practice, 15 assignments, fee $35 ($5 more for out-of-state enrollees). There are no academic requirements for these courses, anybody can enroll. Those who, in the instructor's opinion, prove to be unqualified are advised to switch to an elementary course in grammar and composition.

71   Cecilia Bartholomew, who has taught the short-story course by correspondence for the past twelve years, is herself the author of two novels and numerous short stories. She cringes at the thought of drumming up business for the course: "I'd be a terrible double-dealer to try to *sell* people on it," she said. Like the Famous Writers instructors, Mrs. Bartholomew sends her students a lengthy criticism of each assignment, but unlike them she does not cast herself in the role of editor revising stories for publication: "It's the improvement in their writing technique that's important. The aim of my course is to develop in each student a professional standard of writing. I'll tell him when a piece is good enough to submit to an editor, but I'll never tell him it will sell." Have any of her students sold their pieces? "Yes, quite a few. Some have published in volumes of juvenile stories, some in *Hitchcock Mysteries*. But we don't stress this at all."

72   In contrast, Louis Boggess, who teaches Magazine Article Writing by correspondence in addition to her classes in "professional writing" at the College of San Mateo, exudes go-ahead salesmanship: she believes that most of her students will eventually find a market for their work. The author of several how-to-do-it books (among them *Writing Articles That Sell*, which she uses as the text for her course), she points her students straight toward the mass writing market. In her streamlined, practical lessons the emphasis is unabashedly on formula writing that will sell. Her very first assignment is how to write a "hook," meaning an arresting opening sentence. What does she think of the word "The" for openers? It doesn't exactly grab her, she admitted.

73   During the eighteen months she has been teaching the correspondence course, several of her 102 students have already sold pieces to such magazines as *Pageant, Parents, Ladies Circle, Family Weekly*. She has had but six dropouts, an enviable record by FWS standards.

74   My brief excursion into correspondence-school-land taught me little, after all, that the canny consumer does not already know about the difference between buying and being sold. As Faith Baldwin said, most advertising is

somewhat misleading; as Bennett Cerf said, the crux of mail order selling is a hard pitch to the gullible. We know that the commission sales-man will, if we let him into our homes, dazzle and bemuse us with the beauty, durability, un-excelled value of his product, whatever it is. As for the tens of thousands who sign up with FWS when they could get a better and cheaper correspondence course through the universities (or, if they live in a city, Adult Education Ex-tension courses), we know from reading Vance Packard that people tend to prefer things that come in fancy packages and cost more.

75 There is probably nothing actually illegal in the FWS operation, although the consumer watchdogs have their eye on it.

76 Robert Hughes, counsel for the Federal Trade Commission's Bureau of Deceptive Prac-tices, told me he has received a number of com-plaints about the school, mostly relating to the high-pressure and misleading sales pitch. "The real evil is in the solicitation and enrollment procedures," he said. "There's a basic contra-diction involved when you have profit-making organizations in the field of education. There's pressure to maximize the number of enroll-ments to make more profit. Surgery is needed in the enrollment procedure."

77 There is also something askew with the cast of characters in the foregoing drama which would no doubt be quickly spotted by FWS in-structors in television scriptwriting ("where the greatest market lies for the beginning writer," as the school tells us).

78 I can visualize the helpful comment on my paper: "Good work, Miss Mitford. The Oak-land widow's problem was well thought through. But characterization is weak. You could have made your script more believable had you chosen a group of shifty-eyed huck-sters out to make a buck, one step ahead of the sheriff, instead of these fifteen eminently successful and solidly respectable writers, who are well liked and admired by the American viewing public. For pointers on how to make your characters come to life in a way we can all identify with, I suggest you study Rod Ser-ling's script *The Twilight Zone,* in the kit you received from us. Your grade is D—. It has been a pleasure working with you. Good luck!" ◆

Comment on "Let Us Now Appraise Famous Writers"

Jessica Mitford

A journalism teacher as well as a journalist, Jessica Mitford often shared with her students her techniques of research as well as her thoughts about the satisfactions of investigative reporting. The following comment was published in Poison Penmanship: The Gentle Art of Muckraking.

1   THIS ARTICLE GAVE ME MORE PLEASURE, from start to finish, than any other I have written. Its preparation afforded the opportunity to apply everything I had thus far learned about investigative techniques. My efforts to get it published, a series of dizzying ups and downs, gave me an insight into the policymaking process of magazines that I should never otherwise have acquired. The aftermath of publication filled my normally uneventful life with drama of many months' duration. It was also one of the few clear-cut successes, however temporary, of my muckraking career, so I pray forgiveness if an unseemly note of self-congratulation becomes apparent in what follows.

2   At first it was a mere twinkle in the eye. By some fortunate confluence of the stars, the "Oakland lawyer" (who was in fact my husband, Bob Treuhaft) happened to tell me about his case of the aged widow vs. Famous Writers School on the very same day that Robert Byrne's excellent and amusing book *Writing Rackets* appeared in my mailbox. Lunching soon after with William Abrahams, then West Coast editor of the *Atlantic,* I regaled him with stories of the misdeeds of these Famous Frauds. Why not do a short piece for the *Atlantic,* suggested Abrahams, about seven hundred words, combining an account of the Oakland widow's unhappy experience with a review of Byrne's book? And so it was settled.

3   Here my publishing troubles began. The next day Abrahams called up to say that Rob-

ert Manning, editor of the *Atlantic,* had second thoughts about the piece: while Manning agreed that the Famous Writers School advertising was "probably unethical," the *Atlantic* had profited by it to the tune of many thousands of dollars, hence it would be equally "unethical" for the magazine to run a piece blasting the school. I was aghast at this reasoning; would it not, then, be "unethical" for a magazine to publish an article linking smoking to lung cancer while accepting ads from the tobacco companies? I asked Abrahams. Well, yes, he saw the point. If Manning changed his mind, he would get back to me.

4   A week went by; no word from the *Atlantic.* By now adrenalin was flowing (easily the most effective stimulant for the muckraker); those Famous Writers, I was beginning to see, were a power to be reckoned with if they could so easily influence the policy of a major magazine. Without much hope, I queried the articles editor at *McCall's.* She replied that *McCall's* would welcome a full-scale rundown on the school's operation, six to seven thousand words, no holds barred. This put the matter in an entirely new light; with *McCall's* lavish backing for a piece of that length, I could afford to go all out in pursuit of the story.

5   For weeks thereafter I lived in what turned out to be a fool's paradise, traveling back East at *McCall's* expense to see the school in Westport and to visit its Madison Avenue advertising headquarters in New York, interviewing the Famous ones, poring over the textbooks

Murder in the Schoolroom, Part II

THE   JULY 1970   75 CENTS

Atlantic

"We're looking for people who want to write."

Jessica Mitford:
Let us now appraise Famous Writers

illustration by Edward Sorel. Reprinted with permission from the artist and *The Atlantic Magazine*

and the stockholders' reports. The finished article drew extravagant praise from the articles editor and her associates at *McCall's,* but when the editor-in-chief returned a week later from a trip out of town she rejected it. *Why?* I sternly asked her. "Well—I don't think it's very good," she answered, a comment to which there is, of course, no possible rejoinder. However, she promptly paid not only my large expense account but the full agreed-on fee, rather than the "kill fee" that is usual in such circumstances. Did she have a guilty conscience? Had the Famous Writers got to her? Yes, it turned out, but I only learned this much later.

6   Furious at this turn of events and in a black mood of revenge, I submitted the piece to *Life,* whose editor immediately responded: he would be delighted to have it, photographers would be deployed to take pictures of the school and its Famous Faculty, it would be a major *Life* story. But the next day the editor happened to drop by the office of *Life's* advertising manager, who mentioned that the school had contracted for half a million dollars' worth of advertising over the next six months. End of that pipe dream.

By now the article, Xeroxed copies of which   7 were floating around in New York publishing circles, had achieved a sort of underground notoriety; my editor at Knopf got a wire from

Willie Morris, then editor of *Harper's,* saying he would love to publish it. I was on the point of turning it over to Morris when William Abrahams at last did "get back" to me: the *Atlantic* wanted it after all. Furthermore, Manning had canceled the magazine's advertising contract with FWS.

8   How does one go about researching such an article? My first step, before laying siege to the Famous Faculty, was to accumulate and absorb every available scrap of information about the school, my objective being to know more about its operating methods than did the Famous Writers themselves—which, as I soon discovered, was not hard. Via the *Readers' Guide to Periodical Literature,* I found articles in back issues of *Business Week, Advertising Age,* the *Wall Street Journal* from which I was able to trace the school's phenomenal growth over the years. Robert Byrne lent me his vast file containing among other treasures the school's glossy promotional brochures, its annual financial reports, and the original correspondence between "Louella Mae Burns" and the "registrar."

9   Wishing to make contact with some live ones who had actually enrolled in FWS, I hit on the idea of taking an ad in the *Saturday Review's* classified columns, giving my name and a box number: "Wanted: Experiences, good, bad or indifferent, with Famous Writers School." I choose *SR* for the purpose because it seemed just the kind of middlebrow magazine whose readership might include likely victims. Nor was I disappointed; my ad drew several letters from dissatisfied students. Faced with the agony of selection from these, I decided eventually to use the one that seemed most representative—from the couple in "the boondocks of Arkansas," as they put it, conveying in authentic tones of frustration their earnest expectations of the school and their dashed hopes. (My Yale students, to whom I imparted this story, loved the idea of using the classified columns as a research tool. I was told

that during my stint there as instructor, the advertising revenues of the *Yale Daily* soared as a result of ads placed by members of my journalism seminar.)

10   Thus prepared, I set about interviewing those of the Guiding Faculty whose home addresses were listed in *Who's Who* and whose phone numbers I got from Information. Early one Sunday morning my husband found me at the telephone. "What are you doing?" "Dialing Famous Writers." He insisted I was wasting my time: "They won't talk to you, why should they?" "No harm in trying," I said. "Wait and see." He stood by fascinated as one after another they talked on interminably—it was hard to shut them up. Needless to say, their off-the-cuff comments—and their unanimously admitted ignorance of the school's operating methods—made for some of the most successful passages in the piece.

11   I was now ready to advance on the ultimate stronghold, the school itself. Armed with my list of questions, carefully graduated from Kind to Cruel, I called the director, Mr. John Lawrence, and explained that Miss Faith Baldwin, Mr. Paul Engle, and other faculty members had suggested he could help me with an article I was writing about the value of correspondence schools. He immediately offered to pay my fare, first class, to New York where I would be put up at the hotel of my choice, and to set aside a day to show me around the school. (When I reported this to the articles editor at *McCall's,* she insisted that as a matter of principle *McCall's* should pay. I suppressed the fleeting and unworthy thought that I might collect the price of the fare from both.)

12   My day at the school was long, grueling, and on the whole satisfactory. Late in the afternoon, having elicited through persistent questioning Mr. Lawrence's firm and unqualified assurance that *never* had the school demanded a medical certificate of ill health as the condition of a student's withdrawal, I sprung the final Cruel: Bob's file on the Oakland widow, which contained a letter stating, "It is the pol-

icy of the School that when difficulties such as yours arise that we require a statement from the physician in attendance attesting to the inability of the student to continue on with studies. . . ." After listening to Mr. Lawrence's murky attempt at an explanation—"unfortunate occurrence . . . a slip-up"—I took my leave. There seemed to be nothing more to say.

13 I saved Bennett Cerf for the last. My interview with him in New York went as described in the piece; the high point his illuminating remark about mail order selling: "a very hard sales pitch, an appeal to the gullible," which he immediately regretted and asked me not to quote.

14 How, then, could I justify quoting it? I have been asked this many times by my students, and even by other working journalists. Was it not "unethical" of me? The technical answer is that at no time had Mr. Cerf indicated that his conversation was to be off the record, hence I had violated no agreement. Yet there is more to it than that. I can easily visualize interviewing an average citizen who is unused to dealing with the press, and acceding to his plea not to quote some spontaneous and injudicious comment. But—Bennett Cerf, at the top of the heap in publishing, television star performer, founder of FWS, who was cynically extracting tuition payments from the "gullible" for the augmentation of his already vast fortune? This hard heart felt then, and feels now, not the slightest compunction for having recorded his words as spoken.

15 We had one more brief encounter. I had just submitted the finished article to *McCall's* and was showing a Xerox of it to a friend at Knopf, up on the twenty-first floor of the Random House building. We were giggling away about the Famous Writers when who should pop in but Bennett Cerf. The Random House offices are on the twelfth floor. What was he doing up here, I wondered—has somebody tipped him off to my presence? Genial as ever, Mr. Cerf took a chair and remarked jovially, "So HERE's the archvillain. I hope you're not going to murder us in that piece of yours."

"Murder you? Of course not," I answered. "It's just a factual account of the school, how it operates, and your role in it."

"I don't like the look in your eye as you say that," said Cerf. "Where are you going to publish it?"

Three possible answers flashed through my mind: (1) I haven't decided, (2) I'd rather not say, (3) the truth. I reluctantly settled on the last. "If I tell you, do you promise not to try to stop publication?" I asked. Cerf made pooh-poohing sounds at the very suggestion. "It was commissioned by *McCall's*," I said. He sprang out of his chair: "*McCall's!* They're out of their mind if they think they can get away with this."

By the time the article had finally found safe haven at the *Atlantic,* I was aglow with unbecoming pride which, as we know, precedes a fall. It seemed to me I had diligently and fully explored every facet of the school's operation. The luck factor had been with me all the way; short of reading matter in a motel where I was staying, I had picked up the Gideon Bible, which miraculously fell open at the very passage in St. Luke's gospel quoted in the epigraph, "Beware of the scribes. . . ." And somebody in Robert Manning's office had spotted and forwarded to me the postcard inserts in paperback books, an incomparable example of FWS's sloppy yet devious methods, which I use for the box, "Object Lesson."

The fall came after the piece was published, and it still gives me nightmares. The *Atlantic* ran a letter from Cecelia Holland, a young novelist, who once when in financial straits had taken a job as instructor for FWS. She wrote: "Students are led to believe that each letter of criticism is personally written by the instructor. It is not. The instructor has a notebook full of prewritten paragraphs, identified by number. He consults this book and types out, not personal comments, but a series of numbers. Later, the paragraphs are written out in full by a computer-typewriter."

How could I have missed this stunning bit of chicanery which so neatly epitomized the ultimate swindle perpetrated by the school? I shall ever regret not having set eyes on those automated typewriters, sincerely clacking out "This opening is effective. It captures the reader's interest. . . ." "I can see you made a try at writing a satisfactory ending, but you only partially succeeded. . . ." I had spent much of my day at the school watching the instructors at work—why had I not asked to see some of the "two-page personal letters of criticism and advice" promised in the advertising? Why had I not quizzed Mr. Lawrence as to whether I had been shown the entire premises—was there anything interesting in the basement that I might have overlooked? To this day it pains me to think of this lapse in my investigation, and I only relate it here as a solemn warning to the would-be muckraker to take nothing for granted, and never to be lulled into the assumption that one's research is beyond reproach.

22   Robert Manning scheduled the article for publication in July. Once having taken up arms against the school, he proved himself a most effective ally. It was he who thought of the clever and apposite title, "Let Us Now Appraise Famous Writers," and who commissioned the brilliant cover cartoon by Edward Sorel, depicting Famous Writers William Shakespeare, Oscar Wilde, Samuel Johnson, Gertrude Stein, Voltaire, Ernest Hemingway, Mark Twain, Leo Tolstoy, Edgar Allan Poe, and Dylan Thomas gathered to pose for their publicity photograph.

23   Before the July issue appeared on the newsstands, Manning telephoned to say the *Atlantic* had already received fifty letters about the school from subscribers, who get their copies early. He was amazed—generally, he said, even a controversial article draws no more than a dozen letters during the whole life of the issue. (I can attest to this, having often published in the *Atlantic* on far more important subjects, such as the Spock trial and prisons, which generated maybe six to ten letters apiece. What

stirs up readers to the point of writing letters to the editor will ever remain a mystery to me.) Before the month was over, more than three hundred letters arrived, all of which were forwarded to me and all of which I answered. Most of them were from FWS students who felt they had been swindled and who wanted to get out of the contract. To these I replied, "Don't make any more payments and tell the school I advised this."

24   Developments now came thick and fast. Manning reported that the July issue of the *Atlantic* had the largest newsstand sale of any in the magazine's history—which recalled to me a line in the "registrar's" letter to "Louella Mae Burns": "Just consider how a single article can cause a magazine's newsstand sales to soar. . . ." Both the Washington *Post* and the Des Moines *Register* ran the piece in their Sunday editions, the first and only time one of my magazine articles has been picked up and republished in a daily paper. It was subsequently reprinted in England and West Germany, both countries in which the school was trying to establish a foothold. The state universities of Washington and Indiana ordered reprints for distribution to all secondary-school principals and counselors, and all university directors of independent study. Television producers invited me to discuss the school on programs ranging from the *Dick Cavett Show* to ABC's *Chicago*.

25   As a result of all this, the controversy heated up in the most exhilarating fashion, reaching an audience far beyond the readership of the *Atlantic*. I put up a map of the United States and began shading in the battle areas as they developed: D.C., Virginia, Maryland, covered by the Washington *Post*; Middle Western states, the Des Moines *Register*; and so on.

26   Soon the consumer watchdogs got into the act, and my map filled up accordingly. Congressman Laurence J. Burton of Utah read the whole thing into the *Congressional Record* as a warning to the public. The Attorney General of Iowa filed suit to enjoin the school from sending its literature into that state, charging

use of the mails to defraud. Louis J. Lefkowitz, New York State Attorney General, announced a crackdown on the school's "deceptive practices" and, adding injury to insult, ordered the school to pay $10,000 in costs. The New York City Department of Consumer Affairs demanded "substantial revisions" in FWS advertising and required the school to pay $3,000 to cover the cost of the investigation. The Federal Trade Commission launched a full-scale inquiry, sending investigators around the country to take depositions of the school personnel, the Famous Faculty, and disgruntled students.

27   Cartoonists merrily joined the fray. A drawing in *The New York Times Book Review* portrayed an amply proportioned middle-aged lady writing a letter at her desk: "Dear Bennett Cerf and Faith Baldwin, Yes! I have a strong desire, nay, a *lust* to write. . . ." The *National Lampoon* ran a caricature of a disheveled Cerf, red pencil in hand, captioned: "Unlikely Events of 1971: Bennett Cerf Stays Up All Night Correcting Student Papers from the Famous Writers School." A *New Yorker* cartoon showed a scowling husband at the typewriter, saying to his smirking wife: "Go ahead, scoff. Bennett Cerf and Faith Baldwin say I have writing aptitude, and they know more about it than you do." *Screw* magazine ran a full-page ad for the Famous Fuckers School: "We're Looking for People Who Like to Fuck. Earn money at home. We know that many people who could become professionals—and *should* become professionals—never do."

28   The letters, the media interest, the cartoons filled me with nostalgia—they were so reminiscent of the response to *The American Way of Death,* published seven years earlier. So, too, was the school's counteroffensive, which was not long in coming, its opening shot a letter to the *Atlantic* saying that my article contained "at least twenty-three errors according to our latest count." Famous Writer Bergen Evans repeated this libel on the *Dick Cavett Show,* where he was given equal time to rebut my re-

marks. Pressed for what the errors were, Evans was unable to answer, nor were they ever revealed by the school; although *Time,* in its roundup of the story, said the list was "long but quibbling." The Evans effort drew a sharp comment from Harriet Van Horne, television critic for the New York *Post:* "One might have expected a professor of English to refute Miss Mitford objectively and efficiently. One expected wrong. Dr. Evans leveled a purely personal attack."

29   There was more of the same to come. In October, an outraged employee of Congressman (later Senator) Lowell P. Weicker, Jr., of Connecticut sent me a Xerox copy of a letter to Weicker from John J. Frey, president of FWS. Drawing attention to the fact that I had just been listed by Congressman Ichord, chairman of the House Internal Security Committee, as one of sixty-five radical campus speakers, Mr. Frey suggested that Congressman Weicker should read this information into the *Congressional Record* to counteract the damage done by Congressman Burton: "Most interesting is her association with the Communist Party, USA. We would like to visit you to discuss the nature and depth of damage to our reputation and with a suggestion that may set the *Congressional Record* straight. . . . We feel that this matter has assumed urgent proportions and would like to take counteraction quickly." (Weicker, the employee assured me, had no intention of participating in the "counteraction.")

30   Had Mr. Frey borrowed this idea from the undertaking fraternity, whose response to *The American Way of Death* had been to get an ally in Congress, James B. Utt of Santa Ana, California, to read into the *Record* a lengthy report by the House Committee on Un-American Activities about my subversive background? In any event, it set me thinking about what undertakers and Famous Writers have in common: both promise their customers a measure of immortality, overcharge for it, and then fail to produce.

31   While all the attention lavished on the fracas in the popular press and on television was most gratifying, even more so were accounts of the school's growing financial difficulties as reported in the daily stock market quotations, *The New York Times* financial pages, the *Wall Street Journal,* and *Advertising Age.* Having in the past been a resolute nonreader of stock market reports, I now swooped down on that page in the San Francisco *Chronicle* first thing each morning to see how the school was doing. For some months after my article appeared, FAS International stock declined consistently and precipitately, plunging from 35 to 5. But then it started creeping up again: 5¼, 5⅜, 5½. . . . I was in despair. "What can I *do?*" I wailed to my husband. When the stock reached 6, fearing perhaps for my mental well-being, he presented me with a certificate for ten shares of stock bought in my name as a special surprise: "That way, you won't mind so much if it does go up a bit," he said sympathetically.

32   In May, 1971, I was staying in Washington, doing research for my book on prisons. One morning I got a telegram from my husband: "SORRY, YOUR FAMOUS WRITERS STOCK WIPED OUT. SUSPENDED FROM TRADING ON THE STOCK EXCHANGE." Later, he told me that when he had phoned in the telegram to Western Union, the operator had suggested, "Don't you think you should phrase that more gently? Your wife might do something drastic—jump out of the window—if you tell her she's been wiped out."

33   Early the following year the school filed for bankruptcy. The final windup was reported in *More* magazine's Hellbox column for January, 1972: "Rosebuds (late blooming) to Jessica Mitford, whose devastating dissection of the Famous Writers School in the *Atlantic* has produced what all exposés aim at but so few achieve: tangible results. . . . The Mitford article and all the nosing around it prompted has staggered the school financially. Earnings dropped from $3,466,000 in 1969 to $1,611,000 in 1970. . . ."

34   "A wilted rosebud should also go to the editor-in-chief of *McCall's,* who originally assigned the piece and then rejected it because, she explains, 'I did not want to offend Bennett Cerf at a time when *McCall's* was trying to improve the caliber of its fiction.' "

35   There is, however, a sad addendum: the Famous Writers School is creeping back.

36   I first became aware of this in 1974 when Justin Kaplan, the distinguished biographer and long-time friend of mine, sent me a letter he had received from Famous Writer Robin Moore inviting him to join the Advisory Board of the "new" FWS: "The emoluments are not, inconsiderable," Mr. Moore had written. Justin replied, "I am interested in hearing more about the Advisory Board. I do need to find out how the new operation differs from the old, which as a friend of Jessica Miltford's I followed with more than routine interest." But answer came there none; on this matter, Mr. Moore "stood mute," as lawyers say.

37   More recently friends have clipped and sent me ads for the school—not the huge full-page clarion calls of yore, rather discreet columns headed "Are You One of the 'Quiet Ones' Who Should Be a Writer?"

38   Seeking to make a cursory check of the school's comeback, I asked a friend in San Francisco to write for the Aptitude Test. It arrived: the same old Aptitude Test. She sent it in, and within days a "Field Representative" appeared at her house: same old pitch, almost indistinguishable from the one I described in the article.

39   Some of the "Advisory Board" members listed in the current 1978 brochure are holdrom the same old Guiding Faculty, although as a regular reader of the obit page I have noted that quite a few of these have gone to join the Famous Faculty in the Sky. I mentioned this circumstance to Cecelia Holland, who replied, "Oh—well, but surely you've heard of ghost writers." ◆

RED WINGS IN THE SUNSET

Stephen J. Gould

Stephen Jay Gould, who teaches biology, geology, and the history of science at Harvard University, is obviously a "working scientist." But he is better known to thousands of readers through his column "This View of Life," published in the popular magazine *Natural History*. In the essay below, he reports on the career of artist and naturalist Abbott Thayer, who discovered the key principles of camouflage but then "followed a common path to perdition" by allowing his theory to overwhelm his judgment.

1   TEDDY ROOSEVELT BORROWED AN African proverb to construct his motto: Speak softly, but carry a big stick. In 1912, a critic turned Roosevelt's phrase against him, castigating the old Roughrider for trying to demolish an opponent by rhetoric alone: "Ridicule is a powerful weapon and the temptation to use it unsparingly is a strong one. . . . Even if we don't agree with him [Roosevelt's opponent], it is not necessary either to cut him into little pieces or to break every bone in his body with the 'big stick.' "

2   This criticism appeared in the midst of Roosevelt's presidential campaign (when he split the Republican party by trying to wrest the nomination from William Howard Taft, then formed his own Progressive, or Bull Moose, party to contest the election, thereby scattering the Republican vote and bringing victory to Democrat Woodrow Wilson). Surely, therefore, the statement must record one of Roosevelt's innumerable squabbles during a tough political year. It does not. Francis H. Allen published these words in an ornithological journal, *The Auk*. He was writing about flamingos.

3   When, as a cynical and posturing teenager, I visited Mount Rushmore, I gazed with some approval at the giant busts of Washington, Jefferson, and Lincoln, and then asked as so many others have—what in hell is Teddy Roosevelt doing up there? Never again shall I question his inclusion, for I have just discovered something sufficiently remarkable to warrant a sixty-foot stone likeness all by itself. In 1911, an ex-president of the United States, after seven exhausting years in office, and in the throes of preparing his political comeback, found time to write and publish a technical scientific article, more than one hundred pages long: "Revealing and Concealing Coloration in Birds and Mammals."

4   Roosevelt wrote his article to demolish a theory proposed by the artist-naturalist Abbott H. Thayer (and defended by Mr. Allen, who castigated Roosevelt for bringing the rough language of politics into a scientific debate). In 1896 Thayer, as I shall document in a moment, correctly elucidated the important principle of countershading (a common adaptation that confers near invisibility upon predators or prey). But he then followed a common path to perdition by slowly extending his valid theory to a doctrine of exclusivity. By 1909, Thayer was claiming that *all* animal colors, from the peacock's tail to the baboon's rump, worked primarily for concealment. As a backbreaking straw that sealed his fate and inspired Roosevelt's wrath, Thayer actually argued that natural selection made flamingos red, all the better to mimic the sunset. In the book that will stand forever as a monument to folly, to cockeyed genius, and to inspiration gone askew, Thayer stated in 1909 (in *Concealing-Colora-*

tion in the Animal Kingdom, written largely by his son Gerald H. Thayer and published by Macmillan):

> These traditionally "showy" birds are, at their most critical moments, perfectly "obliterated" by their coloration. Conspicuous in most cases, when looked at from above, as man is apt to see them, they are wonderfully fitted for "vanishment" against the flushed, rich-colored skies of early morning and evening.

5   Roosevelt responded with characteristic vigor in his 1911 article:

> Among all the wild absurdities to which Mr. Thayer has committed himself, probably the wildest is his theory that flamingos are concealingly colored because their foes mistake them for sunsets. He has never studied flamingos in their haunts, he knows nothing personally of their habits or their enemies or their ways of avoiding their enemies. . . . and certainly has never read anything to justify his suppositions; these suppositions represent nothing but pure guesswork, and even to call them guesswork is a little overconservative, for they come nearer to the obscure mental processes which are responsible for dreams.

6   Roosevelt's critique (and many others equally trenchant) sealed poor Thayer's fate. In 1896, Thayer had begun his campaign with praise, promise, and panache (his outdoor demonstrations of disappearing decoys became legendary). He faced the dawn of World War I in despair and dejection (though the war itself brought limited vindication as our armies used his valid ideas in theories of camouflage). He lamented to a friend that his avocation (defending his theory of concealing coloration) had sapped his career:

> Never . . . have I felt less a painter . . . I am like a man to whom is born, willy nilly, a

child whose growth demanded his energies, he the while always dreaming that this growing offspring would soon go forth to seek his fortune and leave him to his profession, but the offspring again and again either unfolding some new faculties that must be nurtured and watched, or coming home and bursting into his parent's studio, bleeding and bruised by an insulted world, continued to need attention so that there was nothing for it but to lay down the brush and take him once more into one's lap.

I must end this preface to my essay with a confession. I have known about Thayer's "crazy" flamingo theory all my professional life—and for a particular reason. It is the standard example always used by professors in introductory courses to illustrate illogic and unreason, and dismissed in a sentence with the ultimate weapon of intellectual nastiness— ridicule that forecloses understanding. When I began my research for this essay, I thought that I would write about absurdity, another comment on unthinking adaptationism. But my reading unleashed a cascade of discovery, leading me to Roosevelt and, more importantly, to the real Abbott Thayer, shorn of his symbolic burden. The flamingo theory is, of course, absurd—that will not change. But how and why did Thayer get there from an excellent start that the standard dismissive anecdote, Thayer's unfortunate historical legacy, never acknowledges? The full story, if we try to understand Abbott Thayer aright, contains lessons that will more than compensate for laughter lost.   7

Who was Abbott Handerson Thayer anyway? I had always assumed, from the name alone, that he was an eccentric Yankee who used wealth and social position to gain a hearing for his absurd ideas. I could find nothing about him in the several scientific books that cite the flamingo story. I was about to give up when I located his name in the *Encyclopedia Britannica.* I found, to my astonishment, that   8

Abbott Thayer was one of the most famous painters of late nineteenth century America (and an old Yankee to be sure, but not of the wealthy line of Thayers—see the biography by Nelson G. White, *Abbot H. Thayer: Painter and Naturalist*). He specialized in ethereal women, crowned with suggestions of halos and accompanied by quintessentially innocent children. Art and science are both beset by fleeting tastes that wear poorly—far be it for me to judge. I had begun to uncover a human drama under the old pedagogical caricature.

9   But let us begin, as they say, at the beginning. Standard accounts of the adaptive value of animal colors use three categories to classify nature's useful patterns (no one has substantially improved upon the fine classic by Hugh B. Cott, *Adaptive Coloration in Animals,* 1940). According to Cott, adaptive colors and patterns may serve as (1) concealment (to shield an animal from predators or to hide the predator in nature's never-ending game); (2) advertisement, to scare potential predators (as in the prominent false eyespots of so many insects), to maintain territory or social position, or to announce sexual receptivity (as in baboon rump patches); and (3) disguise, as animals mimic unpalatable creatures to gain protection, or resemble an inanimate (and inedible) object (numerous leaf and stick insects, or a bittern, motionless and gazing skyward, lost amidst the reeds). Since disguise lies closer to advertisement than to concealment (a disguised animal does not try to look inconspicuous, but merely like something else), we can immediately appreciate Abbott Thayer's difficulty. He wanted to reduce all three categories to the single purpose of concealment—but fully two-thirds of all color patterns, in conventional accounts, serve the opposite function of increased visibility.

10   Abbott Thayer, a native of Boston, began his artistic career in the maelstrom of New York City but eventually retreated to a hermitlike existence in rural New Hampshire, where his old interests in natural history revived and deepened. As a committed Darwinian, he believed that all form and pattern must serve some crucial purpose in the unremitting struggle for existence. He also felt that, as a painter, he could interpret the colors of animals in ways and terms unknown to scientists. In 1896, Thayer published his first, landmark article in *The Auk:* "The Law Which Underlies Protective Coloration."

11   Of course, naturalists had recognized for centuries that many animals blend into their background and become virtually invisible—but scientists had not properly recognized how and why. They tended to think, naively (as I confess I did before my research for this essay), that protection emerged from simple matching between animal and background. But Thayer correctly identified the primary method of concealment as countershading—a device that makes creatures look flat. Animals must indeed share the right color and pattern with their background, but their ghostly disappearance records a loss of dimensionality, not just a matching of color.

12   In countershading, an animal's colors are precisely graded to counteract the effects of sunlight and shadow. Countershaded animals are darkest on top, where most sunlight falls, and lightest on the bottom (Thayer thereby identified the adaptive significance of light bellies—perhaps the most universal feature of animal coloration). The precise reversal between intensity of coloration and intensity of illumination neatly cancels out all shadow and produces a uniform color from top to bottom. As a result, the animal becomes flat, perfectly two-dimensional, and cannot be seen by observers who have, all their lives, perceived the substantiality of objects by shadow and shading. Artists have struggled for centuries to produce the illusion of depth and roundness on a flat canvas; nature has simply done the opposite—she shades in reverse in order to produce an illusion of flatness in a three-dimensional world.

13   Contrasting his novel principle of counter-shading with older ideas about mimicry, Thayer wrote in his original statement of 1896: "Mimicry makes an animal appear to be some other thing, whereas the newly discovered law makes him cease to appear to exist at all."

14   Thayer, intoxicated with the joy of discovery, attributed his success to his chosen profession and advanced a strong argument about the dangers of specialization and the particular value of "outsiders" to any field of study. He wrote in 1903: "Nature has evolved actual art on the bodies of animals, and only an artist can read it." And later, in his 1909 book, but now with the defensiveness and pugnacity that marked his retreat:

> The entire matter has been in the hands of the wrong custodians. . . . It properly belongs to the realm of pictorial art, and can be interpreted only by painters. For it deals wholly in optical illusion, and this is the very gist of a painter's life. He is born with a sense of it; and, from his cradle to his grave, his eyes, wherever they turn, are unceasingly at work on it—and his pictures live by it. What wonder, then, if it was for him alone to discover that the very art he practices is at full—beyond the most delicate precision of human powers—on almost all animals.

15   So far, so good. Thayer's first articles and outdoor demonstrations won praise from scientists. He began with relatively modest claims, arguing that he had elucidated the basis for a major principle of concealment but not denying that other patterns of color displayed quite different selective value. Initially, he accepted the other two traditional categories—revealing coloration and mimicry—though he always argued that concealment would gain a far bigger scope than previously admitted. In his most technical paper, published in the *Transactions of the Entomological Society of London*

(1903), and introduced favorably by the great English Darwinian E. B. Poulton, Thayer wrote:

> Every possible form of advantageous adaptation must somewhere exist. . . . There must be unpalatability accompanied by warning coloration . . . and equally plain that there must be mimicry.

16   Indeed, Thayer sought ways to combine ideas of concealment with other categories that he would later deny. He supported, for example, the ingenious speculation of C. Hart Merriam that white rump patches are normally revealing, but that their true value lies in a deer's ability to "erase" the color at moments of danger—a deer "closes down" the patch by lowering its tail over the white blotch and then disappears, invisible, into the forest. In his 1909 book, however Thayer explicitly repudiated this earlier interpretation and argued for pure concealment—the white patch as "sky mimicking" when seen from below.

17   Thayer's pathway from insight to ridicule followed a distressingly common route among intellectuals. Countershading for concealment, amidst a host of alternatives, was not enough. Thayer had to have it all. Little by little, plausibly at first, but grading slowly to red wings in the sunset, Thayer laid his battle plans (not an inappropriate metaphor for a father of camouflage). As article succeeded article, Thayer progressively invaded the categories of mimicry and revealing coloration to gain, or so he thought, more cases for concealment. Finally, nothing else remained: *All* patterns of color served to conceal. He wrote in his book: "All patterns and colors whatsoever of all animals that ever prey or are preyed upon are under certain normal circumstances obliterative."

18   Thayer made his first fateful step in his technical article of 1903. Here, he claimed a second major category of concealing coloration—what he called "ruptive" (we now call them "disruptive") bars, stripes, splotches, and other

assorted markings. Disruptive markings make an animal "disappear" by a route different from countershading. They break an animal's coherent outline and produce an insubstantial array of curious and unrelated patches (this principle, more than countershading, became important in military camouflage). A zebra, Thayers argues, does not mimic the reeds in which it hides; rather, the stripes break the animal's outline into bars of light and darkness—and predators see no coherent prey at all.

19   Again, Thayer had proposed a good idea for some, even many, cases (though not for zebras, who rarely venture into fields of reeds). His 1903 article argues primarily that butterflies carry disruptive pictures of flowers and background scenery upon their wings: "The general aspect of each animal's environment," Thayer wrote, "is found painted upon his coat, in such a way as to minimize his visibility, by making the beholder think he sees *through* him."

20   But, amidst his good suggestions, Thayer had made his first overextended argument. Countershading could scarcely be mistaken for anything else and offered little scope for claiming too much. But the principle of "ruptive" concealment permitted enormous scope for encompassing other patterns that actually serve to reveal or mimic. Color patches and splotches—the classic domain of warning and revealing patterns (consider the peacock's tail)—could, for an overenthusiast like Thayer, become marks of disruptive concealment. Thus, to cite just one example of overstatement, Thayer argued in a 1909 article, adversarily entitled "An Arraignment of the Theories of Mimicry and Warning Colors," that white patches on a skunk's head mimic the sky when seen by mice from below:

Such . . . victims as can see would certainly have much more chance to escape were not what would be a dark-looming predator's head converted, by its white sky-counterfeiting, into a deceptive imitation of mere sky.

21   Still, by 1903, Thayer was not yet ready to claim concealment for all colors. He admitted one category of obvious conspicuousness: "Only unshiny, bright monochrome is intrinsically a revealing coloration."

22   Now we can finally understand why Thayer was eventually driven to his absurd argument about flamingos and the sunset. (Divorced from the context of Thayer's own personal development, the idea sounds like simple disembodied craziness—as professors always present it for laughs in introductory classes.) Once Thayer decided to go for broke, and to claim that all color works for concealment, flamingos became his crucial test, his do-or-die attempt at exclusivity. As a last shackle before the final plunge, Thayer had admitted that stark monochromes—animals painted throughout with one showy color—were "intrinsically revealing." If he could now show that such monochromes also served for concealment, then his triumph would be complete. Flamingos occupied the center of his daring, not a curious diversion. He had to find a way to fade bright red into ethereal nothingness. Hence the sunset—his as well as the flamingo's.

23   So Thayer visited the West Indies, got down on his belly in the sulfurous muds, and looked at flamingos—not comfortably down from above (as he always accused lazy and uncritical zoologists of doing), but from the side as might a slithering anaconda or a hungry alligator. And he saw red wings fading into the sunset—the entire feeding flock became a pink cloud, a "sky-matching costume":

These birds are largely nocturnal, so that the only sky bright enough to show any color upon them is the more or less rosy and golden one that surrounds them from sunset till dark and from dawn until soon after sunrise. They commonly feed in immense, open lagoons, wading in vast phalanxes, while the entire real sky above them and its reflected duplicate below them constitute either one vast hollow sphere of gold, rose, and salmon, or at least glow, on one side or the other, with these tones. Their whole plumage is a most exquisite duplicate of these scenes. . . . This flamingo, having at his feeding time so nearly only sunrise colors to match, wears, as he does, a wonderful imitation of them.

24   Thayer had finally gone too far and exasperated even his erstwhile supporters. His exaggerations—particularly his flamingos—now brought down a storm of criticism, including Roosevelt's hundred-page barrage. Critics pointed out Thayer's errors in every particular: Flamingos do not concentrate their feeding at dawn and dusk, but are active all day; anacondas and alligators do not inhabit the thin films of saline ponds that flamingos favor; flamingos eat by filtering tiny eyeless animals that cannot enjoy the visual pleasures of sunset.

    Most sadly, Thayer's argument even failed   25 in its own terms—and Thayer, who was overenthusiastic to a fault, but neither dishonest nor dishonorable, had to confess. Any object viewed *against* the fading light will appear dark, whatever its actual color. Thayer admitted this explicitly by painting a dark palm tree against the sunset in his infamous and fanciful painting of fading flamingos (reproduced here, for unfortunate practical reasons, in inappropriate black and white). Thus, he could only

neg no 2A13239, Courtesy Department of Library Services, American Museum of Natural History

White (top) and red (bottom) flamingos fade to invisibility against the sky at sunrise and sunset. From Thayer's 1909 book.

claim that flamingos looked like the sunset in the *opposite* side of the sky: red clouds of sunset in the west, red masses of flamingos in the east. Would any animal be so confused by two "sunsets," with flamingos showing dark against the real McCoy? Thayer admitted in his 1909 book:

> Of course a flamingo seen against dawn or evening sky would look dark, like the palm in the lower left-hand figure, no matter what his colors were. The . . . right-hand figures, then, represent the lighted sides of flamingos at morning or evening, and show how closely these tend to reproduce the sky of this time of day; although always, of course, *in the opposite quarter of the heavens* [Thayer was good enough to underline his admission] from the sunset or dawn itself.

26 As a final, and feeble, parting salvo, Thayer added: "but the rosy hues very commonly suffuse both sides of the sky, so that . . . the flamingos' illuminated ruddy color very often has a true 'background' of illuminated ruddy sky."

27 Teddy Roosevelt was particularly perturbed. As an old big-game hunter, he knew that most of Thayer's "ruptive" patterns did not conceal quarries. How could Thayer have it both ways—how could a lion be concealed in the desert, a zebra amongst the reeds when, in fact, they share the same habitat, often to the zebra's fatal disadvantage? Thus, Roosevelt decided to counterattack and wrote his scientific *magnum opus* during some spare time amidst other chores. He saved his best invective for the poor flamingos. Writing on February 2, 1911, to University of California biologist Charles Kofoid, he stated:

> [Thayer's] book shows such a fantastic quality of mind on his part that it is a matter of very real surprise to me that any scientific observer . . . no matter how much credit he may give to Mr. Thayer for certain discover-

ies and theories, should fail to enter the most emphatic protest against the utter looseness and wildness of his theorizing. Think of being seriously required to consider the theory that flamingos are colored red so that fishes (or oysters for that matter—there is no absurdity of which Mr. Thayer could not be capable) would mistake them for the sunset!

28 The debate between Roosevelt and Thayer developed into an interesting discussion of scientific methodology, not merely some rhetorical sniping about specifics. To grasp Roosevelt's primarily methodological (and cogent) objections to Thayer's work, consider Thayer's most remarkable painting of all—the frontispiece to his 1909 book, showing a peacock obliterated in the foliage. Here, Thayer argues that every nuance of a peacock's coloration increases his concealment in a particular bit of habitat—the combined effect adding to invisibility. Given the usual interpretation of a peacock's color as revealing, and the gaudy impression that he makes both upon us and, one must assume, the peahen, Thayer's interpretation represents quite a departure from tradition and common sense:

> The peacock's splendor is the effect of a marvelous combination of "obliterative" designs, in forest-colors and patterns. . . . All imaginable forest-tones are to be found in this bird's costume; and they "melt" him into the scene to a degree past all human analysis.

29 Thayer then positions his bird so precisely that all features blend with surroundings. He paints the blue neck against a gap in the foliage, so that it may mimic "blue sky seen through the leaves." He matches the golden greens and browns of the back to forest tones. He depicts the white cheek patch as a "ruptive" hole that disaggregates the face. He

A peacock in the woods, showing how, in at least one highly peculiar position, each "showy" feature can help blend the bird into invisibility. From Thayer's 1909 book.

neg no 2A13238, Courtesy Department of Library Services, American Museum of Natural History

paints the celebrated ocelli (eyespots) of the tail feathers as leaf mimics. He also notes that ocelli are smallest and dimmest near the body, grading to larger and brighter toward the rear end: "They inevitably lead the eye away from the bird, till it finds itself straying amid the foliage beyond the tail's evanescent border." The spread tail, he claims, may impress the peahen, but it "looks also very much like a shrub bearing some kind of fruit or flower." Finally, he argues that the tail's coppery brown color rep-

resents perfectly "the bare ground and tree-trunks seen between the leaves."

What a tour de force, but what can we possibly make of such special pleading? Who would doubt that some conceivable habitat might conceal almost any animal? Note how precisely the peacock must choose his spot to receive the cryptic benefit that Thayer wishes to confer upon him. In particular, he must always place his shimmering blue neck in a gap amidst the foliage where it will vanish against

30

a clear sky (but what does he do on a cloudy day, or in a bush so dense that no holes exist, as seen from all relevant directions at once?) Peacocks, in any case, live primarily in open fields. Their spreading display is a glory to behold—and the very opposite of invisible.

31   Thayer, of course, knew all this. He didn't claim (as his critics sometimes charged) that a habitat offering protection by concealment must be the usual, or even a common, haunt of its invisible beneficiary. Thayer simply argued that such protection might be important at critical moments occurring only once or twice in an animal's lifetime—at crucial instants of impending death from a stalking predator.

32   But how could odd and improbable moments shape such complex and intricate patterns as the innumerable details of a peacock's design? With this question, we finally arrive at the key theoretical issue of this debate—the power of natural selection itself. In order to believe that complex designs might be constructed by such rare and momentary benefits as sunsets or particular positions in trees outside an animal's normal habitat, one must have an overarching faith in the power of natural selection. Selection must be so potent that even the rarest of benefits will eventually be engraved into the optimal designs of organisms. Thayer had this faith; Roosevelt, and most biologists then and since, did not. Thayer wrote in 1900: "Of course, to any one who feels the inevitability of natural selection, it is obvious that each organ or structural detail, and likewise each quality of organic forms, owes its existence to the sum of all its uses." Thayer then laid it on the line in stark epitome—patterns of color are built by natural selection, "pure, simple, and omnipotent."

33   Roosevelt and other acute critics correctly identified the central flaw in Thayer's science—not in his numerous factual errors, but in his methodology. Thayer found a hiding place for all his animals but with a method that made his theory untestable and therefore useless to science. Thayer insisted that he had proved his point simply by finding *any* spot that rendered an animal invisible. He didn't need to show that the creature usually frequented such a place or that the location formed part of a natural habitat at all. For the animal might seek its spot only in the rarest moments of need. But how then could we disprove any of Thayer's claims? We might work for years to show that an animal never entered its domain of invisibility, and Thayer would reply: Wait till tomorrow when urgent need arises. Scientists are trained to avoid such special pleading because it exerts a chilling and stupefying effect upon hypotheses, by rendering them invulnerable to test and potential disproof. Doing is the soul of science and we reject hypotheses that condemn us to impotence.

34   T. Barbour, former director of Harvard's Museum of Comparative Zoology (where I now sit composing this piece), and J. C. Phillips emphasized this point in reviewing Thayer's book in 1911:

Acquiescence in Mr. Thayer's views throws a pall over the entire subject of animal coloration. Investigation is discouraged; and we find jumbled together a great mass of fascinating and extremely complicated data, all simply explained by one dogmatic assertion. For we are asked to believe that an animal is protectively clothed whether he is like his surroundings, or whether he is very unlike them (obliteratively marked) or . . . if he falls between these two classes, there is still plenty of space to receive him.

35   Teddy Roosevelt addressed the same issue with more vigor in a letter to Thayer on March 19, 1912 (just imagine any presidential candidate taking time out to pursue natural history more than a month after the New Hampshire primary—oh, I know, campaigns were shorter then):

There is in Africa a blue rump baboon. It is also true that the Mediterranean Sea bounds one side of Africa. If you should make a series of experiments tending to show that if the blue rump baboon stood on its head by the Mediterranean you would mix up his rump and the Mediterranean, you might be illustrating something in optics, but you would not be illustrating anything that had any bearing whatsoever on the part played by the coloration of the animal in actual life. . . . My dear Mr. Thayer, if you would face facts, you might really help in elucidating some of the problems before me, but you can do nothing but mischief, and not very much of that, when conducting such experiments. . . . Your experiments are of no more real value than the experiment of putting a raven in a coal scuttle, and then claiming that he is concealed.

36   Contemporary (and later) accounts of Thayer's debacle rest largely upon a red herring, concealed in more than the sunset, that will not explain his failure and only reinforces a common and harmful stereotype about the intrinsic differences among intellectual styles. In short, we are told that Abbott Thayer ultimately failed because he possessed an artist's temperament—good for an initial insight perhaps, but with no staying power for the hard (and often dull) work of real science.

37   Such charges were often lodged against Thayer, and with undoubted rhetorical effect, but they represent a dangerous use of ad hominem argument with anti-intellectual overtones. Thayer may have laid himself open to such ridicule with a passionate temperament that he made no effort to control in a more formal age. John Jay Chapman, the acerbic essayist, wrote of Thayer (admittedly in a fit of pique when his wife, at his great displeasure, decided to study art in Thayer's studio):

Thayer by the way, is a hipped egoist who paints three hours, has a headache, walks four hours—holds his own pulse, wants to save his sacred light for the world, cares for nobody, and has fits of dejection during which forty women hold his hand and tell him not to despair—for humanity's sake.

But is such passion the exclusive birthright of artists? I have known many scientists equally insufferable.

38   Thayer's scientific critics also raised the charge of artistic temperament. Roosevelt wrote, in a statement that might have attracted more attention in our litigious age: Thayer's misstatements "are due to the enthusiasm of a certain type of artistic temperament, an enthusiasm also known to certain types of scientific and business temperaments, and which when it manifests itself in business is sure to bring the owner into trouble as if he were guilty of deliberate misconduct." Barbour and Phillips argued that "Mr. Thayer, in his enthusiasm, has ignored or glossed over with an artistic haze. . . . This method of peruasion, while it does appeal to the public, is—there is no other word—simple charlatanry however unwitting." Barbour and Phillips then defended the cold light of dispassionate science in a bit of self-serving puffery:

[Our statements] are simply the impressions made upon open-minded observers who have no axe to grind, and who have no reason to take sides on the question, one way or another. They have been written in a friendly spirit, and we hope they will be received in the same way.

Do friendly spirits ever accuse their opponents of "simple charlatanry"?

39   The charge of artistic temperament may be convenient and effective, especially since it appeals to a common stereotype—but it won't wash. The facile interpretation that scientists wouldn't give Thayer a hearing because he was an "outsider" won't work either—for contemporary accounts belie such charges of territoriality and narrowness. Even though Thayer

made such strong claims—quoted above—for scientists' incompetence in a domain accessible only to artists, naturalists welcomed his insights about countershading and enjoyed both his initial articles and his outdoor demonstrations. E. B. Poulton, one of England's greatest evolutionists, warmly supported Thayer and wrote introductions to his publications. Frank M. Chapman, great ornithologist and editor of *The Auk,* wrote in his *Autobiography of a Bird Lover:*

> As an editor, doubtless my most notable contributions to the Auk's pages were Abbott Thayer's classical papers on protective coloration. . . . I knew little of Thayer's eminence as an artist. It was the man himself who impressed me by the overwhelming force of his personality. He made direct and inescapable demands on one's attention. He was intensely vital and lived normally at heights which I reached only occasionally and then only for short periods.

40   Thayer's ultimate failure reflects a more universal tendency, distributed without reference to profession among all kinds of people. Nothing but habit and tradition separate the "two cultures" of humanities and science. The processes of thought and modes of reason are similar—so are the people. Only subject matter differs. Science may usually treat the world's empirical information; art may thrive on aesthetic judgment. But scientists also traffic in ideas and opinions, and artists surely respect fact.

41   The *idée fixe* is a common intellectual fault of all professions, not a characteristic failure of artists. I have often written about scientists as single-mindedly committed to absurd unities and false simplifications as Thayer was devoted to the exclusivity of concealing coloration in nature. Some are charming and a bit dotty—such as old Randolph Kirkpatrick, who thought that all rocks were made of single-celled nummulospheres (see Essay 22 in *The Panda's Thumb,* 1980). Others are devious and more than a bit dangerous—such as Cyril Burt, who fabricated data to prove that all intelligence resided in heredity (see my book *The Mismeasure of Man*).

42   Abbott Thayer had an *idée fixe;* he burned with desire to reduce a messy and complex world to one beautiful, simple principle of explanation. Such monistic schemes never work. History has built irreducible complexity and variety into the bounteous world of organisms. Diversity reigns at the superficial level of overt phenomena—animal colors serve many different functions. The unifying principles are deeper and more abstract—may I suggest evolution itself for starters. ◆

7 Longer Research Papers

THIS CHAPTER FOCUSES ON WHAT IS SOMETIMES CALLED THE LIBRARY paper, the formal research paper, or the term paper: a long essay in which the writer supports assertions by citing the work of several other researchers. The research for such a paper may take several weeks, but if you do it well, it has a reward: your work will make you an apprentice scholar, a specialist on a subject about which you know more than most students—and most professors—ever will.

Like Chapter 6, this chapter will offer a series of hints. You can read as a roadmap now and return to as a detailed guide later. Assuming that you have already read Chapter 6, I'll not repeat advice given there. At the end of this chapter are two appendices that deal with the technical details of manuscript form and documentation: (1) a sample term paper that will show how one writer resolved many of the difficulties you may encounter and (2) some "General Comments on Citation Form" that supplement the examples given in the term paper.

HINT 1:

Lay out a sensible schedule of deadlines.

Some writing projects can succeed even when the writer's procrastination squeezes them into an intense last-minute effort—but not the term paper. The writer who procrastinates will likely discover too late that key sources are unavailable, that the hypothesis is untenable, or that the time needed to ferret information from the books piled on the desk would take the whole project past its deadline.

A common and sensible way to fight this kind of damaging procrastination is to set up and meet a series of "stage" deadlines leading up to the final one. You might, for instance, establish the following:

1. A deadline for finishing preliminary reading and producing a one-page description of the projected paper.

2. A deadline for completing a list of all the sources you intend to use (this deadline must be set early enough to allow time for interlibrary loans or trips to other libraries, if necessary).

3. A deadline for note-taking.

4. A deadline for completing a preliminary draft.

Don't underestimate the amount of time each stage will take; allow some time for the unexpected. Typically, the first stage might be set for five weeks before the paper is due, and a week might be allowed for each of the others.

HINT 2:

Don't commit yourself to a long library-research paper on a subject for which too few sources are available.

In the academic world, the aim of a research project is to make new knowledge, not to reproduce old knowledge. In this respect, library research seems almost a contradiction in terms, since everything found on the shelves is known to at least one earlier researcher. The new knowledge produced by library research is really a novel combination of materials not novel in themselves: the research-based essay is like a "new" dish created from groceries that anyone could have purchased but that no one else has brought together in precisely *this* way and with precisely *this* effect.

Obviously, the opportunities for novel combinations are greatly reduced if a researcher (or a cook) works with very few ingredients. If, for example, you attempt to do a library research paper on the Flat Earth Society's denial that men have landed on the moon, and you discover that your library can offer only a magazine article of moderate length and two ten-line newspaper stories repeating information from the article, you are in a difficult position. Unless you redefine your topic or find a way to do some nonlibrary research (perhaps an interview with a local member of the Society), you will probably produce just a paraphrase of the magazine article.

The problem of finding adequate sources is not merely one of finding a large enough number of them. In some cases, you may find ten or fifteen sources that all seem to say the same thing. What you are looking for are sources that differ from one another *or from you* in their perspective or in the data they present. A difference in perspective (framework) is an especially valuable find, since it allows the researcher to explain the arguments and counterarguments by which experts attempt to establish their versions of the truth.

HINT 3:

Where it is feasible, begin library research at the encyclopedia level.

You may have learned in high school that no respectable research paper would cite a general-reference encyclopedia as a source, and it is certainly true that a supposed research paper that gets most of its information from encyclopedia articles suggests a writer unable or unwilling to locate other (probably more interesting) material. But great encyclopedias (such as *Encyclopaedia Britannica,* available in almost every library) should not be dismissed lightly, particularly in the early stages of research. The longer articles, often written by internationally recognized experts, survey an area of knowledge ("Shakespeare" or "Mitochondria"), giving background information that will be useful to you when you read other sources. They define areas of dispute that may be topics for lively papers. And they usually conclude with a bibliography that can lead you to important scholarly sources.

Though they are in many ways less impressive than *Britannica,* the following general-interest encyclopedias are often worth consulting:

Chambers's Encyclopaedia is useful because it presents subjects from a European and British perspective. It is published in England (unlike *Britannica,* which is—despite its name—American).

Collier's Encyclopedia devotes a higher percentage of its space to modern subjects than *Britannica* does.

The *Encyclopedia Americana* can be particularly useful on scientific and technical subjects.

Larger libraries will ordinarily include a number of specialized encyclopedias you may find useful. An exhaustive list here would be impossible, but the following titles will give you a sense of what is available:

Encyclopedia of Education.
Encyclopedia of Philosophy.
Encyclopedia of Psychology.
International Encyclopedia of the Social Sciences.
McGraw-Hill Dictionary of Art.
McGraw-Hill Dictionary of Science and Technology.

While encyclopedias usually offer good biographical information on major figures from the past, they are less useful for minor figures or—especially—for individuals who are still alive. For additional biographical information, the following sources are particularly valuable:

Current Biography.
Contemporary Authors.
Who's Who (with several variations, including *Who's Who in America*).

If encyclopedia-level research turns up no information on a topic on which you had planned to do a long research paper, ask yourself a few questions: Is this topic too obscure to be researched in a limited time? Is it so current that you will need to rely principally on recent periodicals or on interviews? Would it be wise to change your topic or your approach?

HINT 4:

Save time by locating existing bibliographies.

One of the keys to effective research is learning how to exploit the labors of others. If you are researching a topic that has produced a good deal of earlier research and comment—the sort of topic that gets a full article in *Encyclopaedia Britannica,* for example—there is a good chance that someone else has gone to the trouble of compiling a bibliography for you. The ends of encyclopedia articles and articles in other general reference sources often contain such bibliographies, and some of the works listed there will in turn contain their own bibliographies.

   This route from encyclopedia-level research to bibliographies will not always lead to the most valuable sources. A second course of action is to look for what we might call "general bibliographies," catalogs (usually compiled by scholars) of important works in a given area. Among the heavily used general bibliographies are

   Guide to Historical Literature
   Cambridge Bibliography of English Literature
   Research Guide for Psychology
   A Guide to Philosophical Bibliography and Research

Topics that have received a good deal of scholarly attention often produce more focused bibliographies. Someone researching a paper on Robert Browning, for example, might use *The Victorian Poets: A Guide to Research* or *Readers' Guide to Robert Browning.*

   You can locate both general and focused bibliographies in the card catalog or the on-line catalog of your library. For this purpose, search *by subject.* If the subject heading you choose is a major one, there will be a subheading that lists bibliographies. If you find no bibliographies or are otherwise disappointed in the catalog's listings, you may need to try another subject heading: the catalog may produce nothing under *religion and evolution,* for instance, but may have several entries under *Bible and evolution.* The choice of headings is not arbitrary; almost all libraries in the United

States now use the Library of Congress's system of headings. If you have trouble finding a productive heading, therefore, you can consult the *Library of Congress Subject Headings,* a three-volume reference work that is probably kept very near the catalogue. Or ask your librarian for help.

HINT 5:

Choose a convenient system for keeping bibliographical references and notes, and stick to it.

"I had it in my hands just the other day," I find myself saying too frequently. "It" will be a book from which I copied a passage without noting the page number, or an article that I know would be useful to me today, even though I can't quite remember which issue of which magazine I read it in. The result of letting a source out of your hands without recording the pertinent information could be a loss of vital information but will more likely be a waste of time. An unnecessary trip to the library and the frustration of finding that the book is now checked out to someone else or that the

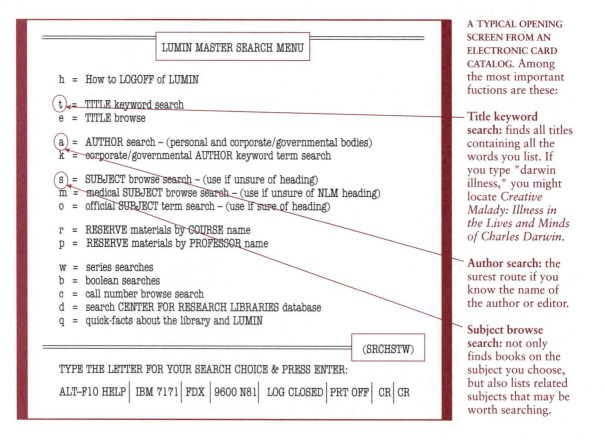

```
═══════════════════════════════╦══════════════════╦═══════════════════
              ┌─────────────────────────────────┐
              │     LUMIN MASTER SEARCH MENU     │
              └─────────────────────────────────┘

     h  =  How to LOGOFF of LUMIN

    (t) =  TITLE keyword search
     e  =  TITLE browse

    (a) =  AUTHOR search – (personal and corporate/governmental bodies)
     k  =  corporate/governmental AUTHOR keyword term search

    (s) =  SUBJECT browse search – (use if unsure of heading)
     m  =  medical SUBJECT browse search – (use if unsure of NLM heading)
     o  =  official SUBJECT term search – (use if sure of heading)

     r  =  RESERVE materials by COURSE name
     p  =  RESERVE materials by PROFESSOR name

     w  =  series searches
     b  =  boolean searches
     c  =  call number browse search
     d  =  search CENTER FOR RESEARCH LIBRARIES database
     q  =  quick-facts about the library and LUMIN
                                                    ┌──────────┐
                                                    │ (SRCHSTW)│
                                                    └──────────┘
═══════════════════════════════════════════════════════════════════════

 TYPE THE LETTER FOR YOUR SEARCH CHOICE & PRESS ENTER:

 ALT–F10 HELP │ IBM 7171 │ FDX │ 9600 N81 │ LOG CLOSED │ PRT OFF │ CR │ CR
```

A TYPICAL OPENING SCREEN FROM AN ELECTRONIC CARD CATALOG. Among the most important fuctions are these:

Title keyword search: finds all titles containing all the words you list. If you type "darwin illness," you might locate *Creative Malady: Illness in the Lives and Minds of Charles Darwin.*

Author search: the surest route if you know the name of the author or editor.

Subject browse search: not only finds books on the subject you choose, but also lists related subjects that may be worth searching.

```
FULL DISPLAY  for Item No.  1                              PROD Files
═══════════════════════════════════════════════════════════════════

     Loc: ELLIS  Call No.: QH31.D2 W5

     TITLE (S)    Darwin's Victorian malady; evidence for its medically
                    induced origin by} John H. Winslow.
     AUTHOR:      Winslow, John H.--1932-
     PUBLISHED:   Philadelphia, American Philosophical Society, 1971.
   DESCRIPTION:   94 p. 24 cm.
     SUBJECTS:    Darwin, Charles--1809-1882.    ◄──────────────┐
                  Naturalists--United States--Biography.         │
                  Chronic diseases--Cases, clinical reports, statistics.
       SERIES:    Memoirs of the American Philosophical Society --v. 88
        NOTES:    Bibliography: p. 87-90.    ◄───────────────────┤
     OCLC NO.:    0C00214907                                     │
                                                                 │
                                                                 │
═════════════════════════════════════════════════════════════════┤
═══════════════════════════════════════════════════════════════════
                                              ┌──────────────┐   │
                                              │  (BF1PREV)   │◄──┘
                                              └──────────────┘

 Type    c  Item No. for CIRCulation information    p  PREVIOUS AUTHOR list
         r  for REVISE search                       u  scan UP display
         n  for NEW search                          d  scan DOWN display

 TYPE  CHOICE & PRESS ENTER:

 ALT-F10 HELP │ IBM 7171 │ FDX │ 9600 N81 │ LOG CLOSED │ PRT OFF │ CR │ CR
```

A TYPICAL SCREEN LISTING A SINGLE BOOK. Found via title, author, or subject search, this screen gives information you will need for your works cited page as well as the call number and other information about the book's location.

Note that punctuation and capitalization on the card may not follow the rules you would use in your paper.

Good researchers pay special attention to the "Subjects" list and bibliography listings in the "Notes." Either of these may give clues that will lead to other valuable sources.

magazine has gone to the bindery: these difficulties take time that would be better spent writing.

More efficient researchers develop and follow a system for keeping track of bibliographic information and notes. For full-scale research projects, a standard operating procedure is to carry two sets of index cards: a 3" × 5" set for bibliographic information and a 4" × 6" set for notes. As soon as you discover a book or magazine (mentioned in a bibliography, let's say) that *may* be useful, you write down all the information that would be necessary to cite it in the final essay. For safety's sake, your bibliography card for a journal or magazine article ought to include the following:

1. The author.
2. The title of the article.
3. The title of the magazine or journal.
4. The volume number (if there is one).
5. The issue number (if there is one).
6. The date of publication (sometimes given only as a year).
7. The pages where the article begins and ends.

A complete book produces a simpler bibliography card:

1. The author.
2. The title.
3. The place of publication.
4. The publisher.
5. The date of publication.

An article contained in an edited book produces a slightly more complex one:

1. The name of the author of the article.
2. The title of the article.
3. The title of the book.
4. The name of the editor of the book.
5. The place of publication.
6. The publisher.
7. The date of publication.
8. The pages where the article begins and ends.

All this information is noted in highly compressed form in a standard bibliography or index or in a library catalog. There is no easier time to write it down than when you are looking at such a source. If you are standing at a card catalog, you may want to write the call number on the 3" × 5" bibliography card. If you are at a computer terminal, it may be possible to print out the bibliographical information you see on the screen.

QH 31
D2 C57
1984

    Clark, Ronald W. The Survival — Title of work
of Charles Darwin: A Biography of
a Man and an Idea. New York:
Random House, 1984.

Call Number

Complete name of author

Title of work

Complete publication information

Sample 3" × 5" bibliography card

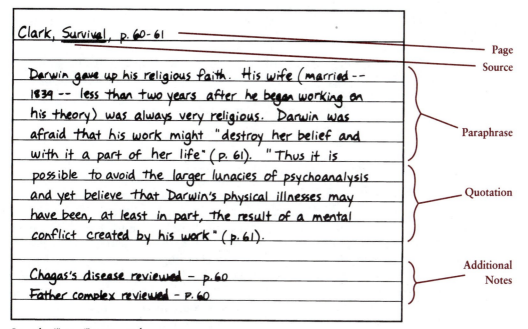

Clark, Survival, p. 60-61 —————— Page
————— Source

Darwin gave up his religious faith. His wife (married --
1839 -- less than two years after he began working on
his theory) was always very religious. Darwin was
afraid that his work might "destroy her belief and ⟩ Paraphrase
with it a part of her life" (p. 61). "Thus it is
possible to avoid the larger lunacies of psychoanalysis
and yet believe that Darwin's physical illnesses may ⟩ Quotation
have been, at least in part, the result of a mental
conflict created by his work" (p. 61).

Chagas's disease reviewed – p. 60 ⟩ Additional
Father complex reviewed – p. 60   Notes

Sample 4" × 6" note card

You will not, however, want to write notes on a small bibliography card or on the back of a computer printout. Instead, file the bibliographic information safely away and write notes on your 4" × 6" cards. Since you know that you have complete bibliographic information safely filed, you can begin each note card by placing the shortest possible identification of the book in the upper-right-hand corner of your note card—perhaps only the author's last name, perhaps this plus a key word from the title: "Johnson, Way" or "Twain, Mississippi."

Barbara Tuchman describes her own approach to note cards, which is a sensible one:

> As to the mechanics of research, I take notes on four-by-six index cards, reminding myself about once an hour of a rule I read long ago in a research manual, "Never write on the back of anything." Since copying is a chore and a bore, use of the cards, the smaller the better, forces one to extract the strictly relevant, to distill from the very beginning, to pass the material through the grinder of one's own mind, so to speak. Eventually, as the cards fall into groups according to subject or person or chronological sequence, the pattern of my story will emerge. Besides, they are convenient, as they can be filed in a shoebox and carried around in a pocketbook. When ready to write I need only take along a packet of them, representing a chapter, and I am

A WRITER AT WORK

"Notecards"
BARBARA TUCHMAN

equipped to work anywhere; whereas if one writes surrounded by a
pile of books, one is tied to a single place, and furthermore likely to be
too much influenced by other authors.

The system using two sizes of index cards has great practical advantages
for major projects. For smaller projects, you may prefer to keep all your
notes and bibliographic entries in a spiral notebook. The important thing
is to keep the information safely and systematically.

HINT 6:

Vary your reading and note-taking style to suit your purpose.

Learning *not* to read is one step toward becoming a researcher, since
searches through bibliographies, indexes, and the library catalogue will
usually produce far more material than there is time to digest. You need
to develop an ability to scan a book or article quickly, estimating its
usefulness without spending much time poring over its individual paragraphs. If you are looking for a particular bit of information, you might
go directly to the index at the back of the book, of course. If you are trying
to get a more general sense of a book's contents, you might examine the
table of contents and chapter titles and sample a few paragraphs before
committing yourself to serious reading. Ordinarily, the introductions and
conclusions of essays and articles give a good indication of their content,
and many scholarly articles begin with an abstract designed to save the
busy researcher the time lost reading irrelevant material.

  Once you have decided that a source is worth a second glance, at
least, you will want to read (or skim) it with note cards or notebook by
your side. For reasons that Barbara Tuchman indicates in the passage just
quoted, most of the notes you take ought to be compressed and put into
your own words. Occasionally, however, you may feel that quoting an
author's exact words will add weight to your paper. Take down the exact
words, then, but be certain to enclose them in large quotation marks on
your note card. Failure to do so has led to many cases of unintentional
plagiarism (see page 197). Occasionally, you will find a source so broadly
significant to your essay that you know you *will* use it, even though you
can't yet foresee where or in how many ways. In such a case, you will
probably want to photocopy it so it will always be on hand.

  Inexperienced researchers tend to make the following mistakes: they
either read sources laboriously or skip them entirely; they exhaust themselves copying long passages from books rather than attempting to separate
essential from inessential material; they photocopy everything, not even
pausing to skim it first, and so end up at home with a briefcase full of bad
material as their only resource. I confess to having made all these errors.
Experienced researchers end up with a lighter briefcase and a clearer mind.
They scan and skim far more material than they read, and they leave the
library with a small cache of high-quality xeroxes and note cards. I seem

to be getting somewhat better at this, but I confess that it is a skill one learns slowly.

HINT 7:

Don't become a slave to your research.

On this subject Barbara Tuchman is once again well worth quoting:

> The most important thing about research is to know when to stop. How does one recognize the moment? When I was eighteen or thereabouts, my mother told me that when out with a young man I should always leave a half-hour before I wanted to. Although I was not sure how this might be accomplished, I recognized the advice as sound, and exactly the same rule applies to research. One must stop *before* one has finished; otherwise, one will never stop and never finish. I had an object lesson in this once in Washington at the Archives. . . . The Archives people introduced me to a lady professor who had been doing research in United States relations with Morocco all her life. She had written her Ph.D. thesis on the subject back in, I think, 1936, and was still coming for six months each year to work in the Archives. She was in her seventies and, they told me, had recently suffered a heart attack. When I asked her what year was her cut-off point, she looked at me in surprise and said she kept a file of newspaper clippings right up to the moment. I am sure she knew more about United States–Moroccan relations than anyone alive, but would she ever leave off her research in time to write that definitive history and tell the world what she knew? I feared the answer. Yet I knew how she felt. I too feel compelled to follow every lead and learn everything about a subject, but fortunately I have an even more overwhelming compulsion to see my work in print. That is the only thing that saves me.

A WRITER AT WORK

"When to Stop"
BARBARA TUCHMAN

Like art, research may have value for its own sake, but as a writer, you need to be a pragmatist. In the course of writing an undergraduate research paper, you cannot expect to become a world-class expert on your subject. You can, however, become well enough informed to be listened to with respect, and you can ordinarily do this in a period of time that will allow you to meet your deadline.

WRITING THE RESEARCH PAPER

Brag (discreetly) about the quality of your sources.   If your readers are going to take you seriously as a researcher, they need to be convinced that you have investigated the subject thoroughly, consulting leading writers on the subject and examining the primary sources[1] available. Lose no

POINTS TO

CONSIDER

---

[1] primary sources: See Chapter 6, page 187, for the distinction between primary and secondary sources.

opportunity, therefore, to show the pedigree of your sources. In Carolyn Douglas's research paper on Darwin's illness (pp. 260–283), she makes it clear that she has examined the great biologist's own writings about his disease, the writings of his son and biographer, and the writings of several physicians and psychoanalysts who have taken an interest in the question. When she finally invokes the authority she will rely on most heavily to make her point, she establishes his credentials meticulously:

> The arsenic theory has been answered by Dr. Ralph Colp, a physician and psychiatrist who studied Darwin's Diary of Health, his letters, and other relevant documents thoroughly.

Later she reinforces the reader's good opinion of Colp with this statement:

> Colp's book is clearly the most complete study of Darwin's illness ever published, and his conclusion seems difficult to refute.

By statements like these, the writer not only tells the reader who is being quoted, but also strengthens her own authority by showing that she is playing, so to speak, with an all-star team.

Let your voice be heard.   Authority in a paper can't be achieved solely by assembling good sources. The writer's voice, too, must be heard, reasoning its way through the tangle of expert opinions, weighing evidence judiciously, drawing conclusions, rising above the data. If you examine the way Douglas's paper opens, you'll see that after a page in which she carefully pegs each assertion to the authority that supports it, she stands on her own feet to make key judgments:

> The precise cause of Darwin's illness remains a mystery, but the best evidence now available suggests that it was caused by the psychological stress of advocating the theory of evolution. The persistent attempt to find a physical cause reveals at least as much about society's reluctance to consider mental disease "real" as it does about what was wrong with Charles Darwin.

The alternation between the voices of "the authorities" and the voice of the writer is one sign of a good research paper. Readers need to hear the writer's voice establishing the overall meaning of the paper. Otherwise, they may feel that they are reading no more than a patchwork collection of quotations and summaries.

QUESTIONS FOR PEER REVIEW

Since authorities and authority are so important in the long research paper, you may want to ask your readers the following questions in addition to the general questions listed on pp. 60–61:

1. Are there points in the paper where I am relying on unimpressive or unidentified authorities? Where?

2. Can you point to passages where I am clearly speaking in my own voice, making my own judgments?

3. In these passages, do I seem to speak with an appropriate mixture of caution and confidence?

The last of these questions may seem odd, but it is very important. Inexperienced writers of research papers tend to speak like mice or like lions: either they refuse to risk a judgment or they write as though theirs are the only voices worth listening to. To speak with quiet and justifiable authority in a paper that is packed with authorities requires practice and maturity.

Assignments for Chapter 7

Because a long research paper requires so much time and effort, you should choose a topic with care. The assignments below may serve as catalysts to your thinking, but you will want to consult with your instructor as you design your actual topic.

ASSIGNMENT 1: **HOMOSEXUALS AND THE MILITARY**

During the early 1990s the United States became embroiled in a controversy about the integration of homosexuals into the armed forces. Some advocates of integration pointed to the successful integration of African Americans and of women into military service as parallel cases. Others pointed to the successful integration of homosexuals into the armed forces of other countries. Write a research paper in which you explore one of these parallel cases, showing what light—if any—it sheds on what has been happening in the United States.

ASSIGNMENT 2: **ONE PRODUCT ENTERS THE WASTE STREAM**

Some environmentalists complain that consumers know nothing about the way products they buy will eventually enter the "waste stream" of our culture. Write a research paper in which you thoroughly investigate the way we are currently dealing with the disposal of automobile tires, motor oil, or disposable diapers. How serious is the problem of disposal? Are adequate solutions to the problem in place or in sight? What can we expect the future to bring?

ASSIGNMENT 3: **THE HILL/THOMAS AFFAIR**

The Senate confirmation hearing on the nomination of Clarence Thomas to the Supreme Court was one of the stormiest in American history. At the heart of the matter was Professor Anita Hill's allegation of sexual harassment. During the hearing, several senators attempted to develop evidence to support or refute Hill's allegation but no one seemed able to present a completely convincing case. After the hearing, the controversy continued to smolder. Write a research paper in which you bring the reader up to date on the Hill/Thomas case by reviewing evidence and arguments that have come to light since Thomas's confirmation. What would a reasonable person *now* conclude about the truth of Hill's allegation?

ASSIGNMENT 4:   ## Canadian and British Health Care

Participants in the current American health-care debate often point either to the Canadian system or the British system to make their points. Yet few Americans really understand how either of these systems works. Write a research paper in which you explain to American readers how, and how successfully, health care is provided in Great Britain or Canada.

ASSIGNMENT 5:   ## The Technology of Cartoon Films

From a technological point of view, computer technology has divided the twentieth century rather neatly in half. Many procedures that were done by hand before midcentury have changed dramatically. The production of animated cartoons is a conspicuous case, though not one that most people understand in detail. Write a research paper in which you contrast the old technology of cartoon-film production with the new. Since the Disney studio has been the leader throughout the century, you may want to contrast the production of an early animated feature film like *Snow White* with the production of a later feature like *The Lion King*.

1.

Carolyn Douglas

Prof. Gene Joy

Humanities 104

24 May 1990

Changing Theories of Darwin's Illness

2.

From 1831-36, Charles Darwin explored South America and several Pacific islands as the naturalist aboard the Beagle. Though he suffered from seasickness, he was healthy and energetic on land. In 1833 he undertook a horseback journey of 400 miles through an unsettled region of Argentina, climbing mountains along the way, hunting with gauchos, and going for "several days without tasting anything besides meat" (C. Darwin, Works 1: 106-21). Soon after his return to England, however, his health broke, and by 1842, at the age of 33, he was living in seclusion in the English countryside, so easily exhausted that he could

3.

work for only a few hours each day and could manage only short walks (F. Darwin, Life 1: 87-102). He was so ill that he could

4.

barely cope with a visit from friends: ". . . my health always suffered from the excitement, violent shivering and vomiting attacks being thus brought on" (C. Darwin, Autobiography 115).

"Many of my friends, I believe, think me a hypochondriac," Darwin wrote in 1845 (F. Darwin, Life 1: 318), and Sir Peter

5.

Medawar[1] has suggested that Darwin's inability to find a physical cause for his disease was "surely a great embarrassment for a man whose whole intellectual life was a marshalling and assay of hard

6.

evidence" (67). About 1857, Darwin told his physician that he believed the illness had been caused by "the extreme sea-sickness

1. Rather than use a cover sheet (which some teachers may require and others dislike), Douglas gives her name, the professor's name, the course, and the date at the head of her paper.

2. Douglas summarizes material from an entire chapter of the first volume of Darwin's collected works to give evidence of his good health. Notice that she paraphrases almost everything but includes one brief quotation. This is a good technique for showing that her comments are closely connected with what Darwin actually said in the book. Notice that the parenthetical citation specifies C. (Charles) Darwin, to avoid confusion with F. (Francis) Darwin, the author of another source listed under Works Cited. The citation also includes *Works* (the briefest convenient form of the title) to avoid confusion since two works by Charles Darwin appear under Works Cited.

3. Francis Darwin is a primary source here. He reported what he saw with his own eyes. Douglas condenses into one sentence material from sixteen pages of her source.

4. Douglas avoids quoting secondary (distant) sources on the state of Darwin's health, choosing instead Darwin's own words, the primary source.

5. The raised number indicates that there is an endnote (see page 279) with explanatory matter that may interest the reader but is not essential.

6. Since the reader will assume that these are Medawar's words, there is no need to give his name in the citation, and since he is the author of only one work under Works Cited, there is no need to give a title. The page number is sufficient.

Douglas 2

7.

he underwent in H.M.S. 'Beagle.'"[2] His son and biographer, Francis Darwin, reported that the "ill health was of a dyspeptic kind, and may probably have been allied to gout, which was to some extent an hereditary malady" ("Darwin" 525). Modern medicine, however, does not recognize long-term effects of seasickness, and it does not associate gout with shivering and vomiting

8.

(Berkow 1: 975-76, 1450). The precise cause of Darwin's illness remains a mystery, but the best evidence now available suggests that it was caused by the psychological stress of advocating the theory of evolution. The persistent attempt to find a physical

9.

cause reveals at least as much about society's reluctance to consider mental disease "real" as it does about what was wrong with Charles Darwin.

The first argument for a psychological origin other than

10.

hypochondria was made in 1901, nearly two decades after Darwin's death, by physician William W. Johnston. Using evidence in Francis Darwin's The Life and Letters of Charles Darwin, Johnston demonstrated that the illness grew more severe when Darwin worked on his theory of evolution and that it subsided when he did other things. Johnston identified the illness as "chronic neurasthenia," caused by a "continued overstrain of exhausted nerve cells"

11.

and the resulting "loss of normal nerve supply to the digestive organs and the heart" (157-58). The notion of neurasthenia, exhaustion of nerve cells as a result of strong emotions, has

12.

essentially been abandoned by modern medicine (Diamond 8: 27-28), but the correlation between Darwin's research on evolution and his illness has continued to fuel speculation.

7. Darwin said this to Dr. Lane; Lane repeated it in a letter to Dr. Richardson; Dr. Richardson repeated it in a lecture; Dr. Colp, who had seen a printed form of the lecture, quoted it in his book, *To Be an Invalid*. Since Douglas can't go back to any source earlier than Colp's book, she puts in an explanatory note to explain that she is quoting indirectly, through Colp. It is always best to quote a source directly, but Douglas's technique is good if direct quotation is impossible.

8. Douglas cites a standard medical reference book, *The Merck Manual*, on the present understanding of seasickness and gout. This information might be treated as common knowledge, but Douglas wants to show a *definitive* medical opinion.

9. Douglas has a two-part thesis, expressed in two sentences. She aims to show both that the disease had a psychological cause *and* that the reluctance or willingness of people to admit this fact is an indication of changing attitudes toward psychosomatic illness.

10. Notice that throughout the paper Douglas is careful to give relevant credentials for her sources. The reader now knows that Johnston is a physician but that his training dates from the nineteenth century.

11. Douglas learned of the existence of Johnston's article by reading another source (Colp's *To Be an Invalid*). Rather than accept Colp's characterization of the article, however, she found it on the library shelf and read it herself.

12. Once again, Douglas went to a standard reference book to verify the present state of thinking about a disease. In this case the book was the *International Encyclopedia of Psychiatry, Psychology, and Neurology*, where she found a signed article on neurasthenia by Leon Diamond.

Douglas 3

For about fifty years, from World War I through the early
1960s, psychoanalytic theories dominated the discussion of

13.   Darwin's illness. Dr. Edward J. Kempf wrote the first study of
this kind for the <u>Psychoanalytic Review</u> in 1918. Arguing from
evidence in <u>The Life and Letters</u>, Kempf suggests that Darwin
suffered from an "anxiety neurosis" caused by his "complete
submission to his father" (191). Kempf believed that this submission prevented Darwin from expressing anger, first toward his
father and then toward others. Darwin, according to Kempf,
feared "being offensive, ungrateful, and unappreciative" and so
he became, on the surface, "hyperappreciative" and extraordinari-

14.   ly kind. Anger, however, was "a repressed emotional impulse that
he had to be incessantly on guard against and which, perhaps,
contributed to wearying him into invalidism" (174).

15.   In 1954, Dr. Rankine Good published an influential explanation of Darwin's psychology, apparently based on the same sources
used by Kempf. Good believed that Darwin felt "aggression, hate,
and resentment . . . at an unconscious level" for his "tyrannical" father. By "reaction-formation," however, his conscious

16.   feeling was a "reverence for his father which was boundless and
most touching." Darwin's illness, according to Good, was

> . . . in part, the punishment Darwin suffered for
> harbouring such thoughts about his father. For Darwin
> <u>did</u> revolt against his father. He did so in a typical
> obsessional way (and like most revolutionaries) by

17.
> transposing the unconscious emotional conflict to a
> conscious intellectual one--concerning evolution.

13. Douglas's own research has shown her that most of the publications about Darwin from 1918 through about 1963 were either psychoanalytic or reacted to psychoanalytic theories. She therefore opens her paragraph with a generalization she does not attribute to any source. It is her own thought. Several sources told her that Kempf wrote the first psychoanalytic study, so she treats this information as common knowledge.

14. The Kempf article is very long. Douglas summarizes it and includes a few key quotations. Since the quotations are widely separated in the text (seventeen pages apart), she pinpoints them with page numbers. Such pinpoint citations are a scholarly courtesy, useful to a reader who may want to examine the quotations in context.

15. Douglas calls Good's explanation "influential" because several of her sources refer to it.

16. Good wrote, "Further, there is a wealth of evidence that unmistakably points to these symptoms as a distorted expression of the aggression, hate, and resentment felt, at an unconscious level, by Darwin towards his tyrannical father, although, at a conscious level, we find the reaction-formation of the reverence for his father which was boundless and most touching." Notice how Douglas shortens and simplifies this material in her paper. The summarized material comes from the same page of Good's article as the extended quotation that follows, so Douglas delays her parenthetical notation until after the long quotation.

17. Quotations longer than four lines are indented one inch (or ten spaces) from the left margin.

Douglas 4

18.
> Thus, if Darwin did not slay his father in the flesh,
> then in his The Origin of Species . . . he certainly
> slew the Heavenly Father in the realm of natural
> history. (106)

Like Oedipus,[3] Darwin suffered greatly for this "unconscious
patricide." Good believes that it accounts for his "almost forty
years of severe and crippling neurotic suffering" (107).

Speculations of this sort irritated some of Darwin's admir-
ers. In 1958 George Gaylord Simpson, an eminent paleontologist
and expert on Darwin's life, disagreed with the "psychiatrists
and psychoanalysts" who "have considered the disease to be purely
psychological." The "psychoneurotic theory," said Simpson, "is
an easy way out with any undiagnosed illness." A great many
illnesses were undiagnosed in Victorian times, Simpson pointed
out, including brucellosis, "an infectious, long-continuing

19.
disease that frequently produces exactly Darwin's symptoms," and
one to which he was "undoubtedly exposed" (121). Soon after, Dr.

20.
Saul Adler, an internationally recognized expert on diseases
transmitted by parasites, also argued against a "purely psychological aetiology." He pointed out that in the Voyage of the
Beagle, Darwin records being attacked by "the great black bug of
the Pampas," a blood-sucking insect Adler believed to be "no
other than Triatoma infestans . . . the causative agent of
Chagas's disease." Chagas's disease, Adler pointed out, matches
many of Darwin's symptoms, including exhaustion and stomach
trouble (Nature 1102). Sir Gavin de Beer's 1963 biography of
Darwin embraced Adler's theory and dismissed the psychoanalytic

18. Good's article actually says, "in his *The Origin of Species, The Descent of Man,* &c., he certainly slew. . . ." To shorten the quotation, Douglas cuts a few words and indicates the cut with three periods, the standard way to mark an ellipsis within a sentence.

19. Since Simpson's entire discussion of the illness is confined to one page of an article, Douglas does not put in a citation after each short quotation. The citation after "undoubtedly exposed" gives the location of all the preceding information and quotation from Simpson. It shows only the page number because the context makes it clear that Simpson is being quoted, and there is only one work by Simpson under Works Cited.

20. Again, Douglas is careful to show that the authority she quotes has good credentials.

Douglas 5

theories with contempt, especially one (clearly Good's, though
Good is not named) suggesting that "Darwin's theories of evolu-
tion and natural selection killed the Heavenly Father, and that
Darwin suffered the remorse of Oedipus." De Beer treated this

21.   diagnosis as if it were an accusation of weakness and attempted
to refute it by showing that Darwin was, after all, <u>manly</u>:

> It must remain a matter of opinion whether this is
> sufficient explanation of the reduction to semi-
> invalidism of a man with the physical stamina, courage,
> fortitude, healthy mind, and good judgment that Darwin
> showed during the voyage of the <u>Beagle</u>, when for five

22.   years he cheerfully endured the hardships of life at
> sea in a little ship and ashore, when he roughed it
> with the gauchos, ate coarse food and enjoyed it,
> climbed mountains, made numerous, lengthy, arduous, and
> dangerous journeys on foot and on horseback, slept out,
> caught venomous snakes, fished, admired Spanish ladies,
> cracked jokes, and took everything in his stride. (115)

De Beer was in a position to make his opinions known. Writing
for <u>Encyclopaedia Britannica</u>, he briefly mentioned the
psychoanalytic theories and announced that "all this specious and
special pleading is unnecessary" in light of Adler's discovery
("Darwin" 496). At this point, it certainly appeared that the
case for psychological causation was weakening. And the case for
physical causation gained still more strength in 1971, when John
H. Winslow published a book demonstrating that Darwin, like other
Victorians, may have taken arsenic for medical reasons and that

21. The tone of de Beer's comments interests Douglas because it suggests that he finds psychosomatic illness unmanly and disgraceful. Therefore she introduces the quotation in a way that draws attention to the tone.

22. Douglas's quotation from de Beer is long. Quotations this long are justifiable only when the precise wording is crucial to making a point. In this case, the wording is important because it reveals the tone of de Beer's discussion.

Douglas 6

23.　there is "a very close match" between his symptoms and the
symptoms of chronic arsenic poisoning (26-34).

　　　But the case for physical causation had weaknesses, and
doubt was soon cast on both the theory of Chagas's disease and
24.　the arsenic theory.　Dr. A. W. Woodruff, a British expert on
tropical diseases, questioned Adler's diagnosis.　He pointed out
that many of Darwin's symptoms (heart palpitations, undue fatigue, and trembling fingers) appeared before Darwin sailed on
the <u>Beagle</u>, and that when they recurred after his return, they
were associated not with physical strain (as would have been
expected with Chagas's disease) but with "mental stress."　He
also pointed out that no other member of the <u>Beagle</u> crew suffered
from Chagas's symptoms, and he questioned the accuracy of Professor Adler's statistics about the high rate of infection with
Chagas's disease in the province of Mendoza, where Darwin was
25.　attacked by the "black bug" (745-50).　Woodruff's diagnosis of
Darwin's illness was "an anxiety state with obsessive features
and psychosomatic manifestations" (749).　After reading
Woodruff's article, Professor Adler continued to believe in the
theory of Chagas's disease, but he pointed out the possibility
that Darwin suffered both from it <u>and</u> from "an innate or acquired
neurosis" (<u>Journal</u> 1250).　The "black bug" theory therefore lies
in limbo, and even its chief proponent did not argue that it
excluded psychological causation of some of Darwin's symptoms.

　　　The arsenic theory has been answered by Dr. Ralph Colp, a
physician and psychiatrist who studied Darwin's <u>Diary of Health</u>,
his letters, and other relevant documents thoroughly.　Colp

23. Once again, Douglas paraphrases many pages and quotes only briefly. The phrase "a very close match" sums up Winslow's point, and Douglas wants to quote it to make the quotation from Colp two paragraphs later comprehensible.

24. Notice again the care with which Douglas notes the credentials of the people she quotes or paraphrases.

25. Because the quotations from Woodruff are spread through a long article, Douglas pinpoints them with citations to particular pages.

points out that, unlike arsenic poisoning, Darwin's disease was intermittent: ". . . acute nausea and vomiting would sometimes abruptly cease, and his stomach would return to normal, or near-normal, function." In addition, with chronic arsenic poisoning the patient ordinarily loses weight and suffers from "disturbances of the lower part of the bowel," but even during his acute periods of illness Darwin maintained his weight and his bowels were unaffected (133). These and other discrepancies between the symptoms of arsenic poisoning and Darwin's actual symptoms led Colp to conclude that "there is not 'a very close match' between the two groups of symptoms" (137).

26.   Dr. Colp's 1977 book <u>To Be an Invalid</u>, which carefully correlates fluctuations in Darwin's health with records of Darwin's activities, confirms what William W. Johnston noted in 1901: work on the theory of evolution made the illness worse, and practically any relief from that work made it better. It was not merely the strain of mental work that brought on a bout of illness; Darwin's health flourished while he wrote a difficult book on a non-evolutionary topic (52) but suffered as <u>The Origin of Species</u> neared completion (65-66). Colp draws a cautious but firm conclusion: "I believe that the evidence shows that Darwin's

27.   feelings about his evolutionary theory were a major cause for his illness." He does not commit himself to a psychoanalytic view

28.   like Good's, but instead emphasizes some of the stresses in Darwin's life: his awareness that his theories offended some of his few friends, his knowledge that other friends who were eminent scientists doubted some of his conclusions, his awareness

26. Douglas has used past tense to refer to the works of other writers because she views these works as bits of past history. Beginning with Colp, she uses present perfect and present tense ("has been answered," "points out") because she views his theory as current. When the history of ideas is not an issue, most writers use these tenses in referring to works by other writers.

27. Douglas chooses a key quotation from Colp that exactly matches one she used from Winslow.

28. Douglas's references to Johnston and later to Good help the reader see the connections between parts of the paper.

Douglas 8

that time spent in society was time taken away from his great work, and an "obsessional" concern with problems in the theory that he could not solve. Darwin did "have a neurotic side," Colp concludes. He sometimes felt "an excessive and inappropriate anxiety" and he "was tortured by obsessional thoughts," many of them related to his work (141-43). Colp's book is clearly the most complete study of Darwin's illness ever published, and his

29. conclusion seems difficult to refute.

The consensus opinion among experts today seems to be that psychological illness could and did reduce the once vigorous

30. Darwin to semi-invalidism, or at least contributed to his suffering. In the most recent book-length biography, Ronald W. Clark reviews earlier theories and rejects both Chagas's disease and Oedipal conflict. He believes, however, that there was a more "straightforward and likely" psychological cause. Darwin's wife

31. Emma was deeply religious, and Darwin feared that his scientific work might "destroy her belief and with it a part of her life." He also must have sensed that his theory would do damage to the "confident world" of the Victorians. "Thus," Clark concludes, "it is possible to avoid the larger lunacies of psychoanalysis and yet believe that Darwin's illnesses may have been, at least in part, the result of a mental conflict created by his work" (61). The 1989 article on Darwin in <u>Encyclopedia</u> <u>Americana</u>,

32. surprisingly, continues to advocate the theory of Chagas's disease, but the article has not been revised in at least 17 years. Its author is Sir Gavin de Beer, who died in 1972. The 1990 edition of <u>Encyclopaedia</u> <u>Britannica</u> reports that "a careful

29. Douglas is stating her own opinion when she says that Colp's conclusion seems hard to refute. Notice, however, that the next paragraph supports her opinion by showing that views like Colp's, to some degree based on his work, now seem to form a "consensus."

30. Notice that Douglas is echoing the words of de Beer, quoted on page 5. She is also reminding us of the first part of her thesis.

31. Douglas is careful to bring her research up to date, quoting the latest biography and two current encyclopedia articles to check current views.

32. Here is a good example of the danger of assuming that an encyclopedia article will give you the indisputable "facts."

Douglas 9

33.   analysis of the attacks [of illness] in the context of his
[Darwin's] activities points to psychogenic origins" (Kevles
980). Clearly, the author is referring to Colp's book.

34.   In the process of giving his now accepted conclusions, Colp
comments that "maturity and neurosis can coexist in the same
person" (142). In the context of the history of the controversy
over Darwin's illness, this sentence seems especially significant. It appears that in Darwin's own time, psychological disease was considered not "disease" at all but mere hypochondria.
In the twentieth century, psychiatrists and psychologists (though
their theories have sometimes sounded bizarre) have gradually
established the reality of psychological illness. Though we can
see in many of Darwin's "defenders" during the 1950s and 1960s a
tendency to treat psychologically caused illness as though it
were some sort of defect in the character of the sufferer, this
view seems to be losing ground--at least in Darwin's case. Most
writers, and perhaps most readers, seem willing to acknowledge

35.   that psychological illness can coexist not only with maturity but
with a greatness like Darwin's.

33. To make the meaning of the quotation clear, Douglas inserts words of her own. Square brackets mark such editorial insertions.

34. In this paragraph, Douglas turns to the second part of her thesis, showing that attitudes to psychosomatic illness have changed through time.

35. The final sentence directly addresses the thesis and has a note of finality.

36.

Douglas 10

Notes

[1] Winner of the Nobel Prize for Medicine, 1960. Medawar believed that Darwin's illness was partly organic and partly psychological.

[2] The source of this quotation is a letter from Darwin's physician, Dr. Edward Lane, to Dr. B. W. Richardson. Because the letter is not available, I have quoted it from Colp's <u>To Be an Invalid</u>, page 59.

[3] Good is clearly thinking of Freud's famous "Oedipus complex."

36. Not every research paper needs a page of Notes. When it is used, it contains only the exploratory notes that the writer feels compelled to add to the text of the paper. Exploratory notes give additional information or clarify something obscure within the text. They should not be used to give the sort of bibliographical information given under Works Cited. Notice that both the Notes section and the Works Cited section begin with a centered heading, then have a double space between heading and first line.

Douglas 11

Works Cited

37.   Adler, Saul. "Darwin's Illness." <u>Nature</u> 10 Oct. 1959: 1102-03.

---. "Darwin's Illness." <u>British Medical Journal</u> 8 May 1965:
          1249-50.

38.   Berkow, Robert, ed. <u>The Merck Manual of Diagnosis and Therapy</u>
          15th ed. 2 vols. Rahway, NJ: Merck, 1987.

Clark, Ronald W. <u>The Survival of Charles Darwin: The Biography</u>
          <u>of a Man and an Idea</u>. New York: Random, 1984.

39.   Colp, Ralph. <u>To Be an Invalid: The Illness of Charles Darwin</u>.
          Chicago: U of Chicago P, 1977.

40.   Darwin, Charles. <u>The Autobiography of Charles Darwin, 1809-1882,</u>
          <u>With Original Omissions Restored</u>. Ed. Nora Barlow. New
          York: Harcourt, 1958.

41.   ---. <u>Journal of Researches, 1839</u>. Vol. 1 of <u>The Works of</u>
          <u>Charles Darwin</u>. 18 vols. New York: AMS Press, 1972.

Darwin, Francis. "Darwin, Charles Robert." <u>Dictionary of</u>
          <u>National Biography</u>. 1888. 1973 ed.

42.   ---, ed. <u>The Life and Letters of Charles Darwin</u>. 2 vols. New
          York: Basic, 1959.

De Beer, Gavin. <u>Charles Darwin: A Scientific Biography</u>. 1963.
          Garden City, NY: Doubleday, 1965.

43.   ---. "Darwin, Charles." <u>Encyclopedia Americana</u>. 1989 ed.

---. "Darwin, Charles." <u>Encyclopaedia Britannica: Macropaedia</u>.
          1974 ed.

Diamond, Leon. "Neurasthenia." <u>International Encyclopedia of</u>
44.   <u>Psychiatry, Psychology, and Neurology</u>. Ed. Benjamin B.
          Wolman. 12 vols. New York: Aesculapius, 1977.

37. In citing weekly or biweekly publications, use the date rather than the volume number.

38. In citing a work of two or more volumes, give the total number of volumes even if you use only one. Indicate in the text of the paper which volume you are citing (see page 286).

39. Notice the abbreviation for University Press.

40. Use this form for a book written by one person and edited by another.

41. If each volume is a series (like *The Works of Charles Darwin*) has its own title, include the title in the citation and indicate which volume it is.

42. When you are focusing more on the editor's words (from the introduction, preface, or notes, for example) than on those of the original author, you may list the work under the editor's name.

43. Notice the brief citation form for standard encyclopedias; include only the name of the encyclopedia and the edition used. Although these articles are signed, many are not; if the article is unsigned, begin with the title of the article.

44. If you are citing a reference work that is not well known, use the form for books in a series and include the editor, the number of volumes, and the complete publication information.

Douglas 12

Good, Rankine. "The Life of the Shawl." The Lancet 9 Jan.
        1954: 106-07.

Johnston, William W. "The Ill Health of Charles Darwin: Its
        Nature and Its Relation to His Work." American
        Anthropologist, n.s. 3 (1901): 139-58.

Kempf, Edward J. "Charles Darwin--The Affective Sources of His
        Inspiration and Anxiety-Neurosis." Psychoanalytic Review 5
        (1918): 151-92.

Kevles, Barbara. "Darwin, Charles." Encyclopaedia Britannica:
        Macropaedia. 1990 ed.

Medawar, Peter. "Darwin's Illness." The Art of the Soluble.
        London: Methuen, 1967. 61-67.

Simpson, George Gaylord. "Charles Darwin in Search of Himself."
        Scientific American Aug. 1958: 117-22.

Winslow, John H. Darwin's Victorian Malady: Evidence for Its
        Medically Induced Origin. Philadelphia: American
        Philosophical Society, 1971.

Woodruff, A. W. "Darwin's Health in Relation to His Voyage to
        South America." British Medical Journal 20 March 1965:
        745-50.

45.

46.

47.

45. Occasionally a publication is issued in more than one series; "n.s." indicates a new series.

46. When using a titled chapter from a book, list the name of the chapter before providing the title and publication information for the whole book.

47. Monthly and bimonthly publications are listed by date rather than by volume number.

General Comments on Citation Form

The technicalities of citation form take some getting used to—more getting used to, in fact, than most people will do in their lifetimes. Even experienced scholars routinely consult manuals or samples when they compose their Works Cited section: almost no one *knows,* without some assistance, precisely how to list a translated article by two authors appearing in a journal with continuous pagination. You should, however, learn the general method of citation well enough to be able to read the citations in scholarly articles. If you learn this much, you will be able to cite sources in your own paper by finding parallel examples in published sources or in handbooks.

In general, citation in scholarly papers uses a two-part system. The major part is the Works Cited section (called in scientific papers the References section). This alphabetical list at the back of the paper contains the bibliographic information necessary to allow readers to identify precisely the sources that a writer has used. The minor part of the system of citation is the series of parenthetical notations in the text of the paper. Each notation follows a quotation, paraphrase, or summary and tells readers (1) which of the sources from the Works Cited section is involved and (2) what pages of that source are referred to. The sometimes complicated rules of citation form are created to allow the writer to use this two-part system as economically and clearly as possible.

THE MLA CITATION STYLE

The style of documentation described at length in *The MLA Handbook for Writers of Research Papers* assumes that the reader who wants to identify, evaluate, or locate a source needs answers to the following questions:

1. Who wrote the work?

2. What is its title?

3. If it appears between the covers of a larger journal or book, what is the title of the larger work?

4. If the work was prepared by an editor or translator, who is he or she?

5. If the work is available in more than one edition or revision, or if it is part of a multivolume work, which edition or volume is used?

6. What is the place of publication? The publisher's name?

7. When was the work published?

8. If the work is included in a larger work, what pages are involved?

It is possible to find (but easier to invent) an example of a Works Cited listing that answers all these questions in order:

```
Doe, Jane. "Her Article." Her Book. Trans. John Q.
    Public. 2nd edition. Baltimore, Md.: Trankebar
    Press, 1990. 10-20.
```

The carefully prescribed form allows the writer to compress a great deal of information into this brief citation.

Many variations in citation form are essentially omissions of unnecessary information or slight necessary additions. Consider the following examples of citations for complete books.

```
Dubois, Kenneth P., and E. M. K. Geiling. Textbook
    of Toxicology. New York: Oxford UP, 1959.
Dobzhansky, Theodosius. Genetics and the Origin of
    Species. 1937. 3rd ed., rev. New York:
    Columbia UP, 1951.
Krause, Ernst. Erasmus Darwin. Trans. W. S.
    Dallas. With a preliminary notice by Charles
    Darwin. London: John Murray, 1879.
```

In the first example, no article or chapter title is needed; there is no editor or translator; there is no other edition, volume, or revision; and there is no need to give page numbers (since we are not dealing with a separate article inside the book). The example shows us how much can be left out of the form in a simple case. The second example is slightly more complicated. It tells the reader that Dobzhansky's book was first published in 1937 but that the paper refers to the "third edition, revised in 1951." Such citations avoid confusion. For instance, it may be possible to find an edition of Darwin's *Origin of Species* that was published in 1990, but it is important to show that the original publication was 1859. In the third example, a comment is added to note that the book includes a section written by Charles Darwin.

When the source cited is not the book but a single article or chapter inside it, more information is needed:

```
Darlington, Cyril D. "Purpose and Particles in the
    Study of Heredity." Science, Medicine and
    History. Ed. E. Ashworth Underwood. 2 vols.
    London: Oxford UP, 1953. 472-81.
Simpson, George Gaylord. Foreword. The Life and
    Letters of Charles Darwin. Ed. Francis Darwin.
    2 vols. New York: Basic Books, 1959. v-xvi.
```

Notice that in the first example, it is necessary to name both the author of the article and the editor of the whole book. The "Ed." before E. Ashworth Underwood's name can be read "edited by." Notice, too, that the citation ends with a listing of the first and last pages of the article. In the second example, Simpson's foreword has no title, so it is simply listed as "Foreword." Introductions, prefaces, appendixes, and other such parts of books ordinarily have Roman-numeral page numbers.

Many academic journals are issued at infrequent intervals—quarterly (four times per year)—or even annually. Such journals are treated essentially as if they were books, so the citation form for them looks very like what we have just discussed:

```
Kempf, Edward J. "Charles Darwin—The Affective
     Sources of His Inspiration and Anxiety-
     Neurosis." Psychoanalytic Review 5 (1918):
     151-92.
Sulloway, Frank. "Darwin's Conversion: The Beagle
     Voyage and Its Aftermath." Journal of the
     History of Biology Fall 1982: 325-96.
```

The first of the above examples is from a journal that numbers its pages continuously through the year. That is, if the first issue of the year ends on page 121, the second issue starts at page 122 rather than page 1. "*Psychoanalytic Review 5* (1918): 151–92" means "pages 151–92 of Volume 5 of *Psychoanalytic Review,* published in 1918." The second example above is for a journal that starts page numbering anew with each issue: it directs the reader to pages 325–96 of the Fall issue.

Journals, magazines, and newspapers that are issued more frequently use a somewhat different form:

```
Provine, W. B. Review of To Be an Invalid, by
     Ralph Colp. Science 24 June 1977: 1431-32.
Silver, John. "Darwin, Too, Saw the Ocean in the
     Andes." New York Times 30 Mar. 1987, late
     ed.: B18.
```

The first example above is from *Science,* a weekly publication, and you'll notice that it gives the date of publication in the same place where our earlier example read "Fall 1982." Since the date clearly identifies which issue is being cited, there is no need to give other identifiers (such as "Volume 33, number 1"). Notice, too, that this particular "title" does not appear in quotation marks: like many other book reviews, Provine's appeared without any title other than the name of the book reviewed. In such circumstances, you should use a description in the title's place. The second example is from a daily newspaper. Notice that the headline is used as a title. Because different material appears in the *Times's* "national" and "late" editions, the edition is specified. Because the paper is numbered by sections, the citation specifies the page as B18 so that no one will look for the article in section A or section C. Had the article appeared without an author's name, the citation would have begun with the title.

Unpublished sources follow forms loosely like those used for published sources:

```
Golomb, Miriam. Lecture on Misapplications of
     Natural Selection. Campus Writing Program
     Workshop. Columbia, Missouri, 10 Jan. 1994.
Perry, Carolyn. Telephone interview. 21 August
     1994.
```

Obviously, these sources are not available to readers of a research paper, but they *are* sources and should be listed in the Works Cited section.

Parenthetical notations in the text.   In the MLA style, parenthetical notations in the text of the paper give the minimal amount of information needed to identify the pertinent listing in the Works Cited section (call this the *identifier*), then give the page numbers referred to. The form is "*identifier,* space, page numbers."

How much identification is necessary will vary. If, for example, your parenthetical notation follows a sentence in which you have identified Edward J. Kempf as your source, and if there is only one Kempf listing in your Works Cited section, then *no* further identification is necessary. Your notation might be simply (**163–64**). If you had quoted without naming Kempf, your notation might be (**Kempf 163–64**). If you had named Kempf in the text, but there are two articles by him, your notation might be (**"Darwin" 163–64**). If you had not named Kempf and there are two articles, your citation might be (**Kempf, "Darwin" 163–64**). The key is to consider the purpose of the parenthetical citation, which is to point the reader to the appropriate listing on the Works Cited page with as little fuss as possible. See the sample research paper in this chapter for additional information on and examples of parenthetical notations and Works Cited entries.

THE APA CITATION STYLE

The style of citation described in the *Publication Manual of the American Psychological Association* is more commonly used for papers in the natural sciences or social sciences than for those in the humanities. Rather than describe it at length here, I will give you examples of some typical citations:

A book with two or three authors:

```
Dubois, K. P., & Geiling, E. M. K. (1959).
```

Textbook of toxicology. New York: Oxford University Press.

A book written by one author and edited by another:

Darwin, C. (1985). The autobiography of Charles Darwin, 1809-1882. With original omissions restored (N. Barlow, Ed.). New York: Harcourt.

A translation:

Krause, E. (1879). Erasmus Darwin (W. S. Dallas, Trans.). London: John Murray.

A work in several volumes:

Darwin, C. (1972). Journal of researches, 1839. Vol. 1 of The works of Charles Darwin (Vols. 1-18). New York: AMS Press.

A new edition and/or revision of a book:

Dobzhansky, T. (1951). Genetics and the origin of species (3rd ed., rev.). New York: Columbia University Press. (Original work published 1937)

An article from a reference book:

Kevles, B. (1990). Darwin, Charles. In Encyclopaedia Britannica: Macropaedia.

An article collected in a book:

Darlington, C. D. (1953). Purpose and particles in the study of heredity. In E. A. Underwood, (Ed.), Science, medicine and history (pp. 472-81). London: Oxford University Press.

An article in a periodical with continuous pagination:

Kempf, E. J. (1918). Charles Darwin—the affective sources of his inspiration and anxiety-neurosis. Psychoanalytic Review, 5, 151-92.

An article in a periodical that paginates each issue separately:

```
Sulloway, F. (1982, Fall). Darwin's conversion:
    the Beagle voyage and its aftermath. Journal
    of the History of Biology, 15(3), 325-96.
```

An article from a weekly or biweekly periodical:

```
Adler, S. (1959, Oct. 10). Darwin's illness.
    Nature, pp. 1102-03.
```

Parenthetical notations in the text.   In APA style, the year of publication is considered more important than it is in the MLA style. Thus a typical parenthetical notation might be (**1982, p. 326**). Notice that there is a comma between the date and the page, and that a **p.** is used to indicate the page number. A **pp.** is used to indicate a group of pages. If the author is not indicated in the text, his or her name precedes the year: (**Sulloway, 1982, p. 326**). Should you have two articles by the same author in the same year, they are distinguished by a letter following the year: (**Sulloway, 1982b, pp. 326–33**). Sometimes the year and page number are noted in separate sets of parentheses, thus: Sulloway (**1982**) has shown that Darwin's conversion to evolutionary views was completed only after his return from the voyage of the *Beagle* (**pp. 326–33**).

PART IV

PERSUASION

"We may convince others by our arguments, but
we can only persuade them by their own."

JOSEPH JOUBERT

8

Proposals

A
T THIS POINT IN THE BOOK, WE ARE MOVING FROM EXPOSITORY
writing—writing that explains or describes—to argumentative writing. Though some textbook writers see a sharp distinction between exposition and argumentation, I confess that I don't. Almost all writing is persuasive. In an autobiographical sketch or a research report, no less than in a proposal, the writer tries to persuade the reader to see the subject his way or her way.

There is, however, an important psychological shift between exposition and argumentation. In exposition, as we have seen, writers work to find differences between themselves and their readers. The writing prospers when the writer knows something the reader doesn't or sees a subject from a perspective the reader has never considered. Thus, a good piece of advice for the expository writer is, "*Build on differences* that separate you from your audience." In argumentative writing, however, differences are obstacles to overcome. The most significant difference, of course, is that the writer has reached a conclusion the reader does not (yet) completely share. As we'll see in the next three chapters, skillful arguers try to overcome this difference by searching out goals and assumptions that they and their readers share. Thus, a good piece of advice for argumentative writers is "*Build on agreement.*"

The essays we will look at in the first of our argument chapters form a loose-knit family that we might refer to either as proposals or as problem-solution papers. Unlike some other forms of persuasive writing, proposals look to the future rather than the past and call for action rather than mere speculation or judgment. For the proposal writer changing the audience's *thinking* is not enough; he or she wants readers to *do* something.

People in many professions live in a world of proposals accepted or rejected: proposals that funds be allocated, plans be implemented, research be conducted. We'll touch on a few of these more elaborate types of proposals, but we'll begin by examining a simpler form—one that allows us to examine closely the crucial match between the problem and the solution.

PROPOSALS IN TWO VOICES: THE ADVICE COLUMN

At its simplest, a proposal is no more than the presentation of a problem and the recommendation of a course of action. In most formal proposals, one writer both articulates the problem and presents the solution, but in the case of advice columns, this labor is divided, allowing us to study one at a time the two central parts of the proposal. In her nationally syndicated column *Miss Manners,* Judith Martin produces one or more of these short question-and-answer proposals each week.

Ms. Martin, I should warn you, often writes as if she were merely the secretary of the long-dead Miss Manners, Victorian expert on etiquette. The advice, however, is usually very down to earth. Consider the following example:

Dear Miss Manners:

My boyfriend and I are getting ready to celebrate our six-month going steady anniversary. He's giving me a present. The problem is that I don't know whether I am "supposed" to give him one also. My mother says that it is incorrect for me to because, as a girl, I am not obliged. I feel somewhat awkward since he has already let me know that he has a gift for me. I don't want to seem ill-mannered. Please let me know the proper thing to do.

Gentle Reader:

Would you and your mother please stop thinking along the lines of "as a girl, I am not obliged"? There really is no such thing as obligatory present giving. One goes by one's instincts, and yours obviously are to commemorate this momentous occasion. The general rule about presents between unmarried people is that one gives or accepts only what can suitably be returned during a breakup. (Married couples have the courts to help them decide this.) "Take back your mink" is, for example, impossible to say, and therefore it would be inadvisable to give your boyfriend a mink coat. Books, records, and small leather goods such as wallets and keycases are considered to be a proper type of present to be exchanged by those in temporary arrangements.

The issue here is hardly the stuff headlines are made of, but it gives us a good opportunity to note that the question that provokes a proposal has two parts. The questioner has a *goal:* "I don't want to seem ill-mannered." She also has a *problem* that hinders her achieving that goal: she doesn't know whether she is "supposed" to give her boyfriend a gift. The problem solver must accept the goal as a valid one and propose a solution more expert or ingenious than the questioner herself is capable of devising.

A WRITER AT WORK

"Gift Giving"
JUDITH MARTIN

Miss Manners, of course, has goals of her own: she must not only propose a sensible solution for the questioner but produce a column that will enlighten and interest a much wider group of readers. Her answer in this case seems to divide its energy about equally between the two goals.

When the questioner poses a more intricate problem, Miss Manners produces a more serious and elaborate answer:

A WRITER AT WORK

*"Daffodil's
Parents"*
JUDITH MARTIN

Dear Miss Manners:

Our son is planning to marry a girl from another city, a distance of four hundred miles. What are our responsibilities? We have met his fiancée, but not her parents. Do we (a) call them and invite them to visit us? (b) call first and then visit them? (c) wait for them to call us? Any visits must be overnight stays because of the distance. However, we have three other children at home and cannot offer house guests a private bath and other conveniences conducive to privacy. If they come to visit, would it be proper to accommodate them in a nearby hotel? If yes, should we pay the bill? Also, if we visit them, should we expect to stay with them or arrange our own accommodations?

Gentle Reader:

If you choose (c), you may wait forever. Society has changed since the rule about the parents of engaged couples was invented, and no one has bothered to revise it to meet such outrageous situations as engagements between couples whose parents live four hundred miles apart. This has resulted in a great deal of confusion and hurt feelings that are better saved for the wedding.

Miss Manners will now come to the rescue. Here is the old rule: The young man's parents call on the young woman's parents. ("Calling" referred to the now defunct custom of arriving at their doorstep for a short surprise visit that would not inconvenience them because everybody was always calling on everyone else all the time, and therefore it was no surprise at all.)

Here is the new rule: The young man's parents initiate the relationship by telephoning or writing the young woman's parents and expressing their desire of becoming acquainted. The details of the two meetings are then worked out with the help of the two people who are in a position to know what would be most convenient for each household—the young couple. All you have to do, then, is call or write the other parents and say, "We're so pleased. Daffodil is such a lovely girl. We're anxious to meet you, and would love to have the pleasure of entertaining you here." Assuming that Daffodil has warned them about your limited bathroom facilities, they can accept or counterinvite you to their hometown. In either case, saying "I'm afraid we don't have room to make you comfortable, so I've made a hotel reservation for you nearby" is proper. Paying the hotel bill of your guests is charming if you can easily afford it but if not, don't worry about it.

This longer exchange between a reader and Miss Manners allows us to examine the etiquette of proposing and solving a problem. The questioner must *make his or her goal clear, either by naming it outright or by implying it unmistakably*. In this case, the questioners' goal is to get the relationship between themselves and Daffodil's parents off on the right foot. The questioner must also *make clear the nature of the problem that prevents his or her reaching the goal, giving all the pertinent details with as few irrelevancies as possible*. In this case and in many others, the problem involves a statement of the *constraints* that make achievement of the goal difficult: 400 miles to be traveled, a crowded home, and no direct acquaintance with the other couple. Clearly, these constraints create a genuine problem, since inviting Daffodil's parents to visit is inviting them to travel 400 miles and stay either in a crowded home or in a hotel room that they may feel obliged to pay for. The etiquette of the advice column also demands that the questioner *describe a problem challenging enough to create interest*.

The young man's parents have clearly held up their end in this respect: they are caught in the sort of danger that invites rescue. Judith Martin is extremely fortunate; she seems to have an endless supply of readers entangled in social difficulties complex enough to produce not only tension, but suspense. One reads the question and wonders briefly whether even Miss Manners will be able to solve this difficulty. The presentation of a thorny and significant problem is, as we will see, one of the keys to writing excellent proposals.

Generally, the columnist's first step is to reframe the problem in a way that (1) *gives readers insight by putting it into a perspective the questioner had not considered* and (2) *opens the way toward a solution*. The framework Miss Manners brings to this problem is one of her familiar themes: "Society has changed since the rule . . . was invented." Since young people now move farther from home than their ancestors did, and since the custom of "calling" has vanished, we need a new custom for this situation. As you read through the various proposals collected in this chapter, you will see that the writer often reframes a problem by giving an expert or ingenious explanation of its cause. Even though the new framework can't eliminate the constraints (Daffodil's parents remain 400 miles away), it allows the reader to see them from a fresh perspective and to begin to hope that there is a way around them. An engineer analyzing a failing bridge may reframe the problem in the same way Miss Manners does when she analyzes a failing custom. "Surfacing materials have changed," the engineer may report, "since the original deck was built, and the problem we face is how to introduce new materials compatible with the old steel plates."

The columnist's next job is, of course, to present a solution that truly fits the problem. You'll notice that the new rule Miss Manners proposes exactly matches the constraints that the questioner listed. It takes into account the travel distance, the "limited bathroom facilities," and the lack of knowledge each couple has of the other. Only if all the constraints are dealt with adequately will the proposal seem satisfying and feasible.

EXERCISE 1

◆ *Responding as Miss Manners.* The following letter elicited from Miss Manners a sixty-one-word reply. Try your hand as an etiquette columnist by providing your own answer of about the same length:

Dear Miss Manners:

One of the things I do for a living is to give lectures. I don't get rich on it, but I give audiences their money's worth, and I have worked up some good speeches that people seem to enjoy.

Word gets around, of course, and I am often asked by small groups, such as clubs and professional organizations, to give luncheon speeches or answer questions at their meetings. But often, when I accept, I find that they have no intention of paying me!

Perhaps I should bring it up when they invite me, but I assume that they know I am a professional, and it seems crass to demand payment while they are telling me how wonderful they've heard I am, how much everyone is looking forward to hearing me, and so on. These same people wouldn't dream of offering me the services or goods they sell for free, of course.

EXERCISE 2

◆ *Writing to Miss Manners.* The following answer was elicited by a sixty-nine-word question to Miss Manners. Like many of her answers, it painstakingly responds to the particulars of the questioner's situation. After reading the answer, try to write a matching question.

Gentle Reader:

Miss Manners is a cucumber sandwich eater in a doughnut world, so don't think she doesn't sympathize with you. But if one wishes to stress one's willingness to work with other people, regardless of gender, one keeps special requests to a minimum, or presents them as if one were the spokeswoman for a faction, as in, "Perhaps we should provide tea at the next meeting for people who would prefer it."

EXERCISE 3

◆ *Writing to and Responding as Miss Manners.* Write a brief question to and answer from Miss Manners. Attempt not only to fulfill each role properly but to amuse a wider readership. In your answer, you may want to imitate not only Miss Manners' way of dealing with substance, but her style and her tone.

THE PROBLEM/SOLUTION ESSAY: AN EXAMPLE FROM SCIENCE

The transition from Miss Manners to scientific writing may seem to you an unlikely one, but publishing scientists know that their business consists largely of asking intriguing questions and then proposing ways to answer them. The research proposal, the lab report, and the article in a scientific journal are all built on a basic problem/solution pattern every reader of an advice column should recognize.

Often this basic pattern is obscured for the nonscientific reader by technical language and the presentation of data in unfamiliar forms, but in the more popular writings of accomplished scientists we can find examples that show the scientist taking the roles of both questioner and problem solver: the scientist must first state a goal and problem that have challenged researchers, then present a matching solution. The following example is taken from entomologist Vincent Dethier's popular book *To Know a Fly* (1962).

The kind of question asked of nature is a measure of a scientist's intellectual stature. Too many research workers have no questions at all to ask, but this does not deter them from doing experiments. They become enamored of a new instrument, acquire it, and then ask only "What can I do with this beauty?" Others ask such questions as "How many leaves are there this year on the ivy at the zoology building?" And having counted them do not know what to do with the information. But some questions can be useful and challenging. And meaningful questions can be asked of a fly.

Between the fly and the biologist, however, there is a language barrier that makes getting direct answers to questions difficult. With a human subject it is only necessary to ask: what color is this? does that hurt? are you hungry? The human subject may, of course, lie; the fly cannot. However, to elicit information from him it is necessary to resort to all kinds of trickery and legerdemain. This means pitting one's brain against that of the fly—a risk some people are unwilling to assume. But then, experimentation is only for the adventuresome, for dreamers, for the brave. . . .

Extracting information from a fly can be . . . challenging. Take the question of taste, for example. Does a fly possess a sense of taste? Is it similar to ours? How sensitive is it? What does it prefer?

The first fruitful experimental approach to this problem began less than fifty years ago with a very shrewd observation; namely, that flies (and bees and butterflies) walked about in their food and constantly stuck out their tongues. The next time you dine with a fly (and modern sanitary practice has not greatly diminished the opportunities), observe his behavior when he gavots across the top of the custard pie. His proboscis, which is normally carried retracted into his head like the landing gear of an airplane, will be lowered, and like a miniature vacuum cleaner he will suck in food. . . .

Proboscis extension has been seen thousands of times by thousands of people but few have been either struck by the sanitary aspects of the act or ingenious enough to figure out how they might put the observation to use to learn about fly behavior.

The brilliant idea conceived by the biologist[1] who first speculated on why some insects paraded around in their food was that they tasted with their feet. In retrospect it is the simplest thing in the world to test this idea. It also makes a fine parlor trick for even the most blasé gathering.

The first step is to provide a fly with a handle since Nature failed to do so. Procure a stick about the size of a lead pencil. (A lead pencil will do nicely. So will an applicator stick, the kind that a physician employs when swabbing a throat.) Dip one end repeatedly into candle wax or paraffin until a fly-sized gob accumulates. Next anesthetize a fly. The least messy method is to deposit him in the freezing compartment of a refrigerator for several minutes. Then, working very rapidly, place him backside down onto the wax and seal his wings onto it with a hot needle.

Now for the experimental proof. Lower the fly gently over a saucer of water until his feet just touch. Chances are he is thirsty. If so, he will lower his proboscis as soon as his feet touch and will suck avidly. When thirst has been allayed, the proboscis will be retracted compactly into the head. This is a neat arrangement because a permanently extended proboscis might flop about uncomfortably during flight or be trod upon while walking.

Next, lower the fly into a saucer of sugared water. In a fraction of a second the proboscis is flicked out again. Put him back into water (this is the control), and the proboscis is retracted. Water, in; sugar, out. The performance continues almost indefinitely. Who can doubt that the fly can taste with his feet? By taking advantage of its automatism, one can learn very subtle things about a fly's sense of taste.

For example, who has the more acute sense of taste, you or the fly? As the cookbooks say, take ten saucers. Fill the first with water and stir in one teaspoon of sugar. Now pour half the contents of the saucer into another which should then be filled with water. After stirring pour half the contents of the second saucer into a third and fill it with water. Repeat this process until you have a row of ten saucers. Now take a fly (having made certain that he is not thirsty) and lower him gradually into the most dilute mixture. Then try him in the next and so on up the series until his proboscis is lowered. This is the weakest sugar solution that he can taste.

Now test yourself. If you are the sort of person who does not mind kissing the dog, you can use the same saucers as the fly. Otherwise make up a fresh series. You will be surprised, perhaps chagrined, to discover that the fly is unbelievably more sensitive than you. In fact, a starving fly is ten million times more sensitive.

---

[1] biologist: The scientist referred to is Dwight E. Minnich. You can read his original article in *Biological Bulletin* (July 1926).

Dethier's account here carefully avoids the special vocabulary of the laboratory and the impersonal tone of a typical article in a scientific journal. Those who know science, however, will recognize that it presents the key components of a scientific paper: an analysis of the problem, a careful description of materials and methods used in the solution to the problem, a statement of results, and a discussion of their significance.

The parallel to an advice column is fairly clear. In the role of *questioner,* the scientist states a goal (to understand the fly's sense of taste) and a problem achieving that goal (an inability to ask the fly directly). Once again, the best problems are the challenging ones, ones that require "all kinds of trickery and legerdemain." Discussing the problem as a *solver* (Mr. Wizard in place of Miss Manners), the scientist reframes it in order to open a way to a solution. The problem is not really an inability to get the fly to reveal its subjective impression of taste, in which case it would be impossible to overcome. The problem as a scientist sees it is our inability (up to now) to identify precisely the nature of the stimulus that leads to feeding and the location of the organs that receive this stimulus. The layperson thinks of taste as a subjective experience; the scientist redefines it in terms of measurable stimuli and observable behavior.

SCIENTIFIC SKEPTICISM ABOUT CAUSES AND EFFECTS

To some degree, the success of a scientific paper is measured in the same terms as the success of an advice column: has the writer managed to present a truly satisfactory solution to an intriguing difficulty? Most of us, when we read Dethier's account of this experimental procedure will say, "Of course he has." At first glance, the proof that flies taste with their feet seems irrefutable.

Scientists, however, are carefully trained skeptics: they learn to examine very carefully the match between the problem and the solution. Do these experiments in fact prove that the fly tastes with its feet? Isn't it possible, for example, that the fly is not *tasting* the sugar water at all, but *smelling* it, and that the organs for smelling are somewhere in the head (or body or wings) rather than the feet? Couldn't we explain the proboscis extension either of the following ways?:

1. Only when the fly's feet touch the water is its nose close enough to the surface to detect the scent; when the *scent* is detected, the fly lowers the proboscis.

2. The fly's proboscis, as Dethier points out, is retracted while the insect is flying. Suspended by its glob of wax, the fly "believes" it is flying and keeps its proboscis tucked up, even though it smells the sugar water

below. When the fly's feet touch the water, though, it "believes" it has landed and immediately extends its proboscis.

On close analysis, it appears that the experimenter may have been guilty of jumping to an oversimple conclusion about the relationship between a cause and an effect. And, as it turns out, another entomologist criticized his paper for faults of this kind, producing a dispute too technical for us to consider here—one eventually resolved by new experiments. In the scientific problem/solution paper, as Dethier points out, the great danger is asserting a badly tested cause-and-effect relationship: ". . . there is the well-known case of the chap who wondered which component in his mixed drink caused his inevitable intoxication. He tried bourbon and water, rum and water, rye and water, gin and water, and concluded, since every drink had water as a constant, that water caused his drunkenness."

EXERCISE 4

◆ *Proposing an Experiment.* Describe an experiment that could be conducted to solve the problem pointed out: that the fly might be smelling the sugar water rather than tasting the water with its feet.

PROPOSALS ABOUT POLICY

Like scientific proposals, proposals about policy involve links between cause and effect. In the debate about gun-control policy, for instance, some disputants argue that there is a direct link between the ease with which Americans can buy "Saturday night specials" and the number of fatal shootings in the country. Others dispute this "fact." Unlike the scientist, the proposer of a policy deals with the causes and effects that can't be studied in the laboratory. Because matters of policy involve humans and because our society frowns on using humans as guinea pigs, neither the proposer's analysis of the problem nor the effectiveness of his or her solution can be rigorously tested. When the facts are so far from speaking for themselves, the success of a proposal depends more heavily on the persuasive powers of its advocates.

In this section, we'll look at two brief policy proposals, both presented on the op-ed (opinion-editorial) page of the *New York Times*. The op-ed pages of newspapers provide a key forum for policy proposals but also require writers to be very succinct. As we'll see, this forces the writers to make strategic decisions about how to divide a few hundred words among the tasks of establishing an acceptable goal, reframing the problem, and discussing the feasibility of the solution.

A PROPOSAL TO END APARTHEID
ON COLLEGE CAMPUSES

The first of our policy proposals appeared in the *Times* on May 28, 1993, soon after Hillary Rodham Clinton had delivered a notable commencement speech at the University of Pennsylvania. Editorialist Brent Staples used Mrs. Clinton's speech as a springboard for his essay "Ending Apartheid at College: First, Dismantle Segregated Housing."

Hillary Rodham Clinton missed an opportunity in her commencement address at the University of Pennsylvania. Responding to recent racial incidents there, Mrs. Clinton urged students to respect free speech, even in the face of hateful utterances. That's sound advice, as far as it goes. But the deeper problem is a pattern of racial alienation that Penn and other colleges accept and perpetuate.

Many campuses today look like America during its Jim Crow period. In some places, blacks have segregated living arrangements, segregated counselors, segregated pages in the newspaper—even segregated graduation ceremonies. Brunetta Wolfman, who teaches at George Washington University, describes this as "the warm, dark cocoon of resegregation" where "black students live, socialize, and interact primarily with one another, remaining at the margins of campus life."

The "cocoon" offers protection but demands conformity in return. Ideas go unchallenged and misgivings about whites are constantly reinforced. The broadening experience of college is all but lost.

The Supreme Court decreed an end to public school segregation in 1954, with Brown *v.* Board of Education, and ordered the process completed "with all deliberate speed." What that meant depended on where one lived. In Boston, desegregation begot hatred and violence that continues to this day. In Chicago, desegregation never happened; the city stalled it until so many whites had fled the system that compliance was impossible.

I grew up in Chester, Pa., a factory town south of Philadelphia. The spirit of Brown reached Chester in the fall of 1962, during the first week of fifth grade. The principal summoned me from class and handed me a folder containing my transcripts. I'd been transferred to a school in the white end of town. I'd never heard of the school, let alone seen it, a telling fact given that it was only a mile away. That mile was a metaphor for upward mobility. It took me from an ancient, run-down school to a gleaming building with the youngest, most energetic teachers I'd ever seen. It took me from a life on a truck route to a quiet street where the Mayor lived. The mile also took me from the black world into the white one.

At first, the playground was tough. Names were called, noses bloodied. But soon we said goodbye to all that and became friends. At college the pattern was virtually the same. Shouting and shoving were part of the freshman bargain. By graduation, our parents had to pry us apart.

Nowadays, blacks and whites don't get close enough for shoving. Twelve years of Republican race-baiting have taken their toll. But so has a system that estranges blacks from campus, and classmates: black counselors, black student centers, black freshman tours and, worst of all, black housing. The process begins during orientation, when blacks are stamped "minority," and remanded to the campus ghetto.

Once, segregation was decried as an evil. Now colleges defend the practice on the grounds that black students demand it. That's a craven response meant to excuse the university's acquiescence to bad policy. Administrators also say segregation "raises the comfort level" for blacks. Perhaps. But what comforts can also smother.

It's time to dismantle apartheid on campus. The first thing colleges can do is abolish segregated housing and assign rooms on a random basis. Beyond that, administrators need to work mightily at drawing black students into the mainstream of campus life. Until they do, diversity remains a myth.

Like most proposals presented to the general public, this one is not packaged as tidily as a scientific paper or an advice column, but it has the same essential components. Staples doesn't formally state his larger *goal,* but his essay makes it clear: he wants black students to have a "broadening experience" that encourages "upward mobility." Like most writers on op-ed pages, Staples has only about 600 words to spend. He spends very few of them explaining or justifying this goal because almost all readers recognize it and share it. But since many readers will know little about racial policies on college campuses, he spends more space on the *problem,* showing how policymakers have framed it and how he reframes it. Paragraphs 2, 7, and 8 tell us that many college administrators define the problem as the discomfort of black students on largely white campuses; they offer designated black housing, counselors, and student centers as the solution. Staples concedes that the administrators are partly right: *one* problem *is* discomfort; but he focuses on a second problem that makes the first one worse: policies that encourage black students to withdraw into "the warm, dark cocoon of resegregation." His *solution* is, of course, to eliminate the cocoon by eliminating separate black institutions on campus, beginning with segregated housing. Since the segregation of housing comes from students' choosing roommates of their own race, he would have administrators "assign rooms on a random basis."

EXERCISE 5

♦ *Talking Back.* Op-ed pages provide readers an opportunity to respond to articles by writing letters to the editor. Letters about proposals tend to come from people whose experience allows them to comment positively or negatively on the writer's goals, analysis of the problem, or solution. As a college student, you should have experience that would allow you to write a good letter to the editor responding to Staples's essay. Do so, remembering that letters longer than about 500 words are rarely published.

A PROPOSAL TO PUT MORE WOMEN ON PEDESTALS

Like Brent Staples, Lynn Sherr and Jurate Kazickas timed their op-ed piece to take advantage of interest created by an event in the news: the commissioning of a statue of Eleanor Roosevelt for New York's Riverside Park. Sherr and Kazickas, co-authors of a guidebook to women's landmarks in America, urge New Yorkers (and Americans generally) to "Put More Women on a Pedestal."

A WRITER AT WORK

"Put More Women on Pedestals"

LYNN SHERR AND JURATE KAZICKAS

Back at the turn of the century, as Susan B. Anthony entered her 80th year, a colleague in the suffrage wars broached the delicate subject of a memorial after her death. She proposed placing a statue of the distinguished women's rights leader in a park near the Anthony home in Rochester, N.Y.

Miss Anthony, as she was known, demurred. "I never can bear to see the statue of a woman exposed to the cold and rain and snow," she explained. "And I don't like to think of one of myself out of doors."

Alas, the same nation that refused to heed her demand for the vote took these sentiments to heart when she died in 1906. Today, there is no public outdoor statue of Susan B. Anthony, the woman who, more than any other, made it possible for American women to participate in public life.

She is not alone. Wander through our public squares and parks and you will find no freestanding likenesses of such authentic American heroines as Amelia Earhart, Abigail Adams, or even Lucy B. Hobbes, the first female dentist (1866). We know of only 40 public outdoor statues of American woman nationwide. Of those, four portray the same woman, Sacajawea, Lewis and Clark's brave Native American guide.

In New York City, only one real American female is so honored, Gertrude Stein, seated Buddha-like in Bryant Park. But the October groundbreaking for an Eleanor Roosevelt statue in Riverside Park (to be dedicated in 1994) will catapult us, with two statues of women, into the top ranks of American cities. (Even London has nearly a dozen.)

Other Americans who have been immortalized in bronze and stone include Helen Keller and her teacher Anne Sullivan, Mary McLeod Bethune (the only African American woman on the list), Mary Ann (Mother) Buckerdyke, a relief worker during the Civil War, two refugees from political persecution (Anne Hutchinson and Mary Dyer), one cowgirl (Annie Oakley), and one 13-year-old ambassador of peace (Samantha Smith, Yuri Andropov's correspondent).

So much for the real women. Far more common are statues representing anonymous or mythological women, idealized as Liberty or Justice or some other figure modestly draped in marble robes. This, of course, is the only way some men can see women, perfect images on a pedestal.

Who cares, you may ask? Do the pigeons really need equal opportunity roosting places? Does anyone really look at those discolored lumps of metal or marble? Well, yes. Statues tell us something about our past. They are a link to someone else's life of accomplishment. At a time when heroism is in short supply, we need daily reminders of the women who made America great.

Model for the Roosevelt statue in Riverside Park

NYT Pictures

Wouldn't you like to picnic in the shadow of Harriet Tubman, the chief engineer of the underground railroad? Jog past a replica of Annie Edson Taylor, the first person to go over Niagara Falls in a barrel and survive? Pose next to Carry Nation wielding her temperance hatchet?

Or perhaps give a grateful nod to Susan B. Anthony the next time you vote? Right now, the only way to acknowledge her is by heading indoors, to the first floor crypt of the Capitol building in Washington. Miss Anthony and suffragists Elizabeth Cady Stanton and Lucretia Mott were chiseled out of marble in 1921 by Adelaide Johnson—the nation's first statue to women, by a woman, for women's service to women.

But while Susan B. Anthony would be comforted to know that she is not exposed to the elements, she would no doubt lament the indignity that has befallen her memory: the three busts, on their rough-hewn base, are still occasionally referred to as the "Ladies in the Bathtub."

Op-ed contributors often use their 600-or-so words to accomplish several things at once. By placing this essay in the *New York Times,* Sherr and Kazickas generated interest in their book, communicated some information interesting in its own right, and pointed to the accomplishments of some of their heroines. At the same time, they advanced a proposal we can analyze in terms of a goal, problem, and solution. The *goal* implied throughout is to alter the public perception in a way that encourages "heroism" in women and discourages stereotyping by men. The *problem,* they say, is that we don't receive "daily reminders of the women who made America great." And the (partial) *solution* is to increase the number of highly visible outdoor statues of important women.

EXERCISE 6

◆ *Expanding the Proposal.* Squeezed into 611 words, the proposal by Sherr and Kazickas is certainly not as detailed and persuasive as a document that might be submitted, for instance, to a government body that actually had the power to commission statues. Suppose that Sherr and Kazickas had the opportunity to write an expanded proposal to such a body: a city council with funds to erect a half-dozen statues. Suppose they asked your advice on what it should contain. Write them a *proposal* about how to prepare the new proposal. Make your goal, your analysis of the problem, and your proposed solution clear.

WHY PROPOSALS FAIL

The great difficulty of writing a successful proposal is that unless it is persuasive in all its parts, the whole proposal will fail. If the reader is unwilling to accept the proposer's goal, for instance, then he or she may reject the proposal without even considering the analysis of the problem and the solution. Writing a successful proposal requires, therefore, intelligent analysis of the audience's attitudes. Sometimes this analysis is simple. Judith Martin can assume that most of her readers accept courteous behavior as an important goal: people who don't value courtesy are unlikely to read a column entitled *Miss Manners*. An entomologist writing in a scientific journal can assume that for most readers, learning about nature is a higher goal than protecting the lives of individual insects, so he or she can propose procedures that many animal-rights activists would find appalling. Some audiences are much more diverse and resistant, and therefore easier to lose at every stage of the proposal.

AN UNACCEPTABLE GOAL

When writers address an audience that is not predisposed to favor a proposal, they are forced to think harder about how to present the goal. Even in its present form, the essay by Lynn Sherr and Jurate Kazickas presents a goal that some readers of the *New York Times* might not endorse wholeheartedly. Some Americans feel that the public perception of women's roles is already changing too dramatically and that if statues will accelerate the change, they *shouldn't* be raised.

Sherr and Kazickas may be able to afford the loss of these few readers, but suppose their essay had advocated a more controversial goal: the elimination from our society of what has sometimes been called the "cult of female beauty," the tendency to see a beautiful face and body as worthwhile in their own right. This goal, too, would seem to call for fewer statues of idealized beauties and more statues of women remarkable for their accomplishments rather than for their looks. But many more readers— male and female—would be uncomfortable with this goal and unwilling to endorse wholeheartedly a proposal based on it. Irritated as they may sometimes be by a constant emphasis on women's appearance, few Americans will enlist eagerly or serve long in a campaign against any form of beauty.

Whenever possible, the wise writer bases his or her proposal a goal that the overwhelming majority of readers endorse wholeheartedly and without much need for persuasion. A proposal to improve medical care will be read more sympathetically than a proposal to lower the rates for medical malpractice insurance, *even though the two advocate precisely the same course of action*. I don't want to encourage any writer to deceive readers about his or her "real" goal, but I do want you to see that acceptable goals grow out of a meeting of minds between writer and audience. Usually the course of action that the writer advocates advances several of his or her goals at once—all of them "real." Good sense dictates that writers choose, as grounds for an argument, goals they and their readers share.

A QUESTIONABLE IDENTIFICATION OF THE PROBLEM

Even when the readers share the writer's goal, they may not agree that he or she has identified an important problem in achieving it. In the 1920s, for example, the NAACP and its allies in Congress proposed a federal law against lynching. To stop lynching was a goal that few members of Congress would have opposed; yet James Weldon Johnson, leader of the NAACP campaign, tells us that the bill failed in the Senate because key *liberals* felt that the NAACP had not identified a valid problem. Lynching, these liberals reasoned, was murder, and murder was against the law in every state; therefore, the cause of lynching was not the absence of a law, and no additional law could help prevent it. The NAACP argued that the absence of a *federal* law was a problem, since some state courts simply would not convict a white lynch mob of murdering a black man. Federal laws and federal courts, they argued, would better protect civil rights. History has shown that the NAACP's analysis was correct, but the analysis didn't convince key senators at the time. The tragic failure of this NAACP initiative contains a reminder for every writer of proposals. It is not enough to be right. You must find a way to persuade an audience that may resist your reframing of the problem for any of a thousand reasons, rational or irrational.

A SOLUTION THAT DOESN'T SEEM FEASIBLE OR THAT CREATES MORE SERIOUS PROBLEMS

Once readers are convinced that the problem is significant, there still remains the need to convince them that the solution is feasible and doesn't create problems more serious than the one it solves. The feasibility of a solution depends on many factors, some highly technical, as in the case of Vincent Dethier's experiments with the flies. In most cases, the reader will at least need to be convinced that the solution truly matches the problem and that it can be achieved in a reasonable period of time with a reasonable expenditure of resources. If Dethier had presented the amateur scientist with a surefire method of testing the fly's sense of taste that required $10,000 worth of equipment and six months of hard labor, his solution would have been technically feasible but practically impossible.

Often new solutions create problems of their own, and then the proposer must devote part of the proposal to showing that these problems are less important than the benefits. Short as Staples's proposal is, he inserts a passage dealing with a problem it creates: increased racial friction when students of various races are *forced* to share the same social institutions and the same dormitory rooms. In paragraphs 5 and 6, he recounts his own experience and argues that it is probably typical: forced integration creates a good deal of initial "shouting and shoving," but the benefits— friendships that cross racial lines, improved education for black students— far outweigh the costs.

CRITICIZING A PROPOSAL

Obviously, a critic can challenge a proposal at any of the points just mentioned: by showing that the goal is unacceptable, the problem analyzed incorrectly, the solution infeasible or fraught with unwanted consequences. A good place to study the craft of criticizing proposals is in the columns of political writers like George Will, who devotes perhaps half of his syndicated columns to advocating or opposing various plans for political and social change.

In the example reprinted below, Will—who was usually very supportive of President Ronald Reagan's political positions—criticizes the President's proposal on prayer in public schools. In presenting his proposal Reagan had told the nation that his goal was "to reawaken America's religious and moral heart, recognizing that a deep and abiding faith in God is the rock upon which this great nation was founded." He believed that a major problem standing between him and this goal was a 1962 Supreme Court ruling that organized prayer in public schools violated the First Amendment guarantee of freedom of religion. In his discussion of the problem, President Reagan implied the nation was suffering from a bad court decision: ". . . current interpretation of our Constitution holds that the minds of our children cannot be free to pray to God in the public schools. No one will ever convince me that a moment of voluntary prayer will harm a child or threaten a school or state." His proposed solution was a new amendment stating that "nothing in this Constitution shall be construed to prohibit individual or group prayer in public schools or other public institutions." Will respectfully disagreed in a *Newsweek* essay.

I stand foursquare with the English ethicist who declared: "I am fully convinced that the highest life can only be lived on a foundation of Christian belief—or some substitute for it." But President Reagan's constitutional amendment concerning prayer in public schools is a mistake.

His proposal reads: "Nothing in this Constitution shall be construed to prohibit individual or group prayer in public schools or other public institutions. No person shall be required by the United States or by any state to participate in prayer." This would restore the *status quo ante* the 1962 Supreme Court ruling that public school prayers violate the ban on "establishment" of religion. The amendment would not settle the argument about prayer; it would relocate the argument. All 50 states, or perhaps all 3,041 county governments, or all 16,214 school districts would have to decide whether to have "voluntary" prayers. But the issue is not really voluntary prayers for individuals. The issue is organized prayers for groups of pupils subject to compulsory school attendance laws. In a 1980 resolution opposing "government authored or sponsored religious exercises in public schools," the Southern Baptist Convention noted that "the Supreme Court has not held that it is illegal for any individual to pray or read his or her Bible in public schools."

This nation is even more litigious than religious, and the school prayer issue has prompted more, and more sophisticated, arguments about constitutional law than about the nature of prayer. But fortunately Senator Jack Danforth is an ordained Episcopal priest and is the only person ever to receive degrees from the Yale Law School and the Yale Divinity School on the same day. Danforth is too polite to pose the question quite this pointedly, but the question is: Is public school prayer apt to serve authentic religion, or is it apt to be mere attitudinizing, a thin gruel of vague religious vocabulary? Religious exercises should arise from a rich tradition, and reflect that richness. Prayer, properly understood, arises from the context of the praying person's particular faith. So, Danforth argues, "for those within a religious tradition, it simply is not true that one prayer is as good as any other."

One person's prayer may not be any sort of prayer to another person whose devotion is to a different tradition. To children from certain kinds of Christian families, a "nondenominational" prayer that makes no mention of Jesus Christ would be incoherent. The differences between Christian and Jewish expressions of piety are obvious; the differences between Protestants and Roman Catholics regarding, for example, Mary and the saints are less obvious, but they are not trivial to serious religious sensibilities. And as Danforth says, a lowest-common-denominator prayer would offend all devout persons. "Prayer that is so general and so diluted as not to offend those of most faiths is not prayer at all. True prayer is robust prayer. It is bold prayer. It is almost by definition sectarian prayer."

Liturgical reform in the Roman Catholic and Episcopal churches has occasioned fierce controversies that seem disproportionate, if not unintelligible, to persons who are ignorant of or indifferent about those particular religious traditions. But liturgy is a high art and a serious business because it is designed to help turn minds from worldly distractions, toward transcendent things. Collective prayer should express a shared inner state, one that does not occur easily and spontaneously. A homogenized religious recitation, perfunctorily rendered by children who have just tumbled in from a bus or playground, is not apt to arise from the individual wills, as real prayer must.

Buddhists are among the almost 90 religious organizations in America that have at least 50,000 members. Imagine, Danforth urges, the Vietnamese Buddhist in a fourth-grade class in, say, Mississippi. How does that child deal with "voluntary" prayer that is satisfactory to the local Baptists? Or imagine a child from America's growing number of Muslims, for whom prayer involves turning toward Mecca and prostrating oneself. Muslim prayer is adoration of Allah; it involves no requests and asks no blessing, as most Christian prayers do. Reagan says: "No one will ever convince me that a moment of voluntary prayer will harm a child . . ." Danforth asks: How is America—or religion—served by the embarrassment of children who must choose between insincere compliance with, or conscientious abstention from, a ritual?

In a nation where millions of adults (biologically speaking) affect the Jordache look or whatever designer's whim is *de rigueur,* peer pressure on children is not a trivial matter. Supporters of Reagan's amendment argue that a nine-year-old is "free" to absent himself or otherwise abstain from a "voluntary" prayer—an activity involving his classmates and led by that formidable authority figure, his teacher. But that argument is akin to one heard a century ago from persons who said child labor laws infringed the precious freedom of children to contract to work 10-hour days in coal mines.

To combat the trivializing of religion and the coercion of children who take their own religious traditions seriously, Danforth suggests enacting the following distinction: "The term 'voluntary prayer' shall not include any prayer composed, prescribed, directed, supervised, or organized by an official or employee of a state or local government agency, including public school principals and teachers." When religion suffers the direct assistance of nervous politicians, the result is apt to confirm the judgment of the child who prayed not to God but for God because "if anything happens to Him, we're properly sunk."

It is, to say no more, curious that, according to some polls, more Americans favor prayers in schools than regularly pray in church. Supermarkets sell processed cheese and instant mashed potatoes, so many Americans must like bland substitutes for real things. But it is one thing for the nation's palate to tolerate frozen waffles; it is another and more serious thing for the nation's soul to be satisfied with add-water-and-stir instant religiosity. When government acts as liturgist for a pluralistic society, the result is bound to be a purée that is tasteless, in several senses.

What is the nature of Will's criticism here? It seems from the first sentence that he agrees, at least in a general way, with President Reagan's goal of fostering religion, but he rejects the proposal as a mistake. One *unwanted consequence* of "nondenominational" prayer in the schools, he tells us, would be the "trivializing of religion." These prayers would have to be written by, or approved by, authorities who would insure that they were sufficiently nondenominational to keep the school system out of court: in effect, they would have to be lawyers' prayers or principals' prayers rather than the "robust" prayers of the devout. Another unwanted consequence cited by both Will and Danforth is the "embarrassment of children who must choose between insincere compliance with, or conscientious abstention from, a ritual." This embarrassment is closely tied to Will's questioning of the *feasibility* of Reagan's plan, which depends on the ability of schoolchildren to choose freely to participate in or abstain from the group prayer. Will simply doesn't believe that the average grade-schooler is capable of resisting the combination of peer pressure and adult leadership in the classroom: as a practical matter, "voluntary" prayer would become required prayer.

The heart of Will's critique of President Reagan's proposal is a quite sharp disagreement about the nature of the problem. Reagan saw the Supreme Court's decision on school prayer as an obstacle to the free exercise of religion. Will takes the opposite view. The court's decision, he argues, actually prevents the required exercise of "add-water-and-stir religiosity" in the schools, and preventing this does no damage to true religion. The problem Reagan raises is, in Will's view, a *nonproblem,* and if we accept Will's analysis, the proposal will not persuade us.

POINTS TO

CONSIDER

WRITING PROPOSALS

When you write a proposal, bear in mind that each of its parts corresponds to a response you hope to elicit from the reader, and that each of these responses is a step toward the decision that you hope the reader will make. In general, the proposal's parts and the reader's path match up as follows:

Parts of Proposal	Reader's Path Toward Decision
Statment of larger goal:	I share this goal.
Identification and discussion of the problem:	I recognize that the problem(s) stated are serious enough to hinder our achieving the goal.
Solution:	I see that the proposed solution fits the problem(s), is feasible, and does not create more serious problems than it solves.

Effective proposal writing requires good judgment about how the parts will actually affect the intended audience.

QUESTIONS FOR PEER REVIEW

When you have completed a draft of your proposal, a good practice is to explain to a friend precisely who the intended readers are and have that reviewer read the draft as if through their eyes. Ask your reviewer how confident he or she is that the audience's responses will be those listed in the right-hand column above.

If you are refuting a proposal, you should once again ask your reviewer to read through the eyes of the intended audience. You must also be certain that he or she (and your ultimate readers, of course) understands what the original proposal was. Then you should ask whether you have broken the right-hand chain of responses by persuading the audience to reject the proposer's goal, the analysis of the problem, or the adequacy of the solution. You need not, of course, break the chain at every point: any break will do.

Because proposals need to motivate the reader to action, their emotional content and tone may be as important as their logic. You may, therefore, want to ask your reader the following questions:

1. Are there passages in my proposal that make you *feel* (as well as understand) the importance of the problem I am trying to solve?

2. Is the tone of my proposal appropriate? Is there a danger that I will alienate readers by seeming too disengaged from the problem to win their sympathy? Is there the opposite danger: that I seem unreasonably concerned or enthusiastic about matters my readers view very calmly?

3. Does my proposal seem well-intentioned? That is, do I sound like a person sincerely committed to solving a problem rather than like a debater eager to score points?

And, of course, you may want your reader to respond to the general peer-review questions listed on pp. 60–61.

Assignments
for Chapter 8

ASSIGNMENT 1: **A Pre-Writing Procedure for Proposals and Other Arguments**

One obstacle to writing successful arguments of any sort is what historian Barbara Tuchman very frankly calls "wooden-headedness." We tend to be so attached to our views that we are unable to think flexibly and understand how matters would seem to people with different backgrounds and different experiences. To guard against your own tendency to be wooden-headed, prepare for your next argumentative paper by writing an informal note according to the following five-step procedure:

1. Explain what it is in your past thinking or experience that makes one side of the argument "naturally" appealing to you.

2. List reasons to doubt this is the right side.

3. List reasons to believe this is the right side.

4. Explain why this is not an open-and-shut question.

5. Explain the consequences, long-term and short-term, of persuading an audience to accept the views of one side or another.

Because it may be unclear exactly what each step of the procedure is asking you to do, you may want to examine the following example, which shows how a student[1] freshened her thought before she wrote a proposal on the following question:

> Should the college adopt the following "affirmative action" policy: Until our faculty is 50 percent female, we will always hire a qualified woman rather than a man with roughly equal qualifications to fill vacant faculty positions.

1. Explain what it is in your past thinking or experience that makes one side of the argument "naturally" appealing to you.

---

[1] student example: This example combines writing from two students and has been retouched in places for clarity's sake. The original versions—brainstormings for an essay—were private documents, filled with peculiar abbreviations and "shorthand" phrases.

Because I am a woman who will soon be looking for a job herself, I'm naturally inclined to favor this policy. Also, I grew up in a fairly liberal family. My parents taught me that affirmative action for blacks, Hispanics, and other minorities was good. I also *like* so many of my female teachers. Naturally, these are the teachers that come to mind when I think about the question, and I want to say "Hire more of them."

2. List reasons to doubt that this is the right side.

   a. From the point of view of a man with "roughly equal qualifications," this could seem terribly unfair. He loses every close call.

   b. Think what would happen when the college tried to enforce this policy. How do they prove that a female candidate has "roughly equal qualifications"? Suppose a man and woman are equal on paper, but when a department talks to the woman, she doesn't seem smart or doesn't seem like she would be a good teacher. Will the college take these subjective considerations into account? If they don't, the policy is bad. If they do, it is unenforceable.

   c. Suppose I got a job at a college that had a policy like this one. Suppose I were to get into an overwhelmingly male department, hired in competition with a man most of the department thought was better, but that the college decided had "roughly equal qualifications." Where would that leave me?

   d. Or suppose the department hired me because they thought I was the greatest thing they'd ever seen. Wouldn't other people, knowing that I was a woman hired under this new policy, *assume* that was just so-so, and that I only got the job because I was a woman?

   e. Where does the 50 percent come from? Is the idea that 50 percent of the pool of professors is female? But what if it really is true that most very good professors (say 70 percent) are male?

   f. Aren't there other ways to go about this? College professors and administrators are rational, well-meaning people (I think). Perhaps the best plan would be just to remind them that there are qualified female applicants who deserve consideration

3. List reasons to believe that this is the right side.

   a. This is not a men's college. Over half the students are women. One problem with being a woman is that when all the authority figures around you are male, your self-confidence is undermined. I *know* this from my own experience. For the sake of the women students there should be more women faculty members.

   b. If you want more women to become college professors, you have to assure them that there will be jobs for them. Supply and demand. I *think* (don't know for sure) that there was a time when women with Ph.D.'s had trouble breaking into the "old boys' network."

c. Letting departments hire on "subjective factors" rather than the objective quality of someone's qualifications *is* the "old boys' network." People hire people who "fit in," their friends' friends. If a department has twelve male professors in it, all of whose best friends are male professors, it's not likely that a female candidate will "fit in."

d. It is true that a woman hired under this new policy would be put in a hard situation. She would have to prove that she *deserved* the job. I just don't think that this would be so hard to do. My mother is an executive in an insurance firm. She says that at first she felt she was on trial as a woman, but pretty soon no one paid attention to this.

e. I'll just bet that if I do some digging in the library, I can defend that 50 percent figure. Perhaps I could find out what percentage of Ph.D.'s graduated in the last ten years are women, or what percentage of professors at other colleges are women.

4. Explain why this is not an open-and-shut question.

One reason it is hard to decide is that the situation looks different to men and women. It is hard to deny that men lose jobs under this plan and woman gain them. Not everyone is better off. Another reason it is hard to decide is that I don't know what "roughly equal qualifications" are, or should be. Are subjective impressions "qualifications"? Should they be? You have to answer these questions before you can get to the real question.

5. Consider the consequences, long term and short term, of persuading an audience to accept the views of one side or another.

The best audience is the faculty and administration of the college, since they could adopt the policy. In the short run, I think we might be better off if they *didn't,* since it is going to create a lot of friction about hiring and it is likely to make the position of the women professors we have even less comfortable. In the long run, I think the rule will make the college into a place with many more women on the faculty, and so it will be a place where both female and male students get used to the idea of women in positions of authority. If a larger audience—all college administrators and faculties—was convinced I think it would encourage a lot of women to get Ph.D.'s because they would know that there are jobs available to them. On the other hand, men might start to be discouraged because they felt their job market was closing. More women would go into college teaching and fewer men, maybe. Would this drive pay down because college teaching would become "women's work," like being a secretary or a nurse? Maybe in the longest run this is a bad policy, after all. *But* the policy would be switched off when the college (or all colleges) reached a 50/50 balance, and the bad effects would be switched off, too.

As you can see from this example, answering a set of questions that slows our judgment somewhat can force our minds to explore channels that otherwise would be untouched. Even though we may arrive at the same conclusion that we would have without the delay, we arrive there better informed, and we tend to reason and write more intelligently. We are prepared to argue rather than to chant the familiar slogans, bully, and offend.

ASSIGNMENT 2:

A Summary of a Proposal

One of the best ways to understand the logic of a proposal is to rephrase it in a compressed form, neatly dividing your summary into parts concentrating on:

1. The goal.
2. The problem or problems (identification and discussion or reframing).
3. The solution (including comments the author may make about feasibility and unwanted consequences).

Attempt such a three-part summary of one of the three essays reprinted at the end of this chapter.

In the process of writing the summary, you will probably rearrange the author's material considerably and change its emphasis. An essay like Clinton's, for instance, is a proposal, but is many other things as well. Your summary will extract the proposal only, making its pattern clearly visible.

ASSIGNMENT 3:

A Summary and Analysis of a Proposal

Summarize a proposal as in Assignment 1, but pause after each of the three parts to analyze the tactics the author uses to make the proposal persuasive. What does the author do to establish common ground with the reader and to establish credibility? What sort of evidence and arguments does the author use? Do you find faults in logic; if so, do they seriously damage the argument? Has the author failed to meet any obvious criticisms of his or her proposal? Your aim in this analysis is not to refute the author's argument but to examine it closely.

ASSIGNMENT 4:

A Refutation of a Proposal

Find a proposal that you feel contains serious weaknesses and write a refutation of it comparable to George Will's response to President Reagan's school prayer amendment. You may use any proposal printed in this book or any proposal you find published in such sources as the opinion-editorial page of your local newspaper, the *My Turn* column in *Newsweek,* or the pages of any other recent periodical, scholarly or popular. Your refutation will necessarily include an adequate summary of the proposal so that your reader can understand what the argument is about.

ASSIGNMENT 5:

A Proposal Suitable for Publication

Write your own proposal on a topic of current interest. Undertake this proposal as a professional might, planning from the outset to see it published in a particular newspaper or magazine. Make its style, form, and argument appropriate for the audience that reads this publication. For comparison's sake, your instructor may ask you to submit a copy of an article printed in the publication to which your article would be submitted.

ASSIGNMENT 6:

A Competitive Proposal

Assume that the trustees of your college have announced a competition with the following rules.

The Board of Trustees is pleased to announce its seventeenth annual competition for proposed improvements to college life. Proposals are invited in three categories:

1. Improving the Classroom Atmosphere. The trustees invite proposals that enhance the effectiveness of classroom teaching not by altering equipment or textbooks, but by improving the interaction between students and teachers. The winning proposal will be distributed to all faculty members and discussed at the faculty pre-school seminar next fall. Proposals will be evaluated on clarity of purpose, feasibility, and capacity to improve learning in a wide range of classes.

2. Improving the Campus Environment. The trustees invite proposals that enhance the campus as a learning and living environment. Proposals should involve costs of no more than $10,000 to the college. The winning proposal will be studied by the Campus Facilities Committee: five winning proposals in the last ten years have been recommended by this committee and undertaken by the college. Proposals will be evaluated on clarity of purpose, feasibility, and capacity to benefit an important segment of the student body.

3. Improving the Community. The trustees invite proposals that allow students or student organizations to perform valuable

services for the community. Proposals should involve voluntary contribution of student labor; they may also involve solicitation of funds from the community. The college will contribute up to $1,000 to aid in the implementation of the winning proposal if the proposal demonstrates a need for such funding. Proposals will be evaluated on clarity of purpose, feasibility, and benefit to the community.

Authors of winning proposals will receive $500 in scholarship aid and will be recognized at the annual awards banquet. Proposals are limited to four double-spaced pages.

U.S. HEALTH CARE SYSTEM: RAMPANT MEDICAL INFLATION

Bill Clinton

Delivered before a joint session of Congress on September 22, 1993, this speech shows the president attempting to present an outline of his controversial proposal for health care reform. The speech (which received generally favorable reviews) presented Clinton with a considerable challenge: he had to deal simultaneously with both an "insider" audience of experts on health care and a much broader audience of television viewers who had not yet developed convictions on the subject.

1   MR. SPEAKER, MR. PRESIDENT, MEMBERS of Congress, distinguished guests, my fellow Americans. Before I begin my words tonight I would like to ask that we all bow in a moment of silent prayer for the memory of those who were killed and those who have been injured in the tragic train accident in Alabama today. Amen.

2   My fellow Americans, tonight we come together to write a new chapter in the American story. Our forebears enshrined the American Dream—life, liberty, the pursuit of happiness. Every generation of Americans has worked to strengthen that legacy, to make our country a place of freedom and opportunity, a place where people who work hard can rise to their full potential, a place where their children can have a better future.

3   From the settling of the frontier to the landing on the moon, ours has been a continuous story of challenges defined, obstacles overcome, new horizons secured. That is what makes America what it is and Americans what we are. Now we are in a time of profound change and opportunity. The end of the Cold War, the Information Age, the global economy have brought us both opportunity and hope and strife and uncertainty. Our purpose in this 0dynamic age must be to change—to make change our friend and not our enemy.

4   To achieve that goal, we must face all our challenges with confidence, with faith, and with discipline—whether we're reducing the deficit, creating tomorrow's jobs and training our people to fill them, converting from a high-tech defense to a high-tech domestic economy, expanding trade, reinventing government, making our streets safer, or rewarding work over idleness. All these challenges require us to change.

5   If Americans are to have the courage to change in a difficult time, we must first be secure in our most basic needs. Tonight I want to talk to you about the most critical thing we can do to build that security. This health care system of ours is badly broken and it is time to fix it.

6   Despite the dedication of literally millions of talented health care professionals, our health care is too uncertain and too expensive, too bureaucratic and too wasteful. It has too much fraud and too much greed.

7   At long last, after decades of false starts, we must make this our most urgent priority, giving every American health security; health care that can never be taken away; health care that

is always there. That is what we must do to-night.

8   On this journey, as on all others of true consequence, there will be rough spots in the road and honest disagreements about how we should proceed. After all, this is a complicated issue. But every successful journey is guided by fixed stars. And if we can agree on some basic values and principles we will reach this destination, and we will reach it together.

9   So tonight I want to talk to you about the principles that I believe must embody our efforts to reform America's health care system—security, simplicity, savings, choice, quality, and responsibility.

10   When I launched our nation on this journey to reform the health care system I knew we needed a talented navigator, someone with a rigorous mind, a steady compass, a caring heart. Luckily for me and for our nation, I didn't have to look very far.

11   Over the last eight months, Hillary and those working with her have talked to literally thousands of Americans to understand the strengths and the frailties of this system of ours. They met with over 1,100 health care organizations. They talked with doctors and nurses, pharmacists and drug company representatives, hospital administrators, insurance company executives and small and large businesses. They spoke with self-employed people. They talked with people who had insurance and people who didn't. They talked with union members and older Americans and advocates for our children. The First Lady also consulted, as all of you know, extensively with governmental leaders in both parties in the states of our nation, and especially here on Capitol Hill.

12   Hillary and the Task Force received and read over 700,000 letters from ordinary citizens. What they wrote and the bravery with which they told their stories is really what calls us all here tonight.

13   Every one of us knows someone who's worked hard and played by the rules and still been hurt by this system that just doesn't work for too many people. But I'd like to tell you about just one.

14   Kerry Kennedy owns a small furniture store that employs seven people in Titusville, Florida. Like most small business owners, he's poured his heart and soul, his sweat and blood into that business for years. But over the last several years, again like most small business owners, he's seen his health care premiums skyrocket, even in years when no claims were made. And last year, he painfully discovered he could no longer afford to provide coverage for all his workers because his insurance company told him that two of his workers had become high risks because of their advanced age. The problem was that those two people were his mother and father, the people who founded the business and still worked in the store.

15   This story speaks for millions of others. And from them we have learned a powerful truth. We have to preserve and strengthen what is right with the health care system, but we have got to fix what is wrong with it.

16   Now, we all know what's right. We're blessed with the best health care professionals on Earth, the finest health care institutions, the best medical research, the most sophisticated technology. My mother is a nurse. I grew up around hospitals. Doctors and nurses were the first professional people I ever knew or learned to look up to. They are what is right with this health care system. But we also know that we can no longer afford to continue to ignore what is wrong.

17   Millions of Americans are just a pink slip away from losing their health insurance, and one serious illness away from losing all their savings. Millions more are locked into the jobs they have now just because they or someone in their family has once been sick and they have what is called the preexisting condition. And on any given day, over 37 million Americans—most of them working people and their little children—have no health insurance at all.

18   And in spite of all this, our medical bills are growing at over twice the rate of inflation, and the United States spends over a third more of its income on health care than any other nation on Earth. And the gap is growing, causing many of our companies in global competition severe disadvantage. There is no excuse for this kind of system. We know other people have done better. We know people in our own country are doing better. We have no excuse. My fellow Americans, we must fix this system and it has to begin with congressional action.

19   I believe as strongly as I can say that we can reform the costliest and most wasteful system on the face of the Earth without enacting new broad-based taxes. I believe it because of the conversations I have had with thousands of health care professionals around the country; with people who are outside this city, but are inside experts on the way this system works and wastes money.

20   The proposal that I describe tonight borrows many of the principles and ideas that have been embraced in plans introduced by both Republicans and Democrats in this Congress. For the first time in this century, leaders of both political parties have joined together around the principle of providing universal, comprehensive health care. It is a magic moment and we must seize it.

21   I want to say to all of you I have been deeply moved by the spirit of this debate, by the openness of all people to new ideas and argument and information. The American people would be proud to know that earlier this week when a health care university was held for members of Congress just to try to give everybody the same amount of information, over 320 Republicans and Democrats signed up and showed up for two days just to learn the basic facts of the complicated problem before us.

22   Both sides are willing to say we have listened to the people. We know the cost of going forward with this system is far greater than the cost of change. Both sides, I think, under

stand the literal ethical imperative of doing something about the system we have now. Rising above these difficulties and our past differences to solve this problem will go a long way toward defining who we are and who we intend to be as a people in this difficult and challenging era. I believe we all understand that.

23   And so tonight, let me ask all of you—every member of the House, every member of the Senate, each Republican and each Democrat— let us keep this spirit and let us keep this commitment until this job is done. We owe it to the American people.

24   Now, if I might, I would like to review the six principles I mentioned earlier and describe how we think we can best fulfill those principles.

25   First and most important, security. This principle speaks to the human misery, to the costs, to the anxiety we hear about every day—all of us—when people talk about their problems with the present system. Security means that those who do not now have health care coverage will have it; and for those who have it, it will never be taken away. We must achieve that security as soon as possible.

26   Under our plan, every American would receive a health care security card that will guarantee a comprehensive package of benefits over the course of an entire lifetime, roughly comparable to the benefit package offered by most Fortune 500 companies. This health care security card will offer this package of benefits in a way that can never be taken away.

27   So let us agree on this: whatever else we disagree on, before this Congress finishes its work next year, you will pass and I will sign legislation to guarantee this security to every citizen of this county.

28   With this card, if you lose your job or you switch jobs, you're covered. If you leave your job to start a small business, you're covered. If you're an early retiree, you're covered. If someone in your family has, unfortunately, had an illness that qualifies as a preexisting condition,

you're still covered. If you get sick or a member of your family gets sick, even if it's a life threatening illness, you're covered. And if an insurance company tries to drop you for any reason, you will still be covered, because that will be illegal. This card will give comprehensive coverage. It will cover people for hospital care, doctor visits, emergency and lab services, diagnostic services like Pap smears and mammograms and cholesterol tests, substance abuse and mental health treatment.

29   And equally important, for both health care and economic reasons, this program for the first time would provide a broad range of preventive services including regular checkups and well-baby visits.

30   Now, it's just common sense. We know— any family doctor will tell you that people will stay healthier and long-term costs of the health system will be lower if we have comprehensive preventive services. You know how all of our mothers told us that an ounce of prevention was worth a pound of cure? Our mothers were right. And it's a lesson, like so many lessons from our mothers, that we have waited too long to live by. It is time to start doing it.

31   Health care security must also apply to older Americans. This is something I imagine all of us in this room feel very deeply about. The first thing I want to say about that is that we must maintain the Medicare program. It works to provide that kind of security. But this time and for the first time, I believe Medicare should provide coverage for the cost of prescription drugs.

32   Yes, it will cost some more in the beginning. But, again, any physician who deals with the elderly will tell you that there are thousands of elderly people in every state who are not poor enough to be on Medicaid, but just above that line and on Medicare who desperately need medicine, who make decisions every week between medicine and food. Any doctor who deals with the elderly will tell you that there are many elderly people who don't get

medicine, who get sicker and sicker and eventually go to the doctor and wind up spending more money and draining more money from the health care system than they would if they had regular treatment in the way that only adequate medicine can provide.

33   I also believe that over time, we should phase in long-term care for the disabled and the elderly on a comprehensive basis.

34   As we proceed with this health care reform, we cannot forget that the most rapidly growing percentage of Americans are those over 80. We cannot break faith with them. We have to do better by them.

35   The second principle is simplicity. Our health care system must be simpler for the patients and simpler for those who actually deliver health care—our doctors, our nurses, our other medical professionals. Today we have more than 1,500 insurers, with hundreds and hundreds of different forms. No other nation has a system like this. These forms are time consuming for health care providers, they're expensive for health care consumers, they're exasperating for anyone who's ever tried to sit down around a table and wade through them and figure them out.

36   The medical care industry is literally drowning in paperwork. In recent years, the number of administrators in our hospitals has grown by four times the rate that the number of doctors has grown. A hospital ought to be a house of healing, not a monument to paperwork and bureaucracy.

37   Just a few days ago, the Vice President and I had the honor of visiting the Children's Hospital here in Washington where they do wonderful, often miraculous things for very sick children. A nurse named Debbie Freiberg told us that she was in the cancer and bone marrow unit. The other day a little boy asked her just to stay at his side during his chemotherapy. And she had to walk away from that child because she had been instructed to go to yet another class to learn how to fill out an-

other form for something that didn't have a lick to do with the health care of the children she was helping. That is wrong, and we can stop it, and we ought to do it.

38   We met a very compelling doctor named Lillian Beard, a pediatrician, who said that she didn't get into her profession to spend hours and hours—some doctors up to 25 hours a week just filling out forms. She told us she became a doctor to keep children well and to help save those who got sick. We can relieve people like her of this burden. We learned— the Vice President and I did—that in the Washington Children's Hospital alone, the administrators told us they spend $2 million a year in one hospital filling out forms that have nothing whatever to do with keeping up with the treatment of the patients.

39   And the doctors there applauded when I was told and I related to them that they spend so much time filling out paperwork, that if they only had to fill out those paperwork requirements necessary to monitor the health of the children, each doctor on that one hospital staff—200 of them—could see another 500 children a year. That is 10,000 children a year. I think we can save money in this system if we simplify it. And we can make the doctors and the nurses and the people that are giving their lives to help us all be healthier and a whole lot happier, too, on their jobs.

40   Under our proposal there would be one standard insurance form—not hundreds of them. We will simplify also—and we must—the government's rules and regulations, because they are a big part of this problem. This is one of those cases where the physician should heal thyself. We have to reinvent the way we relate to the health care system, along with reinventing government. A doctor should not have to check with a bureaucrat in an office thousands of miles away before ordering a simple blood test. That's not right, and we can change it. And doctors, nurses and consumers shouldn't have to worry about the fine print. If

we have this one simple form, there won't be any fine print. People will know what it means.

41   The third principle is savings. Reform must produce savings in this health care system. It has to. We're spending over 14 percent of our income on health care—Canada's at 10; nobody else is over nine. We're competing with all these people for the future. And the other major countries, they cover everybody and they cover them with services as generous as the best company policies here in this country.

42   Rampant medical inflation is eating away at our wages, our savings, our investment capital, our ability to create new jobs in the private sector and this public Treasury. You know the budget we just adopted had steep cuts in defense, a five-year freeze on the discretionary spending, so critical to reeducating America and investing in jobs and helping us to convert from a defense to a domestic economy. But we passed a budget which has Medicaid increases of between 16 and 11 percent a year over the next five years, and Medicare increases of between 11 and 9 percent in an environment where we assume inflation will be at 4 percent or less.

43   We cannot continue to do this. Our competitiveness, our whole economy, the integrity of the way the government works and, ultimately, our living standards depend upon our ability to achieve savings without harming the quality of health care.

44   Unless we do this, our workers will lose $655 in income each year by the end of the decade. Small businesses will continue to face skyrocketing premiums. And a full third of small businesses now covering their employees say they will be forced to drop their insurance. Large corporations will bear vivid disadvantages in global competition. And health care costs will devour more and more and more of our budget. Pretty soon all of you or the people who succeed you will be showing up here, and writing out checks for health care and

interest on the debt and worrying about whether we've got enough defense, and that will be it, unless we have the courage to achieve the savings that are plainly there before us. Every state and local government will continue to cut back on everything from education to law enforcement to pay more and more for the same health care.

45   There rising costs are a special nightmare for our small businesses—the engine of our entrepreneurship and our job creation in America today. Health care premiums for small businesses are 35 percent higher than those of large corporations today. And they will keep rising at double-digit rates unless we act.

46   So how will we achieve these savings? Rather than looking at price control, or looking away as the price spiral continues; rather than using the heavy hand of government to try to control what's happening, or continuing to ignore what's happening, we believe there is a third way to achieve these savings. First, to give groups of consumers and small businesses the same market bargaining power that large corporations and large groups of public employees now have. We want to let market forces enable plans to compete. We want to force these plans to compete on the basis of price and quality, not simply to allow them to continue making money by turning people away who are sick or old or performing mountains of unnecessary procedures. But we also believe we should back this system up with limits on how much plans can raise their premiums year in and year out, forcing people, again, to continue to pay more for the same health care, without regard to inflation or the rising population needs.

47   We want to create what has been missing in this system for too long, and what every successful nation who has dealt with this problem has already had to do: to have a combination of private market forces and a sound public policy that will support that competition, but limit the rate at which prices can exceed the rate of inflation and population growth, if the competition doesn't work, especially in the early going.

48   The second thing I want to say is that unless everybody is covered—and this is a very important thing—unless everybody is covered, we will never be able to fully put the brakes on health care inflation. Why is that? Because when people don't have any health insurance, they still get health care, but they get it when it's too late, when it's too expensive, often from the most expensive place of all, the emergency room. Usually by the time they show up, their illnesses are more severe and their mortality rates are much higher in our hospitals than those who have insurance. So they cost us more.

49   And what else happens? Since they get the care but they don't pay, who does pay? All the rest of us. We pay in higher hospital bills and higher insurance premiums. This cost shifting is a major problem.

50   The third thing we can do to save money is simply by simplifying the system—what we've already discussed. Freeing the health care providers from these costly and unnecessary paperwork and administrative decisions will save tens of billions of dollars. We spend twice as much as any other major country does on paperwork. We spend at least a dime on the dollar more than any other major country. That is a stunning statistic. It is something that every Republican and every Democrat ought to be able to say, we agree that we're going to squeeze this out. We cannot tolerate this. This has nothing to do with keeping people well or helping them when they're sick. We should invest the money in something else.

51   We also have to crack down on fraud and abuse in the system. That drains billions of dollars a year. It is a very large figure, according to every health care expert I've ever spoken with. So I believe we can achieve large savings. And that large savings can be used to cover the unemployed uninsured, and will be used for

people who realize those savings in the private sector to increase their ability to invest and grow, to hire new workers or to give their workers pay raises, many of them for the first time in years.

52   Now, nobody has to take my word for this. You can ask Dr. Koop. He's up here with us tonight, and I thank him for being here. Since he left his distinguished tenure as our Surgeon General, he has spent an enormous amount of time studying our health care system, how it operates, what's right and wrong with it. He says we could spend $200 billion every year, more than 20 percent of the total budget, without sacrificing the high quality of American medicine.

53   Ask the public employees in California, who have held their own premiums down by adopting the same strategy that I want every American to be able to adopt—bargaining within the limits of a strict budget. Ask Xerox, which saved an estimated $1,000 per worker on their health insurance premium. Ask the staff of the Mayo Clinic, who we all agree provides some of the finest health care in the world. They are holding their cost increases to less than half the national average. Ask the people of Hawaii, the only state that covers virtually all of their citizens and has still been able to keep costs below the national average.

54   People may disagree over the best way to fix this system. We may all disagree about how quickly we can do what—the thing that we have to do. But we cannot disagree that we can find tens of billions of dollars in savings in what is clearly the most costly and the most bureaucratic system in the entire world. And we have to do something about that, and we have to do it now.

55   The fourth principle is choice. Americans believe they ought to be able to choose their own health care plan and keep their own doctors. And I think all of us agree. Under any plan we pass, they ought to have that right. But today, under our broken health care system, in spite of the rhetoric of choice, the fact is that that power is slipping away for more and more Americans.

56   Of course, it is usually the employer, not the employee, who makes the initial choice of what health care plan the employee will be in. And if the employer offers only one plan, as nearly three-quarters of small or medium-sized firms do today, you're stuck with that plan, and the doctors that it covers.

57   We propose to give every American a choice among high-quality plans. You can stay with your current doctor, join a network of doctors and hospitals, or join a health maintenance organization. If you don't like your plan, every year you'll have a chance to choose a new one. The choice will be left to the American citizen, the worker—not the boss, and certainly not some government bureaucrat.

58   We also believe that doctors should have a choice as to what plans they practice in. Otherwise, citizens may have their own choices limited. We want to end discrimination that is now growing against doctors, and to permit them to practice in several different plans. Choice is important for doctors, and it is absolutely critical for our consumers. We've got to have it in whatever plan we pass.

59   The fifth principle is quality. If we reformed everything else in health care, but failed to preserve and enhance the high quality of our medical care, we will have taken a step backward, not forward. Quality is something that we simply can't leave to chance. When you board an airplane, you feel better knowing that the plane had to meet standards designed to protect your safety. And we can't ask any less of our health care system.

60   Our proposal will create report cards on health plans, so that consumers can choose the highest quality health care providers and reward them with their business. At the same time, our plan will track quality indicators, so that doctors can make better and smarter choices of the kind of care they provide. We

have evidence that more efficient delivery of health care doesn't decrease quality. In fact, it may enhance it.

61   Let me just give you one example of one commonly performed procedure, the coronary bypass operation. Pennsylvania discovered that patients who were charged $21,000 for this surgery received as good or better care as patients who were charged $84,000 for the same procedure in the same state. High prices simply don't always equal good quality. Our plan will guarantee that high-quality information is available, even in the most remote areas of this country so that we can have high-quality service, linking rural doctors, for example, with hospitals with high-tech urban medical centers. And our plan will ensure the quality of continuing progress on a whole range of issues by speeding the search on effective prevention and treatment measures for cancer, for AIDS, for Alzheimer's, for heart disease, and for other chronic diseases. We have to safeguard the finest medical research establishment in the entire world. And we will do that with this plan. Indeed, we will even make it better.

62   The sixth and final principle is responsibility. We need to restore a sense that we're all in this together and that we all have a responsibility to be a part of the solution. Responsibility has to start with those who profit from the current system. Responsibility means insurance companies should no longer be allowed to cast people aside when they get sick. It should apply to laboratories that submit fraudulent bills, to lawyers who abuse malpractice claims, to doctors who order unnecessary procedures. It means drug companies should no longer charge three times more for prescription drugs made in America here in the United States than they charge for the same drugs overseas.

63   In short, responsibility should apply to anybody who abuses this system and drives up the cost for honest, hard-working citizens and undermines confidence in the honest, gifted health care providers we have.

64   Responsibility also means changing some behaviors in this country that drive up our costs like crazy. And without changing it we'll never have the system we ought to have. We will never.

65   Let me just mention a few and start with the most important—the outrageous cost of violence in this country stems in large measure from the fact that this is the only country in the world where teenagers can roam the streets at random with semi-automatic weapons and be better armed than the police.

66   But let's not kid ourselves, it's not that simple. We also have higher rates of AIDS, of smoking and excessive drinking, of teen pregnancy, of low birth weight babies. And we have the third worst immunization rate of any nation in the western hemisphere. We have to change our ways if we ever really want to be healthy as a people and have an affordable health care system. And no one can deny that.

67   But let me say this—and I hope every American will listen, because this is not an easy thing to hear—responsibility in our health care system isn't just about them, it's about you, it's about me, it's about each of us. Too many of us have not taken responsibility for our own health care and for our own relations to the health care system. Many of us who have had fully paid health care plans have used the system whether we needed it or not without thinking what the costs were. Many people who use this system don't pay a penny for their care even though they can afford to. I think those who don't have any health insurance should be responsible for paying a portion of their new coverage. There can't be any something for nothing, and we have to demonstrate that to people. This is not a free system. Even small contributions, as small as the $10-copayment when you visit a doctor, illustrates that this is something of value. There is a cost to it. It is not free.

68   And I want to tell you that I believe that all of us should have insurance. Why should the

rest of us pick up the tab when a guy who doesn't think he needs insurance or says he can't afford it gets in an accident, winds up in an emergency room, gets good care, and everybody else pays? Why should the small businesspeople who are struggling to keep afloat and take care of their employees have to pay to maintain this wonderful health care infrastructure for those who refuse to do anything?

69   If we're going to produce a better health care system for every one of us, every one of us is going to have to do our part. There cannot be any such thing as a free ride. We have to pay for it. We have to pay for it.

70   Tonight I want to say plainly how I think we should do that. Most of the money we will—will come under my way of thinking, as it does today, from premiums paid by employers and individuals. That's the way it happens today. But under this health care security plan, every employer and every individual will be asked to contribute something to health care.

71   This concept was first conveyed to the Congress about 20 years ago by President Nixon. And today, a lot of people agree with the concept of shared responsibility between employers and employees, and that the best thing to do is to ask every employer and every employee to share that. The Chamber of Commerce has said that, and they're not in the business of hurting small business. The American Medical Association has said that.

72   Some call it an employer mandate, but I think it's the fairest way to achieve responsibility in the health care system. And it's the easiest for ordinary Americans to understand, because it builds on what we already have and what already works for so many Americans. It is the reform that is not only easiest to understand, but easiest to implement in a way that is fair to small business because we can give a discount to help struggling small businesses meet the cost of covering their employees. We should require the least bureaucracy or disruption, and create the cooperation we need to make the system cost-conscious, even as we expand coverage. And we should do it in a way that does not cripple small businesses and low-wage workers.

73   Every employer should provide coverage, just as three-quarters do now. Those that pay are picking up the tab for those who don't today. I don't think that's right. To finance the rest of reform, we can achieve new savings, as I have outlined, in both the federal government and the private sector, through better decision-making and increased competition. And we will impose new taxes on tobacco.

74   I don't think that should be the only source of revenues. I believe we should also ask for a modest contribution from big employers who opt out of the system to make up for what those who are in the system pay for medical research, for health education centers, for all the subsidies to small business, for all the things that everyone else is contributing to. But between those two things, we believe we can pay for this package of benefits and universal coverage and a subsidy program that will help small business.

75   These sources can cover the cost of the proposal that I have described tonight. We subjected the numbers in our proposal to the scrutiny of not only all the major agencies in government—I know a lot of people don't trust them, but it would be interesting for the American people to know that this was the first time that the financial experts on health care in all the different government agencies have ever been required to sit in the room together and agree on numbers. It had never happened before.

76   But, obviously, that's not enough. So then we gave these numbers to actuaries from major accounting firms and major Fortune 500 companies who have no stake in this other than to see that our efforts succeed. So I believe our numbers are good and achievable.

77   Now, what does this mean to an individual American citizen? Some will be asked to pay

more. If you're an employer and you aren't in-
suring your workers at all, you'll have to pay
more, but if you're a small business with fewer
than 50 employees, you'll get a subsidy. If
you're a firm that provides only very limited
coverage, you may have to pay more. But
some firms will pay the same or less for more
coverage.

78   If you're a young, single person in your 20s
and you're already insured, your rates may go
up somewhat because you're going to go into a
big pool with middle-aged people and older
people, and we want to enable people to keep
their insurance even when someone in their
family gets sick. But I think that's fair because
when the young get older, they will benefit
from it, first, and secondly, even those who
pay a little more today will benefit four, five,
six, seven years from now by bringing health
care costs closer to inflation.

79   Over the long run, we can all win. But
some will have to pay more in the short run.
Nevertheless, the vast majority of the Americans watching this tonight will pay the same or
less for health care coverage that will be the
same or better than the coverage they have tonight. That is the central reality.

80   If you currently get your health insurance
through your job, under our plan you still will.
And for the first time, everybody will get to
choose from among at least three plans to belong to. If you're a small business owner who
wants to provide health insurance to your family and your employees, but you can't afford it
because the system is stacked against you, this
plan will give you a discount that will finally
make insurance affordable. If you're already
providing insurance, your rates may well drop
because we'll help you as a small business person join thousands of others to get the same
benefits big corporations get at the same price
they get those benefits. If you're self-employed,
you'll pay less; and you will get to deduct from
your taxes 100 percent of your health care premiums.

If you're a large employer, your health care   81
cost won't go up as fast, so that you will have
more money to put into higher wages and new
jobs and to put into the work of being competitive in this tough global economy.

Now, these, my fellow Americans, are the   82
principles on which I think we should base our
efforts: security, simplicity, savings, choice,
quality and responsibility. These are the guiding stars that we should follow on our journey
toward health care reform.

Over the coming months, you'll be bom-   83
barded with information from all kinds of
sources. There will be some who will stoutly
disagree with what I have proposed—and with
all other plans in the Congress, for that matter.
And some of the arguments will be genuinely
sincere and enlightening. Others may simply be
scare tactics by those who are motivated by
the self-interest they have in the waste the system now generates, because that waste is providing jobs, incomes and money for some
people.

I ask you only to think of this when you   84
hear all of these arguments: Ask yourself
whether the cost of staying on this same course
isn't greater than the cost of change. And ask
yourself when you hear the arguments whether
the arguments are in your interest or someone
else's. This is something we have got to try to
do together.

I want also to say to the representatives in   85
Congress, you have a special duty to look beyond these arguments. I ask you instead to
look into the eyes of the sick child who needs
care; to think of the face of the woman who's
been told not only that her condition is malig-
nant, but not covered by her insurance. To
look at the bottom lines of the businesses
driven to bankruptcy by health care costs. To
look at the "for sale" signs in front of the
homes of families who have lost everything because of their health care costs.

I ask you to remember the kind of people I   86
met over the last year and a half—the elderly

couple in New Hampshire that broke down and cried because of their shame at having an empty refrigerator to pay for their drugs: a woman who lost a $50,000 job that she used to support her six children because her youngest child was so ill that she couldn't keep health insurance, and the only way to get care for the child was to get public assistance; a young couple that had a sick child and could only get insurance from one of the parents' employers that was a nonprofit corporation with 20 employees, and so they had to face the question of whether to let this poor person with a sick child go or raise the premiums of every employee in the firm by $200. And on and on and on.

87   I know we have differences of opinion, but we are here tonight in a spirit that is animated by the problems of those people, and by the sheer knowledge that if we can look into our heart, we will not be able to say that the greatest nation in the history of the world is powerless to confront this crisis.

88   Our history and our heritage tell us that we can meet this challenge. Everything about America's past tells us we will do it. So I say to you, let us write that new chapter in the American story. Let us guarantee every American comprehensive health benefits that can never be taken away.

89   In spite of all the work we've done together and all the progress we've made, there's still a lot of people who say it would be an outright miracle if we passed health care reform. But my fellow Americans, in a time of change, you have to have miracles. And miracles do hap-

pen. I mean, just a few days ago we saw a simple handshake shatter decades of deadlock in the Middle East. We've seen the walls crumble in Berlin and South Africa. We see the ongoing brave struggle of the people of Russia to seize freedom and democracy.

90   And now, it is our turn to strike a blow for freedom in this country. The freedom of Americans to live without fear that their own nation's health care system won't be there for them when they need it. It's hard to believe that there was once a time in this century when that kind of fear gripped old age. When retirement was nearly synonymous with poverty, and older Americans died in the street. That's unthinkable today, because over a half a century ago Americans had the courage to change—to create a Social Security system that ensures that no Americans will be forgotten in their later years.

91   Forty years from now, our grandchildren will also find it unthinkable that there was a time in this country when hardworking families lost their homes, their savings, their businesses, lost everything simply because their children got sick or because they had to change jobs. Our grandchildren will find such things unthinkable tomorrow *if* we have the courage to change today.

92   This is our chance. This is our journey. And when our work is done, we will know that we have answered the call of history and met the challenge of our time.

93   Thank you very much. And God bless America. ◆

FAULTY DIAGNOSIS

Willard Gaylin, M.D.

Willard Gaylin published the following critique of President Clinton's health care proposal in *Harper's* magazine in October 1993. A professor of psychiatry at the Columbia University School of Medicine and an expert on medical ethics, Dr. Gaylin clearly objects to the way that the Clinton adminstration has framed the problem.

1　AS HILLARY CLINTON'S TASK FORCE ON National Health Care Reform completed its deliberations last summer, it sometimes seemed as though the health-care debate we were told the nation was clamoring for had been replaced by a process akin to the selection of a pope. Some five hundred health-care "experts" met behind closed doors over a period of four months, occasionally emitting smoke signals for the media laced with obscure acronyms and buzzwords: HMOs, DRGs, HIPCs (to be pronounced "Hipics," we were instructed), "global budgets," and "managed competition." By now, the public response to the idea of health-care reform is reminiscent of the way most of us feel about our doctors when they begin spouting incomprehensible jargon: we trust that they at least know what they're doing and pray they do no harm.

2　The most unfortunate thing about this shuttered process is that a remarkable opportunity has been missed. What could have been a wide-open, far-ranging public debate about the deeper issues of health care—our attitudes toward life and death, the goals of medicine, the meaning of "health," suffering versus survival, who shall live and who shall die (and who shall decide)—has been supplanted by relatively narrow quibbles over policy. It is a lot easier and safer for politicians and policymakers to talk about delivery systems, health-product-procurement procedures, and third-party payments than about what care to give a desperately ill child or whether a kidney patient over the age of fifty should be eligible for

a transplant. The paradox of our current situation, however, is that unless we address such basic, almost existential questions, we stand little chance of solving our nation's health-care crisis.

3　Partly because of its unwillingness to confront these issues, the Clinton Administration now finds itself tangled in a profound yet largely unacknowledged contradiction. The two key goals of its health-reform plan are (1) to democratize health care—to confront the problem of the 40 million uninsured Americans who can't get adequate care; and (2) to control the ballooning portion of our gross national product that goes to pay for health care. No amount of tinkering with the process of delivery or payment, no number of new tongue-twisting acronyms, can resolve the fundamental contradiction of the Clinton plan: if you promise everyone access to whatever medical care he or she needs or wants, you will enormously increase the total amount the nation spends on health care—the very costs Clinton was elected to bring under control.

4　It is of course cost, and not equity, that has driven health care to the fore of the national debate; injustice has never been as urgent a motivating principle as insolvency. The pressure for health-care reform comes on the heels of a staggering surge in spending that threatens to swamp the federal budget and distort our national purposes, not to mention the bottom lines of America's corporations. Twenty-five years ago, 7.6 percent of the gross domestic product was devoted to health, 6.8 percent to education, and 9.7 percent to defense. Today both defense and education expenditures are roughly 6 percent, whereas health expenditures have climbed to 14 percent of GDP and are likely to reach 18 percent by the end of the decade.

5   It can easily be argued that it is better to spend money to cure cancer or AIDS than to build more bombs and space stations—and, in fact, that's an argument I agree with. But at the rate by which we are increasing our spending on health care, soon the contest for resources will no longer pit the good guys against the bad guys. For however you define the bad guys, we are quickly running out of them. It is becoming a question of good guys versus good guys, as health-care costs gobble up money that ought to go to those authentic needs that are ancillary, yet essential, to a comprehensive conception of health: such things as drug control, education, crime prevention, housing, and poverty.

6   Most students of the economy, and of the medical economy in particular, agree that the need to contain medical costs is absolute and urgent. The questions that divide us involve how it should be done. And the solutions being offered generally depend on how one accounts for the explosion in health-care costs. Most of the experts and policymakers in Washington have been focusing on the deficiencies and failures of modern medicine: greedy pharmaceutical and insurance companies (not to mention physicians); unnecessary procedures; bureaucratic inefficiency and paperwork; expensive technologies; and so forth. These "efficiency experts," as I call them, have taken control of the debate; their ideas have been embraced by the Clinton Administration. They see the solution to our health-care crisis in terms of improving the efficiency of the system. The shibboleths that identify their approach include managed care, HMOs, and managed competition. Implicit in their recommendations is the assumption that the elimination of waste will obviate the need for "rationing" health care.

7   Opposed to this group are those, myself included, who acknowledge that although there is waste in the system, it is incidental to the basic forces driving up costs. I would argue, in fact, that the greatest part of the increase in health-care costs can best be understood as the result not of the failures of medicine but of its successes. The relentless increase in costs is actually a product of the expanding capabilities of medicine. Implicit in this view is the assumption that controlling waste will save money only in the short haul, and that we had best use the limited time such a strategy will buy to figure out a way to confront the deeper and more challenging reasons for escalating health costs: our unbridled appetite for health care and our continuing expansion of the definition of what constitutes health.

8   The efficiency experts generally advocate a few basic, businesslike principles that, if adopted, would supposedly solve the cost crisis. The first is the need to reduce the venality of health-care providers, particularly physicians. (If only they had the same generosity of spirit and humanity as other professionals in our society—say, lawyers, accountants, and bankers.) Another way of putting this is that we must cut the fat out of the health-care system. But what system is there that has no fat? Is our goal to make the health-care industry as efficient as the airlines, the automobile industry, the steel industry? Where can we look to find models of efficient managed competition outside of medicine? And where can we look within medicine?

9   A second bête noire of the efficiency experts is what is called the "halfway technologies"— technologies that extend the life of a patient without actually curing his or her disease. Kidney dialysis is an example. Such technologies sustain people with chronic illnesses at great

expense. But the distinction is artificial: since everyone alive is destined to die, *all* medical technologies are halfway technologies. They sustain the human being in the terminal condition we call life.

10   This leads directly to the third argument made by the efficiency experts. If only more money were spent on preventive medicine, as opposed to therapeutic medicine, we could solve the problem of health-care costs. The data here are misleading. We all are familiar with the examples: a measles shot costs $8, whereas hospitalization for a child with measles costs $5,000; nine months of prenatal care for a pregnant woman costs $600, whereas medical care for a premature baby for one day costs $2,500. But when you try to extend the economic analysis beyond the individual case to the entire system, it becomes clear that the rationale for preventive medicine is not an economic one. The child who would have died from polio or measles or pertussis will grow up to be a very expensive old man or woman. Preventive medicine drives up the ultimate cost of health care to society by enlarging the population of the elderly and infirm. I am certainly not opposed to preventive medicine, only to irrational arguments for its use. The proper argument for preventive medicine is the grief and misery that it averts and the fact that it allows individuals to lead healthy and productive lives.

11   The efficiency experts offer several other explanations for balloning health-care costs, each one based on some other supposed defect in the current system: unnecessary tests, malpractice litigation, bureaucratic waste, profiteering drug companies. Each of these factors adds its penny weight to the scales, but even together they don't begin to account for the sort of quantum leaps in health-care spending we have seen. Even if we were to make angels out of hospital employees and philanthropists out of drug-company executives, we still would not stem the forward march of health-care costs.

12   So what, if not venality and inefficiency, is really driving health costs ever upward into the stratosphere? I would divide the principal causes into four.

13   1. THE INCREASE IN MORBIDITY RATES DUE TO GOOD MEDICINE. It is often difficult for laypeople to appreciate that good medicine does not reduce the percentage of people with illnesses in our population (what is called the morbidity rate); it *increases* that percentage. There are more people wandering the streets of the cities of the United States with arteriosclerotic heart disease, diabetes, essential hypertension, and other expensive chronic diseases than there are in Iraq, Nigeria, or Colombia. Good medicine keeps *sick* people alive, thereby increasing the number of sick people in the population; patients who are killed by their disease are no longer a part of the population. Even outright cures of diseases ultimately add to medical costs. We no longer talk about diphtheria rates or whooping-cough rates, even though those were the two leading causes of death in children for many generations. Those diseases have ceased to exist. But they were rarely expensive. The child either lived or died, and, for the most part, did so quickly and cheaply.

14   2. THE EXPANDING CONCEPT OF HEALTH. Health today does not mean what it did a hundred years ago. If I might begin by casting stones at my own glass house, consider the case of psychiatry, though psychiatry is not the worst offender. The fact is that the patients I deal with in my daily practice would not have been considered mentally ill in the nineteenth century. Mental illness then was rigidly defined. Those considered mentally ill were insane—patently different from you and me—and they were put into hospitals. The leading causes of mental illness were tertiary syphilis and schizophrenia. This, more or less, was psychiatry (a minor branch of neurology) at the turn of the century, before the arrival of its genius, Sigmund Freud. Freud decided that

people did not have to be exclusively either crazy or sane, but that a normal person, like himself or people he knew, could be partly crazy. These "normal" people, who were still in touch with reality, exhibited only isolated symptoms of irrationality—phobias, compulsions, etc. Freud invented a new category of mental diseases now called "neuroses," thereby vastly increasing the population of the mentally ill.

15   Some thirty years later, Wilhelm Reich decided that one does not even have to display mental symptoms to be mentally ill, that one can suffer from "character disorders." The personalities of even completely asymptomatic individuals might so limit their productivity or pleasure in life that we are justified in diagnosing them as mentally ill.

16   Then medicine "discovered" the psychosomatic disorders. There are people with no symptoms of mental illness who have *physical* conditions with psychic roots—peptic ulcers, ulcerative colitis, migraine headache, allergies, and the like. These people, too, were now classified as mentally ill. By such sophisticated expansions of the category, we eventually managed to get some 60 percent to 70 percent (as one serious study found) of the residents of the Upper East Side of Manhattan into the population of the mentally ill.

17   What has happened in mental health has happened across the board in medicine: we have radically altered our concept of what it means to be sick or healthy. Probably the best way to understand this process is to consider how medicine goes about "discovering" new diseases.

18   Most people assume that medical researchers first uncover an illness and then seek a cure for it. This, of course, does happen; the infectious diseases are the paradigm case. What is less familiar, but is becoming more common, is the opposite mechanism: we discover a cure and then invent a disease to go with it.

19   As I am writing this article I am using reading glasses. These reading glasses are paid for by a health insurer, based on the diagnosis of "presbyopia" (an eye "disease") made by an ophthalmologist (a specialty physician). Before the invention of the lens there was no such disease as presbyopia; there were also no ophthalmologists. Old people weren't expected to read. A decline in faculties was simply part of the aging proces; with age, sight would be impaired or lost, as would be hearing, potency, and fertility. As we began to find treatments to delay the aging processes, we reclassified various aspects of aging as "diseases."

20   This vast expansion of the concept of health can be demonstrated in surgery, orthopedics, gynecology—indeed, in any field of medicine. Infertility, for example, was not considered a disease until this generation; before then, it was simply a God-given condition. With the advances of modern medicine—including artificial insemination, in vitro fertilization, and surrogate mothering—new cures were discovered for "illnesses" that now had to be invented. All of them make demands on the health-care dollar. Another example: People do not get their knees or elbows operated on merely to continue to function or be employable; most of us do not work at jobs requiring physical strength. Many operations on the knee are performed strictly so that the patient can continue to play golf or ski; it is the same with elbow operations. Are these justifiable "medical" expenses? If one is free of pain except on the tennis court, is one "ill"? Should "inability to play tennis" be classified as an insurable disease?

21   3. THE SEDUCTION OF TECHNOLOGY AND THE DECEPTION OF MARKETPLACE MODELS. All of us know about how doctors can be seduced by medical technology—how, for example, the ubiquity of delivery-room fetal monitors (which alert obstetricians to the merest hint of fetal distress) has contributed to a surge in cesarean sections. But it is not only the physician who is seduced by technology; the patient and

her family are, too—and not because of an in-
fatuation with gadgetry, but because of the nature of decision-making in matters of life and
death. Decision-making becomes distorted
whenever extreme risks are involved; also, our
perceptions of probability vary significantly depending on the setting.

22   A driver is probably safer in an $80,000
Mercedes than in an $8,000 Isuzu, but few peo-
ple are likely to mortgage the house for the
Mercedes, at least not for reasons of safety.
Similarly, driving 65 miles an hour carries a
greater risk of a fatal accident than driving 55,
yet this well-publicized fact doesn't seem to
keep many drivers under the speed limit. The
possible consequence is too remote; on a drive
to Cape Cod one is thinking about a dip in the
ocean, not the imminence of death. But these
perceptions change in a hospital setting. Imagine if a doctor were to tell a patient that he
sees no sign of a tumor in the X ray and that
though a CAT scan *might* pick up the 1 percent of tumors that X rays miss, he is not sure
it is worth the extra money. The patient
would fire him on the spot. He wants any
edge, however minute, when what is at stake is
the life of his child, his wife, or himself. When
the doctor then tells him, after a negative CAT
scan, that an MRI might still pick up a tumor,
the patient demands the MRI. He will mortgage the house for that, although the statistical
validity of doing so, compared with exercising
prudence on the highway, may make no sense.
Death has a greater reality in the hospital setting. People will pay anything to defend
against the possibility of death, all the more so
when the money involved doesn't come directly out of their own pockets.

23   Because our approach to medical technology
is special, we are wrong to assume that the
marketplace in medical technology will ever follow classical patterns. Generally, as technologies mature and become more prevalent their
costs decline rapidly. I remember once discussing with a brilliant money manager the per-

ilous rise in the cost of medicine. I was being
unduly pessimistic, he claimed—it is in the nature of new technologies to become cheaper
over time, and he cited the ballpoint pen, the
CD player, and the computer as examples.
What he failed to realize is that highly specialized technologies controlled by small groups of
manufacturers do not respond to the marketplace in the same way that mass-produced
items do. Nor did he take into account the fact
that, in health matters, people are willing to
pay substantially more money for relatively minor improvements. When what is being improved is life expectancy rather than, say, the
fidelity of sound coming off of a recording, all
the rules change. Medical technology will continue to be expensive simply because it pays to
market a 1 percent improvement even though
it might be 100 percent more expensive. Armed
with this knowledge, a manufacturer will rush to
market with an expensive procedure or a drug
only marginally superior to one that is already
available at a significantly lower price.

24   4. THE AMERICAN CHARACTER AND APPETITE.
People often ask how nations such as England
and Canada can provide health care comparable to ours for much less money. First of all,
they use a single-party payment system—that
is, the government pays everyone's health-care
costs directly, an option, though highly efficient, that we seem unwilling even to consider.
Second, they are not, in fact, offering comparable services. Their health-care system does not
make nearly as much use of technology, and
they are willing, at least for now, to settle for
less. (But this appears to be changing: most nations with managed care are now accelerating
their health-care spending at a *more* rapid rate
than we are.)

25   The health-care crisis is at its most critical
in America not only because we are the preemi-
nent high-technology culture but also because
of the nature of the American character. I was
reminded of this recently during a seminar at
which a distinguished English Marxist was

holding forth on the venality of the American medical system by citing the higher rates of hernia-repair surgery done in America as compared with England. Since the incidence of hernias is the same in both countries, he interpreted the increased rate of repairs as the product of unnecessary surgery, driven by American greed. It occurred to me that there might be at least two or three other explanations. The simplest, of course, and the one that turns out to be the most accurate, is the funnel effect. Under the medical system in England, health-care services are free and widely distributed. But in order to control costs, and also to save hospital space, voluntary surgery to correct conditions that are not life-threatening is limited to a relatively small number of hospital beds. This results in a long waiting period—a six-lane highway leading to a single tollbooth will allow fewer cars through in an hour than one with six tollbooths. Limited facilities simply mean that the system allows for fewer hernias to be repaired in a given period of time. The disparity does not require the greed of the American surgeon.

26   The deeper explanation, however, is rooted in differences between the American and the British characters. Americans want things solved completely and they want them solved now; they don't want to hear about restrictions, especially on something like health care. I can easily conceive of a typical midland Englishman actually *preferring* to walk around wearing a truss, reflexively moving his hands to his lower abdomen every time he coughs, rather than rushing off for surgery to repair his hernia.

27   The American character is different. Perhaps because of our frontier heritage, Americans refuse to believe there are limits—even to life itself. Consider the struggle in America to define such terms as "death with dignity," which really means death without dying, and "growing old gracefully," a related term that, on closer analysis, means living a long time without aging. Dying in one's sleep at ninety-two after having won three sets of tennis from one's forty-year-old grandson that afternoon and having made love to one's wife twice that same evening—this is about the only scenario I have found most American men will accept as fulfilling their idea of death with dignity and growing old gracefully.

28   Medical costs will bankrupt this country if they continue on their current trajectory. And there are no data to demonstrate that improved mangement techniques will solve the problem. "Managed care" and "managed competition" might save money in the short run (though the examples of some other managed industries—such as the utilities and airlines—do not inspire confidence). But the bulk of the savings achieved by Health Maintenance Organizations has been achieved by cutting back on expensive, unprofitable facilities such as burn centers, neonatal-intensive-care units, emergency rooms, and the like. In other words, HMOs conduct what amounts to a hidden form of health-care rationing—confident in the knowledge that municipal and university hospitals are still around to pick up the slack.

29   As the managers of HMOs know only too well, the surest ways to contain health-care spending are to limit access to health care and to rethink our ever-expanding concept of health. But if we must have allocation, the process should not be hidden from public view or determined by a small group of health-care professionals. It requires open discussion and wide participation. When what we are rationing is life itself, the decisions must be subjected to public scrutiny and debate. The first step is to admit to the cruel necessity of rationing health care. The second is to set limits on health care according to principles of equity and justice.

30   The kinds of questions we will need to debate can be divided into three: issues of access (how do we decide who gets to receive a scarce health resource?), egress (how long may they

receive it?), and allocation (what medical services can the system as a whole provide to everyone?).

31   1. ACCESS. We can no longer leave to the marketplace decisions about access to medical care. We do not want kidneys to be sold to the highest bidder, and yet we now tolerate something perilously close to that. People can still use influence, power, position, and simply money to buy access to life-sustaining services. It is disgraceful to see a parent forced to "advertise" for a liver for her baby on *Oprah* while the governor of Pennsylvania is rushed to the head of the line for his heart and liver transplant. Access to scarce health resources must be organized on some equitable basis— even if equitable does not necessarily mean full coverage for everybody for everything.

32   There are various factors we might consider in evaluating competing claims on scarce and expensive services. One obvious consideration is age. Most of us would agree that a seventy-two-old man, let alone a ninety-two-year-old man, has less of a claim on an organ transplant than a thirty-two-year-old mother or a sixteen-year-old boy, all other things being equal. And yet proponents of such policies are commonly attacked as "ageists."

33   These are never easy decisions. They force us to face our own mortality and demand that we look beyond our own sympathies and interests. But they must be confronted nevertheless. When I recently presented the problem of access to an interdisciplinary class of law, medical, and theology students, the students' first response was that a lottery would be the best way to guarantee fairness. Yet leaving such an important decision to a lottery—precisely because it seeks to avoid questions of justice and fairness—is itself immoral. If my name were put into a drawing for access to a lifesaving resource along with my daughter's or my granddaughter's, and my name were the lucky one drawn, my first act upon recovery would be to throttle the idiot who set up such a system.

Claims on life must be based on enunciated values. Only after we have decided on our priorities and established our categories should we consider using a lottery, as we have done when we have operated a wartime draft.

34   2. EGRESS. The ethical dilemmas do not end with decisions about access to scarce services or technologies; now comes the even trickier (and seldom asked) question of deciding if and when that access should end. Imagine a system in which we have a limited number of artificial-heart devices. We must allocate not only a patient's access but also the amount of time he or she may have on this lifesaving machine. A year might seem insufficient; so might five. But forever until death? Even when someone else, much younger, will be dying while waiting for access to that very machine? So perhaps we pull the plug after an agreed-upon period— say, ten years, or twenty. Now we have been forced out onto the treacherous moral ground of euthanasia—and yet this is precisely where our technology, coupled with our funding crisis, is taking us.

35   It is ludicrous to think we can take away a lifesaving technology once we have introduced it. Since every new medical technology, however expensive, quickly becomes part of the therapeutic norm (and, from the patients' point of view, no longer a privilege but a right), we might be better off deciding in advance not to develop certain new technologies. Such an argument is now being made by bioethicists in debates over the boundaries of future medical research. Some argue, for example, that in view of the health-care system's current economic problems, we ought not develop a left-ventricular pump (essentially, a portable artificial heart). But how can we limit scientific inquiry? We can't—but we can debate what we as a society are willing to fund, just as we now debate whether we really need a supercollider.

36   3. ALLOCATION. What medical services can our society afford to provide to everyone? Here lies the political mine field that the Clinton Administration has apparently decided not

to cross. From all indications, the Clinton plan will offer a very generous package of "basic" health-care benefits to be made available to everyone. Guided by a group of "policy wonks" and quants[1] disdainful of the sticky dilemmas inherent in moral reasoning and terrified by the ambiguities inevitable when dealing with values, the Clinton task force has indulged in the wishful thinking that we *can* have it all—as long as we get the flow charts and systems theory right. By focusing exclusively on cost efficiency, the Clinton plan will do little to disturb the self-deceptive and self-destructive belief that we can meet every American's every "health" need; artificial organs, genetic screening, transplants, unproven AIDS drugs, psychotherapy for unhappiness, surgery for the tennis elbow, intensive care for the infirm elderly as well as for the two-pound fetus.

37   But we cannot do everything for everybody. Limited resources will force us to make tragic choices among competing health needs—if not now, under the Clinton plan, then very soon. To the uninitiated, these may look like medical choices, best made by medical professionals. In fact, they are not medical choices; they are moral and ethical ones, best made by all of us, struggling toward consensus through the usual, sloppy devices of democratic government.

38   Perhaps this is too much to ask of a governmental task force. But there is a precedent for just such a public process. Five years ago the state of Oregon attempted to confront the very dilemma the Clinton task force has chosen to duck. Oregon sought to guarantee a basic health-care package to everyone; at the same time, it acknowledged that doing so would bankrupt the state unless some hard choices were made about what should constitute "basic health care." Not all health services could be included. In other words, Oregon faced up

to the issue of allocation, and it did so out in the open: in a series of town meetings and a statewide "health parliament," issues of access and medical priorities were debated publicly, sometimes fiercely. The state's health commission then published a comprehensive list of medical conditions and treatments, each ranked according to its costs and benefits. More debate ensued; the list was revised. Finally, the legislature decided exactly where on the revised list the state could afford to draw the necessary cutoff line: it would pay for hip replacements and neonatal care, for example, but not liver transplants or in vitro fertilization. (Oregonians who still wanted such treatments were free to pay for them.) By conducting much of this process in public, the health commission was able to develop a consensus behind some otherwise unpopular decisions.

The Oregon plan is by no means perfect.   39 But at least the state has addressed the uncomfortable truth that they cannot have equity in their health-care system without making anguished, even tragic choices. Even more important, the people of Oregon have had a searching public conversation about new technologies and medical priorities, chronic care and cosmetic surgery—about how much health care they can afford and what it really means to be healthy. That is probably a lot more than the rest of us can expect from the narrow, numbing discussion of systems and policies and acronyms that the President insists on calling a health-care debate.

We are now told that the President's health-   40 care plan must be "sold" to the American public. Of course, had the plan been authored by the American public, it would not now have to be sold to it. But the task force was more concerned with secrecy than participation, and little interested in the questions of life and health and death that would have engaged the public's attention. It should come as no surprise that the result of such a process would be bad medicine: a prescription for ineffectual treatment based on a faulty diagnosis. ◆

---

[1] **quants:** slang for *quantifiers*—people who reduce reality to a set of numbers.

BLACK, WHITE OR OTHER?

Deborah A. Thomas

Like several other magazines, *Essence* reserves one page of each issue to allow a writer—professional or amateur—to reach out to the general public with a strong statement of opinion. In July, 1993, New York University student Deborah Thomas used the magazine's "Back Talk" column to advocate a change in the way the U.S. census deals with race.

1 SOMETIMES I CHECK THE BOX MARKED "other" just to mess with people. I did it on my application to Brown University, a college well known for its racially and culturally diverse, yet wealthy, student body, and another time on a job application that listed racial classification as optional. I was forced to justify my decision when the personnel director who knew my family called and asked me why I chose not to help the company fill its affirmative-action requirements.

2 Such is the fate of a mixed-race woman like me who must constantly second-guess the motives of census takers. And there are lots of us. In fact, it has been projected by some experts that, as a result of the doubling of interracial marriages between 1980 and 1990 and the subsequent increase of multiracial children, by the year 2001 lily-white communities will be almost obsolete in this country. By mid-century, if not sooner, the majority of the U.S. population will probably be nonwhite.

3 Yet the United States has denied the reality of racial mixing as fervently as it has upheld the myth of the "melting pot." Miscegenation laws in this country were not repealed until 1967—which makes me, born to a German-American mother and a Jamaican father in 1966, technically "illegal." Because American society adamantly upholds the false concept of racial purity and continues to see racial issues solely in terms of black and white (no pun intended), mixed-race Americans are still not officially represented on demographic information surveys. Put more simply, we have no box to check.

4 Many multicultural organizations, like the San Francisco–based Association of MultiEthnic Americans (AMEA), however, are pushing for the inclusion of a "mixed-race" category in the official census by the year 2000. Founded in 1988 as a confederation of local multiethnic and interracial groups, the AMEA encourages individuals of mixed race to claim their whole identities. It also promotes an awareness of their issues on a societal level.

5 Not surprisingly, many African-American organizations have opposed the AMEA's census category initiative, arguing that it will dilute political unity among Black people. They fear that with the addition of a new racial category, mixed-race persons of the Black and white variety will "shed their skins" and abandon their darker-skinned sisters and brothers and reap the fruits of official differentiation.

6 A new mixed-race category on the census would instead officially expose the fallacious American notion of racial purity. After all, while the "one drop" definition has allowed Black people in this country to create a unified front against white supremacy and cultivate our cultural values and traditions, it has also enabled policies such as segregation to be enforced by perpetuating barriers between the races.

7 One of the most radical and meaningful changes we can make at this time is to force those in power to stop manipulating the bipo-

lar racial system. The reduction of all social analysis to "Black" and "white" categories has unarguably obscured many of the real political, economic and cultural issues that face all oppressed people today—and that includes Blacks, Asians, Hispanics and poor whites.

8   The addition of a new census box will by no means eliminate racism in this country. It also begs the question of what is being mixed with what, or what races are being mixed with what. But at a time when so many Americans are hungry for self-determination, empowerment and liberation, it makes little sense that this country continues to see all of its problems in terms of race rather than class. With the absence of the current "convenient" categories; it is to be hoped that public officials will analyze the deeper issues that confront all of us instead of relying on the racial lip service that is all too prevalent. After all, races *do* mix. We are *all* mixed people: Racial purity is the fantasy of cavemen. ◆

Arguments About Facts

CHAPTER 8 INTRODUCED ARGUMENTATIVE WRITING AND GAVE YOU AN opportunity to practice your skills. The next two chapters will refine the discussion of argument by a close examination of the way people argue when facts are disputed (this chapter) and the way they argue when fairness or justice is the issue (Chapter 10).

Opinions differ about the best way to teach and learn argumentative skills. Some textbooks seem to operate on the assumption that the arguer's mind is like a computer and only needs to be programmed well to get good results. These texts present general rules of argumentation and tell the student that the key to success is to observe the rules. Skeptical about the effectiveness of this approach, I want instead to involve you in a dispute and let you compare your techniques of argumentation and your reactions to arguments with those of your classmates and some professional writers.

Our sample controversy will be the long-standing dispute about who wrote the plays and poems attributed to William Shakespeare. Waged over a period of about 150 years, this dispute has involved not only professors of English but lawyers, historians, X-ray technicians, handwriting experts, statisticians, cryptographers, linguists, and justices of the U.S. Supreme Court. It is a large, complex debate, full of mental gymnastics, but because it doesn't require a great deal of specialized knowledge to understand the issues, we can all plunge into it up to the elbows.

SPECIMEN CASE OF A FACTUAL DISPUTE: THE MAN SHAKSPERE AND THE WORKS OF SHAKESPEARE

Most people assume that William Shakespeare of Stratford wrote such plays as *Romeo and Juliet* and *Hamlet* simply because it has not occurred to them to doubt it: his name always appears on the program or on the title page. Like many of the facts we take for granted, however, this one rests on foundations that appear spongy to the skeptic's eye. During the past two centuries, many intelligent people have doubted that Shakespeare *could* have written the works associated with his name; more than 4,000 books and articles have been published on the question. Among the facts that the skeptics point to are these, none of which are seriously disputed, even by scholars who believe that the Stratford man was the author:

1. The man we call William Shakespeare is called William Shakspere in the records of his christening and burial and apparently signed his name that way as well (the signatures vary from one another and the handwriting is difficult to decipher). He was born in 1564 in the small village of Stratford-on-Avon, England. His father signed documents with an X or cross.

2. If Shakspere attended school (there are no records), it was probably not for long; he married at eighteen and had three children by the time he was twenty-one. He never attended a university.

3. The plays that began to appear soon after Shakspere's moving to London in his early twenties reveal knowledge that would be surprising in an ill-educated person from a small town. *The Comedy of Errors* (1592?) is based on a Latin play that had not then been published in English translation. *Love's Labour's Lost* (1594?) shows an insider's knowledge of life at the royal court. Collectively, the Shakespeare plays display an extraordinary vocabulary and an acquaintance with a wide range of books.

4. While Shakspere was in London, some of the Shakespeare plays were pirated and other plays, now believed not to be Shakespeare's, were attributed to him. There is no evidence that Shakspere protested.

5. Records indicate that Shakspere was an active businessman, a money-lender and real estate investor. In 1597 he bought an expensive house in Stratford, and he seems to have moved there permanently in about 1610.

6. Early in 1616 he made a remarkably detailed will that included mention of such small items as a silver bowl, a sword, and items of clothing. It mentions nothing about books (then very expensive) or manuscripts of the Shakespeare plays, half of which had not yet been published.

7. When Shakspere died, the event went unnoticed in London. Although the deaths of other literary figures of the time were marked by published tributes in prose or verse, none seem to have been published for Shakespeare.

Mark Twain thought it improbable that the man whose life these facts describe could be the author of Shakespeare's works, and he wrote a long manuscript (*Is Shakespeare Dead?*) raising some obvious questions. Is it likely that a man from an illiterate family in a farming village would have acquired the extensive knowledge of books, geography, history, human affairs, and (above all) law that the works display? Is it likely that he would acquire such knowledge without also owning, apparently, a single book? Is it likely that the death of an author whose poems and plays "had been before the London world and in high favor for twenty-five years" would go unnoticed and that no contemporary biographer would have journeyed to Stratford to learn the details of his life? Twain believed all this to be highly unlikely; he accused scholars of perpetuating the "Bard of Avon" myth by "surmising" crucial details of Shakspere's life. Biographers surmised, for instance, that Shakspere learned law by serving as a clerk of Stratford court, although there is no record of his having done so. And they surmised that after he moved to London he "amused himself" by studying law, although no one in Shakspere's lifetime mentioned this studying. Twain compares this surmising to the process by which a paleontologist creates a model brontosaurus from nine bones, a great many assumptions, and tons of plaster of Paris.

Like many other people in the nineteenth and early twentieth centuries, Twain thought the likely author of the poems and plays was Francis Bacon, a writer of demonstrable talent with an extensive knowledge of law, politics, and classical literature. The theory of the "Baconians" was that Bacon had political and social reasons for not wanting a reputation as a playwright and that he persuaded Shakspere to serve as a foster father for the plays. Though during the twentieth century Bacon has had fewer champions, there has been a good deal of support for two other candidates: Christopher Marlowe, a playwright whose production stopped when Shakespeare's began, and—far more significant today—Edward de Vere, the seventeenth earl of Oxford, a patron of acting companies who was praised for his literary talent.

PROBABILISTIC REASONING IN PERSUASION

Twain's objections to the surmisings of Shakespeare's biographers reveal something about the nature of most of the facts we take for granted every day. A "fact" like "William Shakespeare wrote *Hamlet*" obviously doesn't come to us by direct observation: it becomes a fact only when people are persuaded that it is *probable*. And an argument that makes a fact seem probable ordinarily has two parts: (1) a statement of "prior" facts that most people are willing to assume is true and (2) a general statement about probabilities. If the audience believes the prior facts and agrees with the statement of probabilities, it should accept the arguer's conclusion.

As an example, let's begin with two facts that those on every side of the Shakespeare question have been persuaded to accept:

1. The man named Shakspere never studied law formally.

2. Some of the plays attributed to Shakespeare show a remarkably accurate knowledge of law.

"Stratfordians" (those who believe that Shakspere was *the* Shakespeare) apply to these facts a framing assumption we could word this way: "It's likely, isn't it, that a smart person who studies law informally could learn enough to sound like a lawyer?" They conclude that Shakspere must have studied law informally. Anti-Stratfordians apply another statement of probability: "It's unlikely, isn't it that a person without any legal training could write so much about law and make no errors?" They conclude that Shakspere probably was not the author of the plays.

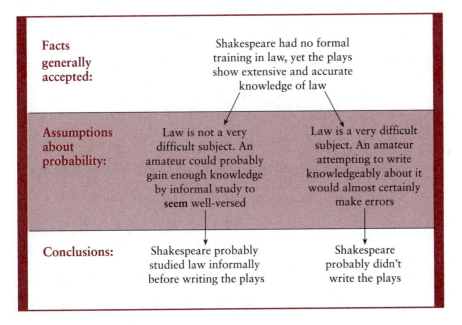

Facts generally accepted:	Shakespeare had no formal training in law, yet the plays show extensive and accurate knowledge of law	
Assumptions about probability:	Law is not a very difficult subject. An amateur could probably gain enough knowledge by informal study to **seem** well-versed	Law is a very difficult subject. An amateur attempting to write knowledgeably about it would almost certainly make errors
Conclusions:	Shakespeare probably studied law informally before writing the plays	Shakespeare probably didn't write the plays

Arguments about facts involve us inevitably in the process of estimating probabilities and drawing inferences from them. The following exercise gives you an opportunity to practice this process of probabilistic reasoning and to compare your thinking with that of your classmates.

◆ *Weighing Evidence.* To complete the following exercise, you will need to write several short notes about probabilities and inferences, so have a pencil and paper ready.

EXERCISE 1

Imagine a scale numbered from 0 to 100, with each point on the scale representing a level of conviction. For this exercise the zero position will indicate absolute certainty that Shakspere did not write the works of Shakespeare. The 100 position will indicate absolute conviction that Shakspere did. Begin by estimating your *present* position on the scale (before reading any of the facts below). Write a brief note explaining the reasoning behind your position: what statement of probability are you relying on? Then recalibrate your position in light of each of the facts, making notes on your reasoning as you go. To benefit most from this exercise, you must recalibrate and rereason after *each* fact. Treat the facts as cumulative: that is, take Fact 1 into consideration as you think about Fact 2, Facts 1 and 2 into consideration as you think about Fact 3, and so on.

Facts That You Can Assume to Be Undisputed

1. One of England's most eminent nineteenth-century lawyers, a man who rose to the office of Lord Chief Justice in 1850 and subsequently became Lord Chancellor, wrote that Shakespeare's plays had to be the work of a man with "a deep technical knowledge of the law" and a thorough acquaintance with "some of the most abstruse proceedings in English jurisprudence." "While novelists and dramatists are constantly making mistakes as to the laws of marriage, of wills, and inheritance, to Shakespeare's law, lavishly as he expounds it, there can be neither demurrer, nor bill of exceptions, nor writ of error."

2. Scholars have located references to Shakespeare's plays in letters, diaries, and other works written by Shakespeare's contemporaries. None of these references suggest in any way that the name *William Shakespeare* was a pseudonym.

3. Mark Twain was the pseudonym of Samuel Clemens, but in ordinary conversation most people refer to Twain's work without mentioning Clemens's real name.

4. Ben Jonson, Shakespeare's contemporary and a well-known playwright, contributed verses praising Shakespeare to the First Folio edition of the plays (1623). He also talked about his friendship with Shakespeare and commented on the virtues and faults of Shakespeare's style in *Timber: or, Discoveries; Made Upon Men and Matter* (1641).

5. Shakspere allowed his name to be rendered "Shagspere" on one marriage document and "Shaxpere" on another.

6. The monument to "Shakspeare" (so spelled) in the parish church at Stratford includes a half-height bust of a man with a pen and paper in his hands and inscriptions in both English and Latin indicating that the man whose life and death are commemorated was a thinker

and writer. Most experts who have examined the monument say that it was erected before 1623.

7. Engravings of the bust that were published in 1656 and 1709 differ in several respects from the present bust, most notably in that the man depicted is not holding a pen and paper.

8. An informal survey of twenty citizens in a city in the American Midwest in 1993 revealed that nineteen believed that the man from Stratford wrote the plays and poems attributed to him.

9. The overwhelming majority of professors of English in the world believe that the man from Stratford wrote the plays and poems.

TEMPERATE AND INTEMPERATE ARGUMENT

Mark Twain argues his case against Shakspere as Shakespeare with combative energy and spices it with a good deal of humor:

> Did Francis Bacon write Shakespeare's Works?
> Nobody *knows*.
> We cannot say we know a thing when the thing has not been proved. *Know* is too strong a word to use when the evidence is not final and absolutely conclusive. We can infer, if we want to, like those slaves . . . No I will not write that word, it is not kind, it is not courteous. The upholders of the Stratford-Shakespeare superstition call us the hardest names they can think of, and they keep doing it all the time; very well, if they like to descend to that level, let them do it, but I will not so undignify myself as to follow them. I cannot call them harsh names; the most I can do is to indicate them by terms reflecting my disapproval; and this without malice, without venom.
> To resume. What I was about to say was, those thugs have built their entire superstition on inferences, not upon known and established facts.

This confrontational stance may work in the hands of a humorist who is willing to parody himself as well as his opponents. It is a risky business for most writers of arguments, however. Generally, the credible arguer is more temperate, carefully weighing one probability against another. Such a balanced, judicious treatment is particularly valued in the academic community, where the unwritten rules of scholarship tell disputants to deal fairly with evidence for the other side. This ethical obligation creates a delicate problem for academic writers, since they must find a middle ground between a cold neutrality and a heated argument. The passage below is the *Encyclopaedia Britannica*'s discussion of the authorship controversy, written by Professor J. R. Brown of the University of Brighton and Professor T. J. B. Spencer of the University of Birmingham. As you read, notice that the professors attempt simultaneously to inform us about views they do not accept and persuade us to accept their views.

Questions of authorship. The idea that Shakespeare's plays and poems were not actually written by William Shakespeare of Stratford has been the subject of many books and is widely regarded as at least an interesting possibility. The source of all doubts about the authorship of the plays lies in the disparity between the greatness of Shakespeare's literary achievement and his comparatively humble origin, the supposed inadequacy of his education, and the obscurity of his life. In Shakespeare's writings, people have claimed to discover a familiarity with languages and literature, with such subjects as law, history, politics, and geography, and with the manners and speech of courts, which they regard as inconceivable in a common player, the son of a provincial tradesman. This range of knowledge, it is said, is to be expected at that period only in a man of extensive education, one who was familiar with such royal and noble personages as figure largely in Shakespeare's plays. And the dearth of contemporary records has been regarded as incompatible with Shakespeare's eminence and as therefore suggestive of mystery. That none of his manuscripts has survived has been taken as evidence that they were destroyed to conceal the identity of their author.

The claims put forward for Bacon. The first suggestion that the author of Shakespeare's plays might be Francis Bacon, Viscount St. Albans, seems to have been made in the middle of the 19th century, inquiry at first centering on textual comparison between Bacon's known writings and the plays. A discovery was made that references to the Bible, the law, and the classics were given similar treatment in both canons. In the later 19th century a search was made for ciphered messages embedded in the dramatic texts. In *Love's Labour's Lost,* for example, it was found that the Latin word "honorificabilitudinitatibus" is an anagram of *Hi ludi F. Baconis nati tuiti orbi* ("These plays, the offspring of F. Bacon, are preserved for the world."). Professional cryptographers of the 20th century, however, examining all the Baconian ciphers, have rejected them as invalid, and interest in the Shakespeare-Bacon controversy has diminished.

Other candidates. A theory that the author of the plays was Edward de Vere, seventeenth earl of Oxford, receives some circumstantial support from the coincidence that Oxford's known poems apparently ceased just before Shakespeare's work began to appear. It is argued that Oxford assumed a pseudonym in order to protect his family from the social stigma then attached to the stage and also because extravagance had brought him into disrepute at court. Another candidate is William Stanley, sixth earl of Derby, who was keenly interested in the theatre and was patron of his own company of actors. Several poems, written in the 1580s and exhibiting signs of an immature Shakespearean style, cannot well have been written by Shakespeare himself. One of these is in Derby's handwriting, and three of them are signed "W.S." These initials are thought by some to have been a concealment for Derby's identity (for some such motives as were attributed to Oxford) and to have been later expanded into "William Shakespeare."

Shakespeare has also been identified with Christopher Marlowe, one theory even going so far as to assert that Marlowe was not killed in a tavern brawl in 1593 (the corpse of another being represented as his own) but was smuggled to France and thence to Italy where he continued to write in exile—his plays being fathered on Shakespeare, who was paid to keep silent.

The case for Shakespeare. In spite of recorded allusions to Shakespeare as the author of many plays in the canon, made by about 50 men during his lifetime, it is arguable that his greatness was not as clearly recognized in his own day as one might expect. But on the other hand, the difficulties are not so great as many disbelievers have held, and their proposals have all too often raised larger problems than they have resolved. Shakespeare's contemporaries, after all, wrote of him unequivocally as the author of the plays. Ben Jonson, who knew him well, contributed verses to the First Folio of 1623, where (as elsewhere) he criticizes and praises Shakespeare as the author. John Heminge and Henry Condell, fellow actors and theatre owners with Shakespeare, signed the dedication and a foreword to the First Folio and described their methods as editors. In his own day, therefore, he was accepted as the author of the plays. Throughout his lifetime, and for long after, no person is known to have questioned his authorship. In an age that loved gossip and mystery as much as any, it seems hardly conceivable that Jonson and Shakespeare's theatrical associates shared the secret of a gigantic literary hoax without a single leak or that they could have been imposed upon without suspicion. Unsupported assertions that the author of the plays was a man of great learning and that Shakespeare of Stratford was an illiterate rustic no longer carry weight, and only when a believer in Bacon or Oxford or Marlowe produces sound evidence will scholars pay close attention to it and to him.

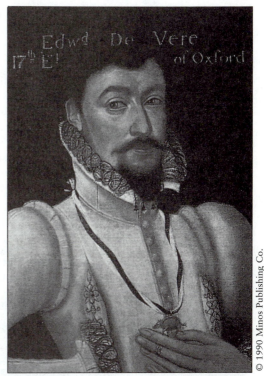

Edward de Vere, seventeenth earl of Oxford (1550–1604). Portrait attributed to Marcus Gheeraedts.

© 1990 Minos Publishing Co.

Advocates of Oxford as the true Shakespeare find a great deal to object to in Brown and Spencer's article, but readers who are not firmly committed to a position when they read it are likely to find it persuasive simply because it doesn't *seem* to be a propaganda piece. Often the most persuasive writing is so low-keyed that we aren't at all aware of being persuaded.

♦ *Weighing Additional Evidence.* Once again, imagine our 0 to 100 scale, with 0 representing an absolute conviction that Shakspere did not write the works and 100 representing an absolute conviction that he did. Begin by placing yourself (as you stand after having read Brown and Spencer, but before considering the facts that follow); note your reasoning. Recalibrate your position on the scale after you have considered each of the following facts and noted why the fact affected your judgment as it did.

Facts That You Can Assume to Be Undisputed

1. Calvin Hoffman, whose book *The Murder of the Man Who Was Shakespeare* (1955) is the cornerstone of the argument for Christopher Marlowe's being the true Shakespeare, was a Broadway press agent.

2. In January 1940, a man named Charles Wisner Barrell published in *Scientific American* the results of his scrutiny of three portraits of William Shakespeare. Barrell's analysis using X-ray and infrared photography revealed that all three were originally portraits of the earl of Oxford, modified later to disguise the true identity of the subject.

3. In a 1940 article for *Harper's* magazine, Oscar James Campbell, a Shakespeare scholar and editor, wrote: "Today a man who makes a cross instead of signing his name gives manifest proof of his illiteracy. But in the sixteenth century, this was not so. When we first find a cross serving as a signature on legal documents it was used because of its significance as a religious symbol. As a representation of the Holy Cross it afforded proof that the man who made it was giving religious sanctity to the ceremony of affixing his name. It was regarded as the written equivalent of an oath."

Portrait of William Shakespeare, 1610, attributed to Cornelius Janssen.

Folger Shakespeare Library Collection

4. In a 1948 letter to the editor of the *Saturday Review of Literature*, Gelett Burgess, a draftsman and designer best known for his suspense fiction and comic poetry, pointed out that the earl of Oxford owned copies of several books that are used as sources for the Shakespeare plays.

5. In a 1955 article for the *New York Times Book Review,* Alfred Harbage, a leading Shakespeare scholar, wrote that "the identity of playwrights then, like that of screen, radio, and television writers now, was a matter of public indifference. . . . The most popular single piece, 'The Spanish Tragedy,' went through eleven editions without mention of the author, and only a late casual allusion lets us assign it to a scrivener's son named Thomas Kyd."

6. In a 1991 article in the *Atlantic Monthly,* Tom Bethel points out that ". . . forty-four years after the Stratford man's death, knowledge of Shakespeare was so poor that the plays bound together for the library of Charles II and labeled 'Shakespeare, Vol. I.' were *Mucedorus, Fair Em,* and *The Merry Devil of Edmonton,* which are not accepted today as Shakespeare's."

7. Most of Shakespeare's sonnets are believed to have been written in the mid–1590s. Some seem concerned with advancing age:

> That time of year thou mayst in me behold
> When yellow leaves, or none, or few, do hang
> Upon those boughs which shake against the cold,
> Bare ruin'd choirs where late the sweet birds sang. . . .
>
> *Sonnet 73*

Shakspere was about thirty in the mid–1590s. Oxford was in his forties.

8. *Shake-speares Sonnets* appeared in 1609 (after Oxford's death, but before Shakspere's) without any prefatory note by the author. The publisher wrote a prefatory note that begins, "To the onlie begetter of these insuing sonnets, Master W.H."

9. Oxford was ward and later son-in-law of Lord Burghley, whom scholars recognize as the model for Polonius (the prince's potential father-in-law) in *Hamlet.*

10. Among those who have doubted Shakspere's authorship of "his" plays are essayist Ralph Waldo Emerson, poets John Greenleaf Whittier and Walt Whitman, the eminent nineteenth-century Shakespeare scholar W. H. Furness, and the novelist Henry James.

The Author's Level of Conviction and the Audience's

Let's consider for a moment the importance of the writer's position relative to the audience on our 100-point scale of conviction. There are, of course, four general possibilities. The writer may address an audience *more skeptical* about Shakspere's being the real Shakespeare than she is (let's say author = 90, audience ranging from 10 to 80), in which case she will presumably try to move them up the scale of conviction. She may address an audience *less skeptical* than she (author = 50, audience 95 to 100), in which case her purpose will be to shake their confidence. She may address a very *mixed* audience, including some more skeptical than she and some more convinced, in which case she may only want to show the unreasonableness of either extreme position. Or she may address an audience that *stands where she stands* on the question, in which case she is not attempting to persuade at all, merely to reassure.

Too often when we think of persuasion or argumentation, we conceive of a situation in which the writer stands at one extreme on a question and tries to win over an audience that stands at the other extreme. This analysis is far too simple. Persuasion more often implies an attempt to adjust an audience's level of conviction about an issue than it does an attempt to win an outright victory, a movement from 0 to 100 or from 100 to 0.

PURPOSE AND STANCE

If a writer's purpose is to sway the audience rather than overcome it, what stance should he or she adopt? Should the writer strive to seem confident, disguising any personal misgivings? Or is it better to take a more tentative stance?

One might ask, as a moral question, whether the writer should ever imply a level of certainty other than the one he or she feels. Doesn't honesty demand that writers 99 percent convinced that a proposition is true express their near certainty by the way they write? Perhaps so, but another sort of honesty tells us that our convictions cannot be so neatly pinpointed. On the Shakespeare authorship question, I am capable of fluctuating, on a given day, from about 85 on our scale to about 99.9. If I were writing an essay on the subject, I would choose to write as an 88 rather than a 99 for at least two reasons. The first is the framework in which I view all such controversies: since I believe that all of us erroneously tend toward extreme and simple answers, I prefer to risk erring on the side of open-mindedness. A second reason is strategic: when the author sounds open-minded, the reader tends to respond open-mindedly. If some of my readers were strong advocates of the earl of Oxford as the true author, I would arouse their resistance and perhaps their anger by treating the case for Shakspere as open-and-shut. I might force some readers who began as 10s to retreat defensively a notch or two *down* the scale of conviction. If my tone were more moderate, I might persuade them to move a notch or two up toward my position. Working at the moderate end of your own range of conviction shows respect and courtesy, at least, toward those who might disagree with you.

One suspects that Brown and Spencer deliberately work at the moderate end of their range of conviction. In private, they might sometimes refer to the advocates of Bacon or Oxford as *crack-pots* or *hare-brains*. In this very public statement, they are more open-minded and conciliatory. They concede that the anti-Stratfordian hypothesis is "at least an interesting possibility," and they admit that there are "difficulties" in reconciling the known facts of Shakspere's life with the magnitude of Shakespeare's literary achievement. At the same time, they are far from neutral on the issue. Look carefully at the first paragraph and the last. The first is filled with expressions like *supposed, claimed, they regard, it is said, has been regarded,* and *has been taken:* Brown and Spencer carefully let us know that they endorse none of these views. The last paragraph, on the other hand, after its conciliatory first sentence, states the authors' views strongly, using expressions that show a high level of confidence: *after all, unequivocally, he was accepted* (not *he seemed to be accepted*), *it seems hardly conceivable, no longer carry weight.* We might say that Brown and Spencer start at the moderate end of their range of conviction and end somewhere nearer its middle or even high end. In most cases, this is both an honest approach and a wise strategy.

Twain's strategy is quite different. At one point in *Is Shakespeare Dead?,* he says that he is neither a "Stratfordian" nor a "Baconian," but a "Brontosaurian"—a person who thinks that the Shakespeare biography is, like a reconstructed brontosaurus, made up largely of questionable assumptions and plaster of Paris. In the hands of another writer, the Brontosaurian position might seem like moderation itself: a detached, impersonal evaluation of the evidence. Twain, however, decides to shock the audience out of its complacent assumption that *of course* Shakespeare (however you spell it) must have written Shakespeare's plays. If anything, he exaggerates his conviction that *of course* "Shakespeare" could not have done so. This strategy is occasionally successful in moving people toward a more moderate position, and it provides the writer with an opportunity to exercise his or her gaudier rhetorical skills, but it is prone to backfire. Readers who feel bullied may dig in their heels and resist all persuasion.

THE NECESSARY LEVEL OF CERTAINTY

Our scale of conviction serves us well when we think about another problem every writer and thinker faces constantly. How certain must we be of supposed facts before we can treat them, in Twain's words, as "verified facts, established facts, undisputed facts"? There is no single answer here, but there are useful ways to think about the difficulty.

To begin with, the writer may be content to leave some "facts" in a state of uncertainty. No biographer of Shakespeare needs to resolve absolutely the question of whether the poet's father could read and write. If the biographer wants to leave the fact of John Shakspere's supposed illiteracy in limbo, he or she can simply move on to other things, being careful to make no argument based on this questionable "fact."

Some facts that stand at a fairly high level of certainty in the minds of the writer and the readers may be left there with little comment. A writer 95 percent certain that the man who wrote *Hamlet* also wrote *Coriolanus* and confident that the audience doesn't dispute this "fact" can usually let the matter rest. That is, he or she can write, "The playwright's imagery in *Coriolanus* is simpler than that in *Hamlet*" without stopping to discuss the possibility that Shakspere wrote one of the plays and the earl of Oxford wrote the other. The discussion of imagery wouldn't be helped by dragging the authorship controversy into it. On the other hand, there are occasions where even a 95 percent level of certainty is not high enough for us to let the matter rest. If investigators report that they are only 95 percent sure that *BrontoSoda* is not highly carcinogenic, we expect the Food and Drug Administration to take it off the shelves. A 5 percent risk of error in this case would be unacceptable.

The level of conviction the writer aims to bring the audience to depends, therefore, on the situation. A fair rule of thumb is that the more serious the consequences of accepting or rejecting a supposed fact, the higher the level of conviction writers must inspire in their audiences.

THE BURDEN OF PROOF

When high levels of conviction are important, the concept usually called "the burden of proof" becomes important. The most familiar example of the burden of proof at work comes from the Anglo-American legal system, which tells jurors in criminal cases that the prosecution must "prove beyond reasonable doubt" that the accused is guilty. Think what this means in terms of our scale of conviction. Use zero to mean that the accused is assuredly innocent and 100 to mean that he or she is assuredly guilty. Under our legal system jurors are instructed to consider the accused "innocent until proven guilty": that is, they must start at the zero point. And if the prosecution is to succeed, the prosecutor must bring them very near the 100 point: a juror 75 percent convinced of the defendant's guilt is expected to vote "not guilty." Unless the prosecution has very strong evidence, this movement from the bottom of the scale to the top will be impossible, *even if the defense says nothing*. The "burden of proof" is on the prosecution.

Rarely does a writer take on so severe a burden of proof as the prosecutor does. But every writer of a persuasive essay needs to think what the audience will or should assume in the absence of any compelling evidence. In the Shakespeare case, most audiences will assume that the man we call Shakespeare (never mind the spelling!) wrote the works, until someone presents them compelling evidence to the contrary. Anti-Stratfordians therefore face a heavy burden. Those who take the conventional view face a lighter burden: if they refute the arguments of someone like Twain, the audience will probably return to its prior assumption that the poet/dramatist we call Shakespeare was the man from Stratford, *even though little or no positive evidence has been presented on that point.* Logically, audiences should distribute the burden of proof equally in a case like this: advocates of Shakspere should have to prove their case just as thoroughly as advocates of Bacon, Marlowe, or Oxford. Psychologically, conventional views generally face a lighter burden of proof.

If you look closely at Twain's argument and that of Professors Brown and Spencer, you'll see that arguers sometimes try to shift the burden of proof to their opponents. Twain relentlessly accuses the Stratfordians of "surmising" and "assuming" with "no evidence." He wants the burden to be on *them.* Brown and Spencer do the same on the other side: "only when a believer in Bacon or Oxford or Marlowe produces sound evidence will scholars pay close attention to him and to it." Reminders of points where the other side has failed to shoulder its burden are legitimate, but we all learn to distrust the arguer who tries to shift the burden *entirely* to the other side.

Some Logical Fallacies That Can (and Should) Hinder Persuasion

As every advertiser knows, persuasion is hardly an exact science, and audiences can sometimes be swayed by entirely irrational appeals. Most audiences, however, include reasonable people who will question a logically flawed argument and view with suspicion the position it is supposed to support. Philosophers have identified more types of logical flaws (or fallacies) than we can possibly discuss here, but we can deal with nine of the most common.

1. Circular Argument. Also known as "begging the question," this fallacy occurs when someone "reaches" a conclusion by a logical route that assumes the conclusion to be true: "We can trust the recommendations of the F.D.A. because the F.D.A.'s recommendations are good ones." A circular argument seems to chase its own tail endlessly, and we may be surprised at first that any writer would fall into one or that any audience would fall for one. But circularity is actually very common. In the Shakespeare debate, Twain justly accuses some of Shakespeare's biographers of circular argument. Shakespeare's plays, one argument goes, show a knowledge of the law, and we know that Shakespeare wrote the plays, and therefore we can assume that Shakespeare studied law informally; and since he studied law informally, there is no disparity between Shakespeare's lack of legal education and the level of legal knowledge shown in the plays, and since there is no disparity, we can continue to assume that Shakespeare wrote the plays. C. S. Lewis mentions a bit of circular reasoning practiced by a friend of his who saw a ghost. She wouldn't deny that she saw the ghost, but she knew that ghosts don't exist, and since ghosts don't exist, this one must have been a hallucination, and since this one was a hallucination, it didn't damage the conclusion that ghosts don't exist.

2. Either/Or Argument.   Also called "false dilemma" or the "black/white" fallacy, this fault in argument oversimplifies a question by saying that there are only two possible views and they are neatly opposed: "The causes of homosexuality are either genetic or social"; "Shakspere was either a university graduate or an uneducated farm boy." In many cases, there is a vast gray area between the extremes where we might look for the truth. Once again, this fallacy is embarrassingly common. Indeed, most participants in the Shakespeare controversy fall into the either/or fallacy by insisting that either Shakspere wrote the works attributed to him or he didn't. It is at least possible that Shakspere wrote some of the works and that other authors wrote the rest, in which case some of the difficulties raised by the author's wide range of knowledge vanish. It is also possible that many of the individual plays were collaborative efforts. Scholars know that some of Shakespeare's plays take plots, characters, settings, and even dialogue from books by other authors. They also suspect that some of Shakespeare's associates in the theater provided him with information from their travels and experience. To say that either Shakspere wrote a play or he didn't is, therefore, to oversimplify the question somewhat. He may have written much of it, taking information when necessary from books and conversations, and relied on his collaborators for other parts.

3. The Bandwagon Fallacy.   This fallacy consists of assuming that the popular position is almost necessarily the correct position. If you are inclined to believe that Shakspere/Shakespeare wrote the works attributed him just because "everyone knows" that this is true (or nineteen of the twenty people polled "knew"), then you have fallen victim to the bandwagon fallacy. Remember that everyone used to "know" that the world is flat and that the best treatment for a heart problem is to cut one of the patient's veins periodically to remove excess blood. The bandwagon fallacy has probably gained strength in recent years because the media now bombard us with the results of public opinion polls, and "expert" commentators present the results as if the opinion of the general public were the most expert opinion of all. The general opinion may or may not be correct; by definition, it is not expert opinion.

4. Ad Hominem Argument.   Also known as "poisoning the well," the *ad hominem* (Latin, "to the person") fallacy consists of attacking the character of those who advocate an opposing view, in a way that is not logically pertinent to the main argument. Someone who argued that Mark Twain's opinion on the Shakespeare question could not be trusted because he was an atheist or an American would clearly be making an *ad hominem* argument. Rarely (unless in politics) are *ad hominem* arguments so obvious. When a

Stratfordian characterized Calvin Hoffman (see exercise 2, Fact 1) as "a Broadway press agent," he was using a more subtle smear tactic. On the one hand, it is fair to consider the credentials of someone who offers an "expert" opinion, and Hoffman was distinctly not a Harvard professor specializing in Shakespeare. On the other hand, he was a graduate of Columbia University and the author of several books of literary criticism and poetry, and his book is the result of nineteen years of research. To label him as "a Broadway press agent" is clearly an attempt to poison the well by suggesting that Hoffman is a shallow sensationalist whose opinions are not worth considering.

5. *The Straw Man.* Closely related to *ad hominem* argument is the setting up of what is called a "straw man," an opponent whose ideas are so clearly wrongheaded that they can easily be refuted. Sometimes the straw man is created by ignoring the strong points of an opponent's position, sometimes by combining the weak points of several opponents who may even disagree among themselves. Mark Twain creates a straw man when he lumps together several unnamed Stratfordian biographers and attributes to all of them the silliest speculations made by any of them. Like the *ad hominem* argument, the straw man fallacy is so common in politics that we almost *expect* to hear Republicans oversimplify and distort "the Democrat position" and Democrats do the same to "the Republican position." Of course, politicians are not generally regarded as trustworthy in such matters.

6. *Hasty Generalization.* This fallacy consists of drawing a broad conclusion from a few unrepresentative examples. It is particularly dangerous when the writer then uses the conclusion as a "fact" in the next stage of an argument. Oscar James Campbell (see exercise 2, Fact 3) offers the generalization that literate men of Shakespeare's time often chose to "sign" documents with a cross rather than their signatures. He uses this "fact" to refute the argument that John Shakspere, William's father, who did sign documents with a cross, was an illiterate man. How legitimate Campbell's argument is depends largely on how many examples of sixteenth-century literate cross-signers his generalization is based on. He gives only one example, thus making the cautious reader wonder whether his generalization is a hasty one.

7. *False Analogy.* Closely related to hasty generalization is false analogy, a fault in reasoning that comes from comparing things that are not truly comparable and so arriving at questionable conclusions. *Is Shakespeare Dead?* contains a magnificent false analogy in which Twain compares Shakespeare's case to his own. On the face of it, the analogy seems logical. Like the supposed Shakspere/Shakespeare, Twain was born in a small village far from any great cultural center, and like Shakspere/Shakespeare, he rose from obscurity to a high literary reputation. Building on the parallels, Twain points out that *his* biography is fairly easy to substantiate and has been largely substantiated by reporters who have interviewed his Hannibal schoolmates and dozens of other people who knew him well. "If Shakespeare had really been celebrated, like me, Stratford could have told things about him; and if my experience goes for anything, they'd have done it."

But do Twain's experiences go for anything here? Twain lived in a country and a period where writers had a high reputation and tended to become celebrities. Apparently writers of Shakespeare's time, particularly playwrights, were not held in high regard; many plays were performed and published without any mention of the author's name. Twain lived in an era when daily and weekly newspapers were eager to fill their columns with stories about celebrities. Shakespeare lived before there were newspapers. Encouraged by his publishers, Twain went on lecture tours that helped spread his fame throughout the country. So far as we know, writers in Shakespeare's time made no such efforts to draw attention to themselves.

8. *Post Hoc Fallacy.* This fallacy draws its name from the Latin phrase *post hoc, ergo propter hoc:* "after this, therefore because of this." It is a pattern of thinking that confuses sequence with causation. A child may discover that every time she watches her favorite football team on television, its players make some dreadful error. She may conclude that because the error followed her sitting down in front of the television, it was her observation of the game that caused the error. I distinctly remember drawing such a conclusion when I was a child, and I remember congratulating myself on one or two Oklahoma University victories that I caused by staying out of the living room.

Of course, it is sometimes true that the thing that comes before causes the thing that comes after, but the writer needs to give the reader strong reason to believe that this cause-and-effect connection is probable. When the advocates of the earl of Oxford point out that his theatrical activities ceased just when Shakespeare's works began to appear, they imply that there is a causal link between the cessation of Oxford and the commencement of Shakespeare. And they are ready to suggest the causal link—that Oxford continued his theater work under the name of Shakespeare. But, as Professors Brown and Spencer point out, the timing of these events may be entirely coincidental. When a writer asserts a causal connection between events, he or she takes on a heavy burden of proof. Showing that one event followed another is simply not enough. The best advocates of Oxford work hard to connect the evidence of timing with other evidence.

9. *Tenuous chain of causation.* This fallacy is essentially a variation of the *post hoc* fallacy. Perhaps the most delightful example comes from a story most of us learned in childhood:

For want of a nail the shoe was lost,
For want of a shoe the horse was lost,
For want of a horse the rider was lost,
For want of a rider the battle was lost,
For want of a battle the kingdom was lost,
And all for the want of a horseshoe nail.

Since the story is fictional, it is hard to challenge its truth, and yet we may be uneasy with the result. Imagine, for example, that a mob enraged at the loss of the kingdom decided to lynch the blacksmith who failed to hammer the nail securely. Surely this would be unjust. To use distinctions familiar to philosophers, the blacksmith's negligence (if it was negligence) may have been a "contributing cause" of the loss. But it was probably not a "sufficient cause" or a "necessary cause." That is, the kingdom could hardly have been lost solely because of the missing nail, and losing the nail would not necessarily lead to losing the kingdom.

Outside of the scientific laboratory, where events can be carefully controlled, almost every event has many causes, and almost every cause has many effects. To identify "the" cause of a great event like the loss of a kingdom is impossible. After all, there may have been other blacksmiths who also failed to hammer in nails properly. Perhaps the absence of other riders from the battle was as important as the absence of the rider who chose our unfortunate blacksmith. Perhaps some of the knights had eaten too heavy a supper or the general used an unwise strategy. The failure of our rider to show up may have been, as we say, the last straw, but it is unfair to call it "the" cause. Ordinarily, when a writer sets out to convince us that X was the cause of Y, we will insist that he or she show that this was the most significant cause, not merely a last straw. Sometimes we will insist that the writer show that his or her proposed cause is the last significant cause in a sequence of events. If, for example, in the final hour of the battle that lost the kingdom, the commanding officer for the losing side directed his knights to charge into an ambush, we surely won't want to hang the unfortunate blacksmith. It may be true that one more rider could have salvaged the situation, but the charge into the ambush contributed more heavily to the loss and contributed nearer to the fatal moment.

◆ *Identifying Flaws in Arguments.* The following statements are taken from published arguments. Removing a statement from its context makes it hard to evaluate, of course, but do your best: decide in each case whether you believe the statement contains a clear logical fallacy, is logically sound, or is in the gray area between. Be prepared to explain your reasoning. If you believe the statement is fallacious, try to identify the fallacy. If it doesn't precisely fit into a category listed above, explain what is illogical about it in your own words.

EXERCISE 3

1. In an essay favoring abortion rights that he published in *Newsweek*, John D. Rockefeller III made the following statement: ". . . those who support legalized abortion—and the opinion polls demonstrate them to be a majority—have been comparatively quiet. After all, they won their case in the Supreme Court decision. Legalized abortion is the law of the land. It is also in the mainstream of world opinion. The number of countries where abortion has been broadly legalized has increased steadily, today covering 60 percent of the world population. In this situation, there is a natural tendency to relax, to assume that the matter is settled and that the anti-abortion clamor will eventually die down. But it is conceivable that the United States could become the first democratic nation to turn back the clock by yielding to the pressure and reversing the Supreme Court decision."

2. In "Letter from Birmingham Jail," Martin Luther King, Jr., justifies his violation of segregationist laws in the following statement: "One may well ask: 'How can you advocate breaking some laws and obeying others?' The answer lies in the fact that there are two types of laws: just and unjust. I would be the first to advocate obeying just laws. One has not only a legal but a moral responsibility to obey just laws. Conversely, one has a moral responsibility to disobey unjust laws."

3. In *The Plug-in Drug: Television, Children, and the Family,* Marie Winn makes the following statement: "The decreased opportunities for simple conversation between parents and children may help explain an observation made by an emergency room nurse at a Boston hospital. She reports that parents just seem to sit there these days when they come in with a sick or seriously injured child, although talking to the child would distract and comfort him. 'They don't seem to know *how* to talk to their own children at any length,' the nurse observes."

4. In an anti-abortion speech before the British House of Commons, Jill Knight made the following statement: "As any doctor knows, depression and rejection of the child is quite a normal phenomenon of early pregnancy. Perhaps the mother-to-be feels sick, perhaps she regrets spoiled holiday plans, perhaps she did not intend to start a baby just then. However, before the Abortion Act it would never have entered her head to go along to her G.P. and ask to have the pregnancy ended. Within a few weeks she would not only accept her condition, but usually begin to look forward with pleasure to her baby. Now, with the knowledge that the highest authority in the land has sanctioned it, and the fact that her temporary period of rejection corresponds with the 'best' time to have an abortion, medically speaking, off she goes."

5. In an essay advocating strict warning labels on alcoholic beverages, Patricia Taylor makes this statement about manufacturers of beer,

wine, and liquor: "Some companies do sponsor occasional ads to remind us to drink 'moderately.' Unfortunately, those ads are designed more to undercut prevention-oriented legislative initiatives than to educate drinkers about health risks. The fact is, the $70 billion-a-year booze industry simply can't afford moderate drinking. Its best customers are heavy drinkers, who account for half of all sales. If those drinkers drank less, sales—and profits—would plummet."

EVALUATING FLAWED ARGUMENTS

There are purists who say that they will reject any argument that contains one of the logical fallacies noted above. If they follow through on this statement, they must find themselves in an odd position—all alone on the logical mountaintop with no argument to keep them company. In the real world, where writers have limited time, space, and information, and readers have limited attention spans, almost all arguments of any complexity are flawed. It is possible that Oscar James Campbell's research had uncovered hundreds of authenticated examples of literate sixteenth-century individuals who signed their names with a cross. Who would want to read twenty pages laboriously explaining these cases? Sometimes it is better to risk the appearance of hasty generalization than to belabor a point. And sometimes writers of short essays are forced to present a complex situation in either/or terms even though they know this is an oversimplification.

Most readers who learn to recognize logical fallacies also learn to evaluate their importance in the context of the whole argument. If the oversimplifying fallacy deals with a minor point or one on which there is little controversy, the reader may simply notice it and move on. If it deals with the center of a controversy, the reader will be more disturbed. If the author seems in general to be a reliable, honest person of good judgment, the reader will be inclined to assume that the oversimplification is innocent and that the writer is merely streamlining the presentation of a thoroughly considered line of thought. If the writer seems to be a bully or a person irrationally committed to a viewpoint, the reader will be more suspicious.

WEIGHING THE EVIDENCE

As we have seen, persuasive essays are ordinarily based on a body of "verified facts, established facts, undisputed facts." We should think briefly about what allows the writer and reader to treat a fact as "established."

There are, of course, philosophers who are willing to doubt everything including their own existence, but let's leave such extreme skepticism aside. Almost everyone will accept the factuality of things that they have encountered with their own senses, particularly if there are other witnesses present who experienced the same thing. If the day comes when I see a flying saucer with my own eyes, turn to my wife and say, "Did you just see a flying saucer?" and hear her say, "Yes," then I will accept as almost certain the fact that at least one flying saucer exists. Direct observation is the strongest sort of evidence, and it ordinarily overrides any of the weaker sorts we will now examine.

When we can't observe something with our own eyes, we will almost certainly be impressed by the testimony of several impartial eyewitnesses we view as reliable, particularly if their testimony is accompanied by documents or photographs dating from or near the moment of observation. If Joan Didion, Maya Angelou, George Will, Annie Dillard, and George Bush were to issue independent statements that they saw a flying saucer hovering over the Washington Monument on the same day, I would reluctantly accept the existence of this saucer as a fact, especially if I had also seen a photograph of it in the newspaper. As the number and the reliability of the eyewitnesses goes down, the certainty of a fact is diminished. If just one of these people reported the sighting and if there were no photograph, I would be more skeptical. If there were only the photograph, I would be very skeptical.

When the number of eyewitnesses from whom we hear directly is very small, we weigh the credibility of the witnesses carefully. If the only eyewitness to a saucer landing is a convicted perjurer who stands to gain money by selling the story, most of us will not accept the landing as an established fact.

PHYSICAL EVIDENCE AND RELIANCE ON AUTHORITIES

Very often, neither the reader nor the writer has direct access to eyewitnesses or their testimony. Now we are dependent on physical evidence, "filtered" testimony, or a combination of the two. Shakespeare's monument in Stratford and his will with its three shaky signatures are physical evidence. No one in the authorship debate seriously disputes their existence, and any argument that does not fit with this physical evidence is unlikely to be convincing.

Three of the five existing Shakespeare signatures.

Folger Shakespeare Library Art Collection

On the other hand, there is a story that Shakspere was the son of a butcher and that "when he was a boy he exercised his father's Trade, but when he kill'd a Calfe, he would doe it in a high style, & make a speech." This story was reported by John Aubrey in 1681 and is, he says, based on an interview with a Mr. Beeston of Stratford. There is physical evidence that Aubrey thought the story worth recording, since we have it in his handwriting, but how reliable is Aubrey? How good is his judgment of Beeston's reliability? From whom did Beeston get the story?

We have now reached a point where we must rely on layers of authority. If experts on Aubrey report that he is a fine judge of a witness's reliability, then we might tentatively elevate this rumor about the speech-making to the level of fact. If the experts who praise Aubrey are themselves unreliable, however, the situation is different: it is possible that Aubrey was a gullible gossipmonger, that Beeston was a liar, and that Shakspere never slaughtered a calf. Every expert is a sort of filter through which evidence passes on its way to us. In effect, experts do some of our thinking for us and give us the result of their deliberation. When the evidence is very complex, this filtering process is essential to our knowing anything, but turning our thinking over to someone else is inherently dangerous.

Careful readers and writers use several tactics to protect themselves from being misinformed by the authorities they rely on. First, they inquire into the credentials of supposed experts. What sort of experience do these experts have, what sort of education? Second, they check for bias. Is there reason to think that the expert stands to benefit from the opinion she or he gives? Third, they consult several authorities, preferably authorities with offsetting biases. If the experts who accept Shakspere as the author of plays in question and the experts who reject him believe the calf-slaughtering story to be true, we will be more likely to believe it ourselves. Fourth, and most important, careful readers and writers attempt to examine for themselves at least some of the evidence on which the expert judgment is based. Evidence that has been filtered through several levels of expertise may be interpreted beyond recognition. Before you accept at second or third hand Charles Wisner Barrell's assertion that three Shakespeare portraits are really retouched portraits of the earl of Oxford, go to the library shelf, find the January 1940 copy of *Scientific American*, and examine the photographs with your own eyes. You may be shocked to discover that the crucial details are mere blurs and that in some cases Barrell has retouched a photograph to make us see what he imagines himself to have seen.

WRITING A PERSUASIVE ESSAY ABOUT DISPUTED FACTS

POINTS TO
CONSIDER

To write persuasively about disputes of fact, you need to have a clear sense of where you stand and good understanding of why reasonable people in your audience might disagree with you. You would do well to set aside a period for self-examination as well as exploration of the issues before you begin to write an essay intended to persuade an audience. (Assignment 1, p. 343, gives you a procedure for this exploration.) Often, exploring the question in this way will show you that you need to do more research and thinking before you commit yourself to a position.

Before you become too deeply involved in arguing your case, gauge your own level of conviction and the level of conviction you aim to inspire in your audience. Must you convince them that some "fact" is virtually certain, or is it enough to convince them that it is more probable than not? Is your aim to raise your readers' confidence in a view they are already inclined to accept, or is it to challenge their view? How heavy a burden of proof are you assuming?

To be sure that you haven't been blinded by your own prejudices, have a draft critiqued by someone who disagrees with your view of the subject. Have your reviewer state his or her own position before and after reading your essay. Did you get the movement you hoped for? Why or why not?

QUESTIONS FOR PEER REVIEW

You might ask your reviewer to respond to the general peer-review questions from Chapter 2 (pp. 60–61), and you may want to add three others:

1. Is my essay entirely free of logical fallacies?

2. Is my evidence, including my use of authorities, unchallengeable?

3. Do I present myself as a reasonable person whose judgment can be trusted in an area of uncertainty?

If your reviewer answers yes to all these questions, you should probably ask for a second opinion before undertaking the final draft. Few arguments are completely untainted by fallacious reasoning, and almost all evidence is challengeable. The best help your reviewer can offer is locating the weakest links in the chain of your argument.

Assignments
for Chapter 9

A TEMPERATE STATEMENT OF YOUR POSITION ON A DISPUTED FACT

Choose one of the "facts" listed below or a "fact" that you choose and that your instructor approves. In an essay about 1500 words long and comparable in tone to Professors Brown and Spencer's discussion of the Shakespeare question, inform your readers about the dispute surrounding the fact and indicate your own position. Your essay should be written with a tone, content, and style appropriate for publication in an encyclopedia. That is, your aim should be both to help readers see why there is some dispute about the fact and to help them arrive at a sensible, balanced position.

1. *Abraham Lincoln believed blacks and whites to be equal.* Separating the mythical Lincoln from the actual one can be difficult. On this question, the best sources are surely Lincoln's own writings, available in every library.

2. *The United States "won" the Cuban missile crisis of October, 1963.* The impression of most Americans who lived through the crisis was certainly that President Kennedy had caught the Cubans and their Soviet allies in an act of secret aggression and forced them to back down. Some historians, journalists, and biographers have questioned this view of what happened.

3. *The United States landed a man on the moon in 1969.* A poll taken in the early 1970s indicated that fewer than half the people in the world believed this to be true, and a January 1990 article in the *Wall Street Journal* indicates that in many parts of the world, skepticism continues to run high.

4. *Reducing serum cholesterol levels will significantly improve the health of Americans.* Though it is the basis of much medical and dietary advice, this "fact" became the subject of some dispute in the late 1980s and early 1990s.

5. *Classification of humans by race has no rational, objective basis.* Racial classifications are used in newspaper accounts, government

363

documents, employment statistics, and everyday conversation, but some biologists and physical anthropologists dismiss all such classifications as bogus.

6. *Widespread burning of fossil fuels and deforestation are causing a global warming trend.* Taken as a truism by some environmentalists, this fact has been challenged by other researchers. Economically and environmentally, this is a high-stakes dispute.

7. *One American woman in eight will be raped during her lifetime.* Though the search for an exact figure may be fruitless, there is a good deal at stake in the approximate figure we take to be accurate. If the figure is more nearly one in three, this nation is a far more sinister place for women than if the figure is nearer one in thirty.

8. *Imprisonment of wrongdoers deters crime.* Recent calls for mandatory sentencing and a massive campaign of prison construction indicate that this "fact" is deeply embedded in the minds of many Americans. Some experts question, however, whether prison time has any significant deterrent effect.

ASSIGNMENT 2:

A Strong Advocacy of an Unpopular Opinion

Write a "minority report" about 1500 words long on a disputed fact you choose. To do this assignment properly, you need to identify a "fact" that most people believe to be true and then argue that there is reason to doubt it. You need not, for this assignment, maintain the careful balancing of views necessary for assignment 1. Be partisan; make your aim to unsettle readers' complacency and move them closer to your view of the question, even though you know some will be reluctant to see you as "right." You might imagine your essay's appearing on the opinion/editorial page of a newspaper with a wide circulation.

ASSIGNMENT 3:

A Balanced Treatment of a Factual Dispute Closer to Home

It is not only questions of national and international interest that produce disputes about facts. Every parent has had to sort through the conflicting stories of children. Every community produces gossip and countergossip about its members. Most of us have faced situations in which we knew from direct observation what someone had done but were forced to speculate about what the true motives were. A college or university newspaper will often include conflicting claims about what a person said or did or about what the actual cause of a campus crisis was. Find one of these local disputes of fact and write an essay in which you explain the dispute clearly and show the reasoning that leads you to accept one version of the truth over another. Strive for the sort of moderate tone that Mary McCarthy achieves in her discussion of her father's alleged drunkenness (see pp. 366–367).

ASSIGNMENT 4: ## AN ANALYSIS OF A PERSUASIVE ESSAY

To get a clearer picture of how the principles discussed in this chapter apply to published persuasive essays, subject one such essay to a three-part analysis. First, comment on the author's tone, level of conviction, and purpose: is this, for example, a cocksure writer attempting to win the reader over completely to one side of the issue? A cautious writer suggesting that the reader be cautious, too? Second, examine the logic of the essay: has the author assumed the burden of proof? Does he or she commit—or come close to committing—any logical fallacies? If the reasoning is sometimes fallacious, how much damage does this do to the argument's credibility? Third, examine the evidence on which the author bases his or her reasoning: does the author refer you to your own experience, write from personal experience, or quote eyewitnesses directly? Does he or she point to physical evidence that you could conceivably examine yourself? Does he or she rely on authorities, and if so, how credible are they? When experts' opinions are cited, does the author describe any of the evidence on which these opinions are based? End your paper by estimating how the essay will affect the opinions of the audience. Consider the different effects the essay will have on readers who are relatively skeptical about the opinion the author advances and on readers who are relatively sympathetic to his or her position. Be sure that your analysis is itself persuasive: cite your evidence and explain your reasoning.

THE TRUTH ABOUT ROY MCCARTHY

Mary McCarthy

In *Memories of a Catholic Girlhood,* Mary McCarthy tells the story of her family's disastrous 1918 railroad journey from Seattle to Minneapolis, during which both her father and her mother developed fatal cases of Spanish influenza. Orphaned at 6, McCarthy entered adult life with only fragmented memories of her mother and father. She remembered, for instance, her father's "coming home one night with his arms full of red roses for my mother, and my mother's crying out, 'Oh, Roy!' reproachfully because there was no food for dinner." Roy's poverty contrasted sharply with the wealth of his parents, who occasionally sent him small sums of money and who eventually insisted that he move from Seattle to Minneapolis so that they could "keep an eye on what was happening and try to curb my father's expenditures." In the preface to *Memories,* McCarthy sorts through conflicting stories about her father's character.

1 AT THIS POINT, I MUST MENTION A THING that was told me, only a few years ago, by my uncle Harry, my father's younger brother. My father, he confided, was a periodical drunkard who had been a family problem from the time of his late teens. Before his marriage, while he was still in Minnesota, a series of trained nurses had been hired to watch over him and keep him off the bottle. But, like all drunkards, he was extremely cunning and persuasive. He eluded his nurses or took them with him (he had a weakness for women, too) on a series of wild bouts that would end, days or weeks later, in some strange Middle Western city where he was hiding. A trail of bad checks would lead the family to recapture him. Or a telegram for money would eventually reveal his whereabouts, though if any money was sent him, he was likely to bolt away again. The nurses having proved ineffective, Uncle Harry was summoned home from Yale to look after him, but my fa-ther evaded him also. In the end, the family could no longer handle him, and he was sent out West as a bad job. That was how he came to meet my mother.

2 I have no idea whether this story is true or not. Nor will I ever know. To me, it seems im-probable, for I am as certain as one can be that my father did not drink when I was a lit-tle girl. Children are sensitive to such things; their sense of smell, first of all, seems sharper than other people's, and they do not like the smell of alcohol. They are also quick to notice when anything is wrong in a household. I do recall my father's trying to make some home-made wine (this must have been just before Prohibition was enacted) out of some grayish-purple bricks that had been sold him as es-sence of grape. The experiment was a failure, and he and my mother and their friends did a good deal of laughing about "Roy's wine." But if my father had been a dangerous drinker, my mother would not have laughed. Moreover, if

he was a drinker, my mother's family seem not to have known it. I asked my mother's brother whether Uncle Harry's story could possibly be true. His answer was that it was news to him. It is just possible, of course, that my father reformed after his marriage, which would explain why my mother's family did not know of his habits, though as Uncle Harry pointed out, rather belligerently: "You would think they could have looked up their future son-in-law's history." Periodical drunkards, however, almost never reform, and if they do, they cannot touch wine. It remains a mystery, an eerie and troubling one. Could my father have been drinking heavily when he came home with those red roses, for my mother, in his arms? It is a drunkard's appeasing gesture, certainly, lordly and off-balance. Was that why my mother said, "Oh, Roy!"?

If my father was a sort of remittance man, sent out West by his family, it would justify the McCarthys, which was, of course, Uncle Harry's motive in telling me. He felt I had defamed his mother, and he wanted me to understand that, from where she sat, my father's imprudent marriage was the last straw. Indeed, from the McCarthy point of view, as given by Uncle Harry, my father's marriage was just another drunkard's dodge for extracting money from his father, all other means having failed. My mother, "your lovely mother," as Uncle Harry always calls her, was the innocent lure on the hook. Perhaps so. But I refuse to believe it. Uncle Harry's derelict brother, Roy, is not the same person as my father. I simply do not recognize him. ♦

White Lies

Sissela Bok

Sissela Bok is an expert on professional ethics and has been a lecturer on medical ethics in the Harvard-M.I.T. Division of Health Sciences and Technology. In this selection from *Lying: Moral Choice in Public and Private Life* (1978), she argues against the apparently self-evident proposition that white lies harm no one. Arguments on moral questions often involve statements of value rather than statements of fact, but Bok's argument here is practical. She attempts to make her case by demonstrating the effects of supposedly benign deception.

Never have I lied in my own interest; but often I have lied through shame in order to draw myself from embarrassment in indifferent matters [. . .] when, having to sustain discussion, the slowness of my ideas and the dryness of my conversation forced me to have recourse to fictions in order to say something.

–JEAN-JACQUES ROUSSEAU, Reveries of
a Solitary Walker

When a man declares that he "has great pleasure in accepting" a vexatious invitation or is the "obedient servant" of one whom he regards as an inferior, he uses phrases which were probably once deceptive. If they are so no longer, Common Sense condemns as overscrupulous the refusal to use them where it is customary to do so. But Common Sense seems doubtful and perplexed where the process of degradation is incomplete and there are still persons who may be deceived: as in the use of the reply that one is "not at home" to an inconvenient visitor from the country.

–HENRY SIDGWICK, Methods of Ethics

HARMLESS LYING

1   WHITE LIES ARE AT THE OTHER END OF the spectrum of deception from lies in a serious crisis. They are the most common and the most trivial forms that duplicity can take. The fact that they are so common provides their protective coloring. And their very triviality, when compared to more threatening lies, makes it seem unnecessary or even absurd to condemn them. Some consider *all* well-intentioned lies, however momentous, to be white; in this book, I shall adhere to the narrower usage: a white lie, in this sense, is a falsehood not meant to injure anyone, and of little moral import. I want to ask whether there *are* such lies; and if there are, whether their cumulative consequences are still without harm; and, finally, whether many lies are not defended as "white" which are in fact harmful in their own right.

2   Many small subterfuges may not even be intended to mislead. They are only "white lies" in the most marginal sense. Take, for example, the many social exchanges: "How nice to see you!" or "Cordially yours." These and a thousand other polite expressions are so much taken for granted that if someone decided, in the name of total honesty, not to employ them, he might well give the impression of an indifference he did not possess. The justification for continuing to use such accepted formulations is that they deceive no one, except possibly those unfamiliar with the language.

3   A social practice more clearly deceptive is that of giving a false excuse so as not to hurt the feelings of someone making an invitation or request: to say one "can't" do what in real-

ity one may not *want* to do. Once again, the false excuse may prevent unwarranted inferences of greater hostility to the undertaking than one may well feel. Merely to say that one can't do something, moreover, is not deceptive in the sense that an elaborately concocted story can be.

4   Still other white lies are told in an effort to flatter, to throw a cheerful interpretation on depressing circumstances, or to show gratitude for unwanted gifts. In the eyes of many, such white lies do no harm, provide needed support and cheer, and help dispel gloom and boredom. They preserve the equilibrium and often the humaneness of social relationships, and are usually accepted as excusable so long as they do not become excessive. Many argue, moreover, that such deception is so helpful and at times so necessary that it must be tolerated as an exception to a general policy against lying. Thus Bacon[1] observed:

5   Doth any man doubt, that if there were taken out of men's minds vain opinions, flattering hopes, false valuations, imaginations as one would, and the like, but it would leave the minds of a number of men poor shrunken things, full of melancholy and indisposition, and unpleasing to themselves?

6   Another kind of lie may actually be advocated as bringing a more substantial benefit, or avoiding a real harm, while seeming quite innocuous to those who tell the lies. Such are the placebos given for innumerable common ailments, and the pervasive use of inflated grades and recommendations for employment and promotion.

7   A large number of lies without such redeeming features are nevertheless often regarded as so trivial that they should be grouped with white lies. They are the lies told

on the spur of the moment, for want of reflection, or to get out of a scrape, or even simply to pass the time. Such are the lies told to boast or exaggerate, or on the contrary to deprecate and understate;[2] the many lies told or repeated in gossip; Rousseau's[3] lies told simply "in order to say something"; the embroidering on facts that seem too tedious in their own right; and the substitution of a quck lie for the lengthy explanations one might otherwise have to provide for something not worth spending time on.

8   Utilitarians often cite white lies as the *kind* of deception where their theory shows the benefits of common sense and clear thinking. A white lie, they hold, is trivial; it is either completely harmless, or so marginally harmful that the cost of detecting and evaluating the harm is much greater than the minute harm itself. In addition, the white lie can often actually be beneficial, thus further tipping the scales of utility. In a world with so many difficult problems, utilitarians might ask: Why take the time to weigh the minute pros and cons in telling someone that his tie is attractive when it is an abomination, or of saying to a guest that a broken vase was worthless? Why bother even to define such insignificant distortions or make mountains out of molehills by seeking to justify them?

9   Triviality surely does set limits to when moral inquiry is reasonable. But when we look more closely at practices such as placebo-giving, it becomes clear that all lies defended as "white" cannot be so easily dismissed. In the first place, the harmlessness of lies is notoriously disputable. What the liar perceives as harmless or even beneficial may not be so in

---

[1] **Bacon:** Francis Bacon (1561–1626), British essayist, philosopher, and statesman.

[2] exaggerate/understate: Aristotle, in *Nicomachean Ethics,* contrasts these as "boasting" and "irony." He sees them as extremes between which the preferable mean of truthfulness is located. [author's note]

[3] **Rousseau:** Jean Jacques Rousseau (1712–78), French philosopher, author, and political theorist, known as the father of French romanticism.

the eyes of the deceived. Second, the failure to look at an entire practice rather than at their own isolated case often blinds liars to cumulative harm and expanding deceptive activities. Those who begin with white lies can come to resort to more frequent and more serious ones. Where some tell a few white lies, others may tell more. Because lines are so hard to draw, the indiscriminate use of such lies can lead to other deceptive practices. The aggregate harm from a large number of marginally harmful instances may, therefore, be highly undesirable in the end—for liars, those deceived, and honesty and trust more generally.

10   Just as the life-threatening cases showed the Kantian analysis[4] to be too rigid, so the cases of white lies show the casual utilitarian calculation to be inadequate. Such a criticism of utilitarianism does not attack its foundations, because it does not disprove the importance of weighing consequences. It merely shows that utilitarians most often do not weigh enough factors in their quick assumption that white lies are harmless. They often fail to look at *practices* of deception and the ways in which these multiply and reinforce one another. They tend to focus, rather, on the individual case, seen from the point of view of the individual liar.

11   In the post-Watergate period, no one need regard a concern with the combined and long-term effects of deception as far-fetched. But even apart from political life, with its peculiar and engrossing temptations, lies tend to spread. Disagreeable facts come to be sugarcoated, and sad news softened or denied altogether. Many lie to children and to those who are ill about matters no longer peripheral but quite central, such as birth, adoption, divorce, and death. Deceptive propaganda and misleading advertising abound. All these lies are often dismissed on the same grounds of harmlessness and triviality used for white lies in general.

12   It is worth taking a closer look at practices where lies believed trivial are common. Triviality in an isolated lie can then be more clearly seen to differ markedly from the costs of an entire practice—both to individuals and to communities. One such practice is that of giving placebos.

PLACEBOS

13   The common practice of prescribing placebos to unwitting patients illustrates the two miscalculations so common to minor forms of deceit: ignoring possible harm and failing to see how gestures assumed to be trivial build up into collectively undesirable practices.[5] Placebos have been used since the beginning of medicine. They can be sugar pills, salt-water injections—in fact, any medical procedure which has no specific effect on a patient's condition, but which can have powerful psychological effects leading to relief from symptoms such as pain or depression.

14   Placebos are prescribed with great frequency. Exactly how often cannot be known, the less so as physicians do not ordinarily talk publicly about using them. At times, self-deception enters in on the part of physicians, so that they have unwarranted faith in the powers of what can work only as a placebo. As with salesmanship, medication often involves unjustified belief in the excellence of what is suggested to others. In the past, most remedies were of a kind that, unknown to the medical profession and their patients, could have only placebic benefits, if any.

----

[4] **Kantian analysis:** based on the belief of Immanuel Kant (1724–1804) that certain rules are essential to our moral consciousness and should under no circumstances be violated.

[5] practices: This discussion draws on my two articles, "Paternalistic Deception in Medicine and Rational Choice: The Use of Placebos," in Max Black, ed., *Problems of Choice and Decision* (Ithaca, N.Y.: Cornell University Program on Science, Technology and Society, 1975), pp. 73–107; and "The Ethics of Giving Placebos," *Scientific American* 231 (1974):17–23. [author's note]

15 The derivation of "placebo," from the Latin for "I shall please," gives the word a benevolent ring, somehow placing placebos beyond moral criticism and conjuring up images of hypochondriacs whose vague ailments are dispelled through adroit prescriptions of beneficent sugar pills. Physicians often give a humorous tinge to instructions for prescribing these substances, which helps to remove them from serious ethical concern. One authority wrote in a pharmacological journal that the placebo should be given a name previously unknown to the patient and preferably Latin and polysyllabic, and added:

16 [I]t is wise if it be prescribed with some assurance and emphasis for psychotherapeutic effect. The older physicians each had his favorite placebic prescriptions—one chose tincture of Condurango, another the Fluidextract of *Cimicifuga migra*.[6]

17 After all, health professionals argue, are not placebos far less dangerous than some genuine drugs? And more likely to produce a cure than if nothing at all is prescribed? Such a view was expressed in a letter to the *Lancet:*

18 Whenever pain can be relieved with a ml of saline, why should we inject an opiate? Do anxieties or discomforts that are allayed with starch capsules require administration of a barbiturate, diazepam, or propoxyphene?[7]

19 Such a simplistic view conceals the real costs of placebos, both to individuals and to the practice of medicine. First, the resort to placebos may actually prevent the treatment of an underlying, undiagnosed problem. And even if the placebo "works," the effect is often short-lived; the symptoms may recur, or crop up in other forms. Very often, the symptoms of which the patient complains are bound to go away by themselves, sometimes even from the mere contact with a health professional. In those cases, the placebo itself is unnecessary; having recourse to it merely reinforces a tendency to depend upon pills or treatments where none is needed.

20 In the aggregate, the costs of placebos are immense. Many millions of dollars are expended on drugs, diagnostic tests, and psychotherapies of a placebic nature. Even operations can be of this nature—a hysterectomy may thus be performed, not because the condition of the patient requires such surgery, but because she goes from one doctor to another seeking to have the surgery performed, or because she is judged to have a great fear of cancer which might be alleviated by the very fact of the operation.

21 Even apart from financial and emotional costs and the squandering of resources, the practice of giving placebos is wasteful of a very precious good: the trust on which so much in the medical relationship depends. The trust of those patients who find out they have been duped is lost, sometimes irretrievably. They may then lose confidence in physicians and even in bona fide medication which they may need in the future. They may obtain for themselves more harmful drugs or attach their hopes to debilitating fad cures.

22 The following description of a case[8] where a placebo was prescribed reflects a common approach:

23 A seventeen-year-old girl visited her pediatrician, who had been taking care of her since infancy. She went to his office without her parents, although her mother had made the appointment for her over the telephone. She told the pediatrician that she was very healthy, but that she thought she had some

---

[6] source: O. H. Pepper, "A Note on the Placebo," *American Journal of Pharmacy* 117 (1945):409–12. [author's note]

[7] source: J. Sice, "Letter to the Editor," *The Lancet* 2 (1972):651. [author's note]

[8] description of a case: I am grateful to Dr. Melvin Levine for the permission to reproduce this case, used in the Ethics Rounds at the Children's Hospital in Boston. [author's note]

emotional problems. She stated that she was having trouble sleeping at night, that she was very nervous most of the day. She was a senior in high school and claimed she was doing quite poorly in most of her subjects. She was worried about what she was going to do next year. She was somewhat overweight. This, she felt, was part of her problem. She claimed she was not very attractive to the opposite sex and could not seem to "get boys interested in me." She had a few close friends of the same sex.

24   Her life at home was quite chaotic and stressful. There were frequent battles with her younger brother, who was fourteen, and with her parents. She claimed her parents were always "on my back." She described her mother as extremely rigid and her father as a disciplinarian, who was quite old-fashioned in his values.

25   In all, she spent about twenty minutes talking with her pediatrician. She told him that what she thought she really needed was tranquilizers, and that that was the reason she came. She felt that this was an extremely difficult year for her, and if she could have something to calm her nerves until she got over her current crises, everything would go better.

26   The pediatrician told her that he did not really believe in giving tranquilizers to a girl of her age. He said he thought it would be a bad precedent for her to establish. She was very insistent, however, and claimed that if he did not give her tranquilizers, she would "get them somehow." Finally, he agreed to call her pharmacy and order medication for her nerves. She accepted graciously. He suggested that she call him in a few days to let him know how things were going. He also called her parents to say that he had a talk with her and he was giving her some medicine that might help her nerves.

27   Five days later, the girl called the pediatrician back to say that the pills were really working well. She claimed that she had calmed down a great deal, and that she was working things out better with her parents, and had a new outlook on life. He suggested that she keep taking them twice a day for the rest of the school year. She agreed.

28   A month later, the girl ran out of pills and called her pediatrician for a refill. She found that he was away on vacation. She was quite distraught at not having any medication left, so she called her uncle who was a surgeon in the next town. He called the pharmacy to renew her pills and, in speaking to the druggist, found out that they were only vitamins. He told the girl that the pills were only vitamins and that she could get them over the counter and didn't really need him to refill them. The girl became very distraught, feeling that she had been deceived and betrayed by her pediatrician. Her parents, when they heard, commented that they thought the pediatrician was "very clever."

29   The patients who do *not* discover the deception and are left believing that a placebic remedy has worked may continue to rely on it under the wrong circumstances. This is especially true with drugs such as antibiotics, which are sometimes used as placebos and sometimes for their specific action. Many parents, for example, come to believe that they must ask for the prescription of antibiotics everytime their child has a fever or a cold. The fact that so many doctors accede to such requests perpetuates the dependence of these families on medical care they do not need and weakens their ability to cope with health problems. Worst of all, those children who cannot tolerate antibiotics may have severe reactions, sometimes fatal, to such unnecessary medication.[9]

30   Such deceptive practices, by their very nature, tend to escape the normal restraints of

---

[9] source: C. M. Kunin, T. Tupasi, and W. Craig, "Use of Antibiotics," *Annals of Internal Medicine* 79 (October 1973):555–60. [author's note]

accountability and can therefore spread more easily than others. There are many instances in which an innocuous-seeming practice has grown to become a large-scale and more dangerous one. Although warnings against the "entering wedge" are often rhetorical devices, they can at times express justifiable caution: especially when there are great pressures to move along the undesirable path and when the safeguards are insufficient.

31   In this perspective, there is much reason for concern about placebos. The safeguards against this practice are few or nonexistent—both because it is secretive in nature and because it is condoned but rarely carefully discussed in the medical literature.[10] And the pressures are very great, and growing stronger, from drug companies, patients eager for cures, and busy physicians, for more medication, whether it is needed or not. Given this lack of safeguards and these strong pressures, the use of placebos can spread in a number of ways.

32   The clearest danger lies in the gradual shift from pharmacologically inert placebos to more active ones. It is not always easy to distinguish completely inert substances from somewhat active ones and these in turn from more active ones. It may be hard to distinguish between a quantity of an active substance so low that it has little or no effect and quantities that have some effect. It is not always clear to doctors whether patients require an inert placebo or possibly a more active one, and there can be the temptation to resort to an active one just in case it might also have a specific effect. It is also much easier to deceive a patient with a

medication that is known to be "real" and to have power. One recent textbook in medicine goes so far as to advocate the use of small doses of effective compounds as placebos rather than inert substances—because it is important for both the doctor and the patient to believe in the treatment! This shift is made easier because the dangers and side effects of active agents are not always known or considered important by the physician.

33   Meanwhile, the number of patients receiving placebos increases as more and more people seek and receive medical care and as their desire for instant, push-button alleviation of symptoms is stimulated by drug advertising and by rising expectations of what science can do. The use of placebos for children grows as well, and the temptations to manipulate the truth are less easily resisted once such great inroads have already been made.

34   Deception by placebo can also spread from therapy and diagnosis to experimentation. Much experimentation with placebos is honest and consented to by the experimental subjects, especially since the advent of strict rules governing such experimentation. But grievous abuses have taken place where placebos were given to unsuspecting subjects who believed they had received another substance. In 1971, for example, a number of Mexican-American women applied to a family-planning clinic for contraceptives. Some of them were given oral contraceptives and others were given placebos, or dummy pills that looked like the real thing. Without fully informed consent, the women were being used in an experiment to explore the side effects of various contraceptive pills. Some of those who were given placebos experienced a predictable side effect—they became pregnant. The investigators neither assumed financial responsibility for the babies nor indicated any concern about having bypassed the "informed consent" that is required in ethical experiments with human beings. One contented himself with the observation that if only

---

10   medical literature: In a sample of nineteen recent, commonly used textbooks, in medicine, pediatrics, surgery, anesthesia, obstetrics, and gynecology, only three even mention placebos, and none detail either medical or ethical dilemmas they pose. Four out of six textbooks on pharmacology mention them; only one mentions such problems. Only four out of eight textbooks on psychiatry even mention placebos; none takes up ethical problems. For references, see Bok, "Paternalistic Deception in Medicine and Rational Choice." [author's note]

the law had permitted it, he could have aborted the pregnant women!

35   The failure to think about the ethical problems in such a case stems at least in part from the innocent-seeming white lies so often told in giving placebos. The spread from therapy to experimentation and from harmlessness to its opposite often goes unnoticed in part *because* of the triviality believed to be connected with placebos as white lies. This lack of foresight and concern is most frequent when the subjects in the experiment are least likely to object or defend themselves; as with the poor, the institutionalized, and the very young.

36   In view of all these ways in which placebo usage can spread, it is not enough to look at each incident of manipulation in isolation, no matter how benevolent it may be. When the costs and benefits are weighed, not only the individual consequences must be considered, but also the cumulative ones. Reports of deceptive practices inevitably leak out, and the resulting suspicion is heightened by the anxiety which threats to health always create. And so even the health professionals who do not mislead their patients are injured by those who do; the entire institution of medicine is threatened by practices lacking in candor, however harmless the results may appear in some individual cases.

37   This is not to say that all placebos must be ruled out; merely that they cannot be excused as innocuous. They should be prescribed but rarely, and only after a careful diagnosis and consideration of non-deceptive alternatives; they should be used in experimentation only after subjects have consented to their use.

LETTERS OF RECOMMENDATION

38   Another deceptive practice where not much may seem to be at stake yet which has high accumulated costs is that of the inflated recommendation. It seems a harmless enough practice, and often an act of loyalty, to give extra praise to a friend, a colleague, a student, a relative. In the harsh competition for employment and advancement, such a gesture is natural. It helps someone, while injuring no one in particular, and balances out similar gestures on the part of many others. Yet the practice obviously injures those who do not benefit from this kind of assistance; and it injures them in a haphazard and inequitable way. Two applicants for work, who are equally capable, may be quite differently rated through no fault of their own.

39   The existing practices also pose many problems for the individuals caught up in them. Take, for instance, a system where all recommendations given to students are customarily exaggerated—where, say, 60 percent of all graduates are classified as belonging to the top 10 percent. If a professor were to make the honest statement to an employer that a student is merely among the top 60 percent, he might severely injure that student's ability to find work, since the statement would not be taken at face value but would be wrongly interpreted to mean that his real standing was very near the bottom.

40   Or consider officer evaluation reports in the U.S. Army. Those who rate officers are asked to give them scores of "outstanding," "superior," "excellent," "effective," "marginal," and "inadequate." Raters know, however, that those who are ranked anything less than "outstanding" (say, "superior" or "excellent") are then at a great disadvantage,[11] and become likely candidates for discharge. Here, superficial verbal harmlessness combines with the harsh realities of the competition for advancement and job retention to produce an inflated set of standards to which most feel bound to conform.

---

11 disadvantage: Form DA 67-7, 1 January 1973, U.S. Army Officer Evaluation Report. [author's note]

41   In such cases, honesty might victimize innocent persons. At the same time, using the evaluations in the accepted manner is still burdensome or irritating to many. And the blurring of the meaning of words in these circumstances can make it seem easier, perhaps even necessary, not to be straightforward in others.

42   It is difficult for raters to know what to do in such cases. Some feel forced to say what they do not mean. Others adhere to a high standard of accuracy and thereby perhaps injure those who must have their recommendations.

43   To make choices on the basis of such inflated recommendations is equally difficult. This is especially true in large organizations, or at great distances, where those who receive the ratings never know who the raters are or by what standards they work.

44   The entire practice, then, is unjust for those rated and bewildering for those who give and make use of ratings. It also robs recommendations of whatever benefits they are intended to bring. No one can know what is meant by a particular rating. Such a practice is fraught with difficulties; the costs to deceivers and deceived alike are great.

45   For this reason, those who give ratings should make every effort to reduce the injustice and to come closer to the standard of accuracy which they would accept were it not for the inflated practice. But if one goes against such a practice, one does have the responsibility of indicating that one is doing so, in order to minimize the effect on those rated. To do so requires time, power, and consistency. A counselor at a school for highly sought-after students, for example, can make it clear to college recruiters that he means every word he uses in his recommendations of students. So can colleagues who know each other well, when they discuss job applicants. But many are caught up in practices where they are nearly anonymous, perhaps transient, and where they have no contact with those who ask them to make out ratings for students or staff members or military personnel. They are then quite powerless: while it may be demeaning to participate in the inflated practices, it is hard to resist them singlehandedly. In verbal inflation as with monetary inflation, more general measures are often necessary. It must, therefore, be more excusable for those individuals to cooperate with the general norm, who cannot establish a different verbal "currency" for what they say.

46   Institutions, on the other hand, do have more leverage, Some can seek to minimize the reliance on such reports altogether. Others can try to work at the verbal inflation itself. But it is very difficult to do so, especially for large organizations. The U.S. Army tried to scale down evaluations by publishing the evaluation report I have cited. It suggested mean scores for the different ranks, but few felt free to follow these means in individual cases, for fear of hurting the persons being rated. As a result, the suggested mean scores once again lost all value.

TRUTHFULNESS AT WHAT PRICE?

47   These examples show that one cannot dismiss lies merely by claiming that they don't matter. More often than not, they do matter, even where looked at in simple terms of harm and benefit. Any awareness of how lies spread must generate a real sensitivity to the fact that most lies believed to be "white" are unnecessary if not downright undesirable. Many are not as harmless as liars take them to be. And even those lies which would generally be accepted as harmless are not needed whenever their goals can be achieved through completely honest means. Why tell a flattering lie about someone's hat rather than a flattering truth about their flowers? Why tell a general white lie about a gift, a kind act, a newborn baby, rather than a more specific truthful statement? If the purpose is understood by both speaker

and listener to be one of civility and support, the *full* truth in such cases is not called for.[12]

48   I would not wish to argue that all white lies should be ruled out. Individuals caught up in the practices of making inflated recommendations, for example, may have no other recourse. In a few cases, placebos may be the only reasonable alternative. And certain marginally deceptive social excuses and conventions are unavoidable if feelings are not to be needlessly injured.

49   But these are very few. And it is fallacious to argue that all white lies are right because a few are. As a result, those who undertake to tell white lies should look hard for alternatives. They should see even these lies as links in much wider practices and should know the ways in which these practices can spread. If they do, white lies, where truly harmless and a last resort—told, for instance, to avoid hurting someone's feelings—can be accepted as policy, but *only* under such limited circumstances.

50   Most of us doubtless come into more frequent contact with white lies than with any

_____

[12] not called for: If, on the other hand, one is asked for one's honest opinion, such partial answers no longer suffice. A flattering truth that conceals one's opinion is then as deceitful as a flattering lie. To avoid deception, one must then choose either to refuse to answer or to answer honestly. [author's note]

other form of deception. To the extent that we train ourselves to see their ramifications and succeed in eliminating them from our speech, the need to resort to them will diminish. If we can then make it clear to others that we stand in no need of white lies from *them,* many needless complications will have been avoided.

51   A word of caution is needed here. To say that white lies should be kept at a minimum is *not* to endorse the telling of truths to all comers. Silence and discretion, respect for the privacy and for the feelings of others must naturally govern what is spoken. The gossip one conveys and the malicious reports one spreads may be true without therefore being excusable. And the truth told in such a way as to wound may be unforgivably cruel, as when a physician answers a young man asking if he has cancer with a curt Yes as he leaves the room. He may not have lied, but he has failed in every professional duty of respect and concern for his patient.

52   Once it has been established that lies should not be told, it still remains to be seen whether anything should be conveyed, and, if so, how this can best be done. The self-appointed removers of false beliefs from those for whom these beliefs may be all that sustains them can be as harmful as the most callous liars. ◆

Warfare Is Only an Invention— Not a Biological Necessity

Margaret Mead

Among the most controversial and basic of the facts we dispute are those that concern human nature. Which of our desires and capabilities are inborn and inescapable, for better or for worse? Which can be altered by a change in culture? Anthropologist Margaret Mead plunges directly into such a question in the essay that follows.

1   IS WAR A BIOLOGICAL NECESSITY, A sociological inevitability or just a bad invention? Those who argue for the first view endow man with such pugnacious instincts that some outlet in aggressive behavior is necessary if man is to reach full human stature. It was this point of view which lay back of William James's famous essay, "The Moral Equivalent of War," in which he tried to retain the warlike virtues and channel them in new directions. A similar point of view has lain back of the Soviet Union's attempt to make competition between groups rather than between individuals. A basic, competitive, aggressive, warring human nature is assumed, and those who wish to outlaw war or outlaw competitiveness merely try to find new and less socially destructive ways in which these biologically given aspects of man's nature can find expression. Then there are those who take the second view: warfare is the inevitable concomitant of the development of the state, the struggle for land and natural resources of class societies springing, not from the nature of man, but from the nature of history. War is nevertheless inevitable unless we change our social system and outlaw classes, the struggle for power, and possessions; and in the event of our success warfare would disappear, as a symptom vanishes when the disease is cured.

2   One may hold a sort of compromise position between these two extremes; one may claim that all aggression springs from the frustration of man's biologically determined drives and that, since all forms of culture are frustrating, it is certain each new generation will be aggressive and the aggression will find its natural and inevitable expression in race war, class war, nationalistic war, and so on. All three of these positions are very popular today among those who think seriously about the problems of war and its possible prevention, but I wish to urge another point of view, less defeatist perhaps than the first and third, and more accurate than the second: that is, that warfare, by which I mean recognized conflict between two groups *as groups,* in which each group puts an army (even if the army is only fifteen pygmies) into the field to fight and kill, if possible, some of the members of the army of the other group—that warfare of this sort is an invention like any other of the inventions in terms of which we order our lives, such as writing, marriage, cooking our food instead of eating it raw, trial by jury or burial of the dead, and so on. Some of this list anyone will grant are inventions: trial by jury is confined to very limited portions of the globe; we know that there are tribes that do not bury their dead but instead expose or cremate them; and we know that only part of the human race has had the knowledge of writing as its cultural inheritance. But, whenever a way of doing things is found universally, such as the use of fire or the practice of some form of marriage, we tend to think at once that it is not an invention at all

377

but an attribute of humanity itself. And yet even such universals as marriage and the use of fire are inventions like the rest, very basic ones, inventions which were perhaps necessary if human history was to take the turn that it has taken, but nevertheless inventions. At some point in his social development man was undoubtedly without the institution of marriage or the knowledge of the use of fire.

3   The case for warfare is much clearer because there are peoples even today who have no warfare. Of these the Eskimo are perhaps the most conspicuous examples, but the Lepchas of Sikkim described by Geoffrey Gorer in *Himalayan Village* are as good. Neither of these peoples understands war, not even defensive warfare. The idea of warfare is lacking, and this idea is as essential to really carrying on war as an alphabet or a syllabary is to writing. But whereas the Lepchas are a gentle, unquarrelsome people, and the advocates of other points of view might argue that they are not full human beings or that they had never been frustrated and so had no aggression to expand in warfare, the Eskimo case gives no such possibility of interpretation. The Eskimo are not a mild and meek people; many of them are turbulent and troublesome. Fights, theft of wives, murder, cannibalism, occur among them—all outbursts of passionate men goaded by desire or intolerable circumstance. Here are men faced with hunger, men faced with loss of their wives, men faced with the threat of extermination by other men, and here are orphan children, growing up miserably with no one to care for them, mocked and neglected by those about them. The personality necessary for war, the circumstances necessary to goad men to desperation are present, but there is no war. When a traveling Eskimo entered a settlement he might have to fight the strongest man in the settlement to establish his position among them, but this was a test of strength and bravery, not war. The idea of warfare, of one *group* organizing against another *group* to

maim and wound and kill them was absent. And without that idea passions might rage but there was no war.

4   But, it may be argued, isn't this because the Eskimo have such a low and undeveloped form of social organization? They own no land, they move from place to place, camping, it is true, season after season on the same site, but this is not something to fight for as the modern nations of the world fight for land and raw materials. They have no permanent possessions that can be looted, no towns that can be burned. They have no social classes to produce stress and strains within the society which might force it to go to war outside. Doesn't the absence of war among the Eskimo, while disproving the biological necessity of war, just go to confirm the point that it is the state of development of the society which accounts for war, and nothing else?

5   We find the answer among the pygmy peoples of the Andaman Islands in the Bay of Bengal. The Andamans also represent an exceedingly low level of society; they are a hunting and food-gathering people; they live in tiny hordes without any class stratification; their houses are simpler than the snow houses of the Eskimo. But they knew about warfare. The army might contain only fifteen determined pygmies marching in a straight line, but it was the real thing none the less. Tiny army met tiny army in open battle, blows were exchanged, casualties suffered, and the state of warfare could only be concluded by a peacemaking ceremony.

6   Similarly, among the Australian aborigines, who built no permanent dwellings but wandered from water hole to water hole over their almost desert country, warfare—and rules of "international law"—were highly developed. The student of social evolution will seek in vain for his obvious causes of war, struggle for lands, struggle for power of one group over another, expansion of population, need to divert the minds of a populace restive under tyranny,

or even the ambition of a successful leader to enhance his own prestige. All are absent, but warfare as a practice remained, and men engaged in it and killed one another in the course of a war because killing is what is done in wars.

7   From instances like these it becomes apparent that an inquiry into the causes of war misses the fundamental point as completely as does an insistence upon the biological necessity of war. If a people have an idea of going to war and the idea that war is the way in which certain situations, defined within their society, are to be handled, they will sometimes go to war. If they are a mild and unaggressive people, like the Pueblo Indians, they may limit themselves to defensive warfare; but they will be forced to think in terms of war because there are peoples near them who have warfare as a pattern, and offensive, raiding, pillaging warfare at that. When the pattern of warfare is known, people like the Pueblo Indians will defend themselves, taking advantage of their natural defenses, the *mesa* village site, and people like the Lepchas, having no natural defenses and no idea of warfare, will merely submit to the invader. But the essential point remains the same. There is a way of behaving which is known to a given people and labeled as an appropriate form of behavior; a bold and warlike people like the Sioux or the Maori may label warfare as desirable as well as possible; a mild people like the Pueblo Indians may label warfare as undesirable; but to the minds of both peoples the possibility of warfare is present. Their thoughts, their hopes, their plans are oriented about this idea, that warfare may be selected as the way to meet some situation.

8   So simple peoples and civilized peoples, mild peoples and violent, assertive peoples, will all go to war if they have the invention, just as those peoples who have the custom of dueling will have duels and peoples who have the pattern of vendetta will indulge in vendetta. And, conversely, peoples who do not know of duel-

ing will not fight duels, even though their wives are seduced and their daughters ravished; they may on occasion commit murder but they will not fight duels. Cultures which lack the idea of the vendetta will not meet every quarrel in this way. A people can use only the forms it has. So the Balinese have their special way of dealing with a quarrel between two individuals: if the two feel that the causes of quarrel are heavy they may go and register their quarrel in the temple before the gods, and, making offerings, they may swear never to have anything to do with each other again. Today they register such mutual "not-speaking" with the Dutch government officials. But in other societies, although individuals might feel as full of animosity and as unwilling to have any further contact as do the Balinese, they cannot register their quarrel with the gods and go on quietly about their business because registering quarrels with the gods is not an invention of which they know.

9   Yet, if it be granted that warfare is after all an invention, it may nevertheless be an invention that lends itself to certain types of personality, to the exigent needs of autocrats, to the expansionist desires of crowded peoples, to the desire for plunder and rape and loot which is engendered by a dull and frustrating life. What, then, can we say of this congruence between warfare and its uses? If it is a form which fits so well, is not this congruence the essential point? But even here the primitive material causes us to wonder, because there are tribes who go to war merely for glory, having no quarrel with the enemy, suffering from no tyrant within their boundaries, anxious neither for land nor loot nor women, but merely anxious to win prestige which within that tribe has been declared obtainable only by war and without which no young man can hope to win his sweetheart's smile of approval. But if, as was the case with the Bush Negroes of Dutch Guiana, it is artistic ability which is necessary to win a girl's approval, the same young man

would have to be carving rather than going out on a war party.

10   In many parts of the world, war is a game in which the individual can win counters—counters which bring him prestige in the eyes of his own sex or of the opposite sex; he plays for these counters as he might, in our society, strive for a tennis championship. Warfare is a frame for such prestige-seeking merely because it calls for the display of certain skills and certain virtues; all of these skills—riding straight, shooting straight, dodging the missiles of the enemy, and sending one's own straight to the mark—can be equally well exercised in some other framework, and, equally, the virtues—endurance, bravery, loyalty, steadfastness—can be displayed in other contexts. The tie-up between proving oneself a man and proving this by a success in organized killing is due to a definition which many societies have made of manliness. And often, even in those societies which counted success in warfare a proof of human worth, strange turns were given to the idea, as when the plains Indians gave their highest awards to the man who touched a live enemy rather than to the man who brought in a scalp—from a dead enemy—because the latter was less risky. Warfare is just an invention known to the majority of human societies by which they permit their young men either to accumulate prestige or avenge their honor or acquire loot or wives or slaves or sago lands or cattle or appease the blood lust of their gods or the restless souls of the recently dead. It is just an invention, older and more widespread than the jury system, but none the less an invention.

11   But, once we have said this, have we said anything at all? Despite a few instances, dear to the hearts of controversialists, of the loss of the useful arts, once an invention is made which proves congruent with human needs or social forms, it tends to persist. Grant that war is an invention, that it is not a biological necessity nor the outcome of certain special types of

social forms, still, once the invention is made, what are we to do about it? The Indian who had been subsisting on the buffalo for generations because with his primitive weapons he could slaughter only a limited number of buffalo did not return to his primitive weapons when he saw that the white man's more efficient weapons were exterminating the buffalo. A desire for the white man's cloth may mortgage the South Sea Islander to the white man's plantation, but he does not return to making bark cloth, which would have left him free. Once an invention is known and accepted, men do not easily relinquish it. The skilled workers may smash the first steam looms which they feel are to be their undoing, but they accept them in the end, and no movement which has insisted upon the mere abandonment of usable inventions has ever had much success. Warfare is here, as part of our thought; the deeds of warriors are immortalized in the words of our poets; the toys of our children are modeled upon the weapons of the soldier; the frame of reference within which our statesmen and our diplomats work always contains war. If we know that it is not inevitable, that it is due to historical accident that warfare is one of the ways in which we think of behaving, are we given any hope by that? What hope is there of persuading nations to abandon war, nations so thoroughly imbued with the idea that resort to war is, if not actually desirable and noble, at least inevitable whenever certain defined circumstances arise?

12   In answer to this question I think we might turn to the history of other social inventions, and inventions which must once have seemed as firmly entrenched as warfare. Take the methods of trial which preceded the jury system: ordeal and trial by combat. Unfair, capricious, alien as they are to our feeling today, they were once the only methods open to individuals accused of some offense. The invention of trial by jury gradually replaced these methods until only witches, and finally not even

witches, had to resort to the ordeal. And for a long time the jury system seemed the one best and finest method of settling legal disputes, but today new inventions, trial before judges only or before commisions, are replacing the jury system. In each case the old method was replaced by a new social invention; the ordeal did not go out because people thought it unjust or wrong, it went out because a method more congruent with the institutions and feelings of the period was invented. And, if we despair over the way in which war seems such an ingrained habit of most of the human race, we can take comfort from the fact that a poor invention will usually give place to a better invention.

13   For this, two conditions at least are necessary. The people must recognize the defects of the old invention, and someone must make a new one. Propaganda against warfare, documentation of its terrible cost in human suffering and social waste, these prepare the ground by teaching people to feel that warfare is a defective social institution. There is further needed a belief that social invention is possible and the invention of new methods which will render warfare as out-of-date as the tractor is making the plow, or the motor car the horse and buggy. A form of behavior becomes out-of-date only when something else takes its place, and in order to invent forms of behavior which will make war obsolete, it is a first requirement to believe that an invention is possible. ◆

10

Arguments About Fairness

THE HINGE ON WHICH ALL PERSUASION TURNS IS AN OUTLOOK OR "framework" shared by the writer and the readers. As we saw in Chapter 9, when the dispute is about facts, the framework is typically a statement about what is probable or improbable:

> We can agree (can't we?) that it's unlikely that the works of Shakespeare could have been written by a man who didn't own a single book.

or

> We can agree (can't we?) that it would be quite possible for someone brilliant enough to write the plays of Shakespeare to learn without formal study as much law as they contain.

In this chapter we'll deal with disputes that are not about facts, but about justice. Now our key framework will be not a statement of probability, but a "rule" of fair play.

The obvious model for disputes about justice is the trial, where people argue cases before an impartial judge and jury. But we aren't concerned solely with what happens at the courthouse. "Courts" don't necessarily include lawyers and black-robed judges. When a high school teacher protests the superintendent's decision not to renew her contract, the school board becomes a court. When a newspaper runs a series of letters on a controversial issue, the readers become the "court of public opinion." An employer who resolves a dispute between employees serves as a one-person court. Think of a "court" as any person or group with the power to decide a dispute about rules, and you will realize that all of us have our days in court.

A MODEL ARGUMENT ANALYZED

A clear example of a courtroom argument about rules occurs in Robert Bolt's *A Man for All Seasons,* a play about the prosecution of Sir Thomas More on a charge that "he did conspire traitorously and maliciously" to deny King Henry VIII's claim to be the Supreme Head of the Church of England.

In case sixteenth-century English history is not your strong suit, let me remind you that Henry VIII was frustrated because the Roman Catholic Church would not grant him a divorce from his first wife. With the help of his advisor Thomas Cromwell, Henry set out to break the power of the Catholic Church in England. This campaign culminated in the Act of Supremacy (1534), which declared that the King, not the Pope, was the head of the Church in England. This done, Henry obtained his divorce from the Church of England despite the Pope's objections and married Anne Boleyn, who became Queen.

Conspicuously absent from Anne's coronation, however, was Sir Thomas More, the chancellor of England. Though More made no statement opposing the Act of Supremacy or denying the validity of the King's divorce, he would not say that he approved of Henry's actions or thought them legal. It was this *silence* that led to the charge of treason. In Bolt's play, Cromwell serves as prosecutor; we will examine a passage in which he questions Sir Thomas:

CROMWELL.   (*Moving to left of MORE.*) Now, Sir Thomas, you stand upon your silence.

MORE.   I do.

CROMWELL.   *(Turning to the Jury.)* But, Gentlemen of the Jury, there are many kinds of silence. Consider first the silence of a man when he is dead. Let us say we go into the room where he is lying: and let us say it is the dead of night—there's nothing like darkness for sharpening the ear—and we listen. What do we hear? (*He listens intently.*) Silence. What does it betoken, this silence? Nothing. This is silence pure and simple. But consider another case. Suppose I were to draw a dagger from my sleeve and make to kill the prisoner with it; and suppose their lordships there,[1] instead of crying out for me to stop or crying out for help to stop me, maintained their silence. That would *betoken.* It would betoken a willingness that I should do it, and under the law they would be guilty with me. So silence can, according to the circumstances, speak. Consider now the circumstances of the prisoner's silence. The oath was put to good and faithful subjects up and down the country and they had declared His Grace's title to be just and good.

A WRITER AT WORK

"A Man for All Seasons"
ROBERT BOLT

---

[1] their lordships: Cromwell refers to the two judges in the case, seated on a platform in sight of the jury.

And when it came to the prisoner, he refused. He calls this silence. Yet is there a man in this court, is there a man in this country, who does not *know* Sir Thomas More's opinion of this title? Of course not. But how can that be? Because this silence betokened—nay, this silence *was*—not silence at all, but most eloquent denial.

MORE.   *(With some of the academic's impatience for a shoddy line of reasoning.)* Not so, Mr. Secretary, the maxim is *"qui tacet consentire"*. *(He turns to the Foreman.)* The maxim of the law is—*(Very carefully.)* "Silence gives consent." If therefore, you wish to construe what my silence "betoken," you must construe that I consented, not that I denied.

CROMWELL.   Is that what the world, in fact, construes from it? Do you pretend that is what you *wish* the world to construe from it?

MORE.   The world must construe according to its wits. This court must construe according to the law.

This scene contains all the key elements of the type of argument that we are considering and that you will soon be writing. First, there is a court, in this case two judges and a jury. Second, there is an opponent[2]: More for Cromwell's argument, Cromwell for More's. Third, there is a fact that the opponents both acknowledge to be beyond dispute: More's silence on the subject of the King's title as Supreme Head of the Church. Fourth, for both Cromwell's argument and More's there are definite conclusions they wish the jury to draw (More's denial of the King's title, or his consent). Fifth, the route to each of these conclusions passes through a rule.

A SIMPLE MAP OF A DISPUTE CONTAINING TWO ARGUMENTS

We can visualize a dispute and the arguments that go with it as a road that forks just before it reaches two gates. The dispute between More and Cromwell is shaped as in the diagram at the top of the next page. From the undisputed fact of More's silence, Cromwell would lead the court along the left-hand route. His rule is that silence can mean *anything* according to the circumstances and that the court should use common sense to understand the meaning of an accused man's silence. He tries to hold this gate of interpretation open, and if the court passes through it, More is a step closer to being convicted of treason. More, of course, attempts to close this gate of interpretation and open another. His rule is a centuries-old

---

2 opponent: I say "an opponent" for simplicity's sake. In some cases there are several parties in a dispute, all proposing different rules or different reasons. Among these parties there are alliances as well as oppositions. But there is always at least *one* opponent.

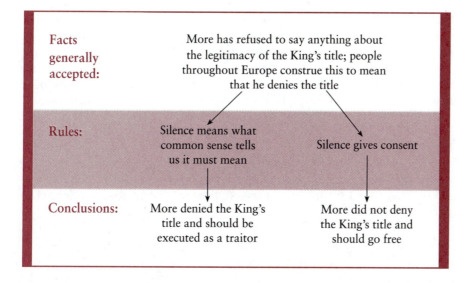

Facts generally accepted:	More has refused to say anything about the legitimacy of the King's title; people throughout Europe construe this to mean that he denies the title	
Rules:	Silence means what common sense tells us it must mean	Silence gives consent
Conclusions:	More denied the King's title and should be executed as a traitor	More did not deny the King's title and should go free

maxim of the law: "Silence gives consent." If the court follows the maxim, More is a step nearer acquittal and release. Ultimately, the court is free to pass through either gate. The arguments of the lawyers can only *incline* it toward one rule or another.

ABOUT RULES

Sir Thomas More's citation of a Latin legal maxim might suggest that all rules comes from books and have an official status. This is not so. A rule is any general statement that *would* logically lead the "court" from the undisputed fact to the conclusion. A *successful* rule is one that *does* lead it to the desired conclusion.

Suppose, for example, that a brother and sister take their dispute about the ownership of a goldfish to their parents (the family court). The sister might argue that she bought the fish with her own money six months ago (a fact her brother can't deny) and that *whoever buys something owns it*. The brother might argue that he, not she, has been feeding the goldfish ever since it arrived (a fact she can't deny) and that *whoever feeds a pet owns it*. These are well-formed arguments based on rules that come partly from custom and partly from the fertile brains of the disputants.

Or suppose that one morning you drive to school and find that every marked place in the lot for which you have purchased a parking sticker is filled, some of them by cars that have no parking stickers. You have to get to class quickly, so you park against a tree in what you know perfectly well is not an official parking place. When you return to the car, you discover under your windshield wiper a $15 ticket for "parking in a nondes-ignated area." You've no intention of paying the ticket, so you send a letter to parking operations arguing that *a person who has bought a parking sticker shouldn't be fined for parking irregularly in a lot where cars with no parking stickers are taking up the designated spaces.* In effect, you have made up a rule that interprets your "violation" as excusable behavior.

The rules in the goldfish and parking ticket cases are clearly not indisputable; if they were, there would be no argument. But the arguers are urging the court to treat their rules *as if* they were universal truths, applicable whenever a similar situation arises. If the director of parking operations accepts your argument and tears up your ticket, she will presum-ably have to void future tickets issued when a sticker-holder is forced to park in an odd place.

EXERCISE 1

◆ *Practice Inventing and Stating Rules.* An essential skill for the suc-cessful arguer is the ability to identify or invent rules that, if accepted, will lead inevitably from the undisputed facts to the disputable conclusion. To exercise this skill, state rules that will lead to each of the conclusions listed in each of the cases that follow. Though the examples are based on actual legal cases, assume that you, unlike a lawyer or judge, are free to use any rules that seem pertinent. Try, however, to make your rule narrow enough that its application to the particular case is obvious. "A person's silence indicates consent rather than objection to what is said or done in the person's presence" is an appropriately narrow rule for the case of Sir Thomas More. "Everybody should do the right thing or else pay the consequences" is too broad to be useful, and you would have difficulty getting it accepted by any court.

1. *Facts beyond dispute:* Tom Piltney, a schoolboy eleven years old, was sitting across the aisle from his friend John Verberg. When he saw John falling asleep during a grammar lesson, he kicked him lightly on the shin, intending only to wake him up. Unfortunately, and unbeknownst to Tom, John's leg had been seriously injured some years before. The kick caused a nick, the nick caused an infection, the infection affected the bone of John's leg, and John was forced to have expensive medical treatments that didn't succeed. He was lamed for life.

> *Conclusion 1:* The Piltneys owe John and his family compensation for the injury.
> *Conclusion 2:* The Verbergs have to bear the cost of the injury them-selves, as Tom and his parents can't be held responsible.

2. *Facts beyond dispute:* Henry Brawny and his wife, Mary, owned an old, boarded-up farmhouse on a piece of property some miles from the town in which they lived. In the farmhouse they stored old bottles and

fruit jars, some of which they considered antiques. Several times over the years the house had been vandalized. The Brawnys posted "no trespassing" signs, but the break-ins continued. Finally, they placed a shotgun trap in one of the bedrooms. At first Henry aimed the gun so that the shot would hit an intruder in the stomach, but Mary insisted that he lower the aim so that it would strike an intruder's legs. A few days after the trap was set, Bill Karko broke into the house intending to steal some of the Brawnys' jars. A blast from the shotgun seriously injured Karko, who will probably never recover the full use of his legs.

Conclusion 1: The Brawnys owe Karko compensation for his injuries.
Conclusion 2: The Brawnys owe Karko no compensation.

3. *Facts beyond dispute:* Ellen Mayer, who was feeling some pain in her right ear, had it examined by Dr. Albert Wilson, who found evidence of disease and recommended an operation. Mayer agreed and signed a form consenting to surgery on the right ear only. On the appointed day she received an anesthetic that rendered her unconscious. Wilson then reexamined the right ear of the unconscious Mayer and decided that its condition was not serious enough to require the surgery. He took the opportunity to examine her left ear closely and discovered that it had a more serious condition than the right, though not one that put her in immediate danger. Without waiting for Mayer to recover consciousness in order to ask her permission, he proceeded to operate on the left ear. The operation was a success. Mayer, however, was not pleased, and sued Wilson.

Conclusion 1: Wilson owes Mayer compensation for performing an operation she did not authorize.
Conclusion 2: Wilson owes Mayer no compensation.

WAYS TO PERSUADE THE "COURT" TO ACCEPT YOUR RULE

As we noted earlier, rules may come from anywhere, including the mind of an arguer desperate to make his or her case. Why should a "court" prefer one rule to another? How does an arguer justify the rule he or she is proposing?

There is no simple answer to these questions. Courts are made up of human beings, and the motives of human beings can be unfathomable. In general, we can say that they will reject any rule that sounds manifestly unfair or unwise and prefer one that is clearly fair and wise. When the fairness or wisdom is not immediately apparent, successful arguers often use three appeals: references to *authority*, calls for *consistency*, and consideration of larger *consequences*.

First, arguers can show that the rule they favor has an authority behind it, that it is not merely a personal opinion, invented in order to make the argument work. This is precisely what Sir Thomas More shows when he refers to the maxim *"qui tacet consentire."* The maxim existed in the law for some centuries before More cited it; it has the weight of authority. When both sides can cite an authority, arguers attempt to show that their rule is derived from a better authority than the one favored by opponents. Thus, a lawyer may argue that where the state Constitution provides one rule and the state legislature another, the Constitution's rule should prevail. Or in ethics, a person might argue that a rule endorsed by Moses, Buddha, Jesus, and Mohammed is preferable to one endorsed by P. T. Barnum.

Second, arguers can show that the rule they favor has consistently been applied to similar situations in the past, so that it would be illogical or unjust to apply a different rule in the present case. Thus a student suspended from high school for a week for wearing a T-shirt with a message the principal found offensive might argue that in seven previous cases involving similar T-shirts students had merely been sent home to change. To switch from the rule that "students wearing offensive shirts will be required to change them" to the rule that "students wearing offensive shirts will be suspended for a week" therefore seems arbitrary and unfair. The student might argue that she would not have risked wearing the shirt if she had known how severe the penalty would be. She had relied on the principal's being consistent in his behavior. The call for consistency obviously makes most sense when it is addressed to an administrator or judge, someone whose decisions in the past people accept as "law" in the present. But then every parent and every employer is sometimes a judge or administrator.

Third, arguers can point to the bad consequences of general application of the rule they oppose or the good consequences of general application of the rule they favor. Consider the argument about the parking ticket, for example. To show that your rule is preferable, you might point out that fining people who have bought parking stickers is no way to encourage lawful behavior: people who know that they can be fined even if they have stickers will very likely stop buying them. Or you might point out that if the present policy is enforced, it could create a "chain reaction" of unauthorized parking. People who find their own "authorized" lots full will conclude that they may as well park in whatever lot they choose, since they are at least as likely to be ticketed in their own lot as in someone else's. Since they will take spaces that properly belong to others, the others will also park in someone else's lot. Eventually, the chance of finding a place in one's proper lot could become very slim, creating just the sort of musical-chairs-parking situation directors are hired to avoid.

Of course, this argument may fail. The director may feel that her present rule that *all* illegally parked cars should be ticketed may be crude, but at least it is workable. To change to your more complicated rule would require the ticketing officer to determine whether legal places were open *at the time you parked,* a virtually impossible task. It would also seem to authorize parking in any odd place—beside hydrants, in fire lanes, blocking exits. If you think the situation over, you may find that the arguments for the present rule are quite strong, and you may decide to write a $15 check rather than a fruitless letter.

The Appeal to Consistency by Way of Analogy

Very often we are forced to plead our case before people who have never passed judgment on a case exactly like it. Under these circumstances an analogy may be an important tool of persuasion. The arguer points to a clearer case (perhaps one already decided), where only one conclusion seems justifiable. He or she then tries to show that the rule that led to that inevitable conclusion also applies to the case at hand.

Consider, for example, an argument made on behalf of Florence Whittaker, a woman who belonged briefly to a religious sect with a colony in Jaffa, Syria. Ms. Whittaker lost her faith in the sect and decided to return to America. She intended to book passage on the next available steamer, but the cult's leader, Frank Sanford (the "second Elijah"), offered to sail her home in his yacht, *Kingdom.* When she expressed a fear that Sanford might refuse to let her off the yacht until she agreed to rejoin the sect, he assured her repeatedly that he would not detain her. On December 28, 1909, she voluntarily boarded the *Kingdom.* When the yacht anchored in the harbor at Portland, Maine, on May 10, however, Sanford would not order a boat to take her ashore. For a month she was unable to escape and had to listen to the preacher's urgings that she return to the flock. Eventually, she was able to get a message to shore and was freed by a court order.

Not surprisingly, Whittaker sued, alleging that Sanford had unjustly imprisoned her and that he owed her compensation for the wrong he had done. Sanford's lawyer argued that there had been no imprisonment. After all, he said, Whittaker had come on board voluntarily, and Sanford had used no violence or physical force to prevent her leaving again. He had merely failed to offer her a means of transportation, and surely the law did not require him to provide boats to anyone who asked. Against this argument, Whittaker's lawyer offered an argument that surrounding a person by a physical barrier like the ocean *was* using "physical force" to imprison her. He developed a compelling analogy, here summarized by Albert R. Savage, Chief Justice of the Maine Supreme Court:

> If one should, without right, turn the key in a door, and thereby prevent a person in the room from leaving, it would be the simplest

form of unlawful imprisonment. The restraint is physical. The four walls
and the locked door are physical impediments to escape. Now is it
different when the one who is in control of a vessel at anchor, within
practical rowing distance from the shore, who has agreed that a guest
on board shall be free to leave, there being no means to leave except by
rowboats, wrongfully refuses the guest the use of a boat? The boat is
the key. By refusing the boat he turns the key. The guest is as effectively
locked up as if there were walls along the side of the vessel. The restraint
is physical. The impassable sea is the physical barrier.

As you can see, the analogy is effective because it neatly matches the case
at hand. The difference between imprisonment on a boat and imprisonment
in a room is not significant with regard to the rule involved: that under
ordinary circumstances no private citizen has a right to physically restrain
the movements of another citizen by surrounding him or her with an
impassable barrier.

In the case of the parking ticket, you might argue that there is an
analogy between buying a parking sticker and buying a theater ticket. A
person who buys a theater ticket and then discovers that all the seats are
taken is presumably entitled to a refund, not a fine. The director of parking
operations, however, might argue that the analogy is a bad one: no theater
owner faces her problem of keeping control over an area without walls,
doors, or locks. She might argue that your parking fee bought only her
effort to have space available to you.

An Extended Example of Persuasive Justification of a Rule

Judges in appellate courts in the United States write "opinions" in which
they give the reasoning behind their rulings. Such opinions reflect the arguments made by the lawyers in the case, but they are also arguments in their
own right, addressed to other judges on the court and to the legal community
at large. These written opinions are often excellent examples of the reasoning one offers to persuade a "court" to adopt a rule.

Consider, for example, the opinion written by Judge Ward Hunt of
the New York Court of Appeals in an 1866 case involving a fire that
destroyed the house of James Ryan. A spark from a steam engine operated
by the New York Central Railroad had set fire to one of the company's
woodsheds and to the wood stored in it. Ryan's house, though it was 130
feet from the shed, "soon took fire from the heat and sparks, and was
entirely consumed, notwithstanding diligent efforts were made to save it."
By the time Judge Hunt heard the case, a lower court had established the
"fact" that the railroad's negligence had caused the fire in the shed. Ryan
and his lawyers argued that if someone's negligence causes a fire (or other

catastrophe), then the negligent party should pay for *all* the resulting damage. The railroad's lawyers (and later Judge Hunt) argued for another rule, that negligent people are responsible only for the "natural" or "ordinary" results of their negligence; they are not responsible for consequences no one could foresee.

Diagrammed as a forking path, the dispute between Ryan and the railroad looks like this:

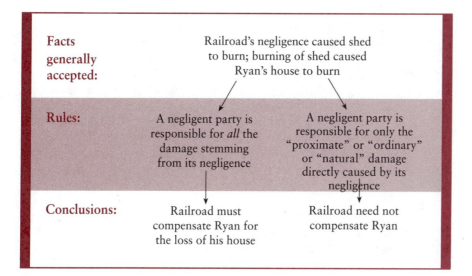

Facts generally accepted:	Railroad's negligence caused shed to burn; burning of shed caused Ryan's house to burn	
Rules:	A negligent party is responsible for *all* the damage stemming from its negligence	A negligent party is responsible for only the "proximate" or "ordinary" or "natural" damage directly caused by its negligence
Conclusions:	Railroad must compensate Ryan for the loss of his house	Railroad need not compensate Ryan

A WRITER AT WORK

"Opinion"
JUDGE WARD HUNT

It is a general principle that every person is liable for the consequences of his own acts. He is thus liable in damages for the proximate results of his own acts, but not for remote damages. It is not easy at all times to determine what are proximate and what are remote damages. In *Thomas v. Winchester* (2 Seld., 408),[3] Judge Ruggles defines the damages for which a party is liable as those which are the natural or necessary consequences of his acts. Thus, the owner of a loaded gun, who puts it in the hands of a child, by whose indiscretion it is discharged, is liable for the injury sustained by a third person from such discharge. (5 Maule & Sel., 198.) The injury is a natural and ordinary result of the folly of placing a loaded gun in the hands of one ignorant of the manner of using it, and incapable of appreciating its effects. The owner of a horse and cart, who leaves them unattended in the street, is liable for an injury done to a person, or his property, by the running away of the horse *(Lynch v. Nurdin,* 1 Adol. & Ellis, N.S., 29; *Illidge v. Goodin,* 5 Car. & P., 190), for the same reason. The injury is the natural result of the

---

[3] (2 Seld., 408): Following standard form for judicial opinions, Hunt cites his sources in parentheses. These parenthetical citations usually refer the reader to pertinent cases decided by other courts.

negligence. If the party thus injured had, however, by the delay or confinement from his injury, been prevented from completing a valuable
contract, from which he expected to make large profits, he could not
recover such expected profits from the negligent party, in the cases
supposed. Such damages would not be the necessary or natural consequences, nor the results ordinarily to be anticipated, from the negligence
committed. (6 Hill, 522; 13 Wend., 601; 3 E. D. Smith, 144.) So if an
engineer upon a steamboat or locomotive, in passing the house of A.,
so carelessly manages its machinery that the coals and sparks from its
fires fall upon and consume the house of A., the railroad company or
the steamboat proprietors are liable to pay the value of the property
thus destroyed. *(Field v. N.Y. Central R.R., 32 N.Y., 339.)* Thus far
the law is settled and the principle is apparent. If, however, the fire
communicates from the house of A. to that of B., and that is destroyed,
is the negligent party liable for his loss? And if it spreads thence to the
house of C., and thence to the house of D., and thence consecutively
through the other houses, until it reaches and consumes the house of
Z., is the party liable to pay the damages sustained by these twenty-six
sufferers? The counsel for the plaintiff does not distinctly claim this, and
I think it would not be seriously insisted that the sufferers could recover
in such case. Where, then, is the principle upon which A. recovers and
Z. fails?

I . . . place my opinion upon the ground that, in the one case, to wit,
the destruction of the building upon which the sparks were thrown by
the negligent act of the party sought to be charged, the result was to
have been anticipated the moment the fire was communicated to the
building; that its destruction was the ordinary and natural result of its
being fired. In the second, third, or twenty-sixth case, as supposed, the
destruction of the building was not a natural and expected result of the
first firing. That a building upon which sparks and cinders fall should
be destroyed or seriously injured must be expected, but that the fire
should spread and other buildings be consumed, is not a necessary or
an usual result. That it is possible, and that it is not unfrequent, cannot
be denied. The result, however, depends, not upon any necessity of a
further communication of the fire, but upon a concurrence of accidental
circumstances, such as the degree of the heat, the state of the atmosphere,
the condition and materials of the adjoining structures and the direction
of the wind. These are accidental and varying circumstances. The party
has no control over them, and is not responsible for their effects.

My opinion, therefore, is, that this action cannot be sustained, for
the reason that the damages incurred are not the immediate but the
remote result of the negligence of the defendants. The immediate result
was the destruction of their own wood and sheds; beyond that, it
was remote.

To sustain such a claim as the present, and to follow the same to its
legitimate consequences, would subject to a liability against which no

prudence could guard, and to meet which no private fortune would be adequate. Nearly all fires are caused by negligence, in its extended sense. In a country where wood, coal, gas and oils are universally used, where men are crowded into cities and villages, where servants are employed, and where children find their home in all houses, it is impossible that the most vigilant prudence should guard against the occurrence of accidental or negligent fires. A man may insure his own house or his own furniture, but he cannot insure his neighbor's building or furniture, for the reason that he has no interest in them. To hold that the owner must not only meet his own loss by fire, but that he must guarantee the security of his neighbors on both sides, and to an unlimited extent, would be to create a liability which would be the destruction of all civilized society. No community could long exist, under the operation of such a principle. In a commercial country, each man, to some extent, runs the hazard of his neighbor's conduct, and each, by insurance against such hazards, is enabled to obtain a reasonable security against loss. To neglect such precaution, and to call upon his neighbor, on whose premises a fire originated, to indemnify him instead, would be to award a punishment quite beyond the offense committed.

The remoteness of the damage, in my judgment, forms the true rule on which the question should be decided, and which prohibits a recovery by the plaintiff in this case.

♦ *Practice Justifying a Rule.* Look again at the three cases beginning on page 386 (Practice Inventing and Stating Rules). Select one case for which you and your classmates have developed plausible rules for both sides. Briefly state the conflicting rules, then write a persuasive case that one rule is preferable. Discuss the bad consequences of following the rule you reject or the good consequences of accepting the rule you favor. Make appeals to consistency and authority by assuming that the court before which you are arguing has made the following statements in earlier cases:

EXERCISE 2

1. In Devlin versus Anglen, the court noted that its "highest goal was to shape the character of the citizenry by rewarding behavior that is socially productive and punishing behavior that is socially destructive."

2. In the case of Molar versus Bump, the court decided that "a person who deliberately touches another person in an offensive or harmful way is liable for whatever physical damage that touching causes." At a cocktail party, Fred Bump had given Bob Molar, a total stranger, a hearty slap on the back that dislodged a loose tooth that found its way into the back of Molar's throat, from which it had to be removed surgically.

3. In the case of Scar versus Striker, the court decided that the rule in Molar versus Bump "applies whether the touching is direct or

indirect." Striker had propped a bucket of water above a door so that it would fall on the next person to enter the room.

4. In the case of Guard versus Center, the court held that "if the person touched gives the person who does the touching reason to believe that the touch is acceptable, the toucher cannot be held liable for the consequences of the touching." George Center, age 15, had tackled John Guard, age 14, in a backyard football game, breaking his leg in the process.

5. In the case of Blush versus Lips, the court decided that "a person who is deliberately touched in an offensive way by another person is entitled to compensation for an offense to his or her dignity, even if no physical damage is done." Fred Lips, a casual friend of Beverly Blush, had given her a noisy, wet, and unsolicited kiss at a meeting of the school board.

6. In the case of Standpat versus Brushby, the court held that "some touching which the person touched may find offensive is so inevitable and customary that it is unreasonable for the toucher to be responsible for its consequences." Professor Standpat had been standing at the front of an elevator. Dr. Brushby had jostled him slightly on the way out and had aggravated the professor's back condition.

7. In the case of Sleeper versus Blade, the court had noted that "a physician has a positive duty to take whatever steps are necessary to preserve the life of a patient, regardless of how offensive and unsolicited the touching involved may be."

THE IMPORTANCE AND NATURE OF "FACTS NO ONE DISPUTES"

The model of argument we have used in this chapter begins in "facts that no one disputes" and leads by way of a rule to a conclusion by the court. This model naturally raises the question of where "facts no one disputes" come from. The simple answer is that some are accepted by general consent and some are arrived at by a process of argument.

General consent is the most significant source of undisputed facts. When all sides in a dispute agree to a fact, it is by definition undisputed. In our imagined argument over ownership of the goldfish, for example, the brother did not deny that the sister had paid for the fish, nor did the sister deny that the brother had fed it. Agreement on these facts created a solid foundation on which the arguments for both sides could be built. In the parking case, you do not deny parking in the illegal space, and the director of parking operations is not likely to deny that the legal spaces were full. In Florence Whittaker's lawsuit against Frank Sanford, Whittaker did not deny that she had boarded the *Kingdom* voluntarily. In most disputes a good many facts are accepted by general consent.

When general consent fails, facts must be established by argument. In Chapter 9, we dealt with one kind of fact established by argument—the probable fact. An audience (or court) can be convinced that Shakespeare probably wrote *Hamlet*. A court may be convinced that the sparks from the New York Central Railroad's engine very probably (or almost certainly) caused the fire that burned Ryan's house.

In addition to such probable facts, there are "facts" established by the application of rules. Indeed, most of the arguments we have examined in this chapter set out to prove such "facts." If the sister wins the goldfish argument, for example, she will have established the "fact" that she owns the goldfish. When the court decided that Ms. Whittaker *had* been held prisoner, this conclusion became a "fact" that allowed her suit to be successful. These facts are created not by an appeal to our sense of what is probable but by an appeal to our sense of what is just or logical.

Obviously, once a fact is established by argument, it can become the starting point for another argument. Suppose, for example, that in the goldfish argument the sister is an enthusiastic amateur biologist and that the reason she wants to establish ownership is so that she can vivisect the pet in order to see how its heart works. Winning the argument about ownership might get her only partway to her goal because her brother might argue that even if she does own the fish, she has no right to cut up a living creature to satisfy her curiosity. Now we have a dispute that looks like this:

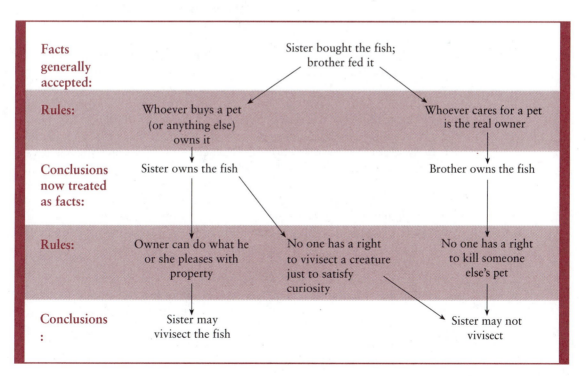

As you can imagine, arguments about issues more complex than the fate of a pet goldfish often involve longer chains of reasoning, each one only as strong as its weakest link.

POINTS TO

CONSIDER

WRITING PERSUASIVELY WHEN RULES ARE DISPUTED

Define the goal of your argument precisely in your own mind.   Keeping a clear head about the whole structure of an argument is crucial. One sort of foggy-headedness comes from becoming so fixated on a portion of the dispute that you lose sight of your goal. If the sister in the goldfish example, for instance, prepared an argument that persuaded her family that she owned the fish but that failed to address the question of whether owners had a right to vivisect, she would fall short of her goal. Another sort of fogginess comes from focusing on beating your opponent rather than on persuading the court. Remember that the court is not judging a contest but attempting to decide which rule is wiser and more just. Don't wrangle over side issues.

Anticipate the rule (or rules) your opponent will offer.   For many writers, this is difficult. We get so caught up in making a case that we forget how the dispute looks from another point of view. The best advocates spend a good deal of effort "working up" the opponent's case, thinking about how *they* would argue if they were in the opponent's shoes. This effort allows them time to discover reasons to reject rules the opponent is likely to propose.

Offer a compelling rule that is narrowly defined.   Broad rules can create great difficulties for those who must apply them: they are often vague, and they may set off a ripple of bad consequences. Offer the court the narrowest rule that covers the situation. Florence Whittaker's lawyer did not argue that *any* means of restricting a person's movement constituted imprisonment—a rule that would include forcing someone to sit in church by threatening her with damnation if she left. He merely argued that confinement by physical barriers constituted imprisonment. An argument based on the broader rule would probably have failed.

Develop persuasive backing.   Look especially for appeals to authority, consistency, and consequences. In many cases, developing an analogy to a more clear-cut case can be an effective strategy, but don't rely on analogy alone, since your case cannot match the comparable case in every detail.

QUESTIONS FOR PEER REVIEW

When you have completed a draft, ask your reviewer to give both general advice (pages 60–61) and reactions to four particular questions:

1. Are the facts that I treat as undisputed actually undisputed? If I rely on a disputed fact, do I establish it by appealing to the reader's sense of what is probable, just, or logical? Does that argument lead back to facts that are *actually* undisputed?

2. Can you identify the general rule from which I am arguing? Does it seem to you to be a valid rule? Is the support I offer for it persuasive? Can you think of other support that would be valuable?

3. If you were my opponent in this argument, what would your argument be? Has my argument taken yours adequately into consideration?

4. Would any bad consequences come from the adoption of my rule in all similar cases? If so, have I persuaded you that the bad consequences are limited enough to make the rule acceptable?

Your reviewer's comments should prepare you to write your final draft.

In some cases, the process of writing the argument will shake your confidence that you are on the right side. If your side is assigned (by the court or by your instructor), you must proceed to make the best argument you can, trusting that the wisdom of the court will insure that the right side prevails. If you are free to change sides, you should do so with enthusiasm, realizing that you have accomplished one of the great goals of a liberal education by losing an argument with yourself.

Assignments
for Chapter 10

PARAGRAPH-LENGTH ARGUMENTS

In his opinion in *Ryan* v. *New York Central Railroad* (pp. 390–393), Judge Ward Hunt says that "every person is responsible for the consequences of his own acts," but only for the "natural" or "ordinary" or "expected" consequences. In each of the following cases, a court might apply Judge Hunt's rule in order to decide what compensation, if any, Drummond (the defendant) owes Podsnap (the plaintiff). For each case, write short arguments on behalf of *both* Podsnap and Drummond.

CASE 1: Drummond, driving at 65 m.p.h. down an interstate highway with a posted maximum speed of 65 and a minimum speed of 40, entered a dense cloud of smoke created by a fire in a field adjoining the highway. She turned on her headlights and slowed to about 60 m.p.h. Almost immediately she smashed into the rear of Podsnap's car, which did not have lights on and had been traveling at about 25 m.p.h. Podsnap, who had slowed to this pace because he felt that higher speeds were dangerous in these conditions, sustained damages to his automobile amounting to $987.50, had a previously existing back condition aggravated (at a medical cost of $531.00, plus considerable pain), and (as a result of the delay) missed a meeting in which he had hoped to make sales that would have netted him $278.00 in commissions. Podsnap sued for $1796.50.

CASE 2: At 2:00 one afternoon, Podsnap was driving his car in one of the westbound lanes of an interstate highway when Drummond's car left an eastbound lane, crossed the grassy median between eastbound and westbound lanes, and smashed into the side of Podsnap's car. Podsnap didn't see Drummond's car until it hit his. He was not injured, but bodywork on the car cost him $987.50, and he sued Drummond for that amount. Investigation revealed that Drummond, an obstetrician who had been up late because of a difficult delivery, had fallen asleep at the wheel. She had never before been involved in an accident and had never before fallen asleep at the wheel. Podsnap sued for $987.50.

CASE 3: Drummond, after a late night at the hospital, was repeatedly awakened by the caterwauling of her neighbor's cat. She had never met her neighbor (Podsnap) and didn't even know his name. At dawn, in exasperation, she snatched up a heavy glass paperweight from her desk, walked round to the side of her house, spied the cat atop a fence, and threw the paperweight at it. The paperweight missed, sailed through the neighbor's window (doing $37.54 worth of damage), and struck an antique Chinese vase worth $20,000, shattering it beyond repair. Podsnap's wife, seeing what had happened, became so angry that she returned fire, throwing a fireplace poker out the broken window like a javelin. In the process, she wrenched her shoulder and incurred medical expenses of $231.34. Podsnap sued for $20,268.88.

ASSIGNMENTS 2–7:   ## ARGUMENTS ABOUT SCHOOL POLICY

Suppose that Mountmonk College is a middle-sized institution (of about 1,500 students) in the heart of an industrial city. It was originally supported by the Presbyterian Church, but this association was terminated in 1960. When the Church's financial support ended, the College searched vigorously for other sources of revenue and was fortunate to find a donor who left it $20 million when she died in 1968. This donor, Mae Westerfield, said in her will that she was "pleased to be able to help insure the continuance of an institution that instilled Judeo-Christian ideals in a society that seemed determined to go to hell in a handcart." Apparently Ms. Westerfield's view of the College's moral effect on its students was encouraged by a series of conversations with the College president, the Reverend C. M. Johnston, who assured her that the end of an official association with a church would not end the College's commitment to produce students who are "in the world, but not of the world." Indeed, there is still a strong religious presence on campus. Many of the most active and generous alumni are clergy or laypersons committed to church work, and every summer the campus is the site of religious retreats and training sessions.

The community surrounding the College is socially and economically complex: relatively affluent neighborhoods adjoin very poor ones; about 40 percent of the people in the community are black, about 40 percent are white, and the rest are principally Hispanic or oriental.

The trustees of the College leave its governance largely in the hands of the president, who in turn entrusts most matters to an array of faculty-student committees. You are a member of the Campus Facilities Committee, along with Professor Susan Brodrick of the Political Science department, an active member of the American Civil Liberties Union; Professor William Hardy, the College chaplain and chairman of the Religious Studies Department; and Professor Al Mendez of the English Department, who describes himself as a born-again feminist. The committee does its work in two short, businesslike meetings per semester. A week or so before each of these meetings, each committee member prepares a brief statement on one or more of the questions the committee must decide. The most difficult decisions usually have to do with the College's long-standing policy of making auditorium and other space available, at little or no charge, for events of interest or importance both to the community and to students.

ASSIGNMENT 2: A flower shop that had been leasing a small space in the Student Union has recently closed. The Democratic Party has approached Mountmonk about leasing this space for three months while it canvasses the area around the College, attempting to gain votes for both the local and the national party tickets. The president of the Young Republicans, having heard of the proposal, objects that "housing the Democrat canvass on campus gives the appearance that Mountmonk College endorses the Democratic Party." Write a brief memo outlining as clearly as possible the best arguments for and against leasing the space to the Democrats. Be certain to make the principle (rule) behind each argument explicit so that the committee can give it due consideration in this and future cases. Conclude your memo by recommending a course of action. (You may use your imagination to add significant details about the physical layout of the Student Union, the conditions of the lease, and other aspects of this scenario.)

ASSIGNMENT 3: Like many other colleges, Mountmonk has both a Women's Center and a Women's Studies department. Next semester both of these organizations are sponsoring several speakers on women's issues, but both decided *not* to invite Shea Slaughter, a prominent local "women's separatist" whose speeches (with titles like "A Frank Message of Hatred for Man-Kind" and "An Argument for Universal Castration") the Women's Center has described as "embarrassing and destructive" and the Women's Studies department has called "concentrated, blind bigotry." Ms. Slaughter's political position is that women should destroy male-dominated institutions by all means "legal and illegal, peaceful and violent," and some of her speeches have been followed by arson attempts and the beating of men. One castration was linked to a recent speech, but Ms. Slaughter has pointed out that she never specifically advocated attacks on individual men, and that her argument for castration was essentially "metaphorical and political." Ms. Slaughter and her supporters (including three students at the College) have now asked Mountmonk to allow them to use a small auditorium to state their views. Write a brief memo outlining as clearly as possible the best argument to be made for allowing Ms. Slaughter and her followers to use the auditorium and the best argument against. Be certain to make the principle (rule) behind each argument explicit so that the committee can give it due consideration in this and future cases. Conclude your memo by recommending a course of action. (You may use your imagination to add significant details about Ms. Slaughter's previous statements and other aspects of this scenario.)

ASSIGNMENT 4: Racial tensions have been running fairly high in the community as a result of some stone-throwing incidents last summer. In one white neighborhood, a group calling itself the Christian White Supremacists (C.W.S.) has acquired a membership of about thirty. The members of the C.W.S. have asked to use the auditorium for a rally and agree to "pay all customary fees." At the rally, they intend to recruit members and hear a speech by Professor Christine Fairly, a sociologist from the state university who claims that blacks, Jews, and orientals haven't the same capacity for moral reasoning that whites do. Fairly's views have been widely reported in the press, but no scholarly journal has been willing to publish any of her articles on the subject. Write a brief memo outlining as clearly as possible the best argument to be made for allowing the use of campus facilities for this rally and the best argument against. Be certain to make the principle (rule) behind each argument explicit so that the committee can give it due consideration in this and future cases. Conclude your memo by recommending a course of action. (You may use your imagination to add significant details about the Christian White Supremacists, Professor Fairly, and other aspects of this scenario.)

ASSIGNMENT 5: Inspired by the success of the controversial 1990 exhibition of Robert Mapplethorpe's photographs, Grace Dawson, a student photographer, has produced a series of photographs that are equally sexually explicit and (to some viewers) equally disturbing. She entered three of these photographs in a student contest this semester and, partly because there were very few entries, won an "honorable mention" ribbon for a photograph that shows a naked, kneeling woman being kicked in the buttocks by a man in a suit while a naked man looks on. Plans had been made to exhibit the ribbon-winning photographs during alumni weekend next semester, but your committee has had requests from both the director of alumni relations and the Women's Center to bar the exhibition of Grace's photo. Write a brief memo outlining as clearly as possible the best argument to be made for barring the display of Grace's photo and the best argument against. Be certain to make the principle (rule) behind each argument explicit so that the committee can give it due consideration in this and future cases. Conclude your memo by recommending a course of action. (You may use your imagination to add significant details about the nature of alumni weekend, the nature of the photo contest, and other aspects of this scenario.)

ASSIGNMENT 6: Jo Ann Winkler, a local sales representative for *WatchYourColour*, a national cosmetics firm, has written to the College requesting the use of a small auditorium or large classroom to conduct a session entitled "Making the Most of Your Beauty Capital." Her letter says that the session would be "useful and beneficial to students"; it also reveals that she would like to display the full line of *WatchYourColour* products and give away free samples. She says that she cannot afford to pay for the use of the facilities.

Write a brief memo outlining as clearly as possible the best argument for allowing her to use the space she requests and the best argument for denying her request. Be certain to make the principle (rule) behind each argument explicit so that the committee can give it due consideration in this and future cases. Conclude your memo by recommending a course of action. (You may use your imagination to add significant details about *WatchYour Colour*'s pricing and mode of operation and about other aspects of this scenario.)

ASSIGNMENT 7:   A photographer for *Ploughboy* magazine is coming to campus next semester to interview and photograph students for an upcoming feature entitled "Coed Madness." *Ploughboy*'s photo features ordinarily present young women with no clothes on and in sexually suggestive postures. The student newspaper has refused to run advertisements for the interviews and photo sessions, and several groups have asked your committee to prevent the photographer from posting handbills on Mountmonk property. Write a brief memo outlining as clearly as possible the best argument for allowing *Ploughboy* to post handbills and the best argument for forbidding it to do so. Be certain to make the principle (rule) behind each argument explicit so that the committee can give it due consideration in this and future cases. Conclude your memo by recommending a course of action. (You may use your imagination to add significant details about *Ploughboy*'s mode of operation, the remuneration of students photographed, and other aspects of this scenario.)

ASSIGNMENT 8:   ## AN ARGUMENT OF YOUR CHOICE

Identify a dispute in which you are interested and write a 1,500- to 2,000-word paper in which you

1. Describe the undisputed facts in the case in such a way that someone unfamiliar with them can understand them. (The explanatory paragraphs in the assignment above can serve as models.)

2. Briefly outline a well-formed argument your opponents have made or might make. Be sure that your identification of their rule or rules is clear.

3. Develop your own argument, advocating a rule or rules that contrast with your opponents' and lead to a different conclusion.

Your paper should be written with a "court" in mind. Your instructor may ask you to identify the nature of this court.

MILLER v. CALIFORNIA

413 US 15[1] (1973)

In 1969, Marvin Miller promoted the sale of four "adult" books and one "adult" movie by mass-mailing brochures that included photographs and drawings suitable to one of the titles: *Sex Orgies Illustrated.* An envelope containing the five brochures was addressed to a restaurant in Newport Beach, California, where it was opened by the manager of the restaurant and his mother. Not having requested these brochures, the two complained to police, and Miller was arrested under a California law making it a misdemeanor to distribute obscene material. After Miller was convicted, he appealed. Eventually his appeal reached the U.S. Supreme Court, which upheld the conviction by a 5 to 4 vote.

In order to follow the legal arguments made by Chief Justice Burger in the majority opinion and Justice Douglas in a dissenting opinion, you need some information on the constitutional and legal issues involved. At the center of the controversy is the First Amendment to the U.S. Constitution: "Congress shall make no law respecting an establishment of religion, or prohibiting the free exercise thereof; or abridging the freedom of speech, or of the press; or the right of the people peaceably to assemble, and to petition the Government for a redress of grievances." The Fourteenth Amendment, by forbidding states to "make or enforce any law which shall abridge the privileges or immunities of citizens of the United States," made the First Amendment apply to state laws as well.

But is the distribution of obscene material protected under the First Amendment? In *Roth* v. *United States* [354 US 476], the majority of the court had said no and defined obscenity as "material which deals with sex in a manner appealing to prurient interest." It had said that such material was not covered by the First Amendment because it was "utterly without redeeming social importance." The precise meaning of "prurient" in the Roth case was to be defined by "contemporary community standards." The minority of the court and many advocates of civil liberties found this decision alarming, partly because of its vagueness: someone who published material dealing with sex might be arrested and discover to his or her surprise that (in the opinion of the judge or jury) he had offended community standards. Thus the publisher might be convicted for a crime he could not have known he was committing.

Subsequent cases altered the meaning of obscenity somewhat. *Memoirs* v. *Massachusetts* [383 US 413] said that only material "utterly without redeeming social value" could be subject to criminal prosecution. But it was so difficult for prosecutors to prove that a work was *utterly* without redeeming social value that it became

---

[1] 413 US 15: By convention, Supreme Court cases are named by stating the name of the party making the appeal (Marvin Miller) and the name of the party on the other side (State of California). The *v.* between is an abbreviation of *versus.* The numbers and letters below tell the reader where the opinions can be found: Volume 413 of the *United States Reports,* page 15.

nearly impossible to prosecute obscenity cases. In *Ginzberg* v. *New York* [383 US 463] the Court decided that some material might be considered obscene if it were distributed to children, even though it would not be obscene if distributed to adults.

This confusion on the Court about how to define obscenity set the stage for the Miller case, in which Chief Justice Burger and the majority of the court attempted to create a clear legal test for obscenity. Justice Douglas found this new definition no more adequate than those that came before, as you will see.

A case mentioned in Douglas's dissenting opinion also needs explanation. *Bouie* v. *City of Columbia* [378 US 347] involved a 1960 sit-in protest in South Carolina. After two protesters were arrested for trespass, the South Carolina courts reinterpreted the trespass statute in a way that made the charges stick. The U.S. Supreme Court, however, threw the conviction out, saying that the Carolina courts had made the sit-in illegal *ex post facto* (after the fact). In the United States, people can be punished only for actions that were illegal at the time they were committed.

MR. CHIEF JUSTICE BURGER, FOR THE MAJORITY

1   THIS CASE INVOLVES THE APPLICATION OF a State's criminal obscenity statute to a situation in which sexually explicit materials have been thrust by aggressive sales action upon unwilling recipients who had in no way indicated any desire to receive such materials. This Court has recognized that the States have a legitimate interest in prohibiting dissemination or exhibition of obscene material when the mode of dissemination carries with it a significant danger of offending the sensibilities of unwilling recipients or of exposure to juveniles.[2] It is in this context that we are called on to define the standards which must be used to identify obscene material that a State may regulate without infringing on the First Amendment. . . . In Roth *v.* United States the court sustained a conviction under a federal statute punishing the mailing of "obscene, lewd, lascivious or filthy . . ." materials. The key to that holding was the Court's rejection of the claim that obscene materials were protected by the First Amendment. Five Justices joined in the opinion stating:

All ideas having even the slightest redeeming social importance—unorthodox ideas, controversial ideas, even ideas hateful to the prevailing climate of opinion—have the full protection of the [First Amendment] guaranties, unless excludable because they encroach upon the limited area of more important interests. But implicit in the history of the First Amendment is the rejection of obscenity as utterly without redeeming social importance. . . . There are certain well-defined and narrowly limited classes of speech, the prevention and punishment of which have never been thought to raise any Constitutional problem. *These include the lewd and obscene. . . . It has been well observed that such utterances are no essential part of any exposition of ideas, and are of such slight social value as a step to truth that any benefit that may be derived from them is clearly outweighed by the social interest in order and morality.*

2

This much has been categorically settled by the Court, that obscene material is unprotected by the First Amendment.[3] We acknowledge, however, the inherent dangers of undertaking

3

---

[2] juveniles: At this point, Burger cites twelve cases, including Ginzberg *v.* New York.

[3] First Amendment: Here Burger cites six cases, including Roth *v.* United States.

to regulate any form of expression. State statutes designed to regulate obscene materials must be carefully limited.[4] As a result, we now confine the permissible scope of such regulation to works which depict or describe sexual conduct. That conduct must be specifically defined by the applicable state law, as written or authoritatively construed. A state offense must also be limited to works which, taken as a whole, appeal to the prurient interest in sex, which portray sexual conduct in a patently offensive way, and which, taken as a whole, do not have serious literary, artistic, political, or scientific value. . . .

4 Under the holdings announced today, no one will be subject to prosecution for the sale or exposure of obscene materials unless these materials depict or describe patently offensive "hard core" sexual conduct specfically defined by the regulating state law, as written or construed. We are satisfied that these specific prerequisites will provide fair notice to a dealer in such materials that his public and commercial activities may bring prosecution.[5] If the inability to define regulated materials with ultimate, god-like precision altogether removes the power of the States or the Congress to regulate, then "hard core" pornography may be exposed without limit to the juvenile, the passerby, and the consenting adult alike, as, indeed, Mr. Justice Douglas contends. . . .

5 The dissenting Justices sound the alarm of repression. But, in our view, to equate the free and robust exchange of ideas and political debate with commercial exploitation of obscene material demeans the grand conception of the First Amendment and its high purpose in the historical struggle for freedom. It is a "misuse of the great guarantees of free speech and free press. . . ."[6] The First Amendment protects works which, taken as a whole, have serious literary, artistic, political, or scientific value, regardless of whether the government or the majority of the people approve of the ideas these works represent. "The protection given speech and press was fashioned to insure unfettered interchange of *ideas* for the bringing about of political and social changes desired by the people."[7] But the public portrayal of hard core sexual conduct for its own sake, and for the ensuing commercial gain, is a different matter.

6 There is no evidence, empirical or historical, that the stern 19th-century American censorship of public distribution and display of material relating to sex, see Roth *v*. United States, 482–485, in any way limited or affected expression of serious literary, artistic, political, or scientific ideas. On the contrary, it is beyond any question that the era following Thomas Jefferson to Theodore Roosevelt was an "extraordinarily vigorous period," not just in economics and politics, but in belles lettres and in "the outlying fields of social and political philosophies."[8] We do not see the harsh hand of censorship of ideas—good or bad, sound or unsound—and "repression" of political liberty lurking in every state regulation of commercial exploitation of human interest in sex.

7 Mr. Justice Brennan finds [that once censorship is introduced] "it is hard to see how state-ordered regimentation of our minds can ever be forestalled."[9] These doleful anticipations assume that courts cannot distinguish commerce in ideas, protected by the First Amendment,

---

[4] limited: Burger cites Interstate Circuit, Inc. *v*. Dallas, 390 US 682–685.
[5] prosecution: Burger cites Roth *v*. United States and Ginzberg *v*. New York.

[6] "free press . . .": Burger cites Breard *v*. Alexandria, 341 US 645.
[7] ". . . people": Burger cites Roth *v*. United States. The emphasis on *"ideas"* is his.
[8] "philosophies": V. Parrington, *Main Currents in American Thought*, ix ff. Burger's original footnote quotes Parrington and also cites several books and articles by other historians.
[9] "forestalled": Burger cites Brennan's dissenting opinion in Paris Adult Theatre I *v*. Slaton.

from commercial exploitation of obscene material. Moreover, state regulation of hard core pornography so as to make it unavailable to nonadults, a regulation which Mr. Justice Brennan finds constitutionally permissible, has all the elements of "censorship" for adults; indeed even more rigid enforcement techniques may be called for with such dichotomy of regulation.[10] One can concede that the "sexual revolution" of recent years may have had useful byproducts in striking layers of prudery from a subject long irrationally kept from needed ventilation. But it does not follow that no regulation of patently offensive "hard core" materials is needed or permissible; civilized people do not allow unregulated access to heroin because it is a derivative of medicinal morphine.

MR. JUSTICE DOUGLAS, DISSENTING

8   Today we leave open the way for California to send a man to prison for distributing brochures that advertise books and a movie under freshly written standards defining obscenity which until today's decision were never the part of any law.

9   The Court has worked hard to define obscenity and concededly has failed. [Douglas here reviews a number of contradictory definitions from earlier Supreme Court rulings.] Today the Court retreats from the earlier formulations and undertakes to make new definitions. This effort, like the earlier ones, is earnest and well intentioned. The difficulty is that we do not deal with constitutional terms, since "obscenity" is not mentioned in the Constitution or Bill of Rights. And the First Amendment makes no such exception from "the press" which it undertakes to protect nor, as I have said on other occasions, is an exception necessarily implied, for there was no recognized exception to the free press at the time

the Bill of Rights was adopted which treated "obscene" publications differently from other types of papers, magazines, and books. So there are no constitutional guidelines for deciding what is and what is not "obscene." The Court is at large because we deal with tastes and standards of literature. What shocks me may be sustenance for my neighbor. What causes one person to boil up in rage over one pamphlet or movie may reflect only his neurosis, not shared by others. We deal here with a regime of censorship which, if adopted, should be done by constitutional amendment after full debate by the people.

10   Obscenity cases usually generate tremendous emotional outbursts. They have no business being in the courts. If a constitutional amendment authorized censorship, the censor would probably be an administrative agency. Then criminal prosecutions could follow as, if, and when publishers defied the censor and sold their literature. Under the regime a publisher would know when he was on dangerous ground. Under the present regime—whether the old standards or the new ones are used—the criminal law becomes a trap. A brand-new test would put a publisher behind bars under a new law improvised by the courts after the publication. That was done in Ginzberg and has all the evils of an ex post facto law.

11   My contention is that until a civil proceeding has placed a tract beyond the pale, no criminal prosecution should be sustained. For no more vivid illustration of vague and uncertain laws could be designed than those we have fashioned. As Mr. Justice Harlan has said:

12   The upshot of all this divergence in viewpoint is that anyone who undertakes to examine the Court's decisions since Roth which have held particular material obscene or not obscene would find himself in utter bewilderment.[11]

---

10   regulation: Burger cites Interstate Circuit, Inc. *v.* Dallas, 390 US 690.

11   bewilderment: Douglas cites Interstate Circuit, Inc. *v.* Dallas, 390 US 676.

13   In Bouie *v.* City of Columbia,[12] we upset a conviction for remaining on property after being asked to leave, while the only unlawful act charged by the statute was entering. We held that the defendants had received no "fair warning, at the time of their conduct" while on the property "that the act for which they now stand convicted was rendered criminal" by the state statute. The same requirement of "fair warning" is due here, as much as in Bouie. The latter involved racial discrimination; the present case involves rights earnestly urged as being protected under the First Amendment. In any case—certainly when constitutional rights are concerned—we should not allow men to go to prison or be fined when they had no "fair warning" that what they did was criminal conduct.

14   If a specific book, play, paper, or motion picture has in a civil proceeding been condemned as obscene and review of that finding has been completed, and thereafter a person publishes, shows, or displays that particular book or film, then a vague law has been made specific. There would remain the underlying question whether the First Amendment allows an implied exception in the case of obscenity. I do not think it does and my views on the issue have been stated over and over again. But at least a criminal prosecution brought at that juncture would not violate the time-honored void-for-vagueness test.

15   No such protective procedure has been designed by California in this case. Obscenity—which even we cannot define with precision—is a hodgepodge. To send men to jail for violating standards they cannot understand, construe, and apply is a monstrous thing to do in a Nation dedicated to fair trials and due process. . . .

16   There is no "captive audience" problem in these obscenity cases. No one is being compelled to look or listen. Those who enter news stands or bookstalls may be offended by what they see. But they are not compelled by the State to frequent those places; and it is only state or governmental action against which the First Amendment, applicable to the States by virtue of the Fourteenth, raises a ban.

17   The idea that the First Amendment permits government to ban publications that are "offensive" to some people puts an ominous gloss on freedom of the press. That test would make it possible to ban any paper or any journal or magazine in some benighted place. The First Amendment was designed "to invite dispute," to induce "a condition of unrest," to "create dissatisfaction with conditions as they are," and even to stir "people to anger."[13] The idea that the First Amendment permits punishment for ideas that are "offensive" to the particular judge or jury sitting in judgment is astounding. No greater leveler of speech or literature has ever been designed. To give the power to the censor, as we do today, is to make a sharp and radical break with the traditions of a free society. The First Amendment was not fashioned as a vehicle for dispensing tranquilizers to the people. Its prime function is to keep debate open to "offensive" as well as "staid" people. The tendency throughout history has been to subdue the individual and exalt the power of government. The use of the standard "offensive" gives authority to government that cuts the very vitals out of the First Amendment.[14] As is intimated by the Court's opinion, the materials before us may be garbage. But so is much of what is said in political campaigns, in the daily press, on TV, or over the radio. By reason of the First Amendment—and solely because of it—speakers and publishers have not

---

12 Bouie *v.* City of Columbia: 378 US 347.

13 anger: Douglas cites Terminiello *v.* Chicago, 337 US 1, 4.
14 First Amendment: Obscenity law has had a capricious history: "The white slave traffic was first exposed by W. T. Snead in a magazine article, 'The Maiden Tribute.' The English law did absolutely nothing to the profiteers in vice, but put Stead in prison for a year for writing about an indecent subject." Z. Chafee, *Free Speech in the United States,* page 151. [Douglas's note, shortened]

been threatened or subdued because their thoughts and ideas may be "offensive" to some.

18   The standard "offensive" is unconstitutional in yet another way. In Coates *v.* City of Cincinnati[15] we had before us a municipal ordinance that made it a crime for three or more persons to assemble on a street and conduct themselves "in a manner annoying to persons passing by." We struck it down, saying: "If three or more people meet together on a sidewalk or street corner, they must conduct themselves so as not to annoy any police officer or other person who should happen to pass by. In our opinion this ordinance is unconstitutionally vague because it subjects the exercise of the right of assembly to an unascertainable standard, and unconstitutionally broad because it authorizes the punishment of constitutionally protected conduct.

19   Conduct that annoys some people does not annoy others. Thus the ordinance is vague, not in the sense that it requires a person to conform his conduct to an imprecise by comprehensive normative standard, but rather in the sense that no standard of conduct is specified at all.

------

[15] Coates *v.* City of Cincinnati: 402 US 611.

20   How can we deny Ohio the convenience of punishing people who "annoy" others and allow California power to punish people who publish materials "offensive" to some people is difficult to square with constitutional requirements.

21   If there are to be restraints on what is obscene, then a constitutional amendment should be the way of achieving the end. There are societies where religion and mathematics are the only free segments. It would be a dark day for America if that were our destiny. But the people can make it such if they choose to write obscenity into the Constitution and define it.

22   We deal with highly emotional, not rational, questions. To many the Song of Solomon is obscene. I do not think that we, the judges, were ever given the constitutional power to make definitions of obscenity. If it is to be defined, let the people debate and decide by a constitutional amendment what they want to ban as obscene and what standards they want the legislatures and the courts to apply. Perhaps the people will decide that the path towards a mature, integrated society requires that all ideas competing for acceptance must have no censor. Perhaps they will decide otherwise. Whatever the choice, the courts will have some guidelines. Now we have none except our predilections. ◆

LET'S PUT PORNOGRAPHY BACK IN THE CLOSET

Susan Brownmiller

Journalist Susan Brownmiller is one of the founders of Women Against Pornography and an organizer of the New York Radical Feminists. In 1975, after four years of research, she published *Against Our Will,* a study of the causes of rape and its effects. She published the following essay in *Newsday* in 1979 as part of her well-publicized crusade against pornography.

1 FREE SPEECH IS ONE OF THE GREAT FOUNdations on which our democracy rests. I am old enough to remember the Hollywood Ten, the screenwriters who went to jail in the late 1940s because they refused to testify before a congressional committee about their political affiliations. They tried to use the First Amendment as a defense, but they went to jail because in those days there were few civil liberties lawyers around who cared to champion the First Amendment right to free speech, when the speech concerned the Communist Party.

2 The Hollywood Ten were correct in claiming the First Amendment. Its high purpose is the protection of unpopular ideas and political dissent. In the dark, cold days of the 1950s, few civil libertarians were willing to declare themselves First Amendment absolutists. But in the brighter, though frantic, days of the 1960s, the principle of protecting unpopular political speech was gradually strengthened.

3 It is fair to say now that the battle has largely been won. Even the American Nazi Party has found itself the beneficiary of the dedicated, tireless work of the American Civil Liberties Union. But—and please notice the quotation marks coming up—"To equate the free and robust exchange of ideas and political debate with commercial exploitation of obscene material demeans the grand conception of the First Amendment and its high purposes in the historic struggle for freedom. It is a misuse of the great guarantees of free speech and free press."

4 I didn't say that, although I wish I had, for I think the words are thrilling. Chief Justice Warren Burger said in 1973, in the United States Supreme Court's majority opinion in *Miller* v. *California.* During the same decades that the right to political free speech was being strengthened in the courts, the nation's obscenity laws also were undergoing extensive revision.

5 It's amazing to recall that in 1934 the question of whether James Joyce's *Ulysses* should be banned as pornographic actually went before the Court. The battle to protect *Ulysses* as a work of literature with redeeming social value was won. In later decades, Henry Miller's *Tropic* books, *Lady Chatterley's Lover* and the *Memoirs of Fanny Hill* also were adjudged not obscene. These decisions have been important to me. As the author of *Against Our Will,* a study of the history of rape that does contain explicit sexual material, I shudder to think how my book would have fared if James Joyce, D. H. Lawrence and Henry Miller hadn't gone before me.

6 I am not a fan of *Chatterley* or the *Tropic* books, I should quickly mention. They are not to my literary taste, nor do I think they represent female sexuality with any degree of accuracy. But I would hardly suggest that we ban them. Such a suggestion wouldn't get very far

anyway. The battle to protect these books is ancient history. Time does march on, quite methodically. What, then, is unlawfully obscene, and what does the First Amendment have to do with it?

7   In the Miller case of 1973 (not Henry Miller, by the way, but a porn distributor who sent unsolicited stuff through the mails), the Court came up with new guidelines that it hoped would strengthen obscenity laws by giving more power to the states. What it did in actuality was throw everything into confusion. It set up a three-part test by which materials can be adjudged obscene. The materials are obscene if they depict patently offensive, hardcore sexual conduct; lack serious scientific, literary, artistic or political value; and appeal to the prurient interest of an average person—as measured by contemporary community standards.

8   "Patently offensive," "prurient interest" and "hard-core" are indeed words to conjure with. "Contemporary community standards" are what we're trying to redefine. The feminist objection to pornography is not based on prurience, which the dictionary defines as lustful, itching desire. We are not opposed to sex and desire, with or without the itch, and we certainly believe that explicit sexual material has its place in literature, art, science and education. Here we part company rather swiftly with old-line conservatives who don't want sex education in the high schools, for example.

9   No, the feminist objection to pornography is based on our belief that pornography represents hatred of women, that pornography's intent is to humiliate, degrade and dehumanize the female body for the purpose of erotic stimulation and pleasure. We are unalterably opposed to the presentation of the female body being stripped, bound, raped, tortured, mutilated and murdered in the name of commercial entertainment and free speech.

10   These images, which are standard pornographic fare, have nothing to do with the hal-lowed right of political dissent. They have everything to do with the creation of a cultural climate in which a rapist feels he is merely giving in to a normal urge and a woman is encouraged to believe that sexual masochism is healthy, liberated fun. Justice Potter Stewart once said about hard-core pornography, "You know it when you see it," and that certainly used to be true. In the good old days, pornography looked awful. It was cheap and sleazy, and there was no mistaking it for art.

11   Nowadays, since the porn industry has become a multimillion dollar business, visual technology has been employed in its service. Pornographic movies are skillfully filmed and edited, pornographic still shots using the newest tenets of good design artfully grace the covers of *Hustler, Penthouse* and *Playboy*, and the public—and the courts—are sadly confused.

12   The Supreme Court neglected to define "hard-core" in the Miller decision. This was a mistake. If "hard-core" refers only to explicit sexual intercourse, then that isn't good enough. When women or children or men—no matter how artfully—are shown tortured or terrorized in the service of sex, that's obscene. And "patently offensive," I would hope, to our "contemporary community standards."

13   Justice William O. Douglas wrote in his dissent to the Miller case that no one is "compelled to look." This is hardly true. To buy a paper at the corner newsstand is to subject oneself to a forcible immersion in pornography, to be demeaned by an array of dehumanized, chopped-up parts of the female anatomy, packed like cuts of meat at the supermarket. I happen to like my body and I work hard at the gym to keep it in good shape, but I am embarrassed for my body and for the bodies of all women when I see the fragmented parts of us so frivolously, and so flagrantly, displayed.

14   Some constitutional theorists (Justice Douglas was one) have maintained that any obscenity law is a serious abridgement of free speech. Others (and Justice Earl Warren was one) have

maintained that the First Amendment was never intended to protect obscenity. We live quite compatibly with a host of free-speech abridgements. There are restraints against false and misleading advertising or statements—shouting "fire" without cause in a crowded movie theater, etc.—that do not threaten, but strengthen, our societal values. Restrictions on the public display of pornography belong in this category.

15   The distinction between permission to pub-lish and permission to display publicly is an essential one and one which I think consonant with First Amendment principles. Justice Burger's words which I quoted above support this without question. We are not saying "Smash the presses" or "Ban the bad ones," but simply "Get the stuff out of our sight." Let the legislatures decide—using realistic and humane contemporary community standards—what can be displayed and what cannot. The courts, after all, will be the final arbiters. ◆

THE OLD ITCH TO CENSOR FINDS A NEW MEDIUM

Alan M. Dershowitz

A professor of law at Harvard University, Alan Dershowitz has become known to the general public through two books he has written about his involvement in high-profile trials. The second book, *Reversal of Fortune,* describing his successful defense of Claus von Bulow against a murder charge, became a best-seller and was made into a popular movie. Also a syndicated columnist, Dershowitz has become one of America's most respected defenders of free speech.

ALAN DERSHOWITZ reprinted by permission of UFS, Inc.

1   SHOULD A COMPUTER NETWORK READ—AND censor—its customers' electronic messages? That new-age variation of an age-old debate is now raging within the computer industry. The impetus for the controversy was a series of anti-Semitic messages carried on the electronic bulletin board and in private person-to-person electronic mail of the Prodigy Computer Network.

2   The messages, declaring that Hitler was right and that Jews "richly deserve" what they experienced during the Holocaust, were deeply offensive to many who read them. Other messages denied that the Holocaust had occurred.

3   The Anti-Defamation League of the B'nai B'rith—the self-appointed watchdog of the Jewish community against anti-Semitism, as they define it—protested to Prodigy, demanding that it censor such messages. Prodigy responded by "amplifying" its existing system, under which its censors decided which messages were sufficiently "repugnant" to warrant censorship. It then decided that although some racist, sexist and anti-Semitic messages should be censored, messages that denied the Holocaust were not sufficiently offensive to justify censorship.

4   This unfortunate episode demonstrates the dangers of censorship.

5   All large institutions—whether they be governments, universities, corporations, libraries or computer networks—must face a fundamental choice: Will they or will they not read the mail and get into the business of deciding what is sufficiently offensive to justify censorship? The simple approach is for the institution to eschew the role of censor and simply let people say whatever they want to each other. This approach is particularly suitable to private communication, such as ordinary mail, telephone calls and conversations. If the recipient of the communication is not offended by its content, then why should the institution declare it offensive?

6   Even that simple rule may not avoid all intervention by the institution. Private messages that are criminal in nature—drug deals, assassination plots, price-fixing schemes and the like—are not entitled to use a legitimate means of communication to achieve an illegal end. That is when our Constitution permits intrusion on the basis of "probable cause" to believe that a crime is being committed. Although this constitutional standard does not govern searches conducted in the private sector, most businesses and universities have their own standards, often akin to probable cause, for intruding on the privacy of their employees or students.

7   But what about open bulletin boards? These boards may be of the old-fashioned kind, on which handwritten or typed messages are

placed. Or they may be of the electronic kind, over which computerized messages are sent. They share the common characteristic that many people will be able to read the message. Inevitably, if the message is controversial, it will offend some who read it. And therein lies the conflict between freedom of speech and the right not to be offended.

8   Our First Amendment generally resolves that conflict in favor of free speech. It tells adult citizens who would be offended by protected speech to turn their heads, close the book, switch the channel or learn to live with the offense. Any other approach would create an "offensiveness veto" by even the most squeamish. If only that speech which offended no one were to be permitted, there would be little public speech, and the vast marketplace of ideas would turn into a mini-mart of pabulum. Although the First Amendment does not apply to private institutions, its policies should govern all institutions dedicated to promoting an open marketplace of ideas.

9   Prodigy should get out of the business of reading and censoring electronic messages unless they are criminal. And the Anti-Defamation League should understand that it aggravated the problem by demanding censorship. What began as an individual bigot sending messages of hate turned into a major computer network concluding that Holocaust denial is not all that offensive. That is not only worse for freedom of speech; it is also worse for the Jews, because it mainstreams what would otherwise have been fringe offensiveness.

10   Whenever an institution institutes a regime of censorship, it not only explicitly disapproves of what it censors, it implicitly approves of what it allows to pass through its system uncensored. Thus, if the U.S. Postal Service were to censor Hustler magazine while allowing Playboy to pass through, it would be placing its imprimatur on Playboy. It is far better for the Post Office and Prodigy to declare that they are in the business of delivering the mail, not reading it. ◆

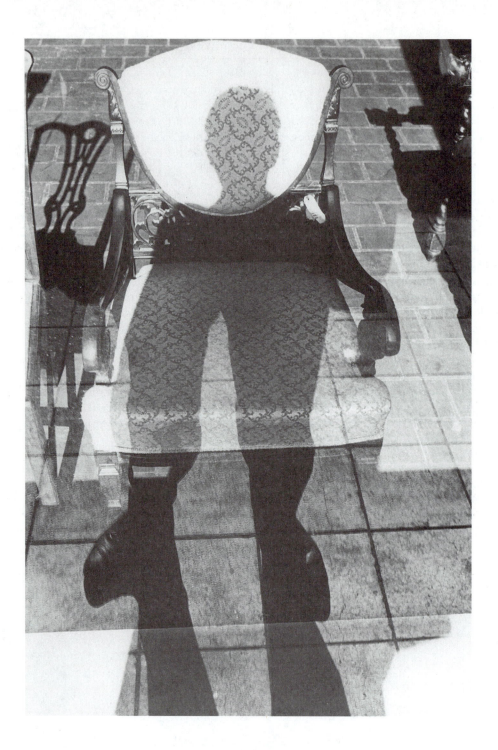

PART V

INTERPRETATION AND EVALUATION

"The voyage of discovery consists not in charting new landscapes, but in having new eyes."

MARCEL PROUST

11

Writing About Literature

TO PRODUCE A CHAPTER ON WRITING ABOUT LITERATURE IS A FOOL'S terrand. There are so many types of literature and so many different approaches that can be taken to it that no chapter can do the job. What this one will attempt is more modest: to present you with an approach to writing one type of paper about one type of literature.

The type of literature will be the narrative, the story. As a member of a society that produces a constant stream of stories—in print, on film, on videotape, and in conversation—you probably know a good deal more about narrative techniques than you are *aware* of knowing. Until we are asked to write about narratives carefully, most of us read them with unconscious ease, just as we ride a bicycle without precisely knowing how we do it. Unconscious ease has its advantages, but it doesn't allow you to hold things up to scrutiny, to analyze or improve your understanding. Writing about narratives is, among other things, an exercise in raising your level of awareness of the storyteller's techniques and your responses to them.

The type of paper that we will be discussing (and that you will be writing) is grounded in a careful analysis of six elements of a narrative: setting (including place and time), character, point of view, plot, theme, and symbolism. Analyzing the way that these elements work in a story often helps you understand the story better. More important, it can help you become conscious of what you *don't* understand. Discovering a *problem* that could prevent readers from understanding a narrative fully is a crucial step toward writing the kind of paper we are discussing here, a paper that presents a solution to a difficulty. The pattern is like the problem-solution pattern we discussed in Chapter 8.

By identifying a problem of interpretation in a narrative and by proposing a solution, you show that you have arrived at an understanding of the work. *An understanding* is not the same thing as *the truth*, of course. Literary works are not puzzles to be solved once and for all, and if your problem is an intriguing one, you can be certain that other readers would arrive at other solutions. Each intelligent solution has its virtues; each teaches us something new about the story or places the emphasis on a new facet. This is not to say, however, that all views of a literary work are equally valuable. An understanding is not the same as an uninformed or slipshod opinion. It is formed from close study and takes into account all significant aspects of the work. It doesn't leave obvious questions unexplored, and it can be listened to with respect by people who disagree with it strongly. Literature teachers often give A's to papers that reveal an *understanding* of a story that is different from their own. Sometimes they are even persuaded to alter their own understandings. But they may give F's to papers that express an unsupported *opinion* about a story, even if that opinion matches their own.

A STORY FOR ANALYSIS

Since analysis is an important step toward understanding, we will begin by analyzing "The Blue Eyes," a very short story by Isak Dinesen.[1]

> I have heard a story . . . of a skipper who named his ship after his wife. He had the figure-head of it beautifully carved, just like her, and the hair of it gilt. But his wife was jealous of the ship. "You think more of the figure-head than of me," she said to him. "No," he answered, "I think so highly of her because she is like you, yes, because she is you yourself. Is she not gallant, full-bosomed; does she not dance in the waves, like you at our wedding? In a way she is really even kinder to me than you are. She gallops along where I tell her to go, and she lets her long hair hang down freely, while you put up yours under your cap. But she turns her back to me, so that when I want a kiss I come home to Elsinore." Now once, when this skipper was trading at Trankebar, he chanced to help an old native King to flee from traitors in his own country. As they parted the King gave him two big blue, precious stones, and these he had set into the face of his figure-head, like a pair of eyes to it. When he came home he told his wife of his adventure, and said: "Now she has your blue eyes too." "You had better give me the stones for a pair of earrings," she said. "No," he said again, "I cannot do that, and you would not ask me to if you understood." Still the wife could not stop fretting about the blue stones, and one day, when her husband was with the skippers' corporation, she had a glazier of the town take them out, and put two

A WRITER AT WORK

"The Blue Eyes"
ISAK DINESEN

---

[1] **Isak Dinesen:** The pen name of Baroness Karen Blixen (1885–1962), the Danish-born author of such notable books as *Seven Gothic Tales, Out of Africa,* and *Winter's Tales,* from which "The Blue Eyes" is taken. "The Blue Eyes" is actually a tale within the tale "Peter and Rosa." See Assignment 4 at the chapter's end.

bits of blue glass into the figure-head instead, and the skipper did not find out, but sailed off to Portugal. But after some time the skipper's wife found that her eyesight was growing bad, and that she could not see to thread a needle. She went to a wise woman, who gave her ointments and waters, but they did not help her, and in the end the old woman shook her head, and told her that this was a rare and incurable disease, and that she was going blind. "Oh, God," the wife then cried, "that the ship was back in the harbor of Elsinore. Then I should have the glass taken out, and the jewels put back. For did he not say that they were my eyes?" But the ship did not come back. Instead, the skipper's wife had a letter from the Consul of Portugal, who informed her that she had been wrecked, and gone to the bottom with all hands. And it was a very strange thing, the Consul wrote, that in broad daylight she had run straight into a tall rock, rising out of the sea.

ANALYSIS OF A STORY: SIX ELEMENTS OF THE NARRATIVE

1. Setting: Place and Time.   Setting is a good starting point in the analysis of a narrative because paying attention to the *place* and *time,* the two subelements of setting, helps us get our bearings. For both of these subelements, I like to begin with a broad identification and then to narrow as much as possible.

Let's begin with place, then. Where shall we say, broadly, that the story is set? Three places are mentioned by name. Elsinore, the skipper's home port; Trankebar, where he assists the native King and is given the blue stones; and Portugal, where he drowns. A few minutes of research in your library's reference section will tell you that Elsinore (or Helsingore) is a city in Denmark and that Trankebar (or Tranquebar) is a city in southeast India. Elsinore, however, is the story's principal setting, and is (for Dinesen and other Danes, at least) an ordinary enough place: it was virtually Dinesen's hometown. If Trankebar sounds like the setting for a romance, Elsinore is as solid as Baltimore.

In many cases the setting can be more exactly identified: the story may be set not only in a particular city but on a particular street, in a particular house, perhaps in a particular room. In this case it is hard to define a setting narrower than the whole of Elsinore. We may suspect that most of the conversations happen inside the skipper's house, but there is no clear evidence.

And in what *time,* broadly, did the story take place? In her first sentence, Dinesen puts the story vaguely in the past: the narrator has heard this story but does not claim to be acquainted personally with any of the people in it. Apparently the story takes place in a time of sailing ships and a time when a person with failing eyes would consult not a physician but a "wise woman." We could say that the date is earlier than, say, 1880, but such literalness seems silly. The general time is the distant past invoked by the "once upon a time" beginning of fairy tales. In some stories we know the day and the hour of each scene. Here we cannot say precisely, but the story must stretch over a period of months or years: even in a fairy tale, there must be time for the voyage to Trankebar and the voyage to Portugal.

2. *Character.* In *Aspects of the Novel* E. M. Forster draws a useful distinction between *flat* characters and *round.* A flat character, he tells us, is one constructed around "a single idea or quality," and the very flattest "can be expressed in one sentence." Round characters more nearly resemble the people we encounter in everyday life. Their personalities have many qualities, and the mixture of qualities sometimes make them behave so that they surprise us, as Forster puts it, "in a convincing way."

We can begin our analysis of the characters in "The Blue Eyes" by ranging them along the continuum from flat to round. The flattest of all surely are the hands on the skipper's ship, so flat that they are not even mentioned separately and so can't be counted characters at all. Next, perhaps, is the "old native King," whose entire "personality" is his gratitude for being saved. But the "wise woman" is perhaps just as flat: her only personality trait is the regret she expresses by shaking her head as she pronounces the wife's eye disease incurable.

Relative to these very flat characters, the skipper seems slightly rounded. We know him to be

1. Adventurous (as shown by the voyage to Trankebar).

2. Deeply in love with his wife.

3. Poetic in speech and artistic in temperament (as shown by his attitude toward the figure-head).

The wife is slightly more rounded still. We know her to be

1. Jealous (of the figure-head).

2. Unimaginative (incapable of understanding the significance of the figure-head).

3. Capable of deceit.

We also know her to be *capable of change.* Once her eyes begin to fail she *sees* the significance of the figure-head and appears to repent of her deception and jealousy. To use two more useful terms borrowed from Forster, she is a *dynamic* (changing) character rather than a *static* (unchanging) one. In my view, but perhaps not in yours, she is a more interesting character than her impossibly wise and virtuous husband: she is recognizably human, and, like most humans, she grows wiser only when she pays dearly for her errors. Her capacity to change is one thing that gives her character roundness.

By comparison to the principal characters of a longer piece of realistic fiction, of course, even the wife is relatively flat. If you have read Toni Cade Bambara's "The Hammer Man" (page 445), for example, you know that Manny and the narrator are far rounder characters than the skipper and his wife.

3. Point of View.   One of the most important tools of the storyteller is the ability to choose the point of view from which events will be described. In their pure form, the principal points of view can be seen as the vertices of a triangle.

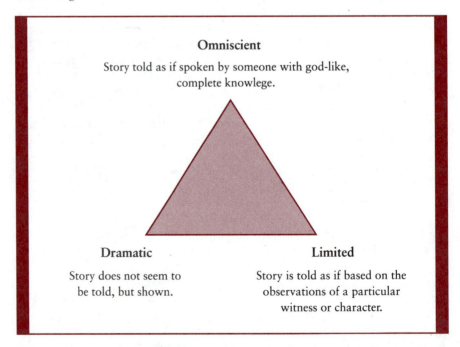

Omniscient

Story told as if spoken by someone with god-like, complete knowlege.

Dramatic

Story does not seem to be told, but shown.

Limited

Story is told as if based on the observations of a particular witness or character.

At one corner is the *omniscient* (all-knowing) point of view, in which the author (or the narrator) places no apparent limit on what is revealed to the audience. Like God, the omniscient narrator can look at will into the minds of all the characters in the story. Often the narrator reveals a knowledge of things that no character involved in the story could possibly know. When the point of view is omniscient, the reader has the impression that the story is being told by someone whose judgments and generalizations are unchallengeable because they are based on a complete knowledge of the world of the story. One sign of omniscient narration is the use of *summaries* of actions or conversations to which no one claims to have been a witness. The creation story in Genesis is told from an omniscient point of view: "In the beginning, God created the heavens and the earth." The author doesn't claim to have been there but does write as someone who *knows* and whose knowledge is not to be questioned.

At another corner of the triangle is the *dramatic* or *objective* point of view, in which everything is viewed as if with a motion picture camera. The actions and words of the characters are recorded but not their unspoken thoughts, and the reader is left with the impression of having witnessed the story as it occurred, with no narrator making judgments or generalizations or summarizing the action. The method here is sometimes called *scenic* to distinguish it from the *summarizing* method available to the omniscient narrator.

At the third corner of the triangle is the *limited* point of view, which restricts itself to the observations of a single witness to the story.[2] The reader seems to view everything from inside the skull of this witness, who becomes the story's *center of consciousness*. Stories with first-person[3] narrators are often restricted in this way: we inhabit the mind of the "I" who speaks in the story. The character who serves as the center of consciousness is a direct witness to events and conversations and may be a participant as well:

> I was glad to hear that Manny had fallen off the roof. I had put out
> the tale that I was down with yellow fever, but nobody paid me no
> mind, least of all Dirty Red who stomped right in to announce that
> Manny had fallen off the roof and that I could come out of hiding
> now. My mother dropped what she was doing, which was the laundry,
> and got the whole story out of Red. "Bad enough you gots to hang
> around with boys," she said. "But fight with them too. And you
> would pick the craziest one at that."

This is the voice of the narrator in "The Hammer Man," and when we hear it we realize that what it tells us is neither an objective rendering of appearances (as in the dramatic point of view) nor an authoritative statement of reality, including both surface appearances and deeper truths (as in the omniscient point of view). Instead, it is a *version* of reality *as perceived by one individual,* who may sometimes be mistaken.

Except for some first-person narratives, few stories are told purely from any one of the three points of view. Usually, some material is presented from an omniscient point of view, some dramatically, and some from the limited perspective of a single character. One way of dealing with this mixture is to say that a story may blend points of view in any proportion and that if we want to characterize its *general* point of view, we might have to locate it somewhere other than at the triangle's corners—perhaps

---

[2] a single witness: Or one witness at a time. Sometimes the author leaps from one limited point of view to another.

[3] first-person narrator: Using, that is, the first-person singular pronoun: "*I* saw," "*I* have heard."

inside, perhaps along one edge. As I discuss the point of view in a story, I will insert a diagram showing where on the triangle it seems to belong.

In "The Blue Eyes," the narrator knows the whole story without having witnessed it, and he begins by summarizing a good deal of action. Though he "heard" the story from someone else, he serves here essentially as if he were the all-knowing author: whatever he says must be taken as the truth. It appears, then, that the narration is from the omniscient point of view. But this classification oversimplifies the situation. Some parts of the story use dialogue, an essentially dramatic technique, and allow us to draw our own conclusions about the characters of the skipper and his wife. At other times in the story we dip into the consciousness of the wife: "his wife was jealous of the ship," "the wife could not stop fretting," and so forth. Never do we dip into the consciousness of the skipper or any other character. On balance, most literary scholars would probably describe the point of view of "The Blue Eyes" as *limited omniscient,* a hybrid form that allows authors to establish one character as the story's center of consciousness but also allows them to escape that consciousness to make observations the character would not.

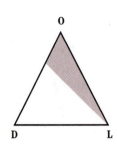

EXERCISE 1

◆ *Identifying Point of View.* Identify the point of view of each of the following passages, and be prepared to discuss the reasons that you classify it as you do.

1. Now once, when this skipper was trading at Trankebar, he chanced to help an old native King to flee from traitors in his own country.

2. When he came home he told his wife of his adventure, and said: "Now she has your blue eyes too." "You had better give me the stones for a pair of earrings," said she. "No," he said again, "I cannot do that, and you would not ask me to if you understood."

3. But after some time the skipper's wife found that her eyesight was growing bad, and that she could not see to thread a needle.

4. Plot. In *Aspects of the Novel* Forster tells us that "the king died and the queen died" is not a plot. "The king died and the queen died of grief," however, Forster does call a plot. What is the difference? A plot is not merely a collection of unconnected events; it is a series of events connected by *causation.* Event 1 causes Event 2, which causes Event 3, and so on until the story ends.[4] A plot synopsis of "The Blue Eyes" stressing causation might read as follows:

A skipper named his ship after his wife and had a figure-head for it carved in her image; into the eyes of the figure-head, he placed pre-

---

[4] Complex stories may have several plots, several separate lines of causally connected events.

cious blue stones. Because she was jealous of the figure-head, the wife had the stones cut out to keep for herself. Because the stones had magically become her eyes, she went blind, and because they had also become the ship's eyes, the ship crashed on a rock in broad daylight, drowning the skipper.

There is, however, another traditional method of analyzing plot. Rather than causation, this method emphasizes a *protagonist* pursuing a goal and confronted with a *problem* or *conflict*. In the case of "The Blue Eyes," this second method presents us with a dilemma. We must decide who the protagonist is, whose problem the story is primarily concerned with. Partly because of the story's point of view, my own feeling is that the wife is the protagonist, and I would summarize the plot as follows:

> A wife wanted her husband to love her completely [the goal], but he seemed to lavish his affection on the figure-head of his ship instead, saying that the figure-head was not only *like* her, it *was* her, an explanation that she could not accept [conflict]. When he acquired some precious blue stones, she wanted them for earrings, but he would not take them out of the eyes of the figure-head where he had placed them, so she cut them out herself [heightened recurrences of the conflict]. When her eyesight began to fail, she realized she had blinded herself by blinding the figure-head. She wished that the ship were in port so that she could replace the stones, but news came that the ship had smashed into a huge rock in broad daylight and her husband had drowned.

It is possible to view the skipper as the story's protagonist, but I think the wife is the more likely choice. We understand the wife's goal better than we do the husband's and the story seems to center on her struggle.

♦ *Summarizing the Plot from Another Perspective.* Assume that the skipper, not the wife, is the protagonist of the story. Write a plot summary that stresses his goal and his struggles.

EXERCISE 2

5. Theme.   The theme is the dominant idea of a literary work, corresponding to what we have been calling the framework of an essay. Generally, literature textbooks define the theme as a general statement about the human condition, expressible in a sentence. By this definition, "jealousy" cannot be the theme of a story, though "jealousy leads to ruin" might be: jealousy might be the subject of a story but cannot be a theme because a theme needs to be a complete statement, a complete sentence. Nor can "the wife betrays her husband" be a theme if it is a statement about two particular people, not a general statement about the human condition.

This rather fussy textbook definition makes the relationship of the theme to the story seem fairly simple: one theme per story, and every competent reader should be able to identify it. In practice, theme is a more difficult element to pin down. When I asked six people with degrees in

English, including two Ph.D.'s with considerable teaching experience, what the theme of "The Blue Eyes" is, I got the following answers:

1. Altering someone's means of expressing love will result in tragedy, *or* we must allow those around us to express their love as they will.

2. The clash of the real and the ideal results in destruction, *or* lack of trust leads to destruction.

3. Jealousy leads to ruin, *or* life is full of mystery.

4. Some objects have a power, either intrinsically or assigned to them by humans, that is undeniable and dangerous.

5. By betraying others, we betray ourselves.

6. Sometimes love should be blind.

Though some of these statements of the theme may be preferable to others, each could be supported in an essay about the story. Like most literary works, "The Blue Eyes" suggests many themes. The difficult question for the person analyzing the story is which theme is most significant, and on that question there is room for reasonable disagreement. Identifying the theme is, therefore, precisely the sort of problem that might produce a good essay.

You'll notice that three of the six respondents above simply couldn't be content with a single theme, apparently feeling that no single one does the story justice. If you follow the convention of assigning a single theme to the story (often a good idea for simplicity's sake), then you will want to choose the one that in your view best holds the story together. And if you are writing an essay on the subject, you will want to show why you take this view, arguing your case as carefully as you would in any other argument.

EXERCISE 3

♦ *Evaluating Arguments About Theme.* Each of the following one-paragraph essays attempts to identify an important theme in "The Blue Eyes" and convince readers that the theme is truly implied in the story. Decide which argument you find most convincing and which you find least convincing. Be prepared to explain the reasons behind your ranking.

1. The theme of "The Blue Eyes" is that there is more mystery in the world than the average person believes possible. The wife in the story represents the average person. Her husband represents the extraordinary person. The wife lives in Elsinore, a small port city near Dinesen's birthplace. Unlike Dinesen, who lived for seventeen years in Africa, however, the wife never leaves home. Her attitude toward life is what

we might expect of a middle-class housewife. She tucks her hair respectably under her cap and wants the blue stones for her earrings. She can't understand why they should be placed in the eyes of the figure-head (an apparently extravagant and poetic gesture), and she can't understand why her husband should be so delighted by a figure made of wood. It never occurs to her that the figure and the stones might have magical powers, and she never comprehends the skipper's romantic and artistic nature. Perhaps it is the skipper's knowledge of a wider world, a world of wonders and adventures, that makes him extraordinary. At any rate, his more poetic, magical view of life turns out to correspond more closely to the truth than her narrow vision does. And by not understanding or at least accepting the mysteries that he knows, she brings disaster to them both.

2. The theme of "The Blue Eyes" is that Karen Blixen wants to be Isak Dinesen; in other words, women often want to be men. This theme is first apparent in the roles Dinesen assigns to her characters. The woman is unimaginative and unadventurous and is ignorant, jealous, and petty. She stays at home, primarily *because* she is a woman, and spends her time finding fault with her husband. Her husband, on the other hand, is full of adventurousness and imagination, and is also loving, courageous, and wise. He travels the world and rescues an old King, but he also shows his wife his devotion by naming the ship after her and carving the figure-head in her image. Throughout her life, Dinesen chose to live like the skipper. Not only did she travel to Africa and manage a coffee plantation for over ten years, she also changed her name to the male name Isak. And by writing in English instead of her native language, she both gave up her identity even more and showed her romantic devotion to her English lover who died in a plane crash just before she began her writing career. The message of the story is clearly that the male life is the one worth living. In fact, when the woman says she wishes to put the eyes back in the ship, she proves that she realizes that her husband really meant that the ship *was* her, and by accepting that fact, she "buys into" the male life of magic and adventure. Furthermore, we can assume that Dinesen's life influenced this story because she set the story in Elsinore; Dinesen grew up, and escaped from, a place very near this city. Also, Dinesen often writes autobiographically, clearly seen in her *Out of Africa* which tells the story of her life in Africa. Finally, Dinesen's sexual confusion has a very real source: she lost her father to suicide and her lover to an accident, and this pattern of dying men and suffering women is reflected in the story, which ends with the woman finally seeing that the male life is the only one worth dying for.

3. The theme of "The Blue Eyes," that trust between a husband and wife must be absolute, is supported by the characters, plot, and symbolism of the story. The characters contrast sharply in their trust for one another.

While the husband finds a creative way of trusting his wife—making her image the figure-head on his ship so that she would guide him in all his travels—the wife stays at home and frets, doubting her husband's love because he enjoys his journeys and his ship so much. So while the skipper maintains his devotion to his wife, his wife grows more and more unhappy, resorting to deception to get back at her husband. The conflict that shapes the plot, then, is caused by the wife's inability to trust her husband's love. The story ends tragically when the wife suffers for her lack of trust: her husband drowns and she goes blind. Finally, the figure-head itself stands for the ideal love that would have included absolute trust. It is a symbol of the wife as she might be, freed of her imperfections. But it is also a symbol of the guiding force that a loving and trusting spouse can be.

6. Symbolism. Probably no element of literature produces more anxiety in the classroom than symbolism. Yet in ordinary life, we are comfortable with the idea that people, places, and objects may signify meanings beyond themselves. Thanks partly to millions of dollars spent on advertising, the "golden arches" have come to symbolize the following things to various people:

1. A McDonald's restaurant.

2. Fast food generally.

3. Wholesomeness (think of all those American-way-of-life advertisements).

4. Mass marketing generally.

5. Mass production of a bland product.

6. The replacement of mom-and-pop businesses by franchises.

7. The ugliness of commercial "strips" in American cities.

The list begins, I think, with the most common meaning of the arches. It could be continued indefinitely with meanings that are strongly present for a few people but not present for others. But which meanings are most present in our minds depends partly on context. Meaning number 2 could be reinforced by a series of photographs showing the logos of McDonald's, Burger King, and Kentucky Fried Chicken. Meaning number 6 could also be reinforced by a series of photographs: one showing a traditional diner on a street corner, one showing the diner being destroyed by bulldozers, one showing a sign (with the "golden arches" logo conspicuously present) announcing the construction of a new McDonald's on the now vacant corner, one showing the newly constructed restaurant with its arches glowing.

Three points are worth making here. The first is that we seem to be inclined by nature to attach meanings to objects: symbolism is not a purely literary phenomenon. The second is that the meaning we attach most strongly to an object will be affected by the context in which the object appears. In a literary work, therefore, the meanings that are most strongly present in the reader's mind ought logically to be those determined by the context of the whole story or poem. The third point is that the meanings of symbols are not mutually exclusive. The golden arches do not stop signifying a McDonald's restaurant at the moment they begin to signify the decline of mom-and-pop businesses.

In "The Blue Eyes," the figure-head with its blue gemstone eyes is the most conspicuous symbol. I asked the same six people who gave us themes for "The Blue Eyes" to tell me what they thought this symbol meant. If they could not be content with a single meaning, they could list more than one. Here are the meanings they listed:

1. The wife.

2. The wife *and* the ship.[5]

3. The love the skipper had for his wife *or* the wife that the skipper wanted to have.[6]

4. The skipper's desire to have his wife with him even when his occupation demanded that he be separated from her.

5. The human tendency to idealize the loved one, to project on him or her the qualities one most desires.

6. A guiding force, similar to the assistance spouses give each other as they "sail through the seas of life."

7. The ideal of beauty *or* love *or* both.

8. The power of imagination *or* of art.

Once again, I have tried to arrange the meanings from the narrowest and most obvious to the broadest and most interpretive. In general, the readers

---

[5] This interpreter refused to rank the two meanings, saying that they are intertwined.
[6] This interpreter said that the figure-head simultaneously symbolized one thing to the skipper and another to the wife.

who chose meanings near the top of the list said that they saw the points of people who chose the later meanings, but they were themselves uncomfortable with such speculations. The readers who chose meanings near the bottom of the list felt that those who chose near the top were right "as far as they went" but that they didn't go nearly far enough: they had not *interpreted* the symbol.

How speculative should one be in assigning a meaning to a literary symbol? There is no fixed rule, but the goal is ordinarily a *plausible interpretation*. To be *plausible* you must be able to develop a strong argument, based on the details of the story, that will support your position. To create an *interpretation,* as was pointed out in Chapter 1, you need to go beyond facts that speak for themselves and take a position with which some reasonable people would disagree. On the list above, I am not convinced that meanings 1 and 2 are interpretations that require argument. The other meanings, however, need demonstration and so might produce interesting essays.

EXERCISE 4   ◆ *Writing Short Arguments for an Interpretation of a Symbol.* Choose a meaning for the figure-head from the list above or suggest a meaning of your own. In a paragraph 100 to 150 words long, explain why you believe your meaning fits the context of the story well.

A POEM FOR ANALYSIS

The analysis of poetry *as poetry* involves many elements that we will not consider in this chapter, including meter, assonance, consonance, and other aspects of sound. Cramped for space and time, we will concentrate on narrative poems and will treat them essentially as we would other stories. Much is lost by this method, but something is gained. When we examine a poem as a narrative, we may learn things about it that would have escaped our notice had we been concentrating specifically on poetic elements.

A 1986 poem by Sharon Olds[7] is particularly suited to such an analysis.

Summer Solstice, New York City

By the end of the longest day of the year he could not stand it,
he went up the iron stairs through the roof of the building
and over the soft, tarry surface
to the edge, put one leg over the complex green tin cornice

---

[7] **Sharon Olds:** born in 1942, Olds won major awards for both her first two volumes of poetry. "Summer Solstice, New York City" first appeared in *The New Yorker* and was later reprinted in her third volume, *The Gold Cell* (1987).

5 and said if they came a step closer that was it.
Then the huge machinery of the earth began to work for his life,
the cops came in their suits blue-grey as the sky on a cloudy evening,
and one put on a bulletproof vest, a
black shell around his own life,
10 life of his children's father, in case
the man was armed, and one, slung with a
rope like the sign of his bounden duty,
came up out of a hole in the top of the neighboring building,
like the gold hole they say is in the top of the head,
15 and began to lurk toward the man who wanted to die.
The tallest cop approached him directly,
softly, slowly, talking to him, talking, talking,
while the man's leg hung over the lip of the next world,
and the crowd gathered in the street, silent, and the
20 dark hairy net with its implacable grid was
unfolded near the curb and spread out and
stretched as the sheet is prepared to receive at birth.
Then they all came a little closer
where he squatted next to his death, his shirt
25 glowing its milky glow like something
growing in a dish at night in the dark in a lab, and then
everything stopped
as his body jerked and he
stepped down from the parapet and went toward them
30 and they closed on him, I thought they were going to
beat him up, as a mother whose child has been
lost will scream at the child when it's found, they
took him by the arms and held him up and
leaned him against the wall of the chimney and the
35 tall cop lit his cigarette
in his own mouth, and gave it to him, and
then they all lit cigarettes, and the
red glowing ends burned like the
tiny campfires we lit at night
40 back at the beginning of the world.

    In the following pages, you'll see first an analysis of the poem and then a short essay discussing the relation of theme and setting in the poem. Both are intended as models for the assignments at the chapter's end. The analysis is, by nature, a rather disjointed set of observations. Such analyses are often written as preparations for more unified, coherent essays. The essay selects some ideas turned up in the analysis and expands on them, leaving other ideas behind. It is less complete, but within its narrowed range, more thorough and (one hopes) more persuasive.

ANALYSIS: THE SIX NARRATIVE ELEMENTS IN "SUMMER SOLSTICE"

1. Setting: Place and Time.   The general *place* is New York City. More narrowly, it is a building in the city, the street below (where the crowd gathers), and an adjacent building (from the top of which one policeman emerges). In fact, most of the action is confined to one edge of the building's roof. The *time,* generally, is the twentieth century (the century of bulletproof vests), perhaps 1986, the year the poem was published. More specifically, it is June 21, the longest day of the year, and it is dusk: the net and the man emerging from the nearby building are still visible in the early part of the narrative, but later the man's white shirt has a "milky glow," and by the time the story ends, the glowing ends of the cigarettes are very visible. The entire story takes place in a very limited time, perhaps an hour.

One curiosity related to setting is Olds's sudden mention, in the last lines of the poem, of a very different place and time: the campsites of our prehistoric ancestors.

2. Character.   The poem includes two groups of people that are not separated into individual characters: the crowd in the street and most of "the cops." Three or four characters in the story do have separate identities: the man who threatens suicide, the "tall cop" who talks to him and eventually gives him a cigarette, the policeman who emerges from the top of a neighboring building with a rope on his shoulder, and the policeman who puts on the bulletproof vest (but the man in the vest may be the "tall cop"). All of these characters are *flat.* The man in the bulletproof vest, for example, has a single trait, the desire to protect his life for his children's sake. We know almost nothing about the near-suicide, only that "he could not stand it." Whether he is *static* or *dynamic* is impossible to say. He comes back from the parapet, but whether he has by then decided that he *can* stand it we will never know.

3. Point of View.   The point of view is difficult to characterize. Only twice do we come close to entering the mind of any character directly involved in the story: when we hear that the man on the roof "could not stand it" and when we are told that one of the policemen puts on the bulletproof vest to protect the "life of his children's father." Neither of these instances seems truly to be a descent into the consciousness of a character, however. Both seem to be the sort of suppositions any observer might draw: isn't a man about to jump from a building likely to be someone who "can't stand it"? And isn't it probable that the man strapping on a bulletproof vest does so partly for the sake of his children? The narrator does not tell the story from the point of view of the suicidal man or the policeman in the vest. Instead, as we discover with a slight shock when the word "I" appears in line 30, she seems to be telling it from her own perspective, as a witness. It now appears that the point of view is *limited* and that the narrator serves as the *center of consciousness.*

This analysis is not strictly accurate, however, since the narrator has shown us at least one thing she could not have observed from any conceivable vantage point: the man walking up the stairs to the roof. Perhaps the best statement that we can make is that the point of view is *limited omniscient,* with more stress on limitation than in "The Blue Eyes."

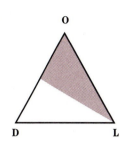

4. Plot. The plot of "Summer Solstice" can be stated fairly simply as a series of events linked by causation, though we have to speculate somewhat about the causes:

> Because he could not stand his life, a man climbed to the top of a building and stepped to the edge, prepared to jump. Because he was seen on the parapet, the police were called. Because one of the policemen talked reassuringly to him, the man stepped back from the parapet, rescued or at least reprieved.

Was the man actually prepared to jump? Were the "tall cop's" words reassuring, and did they bring the man back from the edge? I am not entirely certain, but the conjectures seem plausible.

A *protagonist-conflict* summary is more difficult because it is hard to identify a protagonist. This does not appear to be the story of a man's struggle to kill himself but the story of "the cops'" struggle to prevent his doing so. Somewhat uneasily, therefore, I would offer this as a possible summary:

> The cops [the collective protagonist] want to save [their goal] the life of a man who is poised to commit suicide. He warns them away, saying that he will jump if they come one step closer [the conflict]. They take the usual measures to protect him, including the spreading of a safety net, and attempt to persuade him not to jump. After a time, the persuasion works. He steps back from the parapet; they surround him and share a cigarette with him.

5. Theme. Among the possible themes of this story, the one that strikes me most forcibly is this: the despair we sometimes feel in isolation is weaker than the common bond of humanity that helps us endure. That despair is present in the poem is obvious: the man "could not stand it." But something brings him back from the brink, and the intriguing difficulty of interpreting the poem is to identify the force that counters the despair. It is partly the setting that makes me call the force the "common bond of humanity." New York City has, after all, a reputation for being a gigantic, impersonal, spiritless place. But in Olds's poem, it notices this one man on a ledge, it watches him from the street, it climbs out of a nearby building with a rope to save him, it stretches out a safety net, it approaches him "softly, slowly" in the person of "the tallest cop . . . talking to him, talking, talking." And finally, when the man steps down from the parapet, it encloses him, holds him, lights a cigarette for him, and passes it from mouth to mouth. The poem seems to assert that when the chips are down, we can care for each other as if we were members of one large family.

6. *Symbolism.*   Like many poems, "Summer Solstice" is so dense with meanings that many things in it acquire a symbolic importance. The police might be seen as symbols of the city or the society, for instance, or even as symbols of something larger yet, "the huge machinery of the earth" that works to save each human. New York City might be seen as a symbol of modern life, with its pressures and its apparent lack of concern for the individual. The fire that glows on the ends of the cigarettes when the rescuers and the would-be suicide share a smoke might be a symbol of the bond that holds us together and has held us together since we lit "tiny campfires . . . back at the beginning of the world."

A SAMPLE ESSAY

"Summer Solstice, New York City" presents several difficulties, several obstacles to understanding, and so is a good subject for an essay. Among the difficulties are these:

1. Because of the story's point of view, we don't know what the motivations of the suicidal man are. We don't know what, precisely, he couldn't stand at the poem's beginning, and we don't know what persuaded him to step back from the parapet at the story's end.

2. The theme of the poem is not self-evident. Reasonable people could certainly disagree about it.

3. It is not immediately clear why Olds sets the poem in time as she does. Is there some special significance to the sunset hour of the summer solstice?

4. The sixth line of the poem—"Then the huge machinery of the earth began to work for his life"—sounds especially important, but its meaning is vague. Readers may wonder what, precisely, this "huge machinery" includes.

5. Olds repeatedly introduces similes and metaphors that compare things in the setting to rather unlikely things outside the setting. The police uniforms are compared to "the sky on a cloudy evening," for example, and the glow of the cigarettes is compared to the glow of "tiny campfires" in prehistoric times. The reader may wonder if there is a pattern to these comparisons.

You'll notice that not all these problems are precisely correlated to the six elements used in analyzing narratives. Problems often present themselves in unexpected forms, and part of the challenge of writing a good essay about literature is to relate a nonstandard problem to the standard terms of analysis.

The following short paper focuses on the fifth problem listed above. It attempts to "solve" the problem of Olds's comparisons by showing that they are related to the theme of the poem. The paper handles in a fairly conventional fashion the practical problems of an essay about a literary work: how to introduce quotations, what balance to strike between quotations and commentary, how much summary to include, and other matters of form. To that extent, you may find it useful as a pattern for your own essay. No pattern, however, should be followed slavishly. In practice, essays by literary critics vary tremendously in form, and some assignments will require you to produce a paper of a very different sort.

THE FIRE IN SHARON OLDS'S "SUMMER SOLSTICE, NEW YORK CITY"

The title indicates the essay's focus.

At the end of Sharon Olds's "Summer Solstice, New York City," a man who has been coaxed back from the parapet of the building from which he had threatened to jump is surrounded by a group of policemen. The poem's narrator says, "I thought they were going to/ beat him up, as a mother whose child has been/ lost will scream at the child when it's found . . ," (30–32). Instead, the police "took him by the arms" to a safe place,

The summary is minimal; just enough to make the essay comprehensible to someone unfamiliar with the poem.

> and the
> tall cop lit a cigarette
> in his own mouth, and gave it to him, and
> then they all lit cigarettes, and the
> red glowing ends burned like the
> tiny campfires we lit at night
> back at the beginning of the world. (34–40)

Quotations longer than four lines are indented.

The fire is a symbol of love, of community. It links prehistoric men and the men gathered on the roof of a New York building. In a sense, this link comes as a complete surprise since no mention of prehistoric times has preceded it. But in another sense the link between prehistoric and modern times is implied throughout the poem: in fact, this link points directly to the theme.

The thesis shows the problem—to explain the presence of the campfires. It also uses an element stressed in literary analysis: theme.

The poem's New York City setting would seem to be as far removed from "the beginning of the world" as it is possible to be, but Olds reminds us repeatedly that underneath contemporary life are the ancient experiences of all humanity. The title's mention of the summer solstice, for example, calls to mind astronomical observations older than Stonehenge, older than ancient Greece, older than history. The

"Calls to whose mind?" you may

ask. If this reaction is purely personal, if no other readers share it, then this interpretation is not useful.

The use of very short quotations ties the interpretation to the text. It shows that the assertions have a basis.

calculation of the solstices and equinoxes is one of the earliest great human accomplishments, one of the cornerstones of agriculture and so of civilization. It takes us back—in imagination at least—to the time when there were not cities, but tribes; not strangers living in close proximity, but extended families. The New Yorker who recognizes that this is the longest day of the year is echoing a thought his ancestors had several thousand years ago.

Olds also links the present time to prehistory by comparing objects from the poem's present time to objects and events that are relatively timeless parts of human life. The policemen's suits are "blue-grey as the sky on a cloudy evening" (7). The bulletproof vest is "a/ black shell" (8–9) that may remind the reader of ancient armor. The safety net is "stretched as the sheet is prepared to receive at birth" (22). She repeatedly refers to the timeless relations of family life and the unchanging realities of the body. The man who puts on the vest is protecting the "life of his children's father" (10). The man with the rope comes "out of a hole in the top of the neighboring building,/ like the gold hole they say is in the top of the head" (13–14), a reference to folklore about the fontanel, the soft spot in a baby's skull. And, as we saw, the cops who surround the man at the poem's end are compared to a mother who finds her lost child.

The interpreter should attempt to account for parts of the work that don't seem to fit the interpretation.

Only once does Olds introduce a jarringly modern image—when she compares the man's shirt "glowing its milky glow" to "something growing in a dish at night in the dark in a lab" (25–26). But even this image may fit the pattern. The policemen who save the man are always linked with timeless things, with the family or with nature. But the man in danger, the man "squatted next to his death" (24), is linked to something modern and disconnected from the ancient concerns of human life.

The conclusion reminds the reader of the problem raised in the introduction.

The pattern of images seems to point the way to the poem's theme: that the strongest bond of human life, the love that holds the family or tribe together, is still with us. It may sometimes be obscured. The city may produce isolation or despair, but it is still possible for "the huge machinery of the earth" to work for us. The men sharing their cigarettes on top of a building in New York City are made of essentially the same stuff as their ancestors who gathered around campfires "back at the beginning of the world" (40).

POINTS TO CONSIDER

WRITING ESSAYS ABOUT LITERATURE

Showing an understanding of a work, which is the most common purpose for essays written in college literature classes, requires that you begin with careful reading and analysis. The analysis need not be written for any audience other than yourself, but you will probably find that the process of writing element-by-element notes forces you to see aspects of the work that otherwise would escape your attention.

The following questions can guide you through your analysis of a narrative:

SETTING

Place

Where generally is the story set? (If the story is science fiction, you may need to begin with the planet. Ordinarily the country or city is a good starting point.)

What are the more specific settings? (You may find locations as specific as particular rooms.)

Which is the principal setting?

How does awareness of place affect the way you read the story?

Time

What is the general time period of the story? (The century might be a good starting point.)

What is the more specific time period? (You may be able to narrow to an hour.)

How does awareness of time affect the way you read the story?

CHARACTER

Who are the characters in the story?

Which characters are relatively *round?* Which are relatively *flat?*

What are the qualities or characteristics of the characters?

Are any of the characters ambiguous, hard to figure?

Which characters are *static?* Which are *dynamic?*

What change do you see in the dynamic characters?

POINT OF VIEW

If there is a first-person narrator, is he or she essentially inside the story (a character) or outside it? Does the narrator serve essentially as a witness or as a substitute author?

What passages are presented from an *omniscient* point of view? Which from a *dramatic?* Which from a *limited?*

Does one character serve as the story's *center of consciousness?*

On balance, how would you characterize the point of view? Where would you put it on the point-of-view triangle?

How does consciousness of the point of view affect the way you read the story?

PLOT

How would you summarize the plot as a sequence of causes and effects?

Who is the protagonist of the story?

How would you summarize the plot in terms of the protagonist's *goal* and the *conflicts* he or she becomes involved with?

THEME

What are some statements about the human condition that seem to be suggested by the story?

Which of these statements seems best to match your understanding of the story?

SYMBOLISM

What are the principal symbols in the story?

What do you understand their meaning to be?

Answering these questions will not automatically give you an understanding of the story but will focus your attention on matters that may aid your understanding.

More important, the analysis may reveal a problem that makes your understanding of the narrative incomplete. With thought, such a problem can become an excellent topic for an essay. In fact, one way to search for a topic is to make a list of problems and then discuss the list with a classmate or other person who knows the narrative. If your classmate also finds one of your problems difficult, and if you think you can propose a solution that will improve his or her understanding, then you have probably found a promising paper topic. In writing your draft, remember that your essay is essentially an argument, that you must assemble evidence to back your assertions.

QUESTIONS FOR PEER REVIEW

When your draft is complete, you may benefit by having a peer reviewer answer the following questions:

1. Do I identify a problem that you, too, recognize as a problem? That is, have I found something in the narrative that has been an obstacle to your understanding?

2. Do I propose a solution to the problem that you find plausible? What aspects of my solution are most convincing? What aspects are least convincing?

3. Can you propose a better solution to the problem?

4. Is my argument based on a sound analysis of the narrative elements? If I have made mistakes about elements, what are they?

In addition to these questions, you may want your peer reviewer to answer the general questions on pp. 60–61.

Assignments
for Chapter 11

AN ANALYSIS OF A NARRATIVE

Choose one of the short stories or poems collected on pp. 440–457. Write a detailed analysis using the six narrative elements discussed in this chapter.

AN ESSAY ON A PROBLEM OF INTERPRETATION

After analyzing the narrative elements, write a short essay (500 to 750 words) in which you describe a problem of interpretation in a narrative and propose a solution to that problem. The following questions may serve as problems in themselves, or they may point you toward related problems:

1. What does Leslie Norris gain by having "Blackberries" begin with Mr. Frensham in his shop?

2. How does the point of view in "No One's a Mystery" affect the way the reader sees the relationship between Jack and the girl?

3. Who is the protagonist in "The Hammer Man" and what is the struggle?

4. Can we understand the true character of the Duchess in "My Last Duchess"?

5. Can we account for the suicide in "Richard Cory"?

6. How does the word *swerving* gain special significance in "Traveling Through the Dark"?

A PROBLEM ESSAY WITH SOURCES

A common assignment in literature classes requires you to refer to "outside" or "secondary" sources in a paper that interprets a story or poem. One way to approach such an essay is to begin with a statement of how one or more previous interpreters have attempted to solve the problem you discuss; then describe your own solution. This is the approach taken by Robert Keith Miller in "Mark Twain's Jim" (p. 453) and Charles R. Woodard in "Wilbur's 'Still, Citizen Sparrow'" (p. 456).

Write an essay on this pattern, addressing a problem in "My Last Duchess," "The Hammer Man," "Traveling Through the Dark" or another work that has received enough critical attention to allow you to find a critic interested in your problem. Valuable sources for locating such criticism are the *MLA International Bibliography of Books and Articles on the Modern Languages and Literatures, Contemporary Literary Criticism, Poetry Explication,* and *Twentieth-Century Poetry Explication.*

ASSIGNMENT 4: **A Study of the Effect of Context**

"The Blue Eyes," though Isak Dinesen sometimes recited it (from memory) as a separate story, was originally embedded in the larger story "Peter and Rosa" in her book *Winter's Tales.* Read "Peter and Rosa" and write an essay on the following question: how is our understanding of "The Blue Eyes" affected if we read it in the context of "Peter and Rosa"?

BLACKBERRIES

Leslie Norris

Welsh poet and short story writer Leslie Norris is a meticulous craftsman. As a poet, he once said, he works "slowly and with great pain," producing "about six poems a year." His fiction, too, seems to be the result of great patience, each word and image carefully weighed; three pages from him are likely to suggest more about the lives of his characters than a chapter by a looser novelist.

1   MR. FRENSHAM OPENED HIS SHOP AT eight-thirty, but it was past nine when the woman and the child went in. The shop was empty and there were no footmarks on the fresh sawdust shaken onto the floor. The child listened to the melancholy sound of the bell as the door closed behind him and he scuffed his feet in the yellow sawdust. Underneath, the boards were brown and worn, and dark knots stood up in them. He had never been in this shop before. He was going to have his hair cut for the first time in his life, except for the times when his mother had trimmed it gently behind his neck.

2   Mr. Frensham was sitting in a large chair, reading a newspaper. He could make the chair turn around, and he spun twice about in it before he put down his paper, smiled, and said, "Good morning."

3   He was an old man, thin, with flat white hair. He wore a white coat.

4   "One gentleman," he said, "to have his locks shorn."

5   He put a board across the two arms of his chair, lifted the child, and sat him on it.

6   "How are you, my dear? And your father, is he well?" he said to the child's mother.

7   He took a sheet from a cupboard on the wall and wrapped it about the child's neck, tucking it into his collar. The sheet covered the child completely and hung almost to the floor.

Cautiously the boy moved his hidden feet. He could see the bumps they made in the cloth. He moved his finger against the inner surface of the sheet and made a six with it, and then an eight. He liked those shapes.

8   "Snip, snip," said Mr. Frensham, "and how much does the gentleman want off? All of it? All his lovely curls? I think not."

9   "Just an ordinary cut, please, Mr. Frensham," said the child's mother, "not too much off. I, my husband and I, we thought it was time for him to look like a little boy. His hair grows so quickly."

10   Mr. Frensham's hands were very cold. His hard fingers turned the boy's head first to one side and then to the other and the boy could hear the long scissors snapping away behind him, and above his ears. He was quite frightened, but he liked watching the small tufts of his hair drop lightly on the sheet which covered him, and then roll an inch or two before they stopped. Some of the hair fell to the floor and by moving his hand surreptitiously he could make nearly all of it fall down. The hair fell without a sound. Tilting his head slightly, he could see the little bunches on the floor, not belonging to him any more.

11   "Easy to see who this boy is," Mr. Frensham said to the child's mother. "I won't get redder hair in the shop today. Your father had hair like this when he was young, very much

this color. I've cut your father's hair for fifty years. He's keeping well, you say? There, I think that's enough. We don't want him to dislike coming to see me."

12 He took the sheet off the child and flourished it hard before folding it and putting it on a shelf. He swept the back of the child's neck with a small brush. Nodding his own old head in admiration, he looked at the child's hair for flaws in the cutting.

13 "Very handsome," he said.

14 The child saw his face in a mirror. It looked pale and large, but also much the same as always. When he felt the back of his neck, the new short hairs stood up sharp against his hand.

15 "We're off to do some shopping," his mother said to Mr. Frensham as she handed him the money.

16 They were going to buy the boy a cap, a round cap with a little button on top and a peak over his eyes, like his cousin Harry's cap. The boy wanted the cap very much. He walked seriously beside his mother and he was not impatient even when she met Mrs. Lewis and talked to her, and then took a long time at the fruiterer's buying apples and potatoes.

17 "This is the smallest size we have," the man in the clothes shop said. "It may be too large for him."

18 "He's just had his hair cut," said his mother. "That should make a difference."

19 The man put the cap on the boy's head and stood back to look. It was a beautiful cap. The badge in front was shaped like a shield and it was red and blue. It was not too big, although the man could put two fingers under it, at the side of the boy's head.

20 "On the other hand, we don't want it too tight," the man said. "We want something he can grow into, something that will last him a long time."

21 "Oh, I hope so," his mother said. "It's expensive enough."

22 The boy carried the cap himself, in a brown paper bag that had "Price, Clothiers, High Street" on it. He could read it all except "Clothiers" and his mother told him that. They put his cap, still in its bag, in a drawer when they got home.

23 His father came home late in the afternoon. The boy heard the firm clap of the closing door and his father's long step down the hall. He leaned against his father's knee while the man ate his dinner. The meal had been keeping warm in the oven and the plate was very hot. A small steam was rising from the potatoes, and the gravy had dried to a thin crust where it was shallow at the side of the plate. The man lifted the dry gravy with his knife and fed it to his son, very carefully lifting it into the boy's mouth, as if he were feeding a small bird. The boy loved this. He loved the hot savor of his father's dinner, the way his father cut away small delicacies for him and fed them to him slowly. He leaned drowsily against his father's leg.

24 Afterwards he put on his cap and stood before his father, certain of the man's approval. The man put his hand on the boy's head and looked at him without smiling.

25 "On Sunday," he said, "we'll go for a walk. Just you and I. We'll be men together."

26 Although it was late in September, the sun was warm and the paths dry. The man and his boy walked beside the disused canal and powdery white dust covered their shoes. The boy thought of the days before he had been born, when the canal had been busy. He thought of the long boats pulled by solid horses, gliding through the water. In his head he listened to the hushed, wet noises they would have made, the soft waves slapping the banks, and green tench looking up as the barges moved above them, their water suddenly darkened. His grandfather had told him about that. But now the channel was filled with mud and tall reeds. Bullrush and watergrass grew in the damp passages. He borrowed his father's walking stick

and knocked the heads off a company of seeding dandelions, watching the tiny parachutes carry away their minute dark burdens.

27   "There they go," he said to himself. "There they go, sailing away to China."

28   "Come on," said his father, "or we'll never reach Fletcher's Woods."

29   The boy hurried after his father. He had never been to Fletcher's Woods. Once his father had heard a nightingale there. It had been in the summer, long ago, and his father had gone with his friends, to hear the singing bird. They had stood under a tree and listened. Then the moon went down and his father, stumbling home, had fallen into a blackberry bush.

30   "Will there be blackberries?" he asked.

31   "There should be," his father said. "I'll pick some for you."

32   In Fletcher's Woods there was shade beneath the trees, and sunlight, thrown in yellow patches onto the grass, seemed to grow out of the ground rather than come from the sky. The boy stepped from sunlight to sunlight, in and out of shadow. His father showed him a tangle of bramble, hard with thorns, its leaves just beginning to color into autumn, its long runners dry and brittle on the grass. Clusters of purple fruit hung in the branches. His father reached up and chose a blackberry for him. Its skin was plump and shining, each of its purple globes held a point of reflected light.

33   "You can eat it," his father said.

34   The boy put the blackberry in his mouth. He rolled it with his tongue, feeling its irregularity, and crushed it against the roof of his mouth. Released juice, sweet and warm as summer, ran down his throat, hard seeds cracked between his teeth. When he laughed his father saw that his mouth was deeply stained. Together they picked and ate the dark berries, until their lips were purple and their hands marked and scratched.

35   "We should take some for your mother," the man said.

36   He reached with his stick and pulled down high canes where the choicest berries grew, picking them to take home. They had nothing to carry them in, so the boy put his new cap on the grass and they filled its hollow with berries. He help the cap by its edges and they went home.

37   It was a stupid thing to do," his mother said, "utterly stupid.

38   What were you thinking of?"

39   The young man did not answer.

40   "If we had the money, it would be different," his mother said, "Where do you think the money comes from?"

41   "I know where the money comes from," his father said. "I work hard enough for it."

42   "His new cap," his mother said. "How am I to get him another?"

43   The cap lay on the table and by standing on tiptoe the boy could see it. Inside it was wet with the sticky juice of blackberries. Small pieces of blackberry skins were stuck to it. The stains were dark and irregular.

44   "It will probably dry out all right," his father said.

45   His mother's face was red and distorted, her voice shrill.

46   "If you had anything like a job," she shouted, "and could buy caps by the dozen, then—"

47   She stopped and shook her head. His father turned away, his mouth hard.

48   "I do what I can," he said.

49   "That's not much!" his mother said. She was tight with scorn. "You don't do much!"

50   Appalled, the child watched the quarrel mount and spread. He began to cry quietly, to himself, knowing that it was a different weeping to any he had experienced before, that he was crying for a different pain. And the child began to understand that they were different people; his father, his mother, himself, and that he must learn sometimes to be alone. ◆

NO ONE'S A MYSTERY

Elizabeth Tallent

During her undergraduate years at Illinois State University, Elizabeth Tallent considered becoming an archaeologist. That aspiration may help explain one aspect of her fiction: the way that physical objects—a beat-up truck, a diary with a broken lock, a bottle of tequila—become clues that help us reconstruct the lives of the people who have touched those things.

1   FOR MY EIGHTEENTH BIRTHDAY JACK GAVE me a five-year diary with a latch and a little key, light as a dime. I was sitting beside him scratching at the lock, which didn't want to work, when he thought he saw his wife's Cadillac in the distance, coming toward us. He pushed me down onto the dirty floor of the pickup and kept one hand on my head while I inhaled the musk of his cigarettes in the dashboard ashtray and sang along with Rosanne Cash on the tape deck. We'd been drinking tequila and the bottle was between his legs, resting up against his crotch, where the seam of his Levi's was bleached linen-white, though the Levi's were nearly new. I don't know why his Levi's always bleached like that, along the seams and at the knees. In a curve of cloth his zipper glinted, gold.

2   "It's her," he said. "She keeps the lights on in the daytime. I can't think of a single habit in a woman that irritates me more than that." When he saw that I was going to stay still he took his hand from my head and ran it through his own dark hair.

3   "Why does she?" I said.

4   "She thinks it's safer. Why does she need to be safer? She's driving exactly fifty-five miles an hour. She believes in those signs: 'Speed Monitored by Aircraft.' It doesn't matter that you can look up and see that the sky is empty."

5   "She'll see your lips move, Jack. She'll know you're talking to someone."

6   "She'll think I'm singing along with the radio."

7   He didn't lift his hand, just raised the fingers in salute while the pressure of his palm steadied the wheel, and I heard the Cadillac honk twice, musically; he was driving easily eighty miles an hour. I studied his boots. The elk heads stitched into the leather were bearded with frayed thread, the toes were scuffed, and there was a compact wedge of muddy manure between the heel and the sole—the same boots he'd been wearing for the two years I'd known him. On the tape deck Rosanne Cash sang, "Nobody's into me, no one's a mystery."

8   "Do you think she's getting famous because of who her daddy is or for herself?" Jack said.

9   "There are about a hundred pop tops on the floor, did you know that? Some little kid could cut a bare foot on one of these, Jack."

10   "No little kids get into this truck except for you."

11   "How come you let it get so dirty?"

12   "'How come,'" he mocked. "You even sound like a kid. You can get back into the seat now, if you want. She's not going to look over her shoulder and see you."

13   "How do you know?"

14   "I just know," he said. "Like I know I'm going to get meat loaf for supper. It's in the air. Like I know what you'll be writing in that diary."

15   "What will I be writing?" I knelt on my side of the seat and craned around to look at the butterfly of dust printed on my jeans. Outside the window Wyoming was dazzling in the heat. The wheat was fawn and yellow and

443

parted smoothly by the thin dirt road. I could smell the water in the irrigation ditches hidden in the wheat.

16   "Tonight you'll write, 'I love Jack. This is my birthday present from him. I can't imagine anybody loving anybody more than I love Jack.'"

17   "I can't."

18   "In a year you'll write, 'I wonder what I ever really saw in Jack. I wonder why I spent so many days just riding around in his pickup. It's true he taught me something about sex. It's true there wasn't ever much else to do in Cheyenne.'"

19   "I won't write that."

20   "In two years you'll write, 'I wonder what that old guy's name was, the one with the curly hair and the filthy dirty pickup truck and time on his hands.' "

21   "I won't write that."

22   "No?"

23   "Tonight I'll write, 'I love Jack. This is my birthday present from him. I can't imagine anybody loving anybody more than I love Jack.'"

24   "No, you can't," he says. "You can't imagine it."

25   "In a year I'll write, 'Jack should be home any minute now. The table's set—my grandmother's linen and her old silver and the yel-

low candles left over from the wedding—but I don't know if I can wait until after the trout *à la Navarra* to make love to him.'"

26   "It must have been a fast divorce."

27   "In two years I'll write, 'Jack should be home by now. Little Jack is hungry for his supper. He said his first word today besides "Mama" and "Papa." He said, "Caca." '"

28   Jack laughed. "He was probably trying to fingerpaint with caca on the bathroom wall when you heard him say it."

29   "In three years I'll write, 'My nipples are a little sore from nursing Eliza Rosamund.'"

30   "Rosamund. Every little girl should have a middle name she hates."

31   "'Her breath smells like vanilla and her eyes are just Jack's color of blue.'"

32   "That's nice," Jack said.

33   "So? Which one do you like?"

34   "I like yours," he said. "But I believe mine."

35   "It doesn't matter. I believe mine."

36   "Not in your heart of hearts, you don't."

37   "You're wrong."

38   "I'm not wrong," he said. "And her breath would smell like your milk, and it's kind of a bittersweet smell, if you want to know the truth." ◆

THE HAMMER MAN

Toni Cade Bambara

Toni Cade Bambara was born in New York City in 1939 and raised in Harlem and Bedford-Stuyvesant. A graduate of Queens College (B.A.) and City College of New York (M.A.), she began publishing stories in 1960. "The Hammer Man" first appeared in *The Negro Digest* in 1966 and was reprinted in *Gorilla, My Love* (1972).

1   I WAS GLAD TO HEAR THAT MANNY HAD fallen off the roof. I had put out the tale that I was down with yellow fever, but nobody paid me no mind, least of all Dirty Red who stomped right in to announce that Manny had fallen off the roof and that I could come out of hiding now. My mother dropped what she was doing, which was the laundry, and got the whole story out of Red. "Bad enough you gots to hang around with boys," she said. "But fight with them too. And you would pick the craziest one at that."

2   Manny was supposed to be crazy. That was his story. To say you were bad put some people off. But to say you were crazy, well you were officially not to be messed with. So that was his story. On the other hand, after I called him what I called him and said a few choice things about his mother, his face did go through some piercing changes. And I did kind of wonder if maybe he sure was nuts. I didn't wait to find out. I got in the wind. And then he waited for me on my stoop all day and all night, not hardly speaking to the people going in and out. And he was there all day Saturday, with his sister bringing him peanut-butter sandwiches and cream sodas. He must've gone to the bathroom right there cause every time I looked out the kitchen window, there he was. And Sunday, too. I got to thinking the boy was mad.

3   "You got no sense of humor, that's your trouble," I told him. He looked up, but he didn't say nothing. All at once I was real sorry about the whole thing. I should've settled for hitting off the little girls in the school yard, or waiting for Frankie to come in so we could raise some kind of hell. This way I had to play sick when my mother was around cause my father had already taken away my BB gun and hid it.

4   I don't know how they got Manny on the roof finally. Maybe the Wakefield kids, the ones who keep the pigeons, called him up. Manny was a sucker for sick animals and things like that. Or maybe Frankie got some nasty girls to go up on the roof with him and got Manny to join him. I don't know. Anyway, the catwalk had lost all its cement and the roof always did kind of slant downward. So Manny fell off the roof. I got over my yellow fever right quick, needless to say, and ventured outside. But by this time I had already told Miss Rose that Crazy Manny was after me. And Miss Rose, being who she was, quite naturally went over to Manny's house and said a few harsh words to his mother, who, being who she was, chased Miss Rose out into the street and they commenced to get with it, snatching bottles out of the garbage cans and breaking them on the johnny pumps and stuff like that.

5   Dirty Red didn't have to tell us about this. Everybody could see and hear all. I never figured the garbage cans for an arsenal, but Miss Rose came up with sticks and table legs and things, and Manny's mother had her share of scissor blades and bicycle chains. They got to rolling in the streets and all you could see was pink drawers and fat legs. It was something

445

else. Miss Rose is nutty but Manny's mother's crazier than Manny. They were at it a couple of times during my sick spell. Everyone would congregate on the window sills or the fire escape, commenting that it was still much too cold for this kind of nonsense. But they watched anyway. And then Manny fell off the roof. And that was that. Miss Rose went back to her dream books and Manny's mother went back to her tumbled-down kitchen of dirty clothes and bundles and bundles of rags and children.

6   My father got in on it too, cause he happened to ask Manny one night why he was sitting on the stoop like that every night. Manny told him right off that he was going to kill me first chance he got. Quite naturally this made my father a little warm, me being his only daughter and planning to become a doctor and take care of him in his old age. So he had a few words with Manny first, and then he got hold of the older brother, Bernard, who was more his size. Bernard didn't see how any of it was his business or my father's business, so my father got mad and jammed Bernard's head into the mailbox. Then my father started getting messages from Bernard's uncle about where to meet him for a showdown and all. My father didn't say a word to my mother all this time; just sat around mumbling and picking up the phone and putting it down, or grabbing my stickball bat and putting it back. He carried on like this for days till I thought I would scream if the yellow fever didn't have me so weak. And then Manny fell off the roof, and my father went back to his beer-drinking buddies.

7   I was in the school yard, pitching pennies with the little boys from the elementary school, when my friend Violet hits my brand-new Spaudeen over the wall. She came running back to tell me that Manny was coming down the block. I peeked beyond the fence and there he was all right. He had his head all wound up like a mummy and his arm in a sling and his legs in a cast. It looked phony to me, especially that walking cane. I figured Dirty Red had told

me a tale just to get me out there so Manny could stomp me, and Manny was playing it up with costume and all till he could get me.

8   "What happened to him?" Violet's sisters whispered. But I was too busy trying to figure out how this act was supposed to work. Then Manny passed real close to the fence and gave me a look.

9   "You had enough, Hammer Head," I yelled. "Just bring your crummy self in this yard and I'll pick up where I left off." Violet was knocked out and the other kids went into a huddle. I didn't have to say anything else. And when they all pressed me later, I just said, "You know that hammer he always carries in his fatigues?" And they'd all nod waiting for the rest of a long story. "Well, I took it away from him." And I walked off nonchalantly.

10   Manny stayed indoors for a long time. I almost forgot about him. New kids moved into the block and I got all caught up with that. And then Miss Rose finally hit the numbers and started ordering a whole lot of stuff through the mail and we would sit on the curb and watch these weird-looking packages being carried in, trying to figure out what simpleminded thing she had thrown her money away on when she might just as well wait for the warm weather and throw a block party for all her godchildren.

11   After a while a center opened up and my mother said she'd increase my allowance if I went and joined because I'd have to get out of my pants and stay in skirts, on account of that's the way things were at the center. So I joined and got to thinking about everything else but old Hammer Head. It was a rough place to get along in, the center, but my mother said that I needed to be be'd with and she needed to not be with me, so I went. And that time I sneaked into the office, that's when I really got turned on. I looked into one of those not-quite-white folders and saw that I was from a deviant family in a deviant neighborhood. I showed my mother the word in the

dictionary, but she didn't pay me no mind. It was my favorite word after that. I ran it in the ground till one day my father got the strap just to show how deviant he could get. So I gave up trying to improve my vocabulary. And I almost gave up my dungarees.

12   Then one night I'm walking past the Douglas Street park cause I got thrown out of the center for playing pool when I should've been sewing, even though I had already decided that this was going to be my last fling with boy things, and starting tomorow I was going to fix my hair right and wear skirts all the time just so my mother would stop talking about her gray hairs, and Miss Rose would stop calling me by my brother's name by mistake. So I'm walking past the park and there's ole Manny on the basketball court, perfecting his lay-ups and talking with himself. Being me, I quite naturally walk right up and ask what the hell he's doing playing in the dark, and he looks up and all around like the dark had crept up on him when he wasn't looking. So I knew right away that he'd been out there for a long time with his eyes just going along with the program.

13   "There was two seconds to go and we were one point behind," he said, shaking his head and staring at his sneakers like they was somebody. "And I was in the clear. I'd left the man in the backcourt and there I was, smiling, you dig, cause it was in the bag. They passed the ball and I slid the ball up nice and easy cause there was nothing to worry about. And . . ." He shook his head. "I muffed the goddamn shot. Ball bounced off the rim . . ." He stared at his hands. "The game of the season. Last game." And then he ignored me altogether, though he wasn't talking to me in the first place. He went back to the lay-ups, always from the same spot with his arms crooked in the same way, over and over. I must've gotten hypnotized cause I probably stood there for at least an hour watching like a fool till I couldn't even see the damn ball, much less the basket.

But I stood there anyway for no reason I know of. He never missed. But he cursed himself away. It was torture. And then a squad car pulled up and a short cop with hair like one of the Marx Brothers came out hitching up his pants. He looked real hard at me and then at Manny.

"What are you two doing?"   14

"He's doing a lay-up. I'm watching," I said   15
with my smart self.

Then the cop just stood there and finally   16
turned to the other one who was just getting out of the car.

"Who unlocked the gate?" the big one said.   17

"It's always unlocked," I said. Then we   18
three just stood there like a bunch of penguins watching Manny go at it.

"This on the level?" the big guy asked, tilt-   19
ing his hat back with the thumb the way big guys do in hot weather. "Hey you," he said, walking over to Manny. "I'm talking to you." He finally grabbed the ball to get Manny's attention. But that didn't work. Manny just stood there with his arms out waiting for the pass so he could save the game. He wasn't paying no mind to the cop. So, quite naturally, when the cop slapped him upside his head it was a surprise. And when the cop started counting three to go, Manny had already recovered from the slap and was just ticking off the seconds before the buzzer sounded and all was lost.

"Gimme the ball, man." Manny's face was   20
all tightened up and ready to pop.

"Did you hear what I said, black boy?"   21

Now, when somebody says that word like   22
that, I gets warm. And crazy or no crazy, Manny was my brother at that moment and the cop was the enemy.

"You better give him back his ball," I said.   23
"Manny don't take no mess from no cops. He ain't bothering nobody. He's gonna be Mister Basketball when he grows up. Just trying to get a little practice in before the softball season starts."

"Look here, sister, we'll run you in too,"   24
Harpo said.

25   "I damn sure can't be your sister seeing how I'm a black girl. Boy, I sure will be glad when you run me in so I can tell everybody about that. You must think you're in the South, mister."

26   The big guy screwed his mouth up and let one of them hard-day sighs. "The park's closed, little girl, so why don't you and your boyfriend go on home."

27   That really got me. The "little girl" was bad enough but that "boyfriend" was too much. But I kept cool, mostly because Manny looked so pitiful waiting there with his hands in a time-out and there being no one to stop the clock. But I kept my cool mostly cause of that hammer in Manny's pocket and no telling how frantic things can get what with a bigmouth like me, a couple of wise cops, and a crazy boy too.

28   "The gates are open," I said real quiet-like, "and this here's a free country. So why don't you give him back his ball?"

29   The big cop did another one of those sighs, his specialty I guess, and then he bounced the ball to Manny who went right into his gliding thing clear up to the backboard, damn near like he was some kind of very beautiful bird. And then he swooshed that ball in, even if there was no net, and your couldn't really hear the swoosh. Something happened to the bones in my chest. It was something.

30   "Crazy kids anyhow," the one with the wig said and turned to go. But the big guy watched Manny for a while and I guess something must've snapped in his head, cause all of a sudden he was hot for taking Manny to jail or court or somewhere and started yelling at him and everything, which is a bad thing to do to Manny, I can tell you. And I'm standing there thinking that none of my teachers, from kindergarten right on up, none of them knew what they were talking about. I'll be damned if I ever knew one of them rosy-cheeked cops that smiled and helped you get to school without neither you or your little raggedy dog getting hit by a truck that had a smile on its face, too. Not that I ever believed it. I knew Dick and

Jane was full of crap from the get-go, especially them cops. Like this dude, for example, pulling on Manny's clothes like that when obviously he had just done about the most beautiful thing a man can do and not be a fag. No cop could swoosh without a net.

31   "Look out, man," was all Manny said, but it was the way he pushed the cop that started the real yelling and threats. And I thought to myself, Oh God here I am trying to change my ways, and not talk back in school, and do like my mother wants, but just have this last fling, and now this—getting shot in the stomach and bleeding to death in Douglas Street park and poor Manny getting pistol-whipped by those bastards and whatnot. I could see it all, practically crying too. And it just wasn't no kind of thing to happen to a small child like me with my confirmation picture in the paper next to my weeping parents and schoolmates. I could feel the blood sticking to my shirt and my eyeballs slipping away, and then that confirmation picture again; and my mother and her gray hair; and Miss Rose heading for the precinct with a shotgun; and my father getting old and feeble with no one to doctor him up and all.

32   And I wished Manny had fallen off the damn roof and died right then and there and saved me all this aggravation of being killed with him by these cops who surely didn't come out of no fifth-grade reader. But it didn't happen. They just took the ball and Manny followed them real quiet-like right out of the park into the dark, then into the squad car with his head drooping and his arms in a crook. And I went on home cause what the hell am I going to do on a basketball court, and it getting to be nearly midnight?

33   I didn't see Manny no more after he got into that squad car. But they didn't kill him after all cause Miss Rose heard he was in some kind of big house for people who lose their marbles. And then it was spring finally, and me and Violet was in this very boss fashion show at the center. And Miss Rose bought me my first corsage—yellow roses to match my shoes. ♦

My Last Duchess

Robert Browning

Robert Browning (1812–89) was one of the dominant English poets of the Victorian era. His most remarkable poems are dramatic monologues–poems in which a single speaker reveals setting, conflict, and character. Since the character is talking to another character rather than to the audience, the reader seems to overhear the monologue, and interpreting it presents the reader with the challenge of recreating the context in which it would have taken place. "My Last Duchess" first appeared in *Dramatic Lyrics* (1842).

Ferrara[1]

1   That's my last duchess painted on the wall,
    Looking as if she were alive. I call
    That piece a wonder, now: Frà Pandolf's[2] hands
    Worked busily a day, and there she stands.
5   Will't please you sit and look at her? I said
    "Fra Pandolf" by design, for never read
    Strangers like you that pictured countenance,
    The depth and passion of its earnest glance,
    But to myself they turned (since none puts by
10 The curtain I have drawn for you, but I)
    And seemed as they would ask me, if they durst,
    How such a glance came there; so, not the first
    Are you to turn and ask thus. Sir, 'twas not
    Her husband's presence only, called that spot
15 Of joy into the Duchess' cheek: perhaps
    Frà Pandolf chanced to say "Her mantle laps
    Over my lady's wrist too much," or "Paint
    Must never hope to reproduce the faint
    Half-flush that dies along her throat": such stuff
20 Was courtesy, she thought, and cause enough
    For calling up that spot of joy. She had
    A heart—how shall I say?—too soon made glad,
    Too easily impressed; she liked whate'er
    She looked on, and her looks went everywhere.

---

[1] **Ferrara:** a center of culture during the early Italian Renaissance.

[2] **Frà Pandolf:** an imaginary artist, intended to represent a number of early Renaissance painters; "Fra" (brother) was the title given to monks and friars.

25 Sir, 'twas all one! My favor at her breast,
  The dropping of the daylight in the West,
  The bough of cherries some officious fool
  Broke in the orchard for her, the white mule
  She rode with round the terrace—all and each
30 Would draw from her alike the approving speech,
  Or blush, at least. She thanked men—good! but thanked
  Somehow—I know not how—as if she ranked
  My gift of a nine-hundred-years-old name
  With anybody's gift. Who'd stoop to blame
35 This sort of trifling? Even had you skill
  In speech—which I have not—to make your will
  Quite clear to such an one, and say, "Just this
  Or that in you disgusts me; here you miss,
  Or there exceed the mark"—and if she let
40 Herself be lessoned so, nor plainly set
  Her wits to yours, forsooth, and made excuse,
  —E'en then would be some stooping; and I choose
  Never to stoop. Oh sir, she smiled, no doubt,
  Whene'er I passed her; but who passed without
45 Much the same smile? This grew; I gave commands;
  Then all smiles stopped together. There she stands
  As if alive. Will't please you rise? We'll meet
  The company below, then. I repeat,
  The Count your master's known munificence
50 Is ample warrant that no just pretense
  Of mine for dowry will be disallowed;
  Though his fair daughter's self, as I avowed
  At starting, is my object. Nay, we'll go
  Together down, sir. Notice Neptune,[3] though,
56 Taming a sea-horse, thought a rarity,
  Which Claus of Innsbruck[4] cast in bronze for me! ◆

---

[3] **Neptune:** in Roman mythology, the god of the sea.
[4] **Claus of Innsbruck:** another imaginary artist.

RICHARD CORY

Edwin Arlington Robinson

Edwin Arlington Robinson (1869–1935), an American poet best known for his long narrative poems and for his shorter psychological portraits of New England characters, published "Richard Cory" in his book *The Children of the Night* (1897).

1   Whenever Richard Cory went downtown,
We people on the pavement looked at him:
He was a gentleman from sole to crown,
Clean favored, and imperially slim.

5   And he was always quietly arrayed,
     And he was always human when he talked;
But still he fluttered pulses when he said,
     "Good-morning," and he glittered when he walked.

And he was rich—yes, richer than a king,
10   And admirably schooled in every grace:
In fine, we thought that he was everything
     To make us wish that we were in his place.

So on we worked, and waited for the light,
     And went without the meat, and cursed the bread;
15 And Richard Cory, one calm summer night,
     Went home and put a bullet through his head. ◆

Traveling Through the Dark

William Stafford

Compact with meanings like all good poems, "Traveling Through the Dark" is at the same time a story. Using all the elements discussed in this chapter, Stafford manages a complete narrative—and a complete statement of values—in less than 150 words.

1 Traveling through the dark I found a deer
 dead on the edge of the Wilson River Road.
 It is usually best to roll them into the canyon:
 that road is narrow; to swerve might make more dead.

5 By glow of the tail-light I stumbled back of the car
 and stood by the heap, a doe, a recent killing;
 she had stiffened already, almost cold.
 I dragged her off; she was large in the belly.

 My fingers touching her side brought me the reason—
10 her side was warm; her fawn lay there waiting,
 alive, still, never to be born.
 Beside that mountain road I hesitated.

 The car aimed ahead its lowered parking lights;
 under the hood purred the steady engine.
15 I stood in the glare of the warm exhaust turning red;
 around our group I could hear the wilderness listen.

 I thought hard for all of us—my only swerving—,
 then pushed her over the edge into the river. ◆

MARK TWAIN'S JIM

Robert Keith Miller

Robert Keith Miller is a professor of English at the University of Wisconsin—Stevens Point. He is a frequent contributor to scholarly journals, newspapers, and popular magazines. He is also the author of books on Oscar Wilde and Mark Twain. The following selection from *Mark Twain* (1983) deals with the question of how Twain has portrayed Jim, the runaway slave and faithful companion in *Huckleberry Finn*.

1 IF MODERN CRITICS HAVE BEEN APT TO TAKE Huck too seriously, they have tended to do the same with Jim, celebrating him as a larger-than-life figure. According to Roger Salomon, both Huck and Jim "are related to the demigods of the river, to the barbarous primitivism of the Negro, and beyond that to the archetypal primitives of the Golden Age, instinctively good, uncorrupted by reason, living close to nature and more influenced by its portents than by the conventions of civilization." James Cox is only slightly more moderate. Describing Jim as "the conscience of the novel, the spiritual yardstick by which all men are measured," Cox also turns Jim into a walking myth—the "great residue of primitive, fertile force." So pervasive is this trend that other critics have even praised Jim for being superstitious. Walter Blair believes that when Jim speaks of witches, his "soaring improvisations prove his mastery of supernatural lore." And Gladys Bellamy sounds almost infatuated, admiring Jim for his "manly qualities" and the "dark knowledge that lies in his blood and his nerve ends."

2 There can be no question that Twain intended his readers to feel sympathetic toward Jim. The runaway slave plays a vital role in helping Huck survive. Although it is Huck who discovers the cave on Jackson's Island, it is Jim who insists they make their camp within it, pointing out that it is going to rain. Jim is proved right; it soon begins to rain "like all fury," and Huck is delighted to be comfortably settled in the cave. "Jim, this is nice," he says. "I wouldn't want to be nowhere else but here." And Jim responds by reminding Huck—and the reader—that he is responsible for their well being:

> Well, you wouldn't a ben here, 'f it hadn't a ben for Jim. You'd a ben down dah in de woods widout any dinner, en gittin' mos' drownded, too, dat you would, honey.

3 In a manner of speaking, Jim has provided a home for Huck—something he does once again, after they have left the island for the raft. It is Jim who builds a shelter on the raft, protecting them from bad weather and the lapping of the waves. He knows how to do things and is experienced in the art of survival.

4 Moreover, his loyalty and kindness are remarkable in a book populated mostly with scoundrels. He remains faithful to Huck throughout the book—and, at the end, he is loyal even to Tom Sawyer, a boy who has done nothing but injure him during the last several weeks. And the text makes it clear that Jim is deeply attached to his children. Huck tells us:

> I went to sleep, and Jim didn't call me when it was my turn. He often done that. When I waked up, just at day-break, he was setting there with his head down betwixt his knees, moaning and mourning to himself. I didn't take notice, nor let on. I knowed what it was about. He was thinking about his wife

453

and his children, away up yonder, and he was low and homesick; because he hadn't ever been away from home before in his life; and I do believe he cared just as much for his people as white folks does for their'n. It does not seem natural, but I reckon it's so. He was often moaning and mourning, that way, nights, when he judged I was asleep, and saying, "Po' little 'Lizabeth! po' little Johnny! it's mighty hard; I spec' I ain't ever gwyne to see you no mo'!" He was a mighty good nigger, Jim was.

5   The carefully controlled understatement of Huck's closing line helps drive the point home. Jim is indeed "mighty good."

6   Nonetheless, Jim is portrayed as being extraordinarily gullible and something of a comic figure. Back in St. Petersburg, Jim had been a local celebrity by virtue of his account of how witches had put him in a trance and rode him all over the state. Every time Jim tells his story, it becomes increasingly dramatic. The origin of the tale could hardly be more trivial: Jim had wakened one night to find his hat hanging from a tree—where it had been placed by Tom Sawyer as a practical joke. But he seems to believe his own, more colorful version:

> Jim was monstrous proud about it, and he got so he wouldn't hardly notice the other niggers. Niggers would come from miles to hear Jim tell about it, and he was more looked up to than any nigger in that country. . . . Niggers is always talking about witches in the dark by the kitchen fire; but whenever one was talking and letting on to know all about such things, Jim would happen in and say, "Hm! What you know 'bout witches?" and that nigger was corked up and had to take a back seat. . . . Jim was most ruined, for a servant, because he got so stuck up on account of having seen the devil and been rode by witches.

7   Surely there is nothing admirable about be-

lieving in witchcraft and turning one's delusions into a source of pride. So far from being some sort of wonderful "dark knowledge" worthy of our respect, Jim's belief in witches makes him look foolish. It also links him to the slave on the Phelps plantation who brings him his meals, a pathetic character, with a "chuckle-headed face, and his wool . . . all tied up in little bunches with thread," who is convinced that witches are always after him. Twain's humor is at Jim's expense.

8   More seriously, Jim's passive acceptance of his imprisonment on the Phelps plantation, and his foolish toleration of the punishment the boys inflict upon him, are both perfectly consistent with his behavior throughout the novel. He seems to have been exhausted by his one bold action—his flight to Jackson's Island. Thereafter, he drifts down the river, taking orders from a fourteen-year-old boy and willingly dressing up as "a sick Arab" when told to do so. Although he knows how to cook catfish and make corn bread, he is ultimately helpless when it comes to asserting himself and realizing his own escape from bondage. He entrusts himself to Huck, and when they drift past Cairo—all too significantly—he accepts the situation with disappointing ease.

9   Jim's willingness to go along with the absurdities of Tom Sawyer's grand "evasion" should therefore come as no surprise to critics. Jim has been "going along" throughout most of the book. Had Twain meant Jim to be the hero of the novel, he would have allowed him to escape as the result of his own ingenuity—or at least through Huck's, since Huck is, to an extent, his adopted son. But the ending of *Huckleberry Finn* makes it clear that Jim's flight down the Mississippi lacked any real meaning. Jim has been free for months—not by virtue of his own action, but by the unexpected generosity of Miss Watson. Here is the ultimate indignity. To picture Jim in the last few scenes of the novel is to picture a man dressed in woman's clothing who is about to

discover that he owes his life to the kindness of the mistress he betrayed. But Jim shows no resentment, not even any embarrassment. When Tom Sawyer pays him forty dollars for his trouble, he is absolutely delighted. "*I tole you I bin rich wunst,*" he happily proclaims, "en gwineter to be rich *agin;* en it's come true; en heah she *is!*" The modern reader may be forgiven for wishing that Jim had told all those nice white folk to go to hell. Instead, he dances off the stage like a jolly buffoon, the comic Negro from a nineteenth-century minstrel show.

10   This conclusion would have been inconceivable if Twain had intended the work to celebrate Jim. It is true that Twain was bitterly opposed to slavery. But by the time he wrote *Huckleberry Finn,* he had come to think little of men in general, referring frequently to "the damned human race." Because he considered slavery to be cruel and unjust, it does not follow that he believed the slave superior to the master. Jim has definite limitations. And when Huck bestows upon him his highest praise, saying that he knew Jim was "white inside," it comes as a distinctly mixed blessing in a novel populated with extraordinarily disagreeable whites. Rather than reading *Huckleberry Finn* as a tribute to "the barbarous primitivism of the Negro," and then complaining that Twain wrote a conclusion that betrayed this interpretation, it would be more accurate to see the work as denying any fundamental difference between white and black, by revealing that both are subject to the same follies. . . . ◆

WILBUR'S
"STILL, CITIZEN SPARROW"

Charles R. Woodard

Richard Wilbur is one of America's leading contemporary poets, a winner of both the Pulitzer Prize and the National Book Award. "Still, Citizen Sparrow" is from his 1950 book, *Ceremony and Other Poems*. Charles R. Woodard, a professor at the University of Alabama in Huntsville, published the following essay on Wilbur's poem in *The Explicator*, February 1976.

STILL, CITIZEN SPARROW

Still, citizen sparrow, this Vulture which you call
Unnatural, let him but lumber again to air
Over the rotten office, let him bear
The carrion ballast up, and at the tall

Tip of the sky lie cruising. Then you'll see
That no more beautiful bird is in heaven's height,
No wider more placid wings, no watchfuller
   flight;
He shoulders nature there, the frightfully free,

The naked-headed one. Pardon him, you
Who dart in the orchard aisles, for it is he
Devours death, mocks mutability,
Has heart to make an end, keeps nature new.

Thinking of Noah, childheart, try to forget
How for so many bedlam hours his saw
Soured the song of birds with its wheezy gnaw,
And the slam of his hammer all the day beset

The people's ears. Forget that he could bear
to see the towns like coral under the keel,
And the fields so dismal deep. Try rather to feel
How high and weary it was, on the waters where

He rocked his only world, and everyone's.
Forgive the hero, you who would have died
Gladly with all you knew; he rode that tide
To Ararat; all men are Noah's sons.

—RICHARD WILBUR

RICHARD WILBUR'S "STILL, CITIZEN Sparrow" has given great difficulty to a majority of those readers who have discussed it in print. By general agreement the poem has come to be seen as in some way a commentary upon politics, with the vulture taken to be representative of rotten politicians who are yet somehow superior to the tame "citizen sparrows" who elect them. A careful scrutiny of the language, however, makes it difficult to sustain such an interpretation. The chief stumbling block in the first half of the poem is the phrase "rotten office," which has regularly been taken to refer to corrupt political office. Donald L. Hill, in his book *Richard Wilbur* (New York: Twayne Publishers, 1967), sees the vulture as "a certain political leader, now out of office," who is "unnatural, a monster." The poet, he continues, "defends this vulture, arguing that if he can be given a chance to climb again to the altitude where he is at home, he will be both beautiful and powerful" (p. 72).

Such a reading leads one immediately into

difficulty with the phrase "carrion ballast," however; Hill is puzzled but assumes that it is to be equated with "rotten office" (p. 72). In fact the poem is best understood if we take the word *office* to mean not a post or position but "performance of a duty or function, service, etc." (*The Shorter Oxford English Dictionary*). Wilbur, who has repeatedly affirmed his dedication to the "things of this world," has his eye on the vulture *as* vulture, not as symbol. It is its "office" or function to consume the "rotten," quite literally carrion, with which it is laden or "ballasted" in flight; the image in the first stanza is the quite explicit one of the ungainly vulture's cumbersome launching of himself into the air after feeding. Despite this unsavory function, as the home-keeping bourgeois "citizen" sparrow sees it, the vulture once aloft is a bird of surpassing beauty and freedom, superior to the sparrow in that its function as scavenger is to "keep nature new" through its digestion of carrion.

3   The second part of the poem, seemingly without transition, switches to Noah. The Wilbur is drawing an implied comparison between Noah and the vulture seems inescapable; as the vulture's wings rock on the buoying air far above the range of the disapproving sparrows, so Noah's ark rocked, borne up by water, far above the towns and fields of his disapproving neighbors. The attempt to read an exclusively political import into the poem is most likely to break down here, for Noah is in no sense a politician, certainly not a corrupt one, nor is he simply representative of some Carlylean[1] "hero" or strong man. The vulture and Noah are not characters in an allegory; rather they are the two terms in a comparison sufficiently far-fetched to constitute a conceit. An object of displeasure to his sparrow-like neighbors, Noah had the courage to endure loneliness, to "mock mutability" and keep nature's species alive. We are all his copies, bearing the saved essence of the past on the rising flood of time. If Noah's heroism must be seen in symbolic terms, it is not that of the politician but of the artist, attempting through his work to hold off the flood of man's mortality. ◆

---

[1] **Carlylean:** in *On Heroes, Hero-Worship and the Heroic in History* (1841), Thomas Carlyle (1795–1881) suggests that the strongest and best will rise to the top and should serve as the leaders in war, society, religion, education, and the arts.

12 Reviews and Evaluations

THE NEIGHBOR GIRLS, SEVEN-YEAR-OLD HAILEY W. AND HER THREE-year-old sister Allison, appeared at our door one day carrying a videotape of *Little Nemo's Adventures in Slumberland*, which Hailey described as "a *really* good movie." They sat down in front of the television with our daughter Kate—not yet three—and began to watch the feature-length cartoon. As it turned out, the "adventures" consist of nightmares. Over and over, just at the moment when a train is running over him or a monster is grabbing at his ankles, little Nemo wakes in his bedroom relieved that "it was only a dream." Then he discovers that he hasn't escaped at all. The monster is in the room with him; it all starts again. The nightmare is *real*. I assume that there is a happy ending, but we never got that far. Half an hour from the start, Kate was screaming for me to shut the movie off, and Allison (who had been having nightmares lately) was saucer-eyed. Hailey was grinning like a daredevil who has managed to keep her hands in the air all through a dip on the roller coaster.

Was Hailey right? Was this a really good movie? For her, it may have been. Action-packed and reasonably well drawn, it made her heart pound in the scary parts and, I suspect, gave her the satisfaction of dealing safely with fears she was beginning to overcome. But for Kate and Allison, it was a terrible movie, worse probably than many films with "adult" ratings. It seems calculated to instill the night terrors that can make three-year-olds fear the dark and wake up screaming.

I begin with this story because it reveals something about the difficulties of evaluation. Seven-year-olds are unreliable and uninteresting critics because to them *good* means no more than "fun for me" and *bad* often means no more than "boring for me." No one entirely outgrows this kind of self-centered, unreflective reaction, but more sophisticated critics complicate it with questions seven-year-olds are not likely to ask:

1. *Why might other people react to this movie (or book or gadget or college) differently than I do?* Until you are aware that others' judgments will differ from yours, you have no reason to take pains explaining your views.

2. *How can I explain my judgment of the thing to people who judge it differently?* Explaining your evaluation to people who have evaluated the thing quite differently can create intriguing difficulties. Often it forces you to examine logically reactions that you have never before exposed to the light of reason.

3. *Can I articulate the standards that guided my judgment?* The most striking difference between the snap judgments of seven-year-olds and the mature evaluations of adults is that adults will appeal to standards that go beyond "fun for me." In his reviews of serious films, Roger Ebert, perhaps the most influential movie critic in America, applies a standard beyond any seven-year-old's range: "Does this film expand or devalue my information about human nature?"

4. *How are those standards related to my deeper beliefs about what constitutes good work, good behavior, or the good life?* Deciding whether you prefer Dove Bars to Eskimo Pies is not likely to lead to much soul-searching. Sometimes, however, the reasons that you like or dislike a thing are deeply tied up with your whole system of values—artistic, ethical, even religious or political. When this is true, you may be eager to write in a way that shows readers how much is at stake in whether they judge this thing good or bad.

5. *Is it important that I persuade others to evaluate the thing as I do?* It may not be. Sometimes it is enough to explain your views to people who will never share them. On occasion, however, you may discover in yourself an urge to make readers see things your way. Some Arab-Americans, for instance, were so profoundly offended by the presentation of Arabian culture as "barbaric" in *Aladdin* that they wrote scathing denunciations of the movie. Eventually the Disney studios toned down the most offensive lyrics.

To help you recognize some possibilities open to you when you write your own evaluations, this chapter will begin by examining three types. We'll begin with a pair of "crusading" evaluations—ones where the writer has strong social or political views and uses the evaluation as an opportunity to advance those views. Then we will look at a consumer-product evaluation—one where the writer is much more concerned about giving information to potential buyers than in promoting a cause. Finally, we will look at movie and book reviews, written partly to help readers decide whether to buy a ticket (or a copy) and partly to help them see where the goodness (or badness) of the thing lies.

A Crusading Evaluation from an Environmentalist

When Wendell Berry published the following evaluation of personal computers in *Harper's* magazine, it produced a lively debate about the ethics of being a responsible consumer. Berry, a professional writer, also works a hundred-acre Kentucky farm whose soil was at one time ruined by greedy, short-sighted farming practices. Near his farm lies other farmland destroyed by the strip-mining that produces the coal that produces most of America's electrical power. A good deal of Berry's physical and literary labor goes into undoing the damage created by the consumer society around him. "That I live every hour of every day in an environmental crisis," he says, "I know from all my senses. Why then is it not my duty to reduce, so far as I can, my own consumption?" These facts about Berry's life and views may help you appreciate the framework of his evaluation.

"Why I Am Not Going to Buy a Computer"
WENDELL BERRY

Like almost everybody else, I am hooked to the energy corporations, which I do not admire. I hope to become less hooked to them. In my work, I try to be as little hooked to them as possible. As a farmer, I do almost all of my work with horses. As a writer, I work with a pencil or a pen and a piece of paper.

My wife types my work on a Royal standard typewriter bought new in 1956, and as good now as it was then. As she types, she sees things that are wrong, and marks them with small checks in the margins. She is my best critic because she is the one most familiar with my habitual errors and weaknesses. She also understands, sometimes better than I do, what *ought* to be said. We have, I think, a literary cottage industry that works well and pleasantly. I do not see anything wrong with it.

A number of people, by now, have told me that I could improve things greatly by buying a computer. My answer is that I'm not going to do it. I have several reasons, and they are good ones.

The first is the one I mentioned at the beginning. I would hate to think that my work as a writer could not be done without a direct dependence on strip-mined coal. How could I write conscientiously against the rape of nature if I were, in the act of writing, implicated in the rape? For the same reason, it matters to me that my writing is done in the daytime, without electric light.

I do not admire the computer manufacturers a great deal more than I admire the energy industries. I have seen their advertisements, attempting to seduce struggling or failing farmers into the belief that they can solve their problems by buying yet another piece of expensive equipment. I am familiar with their propaganda campaigns that have put computers into public schools in need of books. That computers are expected to become as common as TV sets in "the future" does not impress me or matter to me. I do not own a TV set. I do not see that computers are bringing us one step nearer to anything that does matter to me: peace, economic justice, ecological health, political honesty, family and community stability, good work.

What would a computer cost me? More money, for one thing, than I can afford, and more than I wish to pay to people whom I do not admire. But the cost would not be just monetary. It is well understood that technological innovation always requires the discarding of the "old model"—the "old model" in this case being not just our old Royal standard, but my wife, my critic, my closest reader, my fellow worker. Thus (and I think this is typical of present day technological innovation), what would be superseded would be not only some thing, but some body. In order to be technologically up-to-date as a writer, I would have to sacrifice an association that I am dependent upon and that I treasure.

My final and perhaps my best reason for not owning a computer is that I do not wish to fool myself. I disbelieve, and therefore strongly resent, the assertion that I or anybody else could write better or more easily with a computer than with a pencil. I do not see why I should not be as scientific about this as the next fellow: When somebody has used a computer to write work that is demonstrably better than Dante's, and when this better is demonstrably attributable to the use of a computer, then I will speak of computers with a more respectful tone of voice, though I still will not buy one.

To make myself as plain as I can, I should give my standards for technological innovation in my own work. They are as follows:

1. The new tool should be cheaper than the one it replaces.
2. It should be at least as small in scale as the one it replaces.
3. It should do work that is clearly and demonstrably better than the one it replaces.
4. It should use less energy than the one it replaces.
5. If possible, it should use some form of solar energy, such as that of the body.
6. It should be repairable by a person of ordinary intelligence, provided that he or she has the necessary tools.
7. It should be purchasable and repairable as near to home as possible.
8. It should come from a small, privately-owned shop or store that will take it back for maintenance and repair.
9. It should not replace or disrupt anything good that already exists, and this includes family and community relationships.

As Berry's essay demonstrates, a crusading evaluation can show the reader the connection between a product and a framework of values. When we choose computers over manual typewriters, we *are* choosing electricity (and electrical power plants) over handwork. We are choosing to eliminate not only the labor of typing from manuscript, but also the jobs of some typists. We are choosing change over custom. We are very likely choosing the purchase of a new product over the continued use of an old one. These choices may seem so natural to us that we aren't *aware* of making them, of course, and one of the best reasons for writing and reading evaluations is to bring unconscious choices to the surface so that they can be consciously scrutinized.

EXERCISE 1

◆ *A Rejoinder to Berry.* Few Americans these days share Wendell Berry's negative evaluation of the personal computer. One *Harper's* subscriber, in fact, said that he "enjoyed reading Berry's declaration of intent never to buy a personal computer in the same way that I enjoy reading about the belief systems of unfamiliar tribal cultures." On behalf of those who prefer the new writing technology to the old, respond to Berry's essay with a more favorable evaluation of the personal computer. Try, like Berry, to make the standards on which you base your evaluation perfectly clear: you may want to include a numbered list like his.

A Crusading Evaluation from a Communitarian

Like several other liberal journalists of the 1990s, Beth Austin resists the American tendency to see life as an essentially private, individual struggle for success and happiness. She encourages readers instead to turn their attention outward, beyond themselves and their families, to pay attention to what is happening to their communities. In "Pretty Worthless," a long article in *Washington Monthly,* she criticizes the filmmakers of the early 1990s because they "confused niceness with morality and ended up creating a moral universe that stops at the front door." The following excerpt focuses criticism on *Pretty Woman.*

A WRITER AT WORK

"Pretty Worthless"
BETH AUSTIN

In the 1954 film *On the Waterfront,* Marlon Brando plays a dockworker named Terry Malloy whose brother is in cahoots with the vicious leader of the dockworkers' local. Although he resists falling in with the crooks, Terry also has no interest in trying to stop them. When an investigator from the crime commission tries to question him, Terry more or less sums up his philosophy of life: "I don't know nothin', I ain't seen nothin', an' I ain't sayin' nothin'."

Enter Edie (Eva Marie Saint). She's educated and has a shot at escaping the docks; if she falls for Terry, she probably never will. But much more threatening to the relationship than Terry's lack of money or brains are Edie's weird ideas. She's putting herself on the line to clean up the waterfront, and she expects no less from Terry. "Shouldn't everybody care about everybody else?" she asks him. He looks amazed. "Boy," he observes, "are you a fruitcake."

As *On the Waterfront* amply demonstrates, Hollywood has never been a hotbed of complex moral thinking. But the past few years have seen a dramatic narrowing of the issues and themes addressed in the movies. . . . [Y]ou don't have to be a graduate of NYU film school to see that the warm, fuzzy movies celebrating friendship, family, and the occasional dog are also lacking morally. In fact, as a moviegoer—and a wife and a mother and a journalist—I find them not just empty, but insidious, because they leave us feeling so good about our insulated selves. The redoubtable Edie would never have settled for such moral interior decorating, as Terry learns to his peril. She flings his offer of a mere relationship right back in his face: "No wonder everybody calls you a bum."

He pursues her, bewildered. "I'm only trying to help you out. I'm trying to keep you from getting hurt," Terry mumbles. "What more do you want me to do?"

"Much more," Edie fires back, almost snarling, "much, much, much more."

. . .

Getting the girl—in other words, doing the right thing—almost costs Terry his life, but by the time 1990's number two movie, *Pretty Woman,* rolled around, the price of a heroine had dropped to $300. Richard Gere—whose ambition is not to work on the docks but to own a shipyard—at first wins the girl, Julia Roberts, by, literally, paying for her. But keeping her, in both senses of the word, is another matter. Like Edie, Roberts wants much more from her man than he is prepared to deliver—but what, exactly? Good legislation? The defenestration of a corrupt union boss? No. She wants "the fairy tale." Roberts's mission is to use her feminine softness and her unstinting sexual healing to turn Gere from a cold corporate raider into a creative entrepreneur and a family man. To its credit, the movie drives home the lesson that Gere's work is not only worthless but dehumanizing. . . . Roberts sets her man straight (at the same time helping him get over his resentment of his capitalist dad). But making the right career move still isn't enough for Gere to win Roberts. He has to realize he doesn't want to live without her and then *commit.*

Gere may turn to more productive work, but he doesn't sacrifice one thread of his thousand-dollar suits—which is fortunate, since, to deliver the fairy tale, he has to prove over and over again that he's Roberts's knight in platinum armor. He changes for her and he fights for her, but in the movie's most thrilling moments, he's always buying for her. He lifts her up from the slums to a luxury suite with a sweeping view. He decks her out in jewels and whisks her away in a private jet to San Francisco for the opera. With his invincible credit card, he vanquishes shopkeepers for her along Rodeo Drive, scooping up every item in sight as Roberts's smiles (and eyes) grow bigger and bigger. Eventually, he chases after her to carry her off—in a silver stretch limousine.

It's a nice nineties fairy tale, but don't try this at home. Today's movies show boys what it takes to win a girl in much the same way Steve Martin famously advised Americans on "How to be a Millionaire and Never Pay Taxes": "First," he said, "get a million dollars." "You know what's wrong with our waterfront?" cries Karl Malden, playing a Catholic priest also shamed by Edie into doing the right thing by the dockworkers. "It's the love of a lousy buck. It's making the love of a buck and a comfy job more important than love of your fellow man."

You'll notice how heavily Austin's critique relies on the contrast between a film she approves of and one she disapproves of. Such a contrast is common in evaluative essays because no product exists in a vacuum. Evaluating the personal computer as a writing tool necessarily involves deciding whether it is substantially better than the pencil and paper or typewriter it might replace. Evaluating a particular notebook computer would naturally involve contrasting it with comparable notebooks. So strong is the necessity for comparison and contrast that many reviews have a teeter-totter structure: when the product under scrutiny is criticized, another product is praised as an alternative; when the product is praised, its competitor is criticized. It is only when we see alternatives that we are in a position to make critical judgments.

EXERCISE 2

♦ *An Update of Austin.* To consider whether movies in which "the moral universe stops at the front door" are as common now as Austin believed them to be earlier in this decade, list five very popular current movies. Write a one- or two-sentence summary of each, revealing whether the film is concerned primarily with private happiness or with the public good. A summary of *Schindler's List,* for example, might go like this: "In the early 1940s Oskar Schindler, a Czech businessman with a seemingly insatiable appetite for luxury and women, leaves his wife at home and comes to Krakow, Poland, to make his fortune manufacturing equipment for the German army. Growing sympathy for the Jewish prisoners whose slave labor he exploits eventually turns him into a rescuer who risks his life and spends his fortune saving 1100 from extermination." (Obviously, this is not a film that "confuses niceness with morality.")

In addition to helping you investigate the current balance between public and private life at the movies, this exercise will give you practice in the reviewer's skill of packing a great deal of summary into a small space.

A CONSUMER PRODUCT REVIEW

Those who chose to live their lives as simply as Wendell Berry spare themselves the complex choices more active consumers make. Whatever the buyer wants—televisions, computers, toys, blue jeans—the marketplace is likely to offer dozens of brands and models. Facing such a range of choices, people look for information and advice that they can trust. The result has been an enormous increase in the number of product reviews published in newspapers and magazines.

Writing these reviews requires a combination of knowledge about the product and intelligence in visualizing the audience and its interests. If we examine the following review of laser-disc players, written by *Rolling Stone* film critic Peter Travers, we get some sense of how an experienced writer manages to convey a great deal of technical information without intimidating those who have no idea in the world what a "digital dropout compensator" might be. It will be consistent with the spirit of Travers's review to stop the motion now and then and analyze his technique:

> There I was; holed up in a *Rolling Stone* conference room with five spiffy new laser-disc players. Each was connected to an AudioSource SS Three/II Dolby Surround Sound Processor, $399, and a thirty-two-inch Sony Trinitron KV-32XBR35 monitor, $1999. My job, the most fun I'd had since tasting pizzas in a national taste-off, was to put these babies to the test. Could a low-priced player match a high-end model in capturing the visual and aural density of the mother ship's landing in Criterion's *Close Encounters of the Third Kind?* Could it slow down or speed up scenes to help you plumb the complexities of MGM-UA's *2001: A Space Odyssey?* Could it cater to prurient interests by freezing an image of Sharon Stone from LIVE's *Basic Instinct?*
>
> Of course, being a film critic doesn't make me any more qualified to judge laser-disc players than it does pizzas. But this report isn't for connoisseurs; it's for consumers who are both seduced and intimidated, as I am, by laser technology. There are two big questions: Can you afford what you like? And can you get past the page in the manual that says to press POWER?

Travers is more concerned than product reviewers for specialist magazines like *Byte* or *Video* are about establishing a modest, conversational tone. He doesn't want to drive readers away by plunging into technical matters too quickly. Nonetheless, he is not wasting time in this opening passage. A reviewer needs to focus on the uses to which a product might be put, and Travers's three examples are cunningly chosen: not only does he hit the key technical features (reproduction of sound and image, playback at various speeds, freeze-framing), he reminds us of reasons users might find these features worthwhile. And his two big questions point to his three major standards: performance ("what you like"), affordability, and ease of use. Notice how cleverly—and humanly—he addresses all three in the next passage:

> During the testing process, visitors stopped by often to play with the gadgets. They ran the most notorious scene from Fox's *Alien* in slo-mo and noted that the monster bursting out of John Hurt's chest resembles an angry penis with teeth. They compared disc with tape and found that the tape of Warner's *Batman Returns* looked like pudding next to the vivid disc. Lasers offer a seventy percent improvement in picture quality over VCRs, with deeper color saturation and sharper definition in outline and detail.
>
> The clarity of the picture got them every time. What sent them running was the jargon—color bleeding, dot crawls, lines of resolution (laser delivers 430 lines to tape's 240 lines). Even more daunting was the sight of the components laid out: the player, the monitor, the sound processor, the five speakers and all those connecting cables.
>
> Take heart. Laser-disc players are not only easier than ever to use; prices are down by more than half in the past few years (not including discounts), and sales are up twenty-three percent over last year. The advent of the combi-player, which plays regular CDs as well as laser discs, is a strong reason for the boom. Adding one of the following combi-players to your existing audio-video system can produce a startling improvement even before getting fancy with rear-channel speakers and surround-sound decoders.

The "visitors" become stand-ins for Travers's readers, reacting as we might imagine our nontechnical selves reacting. Once again, while keeping his tone light and friendly, Travers manages to convey a good deal of detailed information. The second sentence of the second paragraph typifies his method. Even while he comments on how easily people are "sent running" by talk about "lines of resolution," he gives the key ratio of 430 lines to 240, which explains the earlier statement that "lasers offer a seventy percent improvement in picture quality."

The section that follows is the most businesslike, systematically working through the machines from least expensive to most.

> One of the best starter machines is the Sony MDP-455, $599, which incorporates three features usually found only on more expensive models: a digital time-base corrector for reducing picture jitter, a three-line digital comb filter for sharpening color edges and a digital dropout compensator for minimizing imperfections on dirty or scratched discs. There's also an S-video jack, which delivers color and brightness information separately to further improve performance.
>
> The Samsung DV-5100, $700, also performs solid basic service, though it lacks the Sony extras. Curiously, the Samsung remote does

not include the convenience of a shuttle ring (Sony's does), which allows you to scan discs at various speeds. The Samsung one-ups the Sony by also serving as a karaoke machine. But both machines permit you to access individual movie scenes (or CD tracks), repeat them or shuffle the order.

What more could you want? Check out the Marantz LV500, $799, a middle-range machine with some added advantages for those weaned on VCRs. Though videotapes play straight through, discs utilize two sides. That means you have to get off your butt in the middle of a movie, press EJECT, remove the disc, turn it over and resume play. Purists and couch potatoes find this a fierce intrusion. They'll prize the Morantz's autoreversing transport mechanism, which automatically "flips" the disc while you endure about fifteen seconds of black screen. They'll also appreciate this model's THEATER MODE switch, which shuts off the lights on the front panel during play for that darkened-cineplex effect. Unfortunately, there's no digital time-base corrector like the one you get on the Sony. But the Marantz remote does have a shuttle ring, which permits scanning with only occasional dropouts and image fading.

Of the higher-end players, it would be hard to do better than the Panasonic LX-900, $1100, and the Pioneer CLD-D701, $1200. These beauties perform all the functions just enumerated, including autoreversing. They even freeze the final image on side A until side B begins, so you're never left staring at a blank screen. One of the niftier conveniences on both machines is the remote's inner jog dial, which moves the picture one frame at a time, forward or backward, while the outer dial scans in both directions.

Some readers will be irritated by the parade of product names that turn out to be numbers (CLD-D701 could be the name of an asteroid). Others will flinch at the mention of an "autoreversing transport mechanism" or a "shuttle ring." But to be fair to Travers, we need to acknowledge that this is language that comes with the video territory; it is the language used by salespeople and brochures. He would do the reader no favor by avoiding the technical terms entirely. Still, using them presents a constant challenge to his judgment. He must avoid overexplaining them (wasting space and perhaps insulting the reader) or underexplaining them (leaving the reader in the dark). Notice that he decides not to explain what a shuttle ring is, assuming that most people who would consider buying a laser-disc player have encountered this device on a high-end VCR. He does, however, carefully explain what a digital time-base corrector and a digital comb filter do, and he goes to some trouble to explain why anyone would want to pay extra for an autoreversing transport mechanism. In fact, in the space of 375 words, Travers gives a remarkably thorough overview and explanation of the new video technology.

The sprint through the competitive products complete, he moves to a summary that will allow readers to put the details into perspective:

What's important to remember is that there are a number of disc players out there, in every price range, capable of delivering the goods in picture and sound. If all you want to do is watch a movie on laser, there's no need to spend the extra bucks on the bells and whistles. These features are for those of us who want to manipulate the images, to put them under the microscope to see what makes them tick. Freezing a frame for study is an incomparable kick. But most laser players can't do it unless the disc is in the CAV (Constant Angular Velocity) format. The great majority of discs, though, are in the CLV (Constant Linear Velocity) format. Why? Not surprisingly, the answer is money. Most CLV discs cost around $30. CAV discs, such as Criterion's *Raging Bull,* can cost upward of $100.

Only machines with digital field memory, like the Panasonic and the Pioneer, offer flicker-free stills and slow, forward and reverse visual scanning in the CLV format. They can also store a random frame in memory and play it back. In effect, they can turn inexpensive CLV discs into CAV demonstration movies. For those interested in deconstructing movies as well as watching them, players with digital field memory offer the best bargains around. Orson Welles once said that film was "the biggest toy train set any boy ever had." With the right laser-disc player, even those who never get to direct can see what he meant.

Notice that Travers, unlike Berry and Austin, is careful here not to base his evaluation exclusively on his own set of values and interests. Instead, he is encouraging readers to think what use *they* would make of a disc player and how much money *they* want to spend on one. It's true that his visualization of the audience doesn't extend to people who watch videos just for the stories they tell and are relatively indifferent to sound and picture quality, nor to people like Wendell Berry who don't own a television. But how many people in either category are likely to read a *Rolling Stone* column called *Technopop?*

EXERCISE 3

◆ *Identifying Products for a Comparative Review.* Simple addition will tell you that in order to review the products he did, Peter Travers needed access to over $16,000 worth of equipment. Writers for major magazines can sometimes command setups of this sort, but students rarely can. However, this need not prevent you from writing a serious product review, since relatively inexpensive items can pose for consumers dilemmas almost as complex as those posed by high-end electronic gadgetry. (See, for example, Noel Perrin on maple syrup, p. 212, and Consumers Union on ice-cream bars, p. 482.) To begin exploring some possibilities, name five categories of products inexpensive enough (or available enough) that the average student could afford to review the chief competitors. Then, for each product category, list some of the features that could be compared. Remember that you can interpret "product" broadly: housing on campus could be evaluated as a product; so might dinners at local restaurants.

BOOK AND MOVIE REVIEWS

Reviewing a book or movie presents a writer with a number of puzzles and possibilities. A review might be directed at a reader with no prior knowledge of the work, a reader whose main question is "Will looking at this thing be worth my while?" Or it might be directed at a reader who has seen the movie or read the book and wants to put it into perspective. The reviewer might want to serve primarily as an honest broker characterizing the work in a way that allows readers to make their own judgments, or the reviewer might want to be more active in shaping the standards by which readers will judge not only this work, but others. In fact, most published reviews must serve several purposes and audiences at once; and if you read them closely, you can see the ways writers accommodate themselves to this complex situation.

Let's oversimplify all this complexity for now by saying that the reviewer can take either a *reporterly* stance or a *teacherly* one. That is, the review can be devoted largely to giving information about the work reviewed or it can become a kind of seminar exploring questions of taste and judgment. We will look at a short example of each kind.

A REPORTERLY REVIEW

Manuela Hoelterhoff's review of *Travels with Lizbeth* by Lars Eighner seems to assume that the audience (1) has *not* read the book and (2) wants to decide whether it is worth reading. We could say that the review's main mission is to give readers a foretaste of the book, not simply by summarizing the plot but by indicating reasons they could find it interesting. A more negative review would, of course, give reasons readers *wouldn't* be interested in the book. As you read, notice especially the way that Hoelterhoff catches and maintains interest. To be effective, a review has to be more than an efficient machine for giving information; it must be engaging enough to keep the audience reading.

> One thing led to another until one morning Lars Eighner found himself standing on Texas Highway 290 with, among other things, a backpack stuffed with 25 pounds of dog food, a hospital scrub suit, a warm caftan made by a former housemate, and a bedroll. It fast became clear that he had overpacked.

"I could only get the pack on my back by reclining on it, hooking my arms through the straps, and thrashing my limbs like a supine cockroach to right myself," he recalls in *Travels With Lizbeth: Three Years on the Road and on the Streets* (St. Martin's, 271 pages, $19.95).

Lizbeth was and is his mutt—a half-Labrador retriever not too bright but awfully friendly. Mr. Eighner was, but no longer is, homeless. He now lives in a tiny apartment in Austin, ironically right back where this curious tale starts after Mr. Eighner lost his job at the state lunatic asylum and slowly ran out of funds and friends who could, as he would say, "offer him and Lizbeth some hospitality." An elevated manner of address and a rich vocabulary at odds with his impoverished state and deadbeat friends make Mr. Eighner a quirky guide into the homeless condition as he plunges on, through Miracle Miles, desert flea markets and dusty truck stops, surviving en route the complex architecture of highway access ramps, subzero temperatures, psychotic companions and an amazing encounter with the Texas welfare system. Only people with kitchens, he learns to his befuddlement, qualify for food stamps.

But as he stands there on Highway 290 with less than a quarter in his pocket and that mostly in pennies, Mr. Eighner is a hope-filled man heading to Los Angeles with a three-pronged plan. They are probably not the dreams of a Dawn Steel or a Mike Ovitz,[1] but they are his. He hopes to receive some hospitality from his friend Rufus, who should be getting out of jail for "gross and public lewdness"; he hopes an advertised position for assistant editor at a gay men's magazine will be his (several of his stories have been published to much acclaim if little money in this specialized market niche); he hopes he might be useful working with people with AIDS. His employment history, after all, includes an "eleemosynary corporation"[2] where he "stalked the elusive third-party payment."

But Mr. Eighner will turn fat from junk food and, soon thereafter, 40, weeping outside a dog pound where Lizbeth is imprisoned awaiting death, falsely accused by, yes, a blind person, of assault.

The editor of the *Grackle*, a tiny magazine, to which Mr. Eighner had submitted a few small things (in longhand), donates the $100 he needs to save Lizbeth just shortly before the needle is readied. Given the astonishing preponderance of worthless people in the publishing industry, it is heartening to note that a few good souls emerged from their slush piles to assist the author. In his introduction, he thanks Steven Saylor, an agent who conserved scribbled bits and pieces Mr. Eighner had sent him "while he was in no position to keep things as fragile

---

[1] **a Dawn Steel or a Mike Ovitz:** Two of Hollywood's most powerful people—Steel is the president of Columbia Pictures; Ovitz heads the Creative Artists Agency.
[2] **eleemosynary corporation:** In plainer English, a charitable organization.

as ink and paper," and Wendy Lesser, editor of the appropriately named *Threepenny Review,* the best literary magazine west of Dallas.

It was Ms. Lesser who realized the informative beauty of a piece called "On Dumpster Diving," which now serves as the book's centerpiece. Just hulking trash containers to most of us, dumpsters turned into Mr. Eighner's smorgasbord and hobby center. Hoisting himself into the mess, he learned which foods to avoid and which to finish, with abandoned half-eaten pizzas contributing much to his increasing "stoutness." Sadness tinges these excavations as he comes upon pets lying in state, shredded wedding books and, Austin being a college town, many samples of our failing educational system.

"I am horrified," notes Mr. Eighner in his entertaining, deadpan manner, "to discover the kind of paper that now merits an A in an undergraduate course." An enthusiastic needleworker, he passes the time with embroidery-by-number kits abandoned, he imagines, by fumble-fingered sorority sisters. "Do not think I refrain from chuckling as I make gifts from these kits," he says, busily tearing up some nymph's hideous stitching to create his own more flamboyant design.

The boredom weighs heavily nonetheless. "Every life," he notes, "has trivial occurrences, pointless episodes, and unresolved mysteries, but a homeless life has these and virtually nothing else."

Phlebitis briefly takes him off the streets into an emergency room, where his Nixon jokes only serve to convince the staff he is in need of psychiatric care. Obviously the more he insists that he isn't a drunken, druggy lunatic, the more the doctors chatter about "denial."

In truth, Mr. Eighner isn't your usual shiftless bum, and his compelling narrative makes clear that if our social services were not primarily designed to succor bureaucrats, more deserving people like him could be saved from the streets.

Grasping together his shreds of dignity, he neither begs nor steals, though Lizbeth admittedly shows a less resolute character. Not long into their travels, she perfects what her companion calls "The Dying Dog Routine"—a series of feeble twitches of the tail and wan looks that easily extract handouts from the homeless-hardened.

Travels With Lizbeth ends as Mr. Eighner finds a personal computer in a dumpster and sets out to provide them both with a steady source of income by writing this book, the first, I hope, of many.

Several features of Hoelterhoff's review are worth noting if you want to undertake one like it. First, she opens by pointing to a short passage that characterizes the book's subject (homelessness) and its key quality (deadpan humor in adversity). This technique is common in the opening of movie reviews as well; if the passage is well chosen, it can give readers a nutshell version of the whole work, piquing their interest and establishing the review's positive or negative tone. Second, her review contains enough summary to let the reader know what kind of action and information the book will contain (see especially paragraphs 3–6). Third, Hoelterhoff characterizes the style of the book as well as the content. Indeed, it is the style that chiefly impresses her. If you examine the ten brief quotations that she uses, you'll see that each is carefully selected to show that Eighner's writing is simultaneously "elevated" and "deadpan." Of course, by revealing this unusual style so completely, she makes it possible for some readers to object to it ("'eleemosynary corporation,' indeed!" I can imagine advocates of a plainer style snorting). Finally, Hoelterhoff only occasionally injects her personality into the review. We notice her in the final paragraph, when she hopes that Eighner will write more books. We notice her (perhaps unfortunately) when she expresses opinions about "the preponderance of worthless people in the publishing industry" and the social service system "designed to succor bureaucrats." Most of the time, however, our attention is directed toward Eighner and his work, not toward Hoelterhoff and her opinions.

This self-effacing quality might encourage some people to see Hoelterhoff's review as "objective," but it is not. Any attempt to characterize a 271 page book in 900 words will require the reviewer to make decisions about what crucial to report and what can be set aside. Hoelterhoff has chosen to emphasize the book's wit and the insights it gives into the situation of the homeless. She has not emphasized, as other reviewers have, Eighner's frankness about his sexual appetites and activities. Even the most reporterly of reviews will move some aspects of a work into the spotlight and leave others in the dark. Though the reviewer may decide not to discuss his or her values explicitly, they will decide where the spotlight strikes.

A TEACHERLY REVIEW

If Manuela Hoelterhoff writes primarily for a reader who has not encountered the work she reviews and who wants straightforward information about it, Roger Ebert takes a different approach. While he writes in a way that serves such readers, he seems at least as concerned with readers who have already seen the movie he reviews and who want to enter into a broader discussion of what makes films good or bad. Sometimes he writes as if he were sending a message to the the movie's director. Consider, for example, this essay on *Jurassic Park:*

A WRITER AT WORK

"Jurassic Park"
ROGER EBERT

When young Steven Spielberg was first offered the screenplay for *Jaws,* he said he would direct the movie on one condition: that he didn't have to show the shark for the first hour. By slowly building the audience's apprehension, he felt, the shark would be much more impressive when it finally arrived.

He was right. I wish he had remembered that lesson when he was preparing *Jurassic Park,* his new thriller set in a Pacific-island theme park where real dinosaurs have been grown from long-dormant DNA molecules. The movie delivers all too well on its promise to show us dinosaurs. We see them early and often, and they are indeed a triumph of special effects artistry, but the movie is lacking other qualities that it needs even more, such as a sense of awe and wonderment, and strong human story values.

It's clear, seeing this long-awaited project, that Spielberg devoted most of his effort to creating the dinosaurs. The human characters are a ragtag bunch of half-realized, sketched-in personalities who exist primarily to scream, utter dire warnings, and outwit the monsters.

Richard Attenborough, as the millionaire who builds the park, is given a few small dimensions—he loves his grandchildren, he's basically a good soul, he realizes the error of tampering with nature. But there was an opportunity here to make his character grand and original, colorful and oversize, and instead he comes across as unfocused and benign.

As the film opens, two dinosaur experts (Sam Neill and Laura Dern) arrive at the park, along with a mathematician played by Jeff Goldblum, whose function in the story is to lounge about uttering vague philosophical imprecations. Also along are Attenborough's grandchildren, and a lawyer, who is the first to be eaten by a dinosaur.

Attenborough wants the visitors to have a preview of his new park, where actual living prehistoric animals dwell in enclosures behind tall steel fences, helpfully labeled "10,000 volts." The visitors set off on a tour in remote-controlled utility vehicles, which stall when an unscrupulous employee (Wayne Knight) shuts down the park's computer program so he can smuggle out some dinosaur embryos. Meanwhile, a tropical storm hits the island, the beasts knock over the fences, and Sam Neill is left to shepherd the kids back to safety while they're hunted by towering meat-eaters.

The plot to steal the embryos is handled on the level of a TV sitcom. The Knight character, an overwritten and overplayed blubbering fool, drives his Jeep madly through the storm and thrashes about in the forest. If this subplot had been handled cleverly—with skill and subtlety, as in a caper movie—it might have added to the film's effect. Instead, it's as if one of the Three Stooges wandered into the story.

The subsequent events—after the creatures get loose—follow an absolutely standard outline, similar in bits and pieces to all the earlier films in this genre, from *The Lost World* and *King Kong* right up to 1993's *Carnosaur*. True, because the director is Spielberg, there is a high technical level to the execution of the clichés. Two set pieces are especially effective: a scene where a beast mauls a car with screaming kids inside, and another where the kids play hide-and-seek with two creatures in the park's kitchen.

But consider what could have been. There is a scene very early in the film where Neill and Dern, who have studied dinosaurs all of their lives, see living ones for the first time. The creatures they see are tall, majestic leaf-eaters, grazing placidly in the treetops. There is a sense of grandeur to them. And that is the sense lacking in the rest of the film, which quickly turns into a standard monster movie, with screaming victims fleeing from roaring dinosaurs.

Think back to another ambitious special-effects picture by Spielberg, *Close Encounters of the Third Kind* (1977). That was a movie about the *idea* of visitors from outer space. It inspired us to think what an awesome thing it would be if Earth were visited by living alien beings. You left that movie shaken and a little transformed. It was a movie that had faith in the intelligence and curiosity of its audience.

In the sixteen years since it was made, however, big-budget Hollywood seems to have lost its confidence that audiences can share big dreams. *Jurassic Park* throws a lot of dinosaurs at us, and because they look terrific (and indeed they do), we're supposed to be grateful. I have the uneasy feeling that if Spielberg had made *Close Encounters* today, we would have seen the aliens in the first ten minutes, and by the halfway mark they'd be attacking Manhattan with death rays.

Because the movie delivers on the bottom line, I'm giving it three stars.[1] You want great dinosaurs; you got great dinosaurs. Spielberg enlivens the action with lots of nice little touches; I especially liked a sequence where a smaller creature leaps suicidally on a larger one, and they battle to the death. On the monster movie level, the movie works and is entertaining. But with its profligate resources, it could have been so much more.

Unlike Manuela Hoelterhoff, Ebert does not begin by pointing to some passage in the work he reviews. He begins, instead, with a comparison. This opening is characteristic of the entire review, which does more than give and justify the three-star rating. The review attempts to place the movie on a series of mental maps: how does it compare with other, better, Spielberg movies? How does it compare with other monster movies? How does it compare with good movies generally, in its treatment of human characters and human emotions?

Comparison, as we noted earlier, comes naturally in evaluative essays, and the tendency to compare grows stronger when a writer is working in the area of his or her special interest. Roger Ebert estimates that he has seen ten thousand movies and reviewed six thousand.

Sometimes I see two or three movies a day, mostly in the screening room upstairs over the White Hen Pantry. I slip down at noon for a sandwich, blinded by the sunlight, my mind still filled with chases and gun duels, yuks and big boobs, cute dogs and brainy kids, songs and

---

[1] **three stars:** out of a possible four—i.e., "good" but not "great."

dances, amazing coincidences and chance meetings and deep insights into the nature of man. Whatever was in the movies.

While he doesn't assume that his readers are this immersed in film, he clearly assumes that most of them have seen *Jaws* (1975) and *Close Encounters of the Third Kind* (1977) and that many have seen *King Kong* (1933) and *The Lost World* (1925). He also assumes that most of his readers care enough about Hollywood and Spielberg to regret the way they seem, in *Jurassic Park,* to lose faith in "the intelligence and curiosity of [the] audience."

He writes, that is, with "students" of film in mind: people who already know something about what makes movies good or bad and are ready to learn more. But he doesn't abandon those who less informed or less curious. His summary of the plot (paragraphs 5 and 6) and his final paragraph give adequate information to someone whose main concern is whether to shell out seven dollars for a ticket, and he has included enough information about *Jaws* and *Close Encounters* to make his references to these films comprehensible to people who have never seen them. "I can't write as if everybody was born yesterday, and doesn't know anything that is not in today's papers," he says. On the other hand, he knows that some of his readers *were* born yesterday: "To them, I owe the responsibility of writing a review that will be readable—not jargon—and that will give an accurate notion of the movie they are thinking of going to see."[2] If you plan to write a review that both teaches and informs, you would do well to study the way that Ebert reaches out to a wide range of readers.

WRITING REVIEWS AND EVALUATIONS

POINTS TO
CONSIDER

Consider Your Motives As an Evaluator. Since you are writing your evaluation in a course, you may want to protest that your motive is clear enough: to get a good grade. This motive only scratches the surface, of course. The professional writers quoted in this chapter wrote in order to collect a paycheck; but beyond this they had or *developed* other motives. They wanted readers to reconsider their own buying habits (Berry) or view of the good life (Austin). They wanted to help readers benefit from a new technology (Travers) or enjoy a good read (Hoelterhoff) or realize what a movie has failed to deliver (Ebert). Unless you develop a picture of what you would like to accomplish through your review, you are unlikely to write it well.

---

[2] **"an accurate notion"**: See "A Memo to Myself and Certain Other Film Critics," p. 487.

Consider the Motives of Your Target Audience.   If you are writing the kind of review that could appear in a newspaper or popular magazine, your audience will have sundry motives for reading it, some of them at odds with your motive for *writing* it. If, for instance, your strong inclination is to write a crusading review, but many of your potential readers are more interested in getting practical information about a product, you may have to find a way to combine diatribe with information. It's worth remembering that readers of general-interest magazines and newspapers expect to be *engaged* by what they read. This doesn't mean that you need to be a comic, but it does mean that you should ask yourself, as you examine each paragraph, if you have given an unpaid volunteer reader reason to go on to the next paragraph.

QUESTIONS FOR PEER REVIEW

If you have an opportunity for peer review, ask your reviewer for both general comments (see the checklist on pages 60–61) and for answers to four particular questions:

1. Have I shown an awareness that different people are likely to evaluate my subject differently? Where do you see evidence of this awareness?

2. Have I made clear to people who might evaluate the subject differently why I evaluate it as I do? Please state in your own words what you believe the *real* basis of my judgment is.

3. Are my standards of judgment different from yours, and if so, how? Are the standards of my intended audience likely to be different from mine? If so, in what ways?

4. How do you think my review is likely to affect the way my readers evaluate the subject?

If your reviewer answers honestly, you may be surprised by some things he or she says. A wise friend once told me that the *real*, unacknowledged basis of my criticism of a novel was my desire to show that I was more clever than the novelist. I saw, reluctantly, that he was right and that I owed it to the novelist and myself to do the book justice.

Assignments
for Chapter 12

ASSIGNMENT 1:
A CRUSADING EVALUATION

Since crusading evaluations require commitment to a cause or a point of view, this assignment may not be well suited to everyone. Assuming, however, that you are a person with strong convictions—an environmentalist, a feminist, a conservative, a pacifist, a nationalist, or whatever—seek out a subject to evaluate that will help show what these convictions mean in practical application. Wendell Berry's evaluation of the personal computer, Beth Austin's of movies, and Katha Pollitt's of movies, television programs, and books for children (p. 479) may give you ideas about how to start. Remember that such evaluations are really a form of persuasive writing and that the best of them don't merely preach to the converted, but try to win new converts. Naming the magazine or newspaper in which you would like to have your evaluation appear can help you focus your work.

ASSIGNMENT 2:
A CONSUMER PRODUCT REVIEW

Write a review that, like Peter Travers's "Dumb About Disc Players," evaluates several products that compete with one another for the consumer's dollar. Exercise 3 (p. 468) may help you find an appropriate set of products. Remember that the primary aim of such a review is to help potential buyers sort out their thinking. Avoid becoming the champion of a single product unless it is clearly superior for almost every potential consumer.

ASSIGNMENT 3:
A COLLABORATIVE PRODUCT REVIEW

If you have a bent toward scientific evaluation, you may want to try the kind of review published in magazines such as *Consumer Reports* (see, for example, "Ice-Cream Bars for Big Kids," pp. 482–486). Such an undertaking requires you to identify key features of a given class of products, devise tests to demonstrate different levels of performance, and—of course— perform the tests. Because so much labor is required and because scientific evaluation requires you to avoid the prejudices of a single product-tester, such an evaluation is better undertaken by a committee than by a single writer. When the time comes to write the report, the writing can be parceled out by sections for drafting, then edited in committee.

ASSIGNMENT 4:   ## An Evaluation of a Book or Movie

Unless your instructor assigns a specific audience for your review, you should probably assume that you are writing for a broad and mixed audience. Some of your readers will know nothing about the work you are reviewing and will simply want to know if it is something they want to see or read. Others will already have read the book or seen the movie and will be looking for a review that helps them see its merits and defects in a new light.

THE SMURFETTE PRINCIPLE

Katha Pollitt

Katha Pollitt is not a professional media critic but a poet and essayist who regularly writes articles for such magazines as the *Atlantic Monthly, Mother Jones,* the *New Yorker,* and *Nation.* As this essay from the *New York Times Magazine* makes clear, she is also the mother of a young daughter. Her perspective as a parent makes her turn a critical eye on "the sexism in preschool culture."

1   THIS CHRISTMAS, I FINALLY CAVED IN: I gave my 3-year-old daughter, Sophie, her very own cassette of "The Little Mermaid." Now, she, too, can sit transfixed by Ariel, the perky teen-ager with the curvy tail who trades her voice for a pair of shapely legs and a shot at marriage to a prince. ("On land it's much preferred for ladies not to say a word," sings the cynical sea witch, "and she who holds her tongue will get her man." Since she's the villain, we're not meant to notice that events prove her correct.)

2   Usually when parents give a child some item they find repellent, they plead helplessness before a juvenile filibuster. But "The Little Mermaid" was my idea. Ariel may look a lot like Barbie, and her adventure may be limited to romance and over with the wedding bells, but unlike, say, Cinderella or Sleeping Beauty, she's active, brave and determined, the heroine of her own life. She even rescues the prince. And that makes her a rare fish, indeed, in the world of preschool culture.

3   Take a look at the kid's section of your local video store. You'll find that features starring boys, and usually aimed at them, account for 9 out of 10 offerings. Clicking the television dial one recent week—admittedly not an encyclopedic study—I came across not a single network cartoon or puppet show starring a female. (Nickelodeon, the children's cable chan-

nel, has one of each.) Except for the crudity of the animation and the general air of witlessness and hype, I might as well have been back in my own 1950's childhood, nibbling Frosted Flakes in front of Daffy Duck, Bugs Bunny, Porky Pig and the rest of the all-male Warner Brothers lineup.

4   Contemporary shows are either essentially all-male, like "Garfield," or are organized on what I call the Smurfette principle: a group of male buddies will be accented by a lone female, sterotypically defined. In the worst cartoons—the ones that blend seamlessly into the animated cereal commercials—the female is usually a little-sister type, a bunny in a pink dress and hair ribbons who tags along with the adventurous bears and badgers. But the Smurfette principle rules the more carefully made shows, too. Thus, Kanga, the only female in "Winnie-the-Pooh," is a mother. Piggy, of "Muppet Babies," is a pint-size version of Miss Piggy, the camp glamour queen of the Muppet movies. April, of the wildly popular "Teen-Age Mutant Ninja Turtles," functions as a girl Friday to a quartet of male superheroes. The message is clear. Boys are the norm, girls the variation; boys are central, girls peripheral; boys are individuals, girls types. Boys define the group, its story and its code of values. Girls exist only in relation to boys.

5   Well, commercial television—what did I

479

expect? The surprise is that public television, for all its superior intelligence, charm and commitment to worthy values, shortchanges preschool girls, too. Mister Rogers lives in a neighborhood populated mostly by middle-aged men like himself. "Shining Time Station" features a cartoon in which the male characters are train engines and the female characters are passenger cars. And then there's "Sesame Street." True, the human characters are neatly divided between the genders (and among the races, too, which is another rarity). The film clips, moreover, are just about the only place on television in which you regularly see girls having fun together: practicing double Dutch, having a sleep-over. But the Muppets are the real stars of "Sesame Street," and the important ones—the ones with real personalities, who sing on the musical videos, whom kids identify with and cherish in dozens of licensed products—are *all* male. I know one little girl who was so outraged and heartbroken when she realized that even Big Bird—her last hope—was a boy that she hasn't watched the show since.

6   Well, there's always the library. Some of the best children's books ever written have been about girls—Madeline, Frances the badger. It's even possible to find stories with funny, feminist messages, like "The Paper-bag Princess." (She rescues the prince from a dragon, but he's so ungrateful that she decides not to marry him, after all.) But books about girls are a subset in a field that includes a much larger subset of books about boys (12 of the 14 storybooks singled out for praise in last year's Christmas roundup in *Newsweek,* for instance) and books in which the sex of the child is theoretically unimportant—in which case it usually "happens to be" male. Dr. Seuss's books are less about individual characters than about language and imaginative freedom—but, somehow or other, only boys get to go on beyond Zebra or see marvels on Mulberry Street. Frog and Toad, Lowly Worm, Lyle the Crocodile, all *could* have been female. But they're not.

7   Do kids pick up on the sexism in children's culture? You bet. Preschoolers are like medieval philosophers: the text—a book, a movie, a TV show—is more authoritative than the evidence of their own eyes. "Let's play weddings," says my little niece. We grownups roll our eyes, but face it: it's still the one scenario in which the girl is the central figure. "Women are *nurses,*" my friend Anna, a doctor, was informed by her then 4-year-old, Molly. Even my Sophie is beginning to notice the back-seat role played by girls in some of her favorite books. "Who's that?" she asks every time we reread "The Cat in the Hat." It's Sally, the timid little sister of the resourceful boy narrator. She wants Sally to matter, I think, and since Sally is really just a name and a hair ribbon, we have to say her name again and again.

8   The sexism in preschool culture deforms both boys and girls. Little girls learn to split their consciousness, filtering their dreams and ambitions through boy characters while admiring the clothes of the princess. The more privileged and daring can dream of becoming exceptional women in a man's world—Smurfettes. The others are being taught to accept the more usual fate, which is to be a passenger car drawn through life by a masculine train engine. Boys, who are rarely confronted with stories in which males play only minor roles, learn a simpler lesson: girls just don't matter much.

9   How can it be that 25 years of feminist social changes have made so little impression on preschool culture? Molly, now 6 and well aware that women can be doctors, has one theory: children's entertainment is mostly made by men. That's true, as it happens, and I'm sure it explains a lot. It's also true that, as a society, we don't seem to care much what goes on with kids, as long as they are reasonably quiet. Marshmallow cereal, junky toys, endless hours in front of the tube—a society that accepts all that is not going to get in a lather about a little gender stereotyping. It's easier to focus on

the bright side. I had "Cinderella," Sophie has "The Little Mermaid"—that's progress, isn't it?

10 "We're working on it," Dulcy Singer, the executive producer of "Sesame Street," told me when I raised the sensitive question of those all-male Muppets. After all, the show has only been on the air for a quarter of a century; these things take time. The trouble is, our preschoolers don't have time. My funny, clever, bold, adventurous daughter is forming her gender ideas right now. I do what I can to counteract the messages she gets from her entertainment, and so does her father—Sophie watches very little television. But I can see we have our work cut out for us. It sure would help if the bunnies took off their hair ribbons, and if half of the monsters were fuzzy, blue—and female. ◆

ICE-CREAM BARS FOR BIG KIDS

Consumer Reports

Consumer Reports is probably the most familiar example of a publication devoted to "scientific" or "objective" testing of consumer products by panels of product testers working under tightly controlled conditions. The aim of such publications is to get beyond the hype of advertisers and the subjective reactions of isolated users and present the result of carefully benchmarked tests. "Ice-Cream Bars for Big Kids" shows the method at work on a product inexpensive enough that even college students could afford to evaluate it for taste preferences.

1   THIRTYSOMETHING SUMMERS AGO, THE sound of bells coming down the street heralded the arrival of the Good Humor man. From every door, kids poured forth, eagerly proffering their dimes and nickels to this pied piper of *Popsicles* in anticipation of a few minutes of fast-melting pleasure on a stick.

2   Those kids grew up, but they didn't outgrow their love of ice-cream bars. They buy more than a billion dollars worth of frozen novelties (the trade's term for single-serving goodies) each year.

3   That's just fine with ice-cream makers: Adult-oriented frozen novelties fetch profits of 30 percent, compared with margins of 20 percent for products aimed at children. Eager to spur impulse sales, some supermarket managers have added special freezer displays right at the checkout.

4   The products in the freezer cases range from bite-sized bonbons to bars so big and rich they might do for two. Amidst the sandwiches, cones, and sundaes, you'll find fairly plain (if rich) bars—chocolate or vanilla ice cream covered with chocolate. That's what we tested. You'll also see bars adorned with additional sugary substances, from generic "cheesecake" to brand-name cookies. We nibbled at some of those products, too. . . .

IT'S A NASTY JOB, BUT . . .

5   Taste-testing ice cream isn't one long slurpfest, though we encountered few complaints for our panel of trained tasters. For two months, those panelists sampled portions of the bars, whose identity had been concealed, under red lights to keep appearance out of the judgments. The panelists compared the bars with a host of flavor and texture benchmarks that they rechecked before each session. (Example: The benchmark for vanilla intensity was one-half teaspoon of vanilla extract dissolved in a cup of milk, heated to drive off the alcohol, and then cooled.) Our statisticians then compared the panel's descriptions to CU's[1] criteria for excellence, described in the Ratings.

6   The bars the panelists sampled included pricey, heavily advertised brands like *Dove Bar* and *Haagen-Dazs;* entries from such ice-cream perennials as *Good Humor, Eskimo Pie, Dolly Madison,* and *Polar Bar,* and a couple of supermarket economy brands.

7   Four varieties of *Dove Bar* and three of *Haagen-Dazs* earned a rating of excellent. In

---

[1] CU: Consumers Union

fact, while a taster or two may have demurred, by the time we'd averaged all the numbers, five of those bars actually emerged with scores of 100. But if you care about your purse or your poundage, beware. Those bars cost about a dollar apiece and carry a calorie payload of over 300.

8   At the other end of the scale were the seven bars that we rated only fair. Those products—smaller than the premium bars, sometimes by a lot—cost between 16 and 38 cents each; calories range from about 130 to 225. All three supermarket products tested landed in the sensory cellar.

9   The Federal Government sets standards for what may be called ice cream and ice milk. Ice cream must have at least 10 percent butterfat (8 percent for chocolate), ice milk between 2 and 7 percent. The sweetener must be sugar in one of its forms; a product like *Eskimo Pie Sugar Free Frozen Dairy Dessert* cannot call itself ice cream or ice milk, because it uses aspartame. (For our purposes, we treated it as an ice-cream bar.)

10   Beyond Government-imposed minimums, ice-cream makers are free to increase the butterfat content to their heart's content, if not to yours. Within limits, there's a direct relationship between butterfat and rich taste.

11   The ice-cream trade calls products that exceed 18 percent butterfat "superpremium." Those brands, typified by *Dove* and *Haagen-Dazs* bars, further enhance the sensation of luxury by limiting "overrun"—the introduction of air into the mix during processing. The result is ice cream that feels dense and substantial when it melts in your mouth.

12   Too little overrun, though, can be too much of a good thing. Ice cream with no pumped-in air would be a thick, solidly frozen mass, not very refreshing to eat. Even the superpremiums have at least 20 percent overrun.

13   Cheaper, airier ice cream may approach the legal limit of 100 percent overrun. That means

the ice cream in a three-ounce bar, for example, has been fluffed up to twice the volume of its solid ingredients.

14   We also assessed other attributes of the ice-cream bars:

15   ☐ **Thickness of the coating.** A few bars lost points for a paper-thin coating. The thickest approached one-eighth of an inch. The downside of all that chocolate, though, is that thick coatings are more likely to fall off in pieces when you bite them. Solution: Keep plate or wrapper handy.

16   ☐ **How quickly the coating melts in the mouth.** The sooner the chocolate starts to melt on your tongue, the faster the taste comes through. Like butter, a fast-melting chocolate delivers a sharp burst of flavor. Slower coatings, like some margarines, yield less taste.

17   ☐ **The intensity of the flavors.** We looked for the vanilla in the vanilla bars to approach the intensity of the benchmark we've described. The intensity of the chocolate in the chocolate ice cream ought to approximate the intensity of an ordinary milk-chocolate bar. So should the chocolate in the coatings, unless the coating are specified as "dark." Dark coatings could approach the intensity of semisweet baking chocolate without losing points.

18   The cream flavor we looked for in the ice cream was somewhere between whole milk and cream. Diet products could be less creamy.

19   ☐ **Sweetness.** Ice-cream bars ought to taste sweet, at about the level of four to six teaspoons of sugar dissolved in a cup of water.

20   ☐ **Other flavors.** A bit of the flavor of butterscotch or roasted cocoa beans is all right. We knocked off points for oddities such as a marked saltiness or for the off-note we call "freezer taste," the sometimes stale flavor of a food that has been stored too long in the freezer. The taste, closely related to "package taste," can also occur when ice cream has been thawed and refrozen.

21 ☐ **Bitterness.** The ideal chocolate ice cream should have little or none of this attribute. But you'd expect some bitterness in dark chocolate coatings.

22 ☐ **Iciness.** Sherbet feels icy to the tongue; ice cream shouldn't. Some of the lower-rated ice-cream bars had a coarse, icy texture. That flaw is often associated with poor storage—ice cream that has been allowed to thaw and re-freeze, forming ice crystals.

23 ☐ **Gumminess.** Stabilizers and corn sweeteners added to some ice cream help prevent iciness, but can make it gummy. Our benchmark here was marshmallow creme; ice cream shouldn't come close.

NUTRITION FOR DESSERT?

24 The same stuff that makes an ice-cream bar delicious also makes it fattening. Lots of butter-fat and cocoa butter. Lots of sugar. Coconut oil, a tropical oil high in saturated fat, is used in the coatings to help keep the chocolate shell from falling off. Clearly, these are not desserts for the calorie-conscious or for those worried about dietary fats.

25 Or are they? It all depends on how you look at these products. If you're trying to limit your daily fat intake to 30 percent of all calories, as CU's medical consultants recommend, you should aim to eat no more than 67 grams of fat, evenly divided among saturated, mono-unsaturated, and polyunsaturated fats.

26 The superpremium ice-cream bars each contain 20 to 31 grams of fat, most of it saturated and all of it loaded with calories. To the one out of 10 Americans who eats ice cream every day, all that fat makes the 30 percent goal well nigh impossible to achieve. To the once-a-month splurger, however, the extra fat and the extra few hundred calories may not matter.

27 There *are* some useful nutrients in an ice-cream bar along with all the fats and sugars.

Ice-cream bars

1 Product. Listed in order of sensory score; products rated equally listed alphabetically. If a product comes with a choice of chocolate coatings, we note whether it's **dark** or **milk** chocolate. All but the *Baskin Robbins* are sold in supermarkets.

2 Sensory index. Based on tests by a panel of trained tasters. We compared the

1 Product

Chocolate

Dove Bar Dark

Haagen-Dazs Dark

Dove Bar Milk

Klondike Milk

Nestle Quik Milk

Vanilla

Dove Bar Milk

Haagen-Dazs Dark

Haagen-Dazs Milk

Dove Bar Dark

Dreyer's Dark

Polar Bar Milk

Klondike Milk

Nestle Milk

Haagen-Dazs Milk with Almonds

Eskimo Pie Original Dark

Baskin Robbins Dark

Steve's Milk

Weight Watchers (ice milk)

Good Humor

Eskimo Pie Sugar Free

Dolly Madison

Eskimo Pie Dark

Freezer Pleezer

Nestle Crunch Milk

A & P

Pathmark

A & P (ice milk)

panelists' assessments of flavor and texture with CU's criteria for excellence.

3 Cost per bar. The average, based on what CU shoppers paid in New York, Georgia, Texas, and California. The expensive brands typically come only two or three to a package. Cheaper products may come as many as 10 or 12 to a package.

4 Size. Ice cream is measured by volume, in fluid ounces. Because of varying amounts of air pumped into ice cream during processing (known as overrun), this measurement is not a good guide to the weight of the ice cream.

5 Calories per bar. As measured by CU. The ingredients that make some ice-cream bars taste better than others are, sadly, the ones that add the most calories.

6 Fat per fluid ounce. The fat comes mostly from the cream, but also from coconut oil and cocoa butter used in the coating. All three contain highly saturated fats.

7 Sensory comments. The ice cream was expected to be flavorful—rich in dairy and cream flavor with distinct vanilla or chocolate notes as appropriate. The coating was also expected to be appropriately flavored, with the dairy-chocolate blend of milk chocolate or the slightly bitter, more intense taste of dark chocolate if the label so specified. We've noted the sweetness level for each bar. If you find "very sweet" too sweet, try a "sweet."

2 Sensory index (P F G VG E)	3 Cost per bar	4 Size	5 Calories per bar	6 Fat per fl. oz.	7 Sensory comments
	$ .99	4 fl.oz.	358	6 g	Dense, flavorful ice cream; thick, intense, slightly bitter coating melts quickly. Sweet.
	1.07	3.7	385	7	Very dense, very chocolaty ice cream; thick, intense, slightly bitter coating melts quickly. Sweet.
	1.00	4	352	6	Dense, flavorful ice cream; thick, distinct milk-chocolate coating melts quickly. A bit too sweet.
	.50	5	287	4	Somewhat dense, icy ice cream; thin, somewhat coarse coating with a hint of butterscotch melts a bit slowly. Slight freezer taste. Sweet.
	.37	3	225	6	Airy, gummy, icy ice cream low in flavor; thin, somewhat coarse coating a bit low in flavor and melts a bit slowly. Freezer taste. Sweet.
	1.03	4	342	5	Dense flavorful ice cream; thick, smooth, distinct milk-chocolate coating melts quickly. Very sweet.
	1.07	3.7	377	7	Very dense, flavorful ice cream; thick, smooth, slightly bitter, intense coating melts quickly. Sweet.
	1.07	3.7	319	6	Very dense, flavorful ice cream; thick, smooth, distinct milk-chocolate coating melts quickly. Very sweet.
	.97	4	353	6	Dense, flavorful ice cream; thick, smooth, slightly bitter, intense coating melts quickly and falls off in pieces. Sweet.
	.63	4	295	5	Dense, slightly icy, flavorful ice cream; very thick, slightly bitter, intense coating melts quickly. Sweet.
	.33	3.5	234	5	Somewhat dense, slightly icy, flavorful ice cream; somewhat thick coating. Sweet.
	.50	5	294	4	Dense, slightly icy, flavorful ice cream; somewhat thick coating with a hint of butterscotch but a bit low in chocolate flavor, melts a bit slowly. Sweet.
	.97	3.7	286	5	Dense, slightly icy, flavorful ice cream; thick coating with a hint of caramel melts quickly. Very sweet.
	1.08	3.7	377	8	Very dense, flavorful ice cream; thick coating melts quickly. Almonds have intense roasted flavor but leave particles behind. Very sweet.
	.47	2.3	182	6	Somewhat dense, slightly icy ice cream a bit low in flavor; thick, slightly bitter, intense coating. Sweet.
	.84	3.5	310	6	Somewhat dense, slightly icy and gummy ice cream a bit low in dairy flavor; thick, slightly bitter, intense coating melts quickly. Slight freezer taste. Sweet.
	1.23	4.8	439	6	Dense, slightly icy, flavorful ice cream; thick, slightly rough coating a bit low in flavor, melts a bit slowly, and tends to fall off in pieces. Very sweet.
	.25	1.7	111	4	Somewhat dense, icy, gummy ice milk a bit low in flavor; thin, slightly bitter coating low in flavor. Slight freezer taste.
	.50	3	201	5	Somewhat dense, slightly icy, slightly gummy ice cream a bit low in flavor; thin, somewhat intense coating. Sweet.
	.40	2.5	182	5	Somewhat dense, icy ice cream a bit gummy and low in flavor; thin, slightly coarse, gritty, bitter, somewhat intense coating. Slight freezer taste. Sweet.
	.33	3	197	4	Somewhat dense, icy, gummy ice cream a bit low in dairy flavor; thin, slightly bitter, somewhat intense coating melts a bit slowly. Sweet.
	.35	3	209	5	Airy, icy, gummy ice cream a bit low in flavor; thin, slightly bitter, slightly rough, somewhat intense coating. Slight freezer taste. Sweet.
	.17	2.5	147	4	Airy, icy, gummy ice cream a bit low in flavor; thin, somewhat intense coating melts a bit slowly. Slight freezer taste. Somewhat sweet.
	.38	3	190	4	Somewhat dense, icy, gummy ice cream a bit low in flavor; thin, somewhat intense coating melts a bit slowly. Sweet.
	.20	2.5	151	4	Somewhat dense, icy ice cream a bit low in flavor; thin coating a bit low in flavor. slight freezer taste. Sweet.
	.18	2.5	151	4	Airy, very icy, slightly gummy ice cream a bit low in flavor; thin coating with low flavor. Slight freezer taste. Somewhat sweet.
	.16	2.5	131	3	Airy, very icy, gummy, slightly salty ice milk a bit low in flavor, thin coating a bit low in flavor, melts a bit slowly. Freezer taste. Sweet.

Like any dairy product, ice-cream bars provide calcium, a mineral in short supply in many people's diets. Ice cream also provides a bit of protein, which is in ample supply in almost every American's diet. But even the lowest-cal ice-milk bar packs far too many calories with those nutrients to be considered a good source of calcium or protein.

28   Hoping to appeal to the nutrition-conscious, frozen-novelty makers offer many products that sound more wholesome than ice-cream bars. In addition to ice-milk bars, they make frozen yogurt bars, pudding bars, and *Tofutti* bars. Such products, however, are nearly as rich as ice-cream bars. Like the *Weight Watchers* bar . . . they have fewer calories than the best bars, but that's mainly because they're on the small side. ◆

A CRITIC'S METHOD

Roger Ebert

Reviewing the 1991 movie *Cape Fear* created difficulties for Roger Ebert. He recognized a conflict between what *he* found significant in the film and what many of his readers would find significant. Fortunately for those who want to understand how writers work, he analyzed these difficulties in "A Memo to Myself and Certain Other Film Critics." Together, these two essays form an interesting case study in the way writers can combine honesty and diplomacy in their relations with an audience.

A MEMO TO MYSELF AND CERTAIN OTHER FILM CRITICS

1   NOVEMBER 13, 1991—A NEW THRILLER has opened, starring Nick Nolte, Robert DeNiro, and Jessica Lange. There were supporting performances by Robert Mitchum and Gregory Peck. And those are the terms in which 95 percent of moviegoers think of *Cape Fear*. But if you read the critics you would have heard about a man named Martin Scorsese, who directed the film, and maybe something about Bernard Herrmann, who has been dead for fifteen years, but whose musical score was used in the picture.

2   There is a gulf between people who go to the movies (the public) and people whose lives revolve around them (critics, movie buffs, academics, people in the business). For most people with seven bucks in their pocket and an evening free, there is only one question about *Cape Fear* that is relevant: Will I have a good time? The "good time" may depend on whether the moviegoer has an appetite for violence, or is a fan of one of the stars, but it will not depend on whether the film was directed by Martin Scorsese.

3   That's why I question myself when I write a review like the one about *Cape Fear*. I tried to say whether the filmgoer would have a good time, and I had something to say about the actors. But my central concern was with Scorsese, who I think is the best director at work in the world today, and whose career is therefore the most interesting single aspect of my job. I wondered whether it was good news or bad that he had a multipicture deal with Ste-ven Spielberg and Universal, that he was working with a $34 million budget for the first time, and that he could use stars like Nolte, Lange, and De Niro without asking them to defer their usual salaries. Would he gain Hollywood but lose his soul?

4   Those are questions that may not be fascinating to everybody who reads the daily paper. Maybe some were interested in the fact that Mitchum and Peck had starred in the 1962 version of the same film, but I imagine almost nobody was interested in the fact that Scorsese had recycled the original score that Bernard Herrmann wrote for the 1962 movie. And if I had written that Herrmann was also the composer of the music for *Citizen Kane, Psycho,* and *Taxi Driver,* would that have made any difference?

5   Writing daily film criticism is a balancing act between the bottom line and the higher reaches, between the answers to the questions (1) Is this movie worth my money? and (2) Does this movie expand or devalue my information about human nature? Critics who write so everybody can understand everything are actually engaging in a kind of ventriloquism—working as their own dummies. They are pretending to know less than they do. But critics who write for other critics are hardly more honest, since they are sending a message to millions that only hundreds will understand. It's a waste of postage.

6   Writing the *Cape Fear* review, I had to deal with my own fear, that the director who is most important to me seemed to be turning

away from the material he was born to film, big-city life in the second half of this century. Scorsese, whose *GoodFellas* was the best movie of 1990, has for 1991 made a movie that, in the long run, will not be very important to his career. It is a good movie, and he has changed the original story (good versus evil) to reflect his own vision (guilt versus evil). But Scorsese's soul was not on the line here.

7   In taking this director-oriented approach, I went through a sort of self-justification. I've written at length about every one of Scorsese's movies, since I wrote the first newspaper review he ever received. I assume some of my readers have followed along, and share my interest. I can't write as if everybody was born yesterday, and doesn't know anything that is not in today's paper. One of the reasons I like the British papers is because they assume you know who "Thatcher" is, even if they don't preface her name with the words "Former British Prime Minister Margaret."

8   But there are no doubt many readers who could care less about Great American Filmmaker Martin (*Raging Bull*) Scorsese. To them, I owe the responsibility of writing a review that will be readable—not jargon—and will give an accurate notion of the movie they are thinking of going to see. And I need to tell them that *Cape Fear* stands aside from other current thrillers like *Delusion* and *Ricochet* because it is made by a man with an instinctive mastery of the medium.

9   What I do not owe any reader is simplistic populism. Some newspapers have started using panels of "teen critics" as an adjunct to their staff professionals. These panels seem to be an admission of defeat by the editors; they imply that the newspaper has readers who cannot be bothered by the general tone of the editorial product, and must be addressed in self-congratulatory prose by their peers. "Sneak Previews," a television program of movie reviewing, copied this approach by adding their own teen-age experts, on the assumption that a relative lack of experience and background is an asset.

10   What is happening here seems to be endemic in a lot of American journalism: People read the papers not in the hopes of learning something new, but in the expectation of being told what they already know. This is a form of living death. Its apotheosis is the daily poll in *USA Today,* which informs "us" what percentage of a small number of unscientifically selected people called a toll number to vote on questions that cannot possibly be responded to with a "yes" or "no."

11   Back to the movies. What if a poll discovered that less than one in twenty of the people attending *Cape Fear* know or care who Martin Scorsese is? Would that be a good reason why I shouldn't write about him? I ask these questions here because I sometimes ask them of myself. Everybody who works for a mass-circulation publication has to ask them, at one time or another. I guess the answer is halfway between what you want to know and what else I want to tell you. Eventually you'll know more than I do, and then you can have the job.

[REVIEW OF] CAPE FEAR

1   The way he sees the character of Sam Bowden is the key to why Martin Scorsese wanted to remake the 1962 thriller *Cape Fear*. Bowden, played by Nick Nolte, is a defense attorney who is threatened by a man from his past—a rapist who has finished a fourteen-year prison sentence and wants revenge for what he believes (correctly) was a lousy defense. In the original film, Sam Bowden was a good man trying to defend his family from a madman. In the Scorsese version, Bowden is flawed and guilty, and indeed everyone in this film is weak in one way or another, and there are no heroes. That's the Scorsese touch.

2   The movie, filmed near Fort Lauderdale, Florida, shows Nolte at the head of a troubled family. He and his wife (Jessica Lange) have been through counseling because of his infidelities, and now he seems to be in the opening stages of a new affair. They live in a rambling

house on a lot of land, but there isn't space enough for their daughter (Juliette Lewis), who hates it when they fight, and locks herself in her bedroom to brood and watch MTV. This is a family with a lot of problems even before Max Cady arrives on the scene.

3 Cady is played by Robert De Niro, in a role filled by Robert Mitchum in 1962. Covered with tattoos spelling out dire biblical warnings, Cady is an iron-pumping redneck who learned to read in prison ("I started with Dick, Jane, and Spot, and went on to law books"). He drives into town in a Mustang convertible and offers to teach Bowden something about the law. And soon everywhere Bowden looks, he sees the ominous, threatening presence of Max Cady: outside a restaurant, in a movie theater, on the wall bordering his property.

4 But Cady is clever and stays just this side of the law; he doesn't actually trespass, and he doesn't do physical harm to Bowden. It's almost a game with Cady to taunt Bowden to the breaking point. Bowden goes to the cops, to a lawyer, to a private investigator, and as he seeks help we begin to realize that no one in this universe is untainted. Among the corrupt are Robert Mitchum, as a cop who hints that the lawyer should take the law into his own hands, and Gregory Peck, as a lawyer who represents Cady.

5 What we are looking at here is a *film noir* version of the classic Scorsese hero, who in film after film is a man tortured by guilt and the weakness of the flesh, and seeking forgiveness and redemption. And in this new version of Max Cady, Scorsese gives us not simply a bad man, but an evil one—a man whose whole purpose is to show Sam Bowden that he is a criminal, too.

6 A strata of evil underlies the whole film and is dramatized in the character of Danielle, the Bowdens' daugher, who is going on sixteen and is attracted to the menace and implied sexuality of Max Cady. It's as if she likes anybody who can bug her parents. In a tense, disturbing scene, Cady poses as a drama teacher and Danielle goes

along even after she knows who he really is— allowing herself to be verbally seduced because evil and danger are attractive to her.

7 Nolte's character is more complex. He is not a bad man, but not a very good one, and he finally agrees with his private eye (Joe Don Baker) that maybe three guys should be hired to pound some sense into Max Cady. When Cady thrashes the three goons and comes looking for the Nolte character, we realize the complexity of this movie. Unlike the simplistic version of this scene we have seen in a hundred thrillers, what Scorsese gives us is a villain who has been wronged, seeking to harm a hero who has sinned.

8 I think the movie wanders a little toward the end, during a sensational climax in a tempest-tossed houseboat. The final struggle between Bowden and Cady passes beyond the plausible into the apocalyptic, and Cady delivers one-liners and bitter aphorisms long after he should be crazed by pain. But the final struggle between the two men is visually sensational, and once again Scorsese avoids the simplistic moralism of a conventional thriller; the key to the passage is the close-up of Bowden trying to wash the blood from his hands.

9 *Cape Fear* is impressive moviemaking, showing Scorsese as a master of a traditional Hollywood genre, able to mold it to his own themes and obsessions. Yet as I look at this $35 million movie with big stars, special effects, and production values, I wonder if it represents a good omen from the finest director now at work.

10 This is the first film in a production deal Scorsese has with Universal and Steven Spielberg's Amblin Entertainment, and represents his access to budgets much larger than he has worked with in the past. The result seems to be a certain impersonality in a film by this most personal of directors—the scorsese touch on a genre piece, rather than a film torn out of the director's soul. Most directors would distinguish themselves by making a film this good. From the man who made *Taxi Driver, Raging Bull, After Hours,* and *GoodFellas,* this is not an advance. ◆

EMOTIONAL RESCUE

David Denby

Like Roger Ebert, David Denby of *New York* magazine is a critic whose reviews consistently give the reader more to think about than a simple thumbs up or thumbs down. Underlying the following review of *Philadelphia* is a strong conviction about what separates great movies (and perhaps all great works of art) from those that are merely good.

1 IN JONATHAN DEMME'S *PHILADELPHIA,* there's a single scene that is profoundly beautiful—startling, too, since the rest of the movie, which is about a successful young lawyer dying of AIDS, is no more than conventionally effective. Abruptly fired by the white-shoe Philadelphia firm in which he was a rising star, Andrew Beckett (Tom Hanks) becomes convinced that he is the victim of discrimination—that he was canned because he is gay and has AIDS. He tries to find a lawyer to represent him in a damage suit, and winds up with a crass ambulance chaser, Joe Miller (Denzel Washington), who flacks himself in TV ads. Miller, who has just had a baby girl, is a macho African-American contemptuous of homosexuals. Yet Andrew stirs something in him—a memory of racial hostility, perhaps—and he takes the case.

2 Demme and screenwriter Ron Nyswaner do not hesitate to show us the physical disintegration of Andrew Beckett's body: Each time the movie jumps a few weeks or months in time, we're shocked by Andrew's increasing thinness, tiredness, pallor. A jovial and active man—Tom Hanks, with his dancing dark eyes and springy legs—becomes quiet, withdrawn, and immobile. Hanks's deterioration reminded this viewer of similar downward journeys taken unwillingly but bravely by friends, and even though I wound up disliking the way Nyswaner and Demme used the suffering, I was moved by it. Up to the scene I'm thinking of, however, Demme and Nyswaner have not shown us much of Andrew's life as a homosexual. We can see that Andrew has a lover of many years (Antonio Banderas), who looks after him, and a large and supportive family. In some ways, he could be any suffering human being. But then *Philadelphia* takes a surprising leap.

3 In defiance of his condition, Andrew decides to throw a party in his loft. The joyous bash that Demme stages, with most of the guests dressed up wildly, is the first unashamed, uninhibited, and truly entertaining gay party I can think of in a major studio release. Suddenly, Andrew is not any suffering man; he is a specific gay man with specific tastes and pleasures. When the guests go home at last, Andrew and his lawyer, Joe Miller, sit down to discuss Andrew's upcoming testimony in court. But Andrew, who has only a few weeks to live, brushes off the lawyer's questions. Oddly, irrelevantly, he puts on an aria from Giordano's *Andrea Chenier*—Maria Callas singing "La mamma morta." As Joe looks on in dismay, Andrew passionately explicates the aria, translating the Italian, re-creating with his hands and voice the emotional meaning of the words and of Callas's performance.

4 This sequence, which has been written, directed, and played with the utmost daring and emotional commitment, makes clear, with a force I've never seen before, exactly what opera means for its most passionate fans and for gays in particular. "La mamma morta" is an aria about the power of love. The heroine's mother has died in the flames of the French

Revolution. Maddalena (the Callas character) describes the death and then her own resurrection from despair—she has fallen in love with the poet Andrea Chenier. Love, filling her soul as a kind of godlike presence, speaks to her: "Is everything around thee blood and mire? I am divine! I am oblivion. . . . Ah! I am love." As Andrew moves around his loft, dragging his IV stand and declaiming, Demme swings the camera over Hanks's head, and the lighting, in imitation of the flames in the aria, turns an expressionistic flickering red.

5   Demme goes over the top, and why? Because opera, which uses voice and music to clarify and heighten emotion—to produce moments of ecstatic being—regularly breaks into such exaggerated gestures. Opera is about the intensification of feeling, and in this scene, a man who is dying feels rescued from despair (like Maddalena) by the power of love. Shaken, Joe goes home, and, as the aria plays again on the soundtrack, he kisses his daughter and climbs into bed next to his wife. The filmmakers' meaning becomes clear: If there is a power in love, and if transcendence is possible (Maria Callas makes a good case for it), then these things must include all of us. Now, this is not some gooey message of universal brotherhood intended to comfort the unhappy people of the world; it's nothing less than a call to heroism, because heroism is the only force that can overcome the growing American antagonisms, the divisions of race, gender, and class. As a beginning, the movie says, accept the reality of gay sex and gay identity, and don't hold AIDS against homosexuals.

6   Nothing else in *Philadelphia* comes close to that sequence's awkward greatness. The rest of the movie, which is merely sympathetic, intelligent, and shrewd, attempts to raise consciousness and reverse a few clichés. Demme has given us, for instance, a black who is not the victim but the dispenser of prejudice, and a sympathetic-looking female lawyer (Mary Steenburgen) who represents the villainous firm

and who smilingly subjects Hanks to a ruthless cross-examination. Yet despite these attempts to avoid TV-movie p.c., Demme and Nyswaner have got themselves caught up in a conventional and didactic structure. *Philadelphia* is a kind of lecture-demonstration that's meant to improve us. In doing so, Demme is not above using the pathos of Andrew's condition to drive home his points.

7   As Andrew Beckett's civil suit against his old employers comes to trial, the perfidious swine of the prestigious firm get exposed in all their rancid homophobia; and Joe Miller, saddled with a common set of anti-gay prejudices, learns that he is ignorant, and that his true interests as an African-American lie in his making an alliance with fellow outsiders. He sheds his prejudices and becomes a grown-up. And all the while, Andrew is dying, dying right in court. Hanks's performance is wonderful—restrained, dry, precise—but I grew indignant at what amounted to exploitation of the character's suffering. Andrew Beckett literally falls over at the trial, and the juxtaposition of his weakness with the vile testimony of the law partners almost suggests that prejudice, rather than disease, is killing him.

8   And hasn't courtroom drama itself become a pathetic device? A trial may have a natural dramatic shape, but more and more I've come to feel that courtroom drama answers some deeper and sadder American need. In this country, we are now so divided by ethnic, religious, and sexual differences that we can barely talk to one another. Manners in the largest sense have failed. Litigation fills the void, in life and in movies—except, of course, that it can't fill the void. Denzel Washington says during the trial, "This case is not about AIDS. This case is about our hatred and fear of homosexuals." Yes, and so is the movie. But if that is so, then why rely on a courtroom setting, with its obvious and self-important "revelations"? At least the opera scene suggests the possibility of something greater. ◆

PART VI

MATTERS OF FORM AND STYLE

"Most readers are in trouble about half of the time."

E. B. WHITE

Organization

ONE OF THE GREAT CHICKEN-AND-EGG PROBLEMS IN WRITING IS whether essays ought to be organized and then written, or written and then organized. Either view has its dangers. Writers who choose a form first, then decide what content to pour into it, tend to produce regimented essays like "Seat Belts" (p. 36) that "outline" neatly and read dully:

Thesis:	Everyone should use seat belts.
Topic sentence 1:	Young people should use seat belts.
Topic sentence 2:	Older people should also use seat belts.
Topic sentence 3:	The very young should use seat belts.
Conclusion:	As we have seen, all people should use seat belts.

On the other hand, people who write individual sentences without considering larger structures often produce underorganized mazes that no amount of revision will straighten out. Reading one of these essays is like threading your way through a city by flipping a coin at each corner to decide which way to turn.

To avoid the dangers of both regimented organization and underorganization, let's recall something all of us know from experience: nobody reads with steady attention page after page. We are like underwater swimmers who need to come up for air frequently. We look up from the page, stretch, fidget, think about what we have read so far, plunge back in. Since the limits of the reader's attention span will break the essay into parts at any rate, the wise writer organizes the essay as a set of "pocket essays" that fit with the natural rhythm of reading and pausing. The pockets work together, of course, but they must also work *separately*—each having value and interest in its own right. Planning a whole essay may best be conceived as developing a series of pocket essays—making each pocket's subject and framework clear, putting the series of pockets in a logical order, and making connections among them strong.

THE FIRM APPROACH TO ORGANIZATION

Most nineteenth-century textbooks and many from our own time have recommended what we could call the "firm approach" to organization: each pocket in the essay's body should be exactly one paragraph long, and each of these paragraphs should begin with a topic sentence. If all other sentences in a paragraph support the topic sentence, and if the topic sentences support the thesis, then the essay will be well organized. That the firm approach *can* produce essays as dull as "Seat Belts" doesn't mean that it necessarily will. There are far more sophisticated essays that develop each pocket essay in a single paragraph and begin each paragraph with a topic sentence.

Take, for example, the following paragraph written by Theodore White. While White seems to have mixed feelings about the regimentation at the high school he describes, he writes an excellent paragraph according to the firm principles he learned there:

> (1) The Latin School taught the mechanics of learning with very little pretense of culture, enrichment or enlargement of horizons. (2) Mr. Russo, who taught English in the first year, had the face of a prize-fighter—a bald head which gleamed, a pug nose, a jut jaw, hard and sinister eyes which smiled only when a pupil scored an absolute triumph in grammar. (3) He was less interested in the rhymes of *The Idylls of the King,* or "Evangeline," or in the story in *Quentin Durward,* than in drubbing into us the structure of paragraph and sentence. (4) The paragraph began with the "topic sentence"—that was the cornerstone of all teaching in composition. (5) And sentences came with "subjects," "predicates," "metaphors," "similes," and "analogies." (6) Verbs were transitive, intransitive, and sometimes subjunctive. (7) He taught the English language as if he were teaching us to dismantle an automobile engine or a watch and then assemble it again correctly. (8) We learned clean English from him. (9) Mr. Graetsch taught German in the same way, mechanically, so that one remembered all the rest of one's life that six German prepositions take the dative case—*aus-bei-mit, nach-von-zu,* in alphabetical order. (10) French was taught by Mr. Scully. (11) Not only did we memorize passages (*D'un pas encore vaillant et ferme, un vieux prêtre marche sur la route poudreuse*), but we memorized them so well that long after one had forgotten the title of the work, one remembered its phrases; all irregular French verbs were mastered by the end of the second year.

A WRITER AT WORK

"The Latin School"
THEODORE WHITE

Just as Mr. Russo would have wished, White begins this paragraph with a topic sentence. The topic sentence establishes both the subject (the Latin School) and the framework ("mechanics of learning with very little pretense of culture . . ."). In subsequent sentences, White keeps reminding us of the framework while adding pertinent but unexpected details about the subject. The second sentence tells us that Russo looked like a pug-nosed prizefighter rather than a reader of poetry, thus reinforcing the mechanical-rather-than-cultural framework. It shows us Russo's head gleaming and his jaw jutting, details that refresh our sense of the framework by reminding us of the oily, squared-off surfaces of machines. It asserts that only one thing made Russo smile—a triumph of grammar, the most mechanical aspect of English.

So White works, sentence after sentence, fleshing out the paragraph's topic sentence, reinforcing its framework by adding carefully selected details about its subject. Look at the contrast of *rhymes* (cultural) and *drubbing* (mechanical) in sentence 3, or the use of *cornerstone* (matter-of-fact and mechanical) in sentence 4. Look at the number of times that White links teaching to memorization of lists and passages; and look—especially—at the comparison to an automobile engine and a watch in sentence 7. White wants his paragraph to be a pocket essay that leaves a single strong impression on the mind, and it certainly does. Though we may forget many details, we can hardly fail to get the gist.

The Flexible Approach

Throughout his long career Theodore White followed Mr. Russo's advice and took the firm course. Most of his paragraphs are pocket essays that begin with a topic sentence. Not every successful writer engineers an essay this way, however. Consider the following pocket essay from Annie Dillard's *Encounters with Chinese Writers,* which begins with Dillard's memory of a statement made at a writers' conference in China.

"I believe," says one man, "that after several decades we will be able to lead a good life on our soil." He is speaking of his goals as a writer, and he is addressing the point directly.

He is a handsome man, and an elegant one in his trim gray jacket. He sits erect and relaxed, often with a disdainful expression; when he laughs, his face crumples surprisingly into a series of long dimples. He writes scathing criticism of the government. The very contraction and repose of his limbs suggest great passion under great control. He repeats, "I believe that after several decades we will be able to lead a good life on our soil."

Ah, that soil! He has put his finger on it. For the main fact and difficulty of China is its millions of square miles of terrible soil, soil that all the will and cooperation in the world cannot alter. He has put his finger on it, and so have many others—for the soil of his populous region is so clay-like, and the technology for working it is so labor-intensive, that it—the soil—actually has fingerprints on it.

Driving to this meeting we saw fields on the outskirts of the city, and patches of agriculture. There was a field of eggplant. Separating the rows of eggplant were long strips of dried mud, five inches high, like thick planks set on edge. These low walls shield shoots and stems from drying winds. We stopped to look. The walls were patted mud; there were fingerprints. There were fingerprints dried into the loess walls around every building in the western city of Xian. There were fingerprints in the cones of dried mud around every tree's roots in large afforestation plots near Hangzhou, and along the Yangtze river. There is good soil in China, too, on which the peasants raise three and even four crops a year, and there are 2,000-acre fields, and John Deere tractors—but there is not enough. There are only some arable strips in the river valleys—only one-tenth of China's land. If you look at your right palm, you see a map of China: the rivers flow east, and most of the rest is high and dry; the arable land is like dirt collected in the lines of your palm.

Near the eggplant field, two men were pulling a plow. These humans were pulling the iron plow through the baked ground by ropes lashed across their chests. A third man guided the plow's tongue. "The old planet," Maxine Hong Kingston calls China; it is the oldest enduring civilization on earth.

If Dillard had a teacher who insisted that the cornerstone of composition was putting topic sentences at the beginning of paragraphs, she seems to have shaken off his or her influence. In many cases, Dillard's reader moves through a series of paragraphs before the point of a passage becomes clear. The paragraphs introduce a series of images that gradually reveal the focus of the pocket essay. In this case, the key images are in the fourth paragraph and concern hands and dirt: the fingerprints in the mud planks and in the soil around buildings and new-planted trees; the hand with soil in the palm's lines, offered as a map of China. It is these images that establish the connection between Dillard's subject (cultural conditions in China) and her framework (the difficulty of farming in China). The topic sentence, if it can be called that, is a relatively pale thing buried in the middle of the passage. And the passage is broken into paragraphs for reasons that have less to do with changing the subject or framework than with controlling pace and emphasis.

When White ends a paragraph, he seems to be telling us, "There's the completion of the idea stated in my topic sentence; now I'm moving to the next pocket essay, which is related in ways I will make clear to you." When Dillard ends a paragraph, she sometimes seems to tell us, "Let that soak in a bit; we're going to look at something else; eventually *you'll* put the pieces together in a pocket essay." A flexible approach to organization like Dillard's demands more of the reader than a firm approach like White's. When used well, it draws readers in, gets them actively involved in the process of creating an interpretation. But it carries with it the danger of misunderstanding and sheer fatigue, and on some occasions it is simply out of place. The reader of a business letter or scientific report will neither expect nor appreciate flexible organization.

◆ *Converting a Passage to a Firmer Organization.* In the middle of the Dillard passage, there is a general statement that corresponds to a topic sentence and makes "the point" perfectly clear: ". . . the main fact and difficulty of China is its millions of square miles of terrible soil, soil that all the will and cooperation in the world cannot alter." Using that sentence as a topic sentence, rewrite the passage as a single paragraph that would satisfy Mr. Russo's standard of firm organization. Your rewrite should contain only material related to the topic sentence, so you may find yourself either eliminating some of the information from the original passages or changing the way it is presented. When you have finished, compare your version to Dillard's original. What are the advantages and disadvantages of each?

◆ *Reparagraphing an Essay.* The following column by Ellen Goodman is about 650 words long and was originally printed in several short paragraphs suitable for the narrow columns of a newspaper. Ignoring the problem of narrow columns, mark the points where you believe paragraph breaks would be most useful. Then answer the questions that follow.

A Working Community

A WRITER AT WORK

"A Working Community"
ELLEN GOODMAN

(1) I have a friend who is a member of the medical community. (2) It does not say that, of course, on the stationery that bears her home address. (3) This membership comes from her hospital work. (4) I have another friend who is a member of the computer community. (5) This is a fairly new subdivision of our economy, and yet he finds his sense of place in it. (6) Other friends and acquaintances of mine are members of the academic community, or the business community, or the journalistic community. (7) Though you cannot find these on any map, we know where we belong. (8) None of us, mind you, was born into these communities. (9) Nor did we move into them, U-Hauling our possessions along with us. (10) None has papers to prove we are card-carrying members of one such group or another. (11) Yet it seems that more and more of us are identified by work these days, rather than by street. (12) In the past, most Americans lived in neighborhoods. (13) We were members of precincts or parishes or school districts. (14) My dictionary still defines community, first of all in geographic terms, as "a body of people who live in one place." (15) But today fewer of us do our living in that one place; more of us just use it for sleeping. (16) Now we call our towns "bedroom suburbs," and many of us, without small children as icebreakers, would have trouble naming all the people on our street. (17) It's not that we are more isolated today. (18) It's that many of us have transferred a chunk of our friendships, a major portion of our everyday social lives, from home to office. (19) As more of our neighbors work away from home, the workplace becomes our neighborhood. (20) The kaffeeklatsch

of the fifties is the coffee break of the eighties. (21) The water cooler, the hall, the elevator, and the parking lot are the back fences of these neighborhoods. (22) The people we have lunch with day after day are those who know the running saga of our mother's operations, our child's math grades, our frozen pipes, and faulty transmissions. (23) We may be strangers at the supermarket that replaced the corner grocer, but we are known at the coffee shop in the lobby. (24) We share with each other a cast of characters from the boss in the corner office to the crazy lady in Shipping, to the lovers in Marketing. (25) It's not surprising that when researchers ask Americans what they like best about work, they say it is "the shmoose [chatter] factor." (26) When they ask young mothers at home what they miss most about work, it is the people. (27) Not all the neighborhoods are empty, nor is every workplace a friendly playground. (28) Most of us have had mixed experiences in these environments. (29) Yet as one woman told me recently, she knows more about the people she passes on the way to her desk than she does about the people she passes on her way around the block. (30) Our new sense of community hasn't just moved from house to office building. (31) The labels that we wear connect us with members from distant companies, cities, and states. (32) We assume that we have something "in common" with other teachers, nurses, city planners. (33) It's not unlike the experience of our immigrant grandparents. (34) Many who came to this country still identified themselves as members of the Italian community, the Irish community, the Polish community. (35) They sought out and assumed connections with people from the old country. (36) Many of us have updated that experience. (37) We have replaced ethnic identity with professional identity, the way we replaced neighborhoods with the workplace. (38) This whole realignment of community is surely most obvious among the mobile professions. (39) People who move from city to city seem to put roots down into their professions. (40) In an age of specialists, they may have to search harder to find people who speak the same language. (41) I don't think that there is anything massively disruptive about this shifting sense of community. (42) The continuing search for connection and shared enterprise is very human. (43) But I do feel uncomfortable with our shifting identity. (44) The balance has tipped and we seem increasingly dependent on work for our sense of self. (45) If our offices are our new neighborhoods, if our professional titles are our new ethnic tags, then how do we separate our selves from our jobs? (46) Self-worth isn't just something to measure in the marketplace. (47) But in these new communities, it becomes harder and harder to tell who we are without saying what we do.

1. Identify the thesis statement of Goodman's essay. If you feel that no single sentence in the essay expresses Goodman's thesis, write a sentence that you believe adequately summarizes her general idea.

2. Identify a topic sentence for each of the paragraphs you have identified. If you find no adequate topic sentence, write a sentence that adequately summarizes the idea of the paragraph.

3. Discuss the "firm" or "flexible" qualities of Goodman's essay. How does it compare to the Dillard passage about China and the White paragraph about the Latin School?

A Moderate Approach to Organization

To say that a writer's approach to organization is either firm or flexible is an oversimplification. These approaches exist as extremes of a continuum:

Firm   Flexible

White's style is closer to the left end of the continuum than Dillard's, but there are writers far more rigid: Mr. Russo may have been one. Dillard is fairly far to the right, but—in this passage, at least—not so far that her prose ceases to be expository and becomes purely poetic. Most of the writing done by students and by writers on the job (lawyers, nurses, sales representatives, engineers) falls nearer White's position than Dillard's.

A good compromise position for writing college papers is one that allows "fully conscious" deviations from firm organization. You may want to avoid the predictability of making each paragraph into a pocket essay with a topic sentence at the head, but your drift should be clear enough that the reader could mark boundaries between pocket essays and name the subject and framework of each if asked. Vary your reader's experience by an occasional deviation from the standard "firm" pattern if you like, but organize firmly enough to avoid confusion.

In situations where you must write quickly, with little or no time to revise, the prudent thing is to be firm, since you won't want the grader to be even momentarily confused about the organization of the essay.

Connecting Pocket Essays

Once you realize that every essay longer than a page or two is made up of pocket essays, you recognize the problem of connecting these pockets in the minds of readers. The principal techniques are establishing *keynotes* and referring back to them. In "Nuns," for instance, Anna Quindlen's third paragraph sets the keynotes for the rest of the essay:

> I am sure that being under the constant sway of human beings living in a state of enforced employment and chastity must have some blacker reverberations, and I know the nuns attached too much value to our being well behaved, but today it is the good things I remember. I suspect, deep down, that some of those women turned me into a feminist. I wonder what they would think of that? For the nuns were intelligent, most of them, and they seemed in charge. The place where they lived smelled of furniture polish and horsehair-stuffed brocade and reeked of order, and if in the morning there was chalk on their simple yet majestic habits, by afternoon it was gone.

Feminist, in charge, majestic: these key words define Quindlen's attitude toward the nuns. The words prepare the readers to hear the essay's later body paragraphs.

> In paragraphs four and five, Quindlen contrasts those Catholic women who choose a life of "habitual pregnancy" with those who choose "education and advancement . . . peace and quiet . . . a higher way" in the convent. Without exact repetition, this wording echoes the keynotes. How could a reader fail to connect this description of convent life with words like *majestic* and *in charge*? That this majesty is achieved partly by an escape from "habitual pregnancy" makes the connection to *feminist*.
>
> Paragraph 6 begins with the sentence "Nuns seemed sure of themselves." It tells us that "self-confidence must be part of the costume." Again the connection to the keynotes is obvious, even though the exact words are not repeated.
>
> Paragraphs 7–9 show that though the world in which the nuns lived was in some ways controlled by men, the women "took good care of themselves," "were somehow sterner and less warm with the boys than with the girls," and would run "down a hockey field or out on the polished wood floor of the basketball court, driving or dribbling," so that Quindlen was amazed by girls who told her that "athletics were only for boys." How *majestic* the nuns seem here may depend on your view of basketball, but there is little doubt that Quindlen has made her connection with *feminist* and *in charge*.

In an essay as short as Quindlen's (about 1500 words) and with as few pockets to join, adequate connections can be made by returning in each pocket to the keynotes established in or near the introduction.

When an essay is longer, the writer may need to work more systematically on the transitions between pockets. Here again the principal tools are keynotes and references back. In this chapter, for instance, I had to think hard about how to connect one major section to the next. Looking at a few of my transitions will at least show you that subtlety is not everything.

To get the reader from the opening discussion of the pocket essay to the section on the firm approach, for example, I created this transition:

```
    Planning a whole essay may best be conceived
as developing a series of pocket essays—making
each pocket's subject and framework clear, put-
ting the series of pockets in a logical order,
and making connections among them strong.


        The Firm Approach to Organization

    Most nineteenth-century textbooks and many
from our own time have recommended what we could
call the "firm approach" to organization: each
pocket in the essay's body should be exactly one
paragraph long, and each of these paragraphs
should begin with a topic sentence.
```

The sentence before the section break gives the chapter's thesis and previews what is to come. I imagine that at the section break, readers will come up for air, relaxing their concentration for a moment before reading on. Since I want them to connect the material following the break with what has come before, I refer back by repeating the key word *pocket,* hoping that the oddness of the word will sharpen their memory of the introductory section. Had I said, "Each idea in the essay's body should occupy exactly one paragraph," the connection would have been fainter.

The section on the firm approach, you may remember, concluded with a discussion of Theodore White's paragraph about the Latin School's "mechanical" approach to education. Here is the very end of that section:

```
    White wants his paragraph to be a pocket essay
that leaves a single strong impression on the
mind, and it certainly does. Though we may for-
get many details, we can hardly fail to get the
gist.
```

To make a bridge to the next section, I referred back to Theodore White and his paragraph:

```
            The Flexible Approach

    Throughout his long career Theodore White fol-
lowed Mr. Russo's advice and took the firm
```

```
course. Most of his paragraphs are pocket essays
that begin with a topic sentence. Not every suc-
cessful writer engineers an essay this way, how-
ever. Consider the following pocket essay from
Annie Dillard's Encounters with Chinese Writ-
ers. . . .
```

The reference to White and the firm course are the obvious references back, but the one I particularly like is the word *engineers*, which (I hope) reminds the reader simultaneously of two themes from the preceding section: the mechanical nature of Latin School education and the somewhat mechanical nature of the firm approach. Once I have touched these bases, I'm ready to move on, believing that the reader will be prepared to see the contrast between firm and flexible approaches.

One example more, just to show how blunt a writer can be in making transitions. When I finished the sections explaining the firm and flexible approaches, I wanted to refresh the reader's memory of both approaches before launching into the next section. Therefore, I began the section this way: "To say that a writer's approach to organization is either firm or flexible is an oversimplification." The sentence reaches back 1652 words and says to the reader, "Recall this before you go on."

Writers maintain coherence largely by sending readers on mental errands to collect information deposited in earlier pocket essays. The advantage of establishing definite keynotes is that they serve as a bright tag and a convenient handle. The writer doesn't vaguely request the reader to remember what has been said before. Instead he or she tells the reader to recall a *labeled* discussion ("pocket," "engineered," "firm and flexible"). Fetching a labeled parcel is a much more manageable errand.

OUTLINING

Outlining is the traditional method of mapping the relations among an essay's parts. In the early stages of composing, as we noted in Chapter 3, a simple list—without indentations, numbers, or letters—may be an entirely adequate outline. Even if the list means nothing to a stranger who views it, each item on it serves the writer as a memory peg on which thoughts can be hung. Of course, most of us get our thoughts in order in the process of drafting, so there is danger in following such an outline slavishly. A thorough prewriting outline that doesn't change may be the sign of an exceptionally clear mind, but is at least as likely to be evidence of a dull one.

On the other hand, when the goal is fairly firm organization, creating a thorough outline *after* the essay is drafted can be very useful because the process often uncovers faulty relations among the essay's parts. If you follow the conventions of formal outlining, with indentations, lettering and numbering, you make obvious the relative "sizes" of various passages and their relation to one another. Each Roman numeral entry represents a major pocket, each capital letter a smaller one, each Arabic numeral a still smaller, and so on, down to the smallest pocket-within-a-pocket. There is an advantage even in the very artificial rule that there should be no A-entry in an outline without a corresponding B, no 1-entry without a corresponding 2, since the rule insures that the larger pocket is more inclusive than the smaller pockets it contains.

A formal outline of your paper should be a complete summary of the whole; it should be detailed enough that readers could turn to it rather than to the paper itself to refresh their memories. Such outlines are sometimes required on long, formal writing projects. I include one here both as an example and as a way of summarizing the contents of this chapter.

OUTLINE OF CHAPTER 13

I. Whole essays are best seen as a collection of "pocket essays."
   A. The dangers of mechanical organization or chaos.
   B. Developing units of meaning that fit the rhythm of reading.
   C. Preview of concerns about pocket essays.
      1. Making the subjects and frameworks clear.
      2. Putting them in order.
      3. Making connections strong.

II. Many experts recommend the firm approach to organizing these pocket essays.
   A. Definition: For each pocket, a single paragraph; for each paragraph, a topic sentence.
   B. A good example of the firm approach: Theodore White's paragraph.
   C. Analysis of White's paragraph on the Latin School.
      1. Presence and placement of a topic sentence.
      2. Reinforcement of framework and elaboration of subject throughout the paragraph.

III. Some writers prefer a more flexible approach.
   A. Annie Dillard's pocket essay on China.
   B. Analysis of the pocket essay.
      1. Disappearance of the "firm" paragraph headed by a topic sentence.
      2. Reliance on images to connect subject and framework.
   C. Advantages of the flexible approach.
   D. Disadvantages of the flexible approach.

IV. The best approach is often moderately firm.
   A. The continuum between firm and flexible approaches.

B. Recommendation of a firm approach with conscious deviations in most college writing.

C. Recommendation of an undeviatingly firm approach for writing under pressure.

V. The principal tools for connecting pocket essays are previewing and referring back.

A. Example of simple keynote references from a short essay: Anna Quindlen's "Nuns."

B. Example of more calculated transitions from a longer essay: this chapter.

VI. Outlines can reveal the relations among the pockets in an essay.

A. Definition of outline.

B. Use of scratch outlines before writing.

C. Use of formal outlines to check relations among the essay's parts.

D. An outline of this chapter.

VII. The pocket-essay view of organization gives writers three useful points to consider as they draft and revise.

A. The use of pockets in early stages of drafting.

B. The analysis of pockets as a way of checking organization.

C. The use of pockets as a basis for writing summaries.

◆ *A Formal Outline.* Formal outlines are frequently required for term papers, but the paper by Carolyn Douglas on pages 260–283 has none. To gain a clearer view of how she has organized her essay and to practice the conventions of formal outlining, provide an outline that could have been handed in with the paper.

EXERCISE 3

ORGANIZING THE BODY

Most of us are dimly aware when we read or write an essay that we are actually working our way through a series of related pocket essays. A sharper awareness of these pockets of meaning can bear fruit in at least three ways:

POINTS TO

CONSIDER

1. In the early stages of drafting an essay, writers often feel that they have some good "bits" but can't see how these pieces will ever fit together as a whole. Realizing that an essay *necessarily* consists of pocket essays gives a green light to writers in this situation. Go ahead and work up the "bit"; as the pocket essay takes form, you may find ways to bend your overall organization to fit it.

2. In later stages of reviewing and revising, writers often have trouble recognizing organizational problems because their attention wavers between the big picture and the details. Under these circumstances, it is often useful to reread the essay one pocket at a time, drawing lines at the intersections between pockets. This makes it easier for the writer to concentrate on one question at a time: "Is *this* pocket well organized in itself?" and then "Is its relation to the surrounding pockets clear?"

3. A good method of writing a brief summary of an essay is to draw lines between major pockets, then write a sentence summary of each. This method is useful not only in summarizing the essays of other writers, but also in summarizing your own work in order to check its coherence.

Assignment for Chapter 13

A common writing task in the academic and business worlds is what we could call a "formal" summary, one that attempts to condense a long piece of writing into a short space while recreating its basic organization and maintaining the proportions of its various parts. In effect, the formal summary is an attempt to shrink the essay to a specified size. The summarizer may use a few very brief quotations but ordinarily will recast the document in his or her own words. Ideally, the summary should give someone who has never read the original document a clear idea of what it contains. The summary could also serve as an aid to the memory of someone who has read the document.

The shortest of such summaries are called abstracts. Often limited to 100 to 200 words, abstracts squeeze detail out of the document they summarize, noting in generalized form what the largest "pockets" of the organization contain. Longer summaries add more detail. The longest are, essentially, economical paraphrases of the entire document.

Writing a good formal summary almost inevitably requires you to mark up the text, so you may want to photocopy the document you are summarizing before you begin. (If the document is printed in double columns, you may want to cut the columns apart and tape them to separate sheets, thus creating pages with extra-wide margins.) On the photocopy, you can mark bold lines between major pockets of organization and faint or jagged lines between minor pockets, then use the margin to state in your own words what the essence of each pocket is. (See the following sample annotation of the first three pages of W. E. B. Du Bois's "Jacob and Esau." The marginal annotations then become the basis of your summary.

Your assignment here involves two summaries. Choose one of the following essays from *The Riverside Guide to Writing*:

Eileen M. O'Brien, "What Was the Acheulean Hand Ax?" (p. 533)
Margaret Mead, "A Co-operative Society" (p. 511)
Isaac Asimov, "The Shape of Things" (p. 554)
Stephen Jay Gould, "Red Wings in the Sunset" (p. 235)

Write both an abstract (about 250 words) of the article you choose and a fuller summary (about 750 words).

AN EXAMPLE OF AN ESSAY ANNOTATED FOR SUMMARIZING

On the pages below, you'll see the way one reader has divided the opening pages of W. E. B. Du Bois's "Jacob and Esau" into "pocket essays" and written a brief note summarizing each. Following the annotated pages, you'll see the summary the annotations produced.

Jacob and Esau

W. E. B. DU BOIS

Du Bois recalls Sunday-school lessons about J & E; he disliked Jacob.

I remember very vividly the Sunday-school room where I spent the Sabbaths of my early years. It had been newly built after a disastrous fire; the room was large and full of sunlight; nice new chairs were grouped around where the classes met. My class was in the center, so that I could look out upon the elms of Main Street and see the passersby. But I was interested usually in the lessons and in my fellow students and the frail rather nervous teacher, who tried to make the Bible and its ethics clear to us. We were a trial to her, full of mischief, restless and even noisy; but perhaps more especially when we asked questions. And on the story of Jacob and Esau we did ask questions. My judgment then and my judgment now is very unfavorable to Jacob. I thought that he was a cad and a liar and I did not see how possibly he could be made the hero of a Sunday-school lesson. 1

Many days have passed since then and the world has gone through astonishing changes. But basically, my judgment of Jacob has not greatly changed and I have often promised myself the pleasure of talking about him publicly, and especially to young people. This is the first time that I have had the opportunity. 2

He makes the ideas these men represent his subject.

My subject then is "Jacob and Esau," and I want to examine these two men and the ideas which they represent; and the way in which those ideas have come to our day. Of course, our whole interpretation of this age-old story of Jewish mythology has greatly changed. We look upon these Old Testament stories today not as untrue and yet not as literally true. They are simple, they have their truths, and yet they are not by any means the expression of eternal verity. Here were brought forward for the education of Jewish children and for the interpretation of Jewish life to the world, two men: one small, lithe and quick-witted; the other tall, clumsy and impetuous: a hungry, hard-bitten man. 3

The J & E story is based on conflict between the ancient Jews, who had the "Great Plan" of a centralized state, and the Edomites, nomads without such a plan.

Historically, we know how these two types came to be set forth by the Bards of Israel. When the Jews marched north after escaping from slavery in Egypt, they penetrated and passed through the land of Edom; the land that lay between the Dead Sea and Egypt. It was an old center of hunters and nomads and the Israelites, while they admired the strength and organization of the Edomites, looked down upon them as lesser men; 4

Commencement address delivered at Talladega College, Talladega, Tennessee, June 5, 1944. For the story of Jacob and Esau, see Genesis 25–28.

as men who did not have the Great Plan. Now the Great Plan of the Israelites was the building of a strong, concentered state under its own God, Jehovah, devoted to agriculture and household manufacture and trade. It raised its own food by careful planning. It did not wander and depend upon chance wild beasts. It depended upon organization, strict ethics, absolute devotion to the nation through strongly integrated planned life. It looked upon all its neighbors, not simply with suspicion, but with the exclusiveness of a chosen people, who were going to be the leaders of earth.

Esau, though J's twin, was associated with Edomites—hunting, freedom, unorganized appetites.

This called for sacrifice, for obedience, for continued planning. The 5 man whom we call Esau was from the land of Edom, or intermarried with it, for the legend has it that he was twin of Jacob the Jew but the chief fact is that, no matter what his blood relations were, his cultural allegiance lay among the Edomites. He was trained in the free out-of-doors; he chased and faced the wild beasts; he knew vast and imperative appetite after long self-denial, and even pain and suffering; he gloried in food, he traveled afar; he gathered wives and concubines and he represented continuous primitive strife.

E's legacy is a way of life based on strong, uncalculating passions.

The legacy of Esau has come down the ages to us. It has not been 6 dominant, but it has always and continually expressed and re-expressed itself; the joy of human appetites, the quick resentment that leads to fighting, the belief in force, which is war.

As I look back upon my own conception of Esau, he is not nearly as 7 clear and definite a personality as Jacob. There is something rather shadowy about him; and yet he is curiously human and easily conceived. One understands his contemptous surrender of his birthright; he was hungry after long days of hunting; he wanted rest and food, the stew of meat and vegetables which Jacob had in his possession, and determined to keep unless Esau bargained. "And Esau said, Behold, I am at the point to die: and what profit shall this birthright be to me? And Jacob said, Swear to me this day; and he swore unto him: and he sold his birthright unto Jacob."

When he was hungry, he wanted his soup now, even if it cost him his inheritance.

J's legacy is the idea of a disciplined state more important than the desires of individuals.

On the other hand, the legacy of Jacob which has come down through 8 the years, not simply as a Jewish idea, but more especially as typical of modern Europe, is more complicated and expresses itself something like this: life must be planned for the Other Self, for that personification of the group, the nation, the empire, which has eternal life as contrasted with the ephemeral life of individuals. For this we must plan, and for this there must be timeless and unceasing work. Out of this, the Jews as chosen children of Jehovah would triumph over themselves, over all Edom and in time over the world.

We don't see this legacy in the history of the Jews, who were defeated and dispersed.

Now it happens that so far as actual history is concerned, this dream 9 and plan failed. The poor little Jewish nation was dispersed to the ends of the earth by the overwhelming power of the great nations that arose East, North, and South and eventually became united in the vast empire of Rome. This was the diaspora, the dispersion of the Jews. But the idea of the Plan with a personality of its own took hold of Europe with relentless grasp and this was the real legacy of Jacob, and of other men of other peoples, whom Jacob represents.

We see it in European empires built on a central plan: Roman Empire, Catholic Church, European nations that grabbed power and wealth unscrupulously.

There came the attempt to weld the world into a great unity, first 10 under the Roman Empire, then under the Catholic Church. When this attempt failed, the empire fell apart, there arose the individual states of Europe and of some other parts of the world; and these states adapted the idea of individual effort to make each of them dominant. The state was *all*, the individual subordinate, but right here came the poison of the Jacobean idea. How could the state get this power? Who was to wield the power within the state? So long as power was achieved, what difference did it make how it was gotten? Here then was war—but not Esau's war of passion, hunger and revenge, but Jacob's war of cold acquisition and power.

We can praise the J's of the world for putting the family and the nation above the self. We must sometimes condemn them as liars and thieves whose dishonesty brings disaster and undermines reason.

Granting to Jacob, as we must, the great idea of the family, the clan, 11 and the state as dominant and superior in its claims, nevertheless, there is the bitter danger in trying to seek these ends without reference to the great standards of right and wrong. When men begin to lie and steal, in order to make the nation to which they belong great, then comes not only disaster, but rational contradiction which in many respects is worse than disaster, because it ruins the leadership of the divine machine, the human reason, by which we chart and guide our actions.

SUMMARY OF W. E. B. DU BOIS'S "JACOB AND ESAU"

W. E. B. Du Bois's lecture begins with his memories of Sunday-school lessons about these characters and goes on to describe the ideas they represent. Their story reflects the conflict between the ancient Jews, who had developed the "Great Plan" of a centralized state, and the Edomites, who were nomads without such a plan. Esau, though Jacob's twin, was associated with the Edomites and the culture of hunting, freedom, and unorganized appetites.

Esau's legacy is a way of life based on strong, uncalculating passions: when he was hungry he wanted soup immediately, even at the cost of his inheritance. The legacy of Jacob is the idea of a disciplined state that is more important than individuals and their desires. We see this legacy in the history of European empires built on some central plan: the Roman Empire, the Catholic Church, and later the European nations unscrupulously grabbing power and wealth. Though we can praise the Jacobs of the world for putting the family and nation above private desires, we sometimes must condemn them as liars and thieves whose dishonesty brings disaster and undermines reason. . . .

A CO-OPERATIVE SOCIETY

Margaret Mead

Margaret Mead became perhaps the most famous of all American anthropologists and one of the most controversial. Growing up in the early 1900s, when many Americans were inclined to view male aggressiveness and female docility as fixed biological truths, Mead made a career of showing that male and female roles vary sharply from one culture to another and that the variation can be traced to child-rearing practices. Some critics charge that when Mead looked at a culture, she *managed* to find confirmation of her views. Yet as you will see in the following passage from *Sex and Temperament in Three Primitive Societies*, her conclusions are always supported by detailed observation. Unlike some of Mead's writing for newspapers and popular magazines, this passage about life in a remote region of New Guinea is not an "easy read" but a scholarly piece of work that invites you to practice your skills of careful reading, summary, and paraphrase.

1 ARAPESH LIFE IS ORGANIZED ABOUT THIS central plot of the way men and women, physiologically different and possessed of differing potencies, unite in a common adventure that is primarily maternal, cherishing, and oriented away from the self towards the needs of the next generation. It is a culture in which men and women do different things for the same reasons, in which men are not expected to respond to one set of motivations and women to another, in which if men are given more authority it is because authority is a necessary evil that someone, and that one the freer partner, must carry. It is a culture in which if women are excluded from ceremonies, it is for the sake of the women themselves, not as a device to bolster up the pride of the men, who work desperately hard to keep the dangerous secrets that would make their wives ill and deform their unborn children. It is a society where a man conceives responsibility, leadership, public appearance, and the assumption of arrogance as onerous duties that are forced upon him, and from which he is only too glad to escape in middle years, as soon as his eldest child attains puberty. In order to understand a social order that substitutes responsiveness to the concerns of others, and attentiveness to the needs of others, for aggressiveness, initiative, competitiveness, and possessiveness—the familiar motivations upon which our culture depends—it is necessary to discuss in some detail the way in which Arapesh society is organized.

2 There are no political units. Clusters of villages are grouped into localities, and each locality and its inhabitants have names. These names are sometimes used rhetorically at feasts, or to refer to the region, but the localities themselves have no political organization. Marriages, feasting organizations, and occasional semi-hostile clashes between neighbouring groups take place between hamlets or clusters of hamlets across locality lines. Each hamlet belongs theoretically to one patrilineal family line, which again has a name to distinguish it. The patrilineal families, or small localized clans, also possess hunting and gardening land, and located somewhere on their hunting-land is a water-hole or a quicksand or a steep

waterfall that is inhabited by their *marsalai,* a supernatural who appears in the form of a mythical and bizarrely coloured snake or lizard, or occasionally as a larger animal. In the abode of the *marsalai* and along the borders of the ancestral lands live the ghosts of the clan dead, including the wives of the men of the clan, who after death continue to live with their husbands instead of returning to their own clan-lands.

3   The Arapesh do not conceive of themselves as owning these ancestral lands, but rather as belonging to the lands; in their attitude there is none of the proud possessiveness of the land-owner who vigorously defends his rights against all comers. The land itself, the game animals, the timber trees, the sago, and especially the bread-fuit-trees, which are thought of as very old and dear to the ghosts—these all belong to the ghosts. For the feelings and attitudes of the ghosts the *marsalai* is a focusing-point. This being is not exactly an ancestor and not exactly not an ancestor—Arapesh casualness does not attempt to answer the question. The *marsalai* has a special touchiness about a few ritual points; he dislikes menstruating women, pregnant women, and men who come directly from intercourse with their wives. Such trespass he punishes with illness and death to the women or unborn children, unless he is specially placated by a mimic offering of a pig's tusk, an empty betel-sheath, a sago-container, and a taro-leaf, on which one of the ancestor souls will alight as a bird or a butterfly and absorb the spirit of the offering. The ghosts themselves are the residents of the lands, and a man going upon his own inherited land will announce himself, his name and relationship to them, remarking: "It is I, your grandson, of Kanehoibis. I have come to cut some posts for my house. Do not object to my presence, nor to my timber-cutting. As I return pluck back the brambles from my path, and bend back the branches so that I walk easily." This he must do even if he goes alone on the land that he has inherited from his forefathers. More often he has with him someone less directly connected, a relative or a brother-in-law, who is hunting with him or plans to make a garden on his land. Then introductions are in order. "See, my grandfathers, this is my brother-in-law, the husband of my sister. He comes to garden here with me. Treat him as your grandson, do not object to his being here. He is good." If these precautions are neglected, a hurricane will knock down the careless man's house or a landslip destroy his garden. Wind and rain and landslips are sent by the *marsalais,* who employ these means to discipline those who are careless about expressing the proper attitudes towards the land. In all of this there is none of the sense of ownership with which a man bids a stranger welcome to his land or proudly chops down a tree because it is his.

4   On a neighbouring hill-top, the village of Alipinagle was sadly depleted. In the next generation there would not be enough people to occupy the land. The people of Alitea sighed: "Alas, poor Alipinagle, after the present people are gone, who will care for the land, who will there be beneath the trees? We must give them some children to adopt, that the land and the trees may have people when we are gone." Such generosity had, of course, the practical consequences of placing a child or so in a more advantageous position, but it was never phrased in this way, nor did the people recognize any formulations based upon possessiveness about land. There was just one family in the locality that was possessive, and its attitude was incomprehensible to everyone else. Gerud, a popular young diviner and the eldest son of his family, once in a *séance* suggested as a motive for an alleged theft of dirt that the accused grudged to the children of a new-comer in the village a future share in the hunting-grounds. The rest of the community regarded his reasoning as little short of mad. Surely, people belonged to the land, not land to the people. As

a correlate of this point of view, no one is at all particular as to where he lives, and as often as not members of a clan live not in their ancestral hamlets, but in the hamlets of cousins or brothers-in-law. Without political organization, without any fixed and arbitary social rules, it is easy enough for people to do this.

5   As with residence sites, so with gardens. The Arapesh gardening is of two types: taro-gardens and banana-gardens, in which the men do the initial clearing, tree-lopping, and fencing, and the women do the planting, weeding, and harvesting; and yam-gardens, which with the exception of a little help rendered by women in weeding and in carrying the harvest are entirely men's work. Among many New Guinea tribes each married pair clears and fences a patch of land in their own inherited gardening-bush, and cultivates it more or less alone, with the help of their immature children, perhaps calling in other relatives at the harvest. In this way a New Guinea garden becomes a private place, almost as private as a house, and is frequently used for copulation; it is their own place. A man or his wife can go to the garden every day, repair any gaps in the fencing, and so protect the garden from the inroads of bush animals. All the external circumstances of the Arapesh environment would suggest such a gardening method as exceedingly practical. The distances are long and the roads difficult. People often have to sleep in their gardens because they are too far from other shelter, so they build small, badly thatched, uncomfortable huts on the ground, as it is not worth while to build a house on piles for one year's use. The steep slopes make fencing unsatisfactory and the pigs are always breaking in. Food is scarce and poor and it would seem like that under these conditions of hardship and poverty people would be very possessive of and attentive to their own gardens. Instead the Arapesh have evolved a different and most extraordinary system, expensive in time and human effort, but conducive to the

warm co-operation and sociability that they consider to be much more important.

Each man plants not one garden, but several, each one in co-operation with a different group of his relatives. In one of these gardens he is host, in the others he is guest. In each of these gardens three to six men, with one or two wives each, and sometimes a grown daughter or so, work together, fence together, clear together, weed together, harvest together, and while engaged in any large piece of work, sleep together, crowded up in the little inadequate shelter, with the rain dripping down the necks of more than half of the sleepers. These gardening groups are unstable—some individuals are unable to stand the strain of a bad crop; they tend to blame their gardening partners for it, and to seek new alliances the following year. Choice, now of one piece of long-fallow ground, now of another, sometimes makes next year's gardening-plot too far away for some of those who planted together last year. But each year a man's food-stakes lie not in one plot directly under his control, but scattered about, beneath the ghosts and on the land of his relatives, three miles in one direction, five miles in another.

This arrangement of work has several results. No two gardens are planted at the same time and therefore the Arapesh lack the "hungry time" so characteristic of yam-raising peoples where all of the yam-gardens are planted simultaneously. Where several men work together to clear and fence one plot before scattering to co-operate in clearing and fencing other plots, the harvests succeed each other. This method of gardening is not based upon the slightest physical need for co-operative labour. Tall trees are simply ringed, not felled, and the branches are cut off to let in light, so that a garden looks like an army of ghosts, white against the surrounding deep-green of the bush. The fencing is done with saplings that an adolescent boy could cut. But the preference is strong for working in small happy groups in which one man is host and may feast his guest workers with a little meat—if he finds it. And so the people go up and down the mountain sides, from one plot to another, weeding here, staking vines there, harvesting in another spot, called hither and thither by the demands of gardens in different states of maturity.

8   This same lack of individualism obtains in the planting of coconut-trees. A man plants such trees for his young sons, but not upon his own land. Instead, he will walk four or five miles carrying a sprouting coconut in order to plant it by the door-step of his uncle, or of his brother-in-law. A census of the palm-trees in any village reveals a bewildering number of distantly residing owners and bears no relation to the actual residents. In the same way, men who are friends will plant new sago-palms together, and in the next generation their sons become a working unit.

9   In hunting, too, a man does not hunt alone, but with a companion, sometimes a brother, as often a cousin or a brother-in-law; the bush, the ghosts, and the *marsalai* belong to one of the pair or trio. The man, be he host or guest, who sees the game first claims it, and the only tact that is necessary here is the tact of not seeing game very much more often than other people do. Men who make a practice of always claiming first sight are left to hunt by themselves, and may develop into far better hunters, with increasingly unsocial characters. Such a man was Sumali, my self-nominated father, who in spite of his skill was little esteemed in co-operative enterprises. It was his son who divined stinginess about hunting-lands as a motive for imputed sorcery; and when Sumali's house burned accidentally to the ground, Sumali attributed the accident to jealousy over land. His traps yielded more than the traps of anyone else in the region, his tracking skill was greatest and his aim most accurate, but he hunted alone, or with his young son, and presented his game to his relatives almost as for-mally as he might have presented it to strangers.

It is the same also with house-building. The   10 houses are so small that they actually require very little communal labour. Materials from one house or several dilapidated houses are re-assembled into another house; people take their houses down and rebuild them in another orientation; there is no attempt made to cut the rafters the same length or to saw off the ridge-pole if it is too long for the projected house—if it does not fit this house it will un-doubtedly fit the next one. But no man, except one who has failed to help with the house-building of others, builds alone. A man an-nounces his intention of building a house, and perhaps makes a small feast for raising the ridge-pole. Then his brothers and his cousins and his uncles, as they go about the bush upon their several errands, bear his partly completed house in mind, and stop to gather a bundle of creeper to bind the roof, or a bunch of sago-leaves for the thatching. These contributions they bring to the new house when they pass that way, and gradually, casually, a little at a time, the house is built, out of the uncounted labour of many.

But this loosely co-operative fashion in   11 which all work, even the routine of everyday gardening and hunting, is organized means that no man is master of his own plans for many hours together. If anything, he is less able to plan and carry through any consecutive activities than are the women, who at least know that meals and firewood and water must be provided each day. The men spend over nine-tenths of their time responding to other people's plans, digging in other people's gardens, going on hunting-parties initiated by oth-ers. The whole emphasis of their economic lives is that of participation in activities others have initiated, and only rarely and shyly does anyone tentatively suggest a plan of his own.

This emphasis is one factor in the lack of   12 political organization. Where all are trained to a quick responsiveness to any plan, and mild ostracism is sufficient to prod the laggard into co-operation leadership presents a different problem from that in a society where each man pits his own aggressiveness against that of another. If there is a weighty matter to be decided, one that may involve the hamlet or a cluster of hamlets in a brawl or accusations of sorcery, then the decision is arrived at in a quiet, roundabout, and wholly characteristic fashion. Suppose for instance that a young man finds that a pig belonging to a distant village has strayed into his garden. The pig is a trespasser, meat is scarce, he would like to kill it. But would it be wise to do so? Judgment must be made in terms of all kinds of relationships with the pig's owners. Is a feast pending? Or is a betrothal still unsettled? Does some member of his own group depend upon the pig's owner for assistance in some ceremonial plan? All these things the young man has not the judgment to decide. He goes to his elder brother. If his elder brother sees no objection to killing the pig, the two will take counsel with other elder male relatives, until finally one of the oldest and most respected men of the community is consulted. Of such men every locality with a population of one hundred and fifty or two hundred has one or two. If the big man gives his approval, the pig is killed and eaten and no censure will fall upon the young man from his elders; everyone will stand together to defend their bit of legal piracy.

13   Warfare is practically unknown among the Arapesh. There is no head-hunting tradition, no feeling that to be brave or manly one must kill. Indeed, those who have killed men are looked upon with a certain amount of discomfort, as men slightly apart. It is they who must perform the purification ceremonies over a new killer. The feeling towards a murderer and that towards a man who kills in battle are not essentially different. There are no insignia of any sort for the brave. There is only a modicum of protective magic which can be used by those who are going into a fight: they may scrape a little dust from their fathers' bones and eat it with areca-nut and magic herbs. But although actual warfare—organized expeditions to plunder, conquer, kill, or attain glory—is absent, brawls and clashes between villages do occur, mainly over women. The marriage system is such that even the most barefaced elopement of a betrothed or married woman must be phrased as an abduction and, since an abduction is an unfriendly act on the part of another group, must be avenged. This feeling for righting the balance, for paying back evil for evil, not in greater measure, but in exact measure, is very strong among the Arapesh. The beginning of hostilities they regard as an unfortunate accident; abductions of women are really the result of marital disagreements and the formation of new personal attachments, and are not unfriendly acts on the part of the next community. So also with pigs, since people attempt to keep their pigs at home. If the pigs stray, it is a bad accident, but if a pig is killed, it should be avenged.

14   All such clashes between hamlets start in angry conversation, the aggrieved party coming, armed but not committed to fighting, into the village of the offenders. An altercation follows; the offenders may justify or excuse their conduct, disclaim any knowledge of the elopement, or deny having known the ownership of the pig—it had not had its tail cut yet, how could they know it was not a bush pig? and so on. If the aggrieved party is protesting more as a matter of form than from real anger, the meeting may end in a few harsh words. Alternatively, it may progress from reproach to insult, until the most volatile and easily angered person hurls a spear. This is not a signal for a general fracas; instead everyone notes carefully where the spear—which is never thrown to kill—hits, and the next most volatile person of the opposite party throws a spear back at the man who hurled the first one. This in turn is recorded during a moment of attention, and a

return spear thrown. Each reprisal is phrased as a matter of definite choice: "Then Yabinigi threw a spear. He hit my cross-cousin in the wrist. I was angry because my cross-cousin was hit and I threw a spear back and hit Yabinigi in the ankle. Then the mother's brother of Yabinigi, enraged that his sister's son had been wounded, drew back his arm and hurled a spear at me which missed," and so on. This serial and carefully recorded exchange of spears in which the aim is to wound lightly, not to kill, goes on until someone is rather badly wounded, when the members of the attacking party immediately take to their heels. Later, peace is made by an interchange of rings, each man giving a ring to the man whom he has wounded.

15   If, as occasionally happens, someone is killed in one of these clashes, every attempt is made to disavow any intention to kill: the killer's hand slipped; it was because of the sorcery of the Plainsmen. Although always those on the other side are called by kinship terms, and surely no man would willingly have killed a relative. If the relative killed is a near one, an uncle or a first cousin, the assumption that it was unintentional and due to sorcery is regarded as established, and the killer is commiserated with and permitted to mourn wholeheartedly with the rest. If the relative is more distant, and the possibility of genuine intent more open, the killer may flee to another community. No blood feud will follow, although there may be an attempt to subsidize the sorcery of the Plainsmen against him. But in general sorcery deaths are avenged with sorcery deaths, and all killings within the locality or within avenging distance are regarded as too aberrant, too unexpected and inexplicable, for the community to deal with them. And each man who is wounded in a fight has a further penalty to pay, for he must reimburse his mother's brothers, and his mother's brothers' sons, for his own shed blood. All blood comes to the child from its mother; it is therefore the property of the mother's group. The mother's brother has the right to shed a sister's son's blood; it is he who must open a boil, he who scarifies the adolescent girl. So the man who is injured in any way suffers not only in his person but in his supply of valuables: he must pay for having been in any scene in which he is injured. This sanction is extended to cover injuries in hunting, and involvement in a shameful situation.

The general policy of Arapesh society is to   16 punish those who are indiscreet enough to get involved in any kind of violent or disreputable scene, those who are careless enough to get hurt in hunting, or stupid enough to let themselves become the butt of public vituperation from their wives. In this society unaccustomed to violence, which assumes that all men are mild and co-operative and is always surprised by the individuals who fail to be so, there are no sanctions to deal with the violent man. But it is felt that those who stupidly and carelessly provoke violence can be kept in order. In mild cases of offense, as when a man has been one member of a fighting group, his individual mother's brother calls out for payment. After all, the poor sister's son has already suffered a wound and loss of blood. But if instead he has got himself involved in an undignified public disputation with a wife, or with a young relative who has been overheard by others to insult him, then the whole men's group of the hamlet or cluster of hamlets may act, still instigated by the mother's brothers, who are the official executors of the punishment. The men's group will take the sacred flutes, the voice of the *tamberan*—the supernatural monster who is the patron of the men's cult—and going by night to the house of the offender, play his wife and himself off the premises, break into his house, litter his house-floor with leaves and rubbish, cut down an areca-palm or so, and depart. If the man has been steadily falling in the esteem of the community, if he has been uncooperative, given to sorcery, bad-temper, they may take up his fire-place and dump it out, which is practically equivalent to saying that they can dispense with his presence—for a month at least. The victim, deeply shamed by this procedure, flees to distant relatives and does not return until he has obtained a pig with which to feast the community, and so wipe out his offence.

17   But against the really violent man the community has no redress. Such men fill their fellows with a kind of amazed awe; if crossed they threaten to burn down their own houses, break all their pots and rings, and leave that part of the country for ever. Their relatives and neighbours, aghast at the prospect of being deserted in this way, beseech the violent man not to leave them, not to desert them, not to destroy his own property, and placate him by giving him what he wishes. It is only because the whole education of the Arapesh tends to minimize violence and confuse the motivations of the violent that the society is able to operate by disciplining those who provoke and suffer from violence rather than those who actually perpetrate it.

18   With work a matter of amiable co-operation, and the slight warfare so slenderly organized, the only other need that the community has for leadership is for carrying out large-scale ceremonial operations. Without any leadership whatsoever, with no rewards beyond the daily pleasure of eating a little food and singing a few songs with one's fellows, the society could get along very comfortably, but there would be no ceremonial occasions. And the problem of social engineering is conceived by the Arapesh not as the need to limit aggression and curb acquisitiveness, but as the need to force a few of the more capable and gifted men into taking, against their will, enough responsibility and leadership so that occasionally, every three or four years or at even rarer intervals, a really exciting ceremonial may be organized. No one, it is assumed, really wants to be a leader, a "big man." "Big men" have

to plan, have to initiate exchanges, have to strut and swagger and talk in loud voices, have to boast of what they have done in the past and are going to do in the future. All of this the Arapesh regard as most uncongenial, difficult behaviour, the kind of behaviour in which no normal man would indulge if he could possibly avoid it. It is a rôle that the society forces upon a few men in certain recognized ways.

19   While boys are in their early teens, their elders tend to classify their potentialities to become "big men." Native capacity is roughly divided into three categories: "those whose ears are open and whose throats are open," who are the most gifted, the men who understand the culture and are able to make their understanding articulate; "those whose ears are open and whose throats are shut," useful quiet men who are wise but shy and inarticulate; and a group of the two least useful kinds of people, "those whose ears are closed but whose throats are open" and "those whose ears and throats are both shut." A boy of the first class is specially trained by being assigned in early adolescence a *buanyin,* or exchange partner, from among the young males of a clan in which one of his elder male relatives has a *buanyin.* This *buanyin* relationship is reciprocal feast-giving relationship between pairs of males, members of different clans, and preferably of opposite dual organization membership—which is loosely hereditary. It is a social institution that develops aggressiveness and encourages the rare competitive spirit. It is the duty of *buanyins* to insult each other whenever they meet, to inquire sneeringly whether the other *buanyin* ever means to make anything of his life—has he no pigs, no yams, has he no luck in hunting, has he no trade-friends and no relatives, that he never gives feasts or organizes a ceremony? Was he born head first like a normal human being, or perhaps he came feet first from his mother's womb? The *buanyin* relationship is also a training-ground in the kind of hardness that a big man must have, which in

an ordinary Arapesh is regarded as undesirable.

20   The functioning of this *buanyin* relationship must be understood against Arapesh attitudes about the exchange of food. To a people who disguise all their trading as voluntary and casual gift-giving, any rigid accounting is uncongenial. As with trading from village to village, so it is in all exchange between relatives. The ideal distribution of food is for each person to eat food grown by another, eat game killed by another, eat pork from pigs that not only are not his own but have been fed by people at such a distance that their very names are unknown. Under the guidance of this ideal, an Arapesh man hunts only to send most of his kill to his mother's brother, his cousin, or his father-in-law. The lowest man in the community, the man who is believed to be so far outside the moral pale that there is no use reasoning with him, is the man who eats his own kill—even though that kill be a tiny bird, hardly a mouthful in all.

21   There is no encouragement given to any individual to build up a surplus of yams, the strong reliable crop that can be stored and the increase of which depends upon the conservation of seed. Anyone whose yam crop is conspicuously larger than his neighbour's is graciously permitted to give an *abūlū*, a special feast at which, having painted his yams in bright colours and having laid them out on a ratan measuring-tape, which he may keep as a trophy, all of his yams are given away for seed. His relatives and neighbours come bringing a return gift of their own selection, and carry away a bag of seed. Of this seed he may never eat; even when it has multiplied in the fourth or fifth generation, a careful record is kept. In this way, the good luck or the better gardening of one man does not redound to his personal gain, but is socialized, and the store of seed-yams of the entire community is increased.

22   From all of this socialized treatment of food

and property, this non-competitive, unaccounted, easy give and take, the *buanyin* partnership pattern stands out. Within it are definitely encouraged all the virtues of a competitive, cost-accounting system. A *buanyin* does not wait for the stimulus of an insult given in anger; he insults his *buanyin* as a matter of course. He does not merely share with him of his abundance, but he definitely raises pigs or hunts game in order to give it publicly and ostentatiously to his *buanyin*, accompanied by a few well-chosen insults as to his *buanyin's* inability to repay the gift. Careful accounting is kept of every piece of pig or haunch of kangaroo, and a bundle of coconut-leaf rib is used to denote these in the public altercation during which *buanyins* dun each other. Most astonishing of all is the definite convention of stinginess between *buanyins*. A generous *buanyin* will set aside a special basket of choice entrails and his wife will give it secretly to his *buanyin's* wife, after a feast. For this there need be no return. But while good behaviour is expected everywhere else in social life, people are reconciled to their *buanyin's* neglecting to make this generous gesture.

23   Thus in a society where the norm for men is to be gentle, unacquisitive, and co-operative, where no man reckons up the debts that another owes him, and each man hunts that others may eat, there is a definite training for the special contrasting behavior that "big men" must display. The young men on the way to become big men suffer continual pressure from their elders, as well as from their *buanyins*. They are urged to assume the responsibility of organizing the preliminary feasts that will finally culminate in a big initiation ceremony or the purchase of a new dance-complex from the beach. And a few of them yield to all this pressure, learn to stamp their feet and count their pigs, to plant special gardens and organize hunting-parties, and to maintain the long-time planning over several years that is necessary in order to give a ceremony which lasts no longer

than a day or so. But when his eldest child reaches puberty, the big man can retire; he need no longer stamp and shout, he need no longer go about to feasts looking for opportunities to insult his *buanyin;* he can stay quietly at home, guiding and educating his children, gardening, and arranging his children's marriages. He can retire from the active competitive life that his society assumes, usually correctly, to be eminently uncongenial and distasteful to him. ◆

14 *Introductions and Conclusions*

THE MORE YOU WRITE, THE MORE YOU COME TO VALUE THE OPINIONS of friends who recognize your weaknesses as well as your strengths. One of my best friends and most severe critics is greatly amused to picture me writing a chapter on introductions and conclusions. "Your introductions," she tells me, "tend to read like the warning signs around a radioactive area. And your essays never conclude properly; they just find a convenient cliff and jump off." She's right, I'm afraid. I have no instinct for beginnings and endings.

It is precisely my lack of instinct that tells me to devote a short chapter, at least, to studying the subject. I suspect that introductions and conclusions come hard to many other writers and cause far more trouble, word for word, than the body of the essay. The chapter will look closely at the way two good writers in quite different situations handle introductions and conclusions. From these examples we should be able to draw a few lessons to fall back on when our instincts fail.

INTRODUCTIONS: STANCE, AUTHORITY, AND TONE

A good way to calm your nerves before writing an introduction is to remember what practical business this part of the essay has to accomplish. Beyond the obvious function of letting the reader know what the subject is, the introduction needs to establish three things:

1. The writer's stance.
2. The writer's authority.
3. The tone of the essay.

We can get a sense of how these goals are accomplished in a personal essay by looking at the introduction to Brent Staples's "Just Walk On By

(p. 530)." To see the same goals accomplished in a more academic essay, we'll look at the introduction to Eileen O'Brien's "The Projectile Capabilities of an Acheulian Handaxe from Olorgesailie."

Example 1: Personal Essay, General Audience

Brent Staples's "Just Walk On By" appeared in *Ms.* magazine in 1986. We'll classify it as a personal essay because Staples demonstrates his point largely by referring to his own experiences and those of people he knows. You'll notice that Staples, like most writers for popular magazines, works hard to capture the reader's attention in the first paragraph. Since a magazine reader is essentially a browser, the writer has to set the hook early.

> My first victim was a woman—white, well dressed, probably in her early twenties. I came upon her one evening on a deserted street in Hyde Park, a relatively affluent neighborhood in an otherwise mean, impoverished section of Chicago. As I swung onto the avenue behind her, there seemed to be a discreet, uninflammatory distance between us. Not so. She cast back a worried glance. To her, the youngish black man—a broad six feet two inches with a beard and billowing hair, both hands shoved into the pockets of a bulky military jacket—seemed menacingly close. After a few more quick glimpses, she picked up her pace and was soon running in earnest. Within seconds she disappeared into a cross street.
>
> That was more than a decade ago. I was 22 years old, a graduate student newly arrived at the University of Chicago. It was in the echo of that terrified woman's footfalls that I first began to know the unwieldy inheritance I'd come into—the ability to alter public space in ugly ways. It was clear that she thought herself the quarry of a mugger, a rapist, or worse. Suffering a bout of insomnia, however, I was stalking sleep, not defenseless wayfarers. As a softy who is scarcely able to take a knife to a raw chicken—let alone hold it to a person's throat—I was surprised, embarrassed, and dismayed all at once.

Stance.   In Chapter 1, we discussed stance as a matter of contrasting old and new ways of viewing the subject. The writer says to the reader, in effect, "Your vision of the subject may be X, but the subject can also be seen as Y." Staples's introduction uses the conflict between views of the subject brilliantly. Look again at its first paragraph. From the opening line, it depicts the way a young white woman (most readers of *Ms.* in 1986 were young white women) would be likely to view a street encounter with a young black man. With at least part of her mind she would be likely to see herself as a potential victim and the man as a potential mugger and rapist.

In the second paragraph, Staples starts his countercharacterization of the situation by suggesting that the young black man in such a situation can be seen as a victim, too—at least as a victim of surprise, embarrassment, and dismay. Later in the paragraph, he pushes his alternative way of viewing the subject further still: "And I soon gathered that being perceived as dangerous is a hazard in itself."

Authority.   We could define the authority in an essay as everything that gives the reader reason to hope that *this* writer is capable of delivering valuable insight on *this* subject. Experience may establish the authority: someone who has served as president or prime minister can speak authoritatively about how government works. Research can establish another kind of authority: the deeply read political science professor may speak with an authority comparable to that of a former president. Often the writer's authority comes from the way that he or she presents the subject. The writer who sounds reasonable and honest, who seems capable of understanding the views of others, gives us reason to hope that he or she will say something worth hearing.

Staples immediately shows readers that he will speak with the authority of personal experience. He has been there; he has seen the behavior and felt the emotions that he describes. But if we look closely, we'll see that it isn't merely his *experience* that creates the hope that this writer will say something worth listening to. Staples presents himself as a thinker (an insomniac graduate student at the University of Chicago) who has spent a long time ("that was more than a decade ago") contemplating his experience. Later in the essay, Staples will confirm this impression of thoughtfulness by showing that he understands the views of the women who fear him ("the danger they perceive is not a hallucination") and by referring to two earlier essays about street fear.

Tone.   People often use *tone* to mean something like "the emotional flavor of a piece of writing." They talk about an ominous tone, a lighthearted tone, and so forth. Rhetoricians more often use *tone* to mean the writer's attitude toward the audience and the subject. *Tone* in the first sense may vary from sentence to sentence: Staples opens with a sentence alarming in tone (many readers wonder whether they are about to hear the confession of a mugger or rapist), but in the second paragraph he lightens the tone with humor—he is "a softy who is scarcely able to take a knife to a raw chicken."

These shifts in emotional flavor help us predict what Staples's attitude toward the reader and the subject will be throughout the essay. He will not be a distant, detached writer who avoids addressing the emotional side of the audience and the subject. Neither, however, will he let a single emotion dominate. Given the subject, we could imagine an angry tone from first to last, a writer who wants us to feel his sense of outrage. Staples, however, has chosen not to address his readers as if they were his tormentors, but as if they were reasonable people capable of feeling not only terror but humor and compassion.

Example 2: Academic Essay, Academic Audience

Eileen M. O'Brien's "The Projectile Capabilities of an Acheulian Handaxe from Olorgesailie" began as a research paper written for an undergraduate anthropology class at the University of Massachusetts. It was eventually published in the scholarly periodical *Current Anthropology* and republished in a rewritten form for the more popular journal *Natural History*. As this publication history suggests, it is a remarkably successful piece of student writing in a technical academic area.

The introduction below is from the *Current Anthropology* version. Unless you have experience in reading scientific articles, you may feel uneasy with the language and the form. I think, though, that you'll soon see what O'Brien is up to.

> A WRITER AT WORK
>
> *"The Acheulian Handaxe"*
> EILEEN O'BRIEN

The Acheulian handaxe represents a dramatic change in Paleolithic technology—an increase in size and the addition of symmetry and balance to artifact design. Almond to triangular in shape, the "classic" handaxe is basically a stone core or flake intentionally modified bifacially to produce two converging edges all around. While varying in size and shape, it usually maintains an eccentric center of gravity. This results in an almond shape in cross-section (top-to-bottom lengthwise).

In general, this design imposes constraints on transport (weight), increases the cost of production (time, labor, and skill), and depends on the availability of suitably sized, appropriate raw material (large units of fine-grained/faultless stone). Most importantly, in the absence of a safe handhold, this artifact when manipulated with force is capable of inflicting as much damage on the user as on the object. Yet, over a wide area (Africa, the Middle East, Europe, and Asia) and thousands of generations of reproduction, there was no appreciable change in its design except continuous refinement. This continuity speaks of use, success, and reuse—of a design integral to its function, a function adaptable to environmental diversity, and the advantages of both to early humankind's survival.

Several potential functions of the handaxe have been proffered; butchering (Keeley 1977, Semenov 1964), cutting/scraping, digging (Borders 1968; Clark 1967; Clark 1975*a*, 1976; Isaac 1977; Leakey 1960; Oakley 1972; Washburn 1978), and stationary cutting (Kleindienst and Keller 1976). Further, it has been suggested that it was hafted (Clark 1975b, Howell 1965, Leakey 1960) rather than handheld and that the design (degree of refinement) was esthetic in nature and not functional (Clark 1975*b*). The possibility that it was a core from which tools were struck rather than functional in itself (Jelinek 1977, Oakley 1972) has also been suggested. That the handaxe could have been used in these ways is possible. That it was specifically designed for use in these ways has not been determined—particularly since alternative stone artifacts pre-date and continue alongside the handaxe in the archaeological record.

An alternative and hitherto unexplored possibility is that the handaxe was used as a projectile weapon. . . .

Stance.   Here is a very clear example of what we referred to in Chapter 1 as the expert-opinion-notwithstanding stance. O'Brien identifies her subject (the axe) in the first paragraph and comments on some of its peculiarities in the second—notably that having an edge all around it made it likely to cut the hand that held it. The whole third paragraph is devoted to what is often called a review of the literature. This is where O'Brien recognizes the views that experts have taken of her subject: the axe, they say, might have been used to butcher animals, to cut or scrape or dig; it might have had a handle attached, or it might be no more than the remains of a stone from which other tools have been chipped. All these views have one thing in common. They assume that using the tool meant having it in hand. The fourth paragraph begins O'Brien's discussion of her new view: the axe may have done its work by *leaving* the user's hand as a thrown weapon. Here we have an introduction written according to a pattern often seen in academic writing:

Step 1—Describe the subject.

Step 2—Explain why the subject presents an intriguing problem.

Step 3—Review the solutions of other experts (the old framework or frameworks).

Step 4—Present your own hypothesis (the new framework).

Authority.   One of the differences between personal essays and academic papers is that academic writers must establish their authority by showing that they have systematically studied the subject and the discipline. O'Brien does this in two ways. She uses the specialized language of physical anthropology: tools are "artifacts," and a stone that is chipped from both sides to form an edge is "intentionally modified bifacially." More important, she shows that she has studied the views of several experts who dealt with her subject before she did. Though she is a student, she has made herself an expert on the handaxe, and her introduction reveals this expertise in a way that allows other experts to take her work seriously.

Tone.   Unlike Staples, O'Brien does not want to suggest in her introduction that her essay will address the reader person-to-person about matters that have a great deal of emotional force. She wants instead to talk as a professional addressing other professionals about a matter that is *intellectually* engaging. Again, the language of the essay serves her purpose. Can the phrase "intentionally modified bifacially" ever have been used in a moment of passion, even by an anthropologist? Can we imagine a mother warning her child to be careful with a knife because "when manipulated with force" it is "capable of inflicting as much damage on the user as on the object"? The language in O'Brien's essay is deliberately distant from the warmth of emotional conversation.

This is not to say that no personality emerges from the introduction, however. O'Brien presents herself as someone careful not to overstate or oversimplify ("*While varying in size and shape,* it *usually* maintains an eccentric center of gravity") and as someone willing to give previous investigators their due ("That the handaxe could have been used in these ways is possible"). We feel, though, that this is O'Brien's "official" personality, assumed for the sake of professional decorum and not necessarily connected with the Eileen O'Brien of day-to-day life.

CONCLUSIONS: A SENSE OF GROUND COVERED

The worst conclusions often come from writers who have narrow notions of what a conclusion should sound like. Some student writers, especially, seem to believe that every essay should end with an upbeat moralizing sermon:

> Thus we can see that the world would be a better place in which to live if everyone read *Pet Sematary.*

or with a fanfare:

> Philip Freneau, then, far from being the minor rhymester and propagandist that most scholars believe him to have been, was one of the greatest poets who ever wrote in the English language.

By claiming too much, such conclusions may undo an otherwise sensible essay. In general, a modest conclusion is best.

Some essays come to a logical stopping point without a formal conclusion: the last point of the essay's body has an air of finality and closes the discussion naturally. Some very long essays need a detailed summary at the end. More often, however, essays fall between these extremes, needing a brief conclusion that will accomplish these three things:

1. Remind the reader of the writer's stance.

2. Remind the reader of substantial points in the essay's body.

3. Point out the significance of replacing the old view of the subject with the new.

A look at Eileen O'Brien's conclusion shows that these goals can be accomplished indirectly, without producing a paragraph that begins with "In conclusion" or that seems to be awkwardly tacked on to an essay that is already complete.

> As a projectile, the classic handaxe is functionally and efficiently designed. Experiments reveal that it can be used effectively in this way. How other handaxe designs relate to this function needs to be explored, and the physical analyses of the effects of different sizes need to be confirmed. The use of the classic handaxe as a projectile offers an alternative explanation of the archaeological record and opens a new perspective on the Paleolithic. When combined with the superior strength of *H. erectus*[1] and the potential for lifelong training, the handaxe would have been an important weapon.

There's no attempt to be uplifting or moralizing here. Without belaboring the point, O'Brien reminds readers that her subject has been the use of the handaxe and that her thesis (hypothesis) is that the axe was thrown as a weapon. She also reminds them that the body of her paper was devoted to reporting on experiments that prove the axe works well as a thrown weapon. And she shows that her thesis, if accepted, significantly alters anthropologists' picture of human life a million years ago: our small-brained ancestors may not have been rocket scientists, but they knew how to kill at a distance.

Brent Staples's conclusion for "Just Walk On By" is very different in tone but serves similar purposes:

> And on late-evening constitutionals along streets less traveled by, I employ what has proved to be an excellent tension-reducing measure: I whistle melodies from Beethoven and Vivaldi and the more popular classical composers. Even steely New Yorkers hunching toward nighttime destinations seem to relax, and occasionally they even join in the tune. Virtually everyone seems to sense that a mugger wouldn't be warbling bright, sunny selections from Vivaldi's *Four Seasons*. It is my equivalent of the cowbell that hikers wear when they know they are in bear country.

Until you have read Staples's entire essay, you can't appreciate his skillful use of the word *hunching* to remind the reader of language and ideas from the middle of the essay. You can, however, see that the conclusion deliberately takes the reader back to the introduction, contrasting Staples's encounter with the running woman with more relaxed encounters. The effect is to help readers see the essay as a unified whole. The last sentence of the essay is a brilliant reminder of Staples's stance and its significance.

---

[1] **H. erectus** In the more popular version of her article, O'Brien defines *Homo erectus* as "a small-brained but otherwise fairly recognizable form of human."

Before reading the essay, most *Ms.* readers might have been inclined to identify the young black man with the bear that threatens an innocent hiker. By the essay's end, they are prepared to see him as the endangered hiker.

INTRODUCTIONS AND CONCLUSIONS

POINTS TO

CONSIDER

There is no magic formula for writing successful introductions and conclusions. After looking at the examples above, however, we can begin to see that there are some productive questions to ask yourself when you draft these sections:

1. Do you need a formal introduction and conclusion at all? On some occasions (the essay exam and the interoffice memo are good examples), readers already possess much of the information that introductions and conclusions supply. They know what the writer's subject is and what the familiar frameworks are. They know what qualifies the writer to offer fresh insight. In such cases long introductions and conclusions are unnecessary. Single sentences, even single phrases, may do the job.

2. If you need an introduction and conclusion, do you need them primarily for the sake of the general reader, whose interest you may have to court? Or do you need them for a more expert audience, already interested in your subject, that wants to know what qualifies you to address it? The first case, the Staples case, is common in journalistic writing. The second case, the O'Brien case, is common in academic writing.

3. Can you find a way to make your introduction and conclusion work together to create a sense of closure? If your introduction directly raises a question, as O'Brien's does, your conclusion might highlight the answer. If your introduction directs readers' attention to a particular situation or problem, as Staples's does, you might return attention to the same point in the conclusion.

One word more. In Chapter 3, we saw a case of a writer blocked by her attempt to write an introduction that would "grab the reader's attention." If you have time for revision, don't feel that you must start by drafting an ideal introduction. I find that drafting a throwaway introduction is a useful way to search for stance, authority, and tone. Other writers find it best to concentrate their attention *first* on the body of an essay—its essential content. After that content is somewhat settled, they find it easier to see how their introduction and conclusion can work together, shaping the reader's perceptions of who they are and what they are saying.

Assignments for Chapter 14

EVALUATING INTRODUCTIONS

Below you will find three alternative introductions to Carolyn Douglas's research paper "Changing Theories of Darwin's Illness" (pp. 260–283). In a paper 300 to 500 words long, analyze the introductions and discuss their strengths and weaknesses. Your analysis should focus on (1) the writer's apparent visualization of the audience and (2) the writer's stance, authority, and tone.

A. Illness is a source of fascination for everyone. The illnesses of great people are especially fascinating. If the president has a mole removed from his cheek or complains of fatigue, it will be a lead story in the news. Certain illnesses from the past have been the subject of special interest. One of these is the illness of Charles Darwin, the founder of modern evolutionary theory.

B. Everyone knows what a hypochondriac is—a person who complains constantly about pains in the back, in the stomach, in the legs, but who is not really sick at all. The hypochondriac is the woman who calls in sick every time the workload in the office gets heavy or the man who never feels well enough to go camping with the kids, even though he seems energetic enough during his weekly doubles game. Or he is the elderly relative who relieves his loneliness by calling to complain about his entirely imaginary shortness of breath. In short, the hypochondriac is a person whose frequent illnesses correspond conveniently to periods when he wants attention or wants to avoid a distasteful duty, or so the nonhypochondriac believes.

   As a diagnosed hypochondriac myself, I take a different view of the matter. The shooting pains in my back and hips that periodically confine me to my bed are not in the least convenient, nor are they imaginary. It is true that my physicians have not found any physical cause, and it is likely, as they tell me, that the pains are stress-related. It is certainly possible that in some subconscious way I inflict them on myself. But this doesn't mean that they are under my control. I have as little control over them as I have over my pancreas. No amount of self-discipline or logic will eliminate them. I suffer from a disease, not a character flaw. Because of this personal affliction, I have been particularly interested in the illness of Charles Darwin, who was clearly a hypochondriac, though his relatives and biographers resisted admitting this for more than a century.

C. No case more dramatically indicates society's slowly increasing understanding of psychogenic disease processes than that of Charles Darwin. Darwin himself denied charges of hypochondria (F. Darwin, *Life* 1: 318) and suggested to his physician that the decline of his health was the result of "the extreme sea-sickness he underwent in H.M.S. 'Beagle'" (qtd. in Colp 59). For several decades following the great naturalist's death, the etiology of the illness became a subject of contention between psychoanalysts and physicians, each cleaving to one side or the other of the mind/body split. Only in the 1970s did this sharp distinction between "organic" and "mental" illness begin to be displaced by our current, more complex view.

ASSIGNMENT 2: **WRITING CONCLUSIONS TO MATCH INTRODUCTIONS**

Write conclusions to match each of the introductions in Assignment 1. Your conclusions should match the introductions accurately enough to create a sense of closure. They should also show your awareness of the differing assumptions about the audience's interests and the writer's relation to the subject and audience. If you think that an introduction is well done, imitate its strengths. If you think it is badly done, parody its weaknesses.

ASSIGNMENT 3: **WRITING INTRODUCTIONS AND CONCLUSIONS FOR PROJECTED ESSAYS**

Return to the "stance" statements you produced for Exercise 3 on page 520. Select the two most promising statements and write effective introductions and conclusions for essays based on them. Almost inevitably, this process will force you to imagine the content of the whole essays. You may want to make notes of ideas that occur to you, in case you have an opportunity to write on one of these subjects later in the term.

JUST WALK ON BY

Brent Staples

Brent Staples took a Ph.D. in psychology at the University of Chicago in 1982 and immediately turned to journalism. He is now a regular columnist for the *New York Times* and a member of its editorial board. "Just Walk On By" appeared in *Ms.* magazine in September 1986.

1 MY FIRST VICTIM WAS A WOMAN— white, well dressed, probably in her early twenties. I came upon her late one evening on a deserted street in Hyde Park, a relatively affluent neighborhood in an otherwise mean, impoverished section of Chicago. As I swung onto the avenue behind her, there seemed to be a discreet, uninflammatory distance between us. Not so. She cast back a worried glance. To her, the youngish black man— a broad six feet two inches with a beard and billowing hair, both hands shoved into the pockets of a bulky military jacket—seemed menacingly close. After a few more quick glimpses, she picked up her pace and was soon running in earnest. Within seconds she disappeared into a cross street.

2 That was more than a decade ago. I was 22 years old, a graduate student newly arrived at the University of Chicago. It was in the echo of that terrified woman's footfalls that I first began to know the unwieldy inheritance I'd come into—the ability to alter public space in ugly ways. It was clear that she thought herself the quarry of a mugger, a rapist, or worse. Suffering a bout of insomnia, however, I was stalking sleep, not defenseless wayfarers. As a softy who is scarcely able to take a knife to a raw chicken—let alone hold it to a person's throat—I was surprised, embarrassed, and dismayed all at once. Her flight made me feel like an accomplice in tyranny. It also made it clear that I was indistinguishable from the muggers who occasionally seeped into that area from the surrounding ghetto. That first encounter, and those that followed, signified that a vast, unnerving gulf lay between nighttime pedestrians—particularly women—and me. And I soon gathered that being perceived as dangerous is a hazard in itself. I only needed to turn a corner into a dicey situation, or crowd some frightened, armed person in a foyer somewhere, or make an errant move after being pulled over by a policeman. Where fear and weapons meet—and they often do in urban America—there is always the possibility of death.

3 In that first year, my first away from my hometown, I was to become thoroughly familiar with the language of fear. At dark, shadowy intersections in Chicago, I could cross in front of a car stopped at a traffic light and elicit the *thunk, thunk, thunk, thunk* of the driver—black, white, male, or female—hammering down the door locks. On less traveled streets after dark, I grew accustomed to but never comfortable with people who crossed to the other side of the street rather than pass me. Then there were the standard unpleasantries with police, doormen, bouncers, cab drivers, and others whose business it is to screen out troublesome individuals *before* there is any nastiness.

4 I moved to New York nearly two years ago and I have remained an avid night walker. In central Manhattan, the near-constant crowd

cover minimizes tense one-on-one street encounters. Elsewhere—visiting friends in SoHo, where sidewalks are narrow and tightly spaced buildings shut out the sky—things can get very taut indeed.

5 Black men have a firm place in New York mugging literature. Norman Podhoretz in his famed (or infamous) 1963 essay, "My Negro Problem—And Ours," recalls growing up in terror of black males; they "were tougher than we were, more ruthless," he writes—and as an adult on the Upper West Side of Manhattan, he continues, he cannot constrain his nervousness when he meets black men on certain streets. Similarly, a decade later, the essayist and novelist Edward Hoagland extols a New York where once "Negro bitterness bore down mainly on other Negroes." Where some see mere panhandlers, Hoagland sees "a mugger who is clearly screwing up his nerve to do more than just *ask* for money." But Hoagland has "the New Yorker's quick-hunch posture for broken-field maneuvering," and the bad guy swerves away.

6 I often witness that "hunch posture," from women after dark on the warrenlike streets of Brooklyn where I live. They seem to set their faces on neutral and, with their purse straps strung across their chests bandolier style, they forge ahead as though bracing themselves against being tackled. I understand, of course, that the danger they perceive is not a hallucination. Women are particularly vulnerable to street violence, and young black males are drastically overrepresented among the perpetrators of that violence. Yet these truths are no solace against the kind of alienation that comes of being ever the suspect, against being set apart, a fearsome entity with whom pedestrians avoid making eye contact.

7 It is not altogether clear to me how I reached the ripe old age of 22 without being conscious of the lethality nighttime pedestrians attributed to me. Perhaps it was because in Chester, Pennsylvania, the small, angry indus-

trial town where I came of age in the 1960s, I was scarcely noticeable against a backdrop of gang warfare, street knifings, and murders. I grew up one of the good boys, had perhaps a half-dozen fist fights. In retrospect, my shyness of combat has clear sources.

8 Many things go into the making of a young thug. One of those things is the consummation of the male romance with the power to intimidate. An infant discovers that random flailings send the baby bottle flying out of the crib and crashing to the floor. Delighted, the joyful babe repeats those motions again and again, seeking to duplicate the feat. Just so, I recall the points at which some of my boyhood friends were finally seduced by the perception of themselves as tough guys. When a mark cowered and surrendered his money without resistance, myth and reality merged—and paid off. It is, after all, only manly to embrace the power to frighten and intimidate. We, as men, are not supposed to give an inch of our lane on the highway; we are to seize the fighter's edge in work and in play and even in love; we are to be valiant in the face of hostile forces.

9 Unfortunately, poor and powerless young men seem to take all this nonsense literally. As a boy, I saw countless tough guys locked away; I have since buried several, too. They were babies, really—a teenage cousin, a brother of 22, a childhood friend in his mid-twenties—all gone down in episodes of bravado played out in the streets. I came to doubt the virtues of intimidation early on. I chose, perhaps even unconsciously, to remain a shadow—timid, but a survivor.

10 The fearsomeness mistakenly attributed to me in public places often has a perilous flavor. The most frightening of these confusions occurred in the late 1970s and early 1980s when I worked as a journalist in Chicago. One day, rushing into the office of a magazine I was writing for with a deadline story in hand, I was mistaken for a burglar. The office manager called security and, with an ad hoc posse,

pursued me through the labyrinthine halls, nearly to my editor's door, I had no way of proving who I was. I could only move briskly toward the company of someone who knew me.

11   Another time I was on assignment for a local paper and killing time before an interview. I entered a jewelry store on the city's affluent Near North Side. The proprietor excused herself and returned with an enormous red Doberman pinscher straining at the end of a leash. She stood, the dog extended toward me, silent to my questions, her eyes bulging nearly out of her head. I took a cursory look around, nodded, and bade her good night. Relatively speaking, however, I never fared as badly as another black male journalist. He went to nearby Waukegan, Illinois, a couple of summers ago to work on a story about a murderer who was born there. Mistaking the reporter for the killer, police hauled him from his car at gunpoint and but for his press credentials would probably have tried to book him. Such episodes are not uncommon. Black men trade tales like this all the time.

12   In "My Negro Problem—And Ours," Podhoretz writes that the hatred he feels for blacks makes itself known to him through a variety of avenues—one being his discomfort with that "special brand of paranoid touchiness" to which he says blacks are prone. No doubt he is speaking here of black men. In time, I learned to smother the rage I felt at so often being taken for a criminal. Not to do so would surely have led to madness—via that special "paranoid touchiness" that so annoyed Podhoretz at the time he wrote the essay.

13   I began to take precautions to make myself less threatening. I move about with care, particularly late in the evening. I give a wide berth to nervous people on subway platforms during the wee hours, particularly when I have exchanged business clothes for jeans. If I happen to be entering a building behind some people who appear skittish, I may walk by, letting them clear the lobby before I return, so as not to seem to be following them. I have been calm and extremely congenial on those rare occasions when I've been pulled over by the police.

14   And on late-evening constitutionals along streets less traveled by, I employ what has proved to be an excellent tension-reducing measure: I whistle melodies from Beethoven and Vivaldi and the more popular classical composers. Even steely New Yorkers hunching toward nighttime destinations seem to relax, and occasionally they even join in the tune. Virtually everybody seems to sense that a mugger wouldn't be warbling bright, sunny selections from Vivaldi's *Four Seasons*. It is my equivalent of the cowbell that hikers wear when they know they are in bear country. ◆

What Was the Acheulean Hand Ax?

Eileen M. O'Brien

So impressed were the editors of *Natural History* by "The Projectile Capabilities of an Acheulian Handaxe" that they asked her to rewrite it for their magazine. O'Brien's challenge was to retain the academic content of her article but present it in a way better suited to a very mixed audience. Some readers of *Natural History* are trained biologists or anthropologists, but many others are laypersons who *may* have taken an anthropology course in college. As you read O'Brien's essay, note how she attempts to accommodate herself to this broad audience throughout the essay. Then compare the way she handles the introduction and conclusion of this more accessible version with the way she handled the academic introduction and conclusion discussed in the chapter.

1 ABOUT ONE AND ONE-HALF MILLION years ago, a new type of large, symmetrically shaped stone implement entered the prehistoric tool kit, signaling both an advance in early craftsmanship and the advent of *Homo erectus,* a small-brained but otherwise fairly recognizable form of human being. The tool was the hand ax, which these ancestral humans faithfully made for well over one million years. Named for archaeological finds at Saint Acheul, France, examples of the Acheulean hand ax are found from the Vaal River of South Africa to the lakes, bogs, and rivers of Europe, from the shores of the Mediterranean to India and Indonesia. Such continuity over time and space speaks to us of use, success, and reuse—a design integral to some task, a task appropriate or essential to diverse environments. *Homo erectus* needed tools: tools to cut, slice, and chop; to dig, pound, and grind; tools to defend against predators and competitors, to procure and process food or other materials, even tools to make tools. But which task (or tasks) the hand ax performed is still being debated.

2 The average hand ax looks like a giant stone almond, although some are more ovate and others more triangular. Crafted from a stone core or flake, it can range in size from only a few inches to a foot or more, but more are six or seven inches long. Whether roughly finished or as refined as a work of art, the hand ax always has an eccentric center of gravity and a sharp edge around all or most of its perimeter. Thus in cross section lengthwise, it resembles a stretched-out teardrop.

3 Some have speculated that the hand ax's design was not functional but purely aesthetic or that it was a byproduct of the manufacture of the sharp flakes used in butchering. Most anthropologists, however, assume it was a practical implement. Initially, prehistorians thought it was a hafted, multipurpose tool and weapon like the stone hatchet, or ax, of the aboriginal Americans and Australians. But there is no evidence that it was hafted until much later in time, not until after the evolution of *Homo sapiens.* Another proposal, advanced to explain why excavators find some hand axes standing on edge, *in situ,*[1] is that the hand ax acted as a stationary tool, one edge embedded in the earth while the exposed edge cut or scraped an object passed over it. But the common and traditional interpretation is that it was a handheld tool for butchering, cutting, scraping, digging, or as its name implies, chopping.

_____

[1] **in situ:** in its natural location.

4   Experiments show that these important tasks can be accomplished with a hand ax. But *Homo erectus* possessed other tools suitable for these purposes—tools that precede and continue alongside the hand ax in the archaeological record. Compared with these, the hand ax was costly to produce in terms of time, labor, and skill, and required larger blocks of fine-grained, faultless stone such as flint or basalt. The hand ax also presented a hazard. Since a heavy object requires effort to wield and carry, we may assume the mass of the hand ax was important to its function. Force in the form of increased momentum would be useful for chopping, for example, as compared with a task like scraping, where the user exerts all the energy in the form of pressure. But without a safe handhold, the sharp edge of the hand ax, when used with force, was (and is) capable of inflicting as much damage on the user as on the material being worked.

5   Whatever its function, the hand ax represented to its users not only an investment of energy but also a source of raw material. They would have saved and reused a hand ax for as long as possible and retouched it when necessary. With time and repeated repair, it would have become smaller; once irreparably damaged, what remained could then have served as a core in the production of still smaller stone tools. Accordingly, except for those hand axes that were misplaced or lost, the hand ax should not be in the archaeological record. Excavators, however, recover hands axes in abundance, mostly at sites that are within or alongside what were once (and may still be) watercourses or wetland environments. For example, at the Acheulean site of Olorgesailie (one of the East African sites southwest of Nairobi, Kenya, in the Eastern Rift Valley), hundreds of large hand axes were deposited about four hundred thousand years ago in what appears to have been a shallow stream bed. Elsewhere across the landscape, hand axes are rare, although they are occasionally found in some numbers in prehistoric cave sites. This suggests that during some activity that took place near water, hand axes were used and lost with astonishing frequency.

6   If we let the evidence speak for itself, the appropriate question is: What task would require force, call for a tool with a sharp edge around all (or most) of its perimeter but without a safe handhold, occur in or near water, and often result in the loss of a potentially reusable and valuable artifact? The possibility that occurred to me is that the hand ax was a projectile weapon. The idea, I have since discovered, has been thought of before, but not pursued. Use of the hand ax as a weapon has been suggested since at least the sixteenth century, and small hand axes have been proposed as projectiles since the nineteenth century, most enjoyably by H. G. Wells[2] in his *Tales of Time and Space* (1899). More recently, M. D. W. Jeffreys, a South African anthropologist, wrote that the small- to medium-sized Vaal River hand axes would make good bird-hunting weapons if thrown overhand, like a knife ("The Hand-bolt." *Man*, 1965). But the idea that hand axes were in general used as projectiles has not taken hold, probably because it is not obvious how the larger hand axes could have been thrown.

7   By analogy with modern forms, we understand how prehistoric stone arrowheads and spearpoints were propelled and used as weapons or how a stone ball ("spheroid," to archaeologists) could be thrown or used in a bola (a weighted thong or cord thrown to entangle prey). But what about the hand ax? One way might be overhand, as Jeffreys suggested. Other methods of throwing a small- to medium-sized hand ax might be the side/overhand throw used in baseball and perhaps the backhand throw used in both knife and frisbee throwing. To throw a large, heavy hand ax,

---

[2] **H. G. Wells:** novelist and science-fiction writer (1866–1946).

The Acheulean hand ax

however, a sidearm or underhand throw might be preferable. A few years ago, I decided that a practical experiment was what was needed. From my limited knowledge of track and field, I thought that for sidearm throwing, an analogy might be made between a hand ax and the Olympic discus.

8   Like a hand ax, the early discus of the ancient Greeks was unhafted, edged all around, and made of stone. It also varied in size from about half a foot to more than one foot in diameter, and in weight from about two and one-quarter pounds to more than fourteen and one-half pounds. (Actually, the word *discus* means "a thing for throwing" or "a thing thrown"; the discus thrown by Odysseus in Homer's *Odyssey*, for example, is thought by some scholars to refer to a beach cobble.) Unlike a hand ax, the classic Greek discus was perfectly round. (The modern regulation discus, which weighs 2 kilograms, or 4.4 pounds, is made of wood and weighted with metal around the edge to accelerate its spinning motion. The longer and faster it spins, the more

stable the flight pattern and the longer the flight, all else being equal.)

9   The hand ax I chose for the throwing experiment was the largest I could find in the Olorgesailie collection at the National Museums of Kenya, Nairobi (I was in Africa at the time doing fieldwork unrelated to this topic). Because the original could not be used—and raw material for making a "real" hand ax of such size was difficult to obtain—a fiberglass replica was made. The original hand ax is a little more than a foot long, ovate shaped, and edged all around. It is made of basalt and weighs about four pounds, three ounces. J. D. Ambrosse Esa (then head of the museum's casting department) supervised the casting and the accurate weighting of the facsimile to within one and one-half ounces of the original.

10   The experiment took place in 1978, in the discus practice area at the University of Massachusetts, where I was then a student. Two student athletes participated: Karl Nyholm, a discus thrower, and George Peredy, a javelin thrower. One day in late April, and again two

weeks later, both threw the hand ax discus-style. Peredy also threw it overhand. To maximize potential accuracy in the discus throw, the thrower did not whirl.

11   The first to throw the hand ax discus-style was Karl Nyholm. He took the unfamiliar object in his right hand, grasping it every which way before settling on the butt. He tossed it up and down for balance and "feel," then crouched and practiced his swing. Ready, he paced off from the release line. With his back to the field, he spread his legs apart, bent at the knees, and twisted his right arm far behind him. Then he began the throw: his outstretched left hand grasping at air, weight shifting from right foot to left, he rotated to face the field. The burdened right hand swung wide and low and then raced upward. With a great exhalation of breath, he hurled himself out straight and let go. Silently, gracefully spinning, the hand ax soared.

12   Like a discus, the hand ax spun horizontally as it rose, but changed its orientation in mid-air. On reaching its maximum altitude, it rolled onto its edge and descended in a perpendicular position, its spinning motion appearing to decline. Then, with a thud, it landed point first, slicing deeply into the thawing earth. In both throwing bouts, regardless of thrower, the hand ax repeated this flight pattern when thrown discus-style. It landed on edge forty-two out of forty-five throws, thirty-one of which were point first. The average throw was about one-third the length of a football field (almost 102 feet), and usually accurate to within two yards right or left of the line of trajectory.

13   The propensity of the hand ax to pivot onto its edge in mid-flight was unexpected and curious. But, as suggested to me by several track coaches, it may be related to the same factors that can produce the "peel-off" pattern in a thrown discus, some function of the manner of release and the thrower's expertise. A full explanation of the physical principles involved

must await an interpretation by someone with the relevant expertise. What is important is that it does happen. By so doing, it makes on-edge impact of a thrown hand ax predictable. The further tendency of the hand ax to land point first does not appear accidental and adds to the implement's potential to inflict damage. If the hand ax can also be thrown so that it behaves exactly like the discus in both ascent and descent (more recent demonstrations support this possibility), then by simply changing the angle and manner of release it should be possible to strike a target with either a horizontally or vertically directed edge.

14   Modern discus throwing is not known for its accuracy. But in terms of how far a hand ax might ideally be thrown, it is worth noting that the 1980 Olympic record in discus was 218.8 feet. Since the experimental hand ax weighs only two and a half ounces less than the modern Olympic discus, this suggests that as the thrower's skill and/or strength increase, the potential flight distance of the hand ax increases.

15   When grasped and thrown overhand, like a knife, the experimental hand ax performed like one, rotating symmetrically on edge in both ascent and descent. The average throw was just short of discus-style, but more accurate, about half a yard right or left of the line of trajectory. It always landed on edge, but less often point first. Unfortunately, these results are the product of only six throws; owing to its weight and the ovate, broad point, the experimental hand ax was difficult to grasp and throw overhand. George Peredy, who was the thrower, also appeared to tire more quickly using this method and probably could not have used it at all if he had not had large hands, in proportion to his six-foot six-inch frame. This overhand style would probably be more suitable for lighter, more triangular hand axes. In contrast, weight and shape were of no real concern when throwing the hand ax discus-style. Even a significant increase in weight might not

have impeded the throwing motion, although it would have affected the distance of the throw.

16   Further testing is needed (and is currently under way), but these first trials showed that a hand ax could perform appropriately as a projectile. The hand ax demonstrated a propensity to land on edge when thrown overhand or discus-style, a tendency to land point first, and a potential for distant and accurate impact. Its overall shape minimizes the effects of resistance while in flight, as well as at impact. This is not true of an unshaped stone or a spheroid, for example. And despite its sharp edge, the hand ax could be launched without a safe handhold. The only apparent limitations to the hand ax's use as a projectile weapon are the strength, coordination, and skill of the thrower.

17   *Homo erectus* was bipedal, probably dexterous enough to manipulate a hand ax in either of the tested throwing styles, and very much stronger than most modern humans. With their technique perfected over years of practice and use, our ancestors probably surpassed the accuracy shown in the experimental throws. I suspect the hand ax simply reflects a refinement in missile design, one that allowed for successful long-distance offense and defense against larger animals. This is consistent with evidence that big-game hunting appears for the first time in the archaeological record along with *Homo erectus.*

18   Perfected through trial and error, the hand ax would not necessarily have replaced preexisting projectile or handheld weapons, because weapons and strategies probably varied with the predator being deterred or the game being hunted. Hand axes would have been especially effective in a collective strategy, such as a group of hunters bombarding a herd. To overcome any difficulty in transporting hand axes, *Homo erectus* could have used carrying slings made from hide, stockpiled hand axes near hunting areas, or cached them (in caves, for example) prior to seasonal migrations.

19   Hunting near water, where game is relatively predictable and often concentrated, offers a simple explanation of why hand axes are recovered there in abundance—as well as the phenomenon of hand axes embedded on edge *in situ*. Hand axes that missed their mark, landing in water or dense vegetation on the banks of a river, might have been difficult or impossible to retrieve. Over time, with continued exploitation of an area, projectiles would accumulate like golf balls in a water trap. Elsewhere across the landscape, retrieval is more likely and the hand ax should be rare. This distribution pattern, as noted by English archaeologist L. H. Keeley, resembles that of the Indian projectile points across the American Southwest. (Keeley, however, does not believe that the hand ax was a projectile.)

20   *Homo erectus*, like later *Homo sapiens,* was physically defenseless compared with the rest of the animal kingdom. Relatively slow, without canines, claws, tusks, or other natural means of defense, these early humans were easy prey when out of a tree. With handheld weapons they could defend themselves, once attacked. With projectile weapons they could wound, maim, or kill without making physical contact, avoiding assault or retaliation. Modern humans are notoriously expert at killing from a distance. The hand ax may be proof that this behavioral strategy was refined long ago, at a time when truly "giants strode the earth"—when by dint of size the megamammals of the Pleistocene asserted their dominance, when migrating game might pass in a continuous parade for days without a break in their ranks, and humankind struggled to survive, both consumer and consumed. At the other end of time, at the dawn of history, is it possible that the ancient Greeks preserved as a sport a tradition handed down from that distant yesterday? ◆

15 A Practical Approach to Style

I ONCE READ A PAPER THAT BEGAN WITH THIS SENTENCE: "A GOOD DATE is characterized by a congenial atmosphere that is conducive to intimate interpersonal relationships." The writer told me that he had been working on his style, and his sentence told me that what he meant by style was a way of dressing up simple thoughts in elaborate language.

Let's begin our discussion of style by taking a different view of it, one offered by E. B. White, generally recognized as one of the great prose stylists of our century:

> Young writers often suppose that style is a garnish for the meat of prose, a sauce by which a dull dish is made palatable. Style has no such separate entity; it is nondetachable, unfilterable. The beginner should approach style warily, realizing that it is himself he is approaching, no other; and he should begin by turning resolutely away from all devices that are popularly believed to indicate style—all mannerisms, tricks, adornments. The approach to style is by way of plainness, simplicity, orderliness, sincerity.

We'll assume, as White did, that people who attempt to improve their style by too much direct, self-conscious attention to it are likely to do themselves more harm than good. When style is the question, a better place for most writers to focus attention is on the reader, who is—as White once put it—"in trouble about half the time."

THE TROUBLES OF READERS: AN EXPERIMENT

The difficulties readers face have recently become the subject of ingenious investigations by cognitive psychologists. Meredyth Daneman and Patricia Carpenter, for instance, have used a computer to display the words of a passage one at a time, eliminating the possibility of rereading. The reader pushes a button to see the next word, and the computer records the time between pushes. In one experiment, the investigators had university undergraduates read through the following passage on the computer screen:

> There ○ was ○ a ○ strange ○ noise ○ emanating ○ from ○ the ○ dark ○ house. ○ Bob ○ had ○ to ○ venture ○ in ○ to ○ find ○ out ○ what ○ was ○ there. ○ He ○ was ○ terrified; ○ rumor ○ had ○ it ○ that ○ this ○ house ○ was ○ haunted. ○ He ○ would ○ feel ○ more ○ secure ○ with ○ a ○ stick ○ to ○ defend ○ himself ○ and ○ so ○ he ○ went ○ in ○ and ○ looked ○ among ○ his ○ sporting ○ equipment. ○ He ○ found ○ a ○ bat ○ that ○ was ○ very ○ large ○ and ○ brown ○ and ○ was ○ flying

Most readers paused for a beat longer when the word *flying* appeared on the screen, then pushed the button and moved on:

> back ○ and ○ forth ○ in ○ the ○ gloomy ○ room. ○ Now ○ he ○ didn't ○ need ○ to ○ be ○ afraid ○ any ○ longer.

Most readers assumed, until the bat began to fly, that it was the kind associated with Babe Ruth rather than with Count Dracula. Many never changed their minds. Asked at the end of the passage what Bob found in the house, they responded, "A baseball bat." Having read about a "stick" and "sporting equipment," they weren't expecting to read about bats capable of "flying back and forth," so they ignored what they read. They kept their image of a baseball bat and forgot that they had even *seen* a mention of flying. With words, out of sight is truly out of mind. Here's our familiar story once more: the mind is a leaky bucket, attention is a penlight, the old framework determines how new data will be interpreted (or forgotten).

A slight variation of the experiment made the leakiness of the readers' minds more obvious. Daneman and Carpenter put a period after *bat:* "He found a bat. It was very large and brown and was flying back and forth in the gloomy room." Now even more readers clung to the idea that Bob had found a baseball bat. Research shows that readers race through individual sentences, forgetting or ignoring some words as they go. At the end of each sentence, they pause to decide on a meaning and then *flush most of the remaining words from their memory.* Once the words are gone, a wrong impression is hard to correct. This is why writers learn to pay special attention to the connections between sentences. The end of every sentence is a chance for the reader to wander from the path. The beginning of every sentence is an opportunity for the writer to pull the reader back.

The disturbing lesson for writers is this: readers quickly forget most of the words we write. Of course, when they aren't facing one of Daneman and Carpenter's computer screens, readers *could* backtrack to correct mistaken impressions, but ordinarily they don't. They typically read a passage once, taking in *and discarding* words at a speed exceeding two hundred words per minute.

Two-hundred-plus words per minute, a comfortable cruising speed for the reader, appears positively breakneck from the writer's perspective. The sentence we may have struggled for some minutes to compose will flash by the reader in a few seconds, understood or misunderstood, correctly connected to our line of thinking or misconnected. Among the techniques a writer can use to avoid serious misunderstandings are these:

1. Building memorable images.
2. Emphasizing actions and actors.
3. Writing sentences of manageable length.
4. Eliminating clutter.
5. Referring to prior topics before adding new information.

MEMORABLE IMAGES

As the bat experiment suggests, sentences and words vanish quickly from the reader's memory. Fortunately, images have better staying power. The much-praised journalist and essayist George Orwell, who had his own reasons for distrusting words, encouraged writers to compose by thinking of "pictures and sensations" first:

> Afterwards one can choose—not simply *accept*—the phrases that will best cover the meaning, and then switch round and decide what impressions one's words are likely to make on another person.

Orwell practiced what he preached. His paragraphs usually contain at least one striking image likely to outlast in memory the words that presented it. Some paragraphs in his eyewitness essays consist of little more than a topic sentence and a parade of crisp, clear images that report his experience. When he deals with a subject that does not naturally provide images, he finds metaphors, similes, and analogies that give the reader a sensory impression to cling to. Consider the following paragraph on political writing from "Politics and the English Language."

A WRITER AT WORK

"Politics and the English Language"
GEORGE ORWELL

(1) In our time it is broadly true that political writing is bad writing. (2) Where it is not true, it will generally be found that the writer is some kind of rebel, expressing his private opinions and not a "party line." (3) Orthodoxy, of whatever colour, seems to demand a lifeless, imitative style. (4) The political dialects to be found in pamphlets, leading articles, manifestos, White Papers and the speeches of undersecretaries do, of course, vary from party to party, but they are all alike in that one almost never finds in them a fresh, vivid, home-made turn of speech. (5) When one watches some tired hack on the platform mechanically repeating the familiar phrases—*bestial atrocities, iron heel, bloodstained tyranny, free peoples of the world, stand shoulder to shoulder*—one often has a curious feeling that one is not watching

a live human being but some kind of dummy: a feeling which suddenly
becomes stronger at moments when the light catches the speaker's spectacles and turns them into blank discs which seem to have no eyes behind them. (6) And this is not altogether fanciful. (7) A speaker who
uses that kind of phraseology has gone some distance towards turning
himself into a machine. (8) The appropriate noises are coming out of
his larynx, but his brain is not involved as it would be if he were
choosing his words for himself. (9) If the speech he is making is one
that he is accustomed to make over and over again, he may be almost
unconscious of what he is saying, as one is when one utters the responses in church. (10) And this reduced state of consciousness, if not
indispensable, is at any rate favorable to political conformity.

Excellent as Orwell's language may be here, he knew—even before researchers like Daneman and Carpenter proved the point—that most of the words
would fade quickly from memory.

    If you'll look at sentences 5–9, you'll see Orwell creating the image
he hopes to lodge in the reader's memory: the picture of the political speaker
as a kind of machine, mindless and eyeless behind his glinting spectacles.
In a sense, Orwell entrusted his whole paragraph to that image, wagering
that readers would not forget it and that it would carry for them the essence
of his idea. His wager was a good one, as you can confirm by a simple
experiment. Have someone who has never read "Politics and the English
Language" read Orwell's paragraph aloud so that she will notice every
word but not have time to memorize. Tell her before she begins that you
are going to ask her to reproduce the paragraph from memory. After she
has read, take the book from her immediately and give her time to write.
The result will look something like this:

> In our time it is generally supposed that political writing is bad writ-
> ing. When it is not, it is normally supposed that the writer is some
> kind of rebel, stating his own opinions, not that of the political estab-
> lishment. Something about political writing and speakers using hack-
> neyed phrases . . . *bestial atrocities, stand shoulder to shoulder, free
> peoples of the world.* . . . Often when one hears a political speech, one
> can imagine that the speaker is not a man but a robot and the feeling
> becomes stronger when the light catches his glasses and he becomes.
> . . . This is not altogether fanciful. When a man uses standard political
> phrases his mind is not engaged to the extent that it would be if he
> were using his own words to express his thoughts.

In this case, the reader (my wife, a molecular biologist with a good memory)
has done a fair job of recalling the first two sentences, but we see *not a
single word* of sentence 3, the topic sentence, which is essentially imageless.
Sentence 4 is also virtually absent. But the mechanical man with the glaring
glasses and the string of clichés is very much present. Notice that she uses

a word for him that Orwell did not: *robot*. Clearly, she remembers the image rather than the language; and clearly, she connects the image with Orwell's main idea. We needn't worry that she doesn't remember the words of the topic sentence. She has retained the essence of the paragraph.

I don't mean to suggest that every paragraph should have, like Orwell's, a single dominant image: some excellent paragraphs have several strong ones; some have none. Inserting images according to some artificial rule will do no good, but learning to see *opportunities* to use imagery is important. The *right* image can become a powerful link between the mind of the writer and the mind of the reader.

EXERCISE 1

♦ *An Experiment with Imagery.* Repeat the experiment just outlined, using Theodore White's paragraph about the Latin School (p. 495) or Annie Dillard's passage about China (p. 496) instead of the Orwell paragraph. You will, of course, have to find someone who has not yet read the passages to serve as an experimental subject. Report the results of your experiment: what clues does it give about ways in which writers can help readers overcome the limitations of their working memories?

ACTIONS AND ACTORS

Words run quickly off the reader's consciousness; images stick. Similarly, actionless sentences tend to fade quickly from memory, while sentences where people act seem to have greater staying power. Let's examine the difference by contrasting two versions of a passage in which poet and farmer Wendell Berry explains his reasons for not buying a personal computer.

Here is a version in which I have tried to state Berry's ideas in an abstract way, de-emphasizing people and their actions:

(1) Though energy corporations are not considered admirable by most of us, they are something we are connected to. (2) Less connection is my goal. (3) Minimal connection to them in my work is one of my aims. (4) In farming, almost all my work is done with horses. (5) In writing, a pencil or pen and a piece of paper are my tools.

(6) A Royal standard typewriter bought new in 1956, and as good now as it was then, is used by my wife to type my work. (7) While the typing is done, things that are wrong come to light and are marked with small checks in the margins. (8) The best criticism comes from my wife because of her familiarity with my habitual errors and weaknesses. (9) An understanding of what *ought* to be said, sometimes better than my own, is one of her virtues. (10) The literary cottage industry we have works well, I think. (11) Defects in it are not apparent to me.

(12) The opinion expressed by a number of people, by now, is that buying a computer would greatly improve things. (13) My answer is that it won't be done.

There is a fogginess about this passage, as if we were looking at the subject through a hazy window. As we reach the end of a sentence, we may have difficulty recalling precisely what it said. Now compare Berry's original version:

> (1) Like almost everybody else, I am hooked to the energy corporations, which I do not admire. (2) I hope to become less hooked to them. (3) In my work, I try to be as little hooked to them as possible. (4) As a farmer, I do almost all of my work with horses. (5) As a writer, I work with a pencil or a pen and a piece of paper.
>
> (6) My wife types my work on a Royal standard typewriter bought new in 1956, and as good now as it was then. (7) As she types, she sees things that are wrong, and marks them with small checks in the margins. (8) She is my best critic because she is the one most familiar with my habitual errors and weaknesses. (9) She also understands, sometimes better than I do, what *ought* to be said. (10) We have, I think, a literary cottage industry that works well and pleasantly. (11) I do not see anything wrong with it.
>
> (12) A number of people, by now, have told me that I could greatly improve things by buying a computer. (13) My answer is that I'm not going to do it.

Now the haze is gone, and each sentence leaves a clearer impression on us. Rather than beginning his sentences with an abstract noun (*energy corporations, connection, understanding*) or a lifeless object (*pencil or pen, typewriter*), Berry tends to put a person in the subject position. And these person-subjects usually *do* something (*hope, work, type, mark*). As a species, we don't seem well equipped to deal with a series of sentences in which nobody definite does nothing in particular. Being active and social creatures, we crave most, and understand most quickly, sentences where (1) something definite happens and (2) somebody definite does it. Give us a sentence where we can identify clearly both the actor and the action, and our minds are fit to receive it.

Of course, not all writing deals so directly with people and their actions, and one reason for getting a college education is to learn how to deal with the world in more abstract terms. But even when the subject matter is abstract, you can look for opportunities to focus on actions and actors. When there is a chance to show somebody thinking, desiring, or feeling, seize it. When there is a chance to show someone moving, seize it with both hands. If it is impossible to put a person in the subject position, remember that writers sometimes get good results by following abstract nouns with verbs that suggest concrete actions. "Justice too long delayed is justice denied," Martin Luther King, Jr., wrote, making justice sound rather like a foreigner having trouble passing through customs. Had he written, "Untimely justice may not be substantial justice," much would have been lost.

ACTIVE AND PASSIVE VOICE

One way to focus sentences on actors and actions is to use the active voice rather than the passive voice whenever possible. To distinguish between active and passive, you need to know a bit of grammar. In an *active voice* sentence, the grammatical subject does the action described by the verb, and there may be a direct object:

> *The President ordered the pizza.*

> ["Who ordered?" we ask, and the answer is clearly "The president." "Ordered what?" we ask, and the answer is clearly "The pizza." The active voice sentence in normal word order names the actor before naming the thing or person acted on—the direct object.]

In a *passive voice* sentence, the grammatical subject is not the person or thing that acts. To add the actor to the sentence, the writer must add a *by*-phrase:

> *The pizza was ordered.*

> [The pizza did *not* do the ordering, and the sentence does not say who did.]

> *The pizza was ordered by the President.*

> [The person acting is added in a *by*-phrase. Notice that the sentence first names the thing acted on and ends by naming the actor.]

A sentence that never names the actor can sound evasive (does the President not want to be named in this pizza affair?). A sentence that adds the actor in a *by*-phrase is wordier than an active voice sentence and often sounds anticlimactic. There are circumstances where the passive voice works better than the active: when the actor is unknown or unimportant, for instance, or when first naming the thing acted on will help forge a link between sentences. These exceptions aside, good writers use the active voice almost instinctively.

EXERCISE 2

◆ *Spoiling the Focus on Actors and Actions.* Ellen Goodman is a Pulitzer Prize-winning journalist who habitually writes in the active voice and focuses on specific actors. To get a sense of her style, complete both parts of this two-part exercise.

A. Rewrite the following passage from "A Working Community" (p. 498) in a style that uses more passive voice, duller verbs, and more abstract nouns in the subject position.

(1) In the past, most Americans lived in neighborhoods. (2) We were members of precincts or parishes or school districts. (3) My dictionary

still defines community, first of all in geographic terms, as "a body of people who live in one place." (4) But today fewer of us do our living in that one place; more of us just use it for sleeping. (5) Now we call our towns "bedroom suburbs," and many of us, without small children as icebreakers, would have trouble naming all the people on our street. (6) It's not that we are more isolated today. (7) It's that many of us have transferred a chunk of our friendships, a major portion of our everyday social lives, from home to office. (8) As more of our neighbors work away from home, the workplace becomes our neighborhood.

B. Examine all 47 sentences of "A Working Community" and list all that seem to be *without* actors and actions: no activity expressed in any verb *and* no definite person in any subject position. Examine each of these "actionless" sentences carefully and comment on its effectiveness. Is the sentence limp and sluggish, or does it have virtues that compensate for the lack of action?

SENTENCES OF MANAGEABLE LENGTH

Let's remind ourselves once again that the reader's speed is typically faster than two hundred words per minute. It is a good speed for a well-engineered verbal highway, but a road with many curves or frequent stops is bound to cause trouble. Look, for example, at the following three versions of a passage from Jan Morris's "To Everest." Which is the easiest to read?

1. Here's a story about sheer exuberance. The best day of my life was my last on Everest. The mountain had been climbed. I had already begun my race down the glacier. I was racing toward Katmandu. I had left the expedition behind me. It was packing its gear. I had already sent a message. I had done this with a combination of cunning and ingenuity. The message was coded. I had sent it through an Indian Army transmitter. Namche Bazar is located twenty miles south of Everest. The radio operators were unaware of the message's meaning. I did not know if the message had reached London safely. Therefore, I was myself hastening to the cable office. I was carrying my own final dispatch. The cable office was back in Katmandu. How brilliant I felt! I was with a couple of Sherpa porters. I bounded down the glacial moraine toward the green below.

2. I think for sheer exuberance the best day of my life was my last on Everest. The mountain had been climbed, and I had already begun my race down the glacier toward Katmandu, leaving the expedition to pack its gear behind me. By a combination of cunning and ingenuity I had already sent a coded message through an Indian Army radio transmitter at Namche Bazar, twenty miles south of Everest, its operators being unaware of its meaning; but I did not know if it had reached

London safely, so I was myself hastening back to Katmandu and the cable office with my own final dispatch. How brilliant I felt, as with a couple of Sherpa porters I bounded down the glacial moraine toward the green below!

3. I think for sheer exuberance the best day of my life was my last on Everest, after the mountain had been climbed and after I had by a combination of cunning and ingenuity already sent a coded message through an Indian Army radio transmitter at Namche Bazar, twenty miles south of Everest, its operators being unaware of its meaning, when I, not knowing if it had reached London safely, was myself hastening back to Katmandu and the cable office with my own final dispatch. How brilliant I felt leaving the expedition to pack its gear behind me and beginning my race down the glacier toward Katmandu, bounding with a couple of Sherpa guides down the glacial moraine toward the green below!

Most of us find the first version easy to read and understand until we are four or five sentences into it, at which point we begin to be irritated that *every* sentence is so short. Why the irritation? Remember that most readers are used to moving at a pace of two hundred words per minute. At that pace, they could read the Morris passage in about 40 seconds. But as Daneman and Carpenter have shown, readers pause at the ends of sentences to assimilate what they have read. The first version interrupts the reader about every 10 words (every 3 seconds), creating the stop-and-go anxiety drivers often feel in a traffic jam. And with the passage so chopped up, trying to find its whole meaning is like trying to make a clothesline out of shoelaces.

The second version, Morris's original, averages 32 words per sentence (it would have been 21 if she had elected to use periods after *climbed* in the second sentence and *meaning* in the third). Most readers see fairly effortlessly that each sentence contains one or two central statements surrounded by minor statements that demand less attention:

I think for sheer exuberance the best day of my life was my last on Everest. The mountain had been climbed, and I had already begun my race down the glacier toward Katmandu, leaving the expedition to pack its gear behind me. By a combination of cunning and ingenuity I had already sent a coded message through an Indian Army radio transmitter at Namche Bazar, twenty miles south of Everest, its operators being unaware of its meaning; but I did not know if it had reached London safely, so I was myself hastening back to Katmandu and the cable office with my own final dispatch. How brilliant I felt, as with a couple of Sherpa porters I bounded down the glacial moraine toward the green below!

The relations between central and peripheral information are much harder to see in version 3, which stuffs too much material into two sentences. Starting with a behemoth 84-word sentence and following with a stout (though more manageable) 37-worder, the third version also strains the reader's attention span. If it is hard on us to be interrupted every three seconds, it is equally hard to hold all the parts of a minute-long sentence in mind while waiting for the period (or other end mark) that will allow us to relax and absorb the meaning of the whole.

So how long should sentences be? The answer will vary with the audience and the subject, of course, but it is worth considering that sentences in general-interest magazines aimed at well-educated readers average about 20 words. The average reflects a wide range: in a typical paragraph, a writer might go as high as 50 words in a sentence intended to accumulate details and as low as 5 words in a sentence intended to make a point forcefully. Perhaps the best gauge of length is this: most sentences should contain *one* statement the writer thinks is worth emphasizing. (Compound sentences—like Morris's second one—can contain two.) A writer who gives whole sentences, however short, to information too unimportant to deserve emphasis ("The transmitter was located in Namche Bazar") will irritate and confuse the reader. A writer who tries to cram four significant ideas into a single sentence, however long, will probably do the same.

♦ *Choppy, Manageable, and Overly Complicated Sentences.* Select a passage about 200 words long from one of your own papers and create from it three versions: one in which the sentences are so choppy that they interfere with the reader's comprehension, one in which the sentences are so long that they interfere, and one whose meaning and emphasis seem to you quite clear.

EXERCISE 3

ELIMINATING CLUTTER

Remembering the strain that even the plainest prose puts on the attention of the speeding reader, careful writers naturally try to avoid littering the path with unnecessary words or other distractions. One of the reasons that I admire the work of Valerie Sinzdak, the student writer from Chapter 2, is that she writes sentences that are full of interesting thoughts without being at all cluttered. Let's examine a passage she did *not* (thank goodness) write:

(1) On the telephone, Mike and Mary Gerard, just launched upon their fourth decade of life, can communicate verbally to the listener that they have some traditional middle American values. (2) They propagate agricultural commodities and they participate with them in free-market exchange. (3) They disburse their various governmental assessments. (4) The appellation of their enterprise, Heavenly Harvest Sprouts, represents not the fanaticism of some extreme religious group, but only a convenient repetition of the sound of the letter *H*, which begins the first two words.

Had Sinzdak written something this cluttered, she would have invited no end of misunderstanding and irritation. The middle of the first sentence is clogged with unnecessary material: the reader's attention is distracted both by the notion of people being "launched" on a decade as if it were a sea and by the wordy statement of an obvious fact—that talking on the telephone involves speaking. The second sentence forces the reader to puzzle out just what the writer might mean by "agricultural commodities" and "free-market exchange." The third is a mind-boggling way of saying that the Gerards pay their taxes. The fourth might send some readers to the dictionary to look up *appellation,* and it spends fourteen words overexplaining the business about the *H* sound. The result of all this distraction is prose that keeps the reader in trouble *more* than half the time.

Compare the sharper, more economical sentences that Sinzdak actually wrote:

> (1) On the telephone, Mike and Mary Gerard, barely thirtysomething, can communicate traditional middle American values. (2) They grow things, and they sell them. (3) They pay their taxes. (4) The name of their business, Heavenly Harvest Sprouts, represents not religious fanaticism but only convenient alliteration.

This is not risk-free prose. Sinzdak could have said "barely thirty" instead of "barely thirtysomething," for instance, and thereby have avoided the danger of confusing the reader with a peculiar word; but she would have sacrificed an allusion to baby boomers and their usually materialistic values (see the discussion on page 33). By writing *alliteration,* Sinzdak risks puzzling someone unfamiliar with the term, but the danger is not as great as the danger with *appellation* in the other version, and her choice saves her several words. Though Sinzdak's prose isn't risk-free, it doesn't put readers in *pointless* danger of losing the thread.

Which dangers are justified and which are pointless depends on the audience and situation. An anthropology paper written for an academic journal may contain words like *bifacially* and *Paleolithic* and allude casually to "the superior strength of *H. erectus.*" For the layperson, this kind of language might be distracting clutter; but for its intended audience of trained anthropologists, it is clear, simple, and economical.

EXERCISE 4   ◆ *Editing Cluttered Prose.* George Orwell was one of the master prose stylists of the twentieth century, particularly admired for the economy and clarity of his work. The passage below, excerpted from his essay "Why I Write," has been muddied by the addition of unnecessary words and the substitution of obscure expressions for his plainer ones. Rewrite the passage to restore an uncluttered style.

When I embark upon the adventure of a book, I do not ruminate to myself, "I am going to produce a work of art." I write it because there is some prevarication I want to expose, some fact to which I want to draw attention, and my initial concern is to get a hearing. But I could not do the onerous labor of writing a book, or even a protracted magazine article, if it were not also an aesthetic experience. Anyone who cares to put my work under a microscope will see that even when it is downright propaganda it contains much that a full-time politician would consider irrelevant. . . . So long as I remain sentient and disease-free I shall continue to feel strongly about the manner in which articles, books and other materials are written, to love the surface of the earth, and to take a pleasure in solid objects and scraps of useless information. It is no use trying to suppress that side of myself.

> A WRITER AT WORK
>
> *"Why I Write"*
> GEORGE ORWELL

REFERRING TO PRIOR TOPICS

To keep their readers from getting lost in a prose passage, most writers intuitively write sentences that touch base with a prior topic and *then* move on to new information about it. This is the written equivalent of a familiar move in conversation:

> "You know that guy we were talking about yesterday?"
> "Yeah."
> "Well, I saw him outside Murray's last night and. . . ."

In face-to-face talk, we constantly "check in" with listeners, reminding them of previous topics of conversation and waiting for them to acknowledge that they are still with us. Writers can't get the same kind of feedback, so they need to be careful to make the connection of new topics to old ones clear. They can refer to the old topic in any of these ways:

1. *Repetition of a key word or phrase.*
   Abraham Lincoln, even during the darkest periods of the war, maintained a remarkable sense of humor. His *humor* showed. . . .

2. *Pronoun reference.*
   Abraham Lincoln, even during the darkest periods of the war, maintained a remarkable sense of humor. *He* often entertained White House guests by telling jokes he had read in. . . .

3. *Explicit transitional words or phrases.*
   Abraham Lincoln, even during the darkest periods of the war, maintained a remarkable sense of humor. *For example,* even while Lee's army was threatening Washington. . . .

4. *Any other technique that calls the familiar topic back to mind.*

Consider, for example, the opening sentences of T. H. White's paragraph on the Latin School from Chapter 13 (p. 495):

> The Latin School [*White has referred to it in the previous paragraph, so it is now an "old" topic*] taught the mechanics of learning with very little pretense of culture, enrichment, or enlargement of horizons.
>
> Mr. Russo, who taught English in the first year [*"taught" repeats the "taught" of the previous sentence and points to the old topic of the school*], had the face of a prizefighter—a bald head which gleamed, a pug nose, a jut jaw, hard and sinister eyes which smiled only when a pupil scored an absolute triumph of grammar.
>
> He [*points back to Russo*] was less interested in the rhymes of *The Idylls of the King* or "Evangeline," or in the story in *Quentin Durward,* than in drubbing into us the structure of paragraph and sentence.
>
> The paragraph [*a clear repetition from the previous sentence*] began with the "topic sentence"—
>
> that [*pointing back to the previous idea*] was the cornerstone of all teaching in composition.

Obviously, White has gone to some lengths to make all his connections clear. Now suppose that he had reversed the pattern of his ideas, beginning with the new information and ending with the prior topic. Here is what the passage would look like:

> The mechanics of learning, with very little pretense of culture, enrichment, or enlargement of horizons, was what the Latin School taught. A man with the face of a prizefighter—a bald head which gleamed, a pug nose, a jut jaw, hard and sinister eyes which smiled only when a pupil scored an absolute triumph in grammar, Mr. Russo taught English in the first year. The rhymes of *The Idylls of the King* or "Evangeline," or the story in *Quentin Durward,* interested him less than drubbing into us the structure of paragraph and sentence. The cornerstone of all teaching in composition was that the paragraph began with the "topic sentence."

Now the reader flounders at the beginning of each sentence, uncertain of the connection of what he is reading to what has come before.

As I said at the beginning of this section, the movement from a prior topic to new information seems to come instinctively to most writers, but sometimes our instincts break down. Laboring over an individual sentence, we can lose contact with previous sentences and let the new information (on which we are concentrating) drift to the beginning. An occasional sentence that reverses the expected familiar-to-new pattern may pose no problems for the reader, but a long series of them is likely to be confusing. In reading, as in navigating, we have to know where we are coming from in order to evaluate where we are headed.

◆ *Unscrambling a Scrambled Paragraph.* The following sentences form a paragraph in Margaret Mead's *Sex and Temperament in Three Primitive Societies*. Because Mead regularly follows the familiar-to-new pattern of sentence construction, you should be able to return them to very nearly their original order. Attempt to do so. Be prepared to discuss the reasoning behind your arrangement.

EXERCISE 5

1. In later years, this is the greatest claim that he has upon her.

2. An Arapesh boy grows his wife.

3. And in those exceptional cases when the arranged marriage falls through from the death of the betrothed husband, and the girl is betrothed again after she has attained her growth, the tie is never felt to be so close.

4. Upon the young adolescent husband particularly falls the onus of growing his wife.

5. A little girl is betrothed when she is seven or eight to a boy about six years her senior, and she goes to live in the home of her future husband.

6. Here the father-in-law, the husband, and all of his brothers combine to grow the little bride.

7. Similarly when a man inherits the widow of a relative, he may have contributed very little food to her growth—especially if she is older than he—and these marriages, lacking the most important sanction that the culture recognizes, are less stable.

8. As a father's claim to his child is not that he has begotten it but rather that he has fed it, so also a man's claim to his wife's attention and devotion is not that he has paid a bride-price for her, or that she is legally his property, but that he has actually contributed the food which has become flesh and bone of her body.

9. If she is dilatory or sulky or unwilling, he can invoke this claim: "I worked the sago, I grew the yams, I killed the kangaroo that made your body. Why do you not bring in the firewood?"

STYLE THAT ASSISTS THE READER

A careful stylist takes into account the way readers digest and discard words. We know that they move through the text rapidly, forming general impressions as they go and fitting new information into these hastily

POINTS TO

CONSIDER

constructed frameworks as well as they can. Courtesy and self-defense both recommend the following techniques for fending off misunderstanding:

1. Create images that can represent ideas after the words fade from the reader's memory.

2. Present even abstract ideas, so far as possible, in terms of specific actions performed by definite actors.

3. Write sentences of moderate length, neither so short that their ideas seem disconnected, nor so long and complicated that they strain readers' attention.

4. Eliminate the clutter caused by unnecessary words and by phrasing that is exotic without being exact.

5. Connect new sentences to old by referring to prior topics before introducing new information.

I could precede each of these rules with a disclaimer like "Whenever possible," "Unless it creates more problems than it solves," or "Unless you have a better idea." Good judgment and the ability to see a passage from a reader's perspective are what matter.

Assignments
for Chapter 15

ASSIGNMENT 1: **ANALYSIS OF A PROSE STYLE**

Select a prose passage, about a page long, from a writer whose style you particularly admire. Write an analysis (about 500 words long) of the passage's stylistic features that you think other writers could benefit by imitating.

ASSIGNMENT 2: **IMITATION OF A PROSE STYLE**

Write a passage in which you imitate the style of the passage you selected for assignment 1.

THE SHAPE OF THINGS

Isaac Asimov

E. B. White's statement that the reader is "in trouble about half the time" is particularly true when a writer deals with difficult or unfamiliar subject matter, as Isaac Asimov does in "The Shape of Things." A phenomenally productive writer of both science fiction and popular essays, Asimov is often praised for his ability to explain scientific concepts to readers with only a little scientific training. As you read through Asimov's essay, notice passages where he succeeds in presenting potentially difficult concepts in such a way that you grasp them without great effort. Note, too, passages where he fails to do so. What has gone wrong? How might he have made the meaning clearer?

1 EVERY CHILD COMES STAGGERING OUT OF grammar school with a load of misstatements of fact firmly planted in his head. He may forget, for instance, as the years drift by, that the Battle of Waterloo was fought in 1815 or that seven times six is forty-two; but he will never, never forget, while he draws breath, that Columbus proved the world was round.

2 And, of course, Columbus proved no such thing. What Columbus did prove was that it doesn't matter how wrong you are, as long as you're lucky.

3 The fact that the earth is spherical in shape was first suggested in the sixth century B.C. by various Greek philosophers. Some believed it out of sheer mysticism, the reasoning being that the sphere was the perfect solid and that therefore the earth was a sphere. To us, the premise is dubious and the conclusion a *non sequitur*, but to the Greeks it carried weight.

4 However, not all Greek philosophers were mystics and there were rational reasons for believing the earth to be spherical. These were ca-pably summarized by Aristotle in the fourth century B.C. and turned out to be three in number:

5 1) If the earth were flat, then all the stars visible from one point on the earth's surface would be visible from all other points (barring minor distortions due to perspective and, of course, the obscuring of parts of the horizon by mountains). However, as travelers went southward, some stars disappeared beyond the northern horizon, while new stars appeared above the southern horizon. This proved the earth was not flat but had some sort of curved shape. Once that was allowed, one could reason further that all things fell toward earth's center and got as close to it as they could. That solid shape in which the total distance of all parts from the center is a minimum is a sphere, Q.E.D.[1]

6 2) Ships on leaving harbor and sailing off into the open sea seemed to sink lower and lower in the water, until at the horizon only the tops were visible. The most reasonable con-

---

[1] **Q.E.D.:** *Quod erat demonstrandum*—Latin, "which was to be demonstrated."

clusion was that the water surface, though it seemed flat, was a gently curving hill behind which the ships disappeared. Furthermore, since this effect was eqully intense whatever the direction in which the ship sailed, the gently curving hill of the ocean seemed to curve equally in all directions. The only solid shape that curves equally in all directions is a sphere, Q.E.D.

7   3) It was accepted by the Greek philosophers that the moon is eclipsed when it enters the earth's shadow. As darkness crossed over the face of the moon, the encroaching shadow marked off a projection of the shape of the earth, and that shadow was always the segment of a circle. It didn't matter whether the moon were high in the sky or at either horizon. The shadow was always circular. The only solid for which all projections are circular is a sphere, Q.E.D.

8   Now, Aristotle's reasoning carried conviction. All learned men throughout history who had access to Aristotle's books, accepted the sphericity of the earth. Even in the eighth century A.D., in the very depth of the Dark Ages, St. Bede (usually called "the Venerable Bede"), collecting what scraps of physical science were still remembered from Greek days, plainly stated the earth was a sphere. In the fourteenth century Dante's *Divine Comedy,* which advanced a detailed view of the orthodox astronomy of the day, presented the earth as spherical.

9   Consequently, there is no doubt that Columbus knew the earth was a sphere. But so did all other educated men in Europe.

10   In that case, what was Columbus's difficulty? He wanted to sail west from Europe and cross the Atlantic to Asia. If the earth were spherical, this was theoretically possible, and if educated men all agreed with the premise and, therefore, with the conclusion, why the resistance to Columbus's scheme?

11   Well, to say the earth is a sphere is not enough. The question is—how large a sphere?

12   The first person to measure the circumference of the earth was a Greek astronomer, named Eratosthenes of Cyrene, and he did it without ever leaving home.

13   If the earth were a sphere, as Eratosthenes was certain it was, then the sun's rays should, at any one instant of time, strike different parts of the earth's surface at different angles. For instance, on June 21, the sun was just overhead at noon in the city of Syene, Egypt. In Alexandria, Egypt (where Eratosthenes lived), the sun was not quite overhead at that moment but made a small angle with the zenith.

14   Eratosthenes knew the distance between Alexandria and Syene, and it was simple geometry to calculate the curvature of the earth's surface that would account for the displacement of the sun. From that one could further calculate the radius and the circumference of the earth.

15   Eratosthenes worked out this circumference to be 25,000 miles in our modern units of length (or perhaps a little higher—the exact length in miles of the unit he used is uncertain) and this is just about right!

16   About 100 B.C., however, a Greek geographer named Posidonius of Apamea checked Eratosthenes' work and came out with a lower figure—a circumference of 18,000 miles.

17   This smaller figure may have seemed more comfortable to some Greeks, for it reduced the area of the unknown. If the larger figure were accepted, then the known world made up only about one sixth of the earth's surface area. If the smaller figure were accepted, the earth's surface area was reduced by half and the known world made up a third of the earth's surface area.

18   Now the Greek thinkers were much concerned with the unknown portions of the earth (which seemed as unattainable and mysterious to them as, until recently, the other side of the moon seemed to us) and they filled it with imaginary continents. To have less of it to worry about must have seemed a relief, and

the Greek astronomer Claudius Ptolemy, who lived about A.D. 150, was one of those who accepted Posidonius's figure.

19   It so happened that in the latter centuries of the Middle Ages, Ptolemy's books were as influential as Aristotle's, and if the fifteenth-century geographers accepted Aristotle's reasoning as to the sphericity of the earth, many of them also accepted Ptolemy's figure for its circumference.

20   An Italian geographer named Paolo Toscanelli was one of them. Since the extreme distance across Europe and Asia is some 13,000 miles (a piece of knowledge geographers had become acquainted with thanks to Marco Polo's voyages in the thirteenth century) and the total circumference was 18,000 miles or less, then one would have to travel westward from Spain no more than 5000 miles to reach "the Indies." In fact, since there were islands off the eastern coast of Asia, such as the Zipangu (Japan) spoken of by Marco Polo, the distance might be only 4000 miles or even less. Toscanelli drew a map in the 1470s showing this, picturing the Atlantic Ocean with Europe and Africa on one side and Asia, with its offshore islands, on the other.

21   Columbus obtained a copy of the map and some personal encouragement from Toscanelli and was an enthusiastic convert to the notion of reaching Asia by the westward route. All he needed now was government financing.

22   The most logical place to go for such financing was Portugal. In the fifteenth century many of Europe's luxuries (including spices, sugar, and silk) were available only by overland routes from the Far East, and the Turks who straddled the route charged all the traffic could bear in the way of middleman fees. Some alternate route was most desirable, and the Portuguese, who were at the extreme southeastern edge of Europe, conceived the notion of sailing around Africa and reaching the Far East by sea, outflanking the Turks altogether. Throughout the fourteenth century, then, the

Portuguese had been sending out expedition after expedition, farther and farther down the African coast. (The Portuguese "African effort" was as difficult for those days as our "space effort" is for ours.)

23   In 1484, when Columbus appealed to John II of Portugal for financing, Portuguese expeditions had all but reached the southern tip of Africa (and in 1487 they were to do so).

24   The Portuguese, at the time, were the most experienced navigators in Europe, and King John's geographers viewed with distrust the low figure for the circumference of the earth. If it turned out that the high figure, 25,000 miles, were correct, and if the total east-west stretch of Europe and Asia were 13,000 miles—then it followed, as the night the day, that a ship would have to sail 12,000 miles west from Portugal to reach Asia. No ship of that day could possibly make such an uninterrupted ocean voyage.

25   The Portuguese decision, therefore, was that the westward voyage was theoretically possible but, given the technology of the day, completely impractical. The geographers advised King John to continue work on Project Africa and to turn down the Italian dreamer. This was done.

26   Now, mind you, the Portuguese geographers were perfectly right. It *is* 12,000 miles from Portugal west to Asia, and no ship of the day could possibly have made such a voyage. The fact is that Columbus never did reach Asia by the western route, whereas the Portuguese voyagers succeeded, within thirteen years, in reaching Asia by the African route. As a result, tiny Portugal built a rich and far-flung empire, becoming the first of the great European colonialists. Enough of that empire has survived into the 1960s to permit them to be the last as well.

27   And what is the reward of the Portuguese geographers for proving to be right in every last particular? Why, schoolchildren are taught to sneer at them.

28   Columbus obtained the necessary financing from Spain in 1492. Spain had just taken the last Moslem strongholds on the Iberian Peninsula and, in the flush of victory, was reaching for some daring feat of navigation that would match the deeds of the Portuguese. (In the language of today, they needed an "ocean spectacular" to improve their "world image.") So they gave Columbus three foundering hulks and let him have his pick of the prison population for crewmen and sent him off.

29   It would have meant absolutely certain death for Columbus and his men, thanks to his wrongness, were it not for his incredible luck. The Greek dreamers had been right. The unoccupied wastes of the earth did indeed possess other continents and Columbus ran aground on them after only 3000 miles. (As it was, he barely made it; another thousand miles and he would have been gone.)

30   The Portuguese geographers had not counted on what are now known as the American continents (they would have been fools to do so), but neither had Columbus. In fact, Columbus never admitted he had reached anything but Asia. He died 1506 still convinced the earth was 18,000 miles in circumference— stubbornly wrong to the end.

31   So Columbus had not proved the earth was round; that was already known. In fact, since he had expected to reach Asia and had failed, his voyage was an argument *against* the sphericity of the earth.

32   In 1519, however, five ships set sail from Spain under Ferdinand Magellan (a Portuguese navigator in the pay of Spain), with the intention of completing Columbus's job and reaching Asia, and then continuing on back to Spain. Such an expedition was as difficult for its day as orbiting a man is for ours. The expedition took three years and made it by an inch. An uninterrupted 10,000-mile trip across the Pacific all but finished them (and they were far better prepared than Columbus had been). Magellan himself died en route. However, the one

ship that returned brought back a large enough cargo of spices to pay for the entire expedition with plenty left over.

33   This first circumnavigation of the earth was experimental confirmation, in a way, of the sphericity of the planet, but that was scarcely needed. More important, it proved two other things. It proved the ocean was continuous; that there was one great sea in which the continents were set as large islands. This meant that any seacoast could be reached from any other seacoast, which was vital knowledge (and good news) for merchantmen. Secondly, it proved once and for all that Eratosthenes was right and that the circumference of the earth was 25,000 miles.

34   And yet, after all, though the earth is round, it turned out, despite all Aristotle's arguments, that it wasn't a sphere after all.

35   Again we go back to the Greeks. The stars wheel about the earth in a stately and smooth twenty-four-hour cycle. The Greek philosophers realized that this could be explained in either of two ways. It was possible that the earth stood still and the heavens rotated about it in a twenty-four-hour period. Or the heavens might stand still while the earth rotated about itself in twenty-four hours.

36   A few Greeks (notably Aristarchus of Samos) maintained, in the third century B.C., that it was the earth that rotated. The majority, however, held for a stationary earth, and it was the latter who won out. After all, the earth is large and massive, while the heavens are light and airy; surely it is more logical to suppose the latter turned.

37   The notion of the stationary earth was accepted by Ptolemy and therefore by the medieval scholars and by the Church. It was not until 1543, a generation after Magellan's voyage, that a major onslaught was made against the view.

38   In that year Nicolaus Copernicus, a Polish

astronomer, published his views of the universe and died at once, ducking all controversy. According to his views (which were like those of Aristarchus) the sun was the center of the universe, and the eath revolved about it as one planet among many. If the earth were only a minor body circling the sun, it seemed completely illogical to suppose that the stars revolved about our planet. Copernicus therefore maintained that the earth rotated on its axis.

39   The Copernican view was not, of course, accepted at once, and the world of scholarship argued the matter for a century. As late as 1633, Galileo was forced by the Inquisition to abjure his belief that the earth moved and to affirm that it was motionless. However, that was the dying gasp of the motionless-earth view, and there has been no scientific opposition to earth's rotation since. (Nevertheless, it was not until 1851 that the earth's rotation was actually confirmed by experiment, but that is another story.)

40   Now if the earth rotated, the theory that it was spherical in shape suddenly became untenable. The man who first pointed this out was Isaac Newton, in the 1680s.

41   If the earth were stationary, gravitational forces would force it into spherical shape (minimum total distance from the center) even if it were not spherical to begin with. If the earth rotated, however, a second force would be applied to every particle on the planet. This is centrifugal force, which would counter gravity and would tend to move particles *away* from the center of the earth.

42   But the surface of a rotating sphere moves at varying velocities depending upon its distance from the axis of rotation. At the point where the axis of rotation intersects the surface (as at the North and South Poles) the surface is motionless. As distance from the Poles increases, the surface velocity increases; it is at its maximum at the Equator, which is equidistant from the Poles.

43   Whereas the gravitational force is constant (just about) at all points on earth's surface, the centrifugal force increases rapidly with surface velocity. As a result the surface of the earth lifts up slightly away from the center and the lifting is at its maximum at the Equator where the surface velocity is highest. In other words, said Newton, the earth should have an equatorial bulge. (Or, to put it another way, it should be flattened at the Poles.)

44   This means that if an east-west cross-section of the earth were taken at the Equator, that cross-section would have a circular boundary. If, however, a cross-section were taken north-south through the Poles, that cross-section would have an elliptical boundary and the shortest diameter of the ellipse would run from Pole to Pole. Such a solid body is not a sphere but an "oblate spheroid."

45   To be sure, the ellipticity of the north-south cross-section is so small that it is invisible to the naked eye and, viewed from space, the earth would seem a sphere. Nevertheless, the deviation from perfect sphericity is important, as I shall explain shortly.

46   Newton was arguing entirely from theory, of course, but it seemed to him he had experimental evidence as well. In 1673 a French scientific expedition in French Guiana found that the pendulum of their clock, which beat out perfect seconds in Paris, was moving slightly slower in their tropical headquarters—as compared with the steady motion of the stars. This could only mean that the force of gravity (which was what powered the swinging pendulum) was slightly weaker in French Guiana than in Paris.

47   This would be understandable if the scientific expedition were on a high mountain where the distance from the center of the earth were greater than at sea level and the gravitational force consequently weakened—but the expedition *was* at sea level. Newton, however, maintained that, in a manner of speaking, the expedition was not truly at sea level, but was high up on the equatorial bulge and that that accounted for the slowing of the pendulum.

48   In this, Newton found himself in conflict

with an Italian-born French astronomer named Jean Dominique Cassini. The latter tackled the problem from another direction. If the earth were not a true sphere, then the curvature of its surface ought to vary from point to point. (A sphere is the only solid that has equal curvature everywhere on its surface.) By triangulation methods, measuring the lengths of the sides and the size of the angles of triangles drawn over large areas of earth's surface, one could determine the gentle curvature of that surface. If the earth were truly an oblate spheroid, then this curvature ought to decrease as one approached either Pole.

49 Cassini had conducted triangulation measurements in the north and south of France and decided that the surface curvature was less, not in the north, but in the south. Therefore, he maintained, the earth bulged at the Poles and was flattened at the Equator. If one took a cross-section of the earth through the Poles, it would have an elliptical boundary indeed, but the longest (and not the shortest) diameter would be through the Poles. Such a solid is a "prolate spheroid."

50 For a generation, the argument raged. It was not just a matter of pure science either. I said the deviation of the earth's shape from the spherical was important, despite the smallness of the deviation, and that was because ocean voyages had become commonplace in the eighteenth century. European nations were squabbling over vast chunks of overseas real estate, and victory could go to the nation whose ships got less badly lost en route. To avoid getting lost one had to have accurate charts and such charts could not be drawn unless the exact deviation of the earth's shape from the spherical were known.

51 It was decided that the difference in curvature between northern and southern France was too small to decide the matter safely either way. Something more extreme was needed. In 1735, therefore, two French expeditions set out. One went to Peru, near the Equator. The other went to Lapland, near the North Pole.

Both expeditions took years to make their measurements (and out of their difficulties arose a strong demand for a reform in standards of measurement that led, eventually, to the establishment of the metric system a half century later). When the expeditions returned, the matter was settled. Cassini was wrong, and Newton was right. The equatorial bulge is thirteen miles high, which means that a point at sea level on the Equator is thirteen miles farther from the center of the earth than is sea level at either Pole.

52 The existence of this equatorial bulge neatly explained one particular astronomic mystery. The heavens seem to rotate about an axis of which one end (the North Celestial Pole) is near the North Star. An ancient Greek astronomer, Hipparchus of Nicaea, was able to show about 150 B.C. that this celestial axis is not fixed. It marks out a circle in the heavens and takes some 25,800 years to complete one turn of the circle. This is called "the precession of the equinoxes."

53 To Hipparchus, it seemed that the heavenly sphere simply rotated slowly in that fashion. He didn't know why. When Copernicus advanced his theory, he had to say that the earth's axis wobbled in that fashion. He didn't know why, either.

54 Newton, however, pointed out that the moon traveled in an orbit that was not in the plane of the earth's Equator. During half of its revolution about the earth, it was well to the north of the Equator and during the other half it was well to the south. If the earth were perfectly spherical, the moon would attract it in an all-one-piece fashion from any point. As it was, the moon gave a special unsymmetrical yank at the equatorial bulge. Newton showed that this pull at the bulge produced the precession of the equinoxes. This could be shown experimentally by hanging a weight on the rim of a spinning gyroscope. The axis of the gyroscope then precesses.

55 And thus the moon itself came to the aid of scientists interested in the shape of things.

56 An artificial moon was to do the same, two and a half centuries after Newton's time.

57 The hero of the latest chapter in the drama of earth's shape is Vanguard I, which was launched by the United States on March 17, 1958. It was the fourth satellite placed in orbit and is currently the oldest satellite still orbiting and emitting signals. Its path carried it so high above earth's surface that in the absence of atmospheric interference it will stay in orbit for a couple of centuries. Furthermore, it has a solar battery which will keep it delivering signals for years.

58 The orbit of Vanguard I, like that of the moon itself, is not in the plane of the earth's Equator, so Vanguard I pulls on the equatorial bulge and is pulled by it, just as the moon does. Vanguard I isn't large enough to affect the earth's motion, of course, but it is itself affected by the pull of the bulge, much more than the moon is.

59 For one thing, Vanguard I is nearer to the bulge and is therefore affected more strongly. For another, what counts in some ways is the total number of revolutions made by a satellite. Vanguard I revolves about the earth in two and a quarter hours, which means that in a period of fourteen months, it has completed about 4500 revolutions. This is equal to the total number of revolutions that the moon has completed since the invention of the telescope. It follows that the motions of Vanguard I better reveal the fine structure of the bulge than the motions of the moon do.

60 Sure enough, John A. O'Keefe, by studying the orbital irregularities of Vanguard I, was able to show that the earth's equatorial bulge is not symmetrical. The satellite is yanked just a little harder when it is south of the Equator, so that the bulge must be a little bulgier there. It has been calculated that the southern half of the equatorial bulge is up to fifty feet (not miles but *feet!*) farther from the earth's center than the northern half is. To balance this, the South Pole (calculating from sea level) is one hundred feet closer to the center of the earth than the North Pole is.

61 So the earth is not an exact oblate spheroid, either. It is very, very, very slightly egg-shaped, with a bulging southern half and a narrow northern half; with a flattened southern tip and a pointy northern tip.

62 *Nevertheless, to the naked eye, the earth is still a sphere, and don't you forget it.*

63 This final tiny correction is important in a grisly way. Nowadays the national insanity of war requires that missiles not get lost en route, and missiles must be aimed far more accurately than ever a sailing vessel had to be. The exact shape of the earth is more than ever important.

64 Moreover, this final correction even has theoretical implications. To allow such an asymmetry in the bulge against the symmetrical pull of gravity and the push of centrifugal force, O'Keefe maintains, the interior of the earth must be considerably more rigid than geophysicists had thought.

65 One final word: O'Keefe's descriptive adjective for the shape of the earth, as revealed by Vanguard I, is "pear-shaped," and the newspapers took that up at once. The result is that readers of headlines must have the notion that the earth is shaped like a Bartlett pear, or a Bosc pear, which is ridiculous. There are some varieties of pears that are closer to the egg-shaped, but the best-known varieties are far off. However, "pear-shaped" will last, I am sure, and will do untold damage to the popular conception of the shape of the earth. Undoubtedly the next generation of kids will gain the firm conviction that Columbus proved the earth is shaped like a Bartlett pear.

66 But it is an ill wind that blows no good, and I am breathlessly awaiting a certain opportunity. You see, in 1960 a book of mine entitled *The Double Planet* was published. It is about the earth and moon, which are more

nearly alike in size than any other planet-satellite combination in the solar system, so that the two may rightly be referred to as a "double planet."

67 Now someday, someone is going to pick up a copy of the book in my presence (I have my books strategically scattered about my house), and leaf through it and say, "Is this about the earth?"

68 With frantically beating heart, I will say, "Yes."

69 And he will say (I hope, I hope), "Why do you call the earth a double planet?"

70 And then I will say (get this now), "*Because it is pair-shaped!!!*"

71 –Why am I the only one laughing? ◆

CHIVALRY

Barbara Tuchman

Just as Isaac Asimov faced the challenge of explaining scientific ideas in "The Shape of Things," Barbara Tuchman faced the challenge of explaining an unfamiliar period of history in *A Distant Mirror: The Calamitous 14th Century*. The book became a best-seller, so we can assume that she managed to make life five hundred years ago comprehensible and interesting to thousands of readers. One of her techniques for engaging the reader was to focus on the life of a single figure, Eguerrand de Coucy, "the most experienced and successful of all the knights of France." The following excerpt does not discuss Eguerrand directly but tells about the "moral system" of chivalry and courtly love that prevailed during his lifetime. Read the passage with a writer's eye: note the way Tuchman presents her material and be alert to the strengths and weaknesses of her style.

1   OF CHIVALRY, THE CULTURE THAT NURtured him, much is known. More than a code of manners in war and love, chivalry was a moral system, governing the whole of noble life. That it was about four parts in five illusion made it no less governing for all that. It developed at the same time as the great crusades of the 12th century as a code intended to fuse the religious and martial spirits and somehow bring the fighting man into accord with Christian theory. Since a knight's usual activities were as much at odds with Christian theory as a merchant's, a moral gloss was needed that would allow the Church to tolerate the warriors in good conscience and the warriors to pursue their own values in spiritual comfort. With the help of Benedictine thinkers,[1] a code evolved that put the knight's sword arm in the service, theoretically, of justice, right, piety, the Church, the widow, the orphan, and the oppressed. Knighthood was received in the name of the Trinity after a ceremony of purification, confession, communion. A saint's relic was usually embedded in the hilt of the knight's sword so that upon clasping it as he took his oath, he caused the vow to be registered in Heaven. Chivalry's famous celebrator Ramon Lull, a contemporary of St. Louis,[2] could now state as his thesis that "God and chivalry are in concord."

2   But, like business enterprise, chivalry could not be contained by the Church, and bursting through the pious veils, it developed its own principles. Prowess, that combination of courage, strength, and skill that made a chevalier *preux*,[3] was the prime essential. Honor and loyalty, together with courtesy—meaning the kind of behavior that has since come to be called "chivalrous"—were the ideals, and so-called courtly love the presiding genius. Designed to make the knight more polite and to lift the tone of society, courtly love required its disciple to be in a chronically amorous condition, on the theory that he would thus be rendered more courteous, gay, and gallant, and society in consequence more joyous. Largesse was the necessary accompaniment. An open-handed generosity in gifts and hospitality was the mark of a gentleman and had its practical

---

[1] **Benedictine thinkers:** Monks of the Benedictine order were among the most influential teachers of the Middle Ages.

[2] **St. Louis:** King of France from 1226 to 1270.
[3] *preux:* "valiant."

value in attracting other knights to fight under the banner and bounty of the *grand seigneur*.[4] Over-celebrated by troubadours and chroniclers who depended on its flow, largesse led to reckless extravagance and careless bankruptcies.

3 Prowess was not mere talk, for the function of physical violence required real stamina. To fight on horseback or foot wearing 55 pounds of plate armor, to crash in collision with an opponent at full gallop while holding horizontal an eighteen-foot lance half the length of an average telephone pole, to give and receive blows with sword or battle-ax that could cleave a skull or slice off a limb at a stroke, to spend half of life in the saddle through all weathers and for days at a time, was not a weakling's work. Hardship and fear were part of it. "Knights who are at the wars . . . are forever swallowing their fear," wrote the companion and biographer of Don Pero Niño, the "Unconquered Knight" of the late 14th century. "They expose themselves to every peril; they give up their bodies to the adventure of life in death. Moldy bread or biscuit, meat cooked or uncooked; today enough to eat and tomorrow nothing, little or no wine, water from a pond or a butt, bad quarters, the shelter of a tent or branches, a bad bed, poor sleep with their armor still on their backs, burdened with iron, the enemy an arrow-shot off. 'Ware! Who goes there? To arms! To arms!' With the first drowsiness, an alarm; at dawn, the trumpet. 'To horse! To horse! Muster! Muster!' As lookouts, as sentinels, keeping watch by day and by night, fighting without cover, as foragers, as scouts, guard after guard, duty after duty. 'Here they come! Here! They are so many— No, not as many as that—This way—that— Come this side—Press them there—News! News! They come back hurt, they have prisoners—no, they bring none back. Let us go! Let us go! Give no ground! On!' Such is their calling."

Horrid wounds were part of the calling. In 4 one combat Don Pero Niño was struck by an arrow that "knit together his gorget and his neck," but he fought on against the enemy on the bridge. "Several lance stumps were still in his shield and it was that which hindered him most." A bolt from a crossbow "pierced his nostrils most painfully whereat he was dazed, but his daze lasted but a little time." He pressed forward, receiving many sword blows on head and shoulders which "sometimes hit the bolt embedded in his nose making him suffer great pain." When weariness on both sides brought the battle to an end, Pero Niño's shield "was tattered and all in pieces; his sword blade was toothed like a saw and dyed with blood . . . his armor was broken in several places by lance-heads of which some had entered the flesh and drawn blood, although the coat was of great stength." Prowess was not easily bought.

Loyalty, meaning the pledged word, was 5 chivalry's fulcrum. The extreme emphasis given to it derived from the time when a pledge between lord and vassal was the only form of government. A knight who broke his oath was charged with "treason" for betraying the order of knighthood. The concept of loyalty did not preclude treachery or the most egregious trickery as long as no knightly oath was broken. When a party of armed knights gained entrance to a walled town by declaring themselves allies and then proceeded to slaughter the defenders, chivalry was evidently not violated, no oath having been made to the burghers.

Chivalry was regarded as a universal order 6 of all Christian knights, a trans-national class moved by a single ideal, much as Marxism later regarded all workers of the world. It was a military guild in which all knights were theoretically brothers, although Froissart[5] excepted the Germans and Spaniards, who, he said, were too uncultivated to understand chivalry.

---

[4] *grand seigneur:* "great lord"; powerful nobleman.

[5] **Froissart:** French historian Jean Froissart (1333–1400).

7   In the performance of his function, the knight must be prepared, as John of Salisbury wrote, "to shed your blood for your brethren"—he meant brethren in the universal sense—"and, if needs must, to lay down your life." Many were thus prepared, though perhaps more from sheer love of battle than concern for a cause. Blind King John of Bohemia met death in that way. He loved fighting for its own sake, not caring whether the conflict was important. He missed hardly a quarrel in Europe and entered tournaments in between, allegedly receiving in one of them the wound that blinded him. His subjects, on the other hand, said the cause was Divine punishment—not becaue he dug up the old synagogue of Prague, which he did, but because, on finding money concealed beneath the pavement, he was moved by greed and the advice of German knights to dig up the tomb of St. Adelbert in the Prague cathedral and was stricken blind by the desecrated saint.

8   As an ally of Philip VI, at the head of 500 knights, the sightless King fought the English through Picardy, always rash and in the avantgarde. At Crécy[6] he asked his knights to lead him deeper into the battle so that he might strike further blows with his sword. Twelve of them tied their horses' reins together and, with the King at their head, advanced into the thick of the fight, "so far as never to return." His body was found next day among his knights, all slain with their horses still tied together.

9   Fighting filled the noble's need of something to do, a way to exert himself. It was his substitute for work. His leisure time was spent chiefly in hunting, otherwise in games of chess, backgammon and dice, in songs, dances, pageants, and other entertainments. Long winter evenings were occupied listening to the recital of interminable verse epics. The sword offered the workless noble an activity with a purpose,

one that could bring him honor, status, and, if he was lucky, gain. If no real conflict was at hand, he sought tournaments, the most exciting, expensive, ruinous, and delightful activity of the noble class, and paradoxically the most harmful to his true military function. Fighting in tournaments concentrated his skills and absorbed his interest in an increasingly formalized clash, leaving little thought for the tactics and strategy of real battle.

10   Originating in France and referred to by others as "French combat" (*conflictus Gallicus*), tournaments started without rules or lists as an agreed-upon clash of opposing units. Though justified as training exercises, the impulse was the love of fighting. Becoming more regulated and mannered, they took two forms: jousts by individuals, and melees by groups of up to forty on a side, either *à plaisance*[7] with blunted weapons or *à outrance*[8] with no restraints, in which case participants might be severely wounded and not infrequently killed. Tournaments proliferated as the noble's primary occupation dwindled. Under the extended rule of monarchy, he had less need to protect his own fief, while a class of professional ministers was gradually taking his place around the crown. The less he had to do, the more energy he spent in tournaments artificially re-enacting his role.

11   A tournament might last as long as a week and on great occasions two. Opening day was spent matching and seeding the players, followed by days set apart for jousts, for melees, for a rest day before the final tourney, all interspersed with feasting and parties. These occasions were the great sporting events of the time, attracting crowds of bourgeois spectators from rich merchants to common artisans, mountebanks, food vendors, prostitutes, and pickpockets. About a hundred knights usually participated, each accompanied by two

---

[6] **Crécy:** The battle of Crécy (1346) was one of the great English victories of the Hundred Years' War.

[7] *à plaisance:* "for pleasure."
[8] *à outrance:* "to the death."

mounted squires, an armorer, and six servants in livery. The knight had of course to equip himself with painted and gilded armor and crested helmet costing from 25 to 50 livres, with a war-horse costing from 25 to 100 livres in addition to his traveling palfrey, and with banners and trappings and fine clothes. Though the expense could easily bankrupt him, he might also come away richer, for the loser in combat had to pay a ransom and the winner was awarded his opponent's horse and armor, which he could sell back to him or to anyone. Gain was not recognized by chivalry, but it was present at tournaments.

12   Because of their extravagance, violence, and vainglory, tournaments were continually being denounced by popes and kings, from whom they drained money. In vain. When the Dominicans denounced them as a pagan circus, no one listened. When the formidable St. Bernard[9] thundered that anyone killed in a tournament would go to Hell, he spoke for once to deaf ears. Death in a tournament was officially considered the sin of suicide by the Church, besides jeopardizing family and tenantry without cause, but even threats of excommunication had no effect. Although St. Louis condemned tournaments and Philip the Fair prohibited them during his wars, nothing could stop them permanently or dim the enthusiasm for them.

13   With brilliantly dressed spectators in the stands, flags and ribbons fluttering, the music of trumpets, the parade of combatants making their draped horses prance and champ on golden bridles, the glitter of harness and shields, the throwing of ladies' scarves and sleeves to their favorites, the bow of the heralds to the presiding prince who proclaimed the rules, the cry of poursuivants announcing their champions, the tournament was the peak of nobility's pride and delight in its own valor and beauty.

If tournaments were an acting-out of chivalry,   14 courtly love was its dreamland. Courtly love was understood by its contemporaries to be love for its own sake, romantic love, true love, physical love, unassociated with property or family, and consequently focused on another man's wife, since only such an illicit liaison could have no other aim but love alone. (Love of a maiden was virtually ruled out since this would have raised dangerous problems, and besides, maidens of noble estate usually jumped from childhood to marrige with hardly an interval for romance.) The fact that courtly love idealized guilty love added one more complication to the maze through which medieval people threaded their lives. As formulated by chivalry, romance was pictured as extramarital because love was considered irrelevant to marriage, was indeed discouraged in order not to get in the way of dynastic arrangements.

As its justification, courtly love was consid-   15 ered to ennoble a man, to improve him in every way. It would make him concerned to show an example of goodness, to do his utmost to preserve honor, never letting dishonor touch himself or the lady he loved. On a lower scale, it would lead him to keep his teeth and nails clean, his clothes rich and well groomed, his conversation witty and amusing, his manners courteous to all, curbing arrogance and coarseness, never brawling in a lady's presence. Above all, it would make him more valiant, more *preux;* that was the basic premise. He would be inspired to greater prowess, would win more victories in tournaments, rise above himself in courage and daring, become, as Froissart said, "worth two men." Guided by this theory, woman's status improved, less for her own sake than as the inspirer of male glory, a higher function than being merely a sexual object, a breeder of children, or a conveyor of property.

The chivalric love affair moved from wor-   16 ship through declaration of passionate

---

[9] **St. Bernard:** Bernard of Clairvaux, monastic reformer and promoter of the Second Crusade.

devotion, virtuous rejection by the lady, renewed wooing with oaths of eternal fealty, moans of approaching death from unsatisfied desire, heroic deeds of valor which won the lady's heart by prowess, consummation of the secret love, followed by endless adventures and subterfuges to a tragic denouement. The most widely known of all such romances and the last of its kind was the *Châtelain de Coucy,* written about the time of Enguerrand VII's birth when the *chanson de geste* was dying out. Its hero was not a Seigneur de Coucy but a *châtelain* of the castle named Renault, modeled on a real individual and poet of the 12 century.

17   In the legend he falls madly in love with the Dame de Fayel and through an enormous series of maneuvers occupying 8,266 lines of verse is decoyed into the Third Crusade by the jealous husband, covers himself with glory, and when fatally wounded by a poisoned arrow, composes a last song and farewell letter to be dispatched after his death in a box with his embalmed heart and a lock of the lady's hair. Carried by a faithful servant the box is intercepted by the husband, who has the heart cooked and served to his wife. On being informed what she has eaten, she swears that after such a noble food she will never eat again and dies, while the husband exiles himself in a lifelong pilgrimage to obtain pardon for his deed.

18   "Melancholy, amorous and barbaric,"[10] these tales exalted adulterous love as the only true kind, while in the real life of the same society adultery was a crime, not to mention a sin. If found out, it dishonored the lady and shamed the husband, a fellow knight. It was understood that he had the right to kill both unfaithful wife and lover.

19   Nothing fits in this canon. The gay, the elevating, the ennobling pursuit is founded upon sin and invites the dishonor it is supposed to avert. Courtly love was a greater tangle of irreconcilables even than usury. It remained artificial, a literary convention, a fantasy (like modern pornography) more for purposes of discussion than for everyday practice.

20   The realities were more normal. As described by La Tour Landry,[11] his amorous fellow knights were not overly concerned with loyalty and *courtoisie.* He tells how, when he used to ride abroad with his friends as a young man, they would beg ladies for their love and if this one did not accept they would try another, deceiving the ladies with fair words of blandishment and swearing false oaths, "for in every place they would have their sport if they could." Many a gentlewoman was taken in by the "foul and great false oaths that false men use to swear to women." He tells how three ladies who were exchanging opinions of their lovers discovered that the senior Jean le Maingre, Sire de Boucicaut, was the favorite of each, he having made love to all, telling each he loved her best. When they taxed him with his falsity, he was in no way abashed, saying, "For at that time I spake with each of you, I loved her best that I spake with and thought truly the same."

21   La Tour Landry himself, a seigneur of substance who fought in many campaigns, emerges as a domestic gentleman who liked to sit in his garden and enjoy the song of the thrush in April, and loved his books. Contrary to chivalry, he had also loved his wife, "the bell and flower of all that was fair and good," and "I delighted me so much in her that I made for her love songs, ballads, roundels, verelays and divers new things in the best wise that I could." He does not think much of chivalry's favorite theme, that courtly love inspires knights to greater prowess, for though they say they do it for the ladies, "in faith they do it for themselves to win praise and honor." Nor does

---

[10] **barbaric:** Tuchman's notes indicate that she is quoting Gaston Paris (1839–1903), an eminent French scholar.

[11] **La Tour Landry:** Geoffrey La Tour Landry (1330?–1405?), author of a book of cautionary tales for girls.

he approve of love for its own sake, *par amours,* either before or after marriage, for it can cause all kinds of crime, of which he cites the *Châtelain de Coucy* as an example.

22   As suggested by a spectacular scandal of the time, Edward III's[12] rape of the Countess of Salisbury, courtly love was the ideal of chivalry least realized in everyday behavior. Froissart, who believed in chivalry as St. Louis believed in the Trinity, expurgated the story, supposedly after careful inquiries, but more probably out of respect for his beloved first patron, Philippa of Hainault, Edward's Queen. He reports only that the King, on visiting Salisbury Castle after a battle in Scotland in 1342, was "stricken to the heart with a sparkle of fine love" for the beautiful Countess. After she repulsed his advances, Edward is reported (with some historic license) debating with himself about pursuing his guilty passion in words that are a supreme statement of the chivalric theory of love's role: "And if he should be more amorous it would be entirely good for him, for his realm and for all his knights and squires for he would be more content, more gay and more martial; he would hold more jousts, more tourneys, more feasts and more revels than he had before; and he would be more able and more vigorous in his wars, more amiable and more trusting toward his friends and harsher toward his foes."

23   According to another contemporary, Jean le Bel, who had himself been a knight with few illusions before he took orders as a canon and became a chronicler, matters went rather differently. After sending the Earl of Salisbury to Brittany like Uriah,[13] the King revisited the Countess and, on being again rejected, he villainously raped her, "stopping her mouth with such force that she could only cry two or three cries . . . and left her lying in a swoon bleeding from the nose and mouth and other parts." Edward returned to London greatly disturbed at what he had done, and the good lady "had no more joy or happiness again, so heavy was her heart." Upon her husband's return she would not lie with him and, being asked why, she told him what had happened, "sitting on the bed next to him crying." The Earl, reflecting on the great friendship and honor between him and the King, now so dishonored, told his wife he could live in England no more. He went to court and before his peers divested himself of his lands in such a manner that his wife should have her dowry for life, and then went before the King, saying to his face, "You have villainously dishonored me and thrown me in the dung," and afterward left the country, to the sorrow and wonder of the nobility, and the "King was blamed by all."

24   If the fiction of chivalry molded outward behavior to some extent, it did not, any more than other models that man has made for himself, transform human nature. Joinville's[14] account of the crusaders at Damietta[15] in 1249 shows the knights under St. Louis plunged in brutality, blasphemy, and debauchery. Teutonic knights in their annual forays against the unconverted natives of Lithuania conducted manhunts of the peasants for sport. Yet, if the code was but a veneer over violence, greed, and sensuality, it was nevertheless an ideal, as Christianity was an ideal, toward which man's reach, as usual, exceeded his grasp. ◆

---

12 **Edward III:** King of England from 1327 to 1377.
13 **Uriah:** The husband of Bathsheba, whom David sent to the front lines so that he would be killed in battle (2 Samuel 11).

14 **Joinville's:** Jean de Joinville (1224?–1317) was a chronicler of French history.
15 **Damietta:** A city in northeast Egypt.

SINGING WITH THE FUNDAMENTALISTS

Annie Dillard

Annie Dillard is a more self-conscious stylist than either Isaac Asimov or Barbara Tuchman. Less concerned than they are with explanation in the ordinary sense, Dillard often explores familiar subjects, using structure, imagery, and rhythm to make us *see* subjects we may have *glanced at* a thousand times. "Singing with the Fundamentalists" was first published in the *Yale Review* in 1985.

1 IT IS EARLY SPRING, I HAVE A TEMPORARY office at a state university on the West Coast. The office is on the third floor. It looks down on the Square, the enormous open courtyard at the center of campus. From my desk I see hundreds of people moving between classes. There is a large circular fountain in the Square's center.

2 Early one morning, on the first day of spring quarter, I hear singing. A pack of students has gathered at the fountain. They are singing something which, at this distance, and through the heavy window, sounds good.

3 I know who these singing students are: they are the Fundamentalists. This campus has a lot of them. Mornings they sing on the Square; it is their only perceptible activity. What are they singing? Whatever it is, I want to join them, for I like to sing; whatever it is, I want to take my stand with them, for I am drawn to their very absurdity, their innocent indifference to what people think. My colleagues and students here, and my friends everywhere, dislike and fear Christian fundamentalists. You may never have met such people, but you've heard what they do: they pile up money, vote in blocs, and elect right-wing crazies; they censor books; they carry handguns; they fight fluoride in the drinking water and evolution in the schools; probably they would lynch people if they could get away with it. I'm not sure my friends are correct. I close my pen and join the singers on the Square.

4 There is a clapping song in progress. I have to concentrate to follow it:

> Come on, rejoice,
> And let your heart sing,
> Come on, rejoice,
> Give praise to the king.
> Singing alleluia—
> He is the king of kings;
> Singing alleluia—
> He is the king of kings.

Two song leaders are standing on the broad rim of the fountain; the water is splashing just behind them. The boy is short, hard-faced, with a moustache. He bangs his guitar with the backs of his fingers. The blonde girl, who leads the clapping is bouncy; she wears a bit of make-up. Both are wearing blue jeans.

5 The students beside me are wearing blue jeans too—and athletic jerseys, parkas, football jackets, turtlenecks, and hiking shoes or jogging shoes. They all have canvas or nylon book bags. They look like any random batch of seventy or eighty students at this university. They are grubby or scrubbed, mostly scrubbed; they are tall, fair, or red-headed in large proportions. Their paents are white-collar workers, blue-collar workers, farmers, loggers, orchardists, merchants, fishermen; their names are, I'll bet, Olsen, Jensen, Seversen, Hansen, Klokker, Sigurdsen.

6 Despite the vigor of the clapping song, no one seems to be giving it much effort. And no

one looks at anyone else; there are no sentimental glances and smiles, no glances even of recognition. These kids don't seem to know each other. We stand at the fountain's side, out on the broad, bricked Square in front of the science building, and sing the clapping song through three times.

7   It is quarter to nine in the morning. Hundreds of people are crossing the Square. These passersby—faculty, staff, students—pay very little attention to us; this morning singing has gone on for years. Most of them look at us directly, then ignore us, for there is nothing to see: no animal sacrifices, no lynchings, no collection plate for Jesse Helms,[1] no seizures, snake handling, healing, or glossolalia. There is barely anything to hear. I suspect the people glance at us to learn if we are really singing: how could so many people make so little sound? My fellow singers, who ignore each other, certainly ignore passersby as well. Within a week, most of them will have their eyes closed anyway.

8   We move directly to another song, a slower one.

> He is my peace,
> Who has broken down every wall;
> He is my peace,
> He is my peace.
>
> Cast all your cares on him,
> For he careth for you—oo—oo
> He is my peace,
> He is my peace.

9   I am paying strict attention to the song leaders, for I am singing at the top of my lungs and I've never heard any of these songs before. They are not the old American low-church Protestant hymns; they are not the old European high-church Protestant hymns. These hymns seem to have been written just yester-

---

[1] **Jesse Helms:** (1921–   ), an ultraconservative U.S. Senator from North Carolina.

day, apparently by the same people who put out lyrical Christian greeting cards and bookmarks.

10   "Where do these songs come from?" I ask a girl standing next to me. She seems appalled to be addressed at all, and startled by the question. "They're from the praise albums!" she explains, and moves away.

11   The songs' melodies run dominant, subdominant, dominant, tonic, dominant. The pace is slow, about the pace of "Tell Laura I Love Her," and with that song's quavering, long notes. The lyrics are simple and repetitive; there are very few of them to which a devout Jew or Mohammedan could not give wholehearted assent. These songs are similar to the things Catholics sing in church these days. I don't know if any studies have been done to correlate the introduction of contemporary songs into Catholic churches with those churches' decline in membership, or with the phenomenon of Catholic converts' applying to enter cloistered monasteries directly, without passing through parish churches.

> I'm set free to worship,
> I'm set free to praise him,
> I'm set free to dance before the Lord . . .

12   At nine o'clock sharp we quit and scatter. I hear a few quiet "see you"s. Mostly the students leave quickly, as if they didn't want to be seen. The Square empties.

13   The next day we show up again, at twenty to nine. The same two leaders stand on the fountain's rim; the fountain is pouring down behind them.

14   After the first song, the boy with the moustache hollers, "Move on up! Some of you guys aren't paying attention back there! You're talking to each other. I want you to concentrate!" The students laugh, embarrassed for him. He sounds like a teacher. No one moves. The girl

breaks into the next song, which we join at once:

> In my life, Lord,
> Be glorified, be glorified, be glorified;
> In my life, Lord,
> Be glorified, be glorified, today.

At the end of this singularly monotonous verse, which is straining my tolerance for singing virtually anything, the boy with the moustache startles me by shouting, "Classes!"

15   At once, without skipping a beat, we sing, "In my classes, Lord, be glorified, be glorified . . ." I give fleet thought to the class I'm teaching this afternoon. We're reading a little "Talk of the Town"[2] piece called "Eggbag," about a cat in a magic store on Eighth Avenue. "Relationships!" the boy calls. The students seem to sing "In my relationships, Lord," more easily than they sang "classes." They seemed embarrassed by "classes." In fact, to my fascination, they seem embarrassed by almost everything. Why are they here? I will sing with the Fundamentalists every weekday morning all spring; I will decide, tentatively, that they come pretty much for the same reasons I do: each has a private relationship with "the Lord" and will put up with a lot of junk for it.

16   I have taught some Fundamentalists students here, and know a bit of what they think. They are college students above all, worried about their love lives, their grades, and finding jobs. Some support moderate Democrats; some support moderate Republicans. Like their classmates, most support nuclear freeze, ERA, and an end to the draft. I believe they are divided on abortion and busing. They are not particularly political. They read *Christianity Today* and *Campus Life* and *Eternity*—moderate, sensible magazines, I think; they read a lot of

C. S. Lewis. (One such student, who seemed perfectly tolerant of me and my shoddy Christianity, introduced me to C. S. Lewis's critical book on Charles Williams.) They read the Bible. I think they all "believe in" organic evolution. The main thing about them is this: there isn't any "them." Their views vary. They don't know each other.

17   Their common Christianity puts them, if anywhere, to the left of their classmates. I believe they also tend to be more able than their classmates to think well in the abstract, and also to recognize the complexity of moral issues. But I may be wrong.

18   In 1980, the media were certainly wrong about television evangelists. Printed estimates of Jerry Falwell's television audience ranged from 18 million to 30 million people. In fact, according to Arbitron's actual counts, fewer than 1.5 million people were watching Falwell. And, according to an Emory University study, those who did watch television evangelists didn't necessarily vote with them. Emory University sociologist G. Melton Mobley reports, "When that message turns political, they cut it off." Analysis of the 1982 off-year election turned up no Fundamentalist bloc voting. The media were wrong, but no one printed retractions.

19   The media were wrong, too, in a tendency to identify all fundamentalist Christians with Falwell and his ilk, and to attribute to them, across the board, conservative views.

20   Someone has sent me two recent issues of *Eternity: The Evangelical Monthly*. One lead article criticizes a television preacher for saying that the United States had never used military might to take land from another nation. The same article censures Newspeak, saying that government rhetoric would have us believe in a "clean bomb," would have us believe that we "defend" America by invading foreign soil, and would have us believe that the dictator-

---

[2] **"The Talk of the Town":** a regular feature of the *New Yorker*, consisting of short, unsigned essays.

ships we support are "democracies." "When the President of the United States says that one reason to support defense spending is because it creates jobs," this lead article says, "a little bit of *1984* begins to surface." Another article criticizes a "heavy-handed" opinion of Jerry Falwell Ministries—in this case a broadside attack on artifical insemination, surrogate motherhood, and lesbian motherhood. Browsing through *Eternity,* I find a double crostic.[3] I find an intelligent, analytical, and enthusiastic review of the new London Philharmonic recording of Mahler's second symphony—a review which stresses the "glorious truth" of the Jewish composer's magnificent work, and cites its recent performance in Jerusalem to celebrate the recapture of the Western Wall following the Six Day War. Surely, the evangelical Christians who read this magazine are not book-burners. If by chance they vote with the magazine's editors, then it looks to me as if they vote with the American Civil Liberties Union and Americans for Democratic Action.

21   Every few years some bold and sincere Christian student at this university disagrees with a professor in class—usually about the professor's out-of-hand dismissal of Christianity. Members of the faculty, outraged, repeat the stories of these rare and uneven encounters for years on end, as if to prove that the crazies are everywhere, and gaining ground. The notion is, apparently, that these kids can't think for themselves. Or they wouldn't disagree.

22   Now again the moustached leader asks us to move up. There is no harangue, so we move up. (This will be a theme all spring. The leaders want us closer together. Our instinct is to stand alone.) From behind the tall fountain comes a wind; on several gusts we get sprayed. No one seems to notice.

---

[3] **double crostic:** a difficult word puzzle that requires the solver to recreate a long quotation.

We have time for one more song. The   23
leader, perhaps sensing that no one likes him, blunders on. "I want you to pray this one through," he says. "We have a lot of people here from a lot of different fellowships, but we're all one body. Amen?" They don't like it. He gets a few polite Amens. We sing:

> Bind us together, Lord,
> With a bond that can't be broken;
> Bind us together, Lord,
> With love.

Everyone seems to be in a remarkably foul mood today. We don't like this song. There is no one here under seventeen, and, I think, no one here who believes that love is a bond that can't be broken. We sing the song through three times; then it is time to go.

The leader calls after our retreating back,   24
"Hey, have a good day! Praise Him all day!" The kids around me roll up their eyes privately. Some groan; all flee.

The next morning is very cold. I am here   25
early. Two girls are talking on the fountain's rim; one is part Indian. She says, "I've got all the Old Testament, but I can't get the New. I screw up the New." She takes a breath and rattles off a long list, ending with "Jonah, Micah, Nahum, Habakkuk, Zephaniah, Haggai, Zechariah, Malachi." The other girl produces a slow, sarcastic applause. I ask one of the girls to help me with the words to a song. She is agreeable, but says, "I'm sorry, I can't. I just became a Christian this year, so I don't know all the words yet."

The others are coming; we stand and sepa-   26
rate. The boy with the moustache is gone, replaced by a big, serious fellow in a green down jacket. The bouncy girl is back with her guitar; she's wearing a skirt and wool knee socks. We begin, without any preamble, by singing a song that has so few words that we actually stretch one syllable over eleven separate notes. Then

we sing a song in which the men sing one phrase and the women echo it. Everyone seems to know just what to do. In the context of our vapid songs, the lyrics of this one are extraordinary:

> *I was nothing before you found me.*
> *Heartache! Broken people! Ruined lives*
> *Is why you died on Calvary.*

The last line rises in a regular series of half-notes. Now at last some people are actually singing; they throw some breath into the business. There is a seriousness and urgency to it: "Heartache! Broken people! Ruined lives . . . I was nothing."

27   We don't look like nothing. We look like a bunch of students of every stripe, ill-shaven or well-shaven, dressed up or down, but dressed warmly against the cold: jeans and parkas, jeans and heavy sweaters, jeans and scarves and blow-dried hair. We look ordinary. But I think, quite on my own, that we are here because we know this business of nothingness, brokenness, and ruination. We sing this song over and over.

28   Something catches my eye. Behind us, up in the science building, professors are standing alone at opened windows.

29   The long brick science building has three upper floors of faculty offices, thirty-two windows. At one window stands a bearded man, about forty; his opening his window is what caught my eye. He stands full in the open window, his hands on his hips, his head cocked down toward the fountain. He is drawn to look, as I was drawn to come. Up on the building's top floor, at the far right window, there is another: an Asian-American professor, wearing a white shirt, is sitting with one hip on his desk, looking out and down. In the middle of the row of windows, another one, an old professor in a checked shirt, stands sideways to the opened window, stands stock-still, his long, old ear to the air. Now another window cranks open, another professor—or maybe a

graduate student—leans out, his hands on the sill.

30   We are all singing, and I am watching these five still men, my colleagues, whose office doors are surely shut—for that is the custom here: five of them alone in their offices in the science building who have opened their windows on this very cold morning, who motionless hear the Fundamentalists sing, utterly unknown to each other.

31   We sing another four songs, including the clapping song, and one which repeats, "This is the day which the Lord hath made; rejoice and be glad in it." All the professors but one stay by their opened windows, figures in a frieze. When after ten minutes we break off and scatter, each cranks his window shut. Maybe they have nine o'clock classes too.

32   I miss a few sessions. One morning of the following week, I rejoin the Fundamentalists on the Square. The wind is blowing from the north; it is sunny and cold. There are several new developments.

33   Someone has blown up rubber gloves and floated them in the fountain. I saw them yesterday afternoon from my high office window, and couldn't quite make them out: I seemed to see hands in the fountain waving from side to side, like those hands wagging on springs which people stick in the back windows of their cars. I saw these many years ago in Quito and Guayaquil, where they were a great fad long before they showed up here. The cardboard hands said, on their palms, HOLA GENTE, hello people. Some of them just said HOLA, hello, with a little wave to the universe at large, in case anybody happened to be looking. It is like our sending radio signals to planets in other galaxies: HOLA, if anyone is listening. Jolly folk, these Ecuadorians, I thought.

34   Now, waiting by the fountain for the singing, I see that these particular hands are long surgical gloves, yellow and white, ten of them,

tied off at the cuff. They float upright and they wave, *hola, hola, hola;* they mill around like a crowd, bobbing under the fountain's spray and back again to the pool's rim, *hola.* It is a good prank. It is far too cold for the university's maintenance crew to retrieve them without turning off the fountain and putting on rubber boots.

35   From all around the Square, people are gathering for the singing. There is no way I can guess which kids, from among the masses crossing the Square, will veer off to the fountain. When they get here, I never recognize anybody except the leaders.

36   The singing begins without ado as usual, but there is something different about it. The students are growing prayerful, and they show it this morning with a peculiar gesture. I'm glad they weren't like this when I first joined them, or I never would have stayed.

37   Last night there was an educational television special, part of "Middletown."[4] It was a segment called "Community of Praise," and I watched it because it was about Fundamentalists. It showed a Jesus-loving family in the Midwest; the treatment was good and complex. This family attended the prayer meetings, healing sessions, and church services of an unnamed sect—a very low-church sect, whose doctrine and culture were much more low-church than those of the kids I sing with. When the members of this sect prayed, they held their arms over their heads and raised their palms, as if to feel or receive a blessing or energy from above.

38   Now today on the Square there is a new serious mood. The leaders are singing with their eyes shut. I am impressed that they can bang their guitars, keep their balance, and not fall into the pool. It is the same bouncy girl and earnest boy. Their eyeballs are rolled back a

bit. I look around and see that almost everyone in this crowd of eighty or so has his eyes shut and is apparently praying the words of this song or praying some other prayer.

39   Now as the chorus rises, as it gets louder and higher and simpler in melody—

> *I exalt thee,*
> *I exalt thee,*
> *I exalt thee,*
> *Thou art the Lord—*

then, at this moment, hands start rising. All around me, hands are going up—that tall girl, that blond boy with his head back, the red-headed boy up front, the girl with the McDonald's jacket. Their arms rise as if pulled on strings. Some few of them have raised their arms very high over their heads and are tilting back their palms. Many, many more of them, as inconspicuously as possible, have raised their hands to the level of their chins.

40   What is going on? Why are these students today raising their palms in this gesture, when nobody did it last week? Is it because the leaders have set a prayerful tone this morning? Is it because this gesture always accompanies this song, just as clapping accompanies other songs? Or is it, as I suspect, that these kids watched the widely publicized documentary last night just as I did, and are adopting, or trying out, the gesture?

41   It is a sunny morning, and the sun is rising behind the leaders and the fountain, so those students have their heads tilted, eyes closed, and palms upraised toward the sun. I glance up at the science building and think my own prayer: thank God no one is watching this.

42   The leaders cannot move around much on the fountain's rim. The girl has her eyes shut; the boy opens his eyes from time to time, glances at the neck of his guitar, and closes his eyes again.

43   When the song is over, the hands go down, and there is some desultory chatting in the crowd, as usual: can I borrow your library

---

[4] **"Middletown"**: A 1983 PBS series that updated a book published in 1929, *Middletown: A Study in Contemporary American Culture,* by Robert and Helen Merrell Lynd.

card? And, as usual, nobody looks at anybody.

44   All our songs today are serious. There is a feudal theme to them, or a feudal analogue:

I will eat from abundance of your household.
I will dream beside your streams of righteousness.

You are my king.

Enter his gates
with thanksgiving in your heart;
come before his courts with praise.

He is the king of kings.

Thou art the Lord.

45   All around me, eyes are closed and hands are raised. There is no social pressure to do this, or anything else. I've never known any group to be less cohesive, imposing fewer controls. Since no one looks at anyone, and since passersby no longer look, everyone out here is inconspicuous and free. Perhaps the palm-raising has begun because the kids realize by now that they are not on display; they're praying in their closets, right out here on the Square. Over the course of the next weeks, I will learn that the palm-raising is here to stay.

46   The sun is rising higher. We are singing our last song. We are praying. We are alone together.

He is my peace
Who has broken down every wall . . .

47   When the song is over, the hands go down. The heads lower, the eyes open and blink. We stay still a second before we break up. We have been standing in a broad current; now we have stepped aside. We have dismantled the radar cups; we have closed the telescope's vault. Students gather their book bags and go. The two leaders step down from the fountain's rim and pack away their guitars. Everyone scatters. I am in no hurry, so I stay after everyone is gone. It is after nine o'clock, and the Square is deserted. The fountain is playing to an empty house. In the pool the cheerful hands are waving over the water, bobbing under the fountain's veil and out again in the current, *hola.* ◆

HANDBOOK OF GRAMMAR AND USAGE

Grammar and Sentence Structure

This unit covers the forms and the functions of the eight parts of speech, how to use these basic units to build phrases and clauses, and how to combine these word groups to construct clear, complete, smoothly flowing sentences. Understanding grammar will help you use the English language more effectively in your writing.

1.1 PARTS OF SPEECH

The eight parts of speech are nouns, pronouns, verbs, adjectives, adverbs, prepositions, conjunctions, and interjections.

1.1A NOUNS

A **noun** names a person, a place, a thing, or an idea.

Persons	operator	contestant	Louisa May Alcott
Places	kitchen	valley	Wyoming
Things	freighter	aardvark	oxygen
Ideas	obsession	realism	quality

Dates and days of the week are also classified as nouns.

A.D. 1100   Tuesday   November 29, 1984

Common and Proper Nouns

A **common noun** names a class of people, places, things, or ideas. Do not capitalize a common noun unless it begins a sentence. A **proper noun** gives the name or title of a particular person, place, thing, or idea, and it always begins with a capital letter.

Common Noun	A **speedway** is a race track for automobiles.
Proper Noun	The **Indianapolis Speedway** is the site of the Indianapolis 500.

Compound Nouns

A **compound noun** consists of two or more words used together to form a single noun. There are four kinds of compound nouns. One kind is formed by joining two or more words: *football.* A second kind consists of words joined by hyphens: *city-state.* A third kind consists of two words that are often used together: *sugar beet.* The fourth kind is a proper noun that consists of more than one word: *Missouri River.*

Collective Nouns

A **collective noun** refers to a *group* of people, places, things, or ideas.

> A **swarm** of bees buzzed around us!

> Phyllis has an **accumulation** of compositions that show her progress as a writer.

Concrete and Abstract Nouns

Concrete nouns refer to material things, to people, or to places. Some concrete nouns name things that you can perceive with your senses: *traffic, seasoning, barking.* Other concrete nouns name things that can be measured or perceived only with the aid of technical devices. Although you cannot see an atom, *atom* is a concrete noun because it names a material substance. In the following sentences, the nouns in boldface type are concrete.

> In **polo** the **players** ride on **horseback** and hit a **ball** with a long-handled **mallet.**

> You can tell that that is Denise's **car** because of the **noise** that it makes.

> **Penicillin,** which was discovered by **Alexander Fleming** in **1929,** is actually a **mold** that combats disease-carrying **germs.** [Even though you cannot see, hear, smell, taste, or feel germs, they have a definite material existence.]

Abstract nouns name ideas, qualities, emotions, or attitudes.

> Many critics consider the **conflict** between **integrity** and **power** to be the **theme** of *Macbeth.*

> **Disappointment** was visible on the faces of the players, but the crowd, moved by the **intensity** of the team's **effort,** applauded loudly.

> Galileo defended the **freedom** to pursue the **truth.**

Using Nouns Effectively

In writing, you usually need to use both concrete nouns and abstract nouns. Abstract nouns are necessary in most forms of writing. However, if you link them with details and examples that include concrete nouns, your writing will be clearer and more interesting.

Read the following paragraph from *Quite Early One Morning* by the Welsh writer Dylan Thomas. Notice how Thomas relies on concrete nouns to express his impressions and ideas. The concrete nouns are in italic type.

> I was born in a large Welsh *town* at the beginning of the Great War—an ugly, lovely *town* (or so it was and is to me), crawling, sprawling by a

long and splendid curving *shore* where truant *boys* and sandfield *boys* and old *men* from nowhere, beachcombed, idled and paddled, watched the dock-bound *ships* or the ships steaming away into wonder and *India,* magic and *China, countries* bright with *oranges* and loud with *lions;* threw *stones* into the *sea* for the barking outcast *dogs;* made *castles* and *forts* and *harbors* and *race tracks* in the *sand;* and on Saturday summer *afternoons* listened to the brass *band,* watched the *Punch and Judy,* or hung about on the fringes of the *crowd* to hear the fierce religious *speakers* who shouted at the *sea,* as though it were wicked and wrong to roll in and out like that, white-horsed and full of *fishes.*

Quite Early One Morning
—DYLAN THOMAS

Dylan Thomas relies on concrete nouns to evoke certain feelings about childhood. *India, China, oranges,* and *lions* convey a sense of adventure and discovery. *Castles, forts, harbors,* and *race tracks* create a sense of the boys' imaginative play when they were young. Note that Thomas does not completely avoid abstract nouns; *wonder* and *magic* are both abstract.

In your own writing, use concrete nouns to make ideas and impressions more vivid and interesting.

1.1B PRONOUNS

A **pronoun** is a word that is used in place of a noun. A pronoun identifies persons, places, things, or ideas without renaming them. The noun that a pronoun replaces is the **antecedent** of that pronoun. There are eight kinds of pronouns: personal, possessive, demonstrative, reflexive, intensive, interrogative, relative, and indefinite.

Personal Pronouns

Personal pronouns require different forms to express person, number, and gender. **Person** refers to the relationship between the speaker or writer (first person), the individual or thing spoken to (second person), and the individual or thing spoken about (third person). The **number** of a personal pronoun indicates whether the antecedent is singular or plural. The **gender** of a personal pronoun indicates whether the antecedent is masculine, feminine, or neuter.

Tricia and Annette will not soon forget Machiavelli's *The Prince,* for **it** greatly astonished **them.** [*It* replaces *The Prince,* and *them* replaces *Tricia and Annette.*]

Critics who try to interpret *The Prince* are perplexed because **they** find inconsistencies and contradictions. [*They* replaces *critics.*]

Possessive Pronouns

Possessive pronouns are personal pronouns that show ownership or belonging.

> Copies of *The Courtier* have arrived at the bookstore, and we can pick up **ours** at any time. [*Ours* replaces *copies*.]

> Georgina is doing **her** term paper on Sir Francis Bacon. [*Her* refers to *Georgina*.]

The following list shows the common personal pronouns; the possessive pronouns are in parentheses.

	Singular	Plural
First Person	I, me (my, mine)	we, us (our, ours)
Second Person	you (your, yours)	you (your, yours)
Third Person	he, him (his) she, her (her, hers) it (its)	they, them (their, theirs)

Demonstrative Pronouns

Demonstrative pronouns specify the individual or the group that is being referred to. The demonstrative pronouns are *this, that, these,* and *those.*

> **This** is a more interesting collection of photographs than **that.**

> **These** are the clippers that I used to trim the hedge; **those** are too rusty to use.

Reflexive Pronouns

Reflexive pronouns indicate that people or things perform actions to, for, or on behalf of themselves. To form a reflexive pronoun, add the suffix *-self* or *-selves* to the personal pronouns.

First Person	myself, ourselves
Second Person	yourself, yourselves
Third Person	himself, herself, itself, oneself, themselves

Example: Cervantes's Don Quixote convinces **himself** that the world is like the romances that he reads. He rides out to find adventure for **himself.**

Intensive Pronouns

Intensive pronouns are the same words as the reflexive pronouns, but they draw special attention to a person or a thing mentioned in the sentence. Intensive pronouns usually come immediately after the nouns or pronouns that they intensify.

We drove around the grounds of the estate but could not visit the *mansion* **itself,** which was locked. [The pronoun *itself* draws special attention to the word *mansion.*]

Following the play, the *playwright* **herself** appeared for a bow. [The pronoun *herself* draws special attention to the word *playwright.*]

Interrogative Pronouns

Interrogative pronouns introduce questions. The most frequently used interrogative pronouns are *who, whom, which, what,* and *whose.*

We can get tickets for two games next week. **Which** would you like to attend?

Whose is this glove that I just found in our closet?

Relative Pronouns

Relative pronouns introduce adjective clauses (pages 610–611), which modify nouns and pronouns. The relative pronouns are *who, whom, whose, which,* and *that.*

Sir Thomas More's home in Chelsea, **which** was known as the "Great House," was a center of political and scholarly inquiry. [*Home* is the antecedent of *which.*]

We read some writings by More **that** were commissioned by Henry VIII. [*Writings* is the antecedent of *that.*]

[Erasmus, **whose** *Praise of Folly* is well known, was a member of More's circle. [*Erasmus* is the antecedent of *whose.*]

Indefinite Pronouns

Indefinite pronouns refer to people, places, or things in general. Often you can use these pronouns without antecedents. The following list contains commonly used indefinite pronouns.

all	either	most	other
another	enough	much	others
any	everybody	neither	plenty
anybody	everyone	nobody	several
anyone	everything	none	some
anything	few	no one	somebody
both	many	nothing	someone
each	more	one	something

Examples: Margaret More Roper's learning astonished **everyone!** Few thought women capable of intellectual endeavors.

Anyone with an interest in political science should read More's *Utopia*. For a time Henry VIII respected **none** of his statesmen more than he did Lord Chancellor Thomas More.

1.1C VERBS

A **verb** is a word that expresses an action or a state of being. There are three kinds of verbs: action verbs, linking verbs, and auxiliary verbs.

Action Verbs

An **action verb** describes the behavior or action of someone or something. Action verbs may express physical actions or mental activities.

The fire truck **raced** toward the scene of the fire. [*Raced* refers to a physical action.]

A glacier **crawls** forward at a pace of only a few inches a year. [*Crawls* refers to a physical action.]

Philip **memorizes** names and dates easily because he **concentrates** so well. [*Memorizes* and *concentrates* refer to mental activities.]

The archaeologist **believed** that the site contained some very interesting artifacts. [*Believed* refers to a mental activity.]

Linking Verbs

A **linking verb** connects a noun or a pronoun with a word or words that identify or describe the noun or pronoun. Many linking verbs are verbs of being, which you form from the word *be*.

Will Rogers **was** an American humorist of the 1920s and 1930s. [The word *humorist* identifies Will Rogers.]

The Wilkinsons **were** anxious about encountering heavy traffic on the way to the airport. [The word *anxious* describes the Wilkinsons.]

There are several linking verbs in addition to *be*:

appear	grow	seem	sound
become	look	shine	stay
feel	remain	smell	taste

The students standing on the corner **grew** impatient as they waited for the bus. [*Grew* links the descriptive word *impatient* to *students*.]

The howling of the coyote **sounds** rather distant. [*Sounds* links the descriptive word *distant* to *howling*.]

Some verbs can be either action verbs or linking verbs, depending on their use in a sentence.

Action

Lynette **felt** along the wall for the light switch.

Linking

Although Ron studied late all week, he still **felt** energetic by the weekend.

Auxiliary Verbs

Sometimes a verb needs the help of another verb, called an **auxiliary verb** or a **helping verb.** The verb that it helps is called the **main verb.** Together, a main verb and an auxiliary verb form a **verb phrase.** A verb phrase may have more than one auxiliary verb. Common auxiliary verbs appear in the following list:

am, are, be, been, being, is, was, were	may, might
have, has, had	can, could
do, does, did	will, would
shall, should	must

In the following sentences, the auxiliary verbs are in italic type, and the main verbs are in boldface type. *Still* and *never* are not part of the verb phrase.

When Rhonda left, other cast members *were* still **rehearsing.**

The clerk at the warehouse *could* not *have been* wrong when she said that our package *had* **arrived!**

Will you *be* **waiting** for me at the entrance to the art institute?

Characteristics of Verbs

Verbs have several characteristics that you need to understand in order to use them correctly.

Transitive and Intransitive Verbs. All action verbs are either transitive or intransitive. A verb is **transitive** when its action is directed toward someone or something, which is called the **object of the verb** (pages 631–632).

verb   ⌐——— obj. ———⌐
The Chinese **built** the Great Wall of China over a period of several hundred years. [*Great Wall* is the object of the verb *built. Built* is transitive.]

verb   obj.   obj.
By using a timer, Mr. Allen **photographed** himself and his family. [*Himself* and *family* are the objects of the verb *photographed. Photographed* is transitive.]

A verb is **intransitive** when the performer of the action does not direct that action toward someone or something. In other words, an intransitive verb does not have a receiver of the action. Some action verbs, such as *go*, are intransitive. All linking verbs are intransitive.

> Although Bill **knew** about the surprise party ahead of time, he **acted** surprised. [The verbs *knew* and *acted* do not have objects. They are intransitive.]

> The inn at the top of the mountain **seems** empty. [*Seems* is a linking verb. It is intransitive.]

Many verbs can be either transitive or intransitive, depending on whether there is a receiver of the action.

Transitive

> verb   obj.
> **Stop** Sheila because she forgot to take this letter to the mailbox. [The object of *stop* is *Sheila*.]

Intransitive

> verb
> The subway train approached the station and **stopped**. [*Stopped* has no object.]

Changes in Verb Form. An important characteristic of the verb is that its form changes according to how it is used. A verb changes form in order to agree in person and number with its subject. A verb also changes form to express tense and mood. The basic forms of a verb are its **principal parts.** For an explanation of the rules governing changes in verb form, see pages 625–632.

Using Verbs Effectively

Verbs can make the difference between an ordinary piece of writing and one that stirs the reader's imagination. For this reason, good writers use verbs that tell *how* something happened. Consider the verb *ran* and its synonym in the following example.

> The dog **ran** across the field.
> The dog **scampered** across the field.

When you read that a dog scampered, you form a definite image of how the dog was moving.

The following paragraph is from the short story "The Lagoon" by Joseph Conrad. Notice how Conrad uses specific verbs to describe the action. These verbs are in italic type.

> The Malay only *grunted,* and went on looking fixedly at the river. The [other] man *rested* his chin on his crossed arms and *gazed* at the wake of the boat. At the end of the straight avenue of forests cut by the intense glitter of the river, the sun *appeared* unclouded and dazzling, poised low over water that *shone* smoothly like a band of metal. The forests, somber

and dull, *stood* motionless and silent on each side of the broad stream. At the foot of big, towering trees, trunkless nipa palms *rose* from the mud of the bank, in bunches of leaves enormous and heavy, that *hung* unstirring over the brown swirl of eddies. In the stillness of the air every tree, every leaf, every bough, every tendril of creeper and every petal of minute blossoms *seemed to have been bewitched* into an immobility perfect and final.

"The Lagoon"
—JOSEPH CONRAD

With the verb *grunted,* Conrad tells us how the man sounded. The verb *gazed* suggests that the man was lost in thought. Later in the paragraph, the forests *stood,* the palms *rose,* and the leaves *hung.* All of these verbs make the forests seem alive. In your own writing, use verbs that tell the reader *how* an action occurs.

1.1D   ADJECTIVES

An **adjective** is a word that modifies a noun or a pronoun. To modify means to change, and an adjective changes the meaning of a noun or a pronoun by describing it, limiting it, or making it more specific. An adjective answers one of three questions: *Which? What kind?* or *How many?*

Which?

The course focused on **Western** *civilization.* [Which civilization? *Western* civilization.]

What Kind?

The tennis player has an **unorthodox** *serve.* [What kind of serve? An *unorthodox* serve.]

How Many?

Twenty thousand *people* flocked to the stadium. [How many people? *Twenty thousand.*]

Articles. The most frequently used adjectives are the three articles: *a, an,* and *the. A* and *an* are **indefinite articles** because they do not specify a particular person, place, thing, or idea. *The* is a **definite article** because it always specifies a particular person, place, thing, or idea.

Indefinite   Tom took **a** large *supply* of food on his camping trip.

Definite   He ate nearly all of **the** *food* that he brought.

Placement of Adjectives

Adjectives usually appear directly before the nouns or pronouns that they modify. Sometimes a comma separates adjectives from the words that they modify.

Just beyond the hill was a **beautiful** *valley* with **several small** *clusters* of houses.

Illogical and **vague,** the *speech* made the audience restless.

Adjectives may follow linking verbs and modify the subjects of sentences.

The *staff* remained **loyal** throughout the long campaign, and the

candidate was very **proud** of them. [*Remained* and *was* are linking verbs.]

Adjectives sometimes follow the words that they modify and are separated from them by commas.

Our team's offensive *line*, **large** but **mobile,** dominated our opponents' defense during the game.

Proper Adjectives

A **proper adjective** is a name that functions as the modifier of a noun or a pronoun. Proper adjectives are usually capitalized.

Last evening we heard a **Brahms** *symphony.*

The **New Orleans** *harbor* is one of the busiest harbors in the country.

To create many proper adjectives, you use the suffixes *-n, -an, -ian, -ese, -ish,* or *-al,* changing the spelling of the noun as needed.

Proper Noun	Proper Adjective
Elizabeth	Elizabethan
Lebanon	Lebanese
Ireland	Irish
Albania	Albanian

Nouns Used as Adjectives

Some nouns function as adjectives without changing form, as in the following examples.

The office contained **mahogany** *paneling* and tables with **glass** *tops.*

The invention of the **jet** *airplane* has diminished the need for **passenger** *trains,*

but **freight** *trains* have had an increase in business.

Possessive Nouns. **Possessive nouns** are nouns that show possession or ownership; they function as adjectives because they modify nouns or pronouns.

The **tunnel's** *lights* suddenly went out, plunging us into darkness.

Everyone admired the **actor's** *costumes.*

Pronouns Used as Adjectives

A pronoun functions as an adjective when it modifies a noun or a pronoun. Indefinite pronouns, demonstrative pronouns, interrogative pronouns, the relative pronoun *whose,* and the possessive pronouns* in the following list may serve as adjectives.

	Singular	Plural
First Person	my	our
Second Person	your	your
Third Person	his, her, its	their

For **her** *class* in computer science, Donna asked the neighbors whether she

could use **their** *minicomputer.*

Your *guitar* seems to have lost **its** excellent *tone.* [Notice that the possessive pronouns *its* is spelled without an apostrophe.]

The following list contains examples of the other kinds of pronouns that can function as adjectives:

Indefinite	few, many, several, some
Demonstrative	that, this, these, those
Interrogative	what, which, whose
Relative	whose

---

* The words in the following list are called *possessive pronouns* throughout this handbook, but some people call them *pronominal adjectives.* Use the term that your instructor prefers.

Will the person **whose** *car* is blocking the entrance to the hospital please move it?

I would like to know **which** *newspaper* carried **that** *story* about the new amusement park, for **several** *friends* are interested in reading it.

Using Adjectives Effectively

Adjectives provide the means for creating a mood or a lasting impression of a person, a place, or a thing. To create mood, use adjectives that appeal to the senses. Examples of such adjectives include *blue, golden, gigantic, minuscule, tepid,* and *frigid.* However, you can also use adjectives that refer to emotional states and abstract qualities. *Innocent, angry, confusing,* and *hopeful* are examples of such adjectives.

The following passage is from the short story "The Fall of the House of Usher" by Edgar Allan Poe. Notice how Poe uses some adjectives that appeal to the senses and other adjectives that refer to emotional states and abstract qualities. Adjectives that contribute to the mood of the passage are in italic type.

> The room in which I found myself was very *large* and *lofty.* The windows were *long, narrow,* and *pointed,* and at so *vast* a distance from the *black oaken* floor as to be altogether *inaccessible* from within. *Feeble* gleams of *encrimsoned* light made their way through the *trellised* panes and served to render sufficiently *distinct* the more *prominent* objects around; the eye, however, struggled in vain to reach the *remoter* angles of the chamber, or the recesses of the *vaulted* and *fretted* ceiling. *Dark* draperies hung upon the walls. The *general* furniture was *profuse, comfortless, antique,* and *tattered.* Many books and *musical* instruments lay scattered about but failed to give any vitality to the scene. I felt that I breathed an atmosphere of sorrow. An air of *stern, deep,* and *irredeemable* gloom hung over and pervaded all.

Several of Poe's adjectives appeal to the senses: *large, lofty, vast, black, oaken, encrimsoned, trellised, vaulted,* and *dark.* On the other hand, *stern, deep,* and *irredeemable* refer to abstract qualities. The mood is one of gloom and decay.

In your writing, use adjectives that appeal to the senses and those that refer to emotional states or abstract qualities.

1.1E ADVERBS

Like adjectives, adverbs are modifiers. An **adverb** is a word that modifies a verb, an adjective, or another adverb. An adverb answers one of five questions about the word or phrase that it modifies: *How? When? Where? How often?* or *To what extent?*

How?

Tricia *raised* her arms **triumphantly** when she set a school record in the high jump.

When?

The personnel manager *will see* you **now.**

Where?

We *called* **everywhere,** but no room is available for the conference.

How Often?

Sometimes the smoke alarm *sounds* when something on the stove is burning.

To What Extent?

Jeanine is **rather** *doubtful* about getting a part-time job.

Adverbs such as *rather, really, certainly, indeed,* and *truly* are adverbs of extent and are used for emphasis.

Leonardo da Vinci was a **truly** *remarkable* man in both the breadth and the depth of his interests. [To what extent was Leonardo da Vinci remarkable? *Truly* remarkable.]

The words *not* and *never* are adverbs. They tell to what extent (*not at all*) and when (*never*).

Dennis *will* **not** *build* the kitchen cabinets himself because he *has* **never** *had* experience in carpentry.

Many sentences contain nouns that function as adverbs. Such adverbs usually tell when or where.

Yesterday our boss *informed* us that we have Saturday off.

Adverbs Used to Modify Verbs

Adverbs often modify verbs. An adverb does not have to appear next to the verb that it modifies. Notice the different positions of the adverbs *silently* and *slowly* in the following sentences.

Beginning   Silently and slowly, the tide *covered* the narrow strip of land.

Middle   The tide silently and slowly *covered* the narrow strip of land.

End   The tide *covered* the strip of land silently and slowly.

Adverbs Used to Modify Adjectives

Adverbs may modify adjectives. An adverb usually comes directly before the adjective that it modifies.

In spite of its **very** *forbidding* title, the essay was **fairly** *easy* to read.

The Super Bowl drew an audience of **nearly** *one hundred million* viewers.

Adverbs Used to Modify Other Adverbs

Adverbs can modify other adverbs. Such adverbs usually precede the adverbs that they modify.

Rafael is popular because he listens **so** *well* to other people. [*So* emphasizes the fact that Rafael listens well.]

Although the footbridge over the ravine was considered safe, Ed and Mark

crossed it **quite** *slowly*.

1.1F   PREPOSITIONS

A **preposition** is a word that expresses a relationship between a noun or a pronoun and another word in a sentence.

A special pilot **from** *shore* climbed **on** *board* and went **to** the *helm*. [The preposition *from* relates *shore* to *pilot*. The preposition *on* relates *board* to *climbed*. The preposition *to* relates *helm* to *went*.]

The following list contains frequently used prepositions:

along	around	before	below
among	at	behind	beneath

beside	from	past	until
between	in	since	up
beyond	near	through	upon
by	off	till	with
despite	on	to	within
down	onto	toward	without
during	out	under	
except	outside	underneath	
for	over		

A **compound preposition** is a preposition that consists of more than one word.

> When the Lansings got to the store, they bought two easy chairs **instead of** just one.

Frequently used compound prepositions are in the following list:

according to	in addition to	on account of
aside from	in front of	out of
as of	in place of	prior to
as well as	in regard to	with regard to
because of	in spite of	with respect to
by means of	instead of	

A preposition is usually followed by a noun or a pronoun, which is called the **object of the preposition.** Together, the preposition, the object, and the modifiers of that object form a **prepositional phrase.**

> prep.
>
> The referee called a charging foul **against the opposing team's seven-foot-**
>   obj.
>
> **tall center.** [The prepositional phrase consists of the preposition, *against;* the modifiers, *the, opposing, team's,* and *seven-foot-tall;* and the object, *center.*]

In some sentences, particularly interrogative sentences, the preposition follows the object.

> obj.   prep.
>
> **Whom** are you rooting **for** this weekend? [**Think:** *For whom* are you rooting this weekend?]

A prepositional phrase functions as an adjective if it modifies a noun or a pronoun. A prepositional phrase functions as an adverb if it modifies a verb, an adjective, or an adverb.

Used as an Adjective

The *road* on which we live has a picnic *area* for the residents.

Used as an Adverb

The defense attorney *looked* doubtfully at the witness and then

began her cross-examination in a quiet but effective voice.

Some words can function as prepositions or as adverbs, depending on their use in a sentence.

	prep. obj.
Preposition	Larry saw Marilyn standing **outside the stadium.**
	adv.
Adverb	If you *venture* **outside** in the cold weather, wear a coat.

1.1G CONJUNCTIONS

A **conjunction** is a word that connects words or groups of words. In fact, the word *conjunction* literally means "the act of joining" or "combination." There are three kinds of conjunctions: coordinating conjunctions, correlative conjunctions, and subordinating conjunctions.

Coordinating Conjunctions

A **coordinating conjunction** connects individual words or groups of words that perform the same function in a sentence. The coordinating conjunctions are *and, but, for, nor, or, so,* and *yet*. A coordinating conjunction can connect words, phrases, or clauses. For a complete explanation of phrases and clauses, see pages 601–614.

The dolphin next to our boat *surfaced, jumped,* **and** *dived* as we watched. [connects words]

The antiques dealer, *hoping to find a bargain* **but** *not expecting to find one,* went to the auction. [connects phrases]

We may be a few minutes late for the picnic, **for** *the road crews repairing the expressway have slowed traffic considerably.* [connects clauses]

Correlative Conjunctions

A **correlative conjunction** is a conjunction that consists of two or more words that function together. Like coordinating conjunctions, correlative conjunctions connect words that perform equal functions in a sentence. The following list contains correlative conjunctions:

both . . . and	not only . . . but (also)
either . . . or	whether . . . or
neither . . . nor	

Julian said that he had read **neither** *this novel* **nor** *that long poem* before. [connects words]

Not only *did we see a funny show at the club,* **but** *we* **also** *watched comedians doing improvisations after the regular show.* [connects clauses]

Subordinating Conjunctions

A **subordinating conjunction** introduces a subordinate clause (pages 609– 614), which is a clause that cannot stand by itself as a complete sentence. The subordinating conjunction connects the subordinate clause to an independent clause, which *can* stand by itself as a complete sentence.

—— sub. clause ——┐ ┌————————— indep. clause —————————┐
As the months went by, the Smiths grew accustomed to their new home. [The subordinating conjunction *as* introduces the subordinate clause and connects that clause to the independent clause.]

Subordinating conjunctions usually express relationships of time, manner, cause, condition, comparison, or purpose.

Time	after, as, as long as, as soon as, before, since, until, when, whenever, while
Manner	as, as if, as though
Cause	because
Condition	although, as long as, even if, even though, if, provided that, though, unless, while
Comparison	as, than
Purpose	in order that, so that, that

Jerry has been practicing the drums constantly and plays **as though** he has —————— sub. clause ——————┐
had a great deal of experience. [*As though* expresses manner.]

The stores are extremely crowded these days **unless** you go early on a —— sub. clause ——┐
Saturday morning. [*Unless* expresses condition.]

Conjunction or Preposition?   Certain words can function as either conjunctions or prepositions. However, there are two important differences between a word used as a preposition and one used as a conjunction. First, a preposition always has an object, and a conjunction never has one.

Preposition

Before *me* is a book of Renaissance poetry. [The pronoun *me* is the object of the preposition *before.*]

Conjunction

Before we read it, we should learn something about Renaissance poets' use of myth and allegory. [*Before* has no object. Instead, it introduces the subordinate clause *Before we read it.*]

Second, a preposition introduces a prepositional phrase. A conjunction, on the other hand, connects words or groups of words.

Preposition

┌──── prep. phrase ────┐
After much preparation, Renaissance poets made classical allusions with ease. [*After* introduces the prepositional phrase *After much preparation.*]

Conjunction

Spenser's literary career flourished **after** Sir Walter Raleigh presented him to Queen Elizabeth I. [*After* connects the subordinate clause *after Sir Walter Raleigh presented him to Queen Elizabeth I* to the preceding independent clause.]

Conjunctive Adverbs

A **conjunctive adverb** is an adverb that functions somewhat like a coordinating conjunction because it usually connects independent clauses (page 609). A semicolon precedes the conjunctive adverb, and a comma usually follows it.

Conjunctive Adverb

An expert on career planning will speak in the auditorium on Friday; **furthermore,** he will answer your questions after the lecture.

Coordinating Conjunction

An expert on career planning will speak in the auditorium on Friday, **and** he will answer your questions after the lecture.

The following list contains frequently used conjunctive adverbs:

also	furthermore	later	still
besides	however	moreover	then
consequently	indeed	nevertheless	therefore
finally	instead	otherwise	thus

1.1H   INTERJECTIONS

An **interjection** is an exclamatory word or phrase that can stand by itself, although it may also appear in a sentence. Many interjections express strong emotions. They are followed by exclamation points.

Wow! That ball was really hit!

When an interjection appears within a sentence, you should set it off with a comma or commas.

So, you didn't find what you were looking for at the corner store.

My, these grapefruits are truly excellent!

1.2 SENTENCE STRUCTURE

1.2A   FOUR SENTENCE PURPOSES

A **sentence** is a group of words that has a subject and a predicate and that expresses a complete thought. It describes an action or states a condition of a person, a place, or a thing. There are four categories of sentences: declarative, interrogative, exclamatory, and imperative.

A **declarative sentence** makes a statement and ends with a period. An **interrogative sentence** asks a question and ends with a question mark. An **exclamatory sentence** shows strong feeling and ends with an exclamation point. An **imperative sentence** gives an order or makes a request. A mild command or request ends with a period, but a strong command or request ends with an exclamation point. Some imperative sentences take the form of questions but are actually mild commands or polite requests. Such sentences end with periods.

Declarative	Before reading the novel, Stephen read the preface.
Interrogative	Why did Napoleon lose the battle at Waterloo?
Exclamatory	This traffic will make us miss our plane!
Imperative	Lock the door on your way out.
	Don't drink that sour milk!
	Donna, will you please move your car.

1.2B   SUBJECTS AND PREDICATES

Simple Subjects

The **simple subject** is the noun or pronoun that names the person, place, thing, or idea that the sentence is about. The simple subject does not include modifiers. The complete subject (page 597) consists of the simple subject and its modifiers. In this book the term *subject* refers to the simple subject. In the following sentences, the simple subject is in boldface type.

> **Sigmund Freud** is considered one of the founders of modern psychiatry.

> The **last** of the artifacts that the archaeologist discovered was the most interesting.

> Where will the **seminar** on computer education be held?

The simple subject of an imperative sentence is always *you*. Often, *you* is understood rather than stated.

> Be sure to study the history-book chapter about Reconstruction. [**Think:** *You* be sure.]

Compound Subjects

A **compound subject** is a simple subject that consists of two or more nouns or pronouns of equal rank. The term *compound subject* refers to a compound *simple* subject.

> A larger **dining room**, a **den**, and a big **closet** will be added to Mr. Grabowski's house. [*Dining room, den,* and *closet* form the compound subject.]

Simple Predicates

The **simple predicate** is the verb or verb phrase that describes the action or states the condition of the subject. The simple predicate does not include modifiers and words that complete the meaning of the verb. It also does not include the adverb *not* or *never*. The complete predicate (page 597) includes all such modifiers and complements (page 598). It also includes *not* or *never*. In this book the term *predicate* refers to the simple predicate. In the following sentences, the simple predicate is in boldface type.

> subj.   pred.
> For biology class each *student* **collected** samples of forty different kinds of leaves.

> subj.   ⎡— pred. —⎤
> By this time tomorrow, our *family* **will have driven** through Sequoia National Park.

> pred. ⎡— subj. —⎤ pred.
> What **do** *social scientists* **view** as the major trends for cities in the next ten years?

Compound Predicates

A **compound predicate** is a simple predicate that consists of two or more verbs or verb phrases of equal rank. The term *compound predicate* refers to a compound *simple* predicate.

> Julius Caesar **led** the Roman army in one conquest after another and **expanded** the Roman Empire all the way to Britain but **was assassinated** in 44 B.C. [*Led, expanded,* and *was assassinated* form the compound predicate.]

Complete Subjects and Complete Predicates

The **complete subject** consists of the simple subject and all the words that modify it or identify it.

> ┌─────── complete subject ───────┐
> **Brown County, which is in the south-central part of Indiana,** is known for its art galleries. [*Brown County* is the simple subject.]

> ┌─────── complete subject ───────┐
> **Remembered for his courage in battle,** *Chief Crazy Horse* actually had a quiet, unassuming manner. [*Chief Crazy Horse* is the simple subject.]

> ┌─────── complete subject ───────┐
> *Harvard University,* **the oldest university in the United States, and** *Laval University,* **the oldest university in Canada,** were both founded to train people for the clergy. [Included in the complete subject is the compound simple subject, which appears in italic type.]

The **complete predicate** consists of the simple predicate and all the words that modify it or complete its meaning.

> ┌─────── complete predicate ───────┐
> The Vikings, who came from Scandinavia, *made* **raids on other European countries from the eighth century through the eleventh century.** [*Made* is the simple predicate.]

> ┌─────── complete predicate ───────┐
> Film for your camera *can be bought* **at the visitors' center at the zoo.** [*Can be bought* is the simple predicate.]

> ┌─────── complete predicate ───────┐
> Demographers *study* **population trends and** *predict* **that the average age of people in the United States will rise.** [Included in the complete predicate is the compound simple predicate, *study* and *predict*.]

Placement of Subjects and Predicates

Subjects and predicates may be arranged in a variety of ways in sentences. The placement of the subject and the predicate often depends on the purpose of the sentence. In the examples that follow, the complete subjects are underlined once and the complete predicates twice.

Declarative Sentences

Household utensils made of pewter, an alloy consisting primarily of tin, have been used since the fourteenth century. [The subject precedes the predicate.]

Here are the periodicals that you requested from the reference librarian. [The sentence has inverted word order; that is, the subject follows the predicate.]

Into the street rolled the tennis ball. [The sentence has inverted word order.]

Because they had been studying the ancient history of Britain, Sue and Paulette, who were on a tour, were particularly interested in seeing Stonehenge. [The subject is between the two parts of the predicate.]

Interrogative Sentence

How were you able to fix the plugged drain in the kitchen? [**Think:** You were able to fix.]

Imperative Sentence

Try to finish painting the porch by this evening. [**Think:** *You* try to finish. The entire imperative sentence is the complete predicate because the subject, *you,* is understood.]

Exclamatory Sentences

The pictures that you took are beautiful!

What a fascinating exhibit that was!

1.2C   COMPLEMENTS

A **complement** is a word or a group of words that completes the meaning of a verb in a sentence or a clause (page 604). Complements are always part of the complete predicate.

The oranges sent to us from Florida were **delicious.** [The oranges were *what?* Delicious. *Delicious* is a complement.]

This afternoon Chet is chopping **wood** for the winter. [Chet is chopping *what?* Wood. *Wood* is a complement.]

If the preceding sentences did not have complements, their meaning would be incomplete.

The oranges sent to us from Florida were [Were what?]

Chet is chopping [Is chopping what?]

This section covers three types of complements: objects, objective complements, and subject complements.

Objects

Objects are nouns or pronouns that follow action verbs in the active voice (see pages 631–632). There are two kinds of objects: direct objects and indirect objects.

Direct Objects. A **direct object** is a noun or a pronoun that follows an action verb in the active voice and receives the action of the verb. It answers the question *What?* or *Whom?* Verbs that take direct objects are called *transitive verbs* (page 583). Modifiers are not part of the object.

D.O.

The Leggets *visited* the **aunt** of one of their friends. [Visited *whom?* Aunt.]

D.O.

The next-door neighbors *have* a small **tractor** for clearing the snow from the driveway. [Have *what?* Tractor.]

Indirect Objects. An **indirect object** is a noun or a pronoun that names the person or thing *to* whom or *for* whom an action is performed. An indirect object follows an action verb in the active voice. In most cases an indirect object is used with a direct object. The indirect object comes immediately after the verb and before the direct object.

I.O.   D.O.

The men's choir will sing **us** one more *song* to conclude the program. [**Think:** The choir will sing (*for*) us one more song.]

I.O.   D.O.

Will you bring **me** a *couple* of books from the library when you go there? [**Think:** Will you bring (*to*) me a couple of books?]

Compound Objects. Like subjects and predicates, objects may be compound. A **compound object** consists of two or more objects that complete the same predicate.

Compound Direct Object

D.O.   D.O.

Jerry read several **articles** and **books** about the presidency of James Monroe.

Compound Indirect Object

I.O.   I.O.

We will show **Maxine** and **Paulette** as many historical sites as we have time for.

Objective Complements

An **objective complement** is a noun or an adjective that follows a direct object and explains, identifies, or describes that object. Only certain verbs take an objective complement: *make, find, think, elect, choose, appoint, name, consider, call,* and synonyms of these verbs.

Noun as Objective Complement

— D.O. —   — O.C. —

The votes have elected *Alexandra Smith* **state senator**. [*State senator* is the objective complement of the verb phrase *have elected*. It identifies the direct object *Alexandra Smith*.]

Adjective as Objective Complement

D.O.   O.C.

We considered the dancer's *performance* **brilliant**. [*Brilliant* is the objective complement of the verb *considered*. It describes the direct object, *performance*.]

A sentence may have a compound objective complement, which consists of two or more objective complements.

D.O.   O.C.

The board of trustees has appointed *Dan* the **director** of public information

O.C.

and the **coordinator** of the research department. [The nouns *director* and *coordinator* are objective complements.]

Subject Complements

A **subject complement** is a word that comes after a linking verb and identifies or describes the subject of a sentence or a clause. Subject complements often follow forms of the verb *be*. Other verbs that may take subject complements are in the following list:

appear	look	smell
become	remain	sound
feel	seem	stay
grow	shine	taste

There are two kinds of subject complements: predicate nominatives and predicate adjectives.

Predicate Nominatives. A **predicate nominative** is a noun or a pronoun that follows a linking verb and identifies the subject of the sentence. The root of the word *nominative* is *nominate,* which means "to name." In a sense the predicate nominative renames the subject.

P.N.

During the coming year, *Ron* will remain a **volunteer** at the local recycling center. [*Volunteer* identifies the subject *Ron*.]

P.N.

After Mrs. Sampson's expert training, *Butch* has become an obedient **dog.** [*Dog* identifies the subject *Butch.*]

┌───── P.N. ─────┐   P.N.

The *broadcast* will be either a **press conference** or a **speech** by the governor. [The sentence has a compound predicate nominative, *press conference* and *speech*. Both identify *broadcast.*]

Predicate Adjectives. A **predicate adjective** is an adjective that follows a linking verb and modifies the subject of the sentence.

P.A.

The *sound* coming out of the speakers was rather **feeble.** [The predicate adjective *feeble* modifies the subject *sound.*]

P.A.

The *story* that I read last night was quite **difficult** to follow. [The predicate adjective *difficult* modifies the subject *story.*]

P.A.   P.A.

Harrison felt **refreshed** and **relaxed** after his month-long vacation. [The sentence has a compound predicate adjective, *refreshed* and *relaxed.*]

In some sentences the predicate adjective precedes the verb or verb phrase.

P.A.

Fortunate were the *students* who had bought their tickets early. [The predicate adjective *fortunate* modifies the subject *students.*]

1.3 PHRASES AND CLAUSES

Phrases and clauses let you use a variety of sentence structures in your writing. This section explains the functions of both phrases and clauses.

1.3A PHRASES

A **phrase** is a group of related words that functions as a single part of speech but lacks a subject, a predicate, or both. This section deals with three common kinds of phrases: prepositional phrases, appositive phrases, and verbal phrases.

Prepositional Phrases

A **prepositional phrase** consists of a preposition and its object, including any modifiers of that object. In the following sentences, the prepositional phrases are in boldface type.

> An important challenge facing the United States **for the last two hundred years** has been maintaining the proper balance **between the individual's rights and society's rights.** [The second prepositional phrase has a compound object of the preposition.]

> **Which person** are you looking **for?** [**Think:** *For which person* are you looking?]

Prepositional Phrases Used as Adjectives. A prepositional phrase that modifies a noun or a pronoun functions as an adjective. Such a phrase is sometimes called an **adjective phrase.**

Modifies Noun

The *man* **with the brown raincoat** will drive us downtown, where we will

find the *location* **of the meeting.**

Modifies Pronoun

Several **of the students** have entered the chess tournament.

Prepositional Phrases Used as Adverbs. A prepositional phrase functions as an adverb if it modifies a verb, an adjective, or another adverb. This kind of phrase is sometimes called an **adverb phrase.**

Modifies Verb

The impressionist movement *spread* **from Europe** and influenced American artists in the early 1900s.

Modifies Adjective

The entire class was *curious* **about new energy sources.**

Modifies Adverb

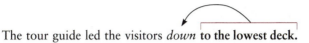

The tour guide led the visitors *down* **to the lowest deck.**

A prepositional phrase can modify the object in another prepositional phrase.

—————— adv. phrase —————— ┌ adj. phrase ┐ adj. phrase

A detour *took* us **around the construction site** **in the middle of the city.**

Appositives and Appositive Phrases

An **appositive** is a noun or a pronoun placed near another noun or pronoun to explain it or identify it.

The senior class *president,* **Amy Jones,** has brought several new ideas into student government.

Will our supervisors show *us* **trainees** the best selling techniques?

Albert Schweitzer, **doctor, missionary,** and **philosopher,** will long be remembered for his humanitarian work in Africa. [The sentence has a compound appositive: *doctor, missionary,* and *philosopher.*]

Like an appositive, an **appositive phrase** explains or identifies a noun or a pronoun. It includes all the words or phrases that modify an appositive.

Colette's *hobby,* **nature and wildlife photography,** will probably lead to an interesting job.

We **listeners with questions** can talk to the professor after the lecture.

A year of fierce snowstorms and widespread drought, *1978* will long be remembered.

An **essential appositive** or an **essential appositive phrase** is an appositive that is necessary to the meaning of the sentence. This kind of appositive should not be separated from the rest of the sentence with a comma or commas.

D. H. Lawrence's *short story* **"The Rocking-Horse Winner"** appears in numerous literature anthologies. [Lawrence wrote more than one story. The appositive is necessary to identify which story.]

A **nonessential appositive** or a **nonessential appositive phrase** is an appositive that is *not* necessary to the meaning of the sentence. Such an appositive should be separated from the rest of the sentence with a comma or commas.

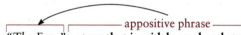

Lawrence also wrote *"The Fox,"* **a story that is widely read and studied.** [The appositive is not necessary to identify the story being discussed.]

Verbals and Verbal Phrases

Verbals are verb forms that function as nouns, adjectives, or adverbs but retain some of the properties of verbs. For instance, they express action or being, and they may take complements. There are three kinds of verbals: participles, gerunds, and infinitives.

Participles. A **participle** is a verb form that can function as an adjective while still keeping some of the properties of a verb. It expresses action or being, and it may take a complement.

Annoyed, *Jane* drove around the block to find a **parking** *place.* [Both *annoyed* and *parking* are participles.]

There are two kinds of participles: present participles and past participles. The present participle and the past participle are two of the four principal parts of a verb. For a complete explanation of the principal parts of verbs, see pages 622–625.

Besides functioning as adjectives, present participles and past participles can form part of a verb phrase. When a participle functions as a verb, it is not a verbal. This section deals with present participles and past participles that function as adjectives. For an explanation of participles used as verbs, see pages 627–632.

To form a present participle, add *-ing* to the infinitive form of a verb.

Did you figure out a solution to that **puzzling** *problem?* [*Puzzling* is a present participle that consists of the verb *puzzle* and the ending *-ing.*]

To form a past participle, first determine whether the verb is regular or irregular (pages 622–625).

1. *Regular verbs.* To form the past participle of a regular verb, add either *-d* or *-ed* to the infinitive form of the verb.

Infinitive	Past Participle
exhaust	exhausted

2. *Irregular verbs.* To form the past participle of an irregular verb, use a special form of the verb. See pages 623–625 for a list of past participles of commonly used irregular verbs.

Infinitive	Past Participle
freeze	frozen
tear	torn

A participle used as an adjective may have one or more auxiliary verbs. The auxiliary verb and the participle function as a unit to modify a noun or a pronoun.

Having been lost, *Jason* vowed never to drive in the city again without a map. [*Having* and *been* are the auxiliary verbs, and *lost* is the participle.]

Participial Phrases. A **participial phrase** consists of a participle and its modifiers and complements. The participial phrase functions as an adjective to modify a noun or a pronoun. Both present participles and past participles may be used to form participial phrases.

There is *Maria* **walking briskly to City Hall.**

Disappointed by the cast's mediocre performance during dress

rehearsal, the *director* emphasized the importance of concentration during a performance.

Having forgotten to send a birthday card, *Ed* sent a telegram to his brother.

Notice that in the preceding sentences, the participial phrases are near the words that they modify. For an explanation of the correct placement of participial phrases, see pages 652–654.

Another kind of phrase that is formed with participles is the absolute phrase. An **absolute phrase** modifies the entire independent clause (page 609) of the sentence; it does not have a direct grammatical connection with any single word in the independent clause. An absolute phrase contains both a participle and the noun or pronoun that is modified by the participle. Consequently, the phrase is "absolute," or complete within itself.

> **The flour having fallen from the top shelf of the pantry,** I had to spend half an hour cleaning the floor. [The absolute phrase modifies the entire independent clause by telling why I had to spend half an hour cleaning.]

Gerunds. A **gerund** is a verbal that ends in *-ing* and functions only as a noun. Although it functions as a noun, a gerund has some of the properties of a verb. It expresses action or being, and it may take a complement such as a direct object or an indirect object.

Used as Subject
According to doctors, **laughing** may be one way to treat certain kinds of illness.

Used as Direct Object
When you study, don't forget **skimming,** which allows you to review a great amount of material quickly.

Used as Indirect Object
Sue gave **skiing** high marks after her first try yesterday.

Used as Object of Preposition
To become an artist, one must first learn the fundamentals of **drawing.**

Used as Predicate Nominative
A good way to gain exercise daily is **walking.**

Used as Appositive
Most children's favorite pastime, **playing,** actually has great educational value.

Be sure that you can distinguish between gerunds and participles. They are identical in form, but participles can function as adjectives, while gerunds always function as nouns.

Gerund Phrase. A **gerund phrase** consists of a gerund and its modifiers and complements.

     — gerund phrase —   — gerund phrase —
The cheering of the crowd all but prevented us from **hearing the conven-**

tion's main speaker.

Like gerunds, gerund phrases may perform all the functions of a noun.

Used as Subject
The marching of the band made the ground tremble.

Used as Direct Object
At this point in the hearings, the committee will avoid **debating specific policy proposals.**

Used as Indirect Object
The city has given **developing new sources of revenue** the greatest importance this year.

Used as Object of Preposition
The council has voted in favor of **setting aside additional land for public parks.**

Used as Predicate Nominative
One way to reduce grocery bills is **planting a garden of tomatoes, lettuce, beans, and cucumbers.**

Used as Appositive
Elaine's summer job, **selling sportswear in a department store,** will prove valuable in her career in merchandising.

Infinitives. An **infinitive** is a verbal that consists of the first principal part (pages 627–628) of the verb. The word *to* usually, though not always, precedes the infinitive. An infinitive may function as a noun, an adjective, or an adverb. Like a participle and a gerund, an infinitive has some of the characteristics of a verb. It expresses action or being and may take a complement.

Functions as Noun
To relax is Greg's goal over spring vacation. [subject]

Because the line for the movie was so long, we decided **to leave.** [direct object]

The purpose of speech class is **to communicate.** [predicate nominative]

Functions as Adjective

Phyllis has an excellent *ability* **to remember.** [What kind of ability? The ability *to remember.*]

Functions as Adverb

At the end of the play, the people *rose* **to applaud.** [Why did the people rise? They rose *to applaud.*]

It looks to me as if the dog is too *lazy* **to run.** [To what extent is the dog lazy? It is too lazy *to run.*]

You may form an infinitive with one or more auxiliary verbs and a past participle. Such infinitives indicate the time of the action.

The *Super Bowl* **to have watched** was the 1969 game between the New York Jets and the Baltimore Colts.

The *route* **to be followed** is marked in red.

Note: Do not confuse infinitives and prepositional phrases. *To* followed by a verb is an infinitive, but *to* followed by a noun or a pronoun is a prepositional phrase.

Infinitive Phrases. An **infinitive phrase** consists of an infinitive and its modifiers and complements. An infinitive phrase can function as a noun, an adjective, or an adverb.

Functions as Noun
   To buy a birthday present is my errand at noon.

Functions as Adjective

The best *time* **to find bargains in the stores** is the last week of December. [Which time? The time *to find bargains in the stores.*]

Functions as Adverb

A crowd *gathered* **to watch the unveiling of the new sculpture.** [Why did a crowd gather? It gathered *to watch the unveiling of the new sculpture.*]

In some sentences an infinitive phrase may be used without the word *to.*

   Will you help me **put up the badminton net?** [**Think:** help me *to* put up the badminton net.]

   Silently, Peg's friends watched her **practice her figure skating.** [**Think:** watched her *to* practice her figure skating.]

Sometimes the infinitive has a subject. Together, the subject of the infinitive and the infinitive make up an **infinitive clause.** If the subject of the infinitive is a pronoun, that pronoun is in the objective case (pages 613–614).

—— infinitive clause ——

The gym teacher told **the class to run one more mile that day.** [*Class* is the subject of the infinitive.]

————————— infinitive clause —————————

Sophie's aunt and uncle asked **her to pay them a visit when she passed
through Cincinnati.**

————————— infinitive clause —————————

Dale wants **us to start a collection of art objects from around the world.**

1.3B CLAUSES

A **clause** is a group of related words that contains both a subject and a
predicate. There are two kinds of clauses: independent clauses and subordinate clauses.

Independent Clauses

An **independent clause** can stand by itself as a sentence. The following
sentence contains two independent clauses, which are in boldface type.
Notice that each clause has a subject and a predicate and that each could
be a separate sentence. In the following example, the subject is underlined
once, and the predicate is underlined twice.

> **Our literary club intended to read *Dune,* by Frank Herbert, but we chose
> Ray Bradbury's *Fahrenheit 451* instead.**

A comma and the coordinating conjunction *but* join the clauses in the
preceding sentence. *But* is not part of either clause. Rather, it coordinates,
or connects, the independent clauses. The other coordinating conjunctions
are *and, or, nor, for, so,* and *yet.*

You can also join independent clauses with either a semicolon or a
semicolon and a conjunctive adverb (pages 615–616).

> Dürer's diary, letters, and memoirs of his family survive today; scholars know
> more about him than about many other Renaissance artists. [semicolon]

> Dürer's diary, letters, and memoirs of his family survive today; **therefore,**
> scholars know more about him than about many other Renaissance artists.
> [semicolon and conjunctive adverb]

Subordinate Clauses

A clause that cannot stand by itself is a **subordinate clause.** This kind of
clause is sometimes called a **dependent clause.** In the following examples,
the subjects are underlined once, and the predicates are underlined twice.
However, the clauses cannot stand by themselves because they do not
express complete thoughts.

> Which is one of the vanishing species in the United States
> While we are waiting for the car to be tuned up
> Although the weather has been mild

Notice that the preceding subordinate clauses begin with the words *which, while,* and *although. Which* is a relative pronoun (page 581), and *while* and *although* are subordinating conjunctions (pages 593–594). Many subordinate clauses begin with either a relative pronoun or a subordinating conjunction. Such introductory words are part of the subordinate clause, and they join the subordinate clause to an independent clause.

——— indep. clause ———   ——— sub. clause ———

Most observers admire the bald eagle, **which** is one of the vanishing species

in the United States.

——— indep. clause ———   ——— sub. clause ———

Why don't we walk around the shopping center **while** we are waiting for

the car to be tuned up?

——— sub. clause ———   ——— indep. clause ———

Although the weather has been mild, forecasters are predicting a harsh

winter.

Clauses Used as Adjectives.   A clause functions as an adjective if it modifies a noun or a pronoun. Such clauses are called **adjective clauses.** Most adjective clauses begin with a relative pronoun: *that, which, who, whom,* and *whose.*

The policy *paper* **that** the candidate issued on city services has some worthwhile ideas. [*Which* paper? The paper *that the candidate issued on city services.*]

I can't remember the name of the *artist* **whose** paintings are being featured

at the art institute. [*Which* artist? The artist *whose paintings are being featured at the art institute.*]

You may also begin adjective clauses with **relative adverbs.** Some of the relative adverbs are *after, before, since, when,* and *where.*

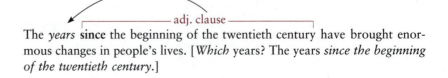

The *years* **since** the beginning of the twentieth century have brought enormous changes in people's lives. [*Which* years? The years *since the beginning of the twentieth century.*]

Sometimes the introductory word in an adjective clause is implied rather than stated.

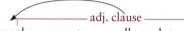

The *bus* the commuters usually took to work was discontinued without any announcement. [**Think:** Bus *that* the commuters usually took.]

Essential and Nonessential Clauses. An adjective clause that is necessary to identify a noun or a pronoun is an **essential clause.** An essential clause is not separated from the rest of the sentence by commas.

Essential Clause

When our car broke down, we were lucky to find the only service

station **that** was open late at night. [The clause is essential in order to identify the station.]

A **nonessential clause** is an adjective clause that is not necessary to identify a noun or a pronoun. A nonessential clause is set off from the rest of the sentence by commas.

Nonessential Clause

The morning classes were shortened because of the

assembly, **which** featured speeches by students running for student council. [The clause is nonessential because without it, the reader would still know which assembly is being discussed.]

Clauses Used as Adverbs. A subordinate clause functions as an adverb when it modifies a verb, an adjective, or an adverb. Such clauses are called **adverb clauses.**

Modifies Verb

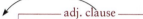

Newspapers *played* a large role in colonial America **because they**
— adv. clause —
supported and publicized the efforts of colonists protesting British rule.

Modifies Adjective

All of the neighbors were *sure* **that Mr. Wallace would recover completely**
— adv. clause —
from his illness.

Modifies Adverb

For her research paper, Evelyn went through the county records more

thoroughly **than anyone else had done before.**

An adverb clause always begins with a subordinating conjunction (pages 592–594), which is a word that shows the relationship between the subordinate clause and the independent clause. A list of frequently used subordinating conjunctions is on page 593.

Adverb clauses tell *how, when, where, to what extent,* and *why.* In the following examples, the subordinating conjunctions are in boldface type.

How

Although nervous, Sharon *greeted* the personnel director **as if** she were

— adv. clause —
completely at ease.

When

——— adv. clause ———
While the tide is coming in, you *should* not *stand* on those low rocks near the ocean.

Where

For lunch we *will meet* you **where** State and Madison streets intersect.

To What Extent

The tourists were so *eager* to see the Washington Monument **that** they

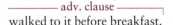

——— adv. clause ———
walked to it before breakfast.

Why

——— adv. clause ———
So that the restaurant can be sure of seating such a large party, you *should*

call ahead of time for a reservation.

Elliptical Clauses. An elliptical clause is an adverb clause in which part of the clause is omitted. Even though the clause is incomplete, its meaning is clear; therefore, it is still classified as a clause.

You deserve more credit for the success of our fund-raising campaign

┌ adv. ┐
│clause│

than I. [**Think:** You deserve more credit than I *deserve. Than I* modifies *more.*]

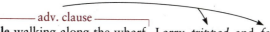

┌─────── adv. clause ───────┐
While walking along the wharf, Larry *tripped* and *fell.* [**Think:** while *he was walking.*]

Clauses Used as Nouns. Clauses that function as nouns in sentences are **noun clauses.** A noun clause may function as a subject, a predicate nominative, a direct object, an indirect object, an object of a preposition, or an appositive.

Functions as Subject

┌─────────── noun clause ───────────┐
Where the city should build a new library is the main item on the agenda at the city council meeting.

Functions as Predicate Nominative

┌─────────── noun clause ───────────┐
The turning point of World War II was **when the Allied forces landed successfully on the shores of Normandy.**

Functions as Direct Object

┌─────────── noun clause ───────────┐
Research scientists are hoping **that the process of nuclear fusion will help solve the world's energy problems in the twenty-first century.**

Functions as Indirect Object

┌─────── noun clause ───────┐
Mr. Pritkin will give **whoever finds his pet poodle** a substantial reward.

Functions as Object of a Preposition

┌─────── noun clause ───────┐
The people in the train station are waiting for **whichever train arrives first.**

Functions as Appositive

┌─── noun clause ───┐
It's after four-thirty, and the pranksters, **whoever they are,** are to return to my office at nine o'clock tomorrow morning.

You may introduce a noun clause with an interrogative pronoun, a subordinating conjunction, or a relative pronoun.

Interrogative Pronouns
who, whom, whose, which, what

Subordinating Conjunctions
how, that, when, where, whether, why

Relative Pronouns
who, whom, whose, which, that

Sometimes you may omit the introductory word in a noun clause.

┌──────────────────── noun clause ────────────────────┐
Has anyone told the reporters **they were the winners of several awards for**

their documentaries this year? [**Think:** informed *that* they were the winners.]

One particular kind of noun clause is the **infinitive clause.** It consists of an infinitive that has a subject. If the subject of the infinitive is a pronoun, that pronoun is in the objective case (pages 607–609) as if it were the direct object of the preceding verb. However, it is not; the entire infinitive clause serves as the direct object of the preceding verb.

┌─────── infinitive clause ───────┐
They built **roads to be wider and stronger.** [*Roads* is the subject of the infinitive.]

┌──────────────────── infinitive clause ────────────────────┐
They designed **them to support the weight of the heavier wagons and artillery.** [*Them* is the subject of the infinitive.]

┌─────── infinitive clause ───────┐
Renaissance engineers developed **pavement to serve this purpose.**

┌──────────────── infinitive clause ────────────────┐
Thus gunpowder caused **Renaissance engineers to build the first paved roads.**

1.3C   SENTENCES CLASSIFIED BY STRUCTURE

Sentences are classified according to the number and kinds of clauses that they contain. The four kinds of sentences are simple, compound, complex, and compound-complex.

Simple Sentences

A sentence containing one independent clause and no subordinate clauses is a **simple sentence.** It may have any number of phrases, and it may have a compound subject, a compound predicate, or both. However, it does not have more than one clause.

Fish, underwater plants, and coral were visible in the crystal blue water.

Myra's car had a flat tire, forcing her off the road.

Compound Sentences

A sentence consisting of two or more independent clauses is a **compound sentence.** A compound sentence never has a subordinate clause. The independent clauses are usually joined with a comma and one of the coordinating conjunctions: *and, but, nor, or, for, so,* or *yet.*

┌──────── indep. clause ────────┐   ┌──── indep. clause ────
Skydiving is an increasingly popular sport, **but** you should be in excellent

physical shape to try it.

Independent clauses may also be joined with a semicolon or with a semicolon and a conjunctive adverb such as *nonetheless, consequently,* or *still* (page 594). A comma always follows the conjunctive adverb.

┌──────── indep. clause ────────┐ ┌──── indep. clause────
A dirigible, a type of aircraft, is lighter than air; the first dirigible was built

in 1884.

┌──────────── indep. clause ────────────
During the 1800s a man named John Chapman traveled throughout the
┌indep. clause
Ohio River valley and planted apple seeds; **consequently,** Chapman is

known to us as Johnny Appleseed.

Complex Sentences

A sentence consisting of one independent clause and one or more subordinate clauses is a **complex sentence.**

┌──────────── sub. clause ────────────
When herders in the mountains of Switzerland want to communicate with
┌──── indep. clause ────
one another across long distances, they use a twelve-foot-long instrument
┌──── sub. clause ────┐
that is called an alpenhorn.

┌──────── sub. clause ────────
Paris's Arc de Triomphe, which commemorates Napoleon's victories, was
┌──── sub. clause ────
not completed until 1836 even though it was started in 1806. [The sentence contains one independent clause: *Paris's Arc de Triomphe was not completed until 1836.* That clause contains a subordinate clause: *which commemorates Napoleon's victories.*]

Compound-Complex Sentences

A sentence consisting of two or more independent clauses and one or more subordinate clauses is a **compound-complex sentence.**

$\overbrace{\hspace{4cm}}^{\text{sub. clause}}$

When the first synthetic fiber, rayon, was developed in 1884, the way was

$\overbrace{\hspace{4cm}}^{\text{indep. clause}} \quad \overbrace{\hspace{3cm}}^{\text{indep. clause}}$

opened for the development of modern textiles, and these textiles have rev-

olutionized the clothing industry.

$\overbrace{\hspace{4cm}}^{\text{sub. clause}}$

Since commercial television became popular in the 1950s, the major net-

$\overbrace{\hspace{4cm}}^{\text{indep. clause}} \quad \overbrace{\hspace{3cm}}^{\text{indep. clause}}$

works have dominated the programming, but recent developments, which

$\overbrace{\hspace{4cm}}^{\text{sub. clause}}$

include cable television and public television, may change the structure of

the industry. [The second independent clause, *recent developments may change the structure of the industry*, is interrupted by the subordinate clause *which include cable television and public television*.]

1.4 WRITING COMPLETE SENTENCES

A **complete sentence** is a group of words that has at least one subject and one predicate and that expresses a complete thought. You should use complete sentences in your writing. Two common errors in writing are the use of sentence fragments and run-on sentences. In this section you will learn how to recognize and correct both kinds of errors.

1.4A AVOIDING SENTENCE FRAGMENTS

A **sentence fragment** is a group of words that lacks a subject or a predicate or does not express a complete thought.

Complete Sentence
    Harriet planned to pick up the reupholstered chair on her way home.

Fragment
    Harriet planned. **To pick up the reupholstered chair on her way home.** [The second group of words lacks a subject and a predicate.]

Fragment
    Harriet, planning to pick up the reupholstered chair on her way home. [The group of words lacks a predicate.]

If the sentence fragment is a phrase, you can correct it by combining the fragment with a related sentence.

Fragment
    During lunch today. I would like to talk about the plans for the panel discussion.

Complete Sentence

┌──prepositional──┐
│   phrase   │
During lunch today I would like to talk about the plans for the panel discussion.

Fragment

The zoo has acquired an anaconda. **A large snake native to South America.**

Complete Sentence

┌────── appositive phrase ──────┐
The zoo has acquired an anaconda, **a large snake native to South America.**

Fragment

To buy an old car and rebuild the engine. That is what Al has decided to do.

Complete Sentence

┌────── infinitive phrase ──────┐
Al has decided **to buy an old car and rebuild the engine.**

Fragment

I think that I saw Uncle Bill. **Waiting in line at the concession stand.**

Complete Sentence

┌────── participial phrase ──────┐
I think I saw Uncle Bill **waiting in line at the concession stand.**

Fragment

Paddling upstream in a canoe. That requires a great expenditure of energy.

Complete Sentence

┌── gerund phrase ──┐
Paddling upstream in a canoe requires a great expenditure of energy.

If the sentence fragment is a subordinate clause used without an independent clause, you can also correct it by combining the fragment with a related sentence.

Fragment

The entire group has decided to go to Palomar Park. **Which is featuring carnival rides at half price over the weekend.**

Complete Sentence

The entire group has decided to go to Palomar Park, **which is featuring**
┌────── subordinate clause ──────┐
carnival rides at half price over the weekend.

Fragment

Before she leaves Florence. Harriet should be sure to see the bronze baptistry doors by Ghiberti.

Complete Sentence

┌── subordinate clause ──┐
Before she leaves Florence, Harriet should be sure to see the bronze baptistry doors by Ghiberti.

Some sentence fragments require additions or rewording to make them complete sentences.

Fragment

The ocean, sparkling under the noonday sun.

Complete Sentence

The ocean sparkled under the noonday sun.

Fragment

The metric system, which is becoming more widely used in the United States.

Complete Sentence

The metric system is becoming more widely used in the United States.

1.4B   AVOIDING RUN-ON SENTENCES

A **run-on sentence** consists of two or more separate sentences written as one sentence. In some run-on sentences, only a comma separates the two sentences. This is called a comma splice. In others, there is no punctuation at all.

Run-on

Radio and television announcers have warned people not to look at the sun during the eclipse tomorrow, doing so could result in blindness. [A comma by itself cannot connect two independent clauses.]

Run-On

Radio and television announcers have warned people not to look at the sun during the eclipse tomorrow doing so could result in blindness. [The sentences are run together without punctuation or a conjunction.]

Correct

Radio and television announcers have warned people not to look at the sun during the eclipse tomorrow, for doing so could result in blindness. [A comma and the coordinating conjunction *for* connect the two clauses.]

There are several ways to correct run-on sentences. Read the following run-on sentence. Then study the five ways in which you can correct that sentence.

Run-on Sentence

The bridge over the river is closed, a ferry will take you to the other side.

1. Separate the run-on sentence into two or more sentences.

Correct

The bridge over the river is closed. **A** ferry will take you to the other side.

2. Join the independent clauses with a comma and a coordinating conjunction (page 592).

Correct

The bridge over the river is closed**, but** a ferry will take you to the other side.

3. Join the independent clauses with a semicolon.

Correct

The bridge over the river is closed; a ferry will take you to the other side.

4. Turn one of the independent clauses into a subordinate clause, and add a subordinating conjunction (pages 593–594) or a relative pronoun (page 581).

Correct

Because the bridge over the river is closed, a ferry will take you to the other side.

5. Join the independent clauses with a semicolon and a conjunctive adverb such as *also, thus,* or *however* (page 594).

Correct

The bridge over the river is closed; **however,** a ferry will take you to the other side.

Usage and Diction

How is the English language used? Logic and long-continued practices have made certain ways of using words and phrases the customary ways. Knowing how to write standard, formal English is useful. In certain writing situations, such as papers and letters of application, you will want to be certain that you are taken seriously. If you use an inappropriate level of formality or nonstandard usage, you may distract, offend, or unintentionally amuse your reader.

2.1 THE SCOPE OF USAGE

The English language is dynamic. It embraces usage ranging from that found in particular occupations or professions (jargon) to that used in particular locales or by particular ethnic groups (dialect); from that used in everyday conversation (colloquial) to that used only on important occasions (ceremonial); from that used only in the past (archaic or obsolete) to that used briefly by cliques or by certain age groups (slang). Moreover, the English language is constantly changing. Words and expressions that are slang today may be accepted as part of formal usage in the future. Expressions and idioms that we commonly use today may one day be obsolete. To communicate effectively, we must learn to recognize and to use the different levels of English usage.

2.1A LEVELS OF USAGE

Formal English

Formal English is the standard English that is used for serious occasions and serious writing. It comprises the words, expressions, grammar, and standards of usage found in formal essays, research papers, scholarly writing, literary criticism, and speeches made on significant or solemn occasions. The sentences used in formal English are often long and precisely structured, sometimes employing parallelism and repetition for rhetorical effect. Formal English uses extensive vocabulary, few contractions, and almost no slang.

Informal English

Informal English is the standard English used in almost all conversation and broadcasting and in many newspapers, magazines, books, letters, and nonceremonial speeches. It is characterized by the sentence variety and length typical of conversation, by vocabulary understood and used in conversation, and by more relaxed standards of usage than those of formal English. Informal English includes contractions, colloquialisms, and slang.

Nonstandard English

Nonstandard English comprises words, expressions, and grammatical constructions that are not generally accepted as correct, although they may be accepted in certain geographic areas or by certain groups of people. Nonstandard English should not normally be used to communicate with a general audience.

2.1B   JARGON AND OCCUPATIONAL LANGUAGE

Originally, **jargon** meant confused speech that was a mixture of several languages or dialects, or any language that sounded strange or incoherent. In some cases, it now refers to the specialized language used by persons in professions or in business.

Occupational language is the technical language used among specialists in the same profession. Although for those outside the profession it is often difficult to understand, technical language can be an efficient, precise means of communication for the specialists themselves. When the audience is more general, however, occupational language quickly becomes jargon—confused, meaningless talk characterized by vague, pretentious language. It not only obscures thought but also can confuse the reader or the listener.

Jargon
> The position afforded much interface, impacting on management objectives.

Jargon
> Our big people need to get into the paint and hit the boards if we're going to shut down their transition game.

2.1C   AVOIDING REDUNDANCY AND VERBOSITY

Redundancy is the practice of saying or writing the same thing in several different ways to no purpose; it usually occurs because of carelessness or ignorance. **Verbosity,** or wordiness, is the practice of saying something in the most complicated way possible.

To eliminate redundancy and verbosity, use concrete words. Never avoid a short, simple word just because it is common. Use specific verbs, such as *grumbling* instead of *talking*. Repeat an idea in a phrase or a sentence only when the idea is made clearer by the repetition.

Inflated Verbosity
Having articulated his well-considered opinion to everyone gathered in the audience to listen, the author reiterated his message and fielded questions adroitly and with acuity.

Redundancy
In my opinion I think that the author expressed her theme and view of the world in what she was saying in her book.

2.2 CORRECT USE OF VERBS

Your ability to communicate increases dramatically with your ability to use verbs correctly. By changing the form of a verb, you can express its tense, the number and the person of its subject, its voice, and its mood.

2.2A   PRINCIPAL PARTS OF VERBS

The four **principal parts** of a verb, the basic forms of a verb, are the infinitive, the present participle, the past, and the past participle. By using these forms alone or with auxiliary verbs, you can express the various tenses of a verb.

The infinitive and the present participle are formed in the same way for all verbs. The **infinitive** is the basic verb form that appears in the dictionary. The word *to* usually precedes the infinitive in a sentence; in some sentences, however, the word *to* is understood but not stated.

Infinitive
Five miles is a long way *to* **walk** in the cold. Raising money for charity, however, will make us all **walk** willingly.

The **present participle** is always a combination of the infinitive and *-ing;* it is used in a sentence with a form of the verb *be* as an auxiliary verb.

Present Participle
Jenny *is* **walking** to prove to herself that she can.

Regular Verbs

Verbs are considered regular or irregular depending on how their past and past participle forms are constructed. You form the **past** and the **past participle** of any regular verb by adding *-d* or *-ed* to the infinitive. In a sentence, the past participle takes a form of the verb *have* as an auxiliary verb.

Past

Margaret **walked** ten miles every week to get ready for the big day.

Past Participle

We *have* **walked** several miles a week to get ready.

Here are the principal parts of two regular verbs. The auxiliary verbs in parentheses remind you that the correct form of the verb *be* is used with the present participle and the correct form of the verb *have* is used with the past participle.

Infinitive	Present Participle	Past	Past Participle
offer	(is) offering	offered	(has) offered
contribute	(is) contributing	contributed	(has) contributed

Irregular Verbs

Irregular verbs are considered irregular because they do not follow the standard rules for forming their past and past participle. Like regular verbs, however, they do use a form of the auxiliary verb *be* with the present participle and a form of the auxiliary verb *have* with the past participle. The following sentences show the correct use of the principal parts of the irregular verb *drink*.

Infinitive

You can lead a horse to water, but you can't make it **drink.**

Present Participle

The horse *is* **drinking** the water now.

Past

The horse **drank** the water when we moved away from its trough.

Past Participle

The horse *has* **drunk** all of the water.

Although no standard rules govern the formation of the past and the past participle of irregular verbs, you should have little trouble mastering their usage. You have probably already developed a good sense of what is correct by what sounds correct. Memorize the principal parts of verbs that you use frequently, and consult your dictionary for those that you do not use as often. The following list contains many common irregular verbs and should serve as a useful reference.

Infinitive	Present Participle	Past	Past Participle
be	(is) being	was	(has) been
become	(is) becoming	became	(has) become
begin	(is) beginning	began	(has) begun

Infinitive	Present Participle	Past	Past Participle
bite	(is) biting	bit	(has) bitten
blow	(is) blowing	blew	(has) blown
burst	(is) bursting	burst	(has) burst
catch	(is) catching	caught	(has) caught
choose	(is) choosing	chose	(has) chosen
come	(is) coming	came	(has) come
dive	(is) diving	dived, dove	(has) dived
do	(is) doing	did	(has) done
draw	(is) drawing	drew	(has) drawn
drive	(is) driving	drove	(has) driven
eat	(is) eating	ate	(has) eaten
fall	(is) falling	fell	(has) fallen
find	(is) finding	found	(has) found
fling	(is) flinging	flung	(has) flung
fly	(is) flying	flew	(has) flown
get	(is) getting	got	(has) gotten
give	(is) giving	gave	(has) given
go	(is) going	went	(has) gone
grow	(is) growing	grew	(has) grown
have	(is) having	had	(has) had
know	(is) knowing	knew	(has) known
lay	(is) laying	laid	(has) laid
lead	(is) leading	led	(has) led
leave	(is) leaving	left	(has) left
lie	(is) lying	lay	(has) lain
lose	(is) losing	lost	(has) lost
ride	(is) riding	rode	(has) ridden
ring	(is) ringing	rang	(has) rung
rise	(is) rising	rose	(has) risen
say	(is) saying	said	(has) said
set	(is) setting	set	(has) set
sit	(is) sitting	sat	(has) sat
speak	(is) speaking	spoke	(has) spoken

Infinitive	Present Participle	Past	Past Participle
swear	(is) swearing	swore	(has) sworn
swim	(is) swimming	swam	(has) swum
tear	(is) tearing	tore	(has) torn
tell	(is) telling	told	(has) told
throw	(is) throwing	threw	(has) thrown
wear	(is) wearing	wore	(has) worn
write	(is) writing	wrote	(has) written

2.2B   VERB TENSE

You use the various forms of a verb to show whether an action or a condition takes place in the present, took place in the past, or will take place in the future. The forms of a verb that express time are called **tenses.** To form tenses, you combine the principal parts with auxiliary verbs. The six English tenses are present, past, future, present perfect, past perfect, and future perfect.

To **conjugate** a verb is to list all of the forms for its six tenses. The **conjugation of a verb** also shows how the verb forms change for the first person, the second person, and the third person and for the singular and the plural.

Conjugation of the Regular Verb *Walk*

	Singular	Plural
Present Tense	I walk	we walk
	you walk	you walk
	he/she/it walks	they walk
Past Tense	I walked	we walked
	you walked	you walked
	he/she/it walked	they walked
Future Tense	I will (shall) walk	we will (shall) walk
	you will walk	you will walk
	he/she/it will walk	they will walk
Present Perfect Tense	I have walked	we have walked
	you have walked	you have walked
	he/she/it has walked	they have walked

	Singular	Plural
Past Perfect Tense	I had walked	we had walked
	you had walked	you had walked
	he/she/it had walked	they had walked
Future Perfect Tense	I will (shall) have walked	we will (shall) have walked
	you will have walked	you will have walked
	he/she/it will have walked	they will have walked

The Six Tenses of Verbs

Present Tense. To form the present tense of a verb, use its infinitive. To form the third-person singular, you usually add *-s* or *-es* to the infinitive.

♦ RULE   Use the present tense to show an action that takes place now, to show an action that is repeated regularly, or to show a condition that is true at any time.

We **walk** four miles to school.

We **walk** every day to increase our endurance.

We found that walking **is** good exercise. [**Think:** Walking is *always* good exercise.]

♦ RULE   Use the present tense in statements about literary works or other works of art.

A Tale of Two Cities **is** one of Charles Dickens's most intriguing novels. Its hero **confronts** a difficult choice.

♦ RULE   Use the present tense occasionally to describe past events with special immediacy. When the present tense is used for this effect, it is called the **historical present.**

In World War II, the English **see** London damaged severely.

In informal communication, you can use the present tense to describe future action if you include a word or a phrase that clearly indicates that the action will occur in the future.

We **walk** in the walkathon *next* Monday.

Past Tense. To form the past tense of a regular verb, add *-d* or *-ed* to the infinitive. To avoid confusion, memorize the principal parts of irregular verbs.

♦ RULE   Use the past tense to express action that occurred in the past and was completed entirely in the past.

We **walked** home from the theater last night.

Future Tense. To form the tense, combine *will* or *shall* with the infinitive form of the main verb.

♦ RULE   Use the future tense to describe action that will occur in the future.

We **will walk** in the walkathon next Monday.

Present Perfect Tense. To form the present perfect tense, use *has* or *have* with the past participle of the main verb.

♦ RULE   Use the present perfect tense to describe action that was completed either in the recent past or at an indefinite time in the past.

We **have** just **walked** farther than we have ever walked before.

Past Perfect Tense. To form the past perfect tense, use *had* with the past participle of the main verb.

♦ RULE   Use the past perfect tense to describe an action that was completed by a certain time in the past or before another action was completed.

past perf.   past

We **had walked** the required distance before we **realized** that we could have stopped to rest.

Future Perfect Tense. To form the future perfect tense, use *will have* or *shall have* with the past participle of the main verb.

♦ RULE   Use the future perfect tense to describe a future action that will be completed before another future action will be completed.

We **will have walked** ten miles before the rest of our group begins.

Tenses of Infinitives and Participles

Infinitives (page 607) and participles (page 604) have two tenses: the present and the perfect.

	Infinitive	Participle
Present	to walk	walking
Perfect	to have walked	having walked

◆ **RULE**   Use infinitives and participles in the present tense to express action that occurs at the same time as the action of the main verb.

Present

⌐ inf. ¬
I wanted **to walk** by myself.

part.
Walking alone, I saw a flock of geese.

◆ **RULE**   Use infinitives and participles in the perfect tense to express action that took place before the action of the main verb.

Perfect

⌐——— inf. ———¬
To have walked in the walkathon makes me feel good.

⌐——— part. ———¬
Having walked by myself most of the way, I gladly joined my friends for the final mile.

Progressive and Emphatic Forms and Modals

Progressive Forms. To form the progressive, use the appropriate tense of the verb *be* with the present participle of the main verb.

◆ **RULE**   Use the progressive form of a verb to describe continuing action.

Present Progressive
We **are walking** to raise money for charity.

Past Progressive
We **were walking** near the coast.

Future Progressive
We **will be walking** for the next two hours.

Present Perfect Progressive
We **have been walking** for two hours.

Past Perfect Progressive
We **had been walking** for two hours when we met the rest of our group.

Future Perfect Progressive
We **will have been walking** for two hours by the time the main group starts.

When communicating informally, you can use the present progressive tense to express future action. Be sure to include a word or a phrase that indicates the future.

We **are walking** in the walkathon *next Monday*.

Emphatic Forms. To use the emphatic form, use the present or the past tense of the verb *do* with the infinitive form of the main verb.

◆ RULE   Use the emphatic form to add emphasis or force to the present and past tenses of a verb.

Present Emphatic	We **do walk** every day when the weather is good.
Past Emphatic	We **did walk** before the snow began to accumulate.

Modals. Modals are the auxiliary verbs *can, could, do, did, may, might, must, shall, will,* and *would.* These auxiliary verbs are used with main verbs to add emphasis to a sentence or to provide shades of meaning.

◆ RULE   Use *can* (present tense) and *could* (past tense) to express ability to perform the action of the main verb.

> We **can** *call* home if we need to.
>
> We **could** have *taken* the car yesterday, but not today.

◆ RULE   Use *do* (present tense) and *did* (past tense) to make negative statements and to ask questions.

> We **do** not *walk* more than four miles without resting.
>
> **Did** you *walk* farther today than you did yesterday?

◆ RULE   Use *may* to mean "have permission to" or to express a possibility.

> His uncle said we **may** *go* now.
>
> We **may** *be* late if we do not hurry.

◆ RULE   Use *might,* the past tense of *may,* to express a possibility that is somewhat less likely than one expressed by *may.*

> There is always a chance that the exam **might** *be canceled.*

◆ RULE   Use *must* to convey the idea that the action of the main verb is required or to suggest a possible explanation.

> We **must** *return* immediately.
>
> We **must** *be* thoughtless to ask for such a favor.

◆ RULE   Use *should,* the past tense of *shall,* to suggest that something ought to happen or that, although something ought to happen, it may not.

> We **should** *call* home right now. [**Think:** We ought to call.]
>
> We **should** *be* home right now. [**Think:** We should be, but we aren't.]

◆ **RULE** Use *would,* the past tense of *will,* to express actions that were repeated in the past or to show that you disapproved of an action in the past.

In the winter we **would** *drive* to school every day. [repeated action]

We were always late. Well, we **would** *leave* everything until the last minute! [disapproval]

Sequence of Tenses

In most sentences, you use verbs that are in the same tense because the time periods described are the same. In some situations, however, you need to use verbs in different tenses to show a difference in time. You can show this difference in time effectively by changing not only the forms of the verbs but also the relationship of one verb to another.

Consistency of Tenses. When two or more actions take place at the same time, you should use verbs that are in the same tense, particularly when you write compound sentences and sentences with compound predicates. Also, remember to use the same verb tense throughout a paragraph unless the meaning of the paragraph requires that you shift tense.

◆ **RULE** Use verbs in the same tense to describe actions occurring at the same time.

	past		pres.
Incorrect	Hugh **held** the clutch in while the rest of us **push** the car.		

	past		past
Correct	Hugh **held** the clutch in while the rest of us **pushed** the car.		

Shifts in Tense. If you need to show a shift from one time period to another, be sure to indicate accurately the relationships between the tenses. By changing forms and tenses, you can express precisely the time sequence that is required.

◆ **RULE** If two actions occurred at different times in the past, use the past perfect tense for the earlier action and the past tense for the later one. To emphasize the closeness in time of two events, however, use the past tense for both.

earlier   later
past perf.   past
I **had waited** in line for hours before I **bought** my ticket. [actions that occurred at different times in the past]

earlier   later
past   past
We **traveled** for many miles and **reached** the coast by dark. [past actions that were close in time]

◆ RULE   If two actions occur in the present but one began in the past, use the present perfect tense for the earlier action and the present tense for the later one.

earlier
pres. perf.

later
pres.

Because she **has been making** calls all afternoon, Meg **feels** a sense of accomplishment.

◆ RULE   If two actions will occur in the future, use the future perfect tense for the action that will take place earlier and the future tense for the action that will occur later.

earlier
future perf.

Because we **will have been working** on this project for several weeks before

later
future

its deadline, we **will want** to finish it correctly.

2.2C ACTIVE VOICE AND PASSIVE VOICE

A verb is in the **active voice** when the subject performs the action of the verb. The active voice is generally a more direct and effective way of expressing action.

The *audience* **applauded** the orchestra's encore.

A verb is in the **passive voice** when the subject receives the action of the verb. Use the passive voice only when you want to emphasize the receiver of the action, or when the person or thing performing the action is unknown, or occasionally when there is no other way to write the sentence. Overuse of the passive voice quickly becomes tedious and weakens your writing.

◆ RULE   To form the passive voice, use a form of the verb *be* and the past participle of the main verb.

The orchestra's *encore* **was applauded** by the audience.

Only transitive verbs (page 583) can be used in the passive voice. Intransitive verbs (page 584) are always in the active voice because they do not take objects. When a verb in the active voice is changed to the passive voice, its direct object becomes the subject of the sentence, and the subject becomes the object of a preposition.

subj.   verb   D.O.

Active   The symphony *orchestra* **played** a Gershwin song.

subj.   verb   obj. of prep.

Passive   A Gershwin *song* **was played** by the symphony orchestra.

When you shift a transitive verb that has both a direct object and an indirect object to the passive voice, either object can become the subject. The other object, however, remains as the complement of the verb. An object that remains as a complement in a passive construction is called a **retained object.**

                subj. verb I.O.   D.O.

Active   His friends **gave** Bill a surprise party.

                subj. verb   D.O.

Passive   Bill **was given** a surprise party by his friends.

                                 retained

                  subj.   verb object

Passive   A surprise party **was given** Bill by his friends.

♦ RULE   Avoid shifting from the active voice to the passive voice when describing a series of events.

Incorrect

                       active   passive

The stable manager **fed** the horses, **was reminded** to change the straw in

              active

their stalls, and **gave** them fresh water.

Correct

                       active   active

The stable manager **fed** the horses, **remembered** to change the straw in

              active

their stalls, and **gave** them fresh water.

2.2D   MOOD

In addition to tense and voice, verbs also express mood. Although you use the indicative mood more frequently, the effective use of the imperative mood and the subjunctive mood will enhance your writing.

The Indicative and the Imperative Moods

♦ RULE   Use the indicative mood to make a statement of fact or to ask a question.

Thunder often **frightens** small children.

Did you **remember** the license plate number?

♦ RULE   Use the imperative mood to make a request or to give a command.

In the imperative mood, the subject of the sentence is often understood rather than stated. Use of the imperative mood adds directness and emphasis to your writing.

Consider taking the train the next time you travel.

Take all your belongings when you leave.

The Subjunctive Mood

Of the three moods, the subjunctive mood is the most infrequently used in conversation and in informal writing. It is primarily used in formal communications, especially in diplomatic statements and in parliamentary procedure. You also use the subjunctive mood, however, to make doubtful, wishful, or conditional statements; to express something that is contrary to fact; or to ask, insist, order, request, or propose in a respectful manner.

You can use verbs in the subjunctive mood in the present tense and in the past tense.

Present Subjunctive
If the truth **be** known, I am to be congratulated.

Past Subjunctive
If the truth **were** known, I should have been congratulated.

The most commonly used verb in the subjunctive mood is the verb *be,* used as a linking verb or as an auxiliary verb. Study the differences between the indicative mood and the subjunctive mood in this partial conjugation of the verb *be.*

	Indicative		Subjunctive	
Present	I am	we are	(if) I be	(if) we be
	you are	you are	(if) you be	(if) you be
	he is	they are	(if) he be	(if) they be
Past	I was	we were	(if) I were	(if) we were
	you were	you were	(if) you were	(if) you were
	he was	they were	(if) he were	(if) they were

◆ RULE   Use *be* for the present subjunctive of the verb *be* regardless of its subject.

Mrs. Penwell asks that her children **be** friendly to their neighbors.

◆ RULE   Use *were* for the past subjunctive of the verb *be* regardless of its subject.

If Rudy **were** a better actor, we wouldn't have known that he forgot a line.

♦ RULE   To form the present subjunctive of verbs other than *be,* use the infinitive form of the verb regardless of its subject.

Professor Art insists that the class **listen** attentively.

♦ RULE   To form the past subjunctive of the verbs other than *be,* use *had* as an auxiliary verb with the past participle of the main verb.

If I **had seen** her, I would have invited her too.

Had I known, I would have told you sooner.

♦ RULE   To express something that is not true or that you doubt will ever be true, use a verb in the subjunctive mood in a clause that begins with *if, as if, as though,* or *that.*

Notice that something that is contrary to fact is often expressed as a wish or a condition.

Because this has been such a long day, I wish *that* I **were** home. [I am not at home.]

If I **were** you, I would ask Diane before I borrowed her book. [I cannot be you; this statement is contrary to fact.]

♦ RULE   Use the subjunctive mood in clauses that begin with *that* and that follow verbs that (1) make requests, such as *ask, prefer,* and *request;* (2) make demands, such as *demand, determine, insist, order,* and *require;* and (3) make proposals, such as *move, propose, recommend,* and *suggest.*

These clauses often appear in formal usage, particularly in standard expressions used in parliamentary procedures.

Morris recommended that the session **be postponed.**

2.3 SUBJECT-VERB AGREEMENT

2.3A   SINGULAR AND PLURAL SUBJECTS AND VERBS

♦ RULE   A subject and its verb must agree in number.

You can change the forms of nouns, pronouns, and verbs to express number. If the subject is singular, the form of the verb should be singular. If the subject is plural, the form of the verb should be plural.

Singular

Grandma Moses **was** a primitive painter who lived on farms all her life.

Plural

> Her *paintings* **are** scenes of rural life.

Verb Phrases

For a verb phrase to agree with its subject, the auxiliary verb must agree in number with the subject.

	verb phrase
Singular	*Marianne* **has tried** some primitive landscapes.
	verb phrase
Plural	*Marianne and I* **have taken** art lessons together.

Intervening Words and Phrases

Sometimes, words and phrases come between a subject and its verb. Such intervening words or phrases do not change the number of the subject, and, as always, the verb must agree in number with the subject. Be sure to make the verb agree in number with the subject of the sentence, not with some word in the intervening phrase.

Singular

> *Grandma Moses,* a latecomer to oils, **was** seventy-six years old when she created her first painting. [**Think:** Grandma Moses *was.*]

Plural

> The *critics* viewing her one-artist show in 1940 **were impressed** with her naive realism. [**Think:** critics *were.*]

Inverted Word Order

In some sentences, especially questions or sentences beginning with *Here* or *There,* you may have difficulty locating the subject because the verb comes before the subject. By mentally rearranging the sentence in its normal subject-verb order, you can find the subject and make the verb agree with it in number.

Singular

> In the landscape **is** a peaceful *farm.* [**Think:** farm *is.*]

Plural

> There **are** many *scenes* of farm life. [**Think:** scenes *are.*]

Singular

> **Is** Uncle George or Aunt Susan meeting us at the exhibit? [**Think:** Aunt Susan *is.*]

Plural

> Here **are** a *painting* and an *embroidery* done by Grandma Moses. [**Think:** a painting and an embroidery *are.*]

2.3B   DETERMINING THE NUMBER OF THE SUBJECT

In some sentences, you may find it troublesome to determine the number of the subject. To avoid confusion, pay special attention to the following types of subjects.

Compound Subjects

A **compound subject** (page 596) is composed of two or more subjects that are connected by *and, or, nor, either . . . or,* or *neither . . . nor.* A compound subject may take a singular or a plural verb, depending on (1) which conjunction is used and (2) whether the words in the compound subject are singular or plural.

♦ RULE   Use a plural verb with most compound subjects connected by *and.*

Plural

The *Prime Minister and the President* **were** to attend the meeting.

♦ RULE   Use a singular verb with a compound subject that refers to one person or one thing or to something that is generally considered as a unit—that is, plural in form but singular in meaning.

Singular

This year's most popular *author and lecturer* **is addressing** our class tomorrow. [The author and lecturer are the same person.]

♦ RULE   Use a singular verb with a compound subject that is composed of singular nouns or pronouns connected by *or* or *nor.*

Singular   Either my *aunt or* my *uncle* **likes** to read poetry.

♦ RULE   Use a plural verb with a compound subject that is composed of plural nouns or pronouns connected by *or* or *nor.*

Plural   Neither the farmer's *goats nor* his *sheep* **have been sold.**

♦ RULE   When a compound subject is composed of a singular subject and a plural subject connected by *or* or *nor,* use a verb that agrees in number with the subject that is closer to the verb in the sentence.

Singular

pl.   — sing —

Neither the *musicians* nor the *conductor* **is** on stage.

Plural

sing.   — pl. —

Neither the team *manager* nor the *players* **agree** on the terms of the contract.

In following this rule, you may discover that some sentences sound awkward. In that case, rephrase the sentence.

The *musicians* **are** not on stage, and neither **is** the *conductor*.

◆ RULE   When the subject is both affirmative and negative, use a verb form that agrees in number with the affirmative part of the subject.

pl.   sing.   pl.
My brothers, not I, **are planning** to travel this summer.

Indefinite Pronouns as Subjects

Indefinite pronouns (pages 581–582) are pronouns that refer to people or things in general. Some indefinite pronouns are always singular and therefore always take singular verbs. The following are examples of singular indefinite pronouns:

anybody	everybody	nobody	other
anyone	everyone	no one	somebody
anything	everything	nothing	someone
each	much	one	something
either	neither		

Singular   Almost *everybody* **watches** television sometime.

Some indefinite pronouns are always plural and therefore always take plural verbs. The most common are *both, few, many,* and *several.*

Plural   *Many* **go** jogging in the park on Saturday morning.

The indefinite pronouns *all, any, enough, more, most, none, plenty,* and *some* may be singular or plural, depending on their antecedents (page 581).

Singular
All the music presented that day **was** enjoyable. [The indefinite pronoun refers to music; it is singular and takes the singular verb *was.*]

Plural
All the band's members **have** exceptional talent. [*All* refers to members; it is plural and takes the plural verb *have.*]

Sometimes an indefinite pronoun refers to a word that is understood rather than stated.

Even though *many* had gone, *most* **were** still at the party when we arrived. [The listener or reader would know that the pronouns refer to guests.]

Collective Nouns as Subjects

A **collective noun** (page 578) is a word that names a group of people or a collection of objects that is singular in form and may be either singular or plural in meaning. Examples include *committee, crowd, fleet, jury,* and *team.*

♦ RULE   If a collective noun refers to a group as a whole, use a singular verb.

Singular

The *crowd* **wants** action. [The crowd is thought of as a whole].

♦ RULE   If a collective noun refers to individual members or parts of a group, use a plural verb.

Plural

The *cast* **know** themselves well. [The members of the cast are acting as individuals.]

Nouns with Plural Form

Nouns such as *economics, mathematics, measles,* and *news* are plural in form but singular in meaning. Although they end in *-s,* they refer to a single thing or to a unit and therefore take a singular verb. (Notice that removing the *-s* does not make a singular noun.)

Singular   *Aeronautics* **is** a subject that I have never studied.

Other nouns, such as *clothes, congratulations, pliers,* and *scissors,* end in *-s* but take a plural verb even though they refer to one thing.

Plural   Your garden *shears* **are** on the workbench.

Some nouns, such as *athletics, dramatics,* and *politics,* end in *-s* but may be singular or plural, depending on their meaning in the sentence. Use your dictionary to find out whether a noun that ends in *-s* takes a singular verb or a plural one.

Singular   In her lecture she told us that *dramatics* **is** her avocation.

Plural   His *dramatics* **are** often ignored by his friends.

Titles and Names as Subjects

Titles of individual books, stories, plays, movies, television programs, musical compositions, and magazines take the singular form of the verb even though the titles may contain plural words. The name of a country or of an organization also takes a singular verb when it refers to an entire country or group. (See pages 661 and 665 for rules regarding capitalization and underlining, or italics, for titles.)

Singular

Hemingway's *A Farewell to Arms* **was made** into a movie.

Singular

The *United Nations* often **sends** peacekeeping forces into troubled areas.

Words of Amount and Time

◆ RULE   Use singular verbs with words and phrases that refer to single units: fractions, measurements, amounts of money, weights, volumes, and intervals of time when the interval refers to a specific unit.

Singular   *One hundred yards* **is** the length of a football field.

◆ RULE   Use a plural verb when the amount or the time is considered to be a number of separate units.

Plural   *Five quarters* **are** all that you need to do the laundry.

When you use *the number* or *the variety* as a subject, you usually use a singular verb. When you use *a number* or *a variety* as a subject, you usually use a plural verb.

Singular   *The variety* of plants at the garden shop **is** amazing.

Plural   *A variety* of plants **are** for sale at the garden shop.

2.3C   PROBLEMS IN AGREEMENT

Inverted Word Order.   In some sentences, especially questions or sentences beginning with *Here* or *There,* you may have difficulty locating the subject because the verb comes before the subject. By mentally rearranging the sentence in its normal subject-verb order, you can find the subject and make the verb agree with it in number.

Singular

Near the building **was** a public park. [**Think:** park **was.**]

Plural

There **are** many ideas to be explored. [**Think:** ideas **are.**]

Singular

Is Uncle George or Aunt Susan meeting us at the restaurant? [**Think:** Aunt Susan **is.**]

Plural

Here **are** the coat and the shirt that you ordered. [**Think:** the coat and the shirt **are.**]

Sentences with Predicate Nominatives.   Using a predicate nominative (page 600) can confuse subject-verb agreement when the subject and the predicate nominative differ in number.

◆ RULE   Use a verb that agrees in number with the subject, not with the predicate nominative.

Incorrect

Violets **is** one of her favorite flowers.

Correct

    subj.   P.N.

Violets **are** one of her favorite flowers. [plural subject; singular predicate nominative]

Agreement in Adjective Clauses. When a relative pronoun, such as *who, which,* or *that,* is the subject of an adjective clause (pages 610–611), decide whether the verb of the adjective clause should be singular or plural by finding the antecedent (see below), of the relative pronoun.

◆ RULE   The verb of an adjective clause and the antecedent of the relative pronoun must agree in number.

Singular

Willie Mays, who **was** one of baseball's greatest center fielders, used to make spectacular catches. [*Who* refers to *Willie Mays,* the singular subject.]

Plural

People who **do** a job well seem to feel better about themselves. [*Who* refers to *People,* the plural subject.]

◆ RULE   When an adjective clause follows the term *one of those,* use a plural verb in the clause.

Plural

Yesterday's assignment is *one of those* that **are** meant to be a challenge.

Every* and *Many a. As adjectives, *every* and *many a* (or *many an*) emphasize separateness when they modify subjects. *Every* teacher means "every single teacher," not "all teachers"; *many a teacher* means that each teacher is separate from all the other teachers.

◆ RULE   Use a singular verb with a single subject and with a compound subject modified by *every, many a,* or *many an.*

Every teacher and student **wants** to be at the meeting.

Many a teacher **corrects** papers every night.

2.4 CORRECT USE OF PRONOUNS

2.4A PRONOUN ANTECEDENTS

All pronouns, whether they are personal, indefinite, relative, reflexive, or intensive (see pages 579–582), must agree with their antecedents in number, gender, and person (page 579).

Agreement in Number

◆ **RULE** Use a singular pronoun to refer to or to replace a singular antecedent; use a plural pronoun to refer to or to replace a plural antecedent.

Singular	Plural
I, me, my, mine	we, us, our, ours
you, your, yours	you, your, yours
he, him, his	they, them, their, theirs
she, her, hers	
it, its	

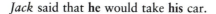

Singular   *Jack* said that **he** would take **his** car.

Plural   Jack's *friends* said that **they** would take **their** cars.

◆ **RULE** Use a plural pronoun to refer to or to replace two or more singular antecedents joined by *and;* use a singular pronoun to refer to or to replace two or more singular antecedents joined by *or* or *nor.*

Jack and Rick went to hear **their** favorite singer.

Neither Jack nor Rick wanted to drive **his** car.

Indefinite Pronouns as Antecedents. The following indefinite pronouns are singular in meaning. Use singular pronouns to refer to or to replace them.

anybody	everybody	nobody	other
anyone	everyone	no one	somebody
anything	everything	nothing	someone
each	much	one	something
either	neither		

Singular   *Each* of the women paid for **her** own ticket.

In sentences where the intended meaning of a singular indefinite pronoun is plural, use a plural pronoun to refer to or to replace the antecedent. For example, it is not sensible to use a singular pronoun in the following sentence.

Unclear

When *everybody* arrived at the theater, **he** or **she** bought a ticket and went inside.

Because the antecedent *everybody* really means *all* and not *each person individually,* you should use a plural pronoun or, preferably, rewrite the sentence to avoid the awkward construction.

Clear

When *everybody* arrived at the theater, **they** bought tickets and went inside.

Better

When *all* of the people arrived at the theater, **they** bought tickets and went inside.

Some indefinite pronouns, such as *several, both, few,* and *many,* are plural in meaning; use plural pronouns to refer to or to replace them.

Plural   *Several* of the students made **their** own lunches.

Some indefinite pronouns, such as *all, any, enough, more, most, none, plenty,* and *some,* can be either singular or plural. Use either singular or plural pronouns to refer to or to replace them, depending on the meaning of the sentence.

Singular

All of the color in the painting had lost **its** vibrancy. [*All* refers to *color,* which is singular; *its* refers to *all.*]

Plural

All of the books need to have **their** bindings replaced. [*All* refers to *books,* which is plural; *their* refers to *all.*]

Collective Nouns as Antecedents. When an antecedent is a collective noun (page 578), you must first determine whether the collective noun is singular or plural in meaning. If it is singular, use a singular pronoun to refer to or to replace it; if it is plural, use a plural pronoun to refer to it.

Singular

The ad hoc *committee* voted to change **its** meeting time. [The meeting time is for the entire committee as a unit.]

Plural

The ad hoc *committee* voted to increase **their** salaries. [The committee voted for individual salaries.]

Agreement in Gender

The gender (page 579) of a noun or a pronoun is either masculine, feminine, or neuter. The masculine pronouns are *he, him,* and *his;* the feminine pronouns are *she, her,* and *hers;* and the neuter pronouns, those referring to neither masculine nor feminine antecedents, are *it* and *its.*

◆ RULE   Use a pronoun that agrees in gender with its antecedent.

Masculine	*Martin Luther King, Jr.,* motivated **his** followers to take action.
Feminine	*Flannery O'Connor* based **her** stories on **her** own experience.
Neuter	A *ship* has to have **its** keel scraped annually.

Sometimes it is unclear whether the gender of a singular antecedent is masculine or feminine. If a neuter pronoun will not work, you can use the phrase *his or her* to show that the antecedent could be either masculine or feminine. This construction, however, is often awkward. If possible, rewrite the sentence so that the antecedent and all words that refer to it or replace it are plural. Sometimes you can repeat the noun that is the antecedent.

Awkward	A *lawyer* has a confidential relationship with **his or her** clients.
Better	*Lawyers* have confidential relationships with **their** clients.

Agreement in Person

Pronouns are in either the first person, the second person, or the third person (page 580).

◆ RULE   Use a pronoun that agrees in person with its antecedent.

First Person	*I* will graduate from college before **my** brother does.
Second Person	Will *you* graduate from college before **your** brother does?
Third Person	*Harriet* will graduate from college before **her** brother does.

When the indefinite pronoun *one* is an antecedent, use a third-person singular pronoun to refer to it or to replace it, or repeat the indefinite pronoun.

One often feels that **he or she** is under a microscope during exam time.

One often feels that **one** is under a microscope during exam time.

Note: In general, do not use *he* to represent both *he* and *she.* You should either repeat the noun or pronoun that is the antecedent or rewrite the sentence to make both the antecedent and the pronoun plural.

Agreement of Reflexive and Intensive Pronouns

Reflexive and intensive pronouns (pages 580–581), formed by adding either *-self* or *-selves* to personal pronouns, must also agree with their antecedents in number, gender, and person. Reflexive and intensive pronouns are always used with antecedents. Do not use them alone to replace a noun or a personal pronoun.

Incorrect
For the first time, Robert and I are filing income tax forms by themselves.

Incorrect
For the first time, Robert and myself are filing income tax forms.

Correct

reflexive
For the first time, Robert and I are filing income tax forms by **ourselves.**

Correct

intensive
The supervisor **herself** authorized the move.

2.4B   PRONOUN CASE

To show the grammatical use of a pronoun in a sentence, you change its form, or **case.** The three cases are nominative, objective, and possessive.

	Singular	Plural
Nominative Case	I	we
	you	you
	he, she, it	they
Objective Case	me	us
	you	you
	him, her, it	them
Possessive Case*	my, mine	our, ours
	your, yours	your, yours
	his, her, hers, its	their, theirs

Pronouns in the Nominative Case

◆ RULE   Use the nominative case when a pronoun acts as a subject (page 597), as a predicate nominative (page 600), or as an appositive to a subject or to a predicate nominative (pages 603–604).

Subject
I would like to speak to Rosalie, please.

Predicate Nominative
This is **she.** To whom am I speaking?

---

* The pronouns *my, your, his, her, its, our,* and *their* are sometimes called pronominal adjectives (page 587).

Appositive to a Subject
Your *friends,* **Sandy and I,** would like you to go to the game with us. [**Think:** Sandy and I would like.]

Appositive to a Predicate Nominative
We are the *friends,* **Sandy and I,** who helped you with your science project. [**Think:** We are Sandy and I.]

Pronouns in the Objective Case

◆ RULE   Use the objective case when a pronoun acts as a direct object (page 599), as an indirect object (page 599), as an objective complement (page 599), as an object of a preposition (page 591), as a subject of the infinitive clause (page 608), as an appositive to a direct or an indirect object (pages 603–604), or as an appositive to an object of a preposition (pages 590–592).

Direct Object
Mara met **her** just before school began.

Indirect Object
She lent **her** a notebook for her first class.

Object of a Preposition
Nancy gave it back to **her** after her class.

Subject of an Infinitive Clause
Mr. Mitchell told **them** to see him after school.

Object of an Infinitive Clause
Mara wanted to ask **him** why he wanted to see **them.**

Appositive to a Direct Object
She liked her *friends,* **Mara and her.**

Appositive to an Indirect Object
She told *them,* **Mara and her,** the whole story.

Appositive to an Object of a Preposition
Mr. Mitchell wanted to read over their papers with both of *them,* **Mara and her.**

Pronouns in the Possessive Case

Possessive pronouns show to whom or to what something belongs. They do not include apostrophes.

◆ RULE   Use the possessive pronouns *mine, yours, his, hers, its, ours,* and *theirs* to refer to or to replace nouns.

You can use these possessive pronouns in the same way that you would use nouns: as subjects, predicate nominatives, direct or indirect objects, objects of prepositions, or appositives.

Subject
> **Hers** is the short story that won first place.

Predicate Nominative
> The second-place short story is **his.**

Direct Object
> After thinking about the plot for a long time, Kathleen wrote **hers** in two hours.

Indirect Object
> Carl gave **hers** a rave review.

Object of a Preposition
> We should really find a publisher for **theirs.**

Appositive
> A publisher has requested that both *stories,* **hers** and **his,** be submitted at once.

◆ RULE   Use the possessive pronouns* *my, your, his, her, its, our,* and *their* to modify nouns.

> Will you visit *your* grandparents this summer?

◆ RULE   Use a possessive pronoun to modify a gerund.

Gerunds (pages 606–607) are *-ing* forms of verbs that are used as nouns. Because they function as nouns, use the possessive forms of nouns and pronouns to modify them.

> **Your** visiting your grandparents will be a great pleasure for them. [*Your* is used instead of *you* because it is the *visiting—your visiting—*that will be a great pleasure for them.]

Compound Constructions with Pronouns

It is sometimes troublesome to choose the correct case for pronouns in compound constructions, such as compound subjects or compound objects of a preposition. To determine which case you should use, say the sentence to yourself, leaving out the conjunction and the noun or the other pronoun in the compound construction. When you have determined how the pronoun functions by itself, you can decide whether to use the nominative case or the objective case.

---

* These possessive pronouns are sometimes called pronominal adjectives (page 587).

Thomas and **they** are responsible for the decorations. [**Think:** *They* are responsible for the decorations.]

Between you and **me**, I think David deserved to win. [Because *you* and *me* are compound objects of the preposition *between,* use a pronoun in the objective case, *me.*]

Who and *Whom*

You can use the forms of the word *who* either as interrogative pronouns (page 581) or as relative pronouns (page 581). As is true of other pronouns, the way that you use the pronoun determines which case or form of the word you should choose. *Who* and *whoever* are in the nominative case; *whom* and *whomever* are in the objective case; *whose* is in the possessive case.

Who and Whom as Interrogative Pronouns. *Who* and *whom* are interrogative pronouns when they introduce questions. To determine whether to use *who* (the nominative case) or *whom* (the objective case), simply turn the question into a statement.

♦ RULE Use *who* when an interrogative pronoun acts as a subject or as a predicate nominative. Use *whom* when an interrogative pronoun acts either as an object of a verb or as an object of a preposition.

Nominative
  Who is singing the lead in *Madame Butterfly?* [*Who* is the subject of the verb *is singing.*]

Objective
  To **whom** did you speak when you telephoned the White House today? [*Whom* is the object of the preposition *to.*]

If the interrogative pronoun *who* or *whom* is followed by an interrupting phrase, such as *do you feel,* you can mentally rearrange the sentence to determine the use of the pronoun in the sentence and which form of the pronoun to use.

Who do you feel will best fill the position of vice president? [**Think:** Who will best fill the position? *Who* is the subject.]

In informal writing and in conversation, *who* is often used to ask a question, regardless of whether the nominative or the objective case is needed. In formal usage, however, you should follow the rules for using the nominative case, *who,* and the objective case, *whom.*

Informal   **Who** do you plan to go with to the movie?

Formal   With **whom** will you attend the plenary session next week?

Who and *Whom* as Relative Pronouns. When forms of the word *who* introduce subordinate clauses (pages 647–648), they are relative pronouns. Choose the form of the word to use by its use in the subordinate clause, *not* by its use in the main clause.

◆ RULE   Use *who* or *whoever* when a relative pronoun is the subject of the subordinate clause; use *whom* or *whomever* when a relative pronoun is an object within the subordinate clause.

> The new teacher, **who** has been here only a week, has made many friends among the students and faculty. [*Who* is the subject of the clause *who has been here only a week.*]

> My mother, **whom** many people respect, was honored at a testimonial dinner. [*Whom* is the direct object of *respect.*]

Pronouns in Appositive Phrases

The pronouns *we* and *us* are often used in appositive phrases, such as *we engineers* or *us pilots.* Because an appositive explains or renames the word with which it is in apposition, you must first determine how the appositive phrase is used in the sentence. If the phrase is a subject or a predicate nominative, use the nominative case of the pronoun. If the phrase is an object, use the objective case.

To determine which case to use, say the sentence to yourself without the noun in the appositive phrase.

Nominative
> **We engineers** attended the computer conference in Los Angeles last April. [**Think:** We attended. Because *we* and *engineers* are subjects, *we* is in the nominative case.]

Objective
> The refresher course for **us pilots** will be given again in the spring. [**Think:** The refresher course for **us.** Because *us* and *pilots* are objects of the preposition *for, us* is in the objective case.]

Pronouns in Comparisons

In some comparisons using *than* or *as,* part of the phrase or clause is not stated but is merely implied. To choose the correct pronoun, mentally supply the missing words to determine how the pronoun is used. Because the case of the pronoun used in an incomplete comparison can alter your intended meaning, make your choice carefully. In the following examples, notice the change in meaning according to the choice of pronoun.

Nominative
> I will walk as far with you as **she.** [**Think:** as far as she will walk. Use the nominative-case pronoun because *she* is the subject of the implied clause, *she will walk with you.*]

Objective

I will walk as far with you as **her**. [**Think:** as far with you as with her. Use the objective-case pronoun *her* because the intended meaning makes *her* the object of the implied preposition *with*.]

2.4C CORRECT PRONOUN REFERENCE

To avoid confusing your listeners or readers, be certain that the pronouns you use refer clearly to their antecedents. If you find an unclear reference, rephrase the sentence.

◆ RULE   Avoid using a pronoun that could refer to more than one antecedent.

Unclear

Jerry picked Bill to be on his team because he knows the game well. [Who knows the game well? The antecedent of *he* is unclear.]

Clear

Jerry picked Bill to be on his team because Bill knows the game well.

◆ RULE   In formal usage, avoid using the pronoun *it, they, you,* or *your* without a clear antecedent.

The following example shows how you can usually replace the pronoun with a noun to eliminate confusion.

Unclear

I forgot my umbrella and my flashlight. When I thought about it, I laughed. [What is *it?* The pronoun has no clear antecedent.]

Clear

I forgot my umbrella and my flashlight. When I thought about my forgetfulness, I laughed.

◆ RULE   Do not use the pronoun *your* in place of an article (*a, an,* or *the*) if possession is not involved.

Avoid   Many of your gymnasts have been training for years.

Use   Many gymnasts have been training for years.

◆ RULE   Avoid using *which, it, this,* and *that* to refer to ideas that are not clearly stated.

The following example demonstrates how you can avoid making such general references.

General

We went to every game in the series, but we didn't see anyone hit a home run, which was quite disappointing. [The pronoun *which* has no clear antecedent; instead, *which* refers generally to an idea in the previous sentence.]

Clear

We went to every game in the series, but we were quite disappointed because we didn't see anyone hit a home run.

2.5 CORRECT USE OF MODIFIERS

2.5A COMPARISON OF MODIFIERS

By using different forms of adjectives and adverbs, you can compare two or more persons or things. The three degrees of comparison are positive, comparative, and superlative.

The Three Degrees of Comparison

You use a modifier in the **positive degree** to assign some quality to a person, a thing, an action, or an idea. You use a modifier in the **comparative degree** to compare a person, a thing, an action, or an idea with another one. You use a modifier in the **superlative degree** to compare a person, a thing, an action, or an idea with at least two others.

	Adjectives
Positive	That line is **long.**
Comparative	That line is **longer** than the one for the other movie.
Superlative	That line is the **longest** one that I have ever seen.

	Adverbs
Positive	Roger behaves **maturely.**
Comparative	Roger behaves **more maturely** than Eric.
Superlative	Of all the students, Roger behaves the **most maturely.**

Using Comparisons Correctly

◆ **RULE** Add the suffix *-er* to form the comparative and the suffix *-est* to form the superlative of modifiers with one or two syllables.

In some cases, to form the comparative modifier correctly, you must drop a final *-e,* double a final consonant, or change a final *-y* to *-i* before adding the suffix.

short, shorter, shortest

funny, funnier, funniest

◆ **RULE**   Use *more* to show the comparative degree and *most* to show the superlative degree in three instances: with all three-syllable words, with two-syllable words that would otherwise be difficult to pronounce, and with adverbs ending in *-ly*.

> serious, more serious, most serious
> dreadful, more dreadful, most dreadful
> restfully, more restfully, most restfully

◆ **RULE**   Use *less* and *least* to form the comparative and superlative degrees of comparisons showing less.

> humorous, less humorous, least humorous
> hopeful, less hopeful, least hopeful
> ambitiously, less ambitiously, least ambitiously

Remember, also, that some modifiers are irregular and do not form comparisons in a standard way. You should memorize them to be able to use them correctly.

bad, worse, worst	little, less, least
far, farther, farthest	many, more, most
far, further, furthest	much, more, most
good, better, best	well, better, best
ill, worse, worst	

◆ **RULE**   Avoid double comparisons. Use either the word *more* or *most* or the appropriate suffix; do not combine the two.

> Incorrect   Jim is **more funnier** than anyone else in the group.
>
> Correct   Jim is **funnier** than anyone else in the group.

◆ **RULE**   Avoid incomplete comparisons by clearly indicating the things being compared.

When you compare one member of a group with the rest of the group, you can avoid being unclear or misleading by using the comparative degree and the word *other* or *else*.

Unclear

> Richard plays the oboe better than anyone in the class. [This sentence says either that Richard plays the oboe better than anyone in the class, including himself, or that Richard plays the oboe better than anyone in a class of which he is not a part.]

Clear

> Richard can play the oboe better than anyone **else** in the class. [Richard is the best oboe player in **his** class.]

♦ **RULE**   Use the words *as . . . as* or *as . . . as . . . than* to complete a compound comparison.

A **compound comparison** really makes two statements by using both the positive and the comparative degrees of a modifier. The positive degree shows that the things being compared are at least equal or similar; the comparative degree shows that they may, in fact, be different. Because you would still have a complete sentence if you removed the second, or parenthetical, part of the comparison, use commas to set off the parenthetical part from the rest of the sentence.

> Being on time to my 8:00 A.M. class is **as** difficult **as,** if not more difficult **than,** being on time to my 7:00 A.M. class.

> Being on time for my 8:00 A.M. class is **as** difficult **as** being on time to my 7:00 A.M. class, if not more difficult.

♦ **RULE**   Avoid making comparisons that are illogical because of missing or faulty elements or because no comparison can be made.

To avoid having your reader or listener misunderstand your meaning, rephrase the comparison to include all the important words.

Illogical
> Sarah writes computer programs that are as complicated as Francine. [Computer programs cannot be compared to Francine. Sarah can write programs; she cannot write Francine.]

Logical
> Sarah writes computer programs that are as complicated as Francine's. [**Think:** Sarah's programs are as complicated as Francine's programs.]

Certain adjectives, such as *perfect, unique, dead, round, full,* and *empty,* do not have a comparative or superlative degree because they express an absolute condition. Because logically nothing can be "more perfect" or "more empty," use the forms *more nearly* or *most nearly* when you use these words in comparisons.

> Jim's plate was the most nearly empty at the end of the meal.

2.5B   PLACEMENT OF PHRASES AND CLAUSES

♦ **RULE**   Place modifying phrases and clauses as close as possible to the words that they modify.

Misplacement of phrases and clauses can create unclear and unintentionally humorous sentences. To avoid misplacing modifiers, identify the word to be modified and place the modifying phrase or clause as close as possible to that word while retaining your intended meaning.

Unclear

    Mrs. Santos decided to support the referendum, persuaded by the editorial. [The phrase *persuaded by the editorial* appears to be modifying *referendum*, thereby distorting the meaning of the sentence.]

Clear

    Mrs. Santos, persuaded by the editorial, decided to support the referendum.

Clear

    Persuaded by the editorial, Mrs. Santos decided to support the referendum.

Notice in the following example that improper placement of the modifying phrase can alter the meaning of the sentence. As you revise your sentences, check to be certain that your intended meaning is still clear.

Unclear

    Strolling by the lake, a family of ducks walked in front of me. [Who was strolling by the lake?]

Clear

    Strolling by the lake, I noticed a family of ducks in front of me. [Meaning: I was strolling by the lake when I noticed the ducks in front of me.]

Clear

    In front of me, I noticed a family of ducks strolling by the lake. [Meaning: The ducks were strolling by the lake.]

◆ RULE To avoid dangling modifiers, provide an antecedent for every modifying phrase or clause to modify.

A **dangling modifier** is a modifying phrase or clause that does not clearly or logically modify any word in the sentence; a dangling modifier can make a sentence unclear or unintentionally humorous.

Unclear

    Before going home, the door must be locked. [Who is going home?]

Clear

    Before going home, you must lock the door. [The adverb phrase *before going home* now modifies the verb phrase *must lock*.]

You can also correct a dangling phrase by changing the phrase to a subordinate clause.

    Clear   Before you go home, the door must be locked.

In current usage some dangling modifiers have become accepted as part of idiomatic expressions. These are usually such present and past participles as *allowing for, based on, considering, concerning, failing, generally speaking, granting, judging,* and *owing to.*

Judging from the cover, the magazine is about computers.

Based on available information, the scholarship committee won't be meeting until July.

You can determine whether an expression is acceptable even though it may seem to be a dangling modifier by asking yourself these questions: "Does the reader expect a word for the phrase to modify, or is the phrase or clause common enough to be considered an idiom? Is the meaning of the sentence clear?"

2.6   USAGE GLOSSARY

a lot, alot   *A lot* means "a great number or amount" and is always two words; avoid using *a lot* in formal usage. *Alot* is not a word.

accept, except   *Accept* is a verb that means "to agree" or "to receive." *Except* is a preposition that means "leaving out" or "but."

> We did not want to **accept** the expensive gift.

> Beth has taken every art course offered by the school, **except** the course on silk screening.

adapt, adopt   *Adapt* means "to change or adjust" or "to make more suitable." *Adopt* means "to take or accept."

> Since he had always lived in a warm climate, it took Jeremy several months to **adapt** to our cold climate.

> The Macintosh family has decided to **adopt** a child.

advice, advise   *Advice* is a noun that means "helpful suggestion or opinion." *Advise* is a verb that means "to give or offer counsel."

> My accountant **advised** me to file my income tax forms on time. Unfortunately, I did not follow that **advice.**

affect, effect   *Affect* is a verb that means "to influence." *Effect* can be a verb that means "to bring about or achieve" or a noun that means "result."

> Because our town was not directly **affected** by the flood, we could offer refuge to several families who were forced out.

> The severe storm **effected** a change in our travel plans. [verb meaning "brought about"]

> The **effects** of the flood were less extreme than we had thought. [noun meaning "results"]

all ready, already   *All ready* functions as a compound adjective that means "entirely ready" or "prepared." *Already* is an adverb that means "before some specified time" or "previously." Do not confuse the two.

> Are you **all ready** to begin the test?

> I can't believe that you've **already** finished that typing!

all right, alright   *All right* means "satisfactory," "unhurt," "correct," or "yes, very well." *Alright* is an incorrect spelling. Do not use it.

> Because we were so late, we telephoned Uncle Jack to let him know that we were **all right.**

> **All right,** who has a better suggestion?

All the farther, as far as   *All the farther* should not be used for *as far as.*

> Two miles is **as far as** I will run today. [not *all the farther*]

among, between   Use *among* for comparisons involving groups of persons or things. Use *between* when only two items are being considered at a time.

> Only one **among** all the race car drivers would win.

> Can you tell the difference **between** a jonquil and a daffodil?

amount, number   Use *amount* with a noun that names something that can be measured or weighed. Use *number* to refer to things that can be counted.

> A large **amount** of snow fell last night.

> A large **number** of snowstorms are expected next winter.

anxious, eager Both words can mean "strongly desirous," but you should use *anxious* to suggest concern or worry.

> Abigail was **anxious** to get to work before the storm broke.

any more, anymore These terms are not interchangeable. The phrase *any more* describes quantity; *any* is an adverb modifying the adjective *more*. *Anymore* is an adverb meaning "at present" or "from now on."

> Is there **any more** traffic on the bridge than there is in the tunnel?

> I don't drive to work **anymore**.

appraise, apprise *Appraise* means "to evaluate"; *apprise* means "to inform."

> Having **appraised** the old desk, the antiques dealer **apprised** its owner that it was worth one thousand dollars.

apt, liable, likely In informal usage, these words are often used interchangeably. In formal usage, only *apt* and *likely* are interchangeable, meaning "tending to" or "inclined to be." Use *liable* to suggest the probability of a harmful, unfortunate, or negative event or to show exposure to legal action.

> Robert is **apt** to be unpleasant when he first awakens in the morning.

> Mark is **liable** to strain a muscle during the game if he doesn't start practicing more regularly.

> Barbara was **liable** for damages when her daughter accidentally knocked over a carton of glassware in the department store.

as, like In formal usage, *like* is most often used as a preposition to introduce a prepositional phrase. *As* is most often used as a conjunction to introduce a subordinate clause.

> Margot thinks **like** her father. [prepositional phrase]

> Margot thinks **as** her father does. [subordinate clause]

In informal usage, *like* is sometimes used as a conjunction. Avoid using *like* as a conjunction in formal usage in place of *as, as if,* or *as though.*

> Avoid   The hikers felt **like** they had walked twenty miles.

> Use   The hikers felt **as if** they had walked twenty miles.

beside, besides *Beside* means "next to." *Besides* means "in addition to."

> I parked the car **beside** our neighbor's truck.

> **Besides** a truck, our neighbor owns a station wagon.

between, among See *among, between.*

between you and me Never use the nominative case *I* as the object of a preposition. *Between* is a preposition.

> The discussion is **between you and me.** [not *between you and I*]

both, either, neither When used to modify compound elements, place *both, either,* and *neither* just before the compound construction. The elements in the compound construction should be parallel or similar in form.

> Incorrect   Nelson intends **both** to study business and engineering.

> Correct   Nelson intends to study **both** *business* and *engineering.*

bring, take Use *bring* when you mean "to carry to." Use *take* when you mean "to carry away."

> **Bring** your swimming suit with you when you come to the party.

> Remember, **take** your swimming suit with you when you go to the party.

compare to, compare with Use *compare to* when pointing out similarities; use *compare with* when pointing out similarities and differences.

> In that metaphor the bright yellow flowers are **compared to** sunshine.

> **Compared with** a tornado, this is a minor windstorm.

credible, creditable, credulous *Credible* means "believable" or "worthy of belief." *Creditable* means "worthy of commendation." *Credulous* applies always to people and means "willing to believe" or "gullible."

> It was a **credible** story; we did not need to force ourselves to become involved in the plot.

> The movie director did a **creditable** job; the movie won three awards.

> Rick is a **credulous** young man; he thought that the science fiction about robots running the Pentagon was true.

data is, data are   *Data* is the plural form of the Latin *datum.* In formal English it should be followed by a plural verb. In informal English a singular verb may be used.

differ from, differ with   Things (or persons) *differ from* each other if they are physically dissimilar. When persons *differ with* each other, they are in disagreement.

>   Children **differ from** adults.

>   I **differ with** Hank about the need for a new stadium.

different from, different than   Use *different from.* Do not use *different than* except to introduce a subordinate clause.

>   My ideas are **different from** hers. [not *different than*]

>   My ideas are **different than** *hers are.*

disinterested, uninterested   *Disinterested* implies a lack of self-interest; it is synonymous with *unbiased* or *impartial. Uninterested* implies a lack of any interest.

>   Although I am **disinterested** in which party wins the court case, I am not **uninterested** in the principles of law that are being challenged by the case.

eager, anxious   See *anxious, eager.*

effect, affect   See *affect, effect.*

e.g., i.e.   *E.g.* stands for the Latin words *exempli gratia,* meaning roughly "an example for free." *E.g.* means "for example" in English. *I.e.* stands for the Latin words *id est,* meaning "that is," and should be used to cite an equivalent. Use both sparingly.

either, both, neither   See *both, either, neither.*

eminent, imminent   *Eminent* means "prominent" or "outstanding in some way." *Imminent* means "about to occur."

>   We were fortunate that the **eminent** historian agreed to visit our school.

>   The heavy, dark clouds indicated that a storm was **imminent.**

et al.   This is a Latin abbreviation for *et alii* and means "and others" (persons, not things). It is used most often in footnotes to refer to other members of a team of authors.

etc.   This Latin abbreviation for *et cetera* means "and other things," "and so forth." Avoid using *etc.* in formal writing; use *and so forth* instead. Do not use *and etc.;* it is redundant.

except, accept   See *accept, except.*

explicit, implicit   These adjectives are antonyms. *Explicit* refers to something that is directly stated. *Implicit* refers to something that is not directly stated.

>   Patty was **explicit** in her description of the swearing-in ceremonies.

>   Betty's feelings about her mother were **implicit** in her willingness to help her in any way she could.

famous, noted, notorious   *Famous* means "renowned or celebrated." *Noted* means "celebrated." *Notorious* means "known widely and regarded unfavorably."

>   The **famous** (*or* **noted**) economist predicted that inflation would continue.

>   The **notorious** prankster was finally caught and punished.

farther, further   These two words are not interchangeable. *Farther* means "more distant in space." *Further* means "more distant in time or degree, additional."

>   Bill swam **farther** than Tom did.

>   The **further** you investigate this story, the more confused the facts seem to be.

>   Conway **further** discussed his ideas about pedestrian safety.

fewer, less   Use *fewer* to refer to things that you can count individually. Use *less* to refer to quantities that you cannot count and to amounts of time, money, or distance when the amount is a single quantity.

>   There were **fewer** requests for help this week than last week.

>   I have **less** trouble with number concepts than he does.

>   I have **less** than three dollars in my pocket.

first, firstly; second, secondly   Use *first* and *second,* not *firstly* and *secondly* to mean "in the first (or second) place."

>   **First,** put the flowers into a vase. [not *Firstly*]

formally, formerly   These two words sometimes sound alike but have distinct spellings and meanings. *Formally* means "in a formal or official manner." *Formerly* means "previously" or "at an earlier time."

> Beth spoke **formally** to the audience.

> He **formerly** was a doctor.

further, farther   See *farther, further.*

good, well   *Good* is an adjective. *Well* can be an adverb or a predicate adjective meaning "satisfactory" or "in good health." The opposite of feeling sick is feeling *well.*

> Fuller is a **good** writer.

> Oliver teaches **well.**

> Are you feeling **well?**

half a   Use *a half* or *half a(n).* Do not use *a half a(n).*

> Will drove by about **a half** hour ago. [not *a half an hour*]

have, of   *Have* and *of* sound similar in rapid speech, but they are different parts of speech. *Have* is a verb; *of* is a preposition. Be careful to say and write *have* when completing a verb phrase, especially after the helping (auxiliary) verbs *should, would,* and *could. Of* is not a verb.

> We **should have** visited him earlier. [not *should of*]

hopefully   *Hopefully* means "with hope," not "I hope."

> **Unclear**   Hopefully, I will deliver my speech. [Do you hope to deliver your speech or will you deliver a hopeful speech?]

> **Improved**   I hope to deliver my speech.

i.e., e.g.   See *e.g., i.e.*

imminent, eminent   See *eminent, imminent.*

implicit, explicit   See *explicit, implicit.*

imply, infer   *Imply* means "to hint at" or "to suggest." *Infer* means "to reach a conclusion based on evidence or deduction." These words are not interchangeable.

> I **implied** in my remarks that the council should approve the plans to build a new school.

> I **inferred** from the applause that followed my remarks that the audience supported my suggestion.

in, into   Use *in* to mean "within" and *into* to suggest movement toward the inside from the outside.

> Ruth walked **into** the store to buy supplies for the camping trip.

> While she was **in** the store, she found the lantern that she wanted.

ingenious, ingenuous   *Ingenious* means "clever"; *ingenuous* means "naive."

> The **ingenious** child was always trying to invent questions that we couldn't answer.

> The newcomer was so **ingenuous** that we had to explain even the most basic things to him.

irregardless, regardless   Do not use *irregardless;* it is a double negative. Use *regardless* instead.

> We will call you when we arrive, **regardless** of the time.

its, it's   *Its* is a possessive pronoun; *it's* is the contraction for *it is.*

> The bear was standing on **its** hind legs, ready to attack.

> **It's** a nice day, so leave your heavy jacket at home.

kind of, sort of   Do not use these terms to mean "somewhat" or "rather." See also *these kinds, this kind.*

> The casserole is **rather** tasty. [not *kind of* or *sort of*]

lay, lie   *Lay* is a transitive verb that means "to put or to place something somewhere." It always takes a direct object. *Lie* is an intransitive verb that means "to be in or to assume a reclining position." It does not take a direct object. (See page 624 for the principal parts of these irregular verbs.)

> **Lay** the placemats on the table before you **lie** down to rest.

leave, let   *Leave* means "to go away" or "to abandon." *Let* means "to permit" or "to allow."

> Will you **let** me **leave** with them on the train tomorrow?

less, fewer   See *fewer, less.*

liable, apt, likely   See *apt, liable, likely.*

lie, lay   See *lay, lie.*

like, as   See *as, like.*

likely, apt, liable   See *apt, liable, likely.*

many, much   Use the adjective *many* to describe things that you can count (pencils, people). Use the adjective *much* to describe things that you cannot count (gas, truth, strength). When used as indefinite pronouns, *much* is singular and *many* is plural.

> **Many** responded to our requests for volunteers.
>
> **Much** was expected, but little was gained.

may, might   See "Modals," pages 629–630.

myself, yourself   Do not use a reflexive pronoun in place of *I, me,* or *you.*

> Incorrect   My brother and **myself** enjoy sightseeing together.
>
> Correct   My brother and **I** enjoy sightseeing together.

neither, both, either   See *both, either, neither.*

noted, notorious, famous   See *famous, noted, notorious.*

nothing like, nowhere near   In formal English, use *nothing like* to mean "not at all like"; use *nowhere near* to mean "not anywhere near."

> This movie is **nothing like** the one that we saw last Saturday. [formal]
>
> The studio is **nowhere near** my house. [formal]
>
> That book was **nowhere near** as suspenseful as I had thought it would be. [informal]

of, have   See *have, of.*

off, off of   *Of* is unnecessary. Do not use *off* or *off of* in place of *from.*

> We lifted the chair **off** the carpet so that we could vacuum. [not *off of*]
>
> Larry got that idea **from** his brother. [not *off*]

only   To avoid confusion, place *only* before the element that it modifies. The placement of *only* can dramatically affect the meaning of your sentence.

> **Only** Dale gave him a watch.
>
> Dale **only** gave him a watch.
>
> Dale gave **only** him a watch.
>
> Dale gave him **only** a watch.

persecute, prosecute   To *persecute* people is to harass or otherwise mistreat them. To *prosecute* is to bring a court action.

> The bullies **persecuted** the small children in the neighborhood.
>
> The store owners **prosecuted** the alleged shoplifter.

precede, proceed   *Precede* means "to exist or come before in time." *Proceed* means "to go forward or onward."

> Tim and Willy **proceeded** with the job, wishing that Max and Sam, who had **preceded** them in the use of the carpentry shop, had sharpened the saws.

raise, rise   *Raise* is a regular transitive verb that means "to lift"; it always takes a direct object. *Rise* is an irregular intransitive verb that means "to move upward." See page 624 for the principal parts of the irregular verb *rise.*

> Adele **raised** her feet from the table when her mother scowled at her.
>
> The moon **rises** early in the afternoon.

real, really   *Real* is an adjective; *really* is an adverb.

> It is **really** fortunate that you found your wallet. [not *real*]
>
> That is a **real** surprise!

reason is because, reason is that   *Reason is because* is redundant. Use *reason is that* or simply *because.*

> Incorrect   The reason that I am late **is because** I missed my bus.
>
> Correct   The reason that I am late **is that** I missed my bus.

refer back   *Refer back* is redundant. Use just *refer.*

> I **refer** to our discussion of this morning. [not *refer back*]

regardless, irregardless   See *irregardless, regardless.*

regretful, regrettable   *Regretful* means "full of sorrow or regret." *Regrettable* means "deserving regret or sorrow."

> Mark was **regretful** over the decision to close the theater.
>
> Closing the theater was a **regrettable** decision.

rise, raise   See *raise, rise.*

said, says, goes, went *Said* is the past tense of the verb *say; says* is a present-tense form. Do not use *says* for *said*. Also, do not use *goes* or *went* for *said*.

> Gary called and **said**, "Do you have a tent for the camping trip, or are you going to rent one?" [not *says* or *goes*]

second, secondly; first, firstly See *first, firstly; second, secondly*.

set, sit *Set* is a transitive verb that means "to place something." *Sit* is an intransitive verb that means "to rest in an upright position"; *sit* does not take a direct object.

> **Sit** down next to the door, please.

> **Set** your books on the floor next to you.

slow, slowly *Slow* is an adjective that can be used as an adverb in informal speech, especially in commands or for emphasis. *Slowly* is an adverb; it is preferred in formal usage.

> Our waiter is very **slow**. [predicate adjective]

> He is walking **slowly** from table to table. [adverb]

> Do you think that someone told him to walk **slow**? [adverb; informal]

some time, sometime, sometimes When you use two words, *some* is an adjective modifying *time*. *Sometime* can be an adverb that means "at an indefinite time," or it can be an adjective that means "occasional." *Sometimes* is an adverb that means "occasionally, now and then."

> adj. noun
> He needs **some time** to be alone.

> adv.
> I would like to go to Peru **sometime**.

> adj.
> Evan is a **sometime** musician.

> adv.
> **Sometimes** I like to go away by myself.

sort of, kind of See *kind of, sort of*.

supposed to, used to *Supposed to* means "expected to" or "required to." *Used to* means "accustomed to, familiar with." Be sure to spell *supposed* and *used* with a final -*d*.

> You were **supposed to** take the children shopping with you. [not *suppose to*]

> They are quite **used to** you now. [not *use to*]

sure, surely *Sure* is an adjective meaning "certain" or "dependable." *Surely* is an adverb meaning "certainly, without doubt."

> Rob was **sure** that the dog was in the house.

> The dog will **surely** return by morning.

take, bring See *bring, take*.

than, then Use *than* as a conjunction in a comparison. Use *then* as an adverb to show a sequence of time or events. Do not use either one as a conjunction between two independent clauses.

> The play was, in my opinion, truer to the book **than** the movie was.

> If we get home in time, **then** you may watch television.

that, which, who Use *that* as a relative pronoun to introduce essential clauses (page 611) that refer to things or to collective nouns referring to people. Because it introduces an essential clause, do not use a comma before *that*.

> The cat **that** was crying at our door has just run away again.

Use *which* as a relative pronoun to introduce nonessential clauses (page 611) that refer to things or to groups of persons. Always use a comma before *which* when it introduces a nonessential clause.

> This book, **which** is one that I received for my birthday, is extremely interesting.

Use *who* or *whom* as a relative pronoun to introduce essential and nonessential clauses that refer to persons. Use a comma before *who* or *whom* when it introduces a nonessential clause.

> The girl **who** won that prize is Cathy's sister.

> Nadia, **who** goes to the same school as I do, is a clerk in this store.

then, than See *than, then*.

these kinds, this kind Use *this* or *that* to modify the singular nouns *kind*, *sort*, and *type*. Use *these* and *those* to modify the plural nouns *kinds*, *sorts*, and *types*. Use the singular form of these nouns when the object of the preposition is singular; use the plural form when the object of the preposition is plural.

sing.

This **kind of** *book* is easy to read.

pl.

These **kinds of** *books* are more difficult.

try and, try to   Use *try to* instead of *try and.*

Please **try to** be on time. [not *try and*]

uninterested, disinterested   See *disinterested, uninterested.*

used to, supposed to   See *supposed to, used to.*

very   Use *very* only sparingly. Overuse diminishes its effect.

well, good   See *good, well.*

where . . . at   Do not use *at* after *where.*

Where is that discount store located? [not *Where is it at?*]

which, that, who   see *that, which, who.*

who, whom   See pages 647–648.

-wise   Avoid using *-wise* on the end of a word to mean "with reference to" or "concerning."

Avoid   **Weatherwise,** it is a pleasant week.

Use   The weather has been pleasant this week.

yourself, myself   See *myself, yourself.*

Punctuation and Mechanics

When you speak, you use pauses and vocal inflections to help convey meaning to your listeners. When you write, you use **mechanics**—capitalization, punctuation, italics, and numbers—to convey meaning to your readers.

In the following passage from *David Copperfield*, the mechanics of capitalization and punctuation have been removed.

> well ill tell you what said mr barkis praps you might be writin to her I shall certainly write to her i rejoined ah he said slowly turning his eyes towards me well if you was writin to her praps youd recollect to say that barkis was willin would you that barkis is willing i repeated innocently is that all the message yees he said considering yees barkis is willin

Here is the same passage with the mechanics correctly in place.

> "Well, I'll tell you what," said Mr. Barkis. "P'raps you might be writin' to her?"
>
> "I shall certainly write to her," I rejoined.
>
> "Ah!" he said, slowly turning his eyes towards me. "Well! If you was writin' to her, p'raps you'd recollect to say that Barkis was willin'; would you?"
>
> "That Barkis is willing," I repeated, innocently. "Is that all the message?"
>
> "Ye—es," he said, considering. "Ye—es. Barkis is willin'."
>
> *David Copperfield*
> —CHARLES DICKENS

You can see that quotation marks, commas, dashes, and other mechanical devices clarify and enliven this passage. In your own writing they will allow your thoughts and opinions to come across clearly.

3.1 CAPITALIZATION

Capital letters are most frequently used to indicate the beginning of a sentence or to show that a word is a proper noun (page 662).

3.1A   CAPITALIZATION IN SENTENCES

◆ **RULE**   Capitalize the first word of a sentence and the first word of a direct quotation that is a complete sentence.

> **Creatures** that normally roam the woods at night are called nocturnal animals. Marcie said, "**Aerial** photographs of the affected region would be extremely helpful."

Begin the second part of an interrupted quotation with a capital letter if it is a new sentence; otherwise use a lower-case letter.

> "The bobsled team has just come around the final curve!" he announced excitedly. "**A** new record has been set on this course."

> "That leaky pipe can be repaired," said Mr. Hobbs, "**if** I replace the worn section with a new piece."

◆ **RULE**   Capitalize the first word of each line of a poem.

> **Fair** daffodils, we weep to see
> **You** haste away so soon;
> **As** yet the early-rising sun
> **Has** not attained his noon.
>
> > *"To Daffodils"*
> > —ROBERT HERRICK

Many modern poets do not capitalize the first word of each line of poetry. When you copy a poem, follow the style of the poet.

> **beauty** is a shell
> **from** the sea
> **where** she rules triumphant
>
> > *"Song"*
> > —WILLIAM CARLOS WILLIAMS

3.1B   PROPER NOUNS

◆ **RULE**   Capitalize the names and initials of people. If a last name begins with *Mc*, *O'*, or *St.*, capitalize the next letter as well. If a last name begins with *Mac*, *de*, *D'*, *la*, *le*, *van*, or *von*, use capitalization according to individual family preference.

> J. **O'**Shea   Hernando de Soto   Robert **La** Follette

Family-Relationship Words. Capitalize a word that shows family relationship if it is part of a particular person's name or if it is used in place of a particular person's name. Usually, if a word is preceded by a possessive pronoun (page 580), or if it is used as a general term, it is not capitalized.

Grandfather Hosmer   Aunt Jeanne   Cousin Rita

Harriet told **Mother** that she would be late for dinner this evening.

Karen hoped that **Uncle Frank** would visit in September.

Her **brother** said that he wished he had a new car.

Personal and Official Titles. Capitalize a personal or official title or its abbreviation when it is used as a name in direct address or precedes a person's name.

Capitalize the names and abbreviations of academic degrees or honors that follow a person's name. Capitalize the abbreviations *Sr.* and *Jr.*

Dean Simpson	**Superintendent** Rossi
Eleanor Brock, **M.D.**	**Governor** Ralston
David Oleson, **Jr.**	Roberta Myers, **Ph.D.**

Yes, **Senator,** the report has been delivered.

I told the **senator** that the report had been delivered.

Do not capitalize a title that follows or substitutes for a person's name unless it is the title of a head of national government.

Title Before Name	Title Following Name
Professor Fischer	Walter Fischer, **professor**
President Wilson	Woodrow Wilson, **President**

The **President** will address the nation at four o'clock this afternoon.

Gods of Mythology. Capitalize the names of gods of mythology, but do not capitalize the word *god* when it refers to one of them.

Myths about the ancient Egyptian **god Osiris** portray the process of cyclic renewal.

♦ RULE   Capitalize the names of particular places, such as continents, countries, cities, parks, and rivers.

Bering Strait	Erie Avenue	Iceland	Ohio
Cooper River	Fairmont Park	Kalamazoo	Paraguay

Compass Points. Capitalize compass points that refer to specific geographic regions. Do not capitalize compass points that simply indicate directions or general regions.

We spent our vacation in the **Southwest** last fall.

They traveled **west,** then **northwest** to reach their destination.

Heavenly Bodies.   Capitalize the names of planets, stars, and constellations. Do not capitalize *sun* and *moon*. Capitalize *Earth* when referring to the planet, except when it is preceded by the word *the*.

Andromeda   Neptune   Sirius   Aquarius

Photographs of **Earth** taken from satellites in space revealed many cloud formations above the planet's surface.

The path of **the earth** around the sun is called **the earth's** orbit.

◆ RULE   Capitalize the names of nationalities, peoples, and languages.

Asian   Melanesian   Finnish

Brazilian   Hopi   Latin

◆ RULE   Capitalize the names of days, months, holidays, and special events. Do not capitalize the name of a season unless it is part of a proper noun.

Tuesday   August   spring

Winter Carnival   Memorial Day   winter

◆ RULE   Capitalize the names of historical events and periods. Capitalize the names of awards and documents.

the Middle Ages   the Treaty of Versailles

the Emancipation Proclamation   the Nobel Prize

◆ RULE   Capitalize the first, the last, and all other important words in the titles of books, newspapers, short stories, poems, television programs, musical works, paintings, and so forth. (See also pages 655 and 661–663.) Capitalize a conjunction, an article, or a preposition only when it is the first or the last word in a title or when a conjunction or a preposition has five or more letters.

"**The** Corn Grows **Up**"   *The Man **Without** a Country*

"Singing **in the** Rain"   *For Whom the Bell Tolls*

◆ RULE   Capitalize the names of academic subjects that are languages or that are followed by a course number. Capitalize proper adjectives in the names of academic subjects.

Latin   science   French literature

Biology II   history   American history

◆ RULE   Capitalize the names of structures and the names of organizations, such as businesses, religions, government bodies, clubs, and schools. Capitalize a word such as *school* or *club* only when it is part of a proper noun.

Abbot Hall	House of Representatives
Taoism	Gordon's Book Store
the Museum of Fine Arts	The Chess Association
the Broadcasters' **Club**	**But** a broadcasters' **club**
Essex **College**	**But** an agricultural **college**

◆ RULE   Capitalize trade names. Do not capitalize a common noun that follows a trade name.

> Tree-Ripe fruit juice   Lyle lamps

◆ RULE   Capitalize names of trains, ships, airplanes, rockets, and spacecraft. (See also page 664.)

> the *Lake Shore Limited*   *Viking II*

3.1C   OTHER USES OF CAPITALIZATION

◆ RULE   Capitalize most proper adjectives (page 662). Use a lower-case letter for a proper adjective that is in common usage.

> **Queen Anne's** lace   **Persian** cat   **Gordian** knot
> **But** oxfords [shoes]

If you are not sure whether to capitalize a proper adjective, consult your dictionary.

◆ RULE   Capitalize both letters in the abbreviations A.D., B.C., A.M., and P.M. Write A.D. before the date; write B.C. following the date.

> 1120 B.C.   A.D. 1970   4:30 P.M.

◆ RULE   Capitalize both letters in the two-letter Postal Service abbreviations of state names.

Use Postal Service abbreviations only in addresses that include the ZIP Code; do not use them in formal writing.

> Minnesota **MN** 55411   Rhode Island **RI** 02915

3.2 PUNCTUATION

Punctuation marks show when to stop, when to pause, and when to pay special attention to a particular part of a sentence. By using punctuation correctly, you help your readers understand what you have written.

3.2A   PERIODS, QUESTION MARKS, AND EXCLAMATION POINTS

The Period

♦ RULE   Use a period at the end of a declarative sentence, a mild command, or a polite suggestion.

A rook is a bird that closely resembles a crow.

Soon the stage lights will dim, and the production will begin.

Wait here until the traffic stops.

Dorothea, would you please lower the volume of the television.

♦ RULE   Use a period after most standard abbreviations, including initials that are used as part of a person's name or title.

Do not use periods after abbreviations for most units of weight, units of measure, or chemical elements. Use the abbreviation *in.* for *inch* to show that you are not writing the preposition *in.*

Do not use periods when the abbreviation of a company or an organization is in all capital letters or when you are writing Postal Service abbreviations of state names.

Use Periods	Do Not Use Periods
Capt. Mario Venditto	**min**—minute
Julia **S.** Drake, **R.N.**	**Kr**—Krypton
Dec.—December	**gal**—gallon
Rte.—route	**AZ**—Arizona
Co.—company	**FAA**—Federal Aviation Administration
Miss.—Mississippi	

Do not confuse standard two-letter state abbreviations (which require periods) with Postal Service abbreviations (which require no periods).

Use Periods	Do Not Use Periods
Preston, **Ga.** [no ZIP Code]	Rhine, **GA** 31077
Casacade, **Ky.** [no ZIP Code]	Clark, **KY** 41011

♦ RULE   When a period in an abbreviation precedes a question mark or an exclamation point in a sentence, use both marks of punctuation.

When is it correct to use Dr.?

Note: Avoid using abbreviations in formal writing. Spell out words instead.

The Question Mark

♦ RULE   Use a question mark at the end of an interrogative sentence.

Has Del applied for the summer internship?

Were those old watches appraised at the jewelry store?

◆ RULE   Use a question mark after a question that is not a complete sentence.

The date? December 30.

◆ RULE   Use a question mark to express doubt about what comes before it.

Josiah Clark (1762?–1809) made furniture that is sturdy and usable even today.

The Exclamation Point

◆ RULE   Use an exclamation point at the end of a sentence that expresses strong feeling or a forceful command or after a strong interjection or other exclamatory expression.

He nearly escaped!

Don't miss the total eclipse!

Congratulations! You are the new assistant.

Wait! Never leave a campfire burning!

3.2B   COMMAS

Commas in Series

◆ RULE   Use commas to separate three or more words, phrases, or clauses in a series. Use a comma after each item except the last.

Donna bought **potting soil, marigold seeds,** and **fertilizer** at the plant store.

The campers **climbed the mountain, selected a campsite,** and **pitched their tents** for the night.

In preparation for the play, **Bert rehearsed his lines, Carla checked the props,** and **Florence tested the sound system.**

Do not use commas to separate items in a series if all of them are joined by conjunctions.

Did you decide to go swimming **or** fishing **or** boating last weekend?

Do not use commas to separate pairs of nouns that are thought of as a single item or as a unit.

unit

For breakfast we ordered juice, cereal, **bacon and eggs,** and milk.

Commas After Introductory Expressions

♦ RULE Use a comma to show a pause after an introductory word or phrase.

Prepositional Phrases. Use a comma after an introductory prepositional phrase (pages 602–603) of four or more words.

After the **management seminar,** the participants handed in their reports.

Participial Phrases. Use a comma after an introductory participial phrase (pages 605–606).

Wondering if she had missed her appointment, Carol raced to the elevator.

Adverb Clauses. Use a comma after an introductory adverb clause (pages 611–612) regardless of its length.

Before she left, Sandra watered the plants.

Interjections. Use a comma to separate *yes, no,* and other interjections, such as *oh* and *well,* from the rest of the sentence.

Yes, Sheila is eligible for the athletic scholarship.

Well, the harvest next year may be more bountiful.

Modifiers. Use commas to separate two or more adjectives that modify the same noun. Do not use commas if the adjectives form a compound with the noun (page 586).

To determine whether to use a comma, ask yourself whether the sentence would sound right if you reversed the adjectives or if you put *and* between them. If it sounds natural, use a comma or commas. If it does not, do not use commas. Do not use a comma between the last adjective and the noun that it modifies.

Natural
Meri manages a successful, innovative business. [comma: *successful* and *innovative* each modify business.]

Natural
Meri manages an innovative, successful business.

Natural
They listened avidly to the first radio broadcast. [no comma: It is the *radio broadcast* that is first; *radio broadcast* is a compound.]

Unnatural
They listened avidly to the radio first broadcast.

Unnatural
They listened avidly to the first and radio broadcast.

Commas to Separate Sentence Parts

◆ RULE   Use a comma to separate sentence parts that might otherwise be read together in a confusing manner.

Later, former senators will gather for a formal group photograph.

Whenever **possible, alternatives** should be researched.

Repeated Words.   Use a comma to separate most words that are repeated.

What little food there **was, was** shared by all.

Rewrite sentences to avoid repeating words, whenever possible.

◆ RULE   Use a comma before a coordinating conjunction (page 592) that joins the independent clauses of a compound sentence (page 615).

Josie never saw a meteor shower, **but** she viewed the Great Meteor Crater in Arizona.

Deliver this message immediately, **and** call Mr. Hutchinson before tomorrow morning.

◆ RULE   Use a comma or a pair of commas to set off words of direct address and parenthetical expressions within a sentence.

Frank, please do not forget the maps.

Her evaluations of the play have, **after all,** been positive.

◆ RULE   Use a comma or a pair of commas to set off nonessential appositives (page 604). Do not set off essential appositives (pages 603–604).

Treat an abbreviated title or a degree following a name as a nonessential appositive.

Nonessential
Karen's brother, **Steve,** will meet her at the airport tonight. [Karen has only one brother.]

Jules Verne, **the author of *Twenty Thousand Leagues Under the Sea,*** was one of the first writers of science fiction.

Wilma Sarkin, **D.D.S.,** will be the guest speaker this afternoon.

Essential

My cousin Tony moved from Boston to Los Angeles fifteen years ago. [I have more than one cousin.]

The American novelist Nathaniel Hawthorne wrote about the duality of human nature. [There is more than one American novelist.]

Julie's cat Tiny Tim purred contentedly. [Julie has more than one cat.]

♦ RULE   Use a comma or a pair of commas to set off a nonessential phrase or a nonessential clause (page 611) from the rest of the sentence. Do not set off an essential phrase or an essential clause (page 611).

Nonessential

The students, **who found the new material difficult,** met in study groups after school. [All of the students found the new material difficult.]

Every week I shop at the same store, **where I often see people whom I know.**

Essential

The students who found the new material difficult met in study groups after school. [Only the students who found the new material difficult met in study groups.]

Every week I shop at the store that is nearest to my home.

♦ RULE   Use commas before and after the year when the year is used with the month and the day. Do not use commas when only the month and the year are given.

Joanne moved into her new apartment on **July 7, 1983,** and she plans to stay there until she graduates from college.

Stuart visited Boston in **May 1979.**

♦ RULE   Use commas before and after the name of a state, province, or country when it is used with the name of a city. Do not use commas between a state and its ZIP Code.

Arlene lives in **Lincoln, Wisconsin,** with her brother and sister-in-law.

Craig carefully wrote the following address on the package: John Saxon, 100 South Street, Waltham **MA 02154.**

♦ RULE   Use a comma after the greeting, or salutation, of a social letter and after the complimentary close of any letter.

Dear Roseann,   Sincerely yours,   Yours truly,

3.2C SEMICOLONS

Semicolons are used to connect independent clauses and to clarify meaning in sentences that contain a number of commas.

♦ RULE Use a semicolon to connect independent clauses.

Without a Coordinating Conjunction. Use a semicolon in a compound sentence to connect closely related independent clauses that are *not* joined by a coordinating conjunction.

> Many times we prepared to turn back; swift rapids nearly tipped the canoes.

With a Conjunctive Adverb or with an Explanatory Expression. Use a semicolon to connect independent clauses that are joined by a conjunctive adverb (page 609) or by an explanatory expression. Use a comma after the conjunctive adverb or after the explanatory expression.

> The members of the diving team were excited about being in the state finals; **however,** each member seemed calm when the event began.

> Hal really enjoyed his trip to Canada; **in fact,** he said that it was the best trip he had ever taken.

♦ RULE Use a semicolon to clarify meaning in a sentence that contains several commas.

Independent Clauses. Use a semicolon to clarify and separate independent clauses that have several commas within them, even when a coordinating conjunction is used.

> I have studied the works of Ralph Waldo Emerson, a neighbor of one of my ancestors; and I would also like to study the works of Henry David Thoreau, Louisa May Alcott, and Bronson Alcott.

Items in a Series. Use semicolons to separate items in a series if those items have internal commas. The semicolons make clear how many items are in the series.

Unclear
> The main characters are Walter, a talented but unrecognized young artist, Pamela, a dedicated art student, Will, a famous art critic, and Harriet, a patron of the arts. [four characters or seven?]

Clear
> The main characters are Walter, a talented but unrecognized young artist; Pamela, a dedicated art student; Will, a famous art critic; and Harriet, a patron of the arts. [four characters]

3.2D COLONS

♦ RULE Use a colon to introduce an explanatory phrase or a statement or a list of items that completes a sentence. The part of a sentence before a list may contain a demonstrative word such as *these* or *those* or an expression such as *the following* or *as follows*.

> The disappointing news was reported to the waiting crowd: **the building would have to be torn down.**

> New legislation will affect the following cities: **Frankfort, Louisville, and Bowling Green.**

> Of the marsupials, he was able to study these: **kangaroos, koalas, and opossums.**

Do *not* use a colon to introduce a list that immediately follows a verb or a preposition.

> The graphic design **includes** triangles, parallelograms, and circles. [not *includes:*]

> What products are made **in** Venezuela, Bolivia, and Brazil? [not *in:*]

♦ RULE Use a colon to separate two independent clauses when the second clause explains or completes the first sentence.

> I think I know why I have read that book three times: I have the same outlook on life that the main character has.

♦ RULE Use a colon to separate the hour and minutes in an expression of time, the chapter and verse in a biblical reference, the title and subtitle of a book, and the volume and page number of a book or magazine reference.

> 3:22 P.M.   *Wheels and Wagons: Early Transportation*
> Genesis 12:2   *Mountaineering Monthly,* 6:72

♦ RULE Use a colon after the salutation of a business letter.

> Dear Mr. Statler: Dear Ms. Fortuna:

♦ RULE Use a colon to introduce a direct quotation.

> Dr. Doneski began her presentation with these words: "I feel honored to be speaking to such a distinguished group."

3.2E QUOTATION MARKS

♦ RULE Use quotation marks to show that you are writing the exact words that someone said, thought, or wrote. Use quotation marks at both the beginning and the end of the quotation.

Do not use quotation marks around an **indirect quotation:** a retelling, in the writer's words, of what another person said, thought, or wrote.

Eliza asked, **"May** I borrow this tape recorder?"

Vic said, **"The** opera *The Magic Flute* was on the radio last night, and I really enjoyed listening to it."

Vic said that he had thoroughly enjoyed listening to *The Magic Flute* on the radio last night. [indirect quotation]

Dialogue. When you are writing dialogue, begin a new paragraph and use a separate set of quotation marks each time the speaker changes.

"Did you check the source of your information?" Dale asked.

"Of course," replied Irene. "I always double-check information concerning a controversial subject."

Brief Quotations. If you are writing a brief quotation that continues for more than one paragraph, use opening quotation marks at the beginning of each paragraph, but use end quotation marks only at the end of the last paragraph.

"No, he had never written about Paris. Not the Paris that he cared about. But what about the rest that he had never **written?** [no quotation marks]
"What about the ranch and the silvered gray of the sage brush, the quick, clear water in the irrigation ditches, and the heavy green of the **alfalfa."**

"The Snows of Kilimanjaro"
—ERNEST HEMINGWAY

Long Quotations. When you are copying a quotation of five or more lines, set it off from the rest of your paper by indenting it five spaces from the left and right margins. Single-space the quotation if you are typing. Do *not* use quotation marks with a quotation that is set off in this way.

♦ RULE Use quotation marks to set off the title of a short story, an article, an essay, a short poem, or a song.

Use quotation marks to set off the title of any piece that forms part of a larger work such as the following: a single television show that is part of a series, a chapter of a book, a section of a newspaper, or a feature in a magazine. (See also page 672.)

Miguel will recite Browning's poem **"My Last Duchess."**

Please rehearse **"The Impossible Dream,"** the second song in the show.

The sixth and final episode, entitled **"Today's Environment,"** was informative.

Luke always reads **"Hints for Hikers"** in *Wilderness* magazine.

♦ RULE   Use quotation marks to call attention to the special nature of such words as nicknames used with a person's full name, technical terms, and odd expressions.

Colonel Edwin E. **"Buzz"** Aldrin, Jr., participated in the historic moon-landing mission.

The bottom of a hydroplane is designed so that the boat **"planes"** on the surface of the water.

Note: The preceding rule is for informal usage only. Avoid such usage in formal writing if possible.

♦ RULE   Use quotation marks to set off a word that defines another word.

I use the word *calculating* to mean **"shrewd."**

Other Punctuation with Quotation Marks.   The following rules will help you to determine where and how to use single quotation marks, commas, periods, colons, semicolons, question marks, and exclamation points with quotation marks.

♦ RULE   Use single quotation marks around a quotation or a title that occurs within a longer quoted passage.

"Watch the episode called **'The Industrial Revolution'** at eight o'clock tonight," said Mr. Creiger.

♦ RULE   Place a comma or a period inside closing quotation marks.

"Return one day and visit," suggested our guide, "for I have enjoyed showing you some of the spectacular sights this city has to offer."

♦ RULE   Place a semicolon or a colon outside closing quotation marks.

Grady reported, "The dam is close to overflowing"; consequently, safety measures were taken immediately.

Now I remember why I carefully read the article "How to Improve Your Memory": I didn't want to forget any of the details.

♦ RULE   Place a question mark or an exclamation point inside the closing quotation marks if it applies only to the material quoted. If the entire sentence is a question or an exclamation, place the question mark or exclamation point outside the closing quotation marks. If both the quotation and the sentence require a question mark or an exclamation point, put the end mark inside the closing quotation marks.

Loren wondered, "Did I miss the appointment?" [The quotation itself is a question.]

Did Alicia say, "I think that I will buy a digital watch"? [The entire sentence, not the quotation, is a question.]

How did you answer the question "What is your job experience?" [Both the quotation and the sentence are questions.]

3.2F APOSTROPHES

Possessives

◆ RULE Use an apostrophe to show possession.

Singular and Plural Nouns. Use an apostrophe and an *-s*(*-'s*) to form the possessive of a singular noun or a plural noun that does not end in *-s.*

> the bear**'s** cubs Keats**'s** poetry the people**'s** choice

Plural Nouns Ending in -s. Use an apostrophe alone to form the possessive of a plural noun that ends in *-s.*

> the settlers**'** land the Elks**'** convention the Davises**'** house

Compound Nouns. Change the last word of a compound noun to the possessive form.

> the passer-**by's** comment the bell**boys'** uniforms

Joint Ownership. Use the possessive form of only the last person's name when a thing is jointly owned. Use the possessive form of each name when two or more people each possess separate items.

> Richard Rodgers and Oscar Hammerstein**'s** musicals
>
> Wallace Stevens**'s** and T. S. Eliot**'s** poetry

Expressions Ending in -s. Use an apostrophe alone to form the possessive of most expressions that end in *-s* or the sound of *s.*

> for goodness**'** sake three years**'** work

Ancient Classical Names Ending in -s. Use an apostrophe alone to form the possessive of ancient classical names that end in *-s.*

> Socrates**'** dialogues Hippocrates**'** oath

Contractions

◆ RULE Use an apostrophe to replace letters or numbers that have been left out in a contraction.

I **can't** lift these barrels by myself.

They'll be ready to leave in less than an hour.

Were the clothing styles of the **'20s** quite different?

Plural Forms

◆ RULE   Use an apostrophe and an *-s(-'s)* to form the plural of letters, numbers, symbols, and words that you are referring to as words or symbols.

Use italics (underlining) correctly in forming plurals with apostrophes. Do not underline the **'s.**

There are three *s*'s in *dissatisfied.*

The vote received twenty-five *yea*'s and three *nay*'s.

She told him to mind his *p*'s and *q*'s.

Note: The plurals of abbreviations that do not include periods are formed by adding just *-s.*

There are several **PTAs** in our school district.

But   The *PTA*'s on the poster were faded. [referring to the letters, not to the organization]

Although names of years are written with numerals, they also usually function as words and should be treated as such.

My grandmother told stories about growing up in New England in the early **1900s.**

Avoiding the Misuse of Apostrophes

◆ RULE   Do not use the apostrophe to form the plurals of nouns. The plural of a noun is generally formed by adding *-s* or *-es*, as in *books, families, tomatoes,* and *atlases.*

Incorrect   Fortunately, we finished our **essay's** on time.

Correct   Fortunately, we finished our **essays** on time.

◆ RULE   Do not add an apostrophe or *-'s* to possessive personal pronouns: *mine, yours, his, hers, its, ours, theirs.* They already show ownership.

Are these lecture notes **yours?**

In addition, do not confuse possessive forms of personal pronouns with contractions.

The cat washed **its** face. [not *it's*]

3.2G HYPHENS, DASHES, AND ELLIPSIS POINTS

The Hyphen

♦ RULE   Use a hyphen to divide a word at the end of a line.

Do not divide a word of one syllable, such as *washed* or *grieve*. Do not divide any word so that one letter stands by itself.

Always divide a word between its syllables and in such a way that the reader will not be confused about its meaning of pronunciation.

Incorrect	Marsha went to the bank Friday and **cash-ed** her paycheck. [*Cashed* is a word of one syllable.]
Correct	Marsha went to the bank Friday and **cashed** her paycheck.
Incorrect	During Jan's vacation trip, the weather was **a-greeable** and the accommodations were satisfactory. [The letter *a* stands by itself.]
Correct	During Jan's vacation trip, the weather was **agree-able** and the accommodations were satisfactory.

Prefixes and Suffixes. Divide a word with a prefix only after the prefix. Divide a word with a suffix only before the suffix.

Paula and Frank told me that they attended an important **inter-national** conference.

The only way to open the lock is to turn the dial in a **clock-wise** direction.

Compound Words. For a compound word that is written as one word, divide it only between the base words. Divide a hyphenated compound word at the hyphen.

If we work quickly, we will be able to finish everything **some-time** in February.

He described his trip to the mountains during the storm as a **hair-raising** experience.

♦ RULE   Use a hyphen after the prefixes *all-*, *ex-*, and *self-*. Use a hyphen to separate any prefix from a proper noun or adjective.

all-purpose	**Neo**-Platonism	But	neophyte
ex-president	**pre**-Alexandrian	But	preview
self-assured	**intra**-Asian	But	intrastate

Note: Do not use a hyphen between most other prefixes and their root words.

entitle   **pre**determine   **sub**standard

◆ RULE Use a hyphen after the prefix of a word that is spelled the same as another word but has a different origin and meaning (a homograph).

re-collect   re-count   re-form
recollect   recount   reform

◆ RULE Use a hyphen after the prefix of a word when the last letter of the prefix is a vowel and is the same as the first letter of the base word.

de-escalate   **pre-**eminent   **re-**educate

◆ RULE Hyphenate a compound adjective when it precedes the noun that it modifies, but not when it follows it. Do not hyphenate a compound adjective when its first word is an adverb that ends in *-ly.*

The moderator introduced **up-to-date** issues.

The issues that the moderator introduced were **up to date.**

A **barely moving** train slowed to a complete stop to avoid an obstruction.

Fractions. Hyphenate a fraction that is used as a modifier. Do not hyphenate a fraction that is used as a noun.

Modifier   The soup was **two-thirds** water.

Noun   **One third** of the soup was vegetables.

◆ RULE Use a hyphen to separate compound numbers from *twenty-one* through *ninety-nine.*

forty-nine   seventy-three
But five hundred   ninety thousand

The Dash

◆ RULE Use a dash to show an interruption in a thought or in a statement. Use a second dash to end the interruption if the sentence continues.

"**If we can just——**"; suddenly he had another idea.

Someone——**I think it's Barbara**——will bring the table decorations.

Appositives and Parenthetical Expressions. Use dashes when appositives or parenthetical expressions have internal commas.

We will need some equipment——**I think that a tent, sleeping bags, back-**

packs, and cooking utensils will do——before we can plan an overnight camping trip.

Several colors——**orange, green, and violet, for example**——are made up of combinations of other colors.

In typing, use two hyphens to represent a dash. Do not type a single hyphen to stand for a dash.

Note: Avoid the overuse of dashes in formal writing.

Ellipsis Points

◆ RULE   Use **ellipsis points,** a set of three spaced periods (. . .), to indicate an omission or a pause in written or quoted material.

A little neglect may breed great mischief . . . for want of a nail the shoe was lost; for want of a shoe the horse was lost; and for want of a horse the rider was lost.

Poor Richard's Almanac
—BENJAMIN FRANKLIN

Other Punctuation Marks. If what precedes the ellipsis points is part of a complete sentence, use a period followed by three ellipsis points (. . . .). If what precedes the ellipsis points is not part of a complete sentence, use only the three ellipsis points, leaving a space before the first point (. . .). If what precedes the ellipsis points is part of a complete sentence ending with a question mark or an exclamation point, retain that mark before the three ellipsis points (? . . .).

Original Passage

None of them knew the colour of the sky. Their eyes glanced level, and were fastened upon the waves that swept toward them. These waves were of the hue of slate, save for the tops, which were of foaming white, and all of the men knew the colours of the sea. The horizon narrowed and widened, and dipped and rose, and at all times its edge was jagged with waves that seemed thrust up in points like rocks.

"The Open Boat"
—STEPHEN CRANE

Abridged Passage

None of them knew the colour of the sky. Their eyes . . . were fastened upon the waves. . . . These waves were of the hue of slate, . . . and all of the men know the colours of the sea. The horizon narrowed and widened, . . . and at all times its edge was jagged with waves. . . .

Sentences and Paragraphs. Use a line of periods to indicate the omission of a stanza of poetry or of an entire paragraph from written material.

3.2H   PARENTHESES AND BRACKETS

Parentheses

♦ RULE   Use parentheses to enclose material that is not basic to the meaning of the sentence.

> Kathleen requested information from the FEC (**Federal Election Commission**) about the campaign funds of the congressional candidates in her district.

> The cardinal (**sometimes called the redbird**) is the state bird of Illinois.

Other Punctuation with Parentheses. Place commas, semicolons, and colons outside parentheses. Place periods outside parentheses unless the parenthetical material is a separate sentence beginning with a capital letter; then place the period inside the parentheses. Place question marks and exclamation points inside the parentheses if they are part of the parenthetical material; otherwise place them outside the parentheses.

Brackets

♦ RULE   Use brackets to enclose explanations or comments that are inserted in a quotation but that are not part of the quotation.

> A guide said, "It [**the Great Salt Lake**] is four to five times as salty as the ocean."

Use brackets to enclose parenthetical information that is part of material already in parentheses.

> Over a dozen oil companies are bidding for the rights to drill in the Atlantic Ocean off the New Jersey shore. (Today's newspaper also contains an article on the environmental risks of off-shore drilling [**see p. 56**].)

Other Punctuation with Brackets.   The only punctuation marks used with brackets are those within the bracketed material.

3.3   USING ITALICS AND NUMBERS IN WRITING

3.3A   ITALICS

In printed material, certain words and symbols are set in italic type *(slanted letters like these)*. In handwriting and typing, you should underline such words and symbols according to the following rules.

♦ RULE   Italicize (underline) the names or titles of books, book-length poems, newspapers, magazines, periodicals, plays, movies, television series, paintings, trains, ships, aircraft, and so forth.

Italicize (underline) an article (*a, an, the*) that comes before a title only if it is part of the title. (See also page 680.)

The Portrait of a Lady   *Paradise Lost*
Casablanca   *Voyager 2*

◆ RULE   Italicize (underline) letters, numbers, symbols, and words when you are referring to them as words or symbols.

I marked a *21* in the last column to complete the store's inventory.

Ryan noticed that *occasionally* was misspelled in the caption.

◆ RULE   Italicize (underline) words from other languages if those words are not commonly used in English. Do not italicize foreign place names or currency.

A spontaneous shout of appreciation followed the singer's solo, the *pièce de résistance* of the evening.

But   Paula spent the day at the Musée de Louvre. This new restaurant has a standard à la carte menu. [À la carte is commonly used in English.]

Italicize (underline) a word or phrase that you wish to emphasize. Avoid overuse of this device.

"After *hours* of work," reported the excited archaeologist, "we finally found evidence of a structure."

3.3B   USING NUMBERS IN WRITING

◆ RULE   Spell out numbers of one hundred or less. Spell out numbers that are rounded to hundreds and that can be written in two words or less.

Ferdinand Magellan's expedition from Spain began with **five** ships, yet only **three** of them continued the trip to the Pacific Ocean.

Were there nearly **one thousand** boxes of hats delivered yesterday?

But   Nina collected **1,250** postcards from around the world.

Note: Do not mix numerals and words when writing two or more numbers in the same category.

Incorrect

Two hundred general practitioners and 350 specialists attended the convention on May 29.

Correct

Two hundred general practitioners and **three hundred fifty** specialists attended the convention on May 29. [Words are used to describe the numbers of people in attendance; numerals are used in the dates.]

◆ RULE   Spell out any number that begins a sentence, or rewrite the sentence.

The word *and* is unnecessary in writing numbers except those numbers between *one hundred* and *one hundred and ten,* and so forth.

Incorrect
106 guardrails will be placed along that steep incline.

Correct
One hundred and six guardrails will be placed along that steep incline.

Correct
Along that steep incline, **106** guardrails will be placed.

Ordinal Numbers. Spell out ordinal numbers (*first, second, third,* and so forth) in your writing. You may write the day of the month as an ordinal number preceding the month, but the month followed by an Arabic numeral is the preferred form.

fifth day   June 8
seventh grade   eighth of June

Compound Numbers. Hyphenate compound numbers from *twenty-one* through *ninety-nine.*

thirty-two   eighty-six   ninety-three

Spell out cardinal numbers (*one, two, three,* and so forth) that occur in a compound with nouns or adjectives.

five-dollar tickets   twenty-pound turkey

◆ RULE   Spell out an expression of time unless it is a specific time using A.M. or P.M. Use numerals and A.M. or P.M. in all technical writing.

Ruth usually leaves her apartment around **eight o'clock.**

But   My computer printout was finished at **3.51** A.M.

◆ RULE   Use numerals to express dates, street numbers, room numbers, apartment numbers, telephone numbers, page numbers, and percentages. Spell out the word *percent*.

July 16, 1925   pages 56–101
122 San Gabriel Avenue   10 percent

Dates. When you write a date, do not add *-st, -nd, -rd,* or *-th* to the numeral.

Incorrect   May 5th, 1971   October 2nd
Correct   May 5, 1971   October 2

3.4 PROOFREADING AND EDITING

3.4A PROOFREADING SYMBOLS

The following symbols are commonly used to identify and correct errors in composition. Learning them will help you revise and proofread your writing.

∧	insert something	lost her ^balance^ walking on stilts
#	space	bought a red#balloon
¶	begin new paragraph	last of the heroes! ¶ In the next century
∼	transpose letter or words	this fab⁀ric⁀made has
ℓ	delete	a mountaintop top℮ retreat
⌒	close up letters	I am happ‿y to introduce
⋯⋯	let it stand (under something crossed out)	consisted of a large℮ percentage ⋯⋯
≡	capitalize	the Department of agriculture≡
/	make lower case	Marlene gazed at the /Portrait.

3.4B   EDITING SYMBOLS

The marks and abbreviations below are common ones that you might use when you edit a friend's draft or that your teacher might use. Page references to this text follow.

adj	adjective, 585	*gl/us*	glossary, usage, 654
adv	adverb, 588	-	hyphen, 677
agr	agreement:	*ital*	italics, 680
	pronoun-antecedent, 640	*j*	jargon, 621
	subject-verb, 634	*mod*	modifier, position of, 668
'	apostrophe, 675	( )	parentheses, 680
cap	capital letters, 661	.	period, 666
c	case, pronoun, 644	" "	quotation marks, 672
:	colon, 672	*ref*	reference, pronoun, 649
,	comma, 667	*r-o*	run-on sentence, 618
cons	consistency	;	semicolon, 671
—	dash, 678	*sl*	slang, 620
dg	dangling modifier, 653	*sub*	subordination, 620
ellip	ellipsis points, 679	*vf*	verb form, 584
frag	fragment, 616	*vt*	verb tense, 625

ABOUT THE PHOTOGRAPHER

Over the past thirty-five years, Lee Friedlander has gained wide acclaim as one of the great photographers of our day. His many award-winning exhibits and books have examined New Orleans jazz musicians, American public monuments, factory life, the cherry blossoms in Japan, the parks of Frederick Law Olmsted, and the faces of friends and family in intimate portraiture. Friedlander is perhaps best known, however, for his witty and insightful black-and-white studies of the modern landscape. He captures with special power the poignant humor of the urban street scene: its maze of shadowy and reflective storefronts, its traffic-filled and vacant spaces, its evocative signage and graffiti. With his art, Friedlander helps us to see the commonplace in fresh, surprising ways.

Self-portrait, 1977, gelatin-silver print courtesy Fraenkel Gallery, San Francisco. When asked once in an interview if there was something that he particularly liked taking pictures of, Friedlander replied, "I've never seen a truck that I wouldn't want to photograph."

For page locations of other photographs by Lee Friedlander, please see the copyright page.

AUTHOR/TITLE INDEX

SUBJECT INDEX

List of Reading Selections

The Riverside Guide to Writing offers 104 diverse, cross-curricular reading selections, 46 of which are new to this edition. The 53 end-of-chapter readings are accompanied by headnotes and linked with the writing assignments. There are also 51 briefer in-chapter readings and excerpts featuring writers at work.